Thinking Critically

Thinking Critically

Boston,
Massachusetts:
Houghton Mifflin, 1997

0395831059

Thinking Critically

Fifth Edition

JOHN CHAFFEE, Ph.D.

Director, Center for Critical Thinking and Language Learning
LaGuardia College, City University of New York

Houghton Mifflin Company   **Boston   New York**

For Jessie and Joshua

Senior Sponsoring Editor: Dean Johnson
Senior Project Editor: Rosemary Winfield
Senior Production/Design Coordinator: Jill Haber
Senior Manufacturing Coordinator: Marie Barnes
Marketing Manager: Pamela Laskey

Acknowledgments
Cover design by Mark Caleb; Cover image: © 1996 M.C. Escher/
Cordon Art-Holland. All rights reserved.

(Acknowledgments continued on page 591.)

Library of Congress Catalog Number: 96-76877
ISBN: 0-395-83105-9

789-QF-00 99 98

Contents

Checklist of Readings

Chapter 6   LANGUAGE AND THOUGHT

Chapter 7   FORMING AND APPLYING CONCEPTS

Chapter 8   RELATING AND ORGANIZING

Chapter 9   REPORTING, INFERRING, AND JUDGING

Preface

Teaching a course in critical thinking is one of the most inspiring and rewarding experiences that a teacher can have. Because the thinking process is such an
integral part of who we are as people, the prospect of expanding students' thinking implies expanding who they are as human beings — the perspective from
which they view the world, the concepts and values they use to guide their
choices, and the impact they have on the world as a result of those choices.
Teaching people to become critical thinkers does not mean simply equipping
them with certain intellectual tools; it involves their personal transformation
and its commensurate impact on the quality of their lives and those around
them. This is truly education at its most inspiring!

Thinking Critically, Fifth Edition, is designed to serve as a comprehensive
introduction to the cognitive process while helping students develop the higher-
order thinking abilities needed for academic study and career success. Based
on a nationally recognized interdisciplinary program in critical and creative
thinking established in 1979 at LaGuardia College (The City University of New
York) and involving more than fifteen hundred students annually, *Thinking Critically* integrates various perspectives on the thinking process drawn from a variety of disciplines such as philosophy, cognitive psychology, linguistics, and the
language arts (English, reading, and oral communication).

Thinking Critically addresses a crucial need in higher education by intro-
ducing students to the rapidly emerging field of critical thinking and fostering
sophisticated intellectual and language abilities. Students apply their evolving
thinking abilities to a variety of subjects drawn from academic disciplines, contemporary issues, and their life experiences. *Thinking Critically* is based on the
assumption, supported by research, that learning to think more effectively is a
synthesizing process, knitting critical thinking abilities together with academic
content and the fabric of students' experiences. Thinking learned in this way
becomes a constitutive part of who students are.

With these considerations in mind, it should be clear that teaching a course
in critical thinking involves embarking on high adventure, a journey that is full
of unanticipated challenges and unexpected triumphs. I have written *Thinking
Critically* to serve as an effective guide for this journey. In the final analysis,
however, you must embark on the journey alone, relying on your experience,
expertise, and critical thinking abilities to provide productive educational experiences for your students.

Features

This book has a number of distinctive characteristics that make it an effective tool for both instructors and students. *Thinking Critically*

- **teaches the fundamental thinking, reasoning, and language abilities that students need for academic success.** By focusing on the major thinking and language abilities needed in all disciplines, and by including a wide variety of readings, the text helps students perform more successfully in other courses.
- **stimulates and guides students to think clearly about complex, controversial issues.** Over forty readings provide in-depth perspectives on significant social issues such as the criminal justice system, racism, euthanasia, AIDS, teen pregnancy, drug and alcohol abuse, date rape, the death penalty, and threats to the earth's ecology. More important, the text helps students develop the thinking and language abilities necessary to understand and discuss intelligently these complex issues.
- **presents foundational thinking, reasoning, and language abilities in a developmentally sequenced way.** The text begins with basic abilities and then carefully progresses to more sophisticated thinking and reasoning skills. Cognitive maps open each chapter to help students understand the thinking process as well as the interrelationship of ideas in that chapter.
- **engages students in the active process of thinking.** Interspersed exercises, discussion topics, readings, and writing assignments encourage active participation, stimulating students to critically examine their own and others' thinking and to sharpen and improve their abilities. *Thinking Critically* provides structured opportunities for students to develop their thinking processes in a progressive, reflective way.
- **provides context by continually relating critical thinking abilities to students' daily lives.** Once students learn to apply critical thinking skills to situations in their own experience, they then apply these skills to more abstract, academic contexts. Additionally, by asking students to think critically about themselves and their experience, the text fosters their personal development as mature, responsible critical thinkers.
- **integrates the development of thinking abilities with the four language skills so crucial to success in college and careers: reading, writing, speaking, and listening.** The abundant writing assignments (short answer, paragraph, and essay), challenging readings, and discussion exercises serve to improve students' language skills.
- **is accompanied by a provocative critical thinking videotape.** A one-hour critical thinking videotape, developed by the author, entitled

"Thinking Towards Decisions," is designed to work in conjunction with Chapter 2, *Thinking Critically.* The tape uses a creative interweaving of a dramatic scenario, expert testimony, and a seminar group to develop students' critical thinking abilities.

- **includes critical thinking test.** The Test of Critical Thinking Abilities, developed by the author, is included in the Instructor's Resource Manual (in a form that can be taken out and reproduced) and provides for a comprehensive evaluation of student thinking and language abilities. Using a court case format arising from a fatal student drinking incident, students are challenged to gather and weigh evidence, ask relevant questions, construct informed beliefs, evaluate expert testimony and summation arguments, reach a verdict, and then view the entire case from a problem-solving perspective.

New to the Fifth Edition

I have made significant changes in the fifth edition of *Thinking Critically,* which reflect my experiences in using the fourth edition, as well as the suggestions of many faculty who used the text in a variety of classes. In addition to rewriting many sections of the text, I have included these features in the new edition:

- **Illustrations.** Forty new illustrations created specifically for this book by the artist Warren Gebert have been added to provoke thoughtful responses, present key concepts, and visually engage the reader.
- **New readings.** New readings added to the many articles already present create a deeply diverse collection of perspectives on important, current themes. As with the previous editions, the readings are carefully integrated into the text, illustrating key concepts and stimulating students to develop their thinking abilities through critical readings and written analysis. New topics include the ethics of corporate "downsizing," college women and alcohol, the nature of religion, and creating our personal myths.
- **Expanded treatment of creative thinking.** A new concluding Chapter 12, "Thinking Critically, Living Creatively," analyzes the creative process, developing creative thinking abilities, and creating a life philosophy through moral choices. The chapter also explains how "creative thinking" is the natural partner to "critical thinking."
- **New section on "Composing Argumentative Essays"** that presents a clear model for researching and writing argumentative essays.

- **New section on "The Critical Thinker's Guide to Reasoning"** that provides an illustrated model that integrates the thinking and reasoning abilities explored in the book.
- **New section on decision making** that includes a versatile decision-making model.
- **New sections on problem solving** that explore solving the problems of "not enough money" and "not enough time."
- **New Thinking Activities,** created for this edition, focus on topics like contrasting historical analyses of the atomic bombings of Hiroshima and Nagasaki.

Instructor's Resource Manual

Major work has produced an enhanced *Instructor's Resource Manual* designed to help instructors tailor this book to their own courses.

- **Critical Thinking courses:** Part 1, "Using *Thinking Critically*," written by John Chaffee, contains an overview of the field of critical thinking as well as suggestions and exercises of interest to teachers using this text. New activities and the Test of Critical Thinking Abilities have been added for the fifth edition.
- **Reading and Writing courses:** Parts 2 and 3 — "*Thinking Critically* and Reading" and "*Thinking Critically* and Writing" — present assignments, useful suggestions, and syllabi for instructors using *Thinking Critically* in reading and writing courses. These materials have been newly revised by Barbara Stout and Christine McMahon of Montgomery College and Bette Kalish of Borough of Manhattan College.
- **Freshman Studies courses and seminars:** Part 4 — "*Thinking Critically* and Freshman Studies" — written and revised by Fred Janzow of Southeast Missouri State University, details how to use the text in courses and seminars explicitly devoted to entering freshmen. This section includes a sample syllabus, specific suggestions, and activities designed for the special needs of freshmen students.

The *Manual* concludes with an extensive bibliography.

Acknowledgments

Many people from a variety of disciplines have contributed to this book at various stages of its development over the past fifteen years, and I would like to thank my colleagues for their thorough scrutiny of the manuscript and their incisive and creative comments.

The following reviewers also provided evaluations that were of great help in preparing the fifth edition:

Linda Buyer, Governors State University, IL

Dan Clurman, Golden Gate University, CA

Sylvia Griego, Colorado Mountain College

Sharon Green, D'Youville College, NY

Bette D. Kalash, Borough of Manhattan Community College, NY

Sarah E. Kreps, Tidewater Community College, VA

Sonia Manuel-Dupont, Utah State University

Rosemary Moore, Iowa Western Community College

Victoria F. Sarkisian, Marist College, NY

Verlyne Starr, Oakland Community College, MI

Martha N. Vaught, Wytheville Community College, VA

Christopher J. Zappe, Bucknell University, PA

My grateful acknowledgment is extended to the National Endowment for the Humanities for their generous support of the Critical Thinking and Reasoning Studies program at LaGuardia. In addition, I would like to offer my deepest gratitude to the faculty members who have participated so creatively in the program, to the administrators at LaGuardia for their steadfast support of the program's development, and to the countless students whose enthusiasm and commitment to learning are the soul of this text.

I have been privileged to work with very special people at Houghton Mifflin Company who have respected the purposes of this book while giving it the kind of wise and imaginative attention that every author hopes for. I would like to express my deep appreciation to Dean Johnson, Rosemary Winfield, and Jill Haber.

Finally, I want to thank my wife, Heide, my children, Jessie and Joshua, and my parents, Charlotte and Hubert Chaffee, for their ongoing love, understanding, and support.

Although this is a published book, it continues to be a work in progress. In this spirit, I invite you to share your experiences with the text by sending me your comments and suggestions. I hope that this book serves as an effective vehicle for your own creative and critical thinking resources. Address your letter to me c/o Marketing Services, College Division, Houghton Mifflin Company, 222 Berkeley Street, Boston, MA 02116-3764.

J.C.

Thinking Critically

CHAPTER

1

THINKING

Working Toward Goals
How do goals function in my life?
What is the appropriate goal?
What are the steps and strategies?

THINKING:
An active, purposeful,
organized process that we use
to make sense of the world

Deciding on a Career
What career should I choose?
What are my interests and abilities?
How do I discover the
appropriate career?

Analyzing Issues
What is the issue?
What is the evidence?
What are the arguments?
What is the conclusion?

Making Decisions
What is the decision?
What are the choices?
What are the pros and cons?
What is the best choice?
What is my plan of action?

Thinking can be developed and improved by becoming aware of,
carefully examining, and practicing the thinking process.

THINKING IS THE EXTRAORDINARY PROCESS we use every waking moment to make sense of our world and our lives. Successful thinking enables us to solve the problems we are continually confronted with, to make intelligent decisions, and to achieve the goals that give our lives purpose and fulfillment. It is an activity that is crucial for living in a meaningful way.

This book is designed to help you understand the complex, incredible process of thinking. You might think of this text as a map to guide you in exploring the way your mind operates. This book is also founded on the conviction that you can *improve* your thinking abilities by carefully examining your thinking process and working systematically through challenging activities. Thinking is an active process, and you learn to do it better by becoming aware of and actually using the thought process, not simply by reading about it. By participating in the thinking activities contained in the text and applying these ideas to your own experiences, you will find that your thinking—and language—abilities are becoming sharper and more powerful.

College provides you with a unique opportunity to develop your mind in the fullest sense. Entering college initiates you into a community of people dedicated to learning, and each discipline, or subject area, represents an organized effort to understand some significant dimension of human experience. As you are introduced to various disciplines, you learn new ways to understand the world, and you elevate your consciousness as a result. This book, in conjunction with the other courses in your college experience, will help you become an "educated thinker," expanding your mind and developing your sensibilities.

Becoming an educated thinker will also help you achieve your career goals. In this rapidly evolving world, it is impossible to predict with precision your exact career (or *careers*) or the knowledge and skills that this career will require. But as an educated thinker you will possess the essential knowledge and abilities that will enable you to adapt to whatever your career situation demands. In addition, becoming an educated thinker will elevate your understanding of the world in which you live and help you develop insight into your "self" and that of others, qualities that are essential to high achievement in most careers.

In this chapter we will examine three areas of our lives in which we use the thinking process to understand our world and make informed decisions:

- Working toward goals
- Making decisions
- Analyzing issues

Working Toward Goals

"Ah, but a man's reach should exceed his grasp, / Or what's a heaven for?"

—Robert Browning

My future career goal is to become a professional photographer, working for <u>National Geographic Magazine</u> and traveling around the world. I originally had different dreams, but gradually drifted away from them and lost interest. Then I enrolled in a photography course and loved it. I couldn't wait until the weekend was over to attend class on Monday or to begin my next class project—reactions that were really quite unusual for me! Not everyone is certain at my age about what they would like to become, and I think it is important to discover a career you will enjoy because you are going to spend the rest of your life doing it. I have many doubts, as I think everyone does. Am I good enough? The main thing I fear is rejection, people not liking my work, a possibility that is unavoidable in life. There is so much competition in this world that sometimes when you see someone better at what you do, you can feel inadequate. These problems and obstacles that interfere with my goals will have to be overcome. Rejection will have to be accepted and looked at as a learning experience, and competition will have to be used as an incentive for me to work at my highest level. But through it all, if you don't have any fears, then what do you have? Lacking competition and the possibility of rejection, there is no challenge to life.

As revealed in this student passage, goals play extremely important functions in your life by organizing your thinking and giving your life order and direction. Whether you are preparing food, preparing for an exam, or preparing for a career, goals suggest courses of action and influence your decisions. By performing these functions, goals contribute meaning to your life. They give

Thinking is the extraordinary process we use to solve problems, make intelligent decisions, achieve the goals that give our lives purpose, and connect us to the people in our world.

you something to aim for and lead to a sense of accomplishment when you reach them, like the satisfaction you may have received when you graduated from high school or entered college. It is your thinking abilities that enable you first to identify what your goals are and then to plan how to reach these goals.

Most of your behavior has a purpose or purposes, a goal or goals, that you are trying to reach. You can begin to discover the goals of your actions by asking the question *why* of what you are doing or thinking. For example, answer the following question as specifically as you can:

Why did you come to this class today?

This question may have stimulated any number of responses:

- Because I want to pass this class.
- Because I was curious about the topics to be discussed.
- Because I woke up early and couldn't get back to sleep.

Whatever your response, it reveals at least one of your goals in attending class.

You attempt to make sense of what people, including yourself, are doing by figuring out the goal or purpose of the behavior, by asking for the reason *why*. Asking *why* about an action usually leads to additional *why* questions because a specific goal is generally part of larger goal patterns. As a result, one approach you can use to try to discover your goal patterns is to ask *why* you did something, and then to ask *why* about the answer, and so on. This approach (reminiscent of the maddening *why* game played by children at grownups' expense), can lead to some interesting results, as revealed in the following activity.

Using your response to the question "Why did you come to class today?" as a starting point, try to discover part of your goal patterns by asking a series of *why* questions. After each response, ask *why* again. (For example: Why did you come to class today? *Because I want to pass this course.* Why do you want to pass this course? *Because . . .*) Try to give thoughtful and specific answers.

As you may have found in completing the activity, this "child's game" begins to reveal the network of goals that structure your experience and leads you to progressively more profound questions regarding your basic goals in life, such as "Why do I want to be successful?" or "Why do I want a happy and fulfilling life?" These are complex issues that require thorough and ongoing exploration. A first step in this direction is to examine the way your mind works to achieve your goals, which is the "goal" of this section. If you can understand the way your mind functions when you think effectively, then you can use this knowledge to improve your thinking abilities. This in turn will enable you to deal more effectively with new situations you encounter. To begin this process, think about an important goal you have achieved in your life, and then complete Thinking Activity 1.1. Thinking Activities are designed to stimulate your thinking process and provide the opportunity to express your ideas about important topics. By sharing these ideas with your teacher and other members of the class, you are not only expanding your own thinking, you are also expanding theirs. Each student in the class has a wealth of experiences and insights to offer to the class community.

Successful thinkers are able to envision a detailed picture of their future goals and construct a specific practical plan to achieve their goals.

THINKING ACTIVITY 1.1

1. Describe an important goal you recently achieved.

2. Identify the steps you had to take to achieve this goal in the order in which they were taken, and estimate the amount of time each step took.

3. Describe how you felt when you achieved your goal. ◀

Achieving Short-term Goals

By examining your response to Thinking Activity 1.1, you can see that thinking effectively plays a crucial role in helping us to achieve our goals by enabling us to perform two distinct, interrelated activities:

1. Identifying the appropriate goals
2. Devising effective plans and strategies to achieve your goals

You are involved in this goal-seeking process in every aspect of your daily life. Some of the goals you seek to achieve are more immediate ("short-term") than others: planning your activities for the day or organizing your activities for an upcoming test.

Although achieving these short-term goals seems like it ought to be a manageable process, the truth is your efforts probably meet with varying degrees of success. You may not always achieve your goals for the day, and you might *occasionally* find yourself inadequately prepared for a test. By improving your mastery of the goal-seeking process, you should be able to improve the quality of every area of your life. Let's explore how to do this.

Identify below five short-term goals you would like to achieve in the next week:

Short-term Goals for Next Week

_____

_____

_____

_____

Now *rank* these goals in order of importance, ranging from the goals that are most essential for you to achieve to those that are less significant.

Once this process of identifying and ranking your goals is complete, you can then focus on devising effective plans and strategies to achieve your goals. In order to complete this stage of the goal-seeking process, select the goal that you ranked 1 or 2, and then *list all of the steps* in the order they need to be taken to achieve your goal successfully. After completing this, *estimate how much time* each step will take and plan the step in your daily/weekly schedule. For example, if your goal is to prepare for a quiz in biology, your steps might include:

Goal: Prepare for biology quiz in 2 days

STEPS TO BE TAKEN	TIME INVOLVED	SCHEDULE
1. Xerox the notes for the class I missed last week	20 minutes	after next class
2. Review reading assignments and class notes	2 hours	tonight
3. Make a summary review sheet	1 hour	tomorrow night
4. Study the review sheet	30 minutes	right before quiz

Goal: _____

STEPS TO BE TAKEN	TIME INVOLVED	SCHEDULE
1. _____	_____	_____
2. _____	_____	_____
3. _____	_____	_____
4. _____	_____	_____

METHOD FOR ACHIEVING SHORT-TERM GOALS

Step 1: Identify the goals.
  Identify the short-term goals.
  Rank the goals in order of importance.
  Select the most important goal(s) to focus on.

Step 2: Devise effective plans to achieve your goals.
  List all of the steps in the order in which they should be taken.
  Estimate how much time each step will take.
  Plan the steps in your daily/weekly schedule.

Although this method may seem a little mechanical the first few times you use it, it will soon become integrated into your thinking processes and become a natural and automatic approach to achieving the goals in your daily life. Much of our failure to achieve our short-term goals is due to the fact we skip one or more of the steps in this process. For example, some common thinking errors in seeking our goals include the following:

- We neglect to explicitly identify important goals.
- We concentrate on less important goals first, leaving insufficient time to work on more important goals.
- We don't identify all of the steps required to achieve our goal, or we approach them in the wrong order.
- We underestimate the time each step will take and/or fail to plan the steps in our schedule.

Achieving Long-term Goals

Identifying immediate or "short-term" goals tends to be a fairly simple procedure. Identifying the appropriate "long-term" goals is a much more complex and challenging process: career aims, plans for marriage, paying for children's college, goals for personal development. Think, for example, about the people you know who have full-time jobs. How many of these people get up in the morning excited and looking forward to going to work that day? The unfortunate fact is that many people have not been successful in identifying the most appropriate career goals for themselves, goals that reflect their true interests and talents.

In many areas of life people are often unaware of the most appropriate goals for themselves. For example, people often have goals that are not really their own but have been inherited from someone else. Have you ever been in this position? Consider the following student's experience:

The goal I inherited was to be a nurse. Since my mother was a nurse, she wanted me to be one. In fact, she wanted all of her daughters to be nurses, but they had all tried it and didn't like it at all. She said I would be very happy but I tried and hated it. It's not that I don't like helping others, it's just that it's not for me. I was very confused and didn't know what to do. I finally spoke to her and explained that being a nurse holds no future for me—I'm not happy in that field of work. She was hurt, but better her than me for the rest of my life.

How do you identify the most appropriate long-term goals for yourself? To begin with, you need to develop an in-depth understanding of yourself: your talents, your interests, the things that stimulate you and bring you satisfaction.

You also need to discover what your possibilities are, either through research or actual experience. Of course, your goals do not necessarily remain the same throughout your life. It is unlikely that the goals you had as an eight-year-old are the ones you have now. As you grow, change, and mature, it is natural for your goals to change and evolve as well. The key point is that you should keep examining your goals to make sure that they reflect your own thinking and current interests.

Research studies have shown that high-achieving people are able to envision a detailed, three-dimensional picture of their future in which their goals and aspirations are clearly inscribed. In addition, they are able to construct a mental plan that includes the sequence of steps they will have to take, the amount of time each step will involve, and strategies for overcoming the obstacles they are likely to encounter. Such realistic and compelling concepts of the future enable these people to make sacrifices in the present to achieve their long-term goals. Of course, they may modify these goals as circumstances change and they acquire more information, but they retain a well-defined flexible plan that charts their life course.

On the other hand, research also reveals that people who are low achievers tend to live in the present and the past. Their concepts of the future are vague and ill defined: "I want to be happy," or "I want a high-paying job." This unclear concept of the future makes it difficult for them to identify the most appropriate goals for them, to devise effective strategies for achieving these goals, and to make the necessary sacrifices in the present that will ensure that the future becomes a reality. For example, imagine that you are faced with the choice of studying for an exam or participating in a social activity, what would you do? If you are focusing mainly on the present rather than the future, then the temptation to go out with your friends may be too strong. On the other hand, if you see this exam as connected to a future that is real and extremely important to you, then you are better equipped to sacrifice a momentary pleasant time for your future happiness.

THINKING ACTIVITY 1.2

Apply some of the insights we have been examining about working toward goals to a situation in your own life.

1. Describe as specifically as possible an important longer-term goal that you want to achieve in your life. Your goal can be academic, professional, or personal.

2. Explain the reasons that led you to select the goal that you did and why you believe that your goal makes sense.

3. Identify both the major and minor steps you will have to take to achieve your goal. List your steps in the order they need to be taken and indicate how much time you think each step will take. Make your responses as specific and precise as possible.

4. Identify some of the sacrifices that you may have to make in the present in order to achieve your future goal. ◀

THINKING PASSAGE

In the following passage from his autobiography, Malcolm X, a civil rights activist and black Muslim leader who was assassinated in 1965, describes the steps he took in pursuit of a significant goal while serving time in prison. During his stay at Norfolk Prison Colony, Malcolm X began writing letters to former friends as well as to various government officials. His frustration in trying to express his ideas led him to a course of self-education.

FROM THE AUTOBIOGRAPHY OF MALCOLM X
by Malcolm X with Alex Haley

I became increasingly frustrated at not being able to express what I wanted to convey in letters that I wrote, especially those to Mr. Elijah Muhammad. In the street, I had been the most articulate hustler out there—I had commanded attention when I said something. But now, trying to write simple English, I not only wasn't articulate, I wasn't even functional. How would I sound writing in slang, the way I would *say* it, something such as, "Look, daddy, let me pull your coat about a cat, Elijah Muhammad—"

Many who today hear me somewhere in person, or on television, or those who read something I've said, will think I went to school far beyond the eighth grade. This impression is due entirely to my prison studies.

It had really begun back in the Charlestown Prison, when Bimbi first made me feel envy of his stock of knowledge. Bimbi had always taken charge of any conversation he was in, and I had tried to emulate him. But every book I picked up had few sentences which didn't contain anywhere from one to nearly all of the words that might as well have been in Chinese. When I just skipped those words, of course, I really ended up with little idea of what the book said. So I had come to the Norfolk Prison Colony still going through only book-reading motions. Pretty soon, I would have quit even these motions, unless I had received the motivation that I did.

I saw that the best thing I could do was get hold of a dictionary—to study, to learn some words. I was lucky enough to reason also that I should try to improve my penmanship. It was sad. I couldn't even write in a straight line. It was both ideas together that moved me to request a dictionary along with some tablets and pencils from the Norfolk Prison Colony school.

I spent two days just riffling uncertainly through the dictionary's pages. I'd never realized so many words existed! I didn't know *which* words I needed to learn. Finally, just to start some kind of action, I began copying. In my slow, painstaking, ragged handwriting, I copied into my tablet everything printed on that first page, down to the punctuation marks. I believe it took me a day. Then, aloud, I read back, to myself, everything I'd written on the tablet. Over and over, aloud, to myself, I read my own handwriting.

I woke up the next morning, thinking about those words—immensely proud to realize that not only had I written so much at one time, but I'd written words that I never knew were in the world. Moreover, with a little effort, I also could remember what many of these words meant. I reviewed the words whose meanings I didn't remember. Funny thing, from the dictionary's first page right now, that "aardvark" springs to my mind. The dictionary had a picture of it, a long-tailed, long-eared, burrowing African mammal, which lives off termites caught by sticking out its tongue as an anteater does for ants.

I was so fascinated that I went on—I copied the dictionary's next page. And the same experience came when I studied that. With every succeeding page, I also learned of people and places and events from history. Actually the dictionary is like a miniature encyclopedia. Finally the dictionary's A section had filled a whole tablet—and I went on into the B's. That was the way I started copying what eventually became the entire dictionary. It went a lot faster after so much practice helped me to pick up handwriting speed. Between what I wrote in my tablet, and writing letters, during the rest of my time in prison I would guess I wrote a million words.

I suppose it was inevitable that as my word-base broadened, I could for the first time pick up a book and read and now begin to understand what the book was saying. Anyone who has read a great deal can imagine the new world that opened. Let me tell you something: from then until I left that prison, in every free moment I had, if I was not reading in the library, I was reading on my bunk. You couldn't have gotten me out of books with a wedge. Between Mr. Muhammad's teachings, my correspondence, my visitors—usually Ella and Reginald—and my reading of books, months passed without my even thinking about being imprisoned. In fact, up to then, I never had been so truly free in my life. ■

Questions for Analysis

In describing how he worked toward the goals of becoming literate and knowledgeable, Malcolm X touches on a variety of important issues related to developing thinking and language abilities. We can analyze some of the issues raised by answering the following questions:

1. Malcolm X states that, although he was an articulate "street hustler," this ability was of little help in expressing his ideas in writing. Explain the differences between expressing your ideas orally and in writing, including the advantages and disadvantages of each form of language expression.

2. Malcolm X envied one of the other inmates, Bimbi, because his stock of knowledge enabled him to take charge of any conversation he was in. Explain why knowledge—and our ability to use it—leads to power in our dealings with others. Describe a situation from your own experience in which having expert knowledge about a subject enabled you to influence the thinking of other people.

3. Malcolm X states about pursuing his studies in prison that "up to then, I never had been so truly free in my life." Explain what you think he means by this statement. ◀

MAKING DECISIONS

In order to reach our goals, we have to learn to make the best decisions for ourselves or our community. Although we all make decisions, we don't always make the most *informed* or *intelligent* decisions possible. In fact, most of us regularly have the experience of mentally kicking ourselves because we made a poor decision. For example, think about a decision you made that you would make differently if you had an opportunity to do it over again.

Many of our poor decisions involve relatively minor issues—for example, selecting an unappealing dish in a restaurant, agreeing to go out on a blind date, taking a course that does not meet our expectations. Although these decisions may result in unpleasant consequences, the discomfort is neither life-threatening nor long lasting (although a disappointing course may *seem* to last forever!). However, there are many more significant decisions in our lives in which poor choices can result in considerably more damaging and far-reaching consequences. For example, one reason that the current divorce rate in the United States stands at 50 percent is the poor decisions people make before or after the vows "till death do us part." Similarly, the fact that many employed adults wake up in the morning unhappy about going to their jobs, anxiously waiting for the end of the day and the conclusion of the week (TGIF!) so they are free to do what they *really* want to do, suggests that somewhere along the line they made poor career decisions, or they felt trapped by circumstances they couldn't control. Our jobs should be much more than a way to earn a paycheck—they should be vehicles for using our professional skills, opportunities for expressing our creative talents, stimulants to our personal growth and intellectual development, and experiences that provide us with feelings of fulfillment and self-esteem. In the final analysis, our careers are central elements of our lives and important dimensions of our life-portraits. Our career decision is one that we better try to get right!

An important part of becoming an educated thinker is learning to make effective decisions. Let's explore the process of making effective decisions and then apply your knowledge to the challenge of deciding on the most appropriate career for yourself.

THINKING ACTIVITY 1.3

1. Think back on an important decision that you made that turned out well, and describe the experience as specifically as possible.

2. Reconstruct the reasoning process that you used to make your decision. Did you:
   - Clearly define the decision to be made and the related issues?
   - Consider various choices and anticipate the consequences of these various choices?
   - Gather additional information to help in your analysis?
   - Evaluate the various pros and cons of different courses of action?
   - Use a chart or diagram to aid in your deliberations?
   - Create a specific plan of action to implement your ideas?
   - Periodically review your decision to make necessary adjustments? ◀

An Organized Approach to Making Decisions

As you reflected on the successful decision you wrote about in Thinking Activity 1.3, you probably noticed your mind working in a more or less systematic way as you thought your way through the decision situation. Of course, we often make important decisions with less thoughtful analysis by acting impulsively or relying on our "intuition." Sometimes these decisions work out well,

People who approach decision situations thoughtfully and analytically tend to be more successful decision makers than people who don't.

but often they don't, and we are forced to live with the consequences of these mistaken choices. People who approach decision situations thoughtfully and analytically tend to be more successful decision-makers than people who don't. Naturally there are no guarantees that a careful analysis will lead to a successful result—there are often too many unknown elements and factors beyond our control. But we can certainly improve our success rate as well as our speed by becoming more knowledgeable about the decision-making process. Expert decision-makers can typically make quick, accurate decisions based on intuitions that are informed, not merely impulsive. However, as with most complex abilities in life, we need to learn to "walk" before we can "run," so let's explore a versatile and effective approach for making decisions.

The decision-making approach we will be using consists of five steps. As you gradually master these steps, they will become integrated into your way of thinking, and you will be able to apply them in a natural and flexible way.

Step 1: Define the Decision Clearly.   This seems like an obvious step, but a lot of decision-making goes wrong at the starting point. For example, imagine that you decide that you want to have a "more active social life" (or perhaps a *"less* active social life"). The problem with this characterization of your decision is it defines the situation too generally and so doesn't give any clear direction for your analysis. Do you want to develop an intimate, romantic relationship? Do you want to cultivate more close friendships? Do you want to engage in more social activities? Do you want to meet new people? In short, there are many ways to define more clearly the decision to have a "more active social life." The more specific your definition of the decision to be made, the clearer will be your analysis and the greater the likelihood of success.

Strategy: *Write a one-page analysis that articulates your decision-making situation as clearly and specifically as possible.*

Step 2: Consider All the Possible Choices.   Successful decision-makers explore all of the possible choices in their situation, not simply the obvious ones. In fact, the less obvious choices often turn out to be the most effective. For example, a student in a recent class of mine couldn't decide whether he should major in accounting or business management. In discussing his situation with other members of the class, he revealed that his real interest was in the area of graphic design and illustration. Although he was very talented, he considered this area to be only a hobby, not a possible career choice. Class members pointed out to him this might turn out to be his best career choice, but he needed first to *see* it as a possibility.

Strategy: *List as many possible choices for your situation as you can, both obvious and not obvious. Ask other people for additional suggestions, and don't censor or prejudge any ideas.*

Step 3: Gather All Relevant Information and Evaluate the Pros and Cons of Each Possible Choice.   In many cases you may lack sufficient information to make an informed choice regarding a challenging, complex decision. Unfortunately, this doesn't prevent people from plunging ahead anyway, making a decision that is often more a gamble than an informed choice. Instead of this questionable approach, it makes a lot more sense to seek out the information you need in order to determine which of the choices you identified has the best chance for success. For example, in the case of the student mentioned in Step 2, there is important information he would need to secure in order to determine whether he should consider a career in graphic design and illustration, including: What are the specific careers within this general field? What sort of academic preparation and experience is required for the various careers? What are the prospects for employment in these areas, and how well do they pay?

Strategy: For each possible choice that you identified, create questions regarding information you need to find out, and then locate that information.

In addition to locating all relevant information, each of the possible choices you identified has certain advantages and disadvantages, and it is essential that you analyze these pros and cons in an organized fashion. For example, in the case of the student described earlier, the choice of pursuing a career in accounting may have advantages like ready employment opportunities, the flexibility of working in many different situations and geographical locations, moderate-to-high income expectations, and job security. On the other hand, disadvantages might include the fact that accounting may not reflect a deep and abiding interest of the student, he might lose interest over time, or the career might not result in the personal challenge and fulfillment that he seeks.

Strategy: Using a format similar to that outlined in the following worksheet, analyze the pros and cons of each of your possible choices.

Define the decision:

_____

Possible choices	Information needed	Pros	Cons
1. _____	_____	_____	_____
2. _____	_____	_____	_____

(Etc.)

Step 4: Select the Choice That Seems to Best Meet the Needs of the Situation. The first four steps of this approach are designed to help you *analyze* your decision situation: to clearly define the decision, generate possible choices, gather relevant information, and evaluate the pros and cons of the choices you identified. In the final step, you must attempt to *synthesize* all that you have learned, weaving together all of the various threads into a conclusion that you believe to be your "best" choice. How do you do this? There is no one simple way to identify your "best" choice, but there are some useful strategies for guiding your deliberations.

Strategy: Identify and prioritize the goal(s) of your decision situation and determine which of your choices best meets these goals. This process will probably involve reviewing and perhaps refining your definition of the decision situation. For example, in the case of the student that we have been considering, some goals might include choosing a career that will:

(a) provide financial security

(b) provide personal fulfillment

(c) make use of special talents

(d) offer plentiful opportunities and job security

Once identified, the goals can be ranked in order of their priority, which will then suggest what the "best" choice will be. For example, if the student ranks goals (a) and (d) at the top of the list, then a choice of accounting or business administration might make sense. On the other hand, if the student ranks goals (b) and (c) at the top, then pursuing a career in graphic design and illustration might be the best selection.

Strategy: Anticipate the consequences of each choice by "preliving" the choices. Another helpful strategy for deciding on the best choice is to project yourself into the future, imagining as realistically as you can the consequences of each possible choice. As with previous strategies, this process is aided by writing your thoughts down and discussing them with others.

Step 5: Implement a Plan of Action and Then Monitor the Results, Making Necessary Adjustments.   Once you have selected what you consider your best choice, you need to develop and implement a specific, concrete plan of action. As was noted in the section on short-term goals, the more specific and concrete your plan of action, the greater the likelihood of success. For example, if the student in the case we have been considering decides to pursue a career in graphic design and illustration, his plan should include reviewing the major that best meets his needs, discussing his situation with students and faculty in that department, planning the courses he will be taking, and perhaps speaking to people in the field.

Strategy: Create a schedule that details the steps you will be taking to implement your decision and a time line for taking these steps.

Naturally your plan is merely a starting point for implementing your decision. As you actually begin taking the steps in your plan, you will likely discover that changes and adjustments need to be made. In some cases, you may find that, based on new information, the choice you selected appears to be the wrong one. For example, as the student we have been discussing takes courses in graphic design and illustration, he may find that his interest in the field is not as serious as he thought, and that although he likes this area as a hobby, he does not want it to be his life work. In this case, he should return to considering his other choices, and perhaps adding additional choices that he did not consider before.

Strategy: *After implementing your choice, evaluate its success by identifying what's working and what isn't, and make the necessary adjustments to improve the situation.*

METHOD FOR MAKING DECISIONS

Step 1: Define the decision clearly.

Strategy: *Write a one-page analysis that articulates your decision-making situation as clearly and specifically as possible.*

Step 2: Consider all the possible choices.

Strategy: *List as many possible choices for your situation as you can, both obvious and not obvious. Ask other people for additional suggestions, and don't censor or prejudge any ideas.*

Step 3: Gather all relevant information and evaluate the pros and cons of each possible choice.

Strategy: *For each possible choice you identified, create questions regarding information you need to find out, and then locate that information.*

Strategy: *Using a format similar to the decision-making worksheet on page 17, analyze the pros and cons of each of your possible choices.*

Step 4: Select the choice that seems to best meet the needs of the situation.

Strategy: *Identify and prioritize the goal(s) of your decision situation and determine which of your choices best meets these goals.*

Strategy: *Anticipate the consequences of each choice by "preliving" the choices.*

Step 5: Implement a plan of action and then monitor the results, making necessary adjustments.

Strategy: *Create a schedule that details the steps you will be taking to implement your decision and a time line for taking these steps.*

Strategy: *After implementing your choice, evaluate its success by identifying what's working and what isn't, and make the necessary adjustments to improve the situation.*

THINKING ACTIVITY 1.4

1. Describe an important decision in your academic or personal life that you will have to make in the near future.

2. Using the five-step decision-making approach we just described, analyze your decision and conclude with your "best" choice.

3. Share your analysis with other members of the class and listen carefully to the feedback they give you. ◀

DECIDING ON A CAREER

> "Work is a search for daily meaning as well as daily bread, for recognition as well as cash . . . in short, for a life rather than a Monday through Friday sort of dying."
>
> —Studs Turkel, *Working*

"What are you going to be when you grow up?" You have undoubtedly been asked this pivotal question many times throughout your life by well intentioned adults. As children, this question is fun to contemplate, because life is an adventure and the future is unlimited. However, now that you are "grown up," this question may elicit more anxiety than enjoyment. "What am I going to be?" *Who* am I going to be?" Enrolling in college is certainly an intelligent beginning. The majority of professional careers require a college education. And the investment is certainly worthwhile in monetary terms: the average college graduate can expect lifetime earnings of $830,000 more than peers who don't go beyond high school—and $600,000 more than those who start college but don't graduate. *(Occupational Outlook Quarterly,* 1995). But having entered college, many students' reaction is "Now what?"

Perhaps you are entering college right out of high school, or perhaps you are returning to college after raising a family, working in a variety of jobs, or serving in the armed forces. The question is the same: "What is the right decision to make about your career future?" Some people have no idea how to answer this question; others have a general idea about a possible career (or careers) but aren't sure exactly which career they want or precisely how to achieve their career goals. Even if you feel sure about your choice, it makes sense to engage in some serious career exploration to ensure that you fully understand your interests and abilities as well as the full range of career choices that match up with your talents.

Most students entering college will change their majors a number of times before graduating. (This author changed his major two weeks after entering college!) Although many students are concerned that these changes reveal instability and confusion, in most cases they are a healthy sign. The changes suggest that students are actively engaged in the process of career exploration: considering possible choices, trying them out, and revising their thinking to try another possibility. Often we learn as much from discovering what we *don't* want as from what we do want. The student who plans to become a veterinarian may end up concluding that "I never want to see a sick animal the rest of my life," as one of my students confided after completing a three-month internship at a veterinary hospital.

The best place to begin an intelligent analysis of your career future is by completing a review of what you already know about your career orientation. Your personal history contains clues regarding which career directions are most appropriate for you. By examining the careers you have considered in your life, and by analyzing the reasons that have motivated your career choices, you can begin creating a picture of yourself that will help you define a fulfilling future. With these considerations in mind, complete the following activity as a way to begin creating your own individual "career portrait. " Start by describing two careers that you have considered for yourself in the past few years along with the reason(s) for your choices, and then complete the following Thinking Activity.

THINKING ACTIVITY 1.5

Describe in a two-page paper your *current* thoughts and feelings about your career plans. Be very honest, and include the following:

1. A specific description of the career(s) you think you might enjoy
2. A description of the history of this choice(s) and the reasons why you think you would enjoy it (them)
3. The doubts, fears, and uncertainties you have concerning your choice(s)
4. The problems you will have to solve and the challenges you will have to overcome in order to achieve your career goal. ◀

Too often, people choose careers for the wrong reasons, including the following:

- They consider only those job opportunities with which they are familiar and fail to discover countless other career possibilities.

- They focus on certain elements—such as salary or job security—while ignoring others—like job satisfaction or opportunities for advancement.
- They choose careers because of pressure from family or peers, rather than selecting careers that they really want.
- They drift into a job by accident or circumstance and never reevaluate their options.
- They fail to understand fully their abilities and long-term interests, and what careers will match these.
- They don't pursue their "dream jobs" because they are afraid that they will not succeed.
- They are reluctant to give up their current unsatisfactory job for more promising possibilities because of the risk and sacrifice involved.

Whatever the reasons, the sad fact is that too many people wind up with dead-end, unsatisfying jobs that seem more like lifetime prison sentences than their "field of dreams." However, such depressing outcomes are not inevitable. This text is designed to help you develop the thinking abilities, knowledge, and insight you will need to achieve the appropriate career.

Where Are You?

Your third grade
teacher said
you had a problem
with math.
You gave up on
math, and you forever
eliminated two-thirds
of the jobs
available in
this world.
Somebody
decided the
Navy needed
a cook.
After your
hitch, you opened
a restaurant.
Mother was a nurse
Now you are.
Why are you
where you are?

Because *you* want
to be there?
Think about it.
Maybe you
ought to be
somewhere else.
Maybe it's
not too late
to figure out
where, and how
to get there.

Source: United Technologies Corporation, Hartford, CT, 1984.

Creating Your Dream Job

One of the powerful thinking abilities you possess is the capacity to think imaginatively. In order to discover the career that is right for you, it makes sense to use your imagination to create an image of the job that you believe would make you feel most fulfilled. Too often people settle for less than they have to, because they don't believe they have any realistic chance to achieve their dreams. Using this self-defeating way of thinking virtually guarantees failure in a career quest. Another thinking error occurs when people decide to pursue a career simply because it pays well, even though they have little interest in the work itself. This approach overlooks the fact that in order to be successful over a long period of time, you must be continually motivated—otherwise you may "run out of gas" when you most need it. Interestingly enough, when people pursue careers that reflect their true interests, their success often results in financial reward because of their talent and accomplishments, even though money wasn't their main goal!

So the place to begin your career quest is with your dreams, not your fears. In order to get started, it's best to imagine an ideal job in as much detail as possible. Of course, any particular job is only one possibility within the field of your career choice. It is likely that you will have a number of different jobs as you pursue your career. However, your imagination works more effectively when conjuring up *specific* images, rather than images in general. Begin this exploratory process by providing a brief but detailed description of your ideal job, including the following dimensions:

1. *Physical setting or environment* in which you would like to spend your working hours.

2. *Types of activities or responsibilities you* would like to spend your time doing.

3. *Kinds of people you* would like to be working with.

4. *Personal goals and accomplishments you* would like to achieve as part of your work.

Of course, these initial responses are merely the first step toward giving your career exploration a genuine and appropriate direction. There is a great deal of thinking, research, and action required in order to transform your dreams into reality. The ancient Chinese proverb advises that the journey of a thousand miles begins with just one step. We might add that in order to reach your desired destination, you must make sure that first step is in the right direction!

THINKING ACTIVITY 1.6

Using your preceding responses as a guide, write a two-page description of your ideal job. Spend time letting your imagination conjure up a specific picture of your job, and don't let negative impulses ("I could never get a job like that!") interfere with your creative vision. Be sure to address each of the four dimensions of your ideal job: (1) physical setting and environment (2) activities and responsibilities (3) people, and (4) personal goals and accomplishments. ◀

Discovering "Who" You Are

Each of us possesses an original combination of interests, abilities, and values that characterizes our personality. Discovering the appropriate career for yourself involves becoming familiar with your unique qualities: the activities that interest you, the special abilities and potentials you have, and the values that define the things you consider to be most important. Once you have a reasonably clear sense of "who" you are and what you are capable of, you can then begin exploring those careers that are a good match for you. However, developing a clear sense of "who" you are is a challenging project and is one of the key goals of this text. Many people are still in the early stages of self-understanding, and this makes identifying the appropriate career particularly difficult.

What Are Your Interests?

In order to find a career that will be stimulating and rewarding to you over the course of many years, you must choose a field that involves activities that you

Discovering the appropriate career for yourself involves becoming familiar with your unique qualities: the activities that interest you, the special abilities you possess, and the values you consider to be most important.

have a deep and abiding interest in performing. If you want to be a teacher, you should find helping people learn to be an inspiring and fulfilling activity. If you want to be an architect, you should find the process of creating designs, working with others, and solving construction problems to be personally challenging activities. When people achieve a close match between their natural interests and the activities that constitute a career, they are assured of working in a profession that will bring them joy and satisfaction.

Achieving a positive match between your natural interests and potential careers means first identifying what your natural interests actually are. Each of us has many interests, and many of these do not appear directly relevant to our career decisions. However, if we examine the situation more closely, we can see that the many interests that we pursue form *patterns* of interests that are very relevant to our career decisions. For example, identify possible careers for the people who list the following interests, and explain your reasons why:

- I enjoy listening to my friends' problems and trying to help them figure out the best thing for them to do.
- I have volunteered to work at an organization devoted to helping young people with substance abuse problems.

- I am particularly interested in the psychology courses I have taken because I find the human personality to be incredibly fascinating.

- When I read the newspaper, I always begin with the business section.
- I have always enjoyed selling products to others—Christmas cards, Girl Scout cookies—and I have always been very successful!
- I have always dreamed of owning my own business and have even drawn up plans for exactly how it's going to work.
- I find that the more business courses I take, the more I want to take.
- I worked on the school newspaper and was responsible for all of the layout and design.

- Art has always been a major interest for me, and I have drawn and painted for as long as I remember. I feel that art enables me to express my creative ideas.
- I am fascinated by the designs of products and advertising for them. I have a large collection of particularly unusual and effective examples.
- I have always excelled in my art courses, particularly design classes. They just seem to come naturally to me.

Although there is not necessarily a direct connection between interests and eventual career, carefully examining your interests should nevertheless provide you with valuable clues in discovering a career that will bring lifelong satisfaction.

THINKING ACTIVITY 1.7

1. Create a listing of the interests in your life, describing each one as specifically as possible. Begin with the present and work backward as far as you can remember, covering the areas of *employment, education,* and *general activities.* Make the listing as comprehensive as you can, including as many interests as you can think of. (Don't worry about duplication.) Ask people who know you how they would describe your interests.

2. Once you have created your list, classify the items into groups based on similarity. Don't worry if the same interest fits in more than one group.

3. For each group you have created, identify possible careers that might be related to the interests described in the group.

4. A student example is included below.

Interest Group #1

- I enjoy helping people solve their problems.
- I am interested in subjects like hypnotism and mental therapy.
- I have always been interested in the behavior of people.
- I enjoy reading books on psychology.

Possible Careers: clinical psychologist, occupational therapist, social worker, gerontologist, behavioral scientist, community mental health worker, industrial psychologist

Interest Group #2

- I am interested in the sciences, especially chemistry and anatomy.
- I like going to hospitals and observing doctors and nurses at work.
- When I was in high school, I always enjoyed biology and anatomy labs.
- I am interested in hearing about people's illnesses and injuries.

Possible Careers: doctor, nurse, physical therapist, paramedic, biomedical worker, chemical technician, mortician, medical laboratory technician

Interest Group #3

- I enjoy going to museums and theaters.
- I enjoy painting and drawing in my free time.
- I enjoy listening to music: classical, jazz, and romantic.
- I enjoy reading magazines like *Vogue, Vanity Fair, Vanidades.*

Possible Careers: actor, publicist, advertising executive, interior designer, fashion designer ◀

What Are Your Abilities?

In general, the activities that you have a sustained interest in over a period of time are activities that you are good at. This is another key question for you to address as you pursue your career explorations: "What are the special abilities and talents that I possess?" Each of us has a unique combination of special talents, and it is to our advantage to select careers that utilize these natural abilities. Otherwise, we will find ourselves competing against people who *do* have natural abilities in that particular area. For example, think of those courses you have taken that seemed extremely difficult despite your strenuous efforts, while other students were successful with apparently much less effort (or, conversely, those courses that seemed easily manageable to you while other students were struggling). There is a great deal of competition for *desirable* careers, and if we are to be successful, we need to be able to use our natural strengths.

I once gave a simulated job interview to a woman who was majoring in business. She possessed wonderful social skills—she was personable, articulate, and engaging—but when reviewing her transcript, it was clear that she had done poorly in most of her business courses while performing very well in a variety of liberal arts courses. When I asked about her academic record, she responded, "I guess I just don't have a head for numbers." Unfortunately, if someone is to excel in business, it is important for her to have a "head for numbers," or she will likely be seriously handicapped in her career growth. On the other hand, the student clearly had exceptional abilities in other areas that her career direction might not make full use of.

How do you go about identifying your natural abilities? One productive approach to begin identifying your abilities is to examine important accomplishments in your life, a strategy described in Thinking Activity 1.8. In addition, there are career counselors, books, and computer software programs that can help you zero in on your areas of interest and strength. However, we sometimes possess unknown abilities that we simply haven't had the opportunity to discover and use. With this in mind, it makes sense for you to explore unfamiliar areas of experience to become aware of your full range of potentials.

THINKING ACTIVITY 1.8

1. Identify the ten most important accomplishments in your life. From this list of ten, select three accomplishments of which you are most proud. Typically, these will be experiences in which you faced a difficult challenge or complex problem that you were able to overcome with commitment and talent.

2. Compose a specific and detailed description (one to two pages) of each of these three accomplishments, paying particular attention to the skills and strategies you used to meet the challenge or solve the problem.

3. After completing the descriptions, identify the abilities which you displayed in achieving your accomplishments. Then place them into groups, based on their similarity to one another. A student example is included below.

Accomplishments:

1. Graduating from high school
2. Getting my real estate license
3. Succeeding at college
4. Owning a dog
5. Winning a swim team championship

6. Moving into my own apartment
7. Finding a job
8. Getting my drivers' license

9. Buying a car
10. Learning to speak another
    language

Accomplishment #1: Graduating from High School

The first accomplishment I would like to describe was graduating from high school. I never thought I would do it. In the eleventh grade I became a truant. I only attended classes in my major, after which I would go home or hang out with friends. I was having a lot of problems with my parents and the guy I was dating, and I fell into a deep depression in the middle of the term. I decided to commit suicide by taking pills. I confided this to a friend, who went and told the principal. I was called out of class to the principal's office. He said he wanted to talk to me, and it seemed like we talked for hours. Suddenly my parents walked in with my guidance counselor, and they joined the discussion. We came to the conclusion that I would live with my aunt for two weeks, and I would also speak with the counselor once a day. If I didn't follow these rules they would place me in a group home. During those two weeks I did a lot of thinking. I didn't talk to anyone from my neighborhood. Through counseling I learned that no problems are worth taking your life. I joined a peer group in my school, which helped me a lot as well. I learned to express my feelings. It was very difficult to get back into my schedule in school, but my teachers' help made it easier. I committed myself to school and did very well, graduating the following year.

Abilities/Skills from Accomplishment #1:

- I learned how to analyze and solve difficult problems in my life.
- I learned how to understand and express my feelings.
- I learned how to work with other people in order to help solve each other's problems.
- I learned how to focus my attention and work with determination for a goal.
- I learned how to deal with feelings of depression and think positively about myself and my future. ◀

Finding the Right Match

The purpose of these past few sections has been to help you use your thinking abilities to begin identifying your interests, abilities, and values. Discovering who you are is one part of identifying an appropriate career. The second part involves researching the careers that are available in order to determine which ones match up with your interests, abilities, and values. There are literally thousands of different careers, most of which you probably have only a vague notion about. How do you find out about them? There are a number of tools at your disposal. To begin with, your college probably has a career resource center that likely contains many reference books, periodical publications, videotapes, and software programs describing various occupations. Career counselors are also available either at your school or in your community. Speaking to people working in various careers is another valuable way to learn about what is really involved in a particular career. Work internships, summer jobs, and volunteer work are other avenues for learning about career possibilities and whether they might be right for you.

As you begin your career explorations, don't lose sight of the fact that your career decisions will likely evolve over time, reflecting your growth as a person and the changing job market. Many people alter their career paths often, so you should avoid focusing too narrowly. Instead, concentrate on preparing for broad career areas and developing your general knowledge and abilities. For example, by learning to think critically, solve problems, make intelligent decisions, and communicate effectively, you are developing the basic abilities needed in virtually any career. As an "educated thinker" you will be able to respond quickly and successfully to the unplanned changes and unexpected opportunities that you encounter as you follow—and create—the unfolding path of your life.

Discovering the right career is an adventure that involves careful analysis, comprehensive research, and patience. For the people who are willing and able to embark on this adventure, the result will be a career which will bring them a lifetime of challenges, accomplishments, and rewards. Instead of saying TGIF, you may actually say TGIM (Thank God it's Monday!).

ANALYZING ISSUES

We live in a complex world filled with challenging and often perplexing issues that we are expected to make sense of. For example, the media informs us every

As educated thinkers we have an obligation to develop informed, intelligent opinions about the complex issues in our lives so that we can function as responsible citizens.

day of issues related to abortion, AIDS, animal experimentation, budget priorities, child custody, crime and punishment, the death penalty, drugs, euthanasia, foreign policy, gender roles, genetic engineering, human rights, insider trading, international conflicts, environmental pollution, poverty, moral values, pornography, individual rights, racism, religion and the state, reproductive technology, right to die, sex education, surrogate motherhood, and many others. Often these broad social issues intrude into our own personal lives, taking them from the level of abstract discussion into our immediate experience. As effective thinkers, we have an obligation to develop informed, intelligent opinions about these issues so that we can function as responsible citizens and also make appropriate decisions when confronted with these issues in our lives.

Almost everyone has opinions about these and other issues. Some opinions, however, are more informed and well supported than others. To make sense of complex issues, we need to bring to them a certain amount of background knowledge and an integrated set of thinking and language abilities. One of the central goals of this book is to help you develop the knowledge and sophisticated thinking and language abilities needed to analyze a range of complex issues.

What Is the Issue?

Many social issues are explored, analyzed, and evaluated through our judicial system. Imagine that you have been called for jury duty and subsequently impaneled on a jury that is asked to render a verdict on the following situation. (*Note:* This fictional case is based on an actual case that was tried in May 1990, in Minneapolis, Minnesota.)

> On January 23, the defendant, Mary Barnett, left Chicago to visit her fiancé in San Francisco. She left her six-month-old daughter, Alison, unattended in the apartment. Seven days later, Mary Barnett returned home to discover that her baby had died of dehydration. She called the police and initially told them that she had left the child with a baby sitter. She later stated that she knew she had left the baby behind, that she did not intend to come back, and that she knew Alison would die in a day or two. She has been charged with the crime of second-degree murder: intentional murder without premeditation. If convicted, she could face up to eighteen years in jail.

As a member of the jury, your role is to hear and weigh the evidence, evaluate the credibility of the witnesses, analyze the arguments presented by the prosecution and defense, determine whether the law applies specifically to this situation, and render a verdict on the guilt or innocence of the defendant. To perform these tasks with clarity and fairness, you will have to use a variety of sophisticated thinking and language abilities. To begin with, describe your initial assessment of whether the defendant is innocent or guilty and explain your reasons for thinking so.

As part of the jury selection process, you are asked by the prosecutor and defense attorney whether you will be able to set aside your initial reactions or preconceptions to render an impartial verdict. Identify any ideas or feelings related to this case that might make it difficult for you to view it objectively. Are you a parent? Have you ever had any experiences related to the issues in this case? Do you have any preconceived views concerning individual responsibility in situations like this? Then evaluate whether you will be able to go beyond your initial reactions to see the situation objectively, and explain how you intend to accomplish this.

What Is the Evidence?

The evidence at judicial trials is presented through the testimony of witnesses called by the prosecution and the defense. As a juror, your job is to absorb the information being presented, evaluate its accuracy, and assess the reliability of the individuals giving the testimony. The following are excerpts of testimony from some of the witnesses at the trial. Witnesses for the prosecution are presented first, followed by witnesses for the defense.

Caroline Hospers: On the evening of January 30, I was in the hallway when Mary Barnett entered the building. She looked distraught and didn't have her baby Alison with her. A little while later the police arrived and I discovered that she had left poor little Alison all alone to die. I'm not surprised this happened. I always thought that Ms. Barnett was a disgrace—I mean, she didn't have a husband. In fact, she didn't even have a steady man after that sailor left for California. She had lots of wild parties in her apartment and that baby wasn't taken care of properly. Her garbage was always filled with empty whiskey and wine bottles. I'm sure that she went to California just to party and have a good time, and didn't give a damn about little Alison. She was thinking only of herself. It's obvious that she is entirely irresponsible and was not a fit mother.

Policeman A: We were called to the defendant's apartment at 11 P.M. on January 30 by the defendant, Mary Barnett. Upon entering the apartment, we found the defendant holding the deceased child in her arms. She was sobbing and was obviously extremely upset. She stated that she had left the deceased with a baby sitter one week before when she went to California, and had just returned to discover the deceased alone in the apartment. When I asked the defendant to explain in detail what had happened before she left, she stated: "I remember making airline reservations for my trip. Then I tried to find a baby sitter, but I couldn't. I knew that I was leaving Alison alone and that I wouldn't be back for a while, but I had to get to California at all costs. I visited my mother and then left. " An autopsy was later performed that determined that the deceased had died of dehydration several days earlier. There were no other marks or bruises on the deceased.

Dr. Parker: I am a professional psychiatrist who has been involved in many judicial hearings on whether a defendant is mentally competent to stand trial and I am familiar with these legal tests. At the request of the district attorney's office, I interviewed the defendant four times during the last three months. Ms. Barnett is suffering from depression and anxiety, possibly induced by the guilt she feels for what she did. These symptoms can be controlled with proper medication. Based on my interview, I believe that Ms. Barnett is competent to stand trial. She understands the charges against her, the roles of her attorney, the prosecutor, judge and jury, and can participate in her defense. Further, I believe that she was mentally competent on January 23, when she left her child unattended. In my opinion she knew what she was doing and what the consequences of her actions would be. She was aware that she was leaving her child unattended and that the child would be in great danger. I think that she feels guilty for the decisions she made, and that this remorse accounts for her current emotional problems.

To be effective critical thinkers, we should not simply accept information as it is presented. We need to try to determine the accuracy of the information and evaluate the credibility of the people providing the information. Evaluate the credibility of the prosecution witnesses by identifying those factors that led you to believe their testimony and those factors that raised questions in your mind about the accuracy of the information presented. You can use these questions to guide your evaluation:

- What information is the witness providing?
- Is the information *relevant* to the charges?
- Is the witness *credible?* What *biases* might influence the witness's testimony?
- To what extent is the testimony accurate?

As a juror, performing these activities effectively involves using many of the higher-order thinking and language abilities explored in the chapters ahead, including Chapter 4, "Perceiving"; Chapter 5, "Believing and Knowing"; Chapter 6, "Language as a System"; and Chapter 9, "Reporting, Inferring, Judging." Based on the testimony you have heard up to this point, do you think the defendant is innocent or guilty of intentional murder without premeditation? Explain the reasons for your conclusion.

Now let's review testimony from the witnesses for the defense.

Alice Jones: I have known the defendant, Mary Barnett, for over eight years. She is a very sweet and decent woman, and a wonderful mother. Being a single parent isn't easy, and Mary has done as good a job as she could. But shortly after Alison's birth Mary got depressed. Then her fiancé, Tim Stewart, was transferred to California. He's a navy engine mechanic. She started drinking to overcome her depression, but this just made things worse. She began to feel trapped in her apartment with little help raising the baby and few contacts with her family or friends. As her depression deepened, she clung more closely to Tim, who as a result became more distant and put off their wedding, which caused her to feel increasingly anxious and desperate. She felt that she had to go to California to get things straightened out, and by the time she reached that point I think she had lost touch with reality. I honestly don't think she realized that she was leaving Alison unattended. She loved her so much.

Dr. Bloom: Although I have not been involved in judicial hearings of this type, Mary Barnett has been my patient, twice a week for the last four months, beginning two months after she returned from California and was arrested. In my professional opinion, she is mentally ill and not capable of standing trial. Further, she was clearly not aware of what she was doing when she left Alison unattended and should not be held responsible for her action. Ms. Barnett's problems began after the birth of Alison. She became caught in the grip of the medical condition known as postpartum depression, a syndrome that affects many women after the birth of their children, some more severely than others. Women feel a loss of purpose, a sense of hopelessness, and a deep depression. The extreme pressures of caring for an infant create additional anxiety. When Ms. Barnett's fiancé left for California, she felt completely overwhelmed by her circumstances. She turned to alcohol to raise her spirits, but this just exacerbated her condition. Depressed, desperate, anxious, and alcoholic, she lapsed into a serious neurotic state and became obsessed with the idea of reaching her fiancé in California. This single hope was the only thing she could focus on, and when she acted on it she was completely unaware that she was putting her daughter in danger. Since the trial has begun, she has suffered two anxiety attacks, the more severe resulting in a near-catatonic state necessitating her hospitalization for several days. This woman is emotionally disturbed. She needs professional help, not punishment.

Mary Barnett: I don't remember leaving Alison alone. I would never do that if I realized what I was doing. I don't remember saying any of the things that they said I said, about knowing I was leaving her. I have tried to put the pieces together through the entire investigation, and I just can't do it. I was anxious and I was real frightened. I didn't feel like I was in control and it felt like it was getting worse. The world was closing in on me, and I had nowhere to turn. I knew that I had to get to Tim, in California, and that he would be able to fix everything. He was always the one I went to, because I trusted him. I must have assumed that someone was taking care of Alison, my sweet baby. When I was in California I knew something wasn't right, I just didn't know what it was.

Based on this new testimony, do you think that the defendant is innocent or guilty of intentional murder without premeditation? Have your views changed? Explain the reasons for your current conclusion. Evaluate the credibility of the defense witnesses by identifying those factors that led you to believe their testimony and those factors that raised questions in your mind about the accuracy of the information being presented. Use the questions on page 34 as a guide.

What Are the Arguments?

After the various witnesses present their testimony through examination and cross-examination questioning, the prosecution and defense then present their final arguments and summation. The purpose of this phase of the trial is to tie together—or raise doubts about—the evidence that has been presented in order to persuade the jury that the defendant is guilty or innocent. Included here are excerpts from these final arguments.

Prosecution Arguments: Child abuse and neglect is a national tragedy. Every day thousands of innocent children are neglected, abused, and even killed. The parents responsible for these crimes are rarely brought to justice because their victims are usually not able to speak in their own behalf. In some sense, all of these abusers are emotionally disturbed, because it takes emotionally disturbed people to torture, maim, and kill innocent children. But these people are also responsible for their actions and they should be punished accordingly. They don't have to hurt these children. No one is forcing them to hurt these children. They can choose not to hurt these children. If they have emotional problems, they can choose to seek professional help. Saying you hurt a child because you have "emotional problems" is the worst kind of excuse.

The defendant, Mary Barnett, claims that she left her child unattended, to die, because she has "emotional problems," and that she is not responsible for what she did. This is absurd. Mary Barnett is a self-centered, irresponsible, manipulative, deceitful mother, who abandoned her six-month-old daughter to die so that she could fly to San Francisco to party all week with her fiancé. She was conscious, she was thinking, she knew exactly what she was doing, and that's exactly what she told the police when she returned from her little pleasure trip. Now she claims that she can't remember making these admissions to the police, nor can she remember leaving little Alison alone to die. How convenient!

You have heard testimony from her neighbor, Caroline Hospers, that she was considerably less than an ideal mother: a chronic drinker who liked to party rather than devoting herself to her child. You have also heard the testimony of Dr. Parker, who stated that Mary Barnett was aware of what she was doing on the fateful day in January and that any emotional disturbance is the result of her feelings of guilt over the terrible thing she did, and her fear of being punished for it.

Mary Barnett is guilty of murder, pure and simple, and it is imperative that you find her so. We need to let society know that it is no longer open season on our children.

After reviewing these arguments, describe those points you find most persuasive and those you find least persuasive, and then review the defense arguments that follow.

Defense Arguments: The district attorney is certainly correct—child abuse is a national tragedy. Mary Barnett, however, is not a child abuser. You heard the police testify that the hospital found no marks, bruises, or other indications of an abused child. You also heard her friend, Alice Jones, testify that Mary was a kind and loving mother who adored her child. But if Mary Barnett was not a child abuser, then how could she have left her child unattended? Because she had snapped psychologically. The combination of postpartum depression, alcoholism, the pressures of being a single parent, and the loss of her fiancé were too much for her to bear. She simply broke under the weight of all that despair and took off blindly for California, hoping to find a way out of her personal hell. How could she leave Alison unattended? Because she was completely unaware that she was doing so. She had lost touch with reality and had no idea what was happening around her.

You have heard the in-depth testimony of Dr. Bloom, who has explained to you the medical condition of postpartum depression and how this led to Mary's emotional breakdown. You are aware that Mary has had two severe anxiety attacks while this trial has taken place, one resulting in her hospitalization. And you have seen her desperate sobbing whenever her daughter Alison has been mentioned in testimony.

Alison Barnett is a victim. But she is not a victim of intentional malice from the mother who loves her. She is the victim of Mary's mental illness, of her emotional breakdown. And in this sense Mary is a victim also. In this enlightened society we should not punish someone who has fallen victim to mental illness. To do so would make us no better than those societies who used to torture and burn mentally ill people whom they thought were possessed by the devil. Mary needs treatment, not blind vengeance.

After reviewing the arguments presented by the defense, identify those points you find most persuasive and those you find least persuasive.

The process of analyzing and evaluating complex arguments like those presented by the prosecution and defense involves using a number of sophisticated thinking and language abilities we will be exploring in the chapters ahead, including Chapter 2, "Thinking Critically"; Chapter 6, "Language and Thought"; Chapter 10, "Constructing Arguments"; and Chapter 11, "Reasoning Critically."

What Is the Verdict?

Following the final arguments and summations, the judge will sometimes give specific instructions to clarify the issues to be considered. In this case the judge reminds the jury that they must focus on the boundaries of the law and determine whether this case falls within these boundaries or outside them. The jury then retires to deliberate the case and render a verdict.

For a defendant to be found guilty of second-degree murder, the prosecution must prove that he or she intended to kill someone, made a conscious decision to do so at that moment (without premeditation), and was aware of the consequences of his or her actions. In your discussion with the other jurors, you must determine whether the evidence indicates, *beyond a reasonable doubt,* that the defendant's conduct in this case meets these conditions. What does the qualification "beyond a reasonable doubt" mean? A principle like this is always difficult to define in specific terms, but in general the principle means that it would not make good sense for thoughtful men and women to conclude otherwise. The whole area of forming, defining, and applying concepts is a key dimension of thinking effectively and is examined in Chapter 7, "Forming and Applying Concepts."

Based on your analysis of the evidence and arguments presented in this case, describe what you think the verdict ought to be and explain your reasons for thinking so.

Verdict: Guilty _____   Not Guilty _____

THINKING ACTIVITY 1.9

Exploring this activity has given you the opportunity to *analyze* the key dimensions of this complex case. Now *synthesize* your thoughts regarding this case by composing a two-page paper in which you explain the reasons and evidence that influenced your verdict. Be sure to discuss the important testimony and your evaluation of the credibility of the various witnesses. ◄

SUMMARY

The first line of this chapter stated, "Thinking is the extraordinary process we use every waking moment to make sense of our world and our lives." Throughout this chapter we have explored the different ways our thinking enables us to make sense of the world by working toward goals, making decisions, and analyzing issues. Of course, our thinking helps us make sense of the world in other ways as well. When we attend a concert, listen to a lecture, or try to understand someone's behavior, it is our thinking that enables us to figure out what is happening. In fact, these attempts to make sense of what is happening are going on all the time in our lives, and they represent the heart of the thinking process.

If we review the different ways of thinking we have explored in this chapter, we can reach several conclusions about thinking:

1. *Thinking is an **active** process.* Whether we are trying to reach a goal, make a decision, or analyze an issue, we are actively using our minds to figure out the situation.
2. *Thinking is directed toward a **purpose.*** When we think, it is usually for a purpose—to reach a goal, make a decision, or analyze an issue.
3. *Thinking is an **organized** process.* When we think effectively, there is usually an order or organization to our thinking. For each of the thinking activities we explored, we saw that there are certain steps or approaches to take that help us reach goals, make decisions, and analyze issues.

We can put together these conclusions about thinking explored in this chapter to form a working definition of the term.

> **Thinking**   An active, purposeful, organized cognitive process that we use to make sense of our world.

At this point, our definition of *thinking* is too general; we need to specify more exactly what thinking involves. We will continue to define *thinking* as we work through this book. Thinking develops with use over a lifetime, whether we are trying to decide what courses to take in school, which career to pursue, or simply how much to bet on a poker hand. By continuing to develop our thinking abilities, we become even better prepared to make sense of our world, to explore the choices available to us, and to make appropriate decisions.

We can improve our thinking in an organized and systematic way by following these three steps:

1. *Becoming aware of our thinking process.* We usually take thinking for granted and do not pay much attention to it. Developing our thinking means that we have to think about the way we think.
2. *Carefully examining our thinking process and the thinking process of others.* In this chapter we have explored various ways in which our thinking works. By focusing our attention on these (and other) thinking approaches and strategies, we can learn to think more effectively.
3. *Practicing our thinking abilities.* To improve our thinking, we actually have to think for ourselves, to explore and make sense of thinking situations by using our thinking abilities. Although it is important to read about thinking and learn how other people think, there is no substitute for actually doing it ourselves.

The ability to think for ourselves by carefully examining the way that we make sense of the world is one of the most satisfying aspects of being a mature human being. We will refer to this ability to think carefully about our thinking as the ability to *think critically.* Using our definition of *thinking* as a starting point, we can define *thinking critically* as follows.

Thinking Critically	An active, purposeful, organized cognitive process we use to carefully examine our thinking and the thinking of others, in order to clarify and improve our understanding.

We are able to think critically because of our natural human ability to *reflect*—to think back on what we are thinking, doing, or feeling. By carefully thinking back on our thinking, we are able to figure out the way our thinking operates and so learn to do it more effectively. In the following chapters we will be systematically exploring many dimensions of the way our minds work, providing the opportunity to deepen our understanding of the thinking process and stimulating us to become more effective thinkers.

Of course, carefully examining the ideas produced by the thinking process assumes that there are ideas that are worth examining. We produce such ideas by *thinking creatively*, an activity we can define as follows.

Thinking Creatively	An active, purposeful, cognitive process we use to develop ideas that are unique, useful, and worthy of further elaboration.

Examining the creative thinking process is a rich and complex enterprise. Although it is not the primary focus of this book, we will nevertheless be addressing important aspects of the creative thinking process as we explore in depth the critical thinking process. In fact, these two dimensions of the thinking process are so tightly interwoven that both must be addressed together in order to understand them individually. For example, when you imagined your "dream job," you were using your creative thinking abilities to visualize an ideal career situation. With this idea as a starting point, you can use your critical thinking abilities to refine your idea and then research existing career opportunities. Once a clear career goal is established, you can use your creative thinking abilities to generate possible ideas for achieving this goal, while your critical thinking abilities will help you evaluate your various options and devise a practical, organized plan.

It is apparent that creative thinking and critical thinking work as partners to produce productive and effective thinking, enabling us to make informed decisions and lead successful lives. As this text unfolds, you will be given the opportunity to become familiar with both of these powerful forms of thought as you develop your abilities to think both critically and creatively.

THINKING PASSAGE

The following article, "Jurors Hear Evidence and Turn It into Stories," describes recent research that gives us insight into the way jurors think and reason during the process of reaching a verdict. The reasoning process of jurors has come under increasing scrutiny with the controversial verdicts in high-profile cases like Rodney King, O.J. Simpson, William Kennedy Smith, and the Menendez brothers. As you read the article, reflect on the reasoning process you engaged in while thinking about the Mary Barnett case, and then answer the questions found at the end of the article.

Jurors Hear Evidence and Turn It into Stories
by Daniel Goleman

Studies Show They Arrange Details to Reflect Their Beliefs

Despite the furor over the verdict in the Rodney G. King beating case, scientists who study juries say the system is by and large sound. Many also believe that it is susceptible to manipulation and bias, and could be improved in various specific ways suggested by their research findings.

If there is any lesson to be learned from the research finding, it is that juries are susceptible to influence at virtually every point, from the moment members are selected to final deliberation.

Much of the newest research on the mind of the juror focuses on the stories that jurors tell themselves to understand the mounds of disconnected evidence, often presented in a confusing order. The research suggests that jurors' unspoken assumptions about human nature play a powerful role in their verdicts.

"People don't listen to all the evidence and then weigh it at the end," said Dr. Nancy Pennington, a psychologist at the University of Colorado. "They process it as they go along, composing a continuing story throughout the trial that makes sense of what they're hearing."

That task is made difficult by the way evidence is presented in most trials, in an order dictated for legal reasons rather than logical ones. Thus, in a murder trial, the first witness is often a coroner, who establishes that a death occurred.

"Jurors have little or nothing to tie such facts to, unless an attorney suggested an interpretation in the opening statement," in the form of a story line to follow, Dr. Pennington said.

In an article in the November 1991 issue of *Cardozo Law Review*, Dr. Pennington, with Dr. Reid Hastie, also a psychologist at the University of Colorado, reported a series of experiments that show just how important jurors' stories are in determining the verdict they come to. In the studies, people called for jury duty but not involved in a trial were recruited for a simulation in which they were to act as jurors for a murder trial realistically re-enacted on film.

In the case, the defendant, Frank Johnson, had quarreled in a bar with the victim, Alan Caldwell, who threatened him with a razor. Later that evening they went outside, got into a fight, and Johnson knifed Caldwell, who died. Disputed points included whether or not Caldwell was a bully who had started the first quarrel when his girlfriend had asked Johnson for a ride to the racetrack, whether Johnson had stabbed Caldwell or merely held his knife out to protect himself, and whether Johnson had gone home to get a knife.

In detailed interviews of the jurors, Dr. Pennington found that in explaining how they had reached their verdicts, 45 percent of the references they made were to events that had not been included in the courtroom testimony. These included inferences about the men's motives and psychological states, and assumptions the jurors themselves brought to the story from their own experience.

The stories that jurors told themselves pieced together the evidence in ways that could lead to opposite verdicts. One common story among the jurors, which led to a verdict of first-degree murder, was that the threat with the razor by Caldwell had so enraged Johnson that he went home to get his knife—a point that was in dispute—with the intention of picking a fight, during which he stabbed him to death.

By contrast, just as many jurors told themselves a story that led them to a verdict of not guilty: Caldwell started the fight with Johnson and threatened him with a razor, and Caldwell ran into the knife that Johnson was using to protect himself.

Role of Jurors' Backgrounds

The study found that jurors' backgrounds could lead to crucial differences in the assumptions they brought to their explanatory stories. Middle-class jurors were more likely to find the defendant guilty than were working-class jurors. The difference mainly hinged on how they interpreted the fact that Johnson had a knife with him during the struggle.

Middle-class jurors constructed stories that saw Johnson's having a knife as strong evidence that he planned a murderous assault on Caldwell in their second confrontation. But working-class jurors said it was likely that a man like Johnson would be in the habit of carrying a knife with him for protection, and so they saw nothing incriminating about his having the knife.

"Winning the battle of stories in the opening statements may help determine what evidence is attended to, how it is interpreted, and what is recalled both during and after the trial," Dr. Richard Lempert, a psychologist at the University of Michigan Law School, wrote in commenting on Dr. Pennington's article.

Verdicts that do not correspond to one's own "story" of a case are shocking. In the King case, "We didn't hear the defense story of what was going on, but only saw the strongest piece of the prosecution's evidence, the videotape," said Dr. Stephen Penrod, a psychologist at the University of Minnesota Law School. "If we had heard the defense theory, we may not have been so astonished by the verdict."

In the contest among jurors to recruit fellow members to one or another version of what happened, strong voices play a disproportionate role. Most juries include some people who virtually never speak up, and a small number who dominate the discussion, typically jurors of higher social status, according to studies reviewed in *Judging the Jury* (Plenum Press, 1986) by two psychologists, Dr. Valerie Hans of the University of Delaware and Dr. Neil Vidmar of Duke University.

The research also reveals that "juries are more often merciful to criminal defendants" than judges in the same cases would be, said Dr. Hans.

Blaming the Victim

In recent research, Dr. Hans interviewed 269 jurors in civil cases and found that many tended to focus on the ability of victims to have avoided being injured. "You see the same kind of blaming the victim in rape cases, too, especially among female jurors," Dr. Hans said. "Blaming the victim is reassuring to jurors because if victims are responsible for the harm that befell them, then you don't have to worry about becoming a victim yourself because you know what to do to avoid it. "

That tendency may have been at work among the King jurors, Dr. Hans said, "when the jurors said King was in control and that if he stopped moving the police would have stopped beating him."

"Of course, the more they saw King as responsible for what happened, the less the officers were to blame in their minds," Dr. Hans said.

Perhaps the most intensive research has focused on the selection of a jury. Since lawyers can reject a certain number of prospective jurors during jury selection without having to give a specific reason, the contest to win the mind of the jury begins with the battle to determine who is and is not on the jury.

The scientific selection of juries began in the early 1970's when social scientists volunteered their services for the defense in a series of political trials, including proceedings arising from the 1971 Attica prison uprising in upstate New York. One method used was to poll the community where the trial was to be held to search for clues to attitudes that might work against the defendant, which the defense lawyers could then use to eliminate jurors.

For example, several studies have shown that people who favor the death penalty are generally pro-prosecution in criminal cases, and so more likely to convict a defendant. Defense lawyers can ask prospective jurors their views on the death penalty, and eliminate those who favor it.

On the basis of such a community survey for a trial in Miami, Dr. Elizabeth Loftus, a psychologist at the University of Washington, found that as a group, whites trust the honesty and fairness of the police far more than blacks. "If you knew nothing else, you'd use that demographic variable in picking a jury in the King case," she said. "But in Ventura County, there's a jury pool with almost no blacks. It was a gift to the defense, in retrospect."

Over the last two decades, such methods have been refined to the point that 300 or more consulting groups now advise lawyers on jury selection. ■

Questions for Analysis

1. Reflect back on your own deliberations of the Mary Barnett case and describe the reasoning process you used to reach a verdict. Did you find that you were composing a continuing story to explain the testimony you were reading? If so, was this story changed or modified as you learned more information or discussed the case with your classmates?

2. Explain how factors from your own personal experience (age, gender, experience with children, etc.) may have influenced your verdict and the reasoning process that led up to it.

3. Explain how your beliefs about human nature and free will may have influenced your analysis of Mary Barnett's motives and behavior.

4. Explain whether you believe that the research strategies lawyers are using to select the "right" jury for their case are undermining the fairness of the justice system. ◀

2

THINKING CRITICALLY

Carefully
Exploring
Situations
withQuestions

Thinking
Independently

Viewing
Situations from
Different
Perspectives

Supporting
Diverse
Perspectives
with Reasons
and Evidence

THINKING CRITICALLY:
Making sense of the world by
carefully examining the thinking
process to clarify and improve
our understanding

Thinking
Actively

Discussing
Ideas in an
Organized Way

BECOMING A CRITICAL THINKER

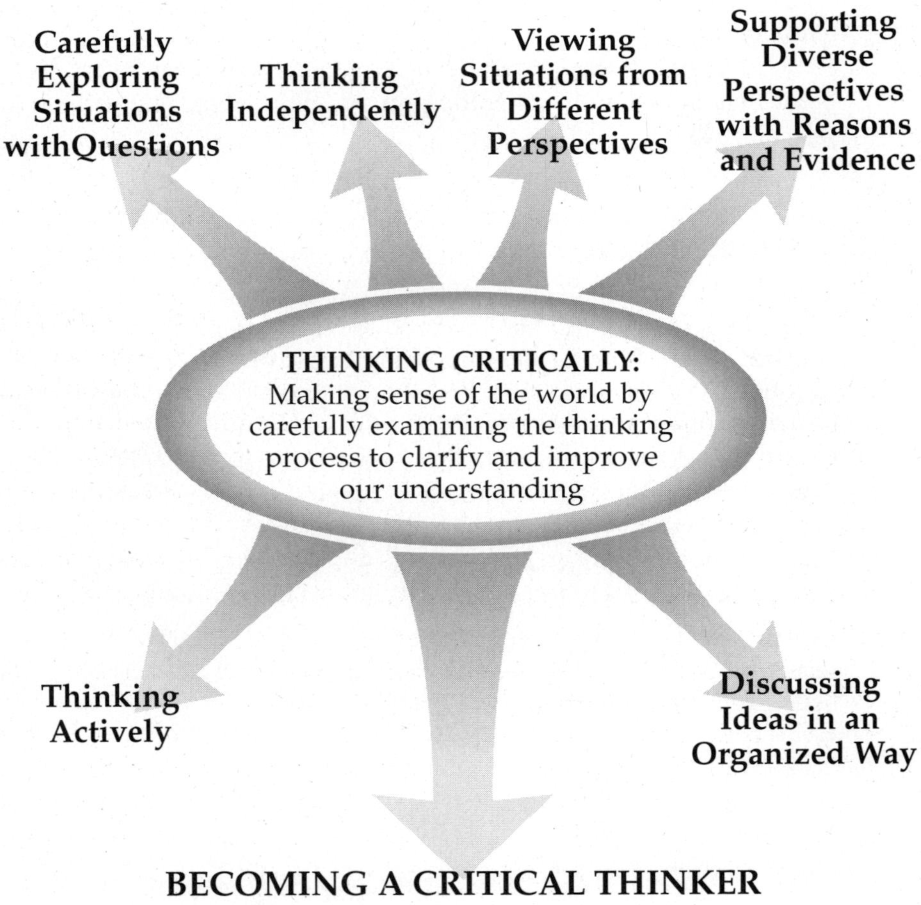

A COLLEGE EDUCATION is the road that can lead you to your life's work, a career that will enable you to use your unique talents to bring you professional fulfillment. However, there are many other benefits to a college education, among them the opportunity to become what we have called an "educated thinker." Becoming an educated thinker is essential for achieving the greatest possible success in your chosen career, and it enriches your life in many other ways as well.

Traditionally, when people refer to an "educated thinker," they mean someone who has developed a knowledgeable understanding of our complex world, a thoughtful perspective on important ideas and timely issues, the capacity for penetrating insight and intelligent judgment, and sophisticated thinking and language abilities. These goals of advanced education have remained remarkably similar for several thousand years. In ancient Greece, most advanced students studied Philosophy in order to achieve "wisdom." (The term *philosophy* in Greek means "lover of wisdom.") In today's world, many college students are hoping through their studies to become the modern-day equivalent: informed, *critical thinkers.*

The word *critical* comes from the Greek word for "critic" *(kritikos)*, which means to question, to make sense of, to be able to analyze. It is by questioning, making sense of situations, and analyzing issues that we examine our thinking and the thinking of others. These critical activities aid us in reaching the best possible conclusions and decisions. The word *critical* is also related to the word *criticize*, which means to question and evaluate. Unfortunately, the ability to criticize is often only used destructively, to tear down someone else's thinking. Criticism, however, can also be *constructive*—analyzing for the purpose of developing a better understanding of what is going on. We will engage in constructive criticism as we develop our ability to think critically.

Thinking is the way you make sense of the world; thinking critically is thinking *about* your thinking so that you can clarify and improve it. If you can understand the way your mind works when you work toward your goals, make informed decisions, and analyze complex issues, then you can learn to think more effectively in these situations. In this chapter you will explore ways to examine your thinking so that you can develop it to the fullest extent possible. That is, you will discover how to *think critically.*

Thinking Critically	An active, purposeful, organized cognitive process we use to carefully examine our thinking and the thinking of others, in order to clarify and improve our understanding.

Critical thinkers possess a knowledgeable understanding of the world, a thoughtful perspective on important ideas, the capacity for intelligent judgment, and sophisticated language abilities.

Becoming a critical thinker transforms you in positive ways by enabling you to become an expert learner, view the world clearly, and make productive choices as you shape your life. Critical thinking is not simply one way of thinking; it is a total approach to understanding how you make sense of a world that includes many parts. This chapter explores the various activities that make up thinking critically, including the following:

- Thinking actively
- Carefully exploring situations with questions
- Thinking independently
- Viewing situations from different perspectives
- Supporting diverse perspectives with evidence and reasons
- Discussing ideas in an organized way

THINKING ACTIVELY

When you think critically, you are *actively* using your intelligence, knowledge, and abilities to deal effectively with life's situations. When you think actively, you are:

- *Getting involved* in potentially useful projects and activities instead of remaining disengaged
- *Taking initiative* in making decisions on your own instead of waiting passively to be told what to think or do
- *Following through* on your commitments instead of giving up when you encounter difficulties
- *Taking responsibility* for the consequences of your decisions rather than unjustifiably blaming others or events "beyond your control"

When you think actively, you are not just waiting for something to happen. You are engaged in the process of achieving goals, making decisions, and solving problems. When you react passively, you let events control you or permit others to do your thinking for you. To make an intelligent decision about your future career, for example, you have to work actively to secure more information, try out various possibilities, speak with people who are experienced in your area of interest, and then critically reflect on all these factors. Thinking critically requires that you think actively—not react passively—to deal effectively with life's situations.

Influences on Your Thinking

As our minds grow and develop, we are exposed to influences that encourage us to think actively. We also, however, have many experiences that encourage us to think passively. For example, some analysts believe that when people, especially children, spend much of their time watching television, they are being influenced to think passively, thus inhibiting their intellectual growth. Listed here are some of the influences we experience in our lives along with space for you to add your own influences. As you read through the list, place an *A* next to those items you believe in general influence you to think *actively*, and a *P* next to those you consider to be generally *passive* influences.

Activities:	*People:*
Reading books	Family members
Writing	Friends
Taking drugs	Employers
Dancing	Advertisers
Drawing/painting	School/college teachers
Playing video games	Police officers
Playing sports	Religious leaders
Listening to music	Politicians

THINKING ACTIVITY 2.1

All of us are subject to powerful influences on our thinking that we are often unaware of. For example, advertisers spend billions of dollars to manipulate our thinking in ways that are complex and subtle.

Select one of your favorite commercials and perform an in-depth analysis of it. If you have a VCR, replay it a number of times, with and without the sound. Explain how each of the commercial's elements—images, language, music—work to influence your thinking. Pay particular attention to the symbolic associations of various images and words, and identify the powerful emotions that these associations elicit. ◀

Of course, in many cases people and activities can act as both active and passive influences, depending on the specifics of situations and our individual responses. For example, consider employers. If we are performing a routine, repetitive job, like the summer I spent in a peanut butter cracker factory hand-scooping 2,000 pounds of peanut butter a day, the very nature of the work tends to encourage passive, uncreative thinking (although it might also lead to creative daydreaming!). We are also influenced to think passively if our employer gives us detailed instructions for performing every task, instructions that permit no exception or deviation. On the other hand, when our employer gives us general areas of responsibility within which we are expected to make thoughtful and creative decisions, then we are being stimulated to think actively and independently.

These contrasting styles of supervision are mirrored in different approaches to raising children. Some parents encourage children to be active thinkers by teaching them to express themselves clearly, make independent decisions, look at different points of view, and choose what they think is right for themselves. Other parents influence their children to be passive thinkers by not letting them do things on their own. These parents give the children detailed instructions they are expected to follow without question, and make the important decisions for them. They are reluctant to give their children significant responsibilities, creating, unintentionally, dependent thinkers who are not well adapted to making independent decisions and assuming responsibility for their lives.

Active learners take initiative in exploring their world, think independently and creatively, and take responsibility for the consequences of their decisions.

Becoming an Active Learner

Critical thinkers actively use their intelligence, knowledge, and abilities to deal with life's situations. Similarly, active thinking is one of the keys to effective learning. Each of us has our own knowledge framework that we use to make sense of the world, a framework that incorporates all that we have learned in our lives. When we learn something new, we have to find ways to integrate this new information or skill into our existing knowledge framework. For example, if one of your professors is presenting material on Sigmund Freud's concept of the unconscious or the role of Heisenberg's uncertainty principle in the theory of quantum mechanics, you need to find ways to relate these new ideas to things you already know in order to make this new information "your own." How do you do this? By actively using your mind to integrate new information into your existing knowledge framework, thereby expanding the framework to include this new information.

For example, when your professor provides a detailed analysis of Freud's concept of the unconscious, you use your mind to call up what you know about Freud's theory of personality and what you know of the concept of the unconscious. You then try to connect this new information to what you already know, integrating it into your expanding knowledge framework. In a way, learning is analogous to the activity of eating: you ingest food (*information*) in one form, actively transform it through digestion (*mental processing*), and then integrate the result into the ongoing functioning of your body.

T HINKING P ASSAGE

Read carefully the passage by Marie Winn located on page 86 at the conclusion of this chapter, which analyzes the processes involved in watching television and reading. Think about whether you agree with the author's analysis, based on your own experiences, and then answer the questions that follow the selection. ◀

C AREFULLY E XPLORING
S ITUATIONS WITH Q UESTIONS

As you have just seen, thinking critically involves actively using your thinking abilities to attack problems, meet challenges, and analyze issues. An important dimension of thinking actively is carefully exploring the situations you are involved in with relevant questions. In fact, the ability to ask appropriate and penetrating questions is one of the most powerful thinking tools you possess, although many people do not make full use of it. Active learners explore the learning situations they are involved in with questions that enable them to understand the material or task at hand, and then integrate this new understanding into their knowledge framework. In contrast, passive learners rarely ask questions. Instead, they try to absorb information like sponges, memorizing what is expected and then regurgitating what they memorized on tests and quizzes.

Questions come in many different forms and are used for a variety of purposes. For instance, questions can be classified in terms of the ways people organize and interpret information, and we can identify six such categories of questions:

1. Fact
2. Interpretation
3. Analysis

4. Synthesis
5. Evaluation
6. Application

Active learners are able to ask appropriate questions from all of these categories in a very natural and flexible way. These various types of questions are closely interrelated and an effective thinker is able to use them in a productive relation to one another. Also, these categories of questions are very general and at times overlap with one another. This means that a given question may be seen to fall into more than one of the six categories of questions. Following is a summary of the six categories of questions along with sample forms of questions from each category.

1. *Questions of Fact:* Questions of fact seek to determine the basic information of a situation: who, what, when, where, how. These questions seek information that is relatively straightforward and objective.

   Who, what, when, where, how _____?

   Describe _____.

2. *Questions of Interpretation:* Questions of interpretation seek to select and organize facts and ideas, discovering the relationships between them. Examples of such relationships include the following:

   - *Chronological relationships:* relating things in time sequence
   - *Process relationships:* relating aspects of growth, development, or change

- *Comparison/contrast relationships:* relating things in terms of their similar/different features
- *Causal relationships:* relating events in terms of the way some events are responsible for bringing about other events

Retell _____ in your own words.

What is the *main idea* of _____?

What is the *time sequence* relating the following events: _____?

What are the steps in the *process of growth* or *development* in _____?

How would you *compare and contrast* the features of _____ and

_____?

What was the *cause* of _____? What was the *effect* of

_____?

3. *Questions of Analysis:* Questions of analysis seek to separate an entire process or situation into its component parts and understand the relation of these parts to the whole. These questions attempt to classify various elements, outline component structures, articulate various possibilities, and clarify the reasoning being presented.

What are the *parts* or *features* of _____?

Classify _____ according to _____.

Outline/diagram/web _____.

What *evidence* can you present to support _____?

What are the *possible alternatives* for _____?

Explain the *reasons why* you think _____.

4. *Questions of Synthesis:* Questions of synthesis have as their goal combining ideas to form a new whole or come to a conclusion, making inferences about future events, creating solutions, and designing plans of action.

What would you *predict/infer* from _____?

What ideas can you *add to* _____?

How would you *create/design* a new _____?

What might happen if you *combined* _____ with

_____?

What *solutions/decisions* would you suggest for_____?

5. *Questions of Evaluation:* The aim of evaluation questions is to help us make informed judgments and decisions by determining the relative value, truth, or reliability of things. The process of evaluation involves identifying the criteria or standards we are using and then determining to what extent the things in common meet those standards.

How would you *evaluate* _____ and what *standards* would you use?

Do you agree with _____? Why or why not?

How would you *decide* about _____?

What *criteria* would you use to *assess* _____?

6. *Questions of Application:* The aim of application questions is to help us take the knowledge or concepts we have gained in one situation and apply them to other situations.

How is _____ *an example* of _____?

How would you *apply* this rule/principle to _____?

Mastering these forms of questions and using them appropriately will serve you as powerful tools in the learning process.

Becoming an expert questioner is an ongoing project, and you can practice it throughout the day. When you are talking to people about even everyday topics, get in the habit of asking questions from all of the different categories. Similarly, when you are attending class, taking notes, reading assignments, make a practice of asking—and trying to answer—appropriate questions. You will find that by actively exploring the world in this way you are discovering a great deal and learning what you have discovered in a meaningful and lasting fashion.

As children, we were natural questioners, but this questioning attitude was often discouraged when we entered the school system. Often we were given the message, in subtle and not so subtle ways, that: "Schools have the questions; your job is to learn the answers." The educator Neil Postman has said: "Children enter schools as question marks and they leave as periods." In order for us to become critical thinkers and effective learners, we have to become question marks again.

THINKING ACTIVITY 2.2

Review the following decision-making situation (based on an incident that happened in Springfield, Missouri, in 1989), and then critically examine it by posing questions from each of the six categories we have considered in this section:

1. Fact   4. Synthesis
2. Interpretation   5. Evaluation
3. Analysis   6. Application

Imagine that you are a member of a student group at your college that has decided to stage the controversial play, *The Normal Heart* by Larry Kramer. The play is based on the lives of real people and dramatizes their experiences in the early stages of the AIDS epidemic. It focuses on their efforts to publicize the horrific nature of this disease and to secure funding from a reluctant federal government to find a cure. The play is considered controversial because of its exclusive focus on the subject of AIDS, its explicit homosexual themes, and the large amount of profanity contained in the script. After lengthy discussion, however, your student group has decided that the educational and moral benefits of the play render it a valuable contribution to the life of the college.

While the play is in rehearsal, a local politician seizes it as an issue and mounts a political and public relations campaign against it. She distributes selected excerpts of the play to the newspapers, religious groups, and civic organizations. She also introduces a bill in the state legislature to withdraw state funding for the college if the play is performed. The play creates a firestorm of controversy, replete with local and national news reports, editorials, and impassioned speeches for and against it. Everyone associated with the play is subjected to verbal harassment, threats, crank phone calls, and hate mail. The firestorm explodes when the house of one of the key spokespersons for the play is burned to the ground. The director and actors go into hiding for their safety, rehearsing in secret and moving from hotel to hotel.

Your student group has just convened to decide what course of action to take. Analyze the situation using the six types of questions listed above and then conclude with your decision and the reasons that support your decision. ◄

THINKING INDEPENDENTLY

Answer the following questions, based on what you believe to be true.

	Yes	No	Not Sure
1. Is the earth flat?			
2. Is there a God?			
3. Is abortion wrong?			
4. Is democracy the best form of government?			
5. Should men be the breadwinners and women the homemakers?			

Your responses to these questions reveal aspects of the way your mind works. How did you arrive at these conclusions? Your views on these and many other issues probably had their beginnings with your family, especially your parents. When we are young, we are very dependent on our parents, and we are influenced by the way they see the world. As we grow up, we learn how to think, feel, and behave in various situations. In addition to our parents, our "teachers" include our brothers and sisters, friends, religious leaders, schoolteachers, books, television, and so on. Most of what we learn we absorb without even being aware of it. Many of your ideas about the issues raised in the

Becoming a critical thinker transforms you in positive ways by enabling you to develop your own well-reasoned viewpoints and to make informed choices.

preceding questions above were most likely shaped by the experiences you had growing up.

As a result of our ongoing experiences, however, our minds—and our thinking—continue to mature. Instead of simply accepting the views of others, we gradually develop the ability to examine this thinking and to decide whether it makes sense to us and whether we should accept it. As we think through such ideas, we use this standard to make our decision: Are there good reasons or evidence that support this thinking? If there are good reasons, we can actively decide to adopt these ideas. If they do not make sense, we can modify or reject them.

Of course, we do not *always* examine our own thinking or the thinking of others so carefully. In fact, we very often continue to believe the same ideas we were brought up with, without ever examining and deciding for ourselves what to think. Or we often blindly reject the beliefs we have been brought up with, without really examining them.

How do you know when you have examined and adopted ideas yourself instead of simply borrowing them from others? One indication of having thought through your ideas is being able to explain *why* you believe them, explaining the reasons that led you to these conclusions.

For each of the views you expressed at the beginning of this section, explain how you arrived at it and give the reasons and evidence that you believe support it.

1. *Example:* Is the earth flat?

   Explanation: I was taught by my parents and in school that the earth was round.

   Reasons/Evidence:

   a. *Authorities:* My parents and teachers taught me this.

   b. *References:* I read about this in science textbooks.

   c. *Factual evidence:* I have seen a sequence of photographs taken from outer space that show the earth as a globe.

   d. *Personal experience:* When I flew across the country, I could see the horizon line changing.

2. Is there a God?

3. Is abortion wrong?

4. Is democracy the best form of government?

5. Should men be the breadwinners and women the homemakers?

Of course, not all reasons and evidence are equally strong or accurate. For example, before the fifteenth century the common belief that the earth was flat was supported by the following reasons and evidence:

- *Authorities:* Educational and religious authorities taught people the earth was flat.
- *References:* The written opinions of scientific experts supported belief in a flat earth.
- *Factual evidence:* No person had ever circumnavigated the earth.
- *Personal experience:* From a normal vantage point, the earth *looks* flat.

Many considerations go into evaluating the strengths and accuracy of reasons and evidence, and we will be exploring these areas in this and future chapters. Let's examine some basic questions that critical thinkers automatically consider when evaluating reasons and evidence by completing Thinking Activity 2.3.

THINKING ACTIVITY 2.3

Evaluate the strengths and accuracy of the reasons and evidence you identified to support your beliefs on the five issues by addressing questions such as the following:

- *Authorities:* Are the authorities knowledgeable in this area? Are they reliable? Have they ever given inaccurate information? Do other authorities disagree with them?
- *References:* What are the credentials of the authors? Are there other authors that disagree with their opinions? On what reasons and evidence do the authors base their opinions?
- *Factual evidence:* What is the source and foundation of the evidence? Can the evidence be interpreted differently? Does the evidence support the conclusion?
- *Personal experience:* What were the circumstances under which the experiences took place? Were distortions or mistakes in perception possible? Have other people had either similar or conflicting experiences? Are there other explanations for the experience? ◀

The opposite of thinking for yourself is when you simply accept the thinking of others without examining or questioning it. Imagine that a friend tells you that a course you are planning to take is very difficult and suggests that you register for a less demanding course. Although the thinking of your friend may have merit, it still makes sense for you to investigate the evidence for that particular view yourself. For example, consider the following situation. Explain how you would respond to the ideas that are being suggested to you, and then give the reasons that support your views.

One of your professors always wears blue jeans and sneakers to class. He says that the clothes you wear have nothing to do with how intelligent or how capable you are or the quality of your work. Other people should judge you on who you are, not on the clothes you wear. Your supervisor at work, however, has just informed you that you have been dressing too casually. How do you respond?

Response:

Reasons that support your response:

Thinking for yourself doesn't always mean doing exactly what you want to; it may mean becoming aware of the social guidelines and expectations of a given situation and then making an informed decision about what is in your best interests. In this situation, even though you may have a legal right to choose whatever clothes you want at the workplace, if your choice doesn't conform to the employer's guidelines or "norms," then you may suffer unpleasant consequences as a result. In other words, thinking for yourself often involves balancing your view of things against those of others, integrating yourself into social structures without sacrificing your independence or personal autonomy.

Learning to become an independent, critical thinker is a complex, ongoing process, that involves all the abilities we have been examining in this chapter to this point:

- Thinking actively
- Carefully exploring situations with questions
- Thinking independently

As you confront the many decisions you have to make in your life, you should try to gather all the relevant information, review your priorities, and then carefully weigh all the factors before arriving at a final decision. One helpful strategy for exploring thinking situations is the one we have been practicing: *identify* the important questions that need to be answered and then try to *answer* these questions.

Critical thinkers are open to new ideas and different view-
points, with the flexibility to explore all sides of an issue
instead of being dogmatic and single-minded.

VIEWING SITUATIONS FROM
DIFFERENT PERSPECTIVES

Although it is important to think for yourself, others may have good ideas from
which you can learn and benefit. A critical thinker is a person who is willing to
listen to and examine carefully other views and new ideas. In addition to your
viewpoint, there may be other viewpoints that are equally important and need
to be taken into consideration if you are to develop a more complete understanding of the situation.

As children we understand the world from only our own point of view. As we grow, we come into contact with people with different viewpoints and begin to realize that our viewpoint is often inadequate, we are frequently mistaken, and our perspective is only one of many. If we are going to learn and develop, we must try to understand and appreciate the viewpoints of others. For example, consider the following situation:

> Imagine that you have been employed at a new job for the past six months. Although you enjoy the challenge of your responsibilities and you are performing well, you find that you simply cannot complete all your work during office hours. To keep up, you have to work late, take work home, and even work occasionally on weekends. When you explain this to your employer, she says that although she is sorry that the job interferes with your personal life, it has to be done. She suggests that you view this as an investment in your future and that you try to work more efficiently. She reminds you that there are many people who would be happy to have your position.

1. Describe this situation from your employer's standpoint, identifying reasons that might support her views.
2. Describe some different approaches that you and your employer might take to help resolve this situation.

For most of the important issues and problems in your life, one viewpoint is simply not adequate to give a full and satisfactory understanding. To increase and deepen your knowledge, you must seek *other perspectives* on the situations you are trying to understand. You can sometimes accomplish this by using your imagination to visualize other viewpoints. Usually, however, you need to seek actively (and *listen* to) the viewpoints of others. It is often very difficult for people to see things from points of view other than their own, and if you are not careful you can make the very serious mistake of thinking that the way you see things is the way things really are. In addition to identifying with perspectives other than your own, you also have to work to understand the *reasons* that support these alternate viewpoints. This approach deepens your understanding of the issues and also stimulates you to evaluate critically your beliefs.

THINKING ACTIVITY 2.4

Describe a belief of yours that you feel very strongly about. Then explain the reasons or experiences that led you to this belief.

Next, describe a point of view that is *different* from your belief. Identify some of the reasons that someone might hold this belief. A student example follows.

A Belief That I Feel Strongly About

I used to think that we should always try everything in
our power to keep a person alive. But now I strongly
believe that a person has a right to die in peace and with
dignity. The reason why I believe this now is because of
my father's illness and death.

It all started on Christmas Day, December 25, when
my father was admitted to the hospital. The doctor's diagnosed his condition as a heart attack. Following this
episode, he was readmitted and discharged from several
different hospitals. On June 18, he was hospitalized for
what was initially thought to be pneumonia but which
turned out to be lung cancer. He began chemotherapy
treatments. When complications occurred, he had to be
placed on a respirator. At first he couldn't speak or eat.
But then they operated on him and placed the tube from
the machine in his throat instead of his mouth. He was
then able to eat and move his mouth. He underwent radiation therapy when they discovered he had three tumors in his head and that the cancer had spread all over
his body. We had to sign a paper which asked us to indicate, if he should stop breathing, whether we would want
the hospital to try to revive him or just let him go. We
decided to let him go because the doctors couldn't guarantee that he wouldn't become brain-dead. At first they
said that there was a forty percent chance that he would
get off the machine. But instead of that happening, the
percentage went down.

It was hard seeing him like that since I was so close
to him. But it was even harder when he didn't want to
see me. He said that by seeing me suffer, his suffering
was greater. So I had to cut down on seeing him. Everybody that visited him said that he had changed dramatically. They couldn't even recognize him.

The last two days of his life were the worst. I prayed
that God would relieve him of his misery. I had come

very close to taking him off the machine in order for him not to suffer, but I didn't. Finally he passed away on November 22, with not the least bit of peace or dignity. The loss was great then and still is, but at least he's not suffering. That's why I believe that when people have terminal diseases with no hope of recovery, they shouldn't place them on machines to prolong their lives of suffering, but instead they should be permitted to die with as much peace and dignity possible.

Somebody else might believe very strongly that we should try everything in our power to keep people alive. It doesn't matter what kind of illness or disease the people have, what's important is that they are kept alive, especially if they are loved ones. Some people want to keep their loved ones alive with them as long as they can, even if it's by a machine. They also believe it is up to God and medical science to determine whether people should live or die. Sometimes doctors give them hope that their loved ones will recover, and many people wish for a miracle to happen. With these hopes and wishes in mind, they wait and try everything in order to prolong a life, even if the doctors tell them that there is nothing that can be done. ◄

Being open to new ideas and different viewpoints means being *flexible* enough to change or modify your ideas in the light of new information or better insight. Each of us has a tendency to cling to the beliefs we have been brought up with and the conclusions we have arrived at. If we are going to continue to grow and develop as thinkers, however, we have to be willing to change or modify our beliefs when evidence suggests that we should. For example, imagine that you have been brought up with certain views concerning an ethnic group—African American, Caucasian, Hispanic, Asian, Native American, or any other. As you mature and your experience increases, you may find that the evidence of your experience conflicts with the views you have been raised with. As critical thinkers, we have to be *open* to receiving this new evidence and *flexible* enough to change and modify our ideas on the basis of it.

In contrast to open and flexible thinking, *un*critical thinking tends to be one-sided and close-minded. People who think this way are convinced they alone see things as they really are and that everyone who disagrees with them is wrong. The words we use to describe this type of person include "dogmatic," "subjective," and "egocentric." It is very difficult for such people to step outside their own viewpoint in order to see things from other people's perspectives. Part of being an educated person is being able to think in an open-minded and flexible way.

SUPPORTING DIVERSE PERSPECTIVES WITH REASONS AND EVIDENCE

When you are thinking critically, what you think makes sense, and you can give good reasons to back up your ideas. As we have seen and will continue to see throughout this book, it is not enough simply to take a position on an issue or make a claim; we have to *back up our views* with other information that we feel supports our position. In other words, there is an important distinction and relationship between *what* you believe and *why* you believe it.

If someone questions *why* you see an issue the way you do, you probably respond by giving reasons or arguments you feel support your belief. For example, take the question of what sort of college to attend: two-year or four-year, residential or commuting. What are some of the reasons you might offer to support your decision to attend the kind of college in which you enrolled?

Although all the reasons you just gave for attending your sort of college support your decision, some are obviously more important to you than others. In any case, even though going to your college may be the right thing for you to do, this decision does not mean that it is the right thing for everyone to do. In order for you fully to appreciate this fact, to see both sides of the issue, you have to put yourself in the position of others and try to see things from their points of view. What are some of the reasons or arguments someone might give for attending a different kind of college?

The responses you just gave demonstrate that, if you are interested in seeing all sides of an issue, you have to be able to give supporting reasons and evidence not just for *your* views, but for the views of *others* as well. Seeing all sides of an issue thus combines these two critical thinking abilities:

- Viewing issues from different perspectives
- Supporting diverse viewpoints with reasons and evidence

Combining these two abilities enables you not only to understand other views about an issue, but also to understand *why* these views are held. Consider the issue of whether seat-belt use should be mandatory. As you try to make sense of this issue, you should attempt to identify not just the reasons that support your view, but also the reasons that support other views. The following are reasons that support each view of this issue.

Issue:

Seat-belt use should be mandatory.   Seat-belt use should not be mandatory.

Supporting Reasons:

1. Studies show that seat belts save lives and reduce injury in accidents.

Supporting Reasons:

1. Many people feel that seat belts may trap them in a burning vehicle.

Now see if you can identify additional supporting reasons for each of these views on making use of seat belts mandatory.

Supporting Reasons:

2.

3.

4.

Supporting Reasons:

2.

3.

4.

THINKING ACTIVITY 2.5

For each of the following issues, identify reasons that support each side of the issue.

Issue:

1. Multiple-choice and true/false exams should be given in college-level courses.

Multiple-choice and true/false exams should not be given in college-level courses.

Issue:

2. It is better to live in a society that minimizes the role of government in the lives of its citizens.

It is better to live in a society in which the government plays a major role in the lives of its citizens.

Issue:

3. The best way to deal with crime is to give long prison sentences.

Long prison sentences will not reduce crime.

4. When a couple divorces, the
   children should choose the
   parent with whom they wish
   to live.

When a couple divorces, the court
should decide all custody issues
regarding the children. ◀

THINKING ACTIVITY 2.6

Working to see different perspectives is crucial in helping you get a more complete understanding of the ideas being expressed in the passages you are reading. Read each of the following passages and then do the following:

1. Identify the main idea of the passage.
2. List the reasons that support the main idea.
3. Develop another view of the main issue.
4. List the reasons that support the other view.

- Most wicked deeds are done because the doer proposes some good to
  himself. The liar lies to gain some end; the swindler and thief want
  things which, if honestly got, might be good in themselves. Even the
  murderer may be removing an impediment to normal desires or gaining possession of something which his victim keeps from him. None of
  these people usually does evil for evil's sake. They are selfish or un-
  scrupulous, but their deeds are not gratuitously evil. The killer for sport
  has no such comprehensible motive. He prefers death to life, darkness
  to light. He gets nothing except the satisfaction of saying, "Something
  which wanted to live is dead. There is that much less vitality, consciousness, and, perhaps, joy in the universe. I am the Spirit that Denies."
  When a human wantonly destroys one of humankind's own works we
  call him Vandal. When he wantonly destroys one of the works of God
  we call him Sportsman.

- More than at any other time in history, America is plagued by the influence of cults, exclusive groups that present themselves as religions devoted to the worship of a single individual. Initially, most Americans
  were not terribly concerned with the growth of cults, but then in 1979
  more than nine hundred cult members were senselessly slaughtered in
  the steamy jungles of a small South American country called Guyana.
  The reason for the slaughter was little more than the wild, paranoid
  fear of the leader, the Reverend Jim Jones, who called himself father
  and savior. Since that time, evidence has increased that another cult

leader, the Reverend Sun Myung Moon, has amassed a large personal fortune from the purses of his followers, male and female "Moonies," who talk of bliss while peddling pins and emblems preaching the gospel of Moon. Cults, with their hypnotic rituals and their promises of ecstasy, are a threat to American youth, and it is time to implement laws that would allow for a thorough restriction of their movements.

- If we want auto safety but continue to believe in auto profits, sales, styling, and annual obsolescence, there will be no serious accomplishments. The moment we put safety ahead of these other values, something will happen. If we want better municipal hospitals but are unwilling to disturb the level of spending for defense, for highways, for household appliances, hospital service will not improve. If we want peace but still believe that countries with differing ideologies are threats to one another, we will not get peace. What is confusing is that up to now, while we have wanted such things as conservation, auto safety, hospital care, and peace, we have tried wanting them without changing consciousness, that is, while continuing to accept those underlying values that stand in the way of what we want. The machine can be controlled at the "consumer" level only by people who change their whole value system, their whole world view, their whole way of life. One cannot favor saving our wildlife and wear a fur coat. ◀

DISCUSSING IDEAS IN AN ORGANIZED WAY

Thinking critically often takes place in a social context, not in isolation. Although it is natural for every person to have his or her perspective on the world, no single viewpoint is adequate for making sense of complex issues, situations, or even people. As we will see in the chapters ahead, we each have our own "lenses" through which we view the world—filters that shape, influence, and often distort the way we see things. The best way to expand one's thinking and compensate for the bias that we all have is to discuss our experiences with other people

This is the way in which thinking develops: being open to the viewpoints of others and willing to listen and exchange ideas with them. This process of give-and-take, of advancing our views and considering those of others, is known as *discussion*. When we participate in a discussion, we are not simply talking; we are exchanging and exploring our ideas in an organized way.

Unfortunately, our conversations with other people about important topics are too often not productive exchanges. They often degenerate into name calling, shouting matches, or worse. Consider the following dialogue.

Person A: I have a friend who just found out she's pregnant and is trying to decide whether she should have an abortion or have the baby. What do you think?

Person B: Well, I think that having an abortion is murder. Your friend doesn't want to be a murderer, does she?

Person A: How can you call her a murderer? An abortion is a medical operation.

Person B: Abortion *is* murder. It's killing another human being, and your friend doesn't have the right to do that.

Person A: Well, you don't have the right to tell her what to do—it's her body and her decision. Nobody should be forced to have a child that is not wanted.

Person B: Nobody has the right to commit murder—that's the law.

Person A: But abortion isn't murder.

Person B: Yes, it is.

Person A: No, it isn't.

Person B: Good-bye! I can't talk to anyone who defends murderers.

Person A: And I can't talk to anyone who tries to tell other people how to run their lives.

If we examine the dynamics of this dialogue, we can see that the two people here are not really:

- Listening to each other
- Supporting their views with reasons and evidence
- Responding to the points being made
- Asking—and trying to answer—important questions
- Trying to increase their understanding rather than simply winning the argument

In short, the people in this exchange are not *discussing* their views, they are simply *expressing* them and trying to influence the other person into agreeing. Contrast this first dialogue with the following one. Although it begins the same way, it quickly takes a much different direction.

Person A: I have a friend who just found that she's pregnant and is trying to decide whether she should have an abortion or have the baby. What do you think?

Person B: Well, I think that having an abortion is murder. Your friend doesn't want to be a murderer, does she?

Person A: Of course she doesn't want to be a murderer! But why do you believe that having an abortion is the same thing as murder?

Person B: Because murder is when we kill another human being, and when you have an abortion, you are killing another human being.

Person A: But is a fetus a human being yet? It certainly is when it is born. But what about before it's born, while it's still in the mother's womb? Is it a person then?

Person B: I think it is. Simply because the fetus hasn't been born doesn't mean that it isn't a person. Remember, sometimes babies are born prematurely, in their eighth or even seventh month of development. And they go on to have happy and useful lives.

Person A: I can see why you think that a fetus in the *last stages* of development—the seventh, eighth, or ninth month—is a person. After all, it can survive outside the womb with special help at the hospital. But what about at the *beginning* of development? Human life begins when an egg is fertilized by a sperm. Do you believe that the fertilized egg is a person?

Person B: Let me think about that for a minute. No, I don't think that a fertilized egg is a person, although many people do. I think that a fertilized egg has the *potential* to become a person—but it isn't a person yet.

Person A: Then at what point in its development do you think a fetus *does* become a person?

Person B: That's a good question, one that I haven't really thought about. I guess you could say that a fetus becomes a person when it begins to look like a person, with a head, hands, feet, and so on. Or you might say that a fetus becomes a person when all of its organs are formed—liver, kidneys, lungs, and so on. Or you might say that it becomes a person when its heart begins to start beating, or when its brain is fully developed. Or you might say that its life begins when it can survive outside the mother. I guess determining when the fetus becomes a person all depends on the *standard* that you use.

Person A: I see what you're saying! Since the development of human life is a continuous process that begins with a fertilized egg and ends with a baby, deciding when the fetus becomes a person depends on what point in the process of development you decide to draw the line. But *how* do you decide where to draw the line?

Person B: That's a good place to begin another discussion. But right now I have to leave for class. See you later.

How would you contrast the level of communication taking place in this dialogue with that in the first dialogue? What are the reasons for your conclusion?

Naturally, discussions are not always quite this organized and direct. Nevertheless, this second dialogue does provide a good model for what can take place in our everyday lives when we carefully explore an issue or a situation with someone else. Let us take a closer look at this discussion process.

Listening Carefully

Review the second dialogue and notice how each person in the discussion *listens carefully* to what the other person is saying and then tries to comment directly on what has just been said. When you are working hard at listening to others, you are trying to understand the point they are making and the reasons for it. This enables you to imagine yourself in their position and see things as they see them. Listening in this way often brings new ideas and different ways of viewing the situation to your attention that might never have occurred to you. An effective dialogue in this sense is like a game of tennis—you hit the ball to me, I return the ball back to you, you return my return, and so on. The "ball" the discussants keep hitting back and forth is the subject they are gradually analyzing and exploring.

Supporting Views with Reasons and Evidence

Critical thinkers support their points of view with evidence and reasons and also develop an in-depth understanding of the evidence and reasons that support other viewpoints. Review the second dialogue and identify some of the reasons used by the participants to support their points of view. For example, Person B expresses the view that "abortion is murder" and supports this view with the reasoning that "murder is killing another human being"; if a fetus is a human being, removing it from the womb prematurely is the same thing as murder.

1. *Viewpoint:*   2. *Viewpoint:*

   Supporting Reason: *Supporting Reason:*

Responding to the Points Being Made

When people engage in effective dialogue, they listen carefully to the people speaking and then respond directly to the points being made instead of simply trying to make their own points. In the second dialogue, Person A responds to Person B's view that "abortion is murder" with the question, "But is a fetus a human being yet?" When you respond directly to other people's views, and they to yours, you extend and deepen the explorations into the issues being discussed. Although people involved in the discussion may not ultimately agree, they should develop more insightful understanding of the important issues and a greater appreciation of other viewpoints. Examine the sample dialogue and notice how each person keeps responding to what the other is saying, creating an ongoing interactive discussion.

Asking Questions

Asking questions is one of the driving forces in your discussions with others. You can explore a subject by raising important questions and, then, trying to answer them together. This questioning process gradually reveals the various reasons and evidence that support each of the different viewpoints involved. For example, although the two dialogues begin the same way, the second dialogue moves in a completely different direction from the first when Person A poses the question: "But *why* do you believe that having an abortion is the same thing as murder?" Asking this question directs the discussion toward a mutual exploration of the issues and away from angry confrontation. Identify some of the other key questions that are posed in the dialogue.

A guide to the various types of questions that can be posed in exploring issues and situations begins on page 52 of this chapter.

Increasing Understanding

When we discuss subjects with others, we often begin by disagreeing with them. In fact, this is one of the chief reasons that we have discussions. In an effective discussion, however, our main purpose should be to develop our understanding—not to prove ourselves right at any cost. If we are determined to prove that we are right, then we are likely not to be open to the ideas of others and to viewpoints that differ from our own.

Imagine that, instead of ending, the second dialogue had continued for a while. Create responses that expand the exploration of the ideas being examined, and be sure to keep the following discussion guidelines in mind as you continue the dialogue.

- When we discuss, we have to listen to each other.
- When we discuss, we keep asking—and trying to answer—important questions.
- When we discuss, our main purpose is to develop a further understanding of the subject we are discussing, not to prove that we are right and the other person wrong.

Person A: I see what you're saying! Since the development of human life is a continuous process that begins with a fertilized egg and ends with a baby, deciding when the fetus becomes a person depends on what point in the process of development you decide to draw the line. But *how* do you decide where to draw the line?

Person B:

Person A:

Person B:

Etc.

Read the following dialogue exploring the issue of capital punishment written by a student and then continue the discussion, creating an additional three or four responses for each person.

Success in college and careers involves expressing ideas clearly and listening to the ideas of others.

Person A: I heard on the news yesterday that a group of prisoners in Virginia took some hostages in one floor of the prison to protest the death sentence of one of their inmates who was going to be executed last night. Nine persons were injured in the revolt.

Person B: Why was the man sentenced to die in the electric chair?

Person A: Because he had killed a pregnant woman and her five-year-old daughter a few years ago.

Person B: Do you believe in the death penalty?

Person A: Well, crime has been on the rise year after year. There has to be a way to regulate the increase, and capital punishment is one way.

Person B: It is true that crime has been on the rise, but to take such an option as capital punishment would make us less civilized and desperate. Capital punishment was used in the past with no positive results.

Person A: It may seem desperate to bring back capital punishment, but what do you suggest instead?

Person B: I think there should be longer prison terms and less plea bargaining. Also, social programs should be available to help prisoners who finish their terms adapt to civilian life.

Person A: That sounds great, but you are talking about a great increase in the budget in correction and social programs. Why not just kill them and save the money?

Person B: Killing them is the easy way out. And if we kill them, that would make us just as bad as the criminals. What gives us the right to take a life?

Person A: Suppose someone kills, serves his prison sentence, and then kills again. What then? If he had been executed the first time, this murder of another innocent person would not have occurred.

Now continue the dialogue.

THINKING ACTIVITY 2.7

Select an important social issue and write a dialogue that analyzes the issue from two different perspectives. As you write your dialogue, keep in mind the qualities of effective discussion: listening carefully to the other person and trying to comment directly on what has been said, asking and trying to answer important questions about the subject, and trying to develop a fuller understanding of the subject instead of simply trying to prove yourself right.

After completing your dialogue, read it to the class (with a classmate as a partner). Analyze the class's dialogues by using the criteria for effective discussions that we have examined. ◀

BECOMING A CRITICAL THINKER

In this chapter we have discovered that critical thinking is not just one way of thinking—it is a total approach to the way we make sense of the world, and it involves an integrated set of thinking abilities and attitudes that include the following:

- *Thinking actively* by using our intelligence, knowledge, and skills to question, explore, and deal effectively with ourselves, others, and life's situations
- *Carefully exploring situations* by asking—and trying to answer—relevant questions
- *Thinking independently* by carefully examining various ideas and arriving at our own thoughtful conclusions
- *Viewing situations from different perspectives* to develop an in-depth, comprehensive understanding and *Supporting viewpoints with reasons and evidence* to arrive at thoughtful, well-substantiated conclusions
- *Discussing ideas in an organized way* in order to exchange and explore ideas with others

These critical thinking qualities are a combination of cognitive abilities, basic attitudes, and thinking strategies that enable you to clarify and improve your understanding of the world. By carefully examining the process and products of your thinking—and the thinking of others—you develop insight into the thinking process and learn to do it better. Becoming a critical thinker does not simply involve mastering certain thinking abilities, however; it affects the entire way that you view the world and live your life. For example, the process of striving to understand other points of view in a situation changes the way you think, feel, and behave. It catapults you out of your own limited way of viewing things, helps you understand others' viewpoints, and broadens your understanding. All of these factors contribute to your becoming a sophisticated thinker and mature human being.

Becoming a critical thinker is a lifelong process. Developing the thinking abilities needed to understand the complex world you live in and make informed decisions requires ongoing analysis, reflection, and practice. The qualities of critical thinking that you have explored in this chapter represent signposts in your journey to become a critical thinker.

Critical thinkers are better equipped to deal with the difficult challenges that life poses: to solve problems, to establish and achieve goals, and to make sense of complex issues. The foundation of thinking abilities and critical attitudes introduced in these first two chapters will be reinforced and elaborated

in the chapters ahead, helping to provide you with the resources to be successful at college, in your chosen career, and throughout the other areas of your life
as well.

THINKING PASSAGES

One useful strategy for developing our critical thinking abilities is to contrast
the views of authors who discuss different sides of the same issue. The two
reading selections that follow argue different viewpoints on the issue of euthanasia (mercy killing). Apply the skills we have been developing in this chapter
by thinking critically about the ideas in the reading selections and then answering the questions that follow.

LIFE SENTENCE: INDIVIDUAL AUTONOMY, MEDICAL TECHNOLOGY, AND THE "COMMON GOOD"
by Howard Moody

Elizabeth Bouvia, a 28-year-old California woman, suffers from severe
cerebral palsy; she is quadriplegic—physically helpless and wholly unable to care for herself, totally dependent on others for all her needs. She
can only lie flat on her back for the rest of her life, for she also suffers from
degenerative arthritis and is in continuous pain.

Our society, using the medical establishment as our surrogate, has
condemned Elizabeth Bouvia to life even though this intelligent, if
despairing, young woman wants to die. The hospital in which she is a
patient, practicing defensive medicine out of fear of liability, denies her
the right to refuse treatment on the grounds that it will result in her death.

Elizabeth Bouvia exposes the underside of the miracle of modern
medical technology. Her predicament threatens our "happy ending" culture which wants to believe that every problem has a solution, every question an answer, and that the admission of complexity and ambiguity are
ways of avoiding progress. She makes it impossible to ignore the fact that
the same technologies that make human life more bearable and bodily
suffering less formidable can also keep alive severely braindamaged
children, the comatose, and others like Bouvia who endure extreme degrees of pain. Her decision to die and her inability to have that decision
honored lay bare our society's attitudes and values about not only modern medical technology but also our most fundamental beliefs about death
and life.

Who Shall Say?

The petitioner for Elizabeth Bouvia in the Court of Appeals in the State of California stated what I believe to be the only morally defensible position:

> Who shall say what the minimum amount of available life must be? Does it matter if it be 15 to 20 years, 15 to 20 months or 15 to 20 days, if such life has been physically destroyed and its quality, dignity and purpose gone? As in all matters, lines must be drawn at some point, somewhere, but the decision must ultimately belong to the one whose life is at issue.

Here Elizabeth Bouvia's decision to forego medical treatment or life support through mechanical means belongs to her. It is not a medical decision for physicians to make. Neither is it a legal question whose soundness is to be resolved by lawyers and judges. It is not a conditional right subject to approval by ethics committees or courts of law. It is a moral and philosophical decision that, being a competent adult, is hers alone.

But Elizabeth Bouvia does not have the right to make that decision. The medical experts and attendants testify that if she is force-fed, she could live 15 or 20 more years in that demoralizing and debilitating condition. The "right-to-lifers" believe she has a duty to endure. The concern about there being no foul play or breaching of medical ethics is legitimate. So too is resistance to the unending pain inflicted on her body and mind until death comes to end her artificially prolonged life. Bouvia's passive acceptance of death is no longer sufficient. Our technology has negated that alternative and forced her to endure a highly invasive therapeutic prolongation of her life against her will. In other words, society is protecting her from the death she prefers to her interminable pain.

The person in our society best protected from death is the one that society has condemned to die. Death row inmates are under meticulous surveillance lest they take their own lives before the appointed hour—namely that time when the state has decided they shall die. Ironically, Bouvia also has no right to end her wretched existence until the state is ready. Only when her body finally revolts against all the new technologies of medicine will the state allow her to die.

If you are a hospital chaplain or Bouvia's pastor, what do you say to her or do for her in her utterly helpless and powerless position? How will you honor her integrity in the face of this massive resistance pitted against her weak will? The only theology germane to her case will be that which is born in and of her pain.

Ancient Beliefs

Many, of course, believe that it is wrong for an individual to commit suicide or at least that the individual decision to terminate life cannot be aided or abetted by the larger community (the public). Such beliefs are as old as the ancient Greeks and continue to influence contemporary medical ethics.

> ". . . [W]e must not participate or assist in taking life, for that would violate what we as a civic community stand for," says Francis I. Kane in a Hastings Center Report ('Keeping Elizabeth Bouvia Alive for the Public Good,' December 1985). "Ironically in demanding her individual autonomy, Elizabeth Bouvia has forced us to reaffirm the common good. In demanding that we help destroy her life, she has led us to profess, not just abstractly, the value of this individual life."

But what is the value of this individual life, and who shall make that determination? Society's harsh moralism against the right of a person to terminate his or her own life makes it difficult to draw any distinctions concerning the reason for such decisions. So of course does the medical professional's (society's surrogate) inordinate preoccupation with prolonging life no matter the quality or the circumstances.

If the Constitution of this nation defends any freedom, it is the fundamental "right to privacy." And in a number of Superior Court cases, a person of adult years and in sound mind has the right to determine whether or not to submit to lawful medical treatment. It follows that such a patient has the right to refuse any medical treatment, even that which may prolong or save her life. This basic right to privacy informed the Presidential Commission for the Study of Ethical Problems in Medicine in its conclusion:

> The voluntary choice of a competent and informed patient should determine whether or not life-sustaining therapy will be undertaken, just as such choices provide the basis for other decisions about medical treatment . . . Health care professionals serve patients best by maintaining a presumption in favor of sustaining life while recognizing that competent patients are entitled to choose to forego any treatments including those that sustain life (*Deciding to Forego Life-Sustaining Treatment*, U.S. Govt. Printing Office).

This right to privacy might enhance an individual's ability to choose life or death. Clearly this has not been the case for Bouvia. Why this is so is

related to our society's view of death. Death is thoroughly institutional-
ized and medicalized. The Enemy or the Grim Reaper, not a welcome
Friend, death is deemed unnatural, and its delay, however briefly, seen as
the triumph of human achievement over the limitations of nature.

This medical warfare against death is highly dramatized in media
events of artificial organ transplants and the heart of a baboon in the body
of a newborn baby. A medical and scientific hubris promises a seemingly
unending and miraculous control of the life process, foretelling the time
when death is a curable disease and immortality a medical commodity.

A "few setbacks" occur. The plague of AIDS is killing off our young
people at alarming rates. But this is but a momentary setback to inevitable
progress; AIDS will be conquered like all the diseases before it. Listen to
the language of "right-to-lifers." In their fanatical semantics God is no
longer ultimate but life is the ultimate. And if life becomes God, then the
death of a life is deicide. A fetus must not be allowed to die no matter
what pain, sorrow, or suffering may result from the consequence of its
birth. Likewise, a brain-dead 80-year-old must be kept alive no matter the
pain and expense to family and society.

The same logic leads to the refusal to let Elizabeth Bouvia die. That
decree does not come from overzealous fundamentalists but from a secular court of law deciding on the values that this society stands for. The
absolutizing of life can occur whether one is religious or not.

But surely, the absolute deification of life is an idolatry for the followers of a Master who said "Greater love hath no man than he who lays
down his life for a friend" or "she who loses life will find it." For people of
faith, life is meaningful and precious (sometimes), but not the only value
in this world. Something more important can cause us to lay it on the line.
Or we may lay it down when it becomes unbearably painful and meaningless.

In our faith, death and life go together. Death may be irrational to
the mind's grasp and irreconcilable to the spirit's longing, but it is natural
to the body's functioning. When we say death and life go together, we
mean that death is written into our bodies—these bodies are the time-
keepers of our lives. A symbol of our finitude and creatureliness, death is
also an integral part of our human existence.

In Stanley Keleman's book *Living Your Dying* he writes, "Our bodies
know about dying and at some point in our lives are irrefutably, absolutely and totally committed to it with the lived experience of the genetic
code." Death is inscribed into the birth of our bodies. We die to uterine life
when we are born into the world, and our dying begins with that birth.

But very quickly our minds deny what our bodies know, and in that repression or denial of the idea of our death grows fear, dread, and anxiety. For a society which values eternal youth and deifies life, thinking and talking about death—not as a morbid distraction from the joy of living, but as part of that living, just like illness and disease—is hard but necessary.

Death Not an End

Death with its mystery and unknown quality sometimes repels us, or scares us with its foreboding. Yet we still affirm that some part of us is unafraid of death; something sometimes is elevated and confirmed by death, something we cherish in the face of death, something we sometimes choose even though it means our death. I find it very hard to name, but I know that only in the presence of death are some things made believable.

Those of us believers, conservative and liberal, who loudly proclaim in our faith that life not death has the last word ought to be able to affirm the wish of an Elizabeth Bouvia. We ought to question seriously the use of a technology that, at incredible cost, might prolong life for a few more weeks or months, when the pain is intolerable or existence is a drugged semiconsciousness. Furthermore, people of faith who declare their belief in the resurrection and another reality that is the promise of God ought, more than most, to know that death is not the last word. Therefore, to grasp one more week or month or year even at unbearable pain and often excessive cost is a kind of act of ultimate distrust in God. The cynic in me conjectures that if Christians really believed in life after death, we could save the billions of dollars in health care spent in the last six months of life, trying to rob death of a few more days, weeks, or months.

We need to resist the very real temptation to idolize life while at the same time we value and affirm life as a precious gift of creation. Not life as some kind of intellectual abstraction but life as a contextual reality where body, mind, and spirit are functioning so as to make it desirable, even with its disabilities and suffering.

The sole determiner of that life's quality and meaning is the one whose life it is. In an earlier time when death gave us no options and came earlier, individuals had no choice. With the advance of medical technology and the institutionalization of death, that choice is as valuable as life itself. That choice in modern society may be the ultimate test of our freedom, and to be able to say no to life is only possible if we have control of our lives. That control is meaningless if finally the state, through its medical surrogates, decides the time of death.

The right to die is as integral a part of our human freedoms as the right to live, and that right should not be hampered by the state's threat to impose penal sanctions on those medical personnel who might be disposed to lend assistance in ending an unbearable life. The medical profession freed from the threat of governmental or legal reprisal would, very likely, have no difficulty in accommodating an individual in Elizabeth Bouvia's situation.

Editor's note: Elizabeth Bouvia has been transferred to a nursing home and has accepted life-sustaining treatment. She dropped her suit against the hospital that denied her request to withdraw treatment. ■

A STEP CLOSER TO MERCY KILLING?
by Robert Barry

Will America legalize mercy killing? The legal foundation for it is quietly being laid.

The Bouvia Case
In the Elizabeth Bouvia case, the California Supreme Court upheld an appellate court decision which permitted her to reject a feeding tube she judged to be too burdensome, but which physicians judged to be life sustaining. The court denied that the medical profession had any duties to preserve life against the wish of patients:

> "It is incongruous, if not monstrous, for medical practitioners to assert ... that someone else must live, or more accurately, endure, for '15 to 20 years.' We cannot conceive it to be the policy of this State to inflict such an ordeal upon anyone."

This decision caused dismay among pro-lifers. Causing even greater dismay was the concurring opinion of Judge Lynn Compton, of the California Second District Appellate Court:

> Elizabeth has apparently made a conscious and informed choice that she prefers death to continued existence in her helpless and, to her, intolerable condition. I believe she has an absolute right to effectuate that decision. The state and the medical profession, instead of frustrating her desire, should be attempting to relieve her suffering by permitting and in fact assisting her to die with ease and dignity. The fact that she is

forced to suffer the ordeal of self-starvation to achieve her objective is in itself inhumane.

The right to die is an integral part of our right to control our own destinies so long as the rights of others are not affected. That right should, in my opinion, include the ability to enlist assistance from others, including the medical profession, in making death as painless and quick as possible. That ability should not be hampered by the state's threat to impose legal sanctions on those who might be disposed to lend assistance.

The medical profession, freed of the threat of government or legal reprisal, would, I am sure, have no difficulty in accommodating an individual in Elizabeth's situation.

An "Absolute" Right

Judge Compton's decision makes it clear that Ms. Bouvia's aim was not merely to reject a "burdensome medical treatment," but to starve herself to death with the cooperation of the medical profession and the approval of the state. Those who recall the early days of the abortion controversy will remember that the right to an abortion also was called "absolute," and it was argued that abortion should be tolerated when it did not affect the rights of others. Judge Compton's decision makes clear that there is a movement to make the "right" to commit suicide as broad as the "fundamental" right to abortion.

Legalizing suicide for those who are medically stable and who are not imminently, certainly and irreversibly dying is morally objectionable not only because it is direct killing, but because of the "educational" value it has for others. When the law against killing is breached so that a certain class of citizens can be allowed to deliberately kill themselves or others, then a "whirlpool" is created which drags others into that breach who do not want to go.

We have seen this happen with pornography. For the most part, those who actually appear in the films and photos are not the wealthy and powerful, but the desperate and impoverished. Just as pornography exploits the weak, so also legalized suicide will exploit the immature, despairing and lonely. They will be the ones who will be dragged into that "whirlpool" because they are most threatened by suicide. They will be the ones who could readily justify their suicide attempts by arguing that their pain, suffering and despair is greater than that of the terminal or hopelessly ill. Suicide is not a threat to people whose lives proceed without trouble, strife or tragedy. But to the sick, lonely, despairing or immature, suicide is a real and present danger, and sometimes it is the prohibitions of the law alone that prevent these unfortunates from ending their lives.

Mercy Killing

Mercy killing by omission is being actively promoted in the United States by the Society for the Right to Die. This organization believes we should have the right to have absolute control over all medical judgments in all circumstances, including the right to reject even food and water when the diagnosis is a "hopeless" condition. A "hopeless" condition is so vaguely defined by this organization that it could include myopia or diabetes.

Positive acts of mercy killing are being promoted by the Hemlock Society of California. This organization is promoting legislation that would permit physicians to assist "terminally ill" patients in their suicides by giving them lethal injections on request. In addition, Hemlock will introduce an amendment to the California state constitution that would permit voluntary suicide for the terminally ill.

One should not underestimate the seductiveness of these organizations' proposals. A person in severe pain or whose family faces large medical expenses could find very attractive a quick and painless death from a lethal injection. America's fixation with autonomy and self-determination makes us vulnerable to claims that a patient can reject any and all treatments. Such claims, however, obscure the fact that people have certain moral obligations to preserve their life, even when they are terminally ill or imminently dying.

Permitting those who decide that their medical condition is "hopeless," or "terminal" to end their lives establishes an elastic criterion that cannot prohibit others from ending their lives. There is no reason to say the sufferings of the terminally ill or dying are more intolerable than those of a lovelorn teenager or a perfectly healthy man who has seen his family killed. If the terminally ill are allowed to kill themselves because of their pain, then all who suffer worse pains should have the same "privilege."

Suicide is not a felony in our country, but those who attempt it can have their freedom extensively restricted by the law to prevent them from harming themselves.

Although America may not legalize mercy killing in the near future, the chances of its happening are very strong now. The American pro-life movement and the nation's Roman Catholic bishops have voiced the only substantial opposition to the removal of life-sustaining, readily-providable food and water from medically stable but not terminally ill patients. Few moral theologians have raised objections to the court decisions in the past three or four years that have allowed feeding to be withdrawn from comatose patients. But the pro-life movement and the bishops have begun to take effective measures to prevent the legalization of mercy killing.

If suicide for the "terminal" or "hopelessly ill" should become legalized, we will probably see a sharp increase in teenage suicide for when adolescents see that it is permissible for the sick or dying to kill themselves, they will judge it to be permissible for themselves. If America legalizes suicide in some circumstances, it might put our young people in serious danger. ■

Questions for Analysis

1. The author of the first article, Howard Moody, states that "the right to die is as integral a part of our human freedoms as the right to live." Explain what Moody means by this statement and identify the reasons he gives to support this view.

2. According to Robert Barry, the author of the second article, "Permitting those who decide that their medical condition is 'hopeless' or 'terminal' to end their lives establishes an elastic criterion that cannot prohibit others from ending their lives." Explain what Barry means by this statement and identify the reasons he gives to support this view.

3. There is an important distinction between "passive euthanasia," which refers to the withdrawal of life-sustaining medical equipment, and "active euthanasia," in which an action is taken to end a person's life who is not on life-sustaining equipment. Identify some of the potential abuses that might occur if society enacts laws legitimizing each of these different forms of euthanasia (as is already beginning to happen) and describe strategies that might be used to avoid these abuses.

4. The patient in the videotape (*Thinking Towards Decisions*) that accompanies this chapter is in a comatose state, being kept alive with a ventilator and feeding tube. Explain how each of these two authors would analyze the family's situation and the choices they ought to make. Be sure to identify the reasons that support their perspectives. ◄

TELEVISION AND READING
by Marie Winn

What Happens When You Read

It is not enough to compare television watching and reading from the viewpoint of quality. Although the quality of the material available in each medium varies enormously, from junky books and shoddy programs to literary masterpieces and fine, thoughtful television shows, the *nature* of the two experiences is different and that difference significantly affects the impact of the material taken in.

Few people besides linguistics students and teachers of reading are aware of the complex mental manipulations involved in the reading process. Shortly after learning to read, a person assimilates the process so completely that the words in books seem to acquire an existence almost equal to the objects or acts they represent. It requires a fresh look at a printed page to recognize that those symbols that we call letters of the alphabet are completely abstract shapes bearing no inherent "meaning" of their own. Look at an "o," for instance, or a "k." The "o" is a curved figure; the "k" is an intersection of three straight lines. Yet it is hard to divorce their familiar figures from their sounds, though there is nothing "o-ish" about an "o" or "k-ish" about a "k." A reader unfamiliar with the Russian alphabet will find it easy to look at the symbol "Ш," and see it as an abstract shape; a Russian reader will find it harder to detach that symbol from its sound, *shch*. And even when trying to consider "k" as an abstract symbol, we cannot see it without the feeling of a "k," sound somewhere between the throat and the ears, a silent pronunciation of "k" that occurs the instant we see the letter.

That is the beginning of reading: we learn to transform abstract figures into sounds, and groups of symbols into the combined sounds that make up the words of our language. As the mind transforms the abstract symbols into sounds and the sounds into words, it "hears" the words, as it were, and thereby invests them with meanings previously learned in the spoken language. Invariably, as the skill of reading develops, the meaning of each word begins to seem to dwell within those symbols that make up the word. The word "dog," for instance, comes to bear some relationship with the real animal. Indeed, the word "dog" seems to *be a dog* in a certain sense, to possess some of the qualities of a dog. But it is only as a result of a swift and complex series of mental activities that the word "dog" is transformed from a series of meaningless squiggles into an idea of something real. This process goes on smoothly and continuously as we read, and yet it becomes no less complex. The brain must carry out all the steps of decoding and investing with meaning each time we read; but it becomes more adept at it as the skill develops, so that we lose the sense of struggling with symbols and meanings that children have when they first learn to read.

But not merely does the mind *hear* words in the process of reading; it is important to remember that reading involves images as well. For when the reader sees the word "dog" and understands the idea of "dog," an image representing a dog is conjured up as well. The precise nature of this "reading image" is little understood, nor is there agreement about what relation it bears to visual images taken in directly by the eyes. Neverthe-less images necessarily color our reading, else we would perceive no mean-ing, merely empty words. The great difference between these "reading images" and the images we take in when viewing television is this: we *create* our own images when reading, based upon our own life experi-ences and reflecting our own individual needs, while we must accept what we receive when watching television images. This aspect of reading, which might be called "creative" in the narrow sense of the word, is present dur-ing all reading experiences, regardless of *what is* being read. When we read it is almost as if we were creating our own small, inner television program. The result is a nourishing experience for the imagination. As Bruno Bettelheim notes,

"Television captures the imagination, but does not liberate it. A good book at once stimulates and frees the mind."

Television images do not go through a complex symbolic transfor-mation. The mind does not have to decode and manipulate during the television experience. Perhaps this is a reason why the visual images re-ceived directly from a television set are strong, stronger, it appears, than the images conjured up mentally while reading. But ultimately they sat-isfy less. A ten-year-old child reports on the effects of seeing television dramatizations of books he has previously read: "The TV people leave a stronger impression. Once you've seen a character on TV, he'll always look like that in your mind, even if you made a different picture of him in your mind before, when you read the book yourself." And yet, as the same child reports, "the thing about a book is that you have so much freedom. You can make each character look exactly the way you want him to look. You're more in control of things when you read a book than when you see something on TV."

It may be that television-bred children's reduced opportunities to indulge in this "inner picture-making" accounts for the curious inability of so many children today to adjust to nonvisual experiences. This is com-monly reported by experienced teachers who bridge the gap between the pretelevision and the television eras. "When I read them a story without showing them pictures, the children always complain—'I can't see.' Their attention flags," reports a first-grade teacher. "They'll begin to talk or wander off. I have to really work to develop their visualizing skills. I tell them that there's nothing to see, that the story is coming out of my mouth, and they can make their own pictures in their 'mind's eye.' They get bet-ter at visualizing, with practice. But children never needed to learn how to visualize before television, it seems to me."

Viewing vs. Reading: Concentration

Because reading demands complex mental manipulations, a reader is required to concentrate far more than a television viewer. An audio expert notes that "with the electronic media it is openness (that counts). Openness permits auditory and visual stimuli more direct access to the brain. . . . Someone who is taught to concentrate will fail to perceive many patterns of information conveyed by the electronic stimuli."

It may be that a predisposition toward concentration, acquired, perhaps, through one's reading experiences, makes one an inadequate television watcher. But it seems far more likely that the reverse situation obtains: that a predisposition toward "openness" (which may be understood to mean the opposite of focal concentration), acquired through years and years of television viewing, has influenced adversely viewers' ability to concentrate, to read, to write clearly—in short, to demonstrate any of the verbal skills literate society requires.

Pace

A comparison between reading and viewing may be made in respect to the pace of each experience, and the relative control we have over that pace, for the pace may influence the ways we use the material received in each experience. In addition, the pace of each experience may determine how much it intrudes upon other aspects of our life. When we read, clearly, we can control the pace. We may read as slowly or as rapidly as we can or wish to read. If we do not understand something, we may stop and reread it, or go in search of elucidation before continuing. If what we read is moving, we may put down the book for a few moments and cope with our emotions without fear of losing anything.

When we view, the pace of the television program cannot be controlled: only its beginning and end are within our control by clicking the knob on and off. We cannot slow down a delightful program or speed up a dreary one. We cannot "turn back" if a word or phrase is not understood. The program moves inexorably forward, and what is lost or misunderstood remains so.

Nor can we readily transform the material we see on television into a form that might suit our particular emotional needs, as we invariably do with material we read. The images move too quickly. We cannot use our own imagination to invest the people and events portrayed on television with the personal meanings that would help us understand and resolve relationships and conflicts in our own life; we are under the power of the imagination of the show's creators. In the television experience the eyes and ears are overwhelmed with the immediacy of sights and sounds. They flash from the television set just fast enough for the eyes and ears to take them in before moving on quickly to the new pictures and sounds . . . so as not *to lose the thread.*

Not to lose the thread . . . it is this need, occasioned by the irreversible direction and relentless velocity of the television experience, that not only limits the workings of the viewer's imagination, but also causes television to intrude into human affairs far more than reading experiences can ever do. If someone enters the room while we're watching television—a friend, a relative, a child, someone, perhaps, we have not seen for some time—we must continue to watch or else we'll lose the thread. The greetings must wait, for the television program will not. A book, of course, can be set aside, with a pang of regret, perhaps, but with no sense of permanent loss.

A grandparent describes a situation that is, by all reports, not uncommon: "Sometimes when I come to visit the girls, I'll walk into their room and they're watching a TV program. Well, I know they love me, but it makes me feel *bad* when I tell them hello, and they say, without even looking up, 'Wait a minute . . . we have to see the end of this program.' It hurts me to have them care more about that machine and those little pictures than about being glad to see me. I know that they probably can't help it, but still . . ."

Can they help it? Ultimately, when we watch television our power to release ourselves from viewing in order to attend to human demands that come up is not altogether a function of the pace of the program. After all, we might *choose* to operate according to human priorities, rather than electronic dictatorship. We might quickly decide "to hell with this program" and simply stop watching when a friend enters the room or a child needs attention.

We might . . . but the hypnotic power of television makes it difficult to shift our attention away, makes us desperate not to lose the thread of the program.

Why Is It So Hard to Stop Watching?

A number of perceptual factors unique to the television experience may play a role in making television more *fascinating* than any other vicarious experience, factors to do with the nature of the electronic images on the screen and the ways the eye takes them in. Whereas in real life we perceive but a tiny part of the visual panorama around us with the fovea, the sharp-focusing part of the eye, taking in the rest of the world with our fuzzy peripheral vision, when we watch television we take in the entire frame of an image with our sharp foveal vision. Let us say that the image on the television screen depicts a whole room or a mountain landscape; if we were there in real life, we would be able to perceive only a very small part of the room or the landscape clearly with any single glance. On television, however, we can see the entire picture sharply. Our peripheral vision is not involved in viewing that scene; indeed, as the eye focuses upon the television screen and takes it all in sharply, the mind blots out the peripheral world entirely. Since in real life the periphery distracts and diffuses our attention, this absence of periphery must serve to abnormally heighten our attention to the television image.

Another unique feature of the television image is the remarkable activity of all contours on the television screen. While the normal contours of real-life objects and people are stationary, the electronic mechanism that creates images on a screen produces contours that are ever moving, although the viewer is hardly aware of the movement. Since the eye is drawn to fixate more strongly on moving than on stationary objects, one result of the activity of television contours is to make them more attention-binding.

Yet another consequence is to make the eye defocus slightly when fixing its attention on the television screen. The reason is this: in viewing television the steadily changing visual activity of the contour causes the eye to have difficulties in fixating properly. Now in real life when the eye does not fixate properly a signal is sent to the visual center of the brain, which then takes corrective steps. Since improper fixation is normally the result of an eye tremor or some physical dysfunction of the viewer rather than of the thing being viewed, the visual system will attempt to make corrections in the eye tremor or in some part of the viewer's visual system. However, in viewing television, it is the visual activity *at the contour of the image* that is causing the difficulties in fixation. Thus the visual system will have increasing difficulty in maintaining its normal fixation. Therefore it may be easier to give up striving for a perfect, focused fixation on a television picture, and to accommodate by a somewhat defocused fixation.

The sensory confusion that occurs as a result of the activity of television images is not unlike the state that occurs when the semicircular canals of the ears, which serve to maintain our balance and help the brain make the necessary adjustments to the body's movements, are confused by motion from external sources (as when one stands still and yet one's ear canals are moved this way and that by the motion of a car or ship or airplane). The unpleasant symptoms of seasickness or carsickness reflect this internal confusion.

The slight defocusing of the eyes while viewing television, while not as unpleasant as seasickness (it is barely perceptible, in fact), may nevertheless have subtle consequences that serve to make the television experience more dysfunctional for the organism than other experiences such as reading. Research shows that defocusing of the eyes normally accompanies various fantasy and daydreaming states. Thus the material perceived on television may take on an air of unreality, a dreamlike quality. Moreover, similar visual-motor conflicts are frequently described as features of many drug experiences by users. This may very well be a reason for the trancelike nature of so many viewers' television experience, and may help to explain why the television image has so strong and hypnotic a fascination. It has even been suggested that "early experiences with electronic displays are predisposing to later enjoyment of psychoactive drugs which produce similar perceptual effects."

All these perceptual anomalies may conspire to fascinate viewers and glue them to the television set.

Of course there are variations in the attention-getting and attention-sustaining powers of television images, many of which depend on such factors as the amount of movement present on the screen at any given moment and the velocity of change from image to image. It is a bit chilling to consider that the producers of the most influential program for preschool children, *Sesame Street,* employed modern technology in the form of a "distractor" machine to test each segment of their program to ensure that it would capture and hold the child's attention to the highest degree possible. With the help of the "distractor," the makers of *Sesame Street* found that fast-paced cartoons and fast-moving stories were most effective in sustaining a child's attention. This attitude toward young children and their television experiences may well be compared to that revealed by Monica Sims of the BBC, who states: "We're not trying to tie children to the television screen. If they go away and play halfway through our programs, that's fine."

The Basic Building Blocks

There is another difference between reading and television viewing that must affect the response to each experience. This is the relative acquaintance of readers and viewers with the fundamental elements of each medium. While the reader is familiar with the basic building blocks of the reading medium, the television viewer has little acquaintance with those of the television medium.

As we read, we have our own writing experience to fall back upon. Our understanding of what we read, and our feelings about it, are necessarily affected, and deepened, by our possession of writing as a means of communicating. As children begin to learn reading, they begin to acquire the rudiments of writing. That these two skills are always acquired together is important and not coincidental. As children learn to read words, they need to understand that a word is something they can write themselves, though their muscle control may temporarily prevent them from writing it clearly. That they wield such power over the words they are struggling to decipher makes the reading experience a satisfying one right from the start for children.

A young child watching television enters a realm of materials completely beyond his control—and understanding. Though the images that appear on the screen may be reflections of familiar people and things, they appear as if by magic. Children cannot create similar images, not even begin to understand how those flickering electronic shapes and forms come into being. They take on a far more powerless and ignorant role in front of the television set than in front of a book.

There is no doubt that many young children have a confused relationship to the television medium. When a group of preschool children were asked, "How do kids get to be on your TV?" only 22 percent of them showed any real comprehension of the nature of the television images. When asked, "Where do the people and kids and things go when your TV is turned off?" only 20 percent of the three-year-olds showed the smallest glimmer of understanding. Although there was an increase in comprehension among the four-year-olds, the authors of the study note that "even among the older children the vast majority still did not grasp the nature of television pictures."

Children's feelings of power and competence are nourished by another feature of the reading experience that does not obtain for television: the nonmechanical, easily accessible, and easily transportable nature of reading matter. Children can always count on a book for pleasure, though the television set may break down at a crucial moment. They may take a book with them wherever they go, to their room, to the park, to their friend's house, to school to read under the desk: they can *control* their use of books and reading materials. The television set is stuck in a certain place; it cannot be moved easily. It certainly cannot be casually transported from place to place by a child. Children must not only watch television wherever the set is located, but they must watch certain programs at certain times, and are powerless to change what comes out of the set and when it comes out.

In this comparison of reading and television viewing a picture begins to emerge that quite confirms the commonly held notion that reading is somehow "better" than television viewing. Reading involves a complex form of mental activity, trains the mind in concentration skills, develops the powers of imagination and inner visualization; the flexibility of its pace lends itself to a better and deeper comprehension of the material communicated. Reading engrosses, but does not hypnotize or seduce the reader from his human responsibilities. Reading is a two-way process: the reader can also write; television viewing is a one-way street: the viewer cannot create television images. And books are ever available, ever controllable. Television controls. ■

Questions for Analysis

1. At the age of four, one of my daughter's first attempts at a "joke" went as follows: "Why did the gorilla watch TV? Because he wanted to get dopey!" (followed by gales of laughter). This "joke" originated in my observation to her that, after watching several hours of television on Saturday morning, she usually became "dopey"—listless, unaware, moody, and not interested in doing anything but watching more television. Explain how the author of this article would explain this transformation of a lively, energetic, inquisitive little child into a hypnotized zombie.

2. Explain how the process of reading differs from the process of watching television, according to the article.

3. Describe evidence the author provides to support her conclusion that watching television instead of reading discourages active thinking, especially in children. Evaluate whether you think these reasons make good sense. If not, explain why.

4. Over the course of several days, reflect on your own experiences of reading and television watching. Describe the differences between these experiences, and explain whether your findings agree with the author's analysis. ◀

3

Solving Problems

AN ORGANIZED
APPROACH TO ANALYZING
DIFFICULT PROBLEMS

**Step One: What Is
the Problem?**
What do I know about the situation?
What results am I aiming for?
How can I define the problem?

**Step Five: How Well Is the
Solution Working?**
What is my evaluation?
What adjustments are necessary?

**Step Two: What Are the
Alternatives?**
What are the boundaries?
What are possible alternatives?

**Step Four: What Is
the Solution?**
Which alternatives(s) will I pursue?
What steps can I take?

**Step Three: What Are the Advantages and/or
Disadvantages of Each Alternative?**
What are the advantages?
What are the disadvantages?
What additional information do I need?

Solving the
Problem of Not
Enough Money

Solving the
Problem of Not
Enough Time

THROUGHOUT YOUR LIFE, you are continually solving problems. As a student, for example, you are faced with a steady stream of academic assignments, quizzes, exams, papers, homework projects, oral presentations. In order to solve these problems effectively—to do well on an exam, for instance—you need to *define* the problem (what areas will the exam cover, and what will be the format?), identify and evaluate various *alternatives* (what are possible study approaches?), and then put all these factors together to reach a *solution* (what will be my study plan and schedule?). Relatively simple problems like preparing for an exam do not require a systematic or complex analysis. We can solve them with just a little effort and concentration. But the difficult and complicated problems in life are a different story.

INTRODUCTION TO SOLVING PROBLEMS

Consider the following problem:

> My best friend is addicted to drugs, but he won't admit it. Jack always liked to drink, but I never thought too much about it. After all, a lot of people like to drink socially, get relaxed, and have a good time. But over the last few years he's started using other drugs as well as alcohol, and it's ruining his life. He's stopped taking classes at the college and will soon lose his job if he doesn't change. Last week I told him that I was really worried about him, but he told me that he has no drug problem and that in any case it really isn't any of my business. I just don't know what to do. I've known Jack since we were in grammar school together and he's a wonderful person. It's as if he's in the grip of some terrible force and I'm powerless to help him.

In working through this problem, the student who wrote this description will have to think carefully and systematically in order to reach a solution. When we think effectively in situations like this, we usually ask ourselves a series of questions, although we may not be aware of the process that our minds are going through.

1. What is the *problem?*
2. What are the *alternatives?*
3. What are the *advantages* and/or *disadvantages* of each alternative?
4. What is the *solution?*
5. How well is the solution *working?*

Let's explore these questions further—and the thinking process that they represent—by applying them to the problem described here. Put yourself in the position of the student whose friend seems to have a serious drug problem.

What Is the Problem?

There are a variety of ways to define the problem facing this student. Describe as specifically as possible what *you* think the problem is.

I would define the problem as:

What Are the Alternatives?

In dealing with this problem, you have a wide variety of possible actions to consider before selecting the best choices. Identify some of the alternatives you might consider.

1. Speak to my friend in a candid and forceful way to convince him that he has a serious problem.
2.
3.
4.

What Are the Advantages and/or Disadvantages of Each Alternative?

Evaluate the strengths and weaknesses of each of the problems you identified so you can weigh your choices and decide on the best course of action.

1. Speak to my friend in a candid and forceful way to convince him that he has a serious problem.

Successful problem solvers are able to deal effectively with the many problems that we encounter in daily life.

Advantage: He may respond to my direct emotional appeal, acknowledge that he has a problem, and seek help.

Disadvantage: He may react angrily, further alienating me from him and making it more difficult for me to have any influence on him.

2.

   Advantage:
   Disadvantage:

3.

   Advantage:
   Disadvantage:

4.

   Advantage:
   Disadvantage:

What Is the Solution?

After evaluating the various alternatives, select what you think is the most effective alternative for solving the problem and describe the sequence of steps you would take to act on the alternative.

Alternative:

Steps:

1.
2.

How Well Is the Solution Working?

The final step in the process is to review the solution and decide whether it is working well. If it is not, you must be able to modify your solution or perhaps choose an alternate solution you had disregarded earlier. Describe what results would inform you that the alternative you selected to pursue was working well or poorly. If you concluded that your alternative was working poorly, describe what your next action would be.

In this situation, trying to figure out the best way to help your friend recognize his problem and seek treatment leads to a series of decisions. This is what the thinking process is all about—trying to make sense of what is going on in our world and acting appropriately in response. When we solve problems effectively, our thinking process exhibits a coherent organization. It follows the general approach we have just explored.

PROBLEM-SOLVING METHOD (BASIC)

1. What is the *problem*?
2. What are the *alternatives* available to me?
3. What are the *advantages* and/or *disadvantages* of each alternative?
4. What is the *solution*?
5. How well is the solution *working*?

If we can understand the way our mind operates when we are thinking effectively, then we can apply this understanding to improve our thinking in new, challenging situations. In the remainder of this chapter we will explore a more sophisticated version of this problem-solving approach and will apply it to a variety of complex, difficult problems.

THINKING ACTIVITY 3.1

1. Describe in specific detail an important problem you have solved recently.
2. Explain how you went about solving the problem. What were the steps, strategies, and approaches you used to understand the problem and make an informed decision?
3. Analyze the organization exhibited by your thinking process by completing the five-step problem-solving method we have been exploring.
4. Share your problem with other members of the class and have them try to analyze and solve it. Then explain the solution you arrived at. ◀

SOLVING COMPLEX PROBLEMS

Imagine yourself in the following situation. What would your next move be, and what are your reasons for it?

You are about to begin your second year of college, following a very successful first year. To this point, you have financed your education through a combination of savings, financial aid, and a part-time job (sixteen hours/week) at a local store. However, you just received a letter from your college reducing your financial aid package by half, due to budgetary problems. The letter concludes, "We hope this aid reduction will not prove to be too great an inconvenience." From your perspective, the loss of aid isn't an inconvenience—it's a disaster! Your budget last year was already tight, and with your job, you had barely enough time to study, participate in a few college activities, and have a modest (but essential) social life. To make matters worse, your mother has been ill, reducing her income and creating financial problems at home. You're feeling panicked—what in the world are you going to do?

When we first approach a difficult problem, it often seems a confused tangle of information, feelings, alternatives, opinions, considerations, and risks. The problem of the college student just described is a complicated situation that does not seem to offer a single simple solution. Without the benefit of a systematic approach, our thoughts might wander through the tangle of issues like this:

I want to stay in school . . . but I'm not going to have enough money. . . . I could work more hours at my job . . . but I might not have enough time to study and get top grades . . . and if all I'm doing is working and studying, what about my social life? . . . and what about mom and the kids—, they

Solving complex problems requires us to **think critically** *about the problem, analyzing it with a thoughtful, organized approach.*

might need my help. . . . I could drop out of school for a while . . . but if I don't stay in school, what kind of future do I have? . . .

Very often when we are faced with difficult problems like this, we simply do not know where to begin in trying to solve them. Every issue is connected to many others. Frustrated by not knowing where to take the first step, we often give up trying to understand the problem. Instead, we may:

1. *Act impulsively* without thought or consideration (e.g., "I'll just quit school").
2. *Do what someone else suggests* without seriously evaluating the suggestion (e.g., "Tell me what I should do—I'm tired of thinking about this").
3. *Do nothing* as we wait for events to make the decision for us (e.g., "I'll just wait and see what happens before doing anything").

None of these approaches is likely to succeed in the long run, and they can gradually reduce our confidence in dealing with complex problems. An alternative to these reactions is to *think critically* about the problem, analyzing it with an organized approach based on the five-step method described earlier.

PROBLEM-SOLVING METHOD (ADVANCED)

1. **Step 1: What is the problem?**
   a. What do I know about the situation?
   b. What results am I aiming for in this situation?
   c. How can I define the problem?

2. **Step 2: What are the alternatives?**
   a. What are the boundaries of the problem situation?
   b. What alternatives are possible within these boundaries?

3. **Step 3: What are the advantages and/or disadvantages of each alternative?**
   a. What are the advantages of each alternative?
   b. What are the disadvantages of each alternative?
   c. What additional information do I need to evaluate each alternative?

4. **Step 4: What is the solution?**
   a. Which alternative(s) will I pursue?
   b. What steps can I take to act on the alternative(s) chosen?

5. **Step 5: How well is the solution working?**
   a. What is my evaluation?
   b. What adjustments are necessary?

Although we will be using an organized method for working through difficult problems and arriving at thoughtful conclusions, the fact is that our minds do not always work in such a logical, step-by-step fashion. Effective problem-solvers typically pass through all the steps we will be examining, but they don't always do so in the sequence we will be describing. Instead, the best problem-solvers have an integrated and flexible approach to the process in which they deploy a repertoire of problem-solving strategies as needed. Sometimes exploring the various alternatives helps them go back and redefine the original problem; similarly, seeking to implement the solution can often suggest new alternatives.

The key point is that although the problem-solving steps are presented in a logical sequence here, you are not locked into following these steps in a mechanical and unimaginative way. At the same time, in learning a problem-solving method like this it is generally not wise to skip steps, because each step deals with an important aspect of the problem. As you become more proficient in using the method, you will find that you can apply its concepts and strategies to problem-solving in an increasingly flexible and natural fashion, just as learning the basics of an activity like driving a car gradually gives way to a more organic and integrated performance of the skills involved.

Before applying a method like the one just outlined above to your problem, however, you need to first ready yourself by *accepting* the problem.

ACCEPTING THE PROBLEM

To solve a problem, you must first be willing to *accept* the problem by *acknowledging* the problem exists, and *committing* yourself to trying to solve the problem. Sometimes you may have difficulty in recognizing there *is* a problem, unless it is pointed out to you. Other times you may actively resist acknowledging a problem, even when it is pointed out to you. The person who confidently states, "I don't really have any problems," sometimes has very serious problems—but is simply unwilling to acknowledge them.

On the other hand, mere acknowledgment is not enough to solve a problem. Once you have identified a problem, you must commit yourself to trying to solve it. Successful problem-solvers are highly motivated and willing to persevere through the many challenges and frustrations of the problem-solving process. How do you find the motivation and commitment that prepare you to enter the problem-solving process? There are no simple answers but a number of strategies may be useful to you.

1. *List the benefits.* Making a detailed list of the benefits you will derive from successfully dealing with the problem is a good place to begin. Such a process helps you clarify why you might want to tackle the problem, motivates you to get started, and serves as a source of encouragement you when you encounter difficulties or lose momentum.

2. *Formalize our acceptance.* When you formalize your acceptance of a problem, you are "going on record," either by preparing a signed declaration or by signing a "contract" with someone else. This formal commitment serves as an explicit statement of your original intentions that you can refer to if your resolve weakens.

3. *Accept responsibility for our lives.* Robert F. Kennedy, the former presidential candidate who was assassinated in 1968, once said, "Some people see things as they are, and ask, 'Why?' I see things as they could be, and ask, 'Why not?'" Each one of us has the potential to control the direction of our lives, but to do so we must accept our freedom to choose and the responsibility that goes with it. As you saw in the last chapter, critical thinkers actively work to take charge of their lives rather than letting themselves be passively controlled by external forces.

4. *Create a "worst-case" scenario.* Some problems persist because you are able to ignore their possible implications. When you use this strategy, you remind yourself, as graphically as possible, of the potentially disastrous consequences of your actions. For example, using vivid color photographs and research conclusions, you can remind yourself that excessive smoking, drinking, or eating can lead to myriad health problems and social and psychological difficulties as well as an early and untimely demise.

5. *Identify the constraints.* If you are having difficulty accepting a problem, it is usually because something is holding you back. For example, you might be concerned about the amount of time and effort involved; you might be reluctant to confront the underlying issues the problem represents; you might be worried about finding out unpleasant things about yourself or others; or you might be inhibited by other problems in your life, such as a tendency to procrastinate. Whatever the constraints, using this strategy involves identifying and describing all of the factors that are preventing you from attacking the problem, and then addressing these factors one at a time.

STEP 1: WHAT IS THE PROBLEM?

The first step in solving problems is to determine exactly what the central is-sues of the problem are. If you do not clearly understand what the problem really is, then your chances of solving it are considerably reduced. You may spend your time trying to solve the wrong problem. For example, consider the different formulations of the following problems. How might these formula-tions lead you in different directions in trying to solve the problems?

"School is boring." vs. "I feel bored in school."

"I'm a failure." vs. "I just failed an exam."

In each of these cases a very general conclusion (left column) has been replaced by a more specific characterization of the problem (right column).

The general conclusions ("I'm a failure") do not suggest productive ways of resolving the difficulties. They are too absolute, too all encompassing. On the other hand, the more specific descriptions of the problem situation ("I just failed an exam") *do* permit us to attack the problems with useful strategies. In short, the way you define a problem determines not only *how* you will go about solv-ing it, but whether you feel that the problem can be solved at all. Correct iden-tification of a problem is essential if you are going to be able to perform a successful analysis and reach an appropriate conclusion. If you misidentify the problem, you can find yourself pursuing an unproductive and even destruc-tive course of action.

Let us return to the problem of the college finances we encountered on page 101 and analyze it using our problem-solving method. *(Note:* As you work through this problem-solving approach, apply the steps and strategies to an unsolved problem in your own life. You will have an opportunity to write up your analysis when you complete Thinking Activity 3.2 on page 118.) In order to complete the first major step of our problem-solving approach, "What is the problem?", we need to address three component questions:

1. What do I know about the situation?
2. What results am I aiming for in this situation?
3. How can I define the problem?

Step 1A: What Do I Know About the Situation?

Solving a problem begins with determining what information you *know* to be the case and what information you *think* might be the case. Your need to have a clear idea of the details of your beginning circumstances to explore the problem successfully. Sometimes a situation may appear to be a problem when it really isn't, simply because your information isn't accurate. For example, you might be convinced that someone you are attracted to doesn't reciprocate your interest. If this belief is inaccurate, however, then your "problem" doesn't really exist.

You can identify and organize what you know about the problem situation by using *key questions*. In Chapter 2, we examined six types of questions that can be used to explore situations and issues systematically: *fact, interpretation, analysis, synthesis, evaluation, application*. By asking—and trying to answer— questions of fact, you are establishing a sound foundation for the exploration of your problem. Answer the following questions of fact—who, what, where, when, how, why—about the problem at the beginning of the chapter.

1. *Who* are the people involved in this situation?

   Who will benefit from solving this problem?
   Who can help me solve this problem?

2. *What* are the various parts or dimensions of the problem?
   What are my strengths and resources for solving this problem?
   What additional information do I need to solve this problem?

3. *Where* can I find people or additional information to help me solve the problem?

4. *When* did the problem begin?
   When should the problem be resolved?

5. *How* did the problem develop or come into being?

6. *Why* is solving this problem important to me?
   Why is this problem difficult to solve?

7. *Additional questions:*

Step 1B: What Results Am I Aiming for in This Situation?

The second part of answering the question, "What is the problem?" consists of identifying the specific *results* or objectives you are trying to achieve. The results are those goals that will eliminate the problem if you are able to attain them. Whereas the first part of Step 1 oriented you in terms of the history of the problem and the current situation, this part encourages you to look ahead to the future. In this respect, it is similar to the process of establishing and working toward your goals that you examined in Chapter 1. To identify your results, you need to ask yourself the question: "What are the objectives that, once achieved, will solve this problem?" For instance, one of the results or objectives in the sample problem might be having enough money to pay for college. Describe additional results you might be trying to achieve in this situation.

1. Having enough money to pay for college
2.
3.
4.

Step 1C: How Can I Define the Problem?

After exploring what you know about the problem and the results you are aiming to achieve, we need to conclude Step 1 by defining the problem as clearly and specifically as possible. Defining the problem is a crucial task in the entire problem-solving process because this definition will determine the direction of the analysis. To define the problem, you need to identify its central issue(s). Sometimes defining the problem is relatively straightforward, such as: "Trying to find enough time to exercise." Often, however, identifying the central issue of a problem is a much more complex process. For example, the statement "My problem is relating to other people" suggests a complicated situation with many interacting variables that resists simple definition. In fact, you may only begin to develop a clear idea of the problem as you engage in the process of trying to solve it. You might begin by believing that our problem is, say, not having the *ability* to succeed and end by concluding that the problem is really a *fear* of success. As you will see, the same insights apply to nonpersonal problems as well. For example, the problem of high school dropouts might initially be defined in terms of problems in the school system, whereas later formulations may identify drug use or social pressure as the core of the problem.

Although there are no simple formulas for defining challenging problems, you can pursue several strategies in identifying the central issue most effectively:

1. *View the problem from different perspectives.* As you saw in Chapter 2, perspective-taking is a key ingredient of thinking critically, and it can help you zero in on many problems as well. For example, when you describe how various individuals might view a given problem—such as the high school dropout rate—the essential ingredients of the problem begin to emerge. In our college finances problem, how would you describe the following perspectives?

    Your perspective:
    College's perspective:
    Your mother's perspective:

Viewing a problem from different perspectives helps us define the problem clearly and generate a variety of possible solutions.

2. *Identify component problems.* Larger problems are often composed of component problems. To define the larger problem, it is often necessary to identify and describe the subproblems that make it up. For example, poor performance at school might be the result of a number of factors, such as ineffective study habits, inefficient time management, and preoccupation with a personal problem. Defining, and dealing effectively with, the larger problem means defining and dealing with the subproblems first. Identify possible subproblems in our sample problem:

Subproblem a:

Subproblem b:

3. *State the problem clearly and specifically.* A third defining strategy is to state the problem as clearly and specifically as possible, based on an examination of the results that need to be achieved to solve the problem. This sort of clear and specific description of the problem is an important step in solving it. For if you state the problem in *very general* terms, you won't have a clear idea of how best to proceed in dealing with it. But if you can describe your problem in more *specific terms,* then your description will begin to suggest actions you can take to solve the problem. Examine the differences between the statements of the following problem:

General: "My problem is money."

More specific: "My problem is budgeting my money so that I won't always run out near the end of the month."

Most specific: "My problem is developing the habit and the discipline to budget my money so that I won't always run out near the end of the month."

Review your analysis of the sample problem and then state the problem as clearly and specifically as possible:

STEP 2: WHAT ARE THE ALTERNATIVES?

Once you have identified your problem clearly and specifically, your next move is to examine each of the possible actions that might help you solve the problem. Before you list the alternatives, however, it makes sense to determine first which actions are possible and which are impossible. You can do this by exploring the *boundaries* of the problem situation.

Step 2A: What Are the Boundaries of the Problem Situation?

Boundaries are the limits in the problem situation that you cannot change. They are a part of the problem, and they must be accepted and dealt with. For example, in our sample situation, the fact that a day has only twenty-four hours must be accepted as part of the problem situation. There is no point in developing alternatives that ignore this fact. At the same time, you must be careful not to identify as boundaries circumstances that can actually be changed. For instance, you might assume that your problem must be solved in your current location without realizing that relocating to another, less expensive, college is one of your options. Identify additional boundaries that might be a part of the sample situation and some of the questions you would want to answer regarding the boundary. For example:

Time limitations: How much time do I need for each of my basic activities—work, school, social life, travel, and sleep? What is the best way to budget this time?

Step 2B: What Alternatives Are Possible Within These Boundaries?

After you have established a general idea of the boundaries of the problem situation, you can proceed to identify the possible courses of action that can take place within these boundaries. Of course, identifying all the possible alternatives is not always easy; in fact, it may be part of your problem. Often we do not see a way out of a problem because your thinking is set in certain ruts, fixed in certain perspectives. We are blind to other approaches, either because we reject them before seriously considering them ("That will never work!") or because they simply do not occur to us. You can use several strategies to overcome these obstacles:

1. *Discuss the problem with other people.* Discussing possible alternatives with others uses a number of the aspects of critical thinking you explored in Chapter 2. As you saw then, thinking critically involves being open to seeing situations from different viewpoints and discussing your ideas with others in an organized way. Both of these abilities are important in solving problems. As critical thinkers we live—and solve problems—in a community, not simply by ourselves. Other people can often suggest possible alternatives that we haven't thought of, in part because they are outside the situation and thus have a more objective perspective, and in part because they naturally view the world differently than we do, based on their past experiences and their personalities. In addition, discussions are often creative experiences that generate ideas the participants would not have come up with on their own. The dynamics of these interactions often lead to products that are greater than the individual "sum" of those involved.

2. *Brainstorm ideas.* Brainstorming, a method introduced by Alex Osborn, builds on the strengths of working with other people to generate ideas and solve

The best approach to solving problems involves generating many different possible alternatives instead of just a few.

problems. In a typical brainstorming session, a group of people work together to generate as many ideas as possible in a specific period of time. As ideas are produced, they are not judged or evaluated, as this tends to inhibit the free flow of ideas and discourages people from making suggestions. Evaluation is deferred until a later stage. People are encouraged to build on the ideas of others, since the most creative ideas are often generated through the constructive interplay of various minds. A useful visual adjunct to brainstorming is creating mind maps, a process described in Chapter 8, "Relating and Organizing."

3. *Change your location.* Your perspective on a problem is often tied into the circumstances in which the problem exists. For example, a problem you may be having in school is tied into your daily experiences and habitual reactions to these experiences. Sometimes what you need is a fresh perspective, get-

ting away from the problem situation so that you can view it with more clarity and in a different light. Using these strategies, as well as your own reflections, identify as many alternatives to help solve the sample problem that you can think of.

1. Attend school part time
2.
3.
Etc.

STEP 3: WHAT ARE THE ADVANTAGES AND/OR DISADVANTAGES OF EACH ALTERNATIVE?

Once you have identified the various alternatives, your next step is to *evaluate* them, using the kinds of evaluation questions described in Chapter 2. Each possible course of action has certain advantages in the sense that if you select that alternative there will be some positive results. At the same time, each of the possible courses of action likely has disadvantages as well, in the sense that if you select that alternative there may be a cost involved or a risk of some negative results. It is important to examine the potential advantages and/or disadvantages in order to determine how helpful each course of action would be in solving the problem.

Step 3A: What Are the Advantages of Each Alternative?

The alternative we listed in Step 2 for the sample problem ("Attend college part time") might include the following advantages:

Alternatives:	*Advantages:*
1. Attend college part time	This would remove some of the immediate time and money pressures I am experiencing while still allowing me to prepare for the future. I would have more time to focus on the courses that I am taking and work additional hours.

Identify the advantages of each of the alternatives that you listed in Step 2. Be sure that your responses are thoughtful and specific.

Step 3B: What Are the Disadvantages of Each Alternative?

You also need to consider the disadvantages of each alternative. The alternative you listed for the sample problem might include the following disadvantages:

Alternatives:	*Disadvantages:*
1. Attend college part time	It would take me much longer to complete my schooling, thus delaying my progress to my goals. Also, I might lose motivation and drop out before completing school because the process was taking so long. Being a part-time student might threaten my eligibility for financial aid.

Now identify the disadvantages of each of the alternatives that you listed above. Be sure that your responses are thoughtful and specific.

Step 3C: What Additional Information Do I Need to Evaluate Each Alternative?

The next part of Step 3 consists of determining what you must know (*information needed*) to best evaluate and compare the alternatives. For each alternative there are questions that must be answered if you are to establish which alternatives make sense and which do not. In addition, you need to figure out where best to get this information (*sources*).

One useful way to identify the information you need is to ask yourself the question, *What if* I select this alternative?" For instance, one alternative in the sample problem was "attend college part time." When you ask yourself the question, *"What if* I attend college part time?" you are trying to predict what will occur if you select this course of action. To make these predictions, you must answer certain questions and find the information to answer them.

- How long will it take me to complete my schooling?
- How long can I continue in school without losing interest and dropping out?
- Will I threaten my eligibility for financial aid if I become a part-time student?

The information—and the sources for it—that must be located for the first alternative in our sample problem might include the following:

Alternative:	*Information Needed and Sources:*
1. Attend college part time	*Information:* How long will it take me to complete my schooling? How long can I continue in school without losing interest and dropping out? Will I threaten my eligibility for financial aid if I become a part-time student? *Sources:* Myself, other part-time students, school counselors, financial aid office.

Identify the information needed and the sources of this information for each of the alternatives that you identified on page 111. Be sure that your responses are thoughtful and specific.

STEP 4: WHAT IS THE SOLUTION?

The purpose of Steps 1 to 3 is to analyze your problem in a systematic and detailed fashion—to work through the problem in order to become thoroughly familiar with it and the possible solutions to it. After breaking down the problem in this way, the final step should be to try to put the pieces back together— that is, to decide on a thoughtful course of action based on your increased understanding. Even though this sort of problem analysis does not guarantee finding a specific solution to the problem, it should *deepen your understanding* of exactly what the problem is about. And in locating and evaluating your alternatives, it should give you some very good ideas about the general direction you should move in and the immediate steps you should take.

Step 4A: Which Alternative(s) Will I Pursue?

There is no simple formula or recipe to tell you which alternatives to select. As you work through the different courses of action that are possible, you may find that you can immediately rule some out. For example, in the sample problem you may know with certainty that you do not want to attend college part time (alternative 1) because you will forfeit your remaining financial aid. However, it may not be so simple to select which of the other alternatives you wish to pursue. How do you decide?

The decisions we make usually depend on what we believe to be most important to us. These beliefs regarding what is most important to us are known

as *values*. Our values are the starting points of our actions and strongly influence our decisions. For example, if we value staying alive (as most of us do),
then we will make many decisions each day that express this value—eating
proper meals, not walking in front of moving traffic, and so on.

Our values help us *set priorities* in life—that is, decide what aspects of our
lives are most important to us. We might decide that for the present going to
school is more important than having an active social life. In this case, going to
school is a higher priority than having an active social life. Unfortunately, our
values are not always consistent with each other—we may have to choose *either*
to go to school or to have an active social life. Both activities may be important
to us; they are simply not compatible with each other. Very often the *conflicts*
between our values constitute the problem. Let's examine some strategies for
selecting alternatives that might help us solve our problem.

1. *Evaluate and compare alternatives.* Although each alternative may have certain
   advantages and disadvantages, not all advantages are equally desirable or
   potentially effective. For example, giving up on college entirely would certainly solve some aspects of the sample problem, but its obvious disadvantages would rule out this solution for most people. Thus it makes sense to
   try to evaluate and rank the various alternatives, based on how effective
   they are likely to be and how they match up with your value system. A good
   place to begin is the "Results" stage, Step 1B. Examine each of the alternatives and evaluate how well it will contribute to achieving the results you
   are aiming for in the situation. You may want to rank the alternatives or
   develop your own rating system to assess their relative effectiveness.

   After evaluating the alternatives in terms of their anticipated *effectiveness*, the next step is to evaluate them in terms of their *desirability*, based on
   your needs, interests, and value systems. Again, you can use either a ranking or a rating system to assess their relative desirability. After completing
   these two separate evaluations, you can then select the alternative(s) that
   seem most appropriate. Review the alternatives you identified in the sample
   problem and then rank or rate them according to their potential effectiveness and desirability, assuming this problem was your own.

2. *Synthesize a new alternative.* After reviewing and evaluating the alternatives
   you generated, you may develop a new alternative that combines the best
   qualities of several options while avoiding the disadvantages some of them
   have if chosen exclusively. In the sample problem, you might combine attending college part time during the academic year with attending school
   during the summer session so that progress toward your degree won't be

impeded. Examine the alternatives you identified and develop a new option that combines the best elements of several of them.

3. *Try out each alternative in your imagination.* Focus on each alternative and try to imagine, as concretely as possible, what it would be like if you actually selected it. Visualize what impact your choice would have on your problem and what the implications would be for your life as a whole. By trying out the alternative in your imagination, you can sometimes avoid unpleasant results or unexpected consequences. As a variation of this strategy, you can sometimes test alternatives on a very limited basis in a practice situation. For example, if you are trying to overcome your fear of speaking in groups, you can practice various speaking techniques with your friends or family until you find an approach you are comfortable with.

After trying out these strategies on the sample problem, select the alternative(s) you think would be most effective and desirable from your standpoint.

Alternative(s):

Step 4B: What Steps Can I Take to Act on the Alternative(s) Chosen?

Once you have decided on the correct alternative(s) to pursue, your next move is to plan the steps you will have to take to put it in action. This is the same process of working toward your goals that we explored in Chapter 1. Planning the specific steps you will take is extremely important. Although thinking carefully about your problem is necessary, it is not enough if you hope to solve the problem. You have to *take action,* and planning specific steps is where we begin. In the sample problem, for example, imagine that one of the alternatives you have selected is "Find additional sources of income that will enable me to work part time and go to school full time." The specific steps you would want to take might include the following:

1. Contact the financial aid office at the school to see what other forms of financial aid are available and what I have to do to apply for them.
2. Contact some of the local banks to see what sort of student loans are available.
3. Look for a higher-paying job so that I can earn more money without working additional hours.

4. Discuss the problem with students in similar circumstances in order to generate new ideas.

Identify the steps you would have to take in pursuing the alternative(s) you identified on page 111.

Of course, plans do not implement themselves. Once you know what actions you have to take, you need to commit yourself to taking the necessary steps. This is where many people stumble in the problem-solving process, paralyzed by inertia or fear. Sometimes, to overcome these blocks and inhibitions, you need to reexamine your original acceptance of the problem, perhaps making use of some of the strategies you explored on pages 102–103. Once you get started, the rewards of actively attacking your problem are often enough incentive to keep you focused and motivated.

STEP 5: HOW WELL IS THE SOLUTION WORKING?

As you work toward reaching a reasonable and informed conclusion, you should not fall into the trap of thinking that there is only one "right" decision and that all is lost if you do not figure out what it is and carry it out. You should remind yourself that any analysis of problem situations, no matter how careful and systematic, is ultimately limited. You simply cannot anticipate or predict everything that is going to happen in the future. As a result, every decision you make is provisional, in the sense that your ongoing experience will inform you if your decisions are working out or if they need to be changed and modified. As you saw in Chapter 2, this is precisely the attitude of the critical thinker— someone who is *receptive* to new ideas and experiences and *flexible* enough to change or modify beliefs based on new information. Critical thinking is not a compulsion to find the "right" answer or make the "correct" decision; it is an ongoing process of exploration and discovery.

Step 5A: What Is My Evaluation?

In many cases the relative effectiveness of your efforts will be apparent. In other cases it will be helpful to pursue a more systematic evaluation, along the lines suggested in the following strategies.

1. *Compare the results with the goals.* The essence of evaluation is comparing the results of your efforts with the initial goals you are trying to achieve. For example, the goals of the sample problem are embodied in the results you specified on page 106. Compare the anticipated results of the alternative(s) you selected. To what extent will your choice meet these goals? Are there goals that are not likely to be met by your alternative(s)? Which ones? Could they be addressed by other alternatives? Asking these and other questions will help you clarify the success of your efforts, and provide a foundation for future decisions.

2. *Get other perspectives.* As you have seen throughout the problem-solving proc–ess, getting the opinions of others is a productive strategy at virtually every stage, and this is certainly true for evaluation. Other people can often pro-vide perspectives that are both different and more objective than yours. Natu-rally, the evaluations of others are not always better or more accurate than your own, but even when they are not, reflecting on these different views usually deepens your understanding of the situation. It is not always easy to receive the evaluations of others, but open-mindedness to outside opinions is a very valuable attitude to cultivate, for it will stimulate and guide you to produce our best efforts.

   To receive specific, practical feedback from others, you need to ask specific, practical questions that will elicit this information. General ques-tions ("What do you think of this?") typically result in overly general, un-helpful responses ("It sounds okay to me"). Be focused in soliciting feedback, and remember: You do have the right to ask people to be *constructive* in their comments, providing suggestions for improvement rather than flatly express-ing what they think is wrong.

Step 5B: What Adjustments Are Necessary?

As a result of your review, you may discover that the alternative you selected is not feasible or is not leading to satisfactory results. For example, in the sample problem, you may find that it is impossible to find additional sources of income so that you can work part time instead of full time. In that case, you simply have to go back and review the other alternatives to identify another possible course of action. At other times you may find that the alternative you selected is working out fairly well but still requires some adjustments as you continue to work toward your desired outcomes. In fact, this is a typical situation that you should expect to occur. Even when things initially appear to be working reasonably well, an active thinker continues to ask questions such as "What might I have overlooked?" and "How could I have done this differently?" Of course, asking—and trying to answer—questions like this is even more essential if solutions are hard to come by (as they usually are in real-world problems) and if you are to retain the flexibility and optimism you need to tackle a new option.

THINKING ACTIVITY 3.2

Select a problem from your own life. It should be one that you are currently grappling with and have not yet been able to solve. After selecting the problem you want to work on, strengthen your *acceptance* of the problem by using one or more of the strategies described on page 102 and describing your efforts. Then analyze your problem using the problem-solving method described in the chapter. Discuss your problem with other class members to generate fresh perspectives and unusual alternatives that might not have occurred to you. Using your own paper, write your analysis in outline style, giving specific responses to the questions in each step of the problem-solving method. Although you might not reach a "guaranteed" solution to your problem, you should deepen your understanding of the problem and develop a concrete plan of action that will help you move in the right direction. Implement your plan of action and then monitor the results. ◄

SOLVING THE PROBLEM OF *NOT ENOUGH MONEY*

The sample problem we are working on is really comprised of several distinct though interrelated problems:

- Not enough time
- Not enough money

These are common problems that many people encounter in their lives. Let's use the method we have been using to explore approaches for solving these problems, beginning with the problem of *not enough money*.

Money difficulties are the number one reason that students drop out of college. Too often, however, students leave college before exploring all of their options for increasing their income or decreasing their expenses.

Effective problem solvers are able to analyze complex problems — like "time" and "money" — in an organized way and then develop creative solutions.

Step 1: What Is the Problem?

A problem like this is actually much more complicated than the simple characterization of "I don't have enough money." If you are like many people, you will live much of your life feeling that you don't have "enough money." Although you will likely be earning more money in the future, you will also probably have more expenses as well. Somehow the amount of money we spend (or want to spend) always seems greater than the money we earn. So the problem isn't merely "not having enough money": the problem is not *managing* your money in a way that enables you to have the things that are most important to you. Managing your money involves both regulating your expenses *and* maximizing your income.

Step 1A: What Do I Know about the Situation (of Not Having Enough Money)?)   Solving a problem begins with determining what information you *know* to be the case and what information you *think* might be the case. Sometimes a situation may appear to be a problem when it really isn't, simply because our information isn't accurate. For example, you might be worried about staying in college because you believe you are not eligible for additional financial assistance. If this belief is inaccurate, however, then your "problem" may not really exist.

The best place to begin the analysis of your money situation is to complete an inventory of where you currently stand. With this information as a foundation, you can then construct an intelligent budget that reflects your priorities, and also engage in some long-range financial planning.

THINKING ACTIVITY 3.3

Analyze your current financial situation by first outlining your sources of *income* by category: for example, paycheck, financial aid, savings, contributions from family. Specify these figures on a weekly and monthly basis. Next, analyze your *expenses* by first making a list of all the categories that you spend money on: rent, utilities, food, tuition, books, transportation, clothes, CDs and tapes, entertainment, and so on. Then organize these expenses on a weekly and monthly basis. Use the Financial Inventory worksheet on page 121 to guide your analysis of both income and expenses.

Having completed your inventories, think about your income and expense patterns. How would you describe your financial situation? Did you find any surprises? How does your total annual income compare to your total annual expenses? ◀

Step 1B: What Results Am I Aiming for in This Situation?   After compiling your income and expense inventory, you need to evaluate your financial situation critically and plan proposed changes if needed. Begin by prioritizing your expenses.

Financial Inventory

Day	INCOME				EXPENSES						
	Paycheck	Financial Aid	Family	Savings	Other	Rent	Utilities	Tuition	Food	Books	Transpor-tation	Entertain-ment
M												
T												
W												
TH												
F												
M												
T												
W												
TH												
F												
M												
T												
W												
TH												
F												
M												
T												
W												
TH												
F												
Totals												

- Identify the expenses that are *essential* and indicate when they are due. Many of these expenses are fixed and recurring, such as rent, utilities, food, and haircuts. Other expenses are intermittent and variable, such as medical fees and car repair.
- Identify the expenses that are *important*, though not necessarily essential, such as new clothes.
- Identify the expenses that are *attractive* but not as important, such as entertainment and vacations.

After completing your work, evaluate whether the amounts you are spending in the various categories are appropriate. If you think that you are spending too much, put a reduced amount in the appropriate column. If you think that you are spending too little, record an increased amount in the appropriate column. These targets represent the expense goals that you will try to achieve.

Next, critically evaluate your income, using the same worksheet. Break down your income into fixed sources—like paychecks or financial aid—and intermittent sources—like working on special projects or occasional contributions from your family.

Identify the areas that you would like to increase your income, and estimate the increased amounts you would *realistically* like to achieve. These amounts represent the income goals that you will try to reach.

As a final step, add all of your proposed expenses on an annual basis and compare this amount to the total income you are planning to achieve. The income figure should be significantly larger than the expense figure, since there are always unexpected emergencies, and we tend to underestimate our expenses and overestimate our income. If your income total is not substantially larger than your expense total, you should probably review your anticipated expenses to try and reduce them!

Step 1C: How Can I Define the Problem?   Using the strategies for defining problems described on page 106, state the problem as clearly and specifically as possible.

Step 2: What Are the Alternatives?

Alternatives for managing your money better fall into the two categories of reducing your expenses and increasing your income. After reviewing the approaches described next, write down additional alternatives that are appropriate to your own individual situation. Use one or more of the strategies described on page 109 to help you break out of your typical ways of thinking. Some possible alternatives follow.

Alternative 1: *Create a weekly and monthly budget.*

Using the expense and income inventories that you completed in Step 1 as a guide, create a weekly and monthly budget for yourself. Do your best to stick to it, and note any unexpected expenses that appear. At the end of each week, revise your monthly budget based on what you have actually earned and spent. A Monthly Budget worksheet to guide you is located on page 124.

Alternative 2: *Avoid credit card purchases whenever possible and pay my total balance each month.*

Institutions that administer credit cards are counting on you to feel that using a credit card is not the same thing as spending money. That's why it's so easy to roll up large amounts on credit cards, amounts you would never spend if you were using cash. Once you charge more than you can pay back at the end of the month, you get drawn into their system of outrageously high interest, typically 18 percent or more. This creates an ongoing balance that never seems to shrink significantly, no matter how hard you try, in part because 20 percent of your spending money is being used for interest.

Alternative 3: *Comparison shop for my purchases.*

There are remarkable discrepancies between what different stores charge for the same items. With a little effort, you can significantly cut your expenses by finding the lowest prices. For example, buy a month's supply of toiletries and cosmetics at a discount drug store. Purchase your computer equipment and software through college-sponsored consortiums. Buy your plane tickets far enough in advance to qualify for discount fares.

Alternative 4: *Limit the spending money in my wallet.*

People tend to find ways to spend the cash that is available to them. Decide in advance how much you want to spend that day or evening, and take along just that amount, with an extra $20 tucked away for emergencies *only.*

Alternative 5: *Avoid impulse buying.*

We often buy things on the spur of the moment that we wouldn't if we had time to think about it. To combat this, wait a day or two to decide on a purchase, asking the question "Do I really *need* this?"

Monthly Budget

Day	INCOME					EXPENSES						
	Paycheck	Financial Aid	Family	Savings	Other	Rent	Utilities	Tuition	Food	Books	Transportation	Entertainment
M												
T												
W												
TH												
F												
M												
T												
W												
TH												
F												
M												
T												
W												
TH												
F												
M												
T												
W												
TH												
F												
Totals												

Alternative 6: *If you are not employed, consider getting a part-time job*

Having a part-time job of less than twenty hours a week not only increases your income, it also helps you structure your time and become more efficient. If you can secure employment in a field related to your career interests, you are gaining valuable experience as well. Many colleges have work/study and internship programs, and many employers offer career opportunities that will sponsor your college study.

Alternative 7: *Create my own job.*

If you can't find a job that suits your needs, consider creating a service that uses your skills. For example, to increase my income in college, I advertised myself as a custom woodworker and began building custom furniture. Since I had no formal experience, I began with simple designs like bookshelves (which everybody needs!) and then branched out to wall units, beds, tables, and drawer units. Eventually I even published a book entitled *Designing and Making Fine Furniture.* Similarly, you may have skills that you can market at the college or in your local area such as hair cutting or braiding, tutoring in specific areas like languages or math, word processing, pet or baby-sitting.

Alternative 8: *Explore all possibilities for financial assistance.*

Although it takes time to research all of the grants and scholarships that you might qualify for, and to complete the required applications, your effort represents a sound investment. If necessary, student loans are also available, through the college and local lending institutions. However, don't lose sight of the fact that these loans must be repaid, usually with interest.

Alternative 9:

Alternative 10:

Step 3: What Are the Advantages and/or Disadvantages of Each Alternative?

Carefully review the alternatives just described, as well as those that you identified, and then for each alternative describe the advantages, disadvantages, and further information needed. For example:

Alternative 1: *Create a weekly and monthly budget*

Advantages: Creating a weekly and monthly schedule will help me orga-nize and control my finances, and become aware of my spending habits. Since it will bring some predictability to my financial situation, a budget will help me feel more relaxed and confident about money, while teaching me important money management skills that I will use throughout my life.

Disadvantages: Trying to stick to a budget can be time-consuming and an-noying. In addition, it is difficult to estimate every expense, and there are often unexpected expenses that throw a budget out of whack.

Information needed: Can I learn to use a budget in a natural and flexible way? Can I learn to adapt to unexpected expenses? Do I have the determina-tion to stick to my budget?

Step 4: What Is the Solution?

Step 4A: Which Alternative(s) Will I Pursue?   Your analysis of the various al-ternatives for managing money should have provided you with some produc-tive ideas you can use. Review the strategies for selecting alternatives explained on page 113, and then identify below one or more alternatives that you plan to implement.

Alternative 1:

Alternative 2:

Alternative 3:

Step 4B: What Steps Can I Take to Act on the Alternative(s) Chosen?   De-velop a plan of action to implement the alternatives that you have selected. Be sure that your plan is realistic and specific. If you find that your resolve is weak-ening, return to the acceptance stage of your analysis to reestablish your cour-age and determination.

Step 5: How Well Is the Solution Working?

Using the strategies described on page 116, evaluate the success of your plan and make any necessary adjustments.

SOLVING THE PROBLEM OF *NOT ENOUGH TIME*

Another problem commonly faced by students is that of "not having enough time." In addition to the demands of school, students must often integrate employment, family responsibilities, athletics, and extracurricular and volunteer activities. Let's apply the method we have been using to analyze the problem of *not enough time.*

Accepting the Problem

Although many people complain about not having enough time, not everyone is ready to acknowledge their responsibility in creating their predicament and committing themselves to improving it through thoughtful analysis and determined action. If you find that you have these sorts of difficulties, perhaps you could use one or more of the strategies described on page 102.

Step 1: What Is the Problem?

Step 1A: What Do I Know about the Situation?   Since we cannot actually *create* time (we're all stuck with twenty-four hours per day, 168 hours per week), we need to think of ways that we can *use* the time we have more efficiently and productively. In order to begin this process it is helpful to analyze how you are currently using the time allocated to you. Complete the time inventory in the following Thinking Activity.

THINKING ACTIVITY 3.4

Describe a typical week in your life, using the following categories: morning preparations, evening preparations, meals, sleep, classes, study, work, travel, socializing, exercise/sports, activities (specify), television/music, reading, other (specify).

Use the Time Inventory worksheet on page 127 as a guide in this task. After completing the worksheet, add up the total hours that you spend in each of the different categories. How would you analyze the result? Did you find any surprises? ◀

Time Inventory

	7:00 am	8:00 am	9:00 am	10:00 am	11:00 am	12:00 pm	1:00 pm	2:00 pm	3:00 pm	4:00 pm	5:00 pm	6:00 pm
Monday												
Tuesday												
Wednesday												
Thursday												
Friday												
Saturday												
Sunday												

	7:00 pm	8:00 pm	9:00 pm	10:00 pm	11:00 pm	12:00 am	1:00 am	2:00 am	3:00 am	4:00 am	5:00 am	6:00 am
Monday												
Tuesday												
Wednesday												
Thursday												
Friday												
Saturday												
Sunday												

Step 1B. What Results Am I Aiming for in This Situation?   Review the time inventory that you just created and think about your own personal situation with respect to time. In which areas of your life do you feel particularly squeezed, where you need more time? On the other hand, in which areas do you feel that you are spending too much time? With these ideas in mind, identify the major "time" results that you would like to achieve.

Result 1:

Result 2:

Result 3:

Step 1C: How Can I Define the Problem?   Based on what you discovered in Step 1A and Step 1B, describe your essential problem with respect to time. Use one or more of the strategies described on page 106 to assist you in defining your problem.

Step 2: What Are the Alternatives?

Beyond chanting the refrain, "I need more time" or cutting down on their sleep, many people have few strategies for better managing their time. Yet there are many successful approaches we can use to create time by living our lives more efficiently. Some strategies are described in this section. After reviewing them, write down additional alternatives that are appropriate to your own individual situation. Use one or more of the strategies described on page 106 to help you break out of your typical ways of thinking.

Alternative 1: *Create a weekly plan to organize my time.*

Using the time inventory that you created in the Thinking Activity, and taking into consideration the changes you proposed after reviewing your inventory, create a proposed weekly schedule for yourself. You can use the Weekly Schedule located on page 130, or you can create your own.

Alternative 2: *Prioritize my activities so that I can concentrate on the most important things.*

Make a daily list on an index card of the things you would like to get done that day. Then prioritize them by using the following key:

+++   Absolutely essential

++   Important

+   Desirable

Weekly Schedule

	7:00 am	8:00 am	9:00 am	10:00 am	11:00 am	12:00 pm	1:00 pm	2:00 pm	3:00 pm	4:00 pm	5:00 pm	6:00 pm
Monday												
Tuesday												
Wednesday												
Thursday												
Friday												
Saturday												
Sunday												

	7:00 pm	8:00 pm	9:00 pm	10:00 pm	11:00 pm	12:00 am	1:00 am	2:00 am	3:00 am	4:00 am	5:00 am	6:00 am
Monday												
Tuesday												
Wednesday												
Thursday												
Friday												
Saturday												
Sunday												

At the end of the day, create a new prioritized list for the following day, placing on the list the things that you didn't get to that day.

Alternative 3: *Synthesize my schedule to make it more efficient.*

Carefully examine your schedule to see how you can organize it more efficiently. For example, try to schedule your classes close together to cut down on extra travel and waiting time between classes (although the extra time in-between classes can be used to study and process the material you just learned, or to prepare for your upcoming classes). Try to locate your key locations—home, school, work, child care—as proximate as possible, in order to save travel time. Combine your shopping trips and errands in order to complete them more efficiently. See if there are other strategies you can use to better synthesize your schedule and so "create" more time.

Alternative 4: *Make use of the small blocks of time in my schedule.*

Although it's best to study in time blocks of one hour or greater, much of our daily schedule has smaller periods of time sandwiched in. Often we don't even attempt to make productive use of these smaller intervals, but they can be valuable resources for us if we approach them creatively. Studying for short, intense intervals can be extremely effective. And if we're prepared to get right to work, we can get things accomplished in as little as fifteen or twenty minutes. After all, three twenty-minute periods does add up to one hour. Similarly, time spent traveling can be used productively, whether riding on public transportation or even driving in our cars, when we listen to tape-recorded versions of the notes we have made.

Alternative 5: *Create a diversely integrated schedule.*

Although it may seem logical to create large time blocks for various activities, like allowing four hours to study history, the fact is this is not the most effective approach. Instead, you work more effectively when you alternate activities in order to stay "fresh." For example, it may make more sense to schedule your four-hour time-block along the following lines:

study history	60 minutes
snack break	15 minutes
philosophy paper	60 minutes
physical exercise	15 minutes

review notes for biology   45 minutes

English reading   45 minutes

This type of diverse scheduling helps you avoid the loss of concentration that often occurs when you are doing one activity for too long. It also encourages you to avoid Parkinson's Law, the observation by C. Northcote Parkinson that work expands to fit the time allotted. By scheduling shorter time periods to complete activities, you are challenged to work in a more focused and efficient mode.

Alternative 6: *Target the "time wasters" in my life and try to reduce or eliminate them.*

Each of us has our own time temptations, activities that we slip into doing and end up wasting precious hours. It may be hanging out with friends, watching the soaps on TV, talking on the phone, or simply daydreaming. Identify your time wasters, and then make a concerted effort to reduce or even eliminate them from your schedule.

Alternative 7: *Avoid perfectionism and procrastination.*

These are distinct though often related time maladies that infect many people. Perfectionism is the need to complete all work to your highest possible standards. It is an admirable goal, but you often don't have the time to meet these high standards in all of your activities. Although some important projects may demand your highest-quality work, you can often use more reasonable standards for many activities.

Procrastination is a more common problem, one in which you postpone responsibilities until you run out of time. Many of the strategies we have described in this chapter will help you overcome procrastination, but you need to exercise your strongest willpower to break these deeply ingrained habits. In fact, procrastination is sometimes so deeply rooted in your personality and way of relating to the world that you need to give it its own individual problem analysis!

Alternative 8:

Alternative 9:

Step 3: What Are the Advantages and/or Disadvantages of Each Alternative?

Carefully review the alternatives just described in the book as well as those that you identified, and then for each alternative list the advantages, disadvantages, and further information needed. For example:

Alternative 1: *Create a weekly plan to organize my time*

Advantages: A weekly schedule will help me create a total design that includes all of the activities I need to accomplish. It will encourage me to plan ahead and also prevent me from spending excessive time on any one activity. It will also discourage time-wasting activities, give my life more stability, and help me feel "in control."

Disadvantages: Weekly schedules can be applied in an overly rigid way. There are also unknown factors and unforeseen circumstances that might interfere with my plans, and if I try to follow the schedule slavishly, I may end up doing more harm than good.

Information needed: Will I be able to stick to the schedule once I have created it? Will I be able to use it flexibly, making the necessary adjustments when the unexpected occurs?

Step 4: What Is the Solution?

4A. Which Alternative(s) Will I Pursue? Your analysis of the various alternatives for managing time should have provided you with some useful ideas which you can use in your own life. Review the strategies for selecting alternatives explained on page 109, and then identify one or more alternatives that you plan to implement.

Alternative 1:

Alternative 2:

Alternative 3:

4B. What Steps Can I Take to Act on the Alternative(s) Chosen? For each of the alternatives that you identified, design a plan of action that specifies the steps that you need to take to implement them. Don't forget to include a *time* schedule with your plans of action!

Step 5: How Well Is the Solution Working?

As you implement the plans of action described in Step 4B, monitor how successfully they are helping you. If you find that you need to make adjustments to improve their effectiveness, then make them. If you find that a plan is not working, go back, review your list of alternatives, and try another one. If you discover that your motivation to manage time is diminishing and find yourself slipping back into some of your old time-wasting habits, review the strategies that you used during the acceptance stage of your analysis (page 102) in an effort to recommit yourself to solving this problem. Additional evaluation strategies are located on page 116.

THINKING ACTIVITY 3.5

Analyze the following problems using the problem-solving approach presented in this chapter.

Problem 1: Background Information

The most important unsolved problem that exists for me is the inability to make that crucial decision of what to major in. I want to be secure with respect to both money and happiness when I make a career for myself, and I don't want to make a mistake in choosing a field of study. I want to make this decision before beginning the next semester so that I can start immediately in my career. I've been thinking about managerial studies. However, I often wonder if I have the capacity to make executive decisions when I can't even decide on what I want to do with my life.

Problem 2: Background Information

One of my problems is my difficulty in taking tests. It's not that I don't study. What happens is that when I get the test I become nervous and my mind goes blank. For example, in my social science class, the teacher told the class on Tuesday that there would be a test on Thursday. That afternoon I went home and began studying for the test. By Thursday I knew most of the work, but when the test was handed out, I got nervous and my mind went blank. For a long time I just stared at the test, and I ended up failing it.

Problem 3: Background Information

My problem is "the weed." I have been smoking cigarettes for over five years. At first I did it because I liked the image and most of my friends were smoking as well. Gradually, I got hooked. It's such a part of my life now, I don't know if I can quit. Having a cup of coffee, studying, talking to people—it just seems natural to have a cigarette in my hand. I know there are a lot of good reasons for me to stop. I've even tried a few times, but I always ended up bumming cigarettes from friends and then giving up entirely. I don't want my health to go up in smoke, but I don't know what to do.

Problem 4: Background Information

One of the serious problems in my life is learning English as a second language. It is not so easy to learn a second language, especially when you live in an environment where only your native language is spoken. When I came to this country three years ago, I could speak almost no English. I have learned a lot, but my lack of fluency is getting in the way of my studies and my social relationships.

Problem 5: Background Information

This is my first year of college and in general I'm enjoying it a great deal. The one disturbing thing I have encountered is the amount of drinking that students engage in when they socialize. Although I enjoy drinking in moderation, most students drink much more than "in moderation" at parties. They want to "get drunk," "lose control," "get wasted." And the parties aren't just on weekends—they're every night of the week! The problem is that there is a lot of pressure for me to join in the drinking and partying. Most of the people I enjoy being with are joining in, and I don't want to be left out of the social life of the college. But it's impossible to party so much and still keep up to date with my course work. And all that drinking certainly isn't good for me physically. But on the other hand, I don't want to be excluded from the social life, and when I try to explain that I don't enjoy heavy drinking, my friends make me feel immature and a little silly. What should I do? ◄

SOLVING NONPERSONAL PROBLEMS

The problems we have analyzed up until this point are "personal" problems in the sense that they represent individual challenges encountered by us as we live our lives. Problems are not only of a personal nature, however. We also face problems as members of a community, society, and the world. As with personal problems, we need to approach these kinds of problems in an organized and thoughtful way in order to explore the issues, develop a clear understanding, and decide on an informed plan of action. For example, racism and prejudice directed toward African Americans, Hispanics, Asians, Jews, homosexuals, and other minority groups seems to be on the rise at many college campuses. There has been an increase of overt racial incidents at colleges and universities during the past several years, a particularly disturbing situation given the lofty egalitarian ideals of higher education. Experts from different fields have offered a variety of explanations to account for this behavior. Describe why you believe these racial and ethnic incidents are occurring with increasing frequency.

Making sense of a complex, challenging situation like this is not a simple process. Although the problem-solving method we have been using in this chapter is a powerful approach, its successful application depends on having sufficient information about the situation we are trying to solve. As a result, it is often necessary for us to research articles and other sources of information to develop informed opinions about the problem we are investigating.

The famous newspaperman H. L. Mencken once said, "To every complex question there is a simple answer—and it's wrong!" We have seen in this chapter that complex problems do not admit simple solutions, whether they concern personal problems in our lives or larger social problems like racial prejudice or world hunger. We have also seen, however, that by working through these complex problems thoughtfully and systematically, we can achieve a deeper understanding of their many interacting elements, as well as develop strategies for solving them.

Becoming an effective problem-solver does not merely involve applying a problem-solving method in a mechanical fashion, any more than becoming a mature critical thinker involves mastering a set of thinking skills. Rather, solving problems, like thinking critically, reflects a total approach to making sense of experience. When we think like problem-solvers, we approach the world in a distinctive way. Instead of avoiding difficult problems, we have the courage to meet them head-on and the determination to work through them. Instead of acting impulsively or relying exclusively on the advice of others, we are able to make sense of complex problems in an organized way and develop practical solutions and initiatives.

A sophisticated problem-solver employs all of the critical thinking abilities that we have examined so far and those we will explore in the chapters ahead. And while we might agree with H. L. Mencken's evaluation of simple answers to complex questions, we might endorse a rephrased version: "To many complex questions there are complex answers—and these are worth pursuing!"

Thinking Activity 3.6

Identify an important local, national, or international problem that needs to be solved. Locate two or more articles that provide background information and analysis of the problem. Using these articles as a resource, analyze the problem using the problem-solving method developed in this chapter. ◀

Thinking Passages

The final section of this chapter comprises two articles dealing with significant social problems in our lives today. The first, "Young Hate" by David Shenk, examines the problem of intolerance on college campuses. This information provides a foundation from which we can construct a thoughtful analysis of this troubling problem and perhaps develop some productive solutions. The second article, "When Is It Rape?" by Nancy Gibbs, addresses another very current and complicated problem on college campuses. After reading each article, identify and analyze the problem being discussed using the problem-solving method developed in this chapter.

Young Hate
by David Shenk

Death to gays. Here is the relevant sequence of events: On Monday night Jerry Mattioli leads a candlelight vigil for lesbian and gay rights. *Gays are trash.* On Tuesday his name is in the school paper and he can hear whispers and feel more, colder stares than usual. On Wednesday morning a walking bridge in the middle of the Michigan State campus is found to be covered with violent epithets warning campus homosexuals to *be afraid, very afraid,* promising to *abolish faggots from existence,* and including messages specifically directed at Mattioli. Beginning Friday morning fifteen of the perpetrators, all known to Mattioli by name and face, are rounded up and quietly disciplined by the university. *Go home faggots.* On Friday afternoon Mattioli is asked by university officials to leave campus for the weekend, for his own safety. He does, and a few hours later receives a phone call from a friend who tells him that his dormitory room has been torched. MSU's second annual "Cross-Cultural Week" is over.

"Everything was ruined," Mattioli says. "What wasn't burned was ruined by smoke and heat and by the water. On Saturday I sat with the fire investigator all day, and we went through the room, literally ash by ash. . . . The answering machine had melted. The receiver of the telephone on the wall had stretched to about three feet long. That's how intense the heat was."

"Good news!" says Peter Jennings. *A recent Washington Post/*ABC News poll shows that integration is up and racial tension is down in America, as compared with eight years ago. Of course, in any trend there are fluctuations, exceptions. At the University of Massachusetts at Amherst, an estimated two thousand whites chase twenty blacks in a clash after a 1986 World Series game, race riots break out in Miami in 1988 and in Virginia Beach in 1989; and on college campuses across the country, our nation's young elite experience an entire decade's aberration from the poll's findings: incidents of ethnic, religious, and genderrelated harassment surge throughout the eighties.

Greatest hits include Randy Bowman, a black student at the University of Texas, having to respectfully decline a request by two young men wearing Ronald Reagan masks and wielding a pistol to exit his eighth-floor dorm room through the window; homemade T-shirts, *Thank God for AIDS* and *Aryan by the Grace of God,* among others, worn proudly on campus; Jewish student centers shot at, stoned, and defaced at Memphis State, University of Kansas, Rutgers (*Six million, why not*), and elsewhere; the black chairperson of United Minorities Council at U Penn getting a dose of hi-tech hate via answering machine: *We're going to lynch you, nigger shit. We are going to lynch you.*

The big picture is less graphic, but just as dreadful: reports of campus harassment have increased as much as 400 percent since 1985. Dropout rates for black students in predominantly white colleges are as much as five times higher than white dropout rates at the same schools and black dropout rates at black schools. The Anti-Defamation League reports a sixfold increase in anti-Semitic episodes on campuses between 1985 and 1988. Meanwhile, Howard J. Ehrlich of the National Institute Against Prejudice and Violence reminds us that "up to 80 percent of harassed students don't report the harassment." Clearly, the barrage of news reports reveals only the tip of a thoroughly sour iceberg.

Colleges have responded to incidents of intolerance—and the subsequent demands of minority rights groups—with the mandatory ethnic culture classes and restrictions on verbal harassment. But what price tranquility? Libertarian and conservative student groups, faculty, and political advisors lash out over limitations on free speech and the improper embrace of liberal political agendas. "Progressive academic administrations," writes University of Pennsylvania professor Alan Charles Kors in the *Wall Street Journal*, "are determined to enlighten their morally benighted students and protect the community from political sin."

Kors and kind bristle at the language of compromise being attached to official university policy. The preamble to the University of Michigan's new policy on discriminatory behavior reads, in part, "Because there is tension between freedom of speech, the right of individuals to be free from injury caused by discrimination, and the University's duty to protect the educational process . . . it may be necessary to have varying standards depending on the locus of regulated conduct." The policy tried to "strike a balance" by applying different sets of restrictions to academic centers, open areas, and living quarters, but in so doing, hit a wall. Before the policy could go into effect, it was struck down in a Michigan court as being too vague. At least a dozen schools in the process of formulating their own policies scurried in retreat as buoyant free-speech advocates went on the offensive. Tufts University president Jean Mayer voluntarily dismissed his school's "Freedom of Speech versus Freedom from Harassment" policy after a particularly inventive demonstration by late-night protesters, who used chalk, tape, and poster board to divide the campus into designated free speech, limited speech, and non-free speech zones. "We're not working for a right to offensive speech," says admitted chalker Andrew Zappia, co-editor of the conservative campus paper, *The Primary Source*. "This is about protecting free speech, in general, and allowing the community to set its own standards about what is appropriate. . . .

"The purpose of the Tufts policy was to prosecute people for what the university described as 'gray area'—meaning unintentional—harassment." Zappia gives a hypothetical example: "I'm a Catholic living in a dorm, and I put up a poster in my room [consistent with my faith] saying that homosexuality is bad. If I have a gay roommate or one who doesn't agree with me, he could have me prosecuted, not because I hung it there to offend him, but because it's gray area harassment. . . . The policy was well intended, but it was dangerously vague. They used words like *stigmatizing, offensive,* harassing—words that are very difficult to define."

Detroit lawyer Walter B. Connolly, Jr., disagrees. He insists that it's quite proper for schools to act to protect the victims of discrimination as long as the restrictions stay out of the classroom. "Defamation, child pornography, fighting words, inappropriate comments on the radio—there are all sorts of areas where the First Amendment isn't the preeminent burning omnipotence in the sky. . . . Whenever you have competing interests of a federal statute [and] the Constitution, you end up balancing."

If you want to see a liberal who follows this issue flinch, whisper into his or her ear the name Shelby Steele. Liberals don't like Steele, an (African American) English professor at California's San Jose State; they try to dismiss him as having no professional experience in the study of racial discrimination. But he's heavily into the subject, and his analyses are both lucid and disturbing. Steele doesn't favor restrictions on speech, largely because they don't deal with what he sees as the problem. "You don't gain very much by trying to legislate the problem away, curtailing everyone's rights in the process," he says. In a forum in which almost everyone roars against a shadowy, usually nameless contingent of racist thugs, Steele deviates, choosing instead to accuse the accusers. He blames not the racists, but the weak-kneed liberal administrators and power-hungry victims' advocates for the mess on campuses today.

"Racial tension on campus is the result more of racial equality than inequality," says Steele. "On campuses today, as throughout society, blacks enjoy equality under the law—a profound social advancement. . . . What has emerged in recent years . . . in a sense as a result of progress . . . is *a politics of difference*, a troubling, volatile politics in which each group justifies itself, its sense of worth and its pursuit of power, through difference alone." On nearly every campus, says Steele, groups representing blacks, Hispanics, Asians, gays, women, Jews, and any combinations therein solicit special resources. Asked for—often demanded, in intense demonstrations—are funds for African-American (Hispanic . . .) cultural centers, separate (face it, segregated) housing, ethnic studies programs, and even individual academic incentives—at Penn State, minority students are given $275 per semester if they earn a C average, twice that if they do better than 2.75.

These entitlements, however, do not just appear *deus ex machina*. Part two of Steele's thesis addresses what he calls the "capitulation" of campus presidents. To avoid feelings of guilt stemming from past discrimination against minority groups, Steele says, "[campus administrators have] tended to go along with whatever blacks put on the table, rather than work with them to assess their real needs. . . . Administrators would never give white students a theme house where they could be 'more comfortable with people of their own kind,' yet more and more universities are doing this for black students." Steele sees white frustration as the inevitable result.

"White students are not invited to the negotiating table from which they see blacks and others walk away with concessions," he says. "The presumption is that they do not deserve to be there, because they are white.

So they can only be defensive, and the less mature among them will be aggressive."

Course, some folks see it another way. The students fighting for minority rights aren't wicked political corruptors, but champions of a cause far too long suppressed by the white male hegemony. Responsive administrators are engaged not in capitulation, but in progress. And one shouldn't look for the cause of this mess on any campus, because he doesn't live on one. His address used to be the White House, but then he moved to 666 St. Cloud Road. Ronald Reagan, come on down.

Dr. Manning Marble, University of Colorado: "The shattering assault against the economic, social, and political status of the black American community as a whole [is symbolized by] the Reagan Administration in the 1980s. The Civil Rights Commission was gutted; affirmative action became a 'dead letter'; social welfare, health care, employment training, and educational loans were all severely reduced. This had a disproportionately more negative impact upon black youth."

The "perception is already widespread that the society at large is more permissive toward discriminatory attitudes and behaviors, and less committed to equal opportunity and affirmative action," concluded a 1988 conference at Northern Illinois University. John Wiener, writing in *The Nation,* attacks long-standing institutions of bigotry, asserting, for example, that "racism is endemic to the fraternity subculture," and praises the efforts of some schools to double the number of minority faculty and increase minority fellowships. On behalf of progressives across the land, Wiener writes off Shelby Steele as someone who is content to "blame the victim."

So the machine has melted, the phone has stretched to where it is useless. This is how intense the heat is. Liberals, who largely control the administration, faculty, and students' rights groups of leading academic institutions, have, with virtually no intensive intellectual debate, inculcated schools with their answers to the problem of bigotry. Conservatives, with a long history of insensitivity to minority concerns, have been all but shut out of the debate, and now want back in. Their intensive pursuit of the true nature of bigotry and the proper response to it—working to assess the "real needs" of campuses rather than simply bowing to pressure— deserves to be embraced by all concerned parties, and probably would have been by now but for two small items: (a) Reagan, their fearless leader, clearly *was* insensitive to ethnic/feminist concerns (even Steele agrees with this); and (b) some of the more coherent conservative pundits *still* show a blatant apathy to the problems of bigotry in this country. This has been

sufficient ammunition for liberals who are continually looking for an excuse to keep conservatives out of the dialogue. So now we have clashes
rather than debates: on how much one can say, on how much one should
have to hear. Two negatives: one side wants to crack down on expression,
the other on awareness. The machine has melted, and it's going to take
some consensus to build a new one. Intellectual provincialism will have
to end before young hate ever will.

A Month in the Life of Campus Bigotry

April 1.
Vandals spray-paint "Jewhaters will pay" and other slogans on the office
walls of *The Michigan Daily* (University of Michigan) in response to editorials condemning Israel for policies regarding the Palestinians. Pro-Israeli
and pro-Palestinian shanties defaced; one is burned.

U of M: Fliers circulated over the weekend announce "White Pride
Month."

Southern Connecticut State University reportedly suspends five fraternity officers after racial brawl.

April 2.
Several gay men of the University of Connecticut are taunted by two students, who yell "faggot" at them.

April 3.
The University of Michigan faculty meet to discuss a proposal to require
students to take a course on ethnicity and racism.

April 4.
Students at the University of California at Santa Barbara suspend hunger
strike after university agrees to negotiate on demands for minority faculty hiring and the changed status of certain required courses.

April 5.
The NCAA releases results of survey on black student athletes, reporting
that 51 percent of black football and basketball players at predominantly
white schools express feelings of being different; 51 percent report feelings of racial isolation; 33 percent report having experienced at least six
incidents of individual racial discrimination.

The *New York Times* prints three op-ed pieces by students on the subject
of racial tension on campus.

Charges filed against a former student of Penn State for racial harassment of a black woman.

April 6.

University of Michigan: Hundreds of law students wear arm bands, boycott classes to protest lack of women and minority professors.

Michigan State University announces broad plan for increasing the number of minority students, faculty, and staff; the appointment of a senior advisor for minority affairs; and the expansion of multicultural conferences. "It's not our responsibility just to mirror society or respond to mandates," President John DiBioggio tells reporters, "but to set the tone."

April 7.

Wayne State University (Detroit, Michigan) student newspaper runs retraction of cartoon considered offensive following protest earlier in the week.

Controversy develops at the State University of New York at Stony Brook, where a white woman charges a popular black basketball player with rape. Player denies charges. Charges are dismissed. Protests of racism and sexual assault commence.

April 12.

Twelve-day sit-in begins at Wayne State University (Michigan) over conditions for black students on campus.

April 14.

Racial brawl at Arizona State.

April 20.

Demonstrations at several universities across the country (Harvard, Duke, Wayne State, Wooster College, Penn State, etc.) for improvements in black student life.

Separate escort service for blacks started at Penn State out of distrust of the regular service.

April 21.

200-student sit-in ends at Arizona State University when administrators agree to all thirteen demands.

April 24.

Proposed tuition increase at City Universities of New York turns into racial controversy.

April 25.

After eighteen months in office, Robert Collin, Florida Atlantic University's first black dean, reveals he has filed a federal discrimination complaint against the school.

Two leaders of Columbia University's Gay and Lesbian Alliance receive death threat. "Dear Jeff, I will kill you butt fucking faggots. Death to COLA!"

April 26.
A black Smith College (Massachusetts) student finds note slipped under door, ". . . African monkey do you want some bananas? Go back to the jungle . . .".

"I don't think we should have to constantly relive our ancestors' mistakes, " a white student at the University of North Carolina at Greensboro tells a reporter. "I didn't oppress anybody. Blacks are now equal. You don't see any racial problems anymore."

White Student Union is reported to have been formed at Temple University in Philadelphia, "City of Brotherly Love."

April 28.
Note found in Brown University (Rhode Island) dorm. "Once upon a time, Brown was a place where a white man could go to class without having to look at little black faces, or little yellow faces or little brown faces, except when he went to take his meals. Things have been going downhill since the kitchen help moved into the classroom. Keep white supremecy [sic] alive!!! Join the Brown chapter of the KKK today." Note is part of series that began in the middle of the month with "Die Homos." University officials beef up security, hold forum.

April 29.
Controversy reported over proposed ban on verbal harassment at Arizona State.

April 30.
Anti-apartheid shanty at University of Maryland, Baltimore County, is defaced. Signs read "Apartheid now," and "Trump Plaza."

University of California at Berkeley: Resolution is passed requiring an ethnic studies course for all students.

University of Connecticut: Code is revised to provide specific penalties for acts of racial intolerance.

When Is It Rape?
Nancy Gibbs

Be careful of strangers and hurry home, says a mother to her daughter, knowing that the world is a frightful place but not wishing to swaddle a child in fear. Girls grow up scarred by caution and enter adulthood eager to shake free of their parents' worst nightmares. They still know to be wary of strangers. What they don't know is whether they have more to fear from their friends.

Most women who get raped are raped by people they already know—like the boy in biology class, or the guy in the office down the hall, or their friend's brother. The familiarity is enough to make them let down their guard, sometimes even enough to make them wonder afterward whether they were "really raped." What people think of as "real rape"—the assault by a monstrous stranger lurking in the shadows—accounts for only one out of five attacks.

So the phrase "acquaintance rape" was coined to describe the rest, all the cases of forced sex between people who already knew each other, however casually. But that was too clinical for headline writers, and so the popular term is the narrower "date rape," which suggests an ugly ending to a raucous night on the town.

These are not idle distinctions. Behind the search for labels is the central mythology about rape; that rapists are always strangers, and victims are women who ask for it. The mythology is hard to dispel because the crime is so rarely exposed. The experts guess—that's all they can do under the circumstances—that while one in four women will be raped in her lifetime, less than 10 percent will report the assault, and less than 5 percent of the rapists will go to jail.

Women charge that date rape is the hidden crime; men complain it is hard to prevent a crime they can't define. Women say it isn't taken seriously; men say it is a concept invented by women who like to tease but not take the consequences. Women say the date-rape debate is the first time the nation has talked frankly about sex; men say it is women's unconscious reaction to the excesses of the sexual revolution. Meanwhile, men and women argue among themselves about the "gray area" that surrounds the whole murky arena of sexual relations, and there is no consensus in sight.

In court, on campus, in conversation, the issue turns on the elasticity of the word *rape,* one of the few words in the language with the power to summon a shared image of a horrible crime.

At one extreme are those who argue that for the word to retain its impact, it must be strictly defined as forced sexual intercourse: a gang of thugs jumping a jogger in Central Park, a psychopath preying on old women in a housing complex, a man with an ice pick in a side street. To stretch the definition of the word risks stripping away its power. In this view, if it happened on a date, it wasn't rape. A romantic encounter is a context in which sex *could* occur, and so what omniscient judge will decide whether there was genuine mutual consent?

Others are willing to concede that date rape sometimes occurs, that sometimes a man goes too far on a date without a woman's consent. But this infraction, they say, is not as ghastly a crime as street rape, and it should not be taken as seriously. The New York *Post*, alarmed by the Willy Smith case, wrote in a recent editorial, "if the sexual encounter, *forced or not*, has been preceded by a series of consensual activities—drinking, a trip to the man's home, a walk on a deserted beach at three in the morning—the charge that's leveled against the alleged offender should, it seems to us, be different than the one filed against, say, the youths who raped and beat the jogger."

This attitude sparks rage among women who carry scars received at the hands of men they knew. It makes no difference if the victim shared a drink or a moonlit walk or even a passionate kiss, they protest, if the encounter ended with her being thrown to the ground and forcibly violated. Date rape is not about a misunderstanding, they say. It is not a communications problem. It is not about a woman's having regrets in the morning for a decision she made the night before. It is not about a "decision" at all. Rape is rape, and any form of forced sex—even between neighbors, co-workers, classmates and casual friends—is a crime.

A more extreme form of that view comes from activists who see rape as a metaphor, its definition swelling to cover any kind of oppression of women. Rape, seen in this light, can occur not only on a date but also in a marriage, not only by violent assault but also by psychological pressure. A Swarthmore College training pamphlet once explained that acquaintance rape "spans a spectrum of incidents and behaviors, ranging from crimes legally defined as rape to verbal harassment and inappropriate innuendo." No wonder, then, that the battles become so heated. When innuendo qualifies as rape, the definitions have become so slippery that the entire subject sinks into a political swamp. The only way to capture the hard reality is to tell the story.

A 32-year-old woman was on business in Tampa last year for the Florida supreme court. Stranded at the courthouse, she accepted a lift from a lawyer involved in her project. As they chatted on the ride home, she recalls, "he was saying all the right things, so I started to trust him." She agreed to have dinner, and afterward, at her hotel door, he convinced her to let him come in to talk. "I went through the whole thing about being old-fashioned," she says. "I was a virgin until I was twenty-one. So I told him talk was all we were going to do."

But as they sat on he couch, she found herself falling asleep. "By now, I'm comfortable with him, and I put my head on his shoulder. He's not tried anything all evening, after all." Which is when the rape came. "I woke up to find him on top of me, forcing himself on me. I didn't scream or run. All I could think about was my business contacts and what if they saw me run out of my room screaming rape.

"I thought it was my fault. I felt so filthy, I washed myself over and over in hot water. Did he rape me?, I kept asking myself. I didn't consent. But who's gonna believe me? I had a man in my hotel room after midnight." More than a year later, she still can't tell the story without a visible struggle to maintain her composure. Police referred the case to the state attorney's office in Tampa, but without more evidence it decided not to prosecute. Although her attacker has admitted that he heard her say no, maintains the woman, "he says he didn't know that I meant no. He didn't feel he'd raped me, and he even wanted to see me again."

Her story is typical in many ways. The victim herself may not be sure right away that she has been raped, that she had said no and been physically forced into having sex anyway. And the rapist commonly hears but does not heed the protest. "A date rapist will follow through no matter what the woman wants because his agenda is to get laid," says Claire Walsh, a Florida-based consultant on sexual assaults. "First comes the dinner, then a dance, then a drink, then the coercion begins." Gentle persuasion gives way to physical intimidation with alcohol as the ubiquitous lubricant. "When that fails, force is used," she says. "Real men don't take no for an answer."

The Palm Beach case serves to remind women that if they go ahead and press charges, they can expect to go on trial along with their attacker, if not in a courtroom then in the court of public opinion. The New York *Times* caused an uproar on its own staff not only for publishing the victim's name but also for laying out in detail her background, her high-school grades, her driving record, along with an unattributed quote from a school official about her "little wild streak." A freshman at Carleton College in Minnesota, who says she was repeatedly raped for four hours by a fellow student, claims that she was asked at an administrative hearing if she performed oral sex on dates. In 1989 a man charged with raping at knife point a woman he knew was acquitted in Florida because his victim had been wearing lace shorts and no underwear.

From a purely legal point of view, if she wants to put her attacker in jail, the survivor had better be beaten as well as raped, since bruises become a badge of credibility. She had better have reported the crime right away, before taking the hours-long shower that she craves, before burning her clothes, before curling up with the blinds down. And she would

do well to be a woman of shining character. Otherwise the strict construc-
tionist definitions of rape will prevail in court. "Juries don't have a great
deal of sympathy for the victim if she's a willing participant up to the
nonconsensual sexual intercourse," says Norman Kinne, a prosecutor in
Dallas. "They feel that many times the victim has placed herself in the
situation." Absent eyewitnesses or broken bones, a case comes down to
her word against his, and the mythology of rape rarely lends her the benefit of the doubt.

She should also hope for an all-male jury, preferably composed of
fathers with daughters. Prosecutors have found that women tend to be
harsh judges of one another—perhaps because to find a defendant guilty
is to entertain two grim realities: that anyone might be a rapist, and that
every woman could find herself a victim. It may be easier to believe, the
experts muse, that at some level the victim asked for it. "But just because
a woman makes a bad judgment, does that give the guy a moral right to
rape her?" asks Dean Kilpatrick, director of the Crime Victim Research
and Treatment Center at the Medical University of South Carolina. "The
bottom line is, Why does a woman's having a drink give a man the right
to rape her?"

Last week the Supreme Court waded into the debate with a 7-to-2
ruling that protects victims from being harassed on the witness stand with
questions about their sexual history. The Justices, in their first decision on
"rape shield laws," said an accused rapist could not present evidence about
a previous sexual relationship with the victim unless he notified the court
ahead of time. In her decision, Justice Sandra Day O'Connor wrote that
"rape victims deserve heightened protection against surprise, harassment,
and unnecessary invasions of privacy."

That was welcome news to prosecutors who understand the reluctance of victims to come forward. But there are other impediments to justice as well. An internal investigation of the Oakland police department
found that officers ignored a quarter of all reports of sexual assaults or
attempts, though 90 percent actually warranted investigation. Departments
are getting better at educating officers in handling rape cases, but the courts
remain behind. A New York City task force on women in the courts charged
that judges and lawyers were routinely less inclined to believe a woman's
testimony that a man's.

The present debate over degrees of rape is nothing new; all through
history, rapes have been divided between those that mattered and those
that did not. For the first few thousand years, the only rape that was punished was the defiling of a virgin, and that was viewed as a property crime.

A girl's virtue was a marketable asset, and so a rapist was often ordered to pay the victim's father the equivalent of her price on the marriage market. In early Babylonian and Hebrew societies, a married woman who was raped suffered the same fate as an adulteress—death by stoning or drowning. Under William the Conqueror, the penalty for raping a virgin was castration and loss of both eyes—unless the violated woman agreed to marry her attacker, as she was often pressured to do. "Stealing an heiress" became a perfectly conventional means of taking—literally—a wife.

It may be easier to prove a rape case now, but not much. Until the 1960s it was virtually impossible without an eyewitness; judges were often required to instruct jurors that "rape is a charge easily made and hard to defend against; so examine the testimony of this witness with caution." But sometimes a rape was taken very seriously, particularly if it involved a black man attacking a white woman—a crime for which black men were often executed or lynched.

Susan Estrich, author of *Real Rape,* considers herself a lucky victim. This is not just because she survived an attack 17 years ago by a stranger with an ice pick, one day before her graduation from Wellesley. It's because police, and her friends, believed her. "The first thing the Boston police asked was whether it was a black guy," recalls Estrich, now a University of Southern California law professor. When she said yes and gave the details of the attack, their reaction was, "So you were really raped." It was an instructive lesson, she says, in understanding how racism and sexism are factored into perceptions of the crime.

A new twist in society's perception came in 1975, when Susan Brownmiller published her book *Against Our Will: Men, Women and Rape.* In it she attacked the concept that rape was a sex crime, arguing instead that it was a crime of violence and power over women. Throughout history, she wrote, rape has played a critical function. "It is nothing more or less than a conscious process of intimidation, by which *all men* keep *all women* in a state of fear."

Out of this contention was born a set of arguments that have become politically correct wisdom on campus and in academic circles. This view holds that rape is a symbol of women's vulnerability to male institutions and attitudes. "It's sociopolitical," insists Gina Rayfield, a New Jersey psychologist. "In our culture men hold the power, politically, economically. They're socialized not to see women as equals."

This line of reasoning has led some women, especially radicalized victims, to justify flinging around the term rape as a political weapon, referring to everything from violent sexual assaults to inappropriate innuendos. Ginny, a college senior who was really raped when she was sixteen, suggests that false accusations of rape can serve a useful purpose. "Penetration is not the only form of violation," she explains. In her view, rape is a subjective term, one that women must use to draw attention to other, nonviolent, even nonsexual forms of oppression. "If a woman did falsely accuse a man of rape, she may have had reasons to," Ginny says. "Maybe she wasn't raped, but he clearly violated her in some way."

Catherine Comins, assistant dean of student life at Vassar, also sees some value in this loose use of "rape." She says angry victims of various forms of sexual intimidation cry rape to regain their sense of power. "To use the word carefully would be to be careful for the sake of the violator, and the survivors don't care a hoot about him." Comins argues that men who are unjustly accused can sometimes gain from the experience. "They have a lot of pain, but it is not a pain that I would necessarily have spared them. I think it ideally initiates a process of self-exploration. 'How do I see women?' 'If I didn't violate her, could I have?' 'Do I have the potential to do to her what they say I did?' Those are good questions."

Taken to extremes, there is an ugly element of vengeance at work here. Rape is an abuse of power. But so are false accusations of rape, and to suggest that men whose reputations are destroyed might benefit because it will make them more sensitive is an attitude that is sure to backfire on women who are seeking justice for all victims. On campuses where the issue is most inflamed, male students are outraged that their names can be scrawled on a bathroom-wall list of rapists and they have no chance to tell their side of the story.

"Rape is what you read about in the New York *Post* about seventeen little boys raping a jogger in Central Park," says a male freshman at a liberal-arts college, who learned that he had been branded a rapist after a one-night stand with a friend. He acknowledges that they were both very drunk when she started kissing him at a party and ended up back in his room. Even through his haze, he had some qualms about sleeping with her: "I'm fighting against my hormonal instincts, and my moral instincts are saying, 'This is my friend and if I were sober, I wouldn't be doing this.'" But he went ahead anyway. "When you're drunk, and there are all sorts of ambiguity, and the woman says 'Please, please' and then she says no sometime later, even in the middle of the act, there still may very well be some kind of violation, but it's not the same thing. It's not rape. If you don't hear her say no, if she doesn't say it, if she's playing around with you—oh, I could get squashed for saying it—there is an element of say no, mean yes."

The morning after their encounter, he recalls, both students woke up hung over and eager to put the memory behind them. Only months later did he learn that she had told a friend that he had torn her clothing and raped her. At this point in the story, the accused man starts using the language of rape. "I felt violated," he says, "I felt like she was taking advantage of me when she was very drunk. I never heard her say 'No!,' 'Stop!,' anything." He is angry and hurt at the charges, worried that they will get around, shatter his reputation and force him to leave the small campus.

So here, of course, is the heart of the debate. If rape is sex without consent, how exactly should consent be defined and communicated, when and by whom? Those who view rape through a political lens tend to place all responsibility on men to make sure that their partners are consenting at every point of a sexual encounter. At the extreme, sexual relations come to resemble major surgery, requiring a signed consent form. Clinical psychologist Mary P. Koss of the University of Arizona in Tucson, who is a leading scholar on the issue, puts it rather bluntly: "It's the man's penis that is doing the raping, and ultimately he's responsible for where he puts it."

Historically, of course, this has never been the case, and there are some who argue that it shouldn't be—that women too must take responsibility for their behavior, and that the whole realm of intimate encounters defies regulation from on high. Anthropologist Lionel Tiger has little patience for trendy sexual politics that make no reference to biology. Since the dawn of time, he argues, men and women have always gone to bed with different goals. In the effort to keep one's genes in the gene pool, "it is to the male advantage to fertilize as many females as possible, as quickly as possible and as efficiently as possible." For the female, however, who looks at the large investment she will have to make in the offspring, the opposite is true. Her concern is to "select" who "will provide the best set-up for their offspring." So, in general, "the pressure is on the male to be aggressive and on the female to be coy."

No one defends the use of physical force, but when the coercion involved is purely psychological, it becomes hard to assign blame after the fact. Journalist Stephanie Gutmann is an ardent foe of what she calls the date-rape dogmatists. "How can you make sex completely politically correct and completely safe?" she asks. "What a horribly bland, unerotic thing that would be! Sex is, by nature, a risky endeavor, emotionally. And desire is a violent emotion. These people in the date-rape movement have erected so many rules and regulations that I don't know how people can have erotic or desire-driven sex."

Nonsense, retorts Cornell professor Andrea Parrot, co-author of *Acquaintance Rape: The Hidden Crime.* Seduction should not be about lies, manipulation, game playing or coercion of any kind, she says. "Too bad that people think that the only way you can have passion and excitement and sex is if there are miscommunications, and one person is forced to do something he or she doesn't want to do." The very pleasures of sexual encounters should lie in the fact of mutual comfort and consent: "You can hang from the ceiling, you can use fruit, you can go crazy and have really wonderful sensual erotic sex, if both parties are consenting."

It would be easy to accuse feminists of being too quick to classify sex as rape, but feminists are to be found on all sides of the debate, and many protest the idea that all the onus is on the man. It demeans women to suggest that they are so vulnerable to coercion or emotional manipulation that they must always be escorted by the strong arm of the law. "You can't solve society's ills by making everything a crime," says Albuquerque attorney Nancy Hollander. "That comes out of the sense of overprotection of women, and in the long run that is going to be harmful to us."

What is lost in the ideological debate over date rape is the fact that men and women, especially when they are young, and drunk, and aroused, are not very good at communicating. "In many cases," says Estrich, "the man thought it was sex, and the woman thought it was rape, and they are both telling the truth." The man may envision a celluloid seduction, in which he is being commanding, she is being coy. A woman may experience the same event as a degrading violation of her will. That some men do not believe a woman's protests is scarcely surprising in a society so drenched with messages that women have rape fantasies and a desire to be overpowered.

By the time they reach college, men and women are loaded with cultural baggage, drawn from movies, television, music videos and "bodice ripper" romance novels. Over the years they have watched Rhett sweep Scarlett up the stairs in *Gone With the Wind*; or Errol Flynn, who was charged twice with statutory rape, overpower a protesting heroine who then melts in his arms; or Stanley rape his sister-in-law Blanche du Bois while his wife is in the hospital giving birth to a child in *A Streetcar Named Desire.* Higher up the cultural food chain, young people can read of date rape in Homer or Jane Austen, watch it in *Don Giovanni* or *Rigoletto.*

The messages come early and often, and nothing in the feminist revolution has been able to counter them. A recent survey of sixth- to ninthgraders in Rhode Island found that a fourth of the boys and a sixth of the girls said it was acceptable for a man to force a woman to kiss him or have sex if he has spent money on her. A third of the children said it would not be wrong for a man to rape a woman who had had previous sexual experiences.

Certainly cases like Palm Beach, movies like *The Accused* and novels like Avery Corman's *Prized Possessions* may force young people to reexamine assumptions they have inherited. The use of new terms, like acquaintance rape and date rape, while controversial, has given men and women the vocabulary they need to express their experiences with both force and precision. This dialogue would be useful if it helps strip away some of the dogmas, old and new, surrounding the issue. Those who hope to raise society's sensitivity to the problem of date rape would do well to concede that it is not precisely the same sort of crime as street rape, that there may be very murky issues of intent and degree involved.

On the other hand, those who downplay the problem should come to realize that date rape is a crime of uniquely intimate cruelty. While the body is violated, the spirit is maimed. How long will it take, once the wounds have healed, before it is possible to share a walk on a beach, a drive home from work or an evening's conversation without always listening for a quiet alarm to start ringing deep in the back of the memory of a terrible crime? ■

Organizing
sensations into a
design or pattern

Selecting
sensations to pay
attention to

Interpreting
what this pattern or
event means

PERCEIVING:
Actively selecting, organizing,
and interpreting what is
experienced by our senses

Experiences shape our
perceptions.

We construct beliefs based
on our perceptions.

We view the world through
our own unique "lenses,"
which shape and influence
our perceptions.

We construct
knowledge based on
our beliefs.

Thinking Critically involves understanding how "lenses"
influence perceptions, beliefs, and knowledge.

THINKING IS THE WAY you make sense of the world. By thinking in an active, purposeful, and organized way, you are able to solve problems, work toward your goals, analyze issues, and make decisions. Your experience of the world comes to you by means of your *senses:* sight, hearing, smell, touch, and taste. These senses are your bridges to the world, making you aware of what occurs outside you, and the process of becoming aware of your world through your senses is known as *perceiving.*

In this chapter you will explore the way your perceiving process operates and how it relates to your ability to think effectively. In particular, you will discover the way you shape your personal experience by actively selecting, organizing, and interpreting the sensations provided by the senses. In a way, each of us views the world through a pair of individual "eyeglasses" or "contact lenses," that reflect our past experiences and unique personalities. As a critical thinker, you want to become aware of the nature of your own "lenses" to help eliminate any bias or distortion they may be causing. You also want to become aware of the "lenses" of others so that you can better understand why they view things the way they do.

At almost every waking moment of your life, your senses are being bombarded by a tremendous number of stimuli: images to see, noises to hear, odors to smell, textures to feel, and flavors to taste. The experience of all these sensations happening at once creates what the nineteenth-century American philosopher William James called "a bloomin' buzzin' confusion." Yet for us, the world usually seems much more orderly and understandable. Why is this so?

In the first place, your sense equipment can receive sensations only within certain limited ranges. For example, there are many sounds and smells that animals can detect but you cannot because their sense organs have broader ranges in these areas than yours do.

A second reason you can handle this sensory bombardment is that from the stimulation available, you *select* only a small amount on which to focus our attention. To demonstrate this, try the following exercise. Concentrate on what you can *see,* ignoring your other senses for the moment. Focus on sensations that you were not previously aware of and then answer the first question. Concentrate on each of your other senses in turn, following the same procedure.

1. What can you *see?* (For example, the shape of the letters on the page, the design of the clothing on your arm.)
2. What can you *hear?* (For example, the hum of the air circulator, the rustling of a page.)
3. What can you *feel?* (For example, the pressure of the clothes against your skin, the texture of the page on your fingers.)

4. What can you *smell?* (For example, the perfume or cologne someone is wearing, the odor of stale cigarette smoke.)

5. What can you *taste?* (For example, the after effects of your last meal.)

Compare your responses with those of the other students in the class. Do your classmates perceive sensations that are different from the ones you perceived? If so, how do you explain these differences?

By practicing this simple exercise, it should be clear that for every sensation that you focus your attention on there are countless sensations that you are simply ignoring. If you were aware of *everything* that is happening at every moment, you would be completely overwhelmed. By selecting certain sensations, you are able to make sense of your world in a relatively orderly way. The activity of using your senses to experience and make sense of your world is known as *perceiving*.

Perceiving   Actively selecting, organizing, and interpreting what is experienced by our senses.

ACTIVELY SELECTING, ORGANIZING, AND INTERPRETING SENSATIONS

It is tempting to think that your senses simply record what is happening out in the world, as if you were a human camera or tape recorder. You are not, however, a passive receiver of information, a "container" into which sense experience is poured. Instead, you are an *active participant* who is always trying to understand the sensations you are encountering. As you perceive your world, your experience is the result of combining the sensations you are having with the way you understand these sensations. For example, examine the following collection of markings. What do you see?

If all you see is a collection of black spots, try looking at the group sideways. After a while, you will probably perceive a familiar animal.

From this example you can see that when you perceive the world you are doing more than simply recording what your senses experience. Besides experiencing sensations, you are also actively making sense of these sensations. That is why this collection of black spots suddenly became the figure of an animal— because you were able actively to organize these spots into a pattern you recognized. Or think about the times you were able to look up at the white, billowy clouds in the sky and see different figures and designs. The figures you were perceiving were not actually in the clouds but were the result of your giving a meaningful form to the shapes and colors you were experiencing.

The same is true for virtually everything you experience. Your perception of the world results from combining the information provided by your senses with the way you actively make sense of this information. And since making sense of information is what you are doing when you are thinking, you can see that perceiving your world involves using your mind in an active way. Of course, you are usually not aware that you are using your mind to interpret the sensations you are experiencing. You simply see the animal or the figures in the clouds as if they were really there.

When you actively perceive the sensations you are experiencing, you are usually engaged in three distinct activities:

1. *Selecting* certain sensations to pay attention to
2. *Organizing* these sensations into a design or pattern
3. *Interpreting* what this design or pattern means to you

In the case of the figure on page 156 you were able to perceive an animal because you *selected* certain of the markings to concentrate on, *organized* these markings into a pattern, and *interpreted* this pattern as representing a familiar animal.

Of course, when you perceive, these three operations of selecting, organizing, and interpreting are usually performed quickly, automatically, and often at the same time. Also, you are normally unaware that you are performing these operations, they are so rapid and automatic. This chapter is designed to help you slow down this normally automatic process of perceiving so that you can understand how the process works.

Let's explore more examples that illustrate how you actively select, organize, and interpret your perceptions of the world. Carefully examine the figure on page 158.

Do you see both the young woman and the old woman? If you do, try switching back and forth between the two images. As you switch back and forth, notice how for each image you are:

- *Selecting* certain lines, shapes, and shadings on which to focus your attention
- *Organizing* these lines, shapes, and shadings into different patterns
- *Interpreting* these patterns as representing things that you are able to recognize—a hat, a nose, a chin

Another way for you to become aware of your active participation in perceiving your world is to consider how you see objects. Examine the illustration below. Do you perceive different-sized people, or the same-sized people at different distances?

When you see someone who is far away, you usually do not perceive a tiny person. Instead, you perceive a normal-sized person who is far away from you. Your experience in the world has enabled you to discover that the farther things are from you, the smaller they look. The moon in the night sky appears about the size of a quarter, yet you perceive it as being considerably larger. As you look down a long stretch of railroad tracks or gaze up at a tall building, the boundary lines seem to come together. Even though these images are what your eyes "see," however, you do not usually perceive the tracks meeting or the building coming to a point. Instead, your mind actively organizes and interprets a world composed of constant shapes and sizes, even though the images you actually see usually vary, depending on how far you are from them and the angle from which you are looking at them.

Examine carefully the engraving pictured on page 160 entitled "Satire on False Perspective," completed by William Hogarth in 1754. In this engraving, the artist has changed many of the clues you use to perceive a world of constant shapes and sizes, thus creating some unusual effects. By analyzing how the artist has created these unusual perspectives, you gain insight into the way your mind actively takes fragmentary information and transforms it into the predictable, three-dimensional world that is so familiar to you.

So far, we have been exploring how your mind actively participates in the way you perceive the world. By combining the sensations you are receiving with the way your mind selects, organizes, and interprets these sensations, you perceive a world of things that is stable and familiar, a world that usually makes sense to you.

The process of perceiving takes place at a variety of different levels. At the most basic level, the concept of "perceiving" refers to the selection, organization, and interpretation of sensations: for example, being able to perceive the various objects in your experience, like a basketball. However, you also perceive larger patterns of meaning at more complex levels, as in watching the action of a group of people engaged in a basketball game. Although these are very different contexts, both engage you in the process of actively selecting, organizing, and interpreting what is experienced by your senses—in other words, "perceiving."

People's Perceptions Differ

Your *active* participation in perceiving your world is something you are not usually aware of. You normally assume that what you are perceiving is what is actually taking place. Only when you find that your perception of the same event differs from the perceptions of others are you forced to examine the

manner in which you are selecting, organizing, and interpreting the events in
your world. For example, consider the contrasting perceptions of the various
characters in the cartoon on page 161. How do you think each individual arrived at his or her (or its) perception?

THINKING ACTIVITY 4.1

Carefully examine the picture of the boy sitting at the desk on page 162. What
do you think is happening in this picture?

1. Describe as specifically as possible what you perceive is taking place in the
   picture.
2. Describe what you think will take place next.

© John Jonik. *Reproduced with permission. This cartoon first appeared in* Psychology Today, *February 1984.*

3. Identify the details of the picture that led you to your perceptions.
4. Compare your perceptions with the perceptions of other students in the class. List several perceptions that differ from yours. ◀

In most cases, people in a group will have a variety of perceptions about what is taking place in the picture in Thinking Activity 4.1. Some will see the boy as frustrated because the work is too difficult. Others will see him concentrating on what has to be done. Still others may see him as annoyed because he is being forced to do something he does not want to do. In each case, the perception depends on how the person is actively using his or her mind to organize and

interpret what is taking place. Since the situation pictured is by its nature somewhat puzzling, different people perceive it in different ways.

   Thinking Activity 4.2 reveals another example of how people's perceptions can differ.

THINKING ACTIVITY 4.2

Closely examine the photograph on page 163.

1. Describe as specifically as possible what you think is taking place in the photograph.
2. Now describe what you think will take place next.
3. Identify the details of the picture that led you to your perceptions.
4. Compare your perceptions with the perceptions of other students in the class.
   List several perceptions that differ from yours. ◀

Viewing the World Through "Lenses"

To understand how various people can be exposed to the same stimuli or events
and yet have different perceptions, it helps to imagine that each of us views the

world through our own pair of "contact lenses." Of course, we are not usually aware of the lenses we are wearing. Instead, our lenses act as *filters* that select and shape what we perceive without our realizing it.

This image of "lenses" helps explain why people can be exposed to the same stimuli or events and yet perceive different things. This happens because people are wearing *different lenses,* which influence what they are perceiving. For example, in "The Investigation" on page 161, each witness is giving what he or she (or it!) believes is an accurate description of the man in the center, unaware that their descriptions are being influenced by who they are and the way that they see things. When members of your class had different perceptions of the boy at the desk in Thinking Activity 4.1 and of the photograph in Thinking Activity 4.2, their different perceptions were the result of the different lenses through which each views the world.

To understand the way people perceive the world, you have to understand their individual lenses, which influence how they actively select, organize, and interpret the events in their experience. A diagram of the process might look like this:

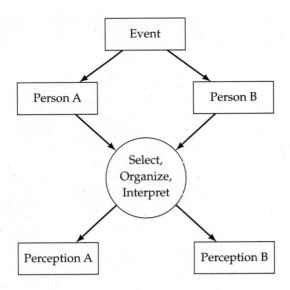

Consider the following pairs of statements. In each of these cases, both people are being exposed to the same basic *stimulus* or event, yet each has a totally different *perception* of the experience. Explain how you think the various perceptions might have developed.

1. a. That chili was much too spicy to eat.
   Explanation:

   b. That chili needed more hot peppers and chili powder to spice it up a little.
   Explanation:

2. a. People who wear lots of makeup and jewelry are very sophisticated.
   Explanation:

   b. People who wear lots of makeup and jewelry are ostentatious and over-dressed.
   Explanation:

3. a. The music that young people enjoy listening to is a very creative cultural expression.
   Explanation:

   b. The music that young people enjoy listening to is obnoxious noise.
   Explanation:

To become an effective critical thinker, you have to become aware of the lenses that you—and others—are wearing. These lenses aid you in actively selecting, organizing, and interpreting the sensations in your experience. If you are un-aware of the nature of your own lenses, you can often mistake your own perceptions for objective truth without bothering to examine either the facts or others' perceptions on a given issue.

Selecting Perceptions

We spend much of the time experiencing the world in a very general way, not aware of many of the details of the events that are taking place. For example, try to draw a picture of the face of a push-button phone, complete with numbers and letters. Then compare your drawing with an actual phone. Did you have any difficulty? Why? We also tend to select perceptions about subjects that have been called to our attention for some reason. For instance, at the age of three, the author's daughter suddenly became aware of beards. On entering a subway car, she would ask in a penetrating voice, "Any beards here?" and then proceed to count them out loud. In doing this, she naturally focused my attention—as well as the attention of many of the other passengers—on beards.

As another aspect of our "perceiving" lenses, we tend to notice what we need, desire, or find of interest. When we go shopping, we focus on the items we are looking for. Walking down the street, we tend to notice certain kinds of people or events while completely ignoring others. Even watching a movie or reading a book, we tend to concentrate on and remember the elements we find of interest. Another person can perform *exactly* the same actions—shop at the same store, walk down the same street with you, read the same book, or go to the same movie—and yet see and remember entirely different things. In other words, what you see and do not see depends largely on your interests, needs, and desires.

The way you are feeling—your mood or emotional state—can also affect the perceptions you select. For example, think back on the times when you have felt cranky, perhaps because you did not get enough sleep or were under pressure, and recall how you behaved. When we are in a bad mood, we often seem ready to focus our attention on every potential insult or criticism by others—and ready to respond the same way.

Although we tend to focus on what is familiar to us, we are normally not aware that we are doing so. In fact, we often take for granted what is familiar to us—the taste of chili or eggs, the street that we live on, our family or friends—and normally do not think about our perception of it. But when something happens that makes the familiar seem strange and unfamiliar, we become aware of our perceptions and start to evaluate them.

To sum up, you actively select your perceptions, based on what has been called to your attention, your needs or interests, your mood or feelings, and what seems familiar or unfamiliar. The way you select your perceptions is an important factor in shaping the lenses through which you view the world.

Organizing Perceptions

Not only do you actively *select* certain perceptions, you also actively *organize* these perceptions into meaningful relationships and patterns. Consider the following series of lines:

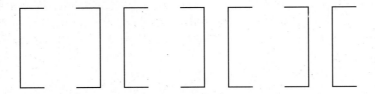

Did you perceive them as individual lines or did you group them into pairs? We seem naturally to try to organize our perceptions to create order and meaning. Consider the items pictured here and try to organize them into a pattern that is familiar to you:

As you perceive the world, you naturally try to order and organize what you are experiencing into patterns and relationships that make sense to you. And when you are able to do so, the completed whole means more to you than the sum of the individual parts. You are continually organizing your world in this way at virtually every waking moment.

We do not live in a world of isolated sounds, patches of color, random odors, and individual textures. Instead, we live in a world of objects and people, language and music—a world in which all these individual stimuli are woven together. We are able to perceive this world of complex experiences because we are able to organize the individual stimuli we are receiving into relationships that have meaning to us.

The way you organize your experience is an important part of the lenses through which you perceive the world. You are able to perceive objects, human expressions, and potential human action because of your ability to organize the lines, shapes, and shadings into meaningful patterns and complex relationships.

Interpreting Perceptions

Besides selecting and organizing your perceptions, you also actively *interpret* what you perceive. When you interpret, you are figuring out what something means. One of the elements that influences your interpretations of what you are perceiving is the *context,* or overall situation, within which the perception is occurring. For example, imagine that you see a man running down the street. Your interpretation of his action will depend on the specific context. For example, is there a bus waiting at the corner? Is a police officer running behind him? Is he wearing a jogging suit?

You are continually trying to interpret what you perceive, whether it is a design, someone's behavior, or a social situation. Like the example of someone running down the street, many of the perceptions you experience can be interpreted in more than one way. When a situation has more than one possible interpretation, you say that it is *ambiguous.* The more ambiguous a situation is, the greater the number of possible meanings or interpretations it has.

Think again about the pictures you examined in Thinking Activities 4.1 and 4.2. In each instance, your description of what was happening—and what was about to happen—was based on your interpretation of the situation. Other members of the class may have given different descriptions of what was occurring because they interpreted the situation differently. Since these two pictures are by their nature puzzling and ambiguous, no one interpretation is necessarily more correct than another. Instead, each interpretation simply reveals the lenses through which this person views the world. Of course, you may feel that some interpretations make more sense than others, based on the details and the relationships that you perceive in the situation.

Your perceptions reveal the lenses through which you are viewing the event. Watching your team play baseball, for example, you may really believe that the opposing runner was "out by a mile"—even though the replay may show otherwise. Or imagine that you are giving a speech to the class and that you are being evaluated by two people—someone who likes you and someone who does not. Do you believe that different perceptions of your performance may result?

Similarly, the way you are feeling can influence your interpretations of what you are experiencing. When you feel happy and optimistic, the world often seems friendly and the future full of possibilities, and you interpret the problems you encounter as challenges to be overcome. On the other hand, when you are depressed or unhappy, you may perceive your world entirely differently. The future can appear full of problems that are trying to overcome you. In both cases the outer circumstances may be very similar; it is your own interpretation of the world through your lenses that varies so completely.

Your perceptions of the world are dramatically influenced by your past experiences: the way you were brought up, the relationships you have had, and the training and education you have undergone. Take the case of two people who are watching a football game. One person, who has very little understanding of football, sees merely a bunch of grown men hitting each other for no apparent reason. The other person, who loves football, sees complex play patterns, daring coaching strategies, effective blocking and tackling techniques, and zone defenses with "seams" that the receivers are trying to "split." Both have their eyes focused on the same event, but they are perceiving two entirely different situations. Their perceptions differ because each person is actively selecting, organizing, and interpreting the available stimuli in different ways. The same is true of any situation in which you are perceiving something about which you have special knowledge or expertise. The following are examples:

- A builder examining the construction of a new house
- A music lover attending a concert
- A naturalist experiencing the outdoors
- A cook tasting a dish just prepared
- A lawyer examining a contract
- An art lover visiting a museum

Think about a special area of interest or expertise that you have and how your perceptions of that area differ from those who don't share your knowledge. Ask other class members about their areas of expertise. Notice how their perceptions of that area differ from your own because of their greater knowledge and experience.

In all these cases, the perceptions of the knowledgeable person differ substantially from the perceptions of a person who lacks knowledge of that area. Of course, you do not have to be an expert to have more fully developed perceptions. It is a matter of degree. In general, the more understanding you have of a particular area, the more detailed and complete your perceptions can be of all matters related to it.

THINKING ACTIVITY 4.3

Let's examine a situation in which a number of different people had somewhat different perceptions about an event they were describing. The first chapter of this book contains a passage by Malcolm X (page 11) written when he was just beginning his life's work. A few years later, this work came to a tragic end with his assassination at a meeting in Harlem. The following are five different accounts of what took place on that day. As you read through the various accounts, pay particular attention to the different perceptions each one presents of this event. After you have completed reading the accounts, analyze some of the differences in these perceptions by answering the questions that follow.

FIVE ACCOUNTS OF THE ASSASSINATION OF MALCOLM X

The New York Times (February 22, 1965)

Malcolm X, the 39-year-old leader of a militant Black Nationalist movement, was shot to death yesterday afternoon at a rally of his followers in a ballroom in Washington Heights. The bearded Negro extremist had said only a few words of greeting when a fusillade rang out. The bullets knocked him over backwards.

A 22-year-old Negro, Thomas Hagan, was charged with the killing. The police rescued him from the ballroom crowd after he had been shot and beaten.

Pandemonium broke out among the 400 Negroes in the Audubon Ballroom at 160th Street and Broadway. As men, women and children ducked under tables and flattened themselves on the floor, more shots were fired. The police said seven bullets struck Malcolm. Three other Negroes were shot. Witnesses reported that as many as 30 shots had been fired. About two hours later the police said the shooting had apparently been a result of a feud between followers of Malcolm and members of the extremist group he broke with last year, the Black Muslims. . . .

Life (March 5, 1965)

His life oozing out through a half dozen or more gunshot wounds in his chest, Malcolm X, once the shrillest voice of black supremacy, lay dying on the stage of a Manhattan auditorium. Moments before, he had stepped up to the lectern and 400 of the faithful had settled down expectantly to hear the sort of speech for which he was famous—flaying the hated white man. Then a scuffle broke out in the hall and Malcolm's bodyguards bolted from his side to break it up—only to discover that they had been faked out. At least two men with pistols rose from the audience and pumped bullets into the speaker, while a third cut loose at close range with both barrels of a sawed-off shotgun. In the confusion the pistol man got away. The shotgunner lunged through the crowd and out the door, but not before the guards came to their wits and shot him in the leg. Outside he was swiftly overtaken by other supporters of Malcolm and very likely would have been stomped to death if the police hadn't saved him. Most shocking of all to the residents of Harlem was the fact that Malcolm had been killed not by "whitey" but by members of his own race.

The New York Post (February 22, 1965)

They came early to the Audubon Ballroom, perhaps drawn by the expectation that Malcolm X would name the men who firebombed his home last Sunday. . . . I sat at the left in the 12th row and, as we waited, the man next to me spoke of Malcolm and his followers: "Malcolm is our only hope. You can depend on him to tell it like it is and to give Whitey hell.". . .

There was a prolonged ovation as Malcolm walked to the rostrum. Malcolm looked up and said "A salaam aleikum (Peace be unto you)" and the audience replied "We aleikum salaam (And unto you, peace). "

Bespectacled and dapper in a dark suit, sandy hair glinting in the light, Malcolm said: "Brothers and sisters . . ." He was interrupted by two men in the center of the ballroom, who rose and, arguing with each other, moved forward. Then there was a scuffle at the back of the room. I heard Malcolm X say his last words: "Now, brothers, break it up," he said softly. "Be cool, be calm."

Then all hell broke loose. There was a muffled sound of shots and Malcolm, blood on his face and chest, fell limply back over the chairs behind him. The two men who had approached him ran to the exit on my side of the room, shooting wildly behind them as they ran. I heard people screaming, "Don't let them kill him." "Kill those bastards."At an exit I saw some of Malcolm's men beating with all their strength on two men. I saw a half dozen of Malcolm's followers bending over his inert body on the stage. Their clothes stained with their leader's blood.

Four policemen took the stretcher and carried Malcolm through the crowd and some of the women came out of their shock and one said: "I hope he doesn't die, but I don't think he's going to make it."

Associated Press (February 22, 1965)

A week after being bombed out of his Queens home, Black Nationalist leader Malcolm X was shot to death shortly after 3 (P.M.) yesterday at a Washington Heights rally of 400 of his devoted followers. Early today, police brass ordered a homicide charge placed against a 22-year-old man they rescued from a savage beating by Malcolm X supporters after the shooting. The suspect, Thomas Hagan, had been shot in the left leg by one of Malcolm's bodyguards as, police said, Hagan and another assassin fled when pandemonium erupted. Two other men were wounded in the wild burst of firing from at least three weapons. The firearms were a .38, a .45 automatic and a sawed-off shotgun. Hagan allegedly shot Malcolm X with the shotgun, a double-barrelled sawed-off weapon on which the stock also had been shortened, possibly to facilitate concealment. Cops charged Reuben Frances, of 871 E. 179th St., Bronx, with felonious assault in the shooting of Hagan, and with Sullivan Law violation—possession of the .45. Police recovered the shotgun and the .45.

The Amsterdam News (February 27, 1965)

"We interrupt this program to bring you a special newscast . . . ," the announcer said as the Sunday afternoon movie on the TV set was halted temporarily. "Malcolm X was shot four times while addressing a crowd at the Audubon Ballroom on 166th Street." "Oh no!" That was my first reaction to the shocking event that followed one week after the slender, articulate leader of the Afro-American Unity was routed from his East Elmhurst home by a bomb explosion. Minutes later we alighted from a cab at the corner of Broadway and 166th St. just a short 15 blocks from where I live on Broadway. About 200 men and women, neatly dressed, were milling around, some with expressions of awe and disbelief. Others were in small clusters talking loudly and with deep emotion in their voices. Mostly they were screaming for vengeance. One woman, small, dressed in a light gray coat and her eyes flaming with indignation, argued with a cop at the St. Nicholas corner of the block. "This is not the end of it. What they were going to do to the Statue of Liberty will be small in comparison. We black people are tired of being shoved around." Standing across the street near the memorial park one of Malcolm's close associates commented: "It's a shame." Later he added that "if it's war they want, they'll get it." He would not say whether Elijah Muhammed's followers had anything to do with the assassination. About 3:30 p.m. Malcolm X's wife, Betty, was escorted by three men and a woman from the Columbia Presbyterian Hospital. Tears streamed down her face. She was screaming, "They killed him!" Malcolm X had no last words. . . . The bombing and burning of the No. 7 Mosque early Tuesday morning was the first blow by those who are seeking revenge for the cold-blooded murder of a man who at 39 might have grown to the stature of respectable leadership. ■

Questions for Analysis

1. What details of the events has each writer *selected* to focus on?

2. How has each writer *organized* the details that have been selected? Remember that most newspapers present what they consider the most important information first and the least important information last.

3. How does each writer *interpret* Malcolm X, his followers, the gunmen, and the significance of the assassination?

4. How has each author used *language* to express his/her perspective and to influence the thinking of the reader? ◀

THINKING ACTIVITY 4.4

Locate three different newspaper or magazine accounts of an important event— a court decision, a crime, and a political demonstration are possible topics. Analyze the perceptual "lenses" of each of the writers by answering the questions in Thinking Activity 4.3. ◀

EXPERIENCES SHAPE YOUR PERCEPTIONS

Your ways of viewing the world are developed over a long period of time through the experiences you have and your thinking about these experiences. As you think critically about your perceptions, you learn more from your experiences and about how you make sense of the world. Your perceptions may be strengthened by this understanding, or they may be changed by this understanding. For example, read the following student passage and consider the way her experiences—and her reflection on these experiences—contributed to shaping her perspective on the world.

Acquired Knowledge

When news of the Acquired Immune Deficiency Syndrome first began to spread, it was just another one of those issues on the news that I felt did not really concern me. Along with cancer, leukemia, and kidney failure, I knew

Your world, and your perception of it, is created by your ongoing experiences and your reflections on these events.

these diseases ran rampant across the country, but they didn't affect me.

Once the AIDS crisis became a prevalent problem in society, I began to take a little notice of it, but my interest only extended as far as taking precautions to insure that I would not contract the disease. Sure, I felt sorry for all the people who were dying from it, but again, it was not my problem.

My father was an intravenous drug user for as long as I can remember. This was a fact of life when I was growing up. I knew that what he was doing was wrong, and that eventually he would die from it, but I also knew that he would never change.

On July 27th, my father died. An autopsy showed his cause of death as pneumonia and tuberculosis, seemingly natural causes. However, I was later informed that these were two very common symptoms related to carriers of the HIV virus. My father's years of drug abuse had finally caught up with him. He had died from AIDS.

My father's death changed my life. Prior to that, I had always felt that as long as a situation did not directly affect me, it was really no concern of mine. I felt that somewhere, someone would take care of it. Having a crisis strike so close to me made me wake up to reality. Suddenly I became acutely aware of all the things that are wrong in the world. I began to see the problems of AIDS, famine, homelessness, unemployment, and others from a personal point of view, and I began to feel that I had an obligation to join the crusade to do something about these problems.

I organized a youth coalition called UPLIFT INC. In this group, we meet and talk about the problems in society, as well as the everyday problems that any of our members may have in their lives. We organize shows (talent shows, fashion shows) and give a large portion of our proceeds to the American Foundation for AIDS Research, the Coalition for the Homeless, and many other worthy organizations.

Now I feel that I am doing my duty as a human being by trying to help those who are less fortunate than myself. My father's death gave me insight into my own mortality. Now I know that life is too short not to only try to enjoy it, but to really achieve something worthwhile out of it. Material gains matter only if you are willing to take your good fortune and spread it around to those who could use it.

In the reading selection located on page 191, a former migrant worker and current union organizer named Roberto Acuna describes changes in his perceptions of his world. Acuna's story illustrates the main purpose of our ongoing attempts to think critically about the way our experiences shape our perceptions. By engaging in this process, we are continually trying to develop a clearer and more complete understanding of what is taking place so that we can make the most effective decisions in our lives. Because our perceptions are based on our experiences, they often change and evolve based on new experiences. Analyzing Roberto Acuna's personal odyssey will illustrate how experiences can shape and reshape our perceptions.

THINKING ACTIVITY 4.5

Think of an experience that has shaped your life. Write an essay describing the experience and the ways it changed your life and how you perceive the world. After writing, analyze your experience by answering the following questions.

1. What were your *initial* perceptions about the situation? As you began the experience, you brought into the situation certain perceptions about the experience and the people involved.

2. What previous experiences had you undergone? Identify some of the influences that helped to shape these perceptions. Describe the actions that you either took or thought about taking.

3. As you became involved in the situation, what experiences in the situation influenced you to question or doubt your initial perceptions?

4. In what new ways did you view the situation that would better explain what was taking place? Identify the revised perceptions that you began to form about the experience. ◀

THINKING CRITICALLY ABOUT PERCEPTIONS

So far, we have emphasized the great extent to which you actively participate in what you perceive by selecting, organizing, and interpreting. We have suggested that each of us views the world through our own unique lenses. This means that no two of us perceive the world in exactly the same way.

Because we actively participate in selecting, organizing, and interpreting the sensations we experience, however, our perceptions are often incomplete, inaccurate, or subjective. To complicate the situation even more, our own limitations in perceiving are not the only ones that can cause us problems. Other people often purposefully create perceptions and misperceptions. An advertiser who wants to sell a product may try to create the impression that your life will be changed if you use this product. Or a person who wants to discredit someone else may spread untrue rumors about her, in order to influence others' perceptions of her.

The only way you can correct the mistakes, distortions, and incompleteness of your perceptions is to *become aware* of this normally unconscious proc–ess by which you perceive and make sense of your world. By becoming aware of this process, you can think critically about what is going on and then correct your mistakes and distortions. In other words, you can use your critical thinking abilities to create a clearer and more informed idea of what is taking place. Perception alone cannot be totally relied on, and if you remain unaware of how it operates and of your active role, then you will be unable to exert any control over it. And in that case, you will be convinced that the way *you see* the world is the way the world is, even when your perceptions are mistaken, distorted, or incomplete.

The first step in critically examining your perceptions is to be willing to *ask questions* about what you are perceiving. As long as you believe that the way you see things is the only way to see them, you will be unable to recognize when your perceptions are distorted or inaccurate. For instance, if you are certain that your interpretation of the boy at the computer in Thinking Activity 4.1 or the photograph in Thinking Activity 4.2 is the only correct one, then you will not be likely to try and see other possible interpretations. But if you are willing to question your perception ("What are some other possible interpretations?"), then you will open the way to more fully developing your perception of what is taking place.

Besides asking questions, you have to try to become aware of the personal factors your lenses bring to your perceptions. As you have seen, each of us brings to every situation a whole collection of expectations, interests, fears, and hopes that can influence what we are perceiving. Consider the following situations:

You've been fishing all day without a nibble. Suddenly you get a strike! You reel it in, but just as you're about to pull the fish into the boat, it frees itself from the hook and swims away. When you get back home later that night, your friends ask you: "How large was the fish that got away?"

The teacher asks you to evaluate the performance of a classmate who is giving a report to the class. You don't like this other student because he

Perceptions are often incomplete or inaccurate, and we need to use our critical thinking abilities to create a clearer, more informed idea of what is taking place.

acts as if he's superior to the rest of the students in the class. How do you evaluate his report?

You are asked to estimate the size of an audience attending an event that your organization has sponsored. How many people are there?

In each of these cases, you can imagine that your perceptions might be influenced by certain hopes, fears, or prejudices that you brought to the situation, causing your observations to become distorted or inaccurate. Although you usually cannot eliminate the personal feelings that are influencing your perceptions, you can become aware of them and try to control them. For instance, if you are asked to evaluate a group of people, one of whom is a good friend, you should try to keep these personal feelings in mind when making your judgment in order to make your perceptions as accurate as possible.

As you saw in Chapter 2, critical thinkers strive to see things from different perspectives. One of the best ways to do so is by communicating with others and engaging in *dialogue* with them. This means exchanging and critically examining ideas in an open and organized way. Similarly, dialogue is one of the main ways that you check out your perceptions—by asking others what their perceptions are and then comparing and contrasting these with your own. This is exactly what you did when you discussed the different possible interpretations of the boy at the computer and the ambiguous photograph. By exchanging your perceptions with the perceptions of other class members, you developed a more complete sense of how these different events could be viewed, as well as the reasons that support these different perspectives.

Looking for reasons that support various perceptions also involves trying to discover any independent proof or evidence regarding the perception. When evidence is available in the form of records, photographs, videotapes, or experimental results, this will certainly help you evaluate the accuracy of your perceptions. For example, consider the situations just described. What are some of the independent forms of evidence you could look for in trying to verify your perceptions?

Thinking critically about your perceptions means trying to avoid developing impulsive or superficial perceptions that you are unwilling to change. As you saw in Chapter 2, a critical thinker is *thoughtful* in approaching the world and *open* to modifying his or her views in the light of new information or better insight. Consider the following perceptions:

- Women are very emotional.
- Politicians are corrupt.
- Teenagers are wild and irresponsible.
- People who are good athletes are usually poor students.
- Men are thoughtless and insensitive.

These types of general perceptions are known as *stereotypes* because they express a belief about an entire group of people without recognizing the individual differences between members of the group. For instance, it is probably accurate to say that there are *some* politicians who are corrupt, but this is not the same thing as saying that all, or even most, politicians are corrupt. Stereotypes affect your perception of the world because they encourage you to form an inaccurate and superficial idea of a whole group of people ("All teenagers are reckless drivers"). When you meet someone who falls into this group, you automatically perceive that person as having these stereotyped qualities ("This person is a teenager, so he is a reckless driver"). Even if you find that this person does not fit your stereotyped perception ("This teenager is not a reckless driver"), this sort of superficial and unthoughtful labeling does not encourage you to change your perception of the group as a whole. Instead, it encourages you to overlook the conflicting information in favor of your stereotyped perception ("All teenagers are reckless drivers—except for this one"). On the other hand, when you are perceiving in a thoughtful fashion, you try to see what a person is like as an individual, instead of trying to fit him or her into a preexisting category.

THINKING ACTIVITY 4.6

1. Describe an incident in which you were perceived as a stereotype because of your age, ethnic or religious background, employment, accent, or place of residence.
2. Describe how it felt to be stereotyped in this way.
3. Explain what you think are the best ways to overcome stereotypes such as these. ◀

SUMMARY

As your mind develops through the experiences you have and your reflection on these experiences, your perceptions of the world should continue to develop as well. By thinking critically about your perceptions, by seeking to view your world from perspectives other than your own and to understand the reasons that support these perspectives, your understanding of the world should become increasingly accurate and complete. You can view your efforts to think critically about what you are perceiving as a problem-solving process, as you continually attempt to interpret your experiences.

As you have seen in this chapter, much of your knowledge of the world begins in perceiving. But to develop knowledge and understanding, you must

make use of your thinking abilities in order to examine this experience critically. Increased understanding of the way the world operates thus increases the
accuracy and completeness of your perceptions and leads you to informed beliefs about what is happening. In the next chapter we will be exploring further
how to develop informed beliefs and knowledge of the world by combining
perceptions with critical thinking.

Thinking Activity 4.7

This chapter has emphasized the extent to which people's perceiving "lenses"
shape and influence the way they see things, the conclusions they reach, and
the decisions they make. Thinking critically involves becoming aware of these
perceiving lenses and evaluating their validity in order to develop the most
accurate, best substantiated conclusions. One of the most powerful strategies
for achieving this goal is to perform a comparative analysis of different perspectives. For example, one of the most controversial and still hotly debated
events in U.S. history was our country's atomic bombing of the Japanese cities
of Hiroshima and Nagasaki. Although the bombings ended World War II, they
killed over 100,000 civilians and resulted in radiation poisoning that affected
many thousands more then and in subsequent generations. In 1995 the
Smithsonian Museum planned an exhibit to commemorate the fiftieth anniver-
sary of the bombings, but controversy over whether the perspective of the exhibit was unbalanced led to its cancellation and the resignation of the Air and
Space Museum's director.

The following activity developed by the historian Kevin O'Reilly presents
two contrasting analyses of this event, each supported by historical documentation. After reviewing the two accounts, answer the questions that follow.

Was the United States Justified in Dropping Atomic Bombs on Japan?

Background Information

For the United States, World War II began with a sneak attack by Japanese
planes on American naval forces at Pearl Harbor. The war was fought in
Europe against the Germans and their allies, and in the Pacific against the
Japanese. During the war the secret Manhattan Project was commissioned
to develop an atomic bomb for the United States. Germany surrendered
(May 1945) before the bombs were completed, but on August 6, 1945, a

The dropping of atomic bombs on Hiroshima and Nagasaki ended World War II but also killed over 100,000 civilians and resulted in radiation poisoning that affected subsequent generations.

single atomic bomb destroyed Hiroshima, and on the ninth, another atomic bomb destroyed Nagasaki.

In this lesson two viewpoints are presented on the controversial use of the atomic bombs. Read and evaluate them according to the criteria of critical thinking. Consider the relevant information that follows the two viewpoints.

Historian A

Some historians argue that dropping atomic bombs on Japan was justified because it shortened the war, thus saving lives in the end. This view is wrong. The United States was not justified in dropping the bombs.

In the summer of 1945, the Japanese were almost totally defeated. American ships and planes pounded the island without any response by the Japanese. Leaders in Japan were trying to surrender and American leaders knew it. Several times the Japanese went to the Russians to ask them to mediate a peace settlement with the United States.[1] (It is not unusual for a country that wants to surrender to ask another country to speak for it at first and help negotiate a settlement.) There was only one condition that the Japanese insisted on—they wanted to keep their emperor, the symbol of Japanese culture. The United States never even talked with the Japanese about surrender terms—American leaders kept demanding unconditional surrender. After we used the bombs and the Japanese surrendered, we let them keep their emperor anyway. We could have allowed the Japanese to surrender earlier and saved all those lives obliterated by the bombs by letting them have their one condition in the first place.

If the bombs were not used to bring about surrender, then why were they used? The plain truth is that they were used to scare Russia. In 1945 the United States disagreed with the Soviet Union in regard to Russia's actions in Europe. Our leaders felt that by showing the Russians we had a powerful weapon, we could get them to agree to our terms in Europe and Asia. As Secretary of War Stimson said in his diary, in diplomacy the bomb would be a "master card."[2]

President Truman had an important meeting scheduled with the Russian leader, Josef Stalin, at Potsdam, Germany in July 1945. He wanted to have the bomb completed and successfully tested when he went into that meeting. Atomic scientist J. Robert Oppenheimer said, "We were under incredible pressure to get it [the bomb] done before the Potsdam meeting."[3] Truman hoped to have the bomb sticking out of his hip pocket, so to speak, when he negotiated with Stalin. Then he could make new demands of the Russians regarding eastern Europe. He told some of his friends at Potsdam before the final test, "If it explodes as I think it will, I'll certainly have a hammer on those boys."[4]

While Truman was negotiating in Potsdam, the bomb was successfully tested in New Mexico, and he became more demanding with Stalin. Secretary of War Stimson stated, "He [Truman] said it [the bomb] gave him an entirely new feeling of confidence. . . ."[5]

But the Russians had to see the power of the bomb before the United States could intimidate them with it. This was accomplished at Hiroshima. Truman remarked, "This is the greatest thing in history!"[6]

A second motive for dropping the bomb was to end the war in Asia before the Russians could get involved. The Japanese were talking of surrender, but the United States wanted surrender within days, not a negotiated surrender taking weeks to complete. The Russians had agreed at Yalta to enter the war against Japan three months after the end of the war in Europe. This would be three months after May 9, or somewhere around August 9. If the Russians got involved in the war in Asia, they could spread

Communism to China and other countries and possibly to Japan itself. American leaders did not want to see this happen.[7]

If the United States could speed up the Japanese surrender, we could avoid all these problems. We dropped the first bomb on August 6; Russia entered the war on the eighth, and we dropped the second bomb on the ninth. Don't these dates look suspicious? No country could surrender in only three days—it takes longer than that to make such an important decision. We would not wait longer because we wanted Japan to surrender before the Russians could get involved.

Some scientists who worked on the bomb recommended that it not be dropped on people. They proposed that the United States demonstrate the bomb's power to Japanese leaders by dropping it on an uninhabited island. American political leaders rejected this idea. The devastating effect of the bomb had to be shown by destroying a city.

Even top military leaders opposed the use of the atomic bomb.[8] The bomb would have little effect on the war, they argued, since the Japanese were already trying to surrender.

All this evidence shows that the atomic bombs were not used to end the war and save lives, but rather to scare the Russians and speed up the end of the war before Russian influence spread further into Asia. The killing of over 100,000 civilians in one country in order to scare the leaders of another country was wrong. The United States was not justified in dropping the atomic bombs.

Endnotes for Historian A

(All are quotes from the sources cited except bracketed portions.)

[1] Gar Alperovitz (a historian), *Atomic Diplomacy* (1965). (Direct quotations from *Foreign Relations Papers of the United States: Conference at Berlin*, Vol. II, pp. 1249, 1250, 1260, 1261.)

> "On July 17, the day of the first plenary session, another intercepted Japanese message showed that although the government felt that the unconditional surrender formula involved too great a dishonor, it was convinced that 'the demands of the times' made Soviet mediation to terminate the war absolutely essential. Further cables indicated that the one condition the Japanese asked was preservation of 'our form of government.' A message of July 25 revealed instructions to the [Japanese] Ambassador in Moscow to go anywhere to meet with [Soviet Foreign Minister] Molotov during the recess of the Potsdam meeting so as to 'impress them with the sincerity of our desire' to terminate the war. He was told

to make it clear that 'we should like to communicate to the other party [the United States] through appropriate channels that we have no objection to a peace based on the Atlantic Charter.' The only 'difficult point is the . . . formality of unconditional surrender.'"

James F. Byrnes (Secretary of State), *All in One Lifetime*, p. 297:

"July 28: Secretary Forrestal arrived and told me in detail of the intercepted messages from the Japanese government to Ambassador Sato in Moscow, indicating Japan's willingness to surrender."

[2] Stimson (Secretary of War) Diary, May 15:

"The trouble is that the President has now promised apparently to meet Stalin and Churchill on the first of July [at Potsdam] and at that time these questions will become burning and it may become necessary to have it out with Russia on her relations to Manchuria and Port Arthur and various other parts of North China, and also the relations of China to us. Over any such tangled web of problems the S-1 secret [the atomic bomb] would be dominant and yet we will not know until after . . . that meeting, whether this is a weapon in our hands or not. We think it will be shortly afterwards, but it seems a terrible thing to gamble with such big stakes in diplomacy without having your master card in your hand."

Leo Szilard (an atomic scientist who opposed use of the bombs on Japan), Conversation with Secretary of State Byrnes. Recorded on August 24, 1944, in Stewart to Bush, Atomic Energy Commission Document 200. Manhattan Engineering District—Top Secret, National Archives, Record Group 77, Box 7, folder 12; Box 14, folder 4:

[Szilard argued that we should not use the bomb.]

"Byrnes – Our possessing and demonstrating the bomb would make Russia more manageable in Europe."

"Szilard – [The] interests of peace might best be served and an arms race avoided by not using the bomb against Japan, keeping it secret, and letting the Russians think that our work on it had not succeeded."

"Byrnes – How would you get Congress to appropriate money for atomic energy research if you do not show results for the money which has been spent already?"

[3] Atomic Energy Commission, Oppenheimer Hearings, p. 31.

[4] Jonathan Daniels (biographer), *The Man of Independence* (1950), p. 266.

[5] *Foreign Relations Papers of the United States: Conference at Berlin*, 1945, Vol. II, p. 1361.

Stimson Diary, July 22:

"Churchill read Grove's report [on the successful testing of the atomic bomb in New Mexico] in full. . . . He said, 'Now I know what happened to Truman yesterday. I couldn't understand it. When he got to the meeting after having read this report he was a changed man. He told the Russians just where they got on and off and generally bossed the whole meeting."

[6] Harry S. Truman, *Year of Decisions*, p. 421.

[7] Byrnes, *All in One Lifetime*, p. 300:

"Though there was an understanding that the Soviets would enter the war three months after Germany surrendered, the President and I hoped that Japan would surrender before then."

Secretary of War Stimson stated in his diary on August 10, 1945, that he urged the President that:

"The thing to do was to get this surrender through as quickly as we can before Russia should get down in reach of the Japanese homeland. . . . It was of great importance to get the homeland into our hands before the Russians could put in any substantial claim to occupy and help rule it."

[8] General Dwight Eisenhower, statement in "Ike on Ike," *Newsweek*, November 11, 1963, p. 107:

"I voiced to him [Secretary of War Stimson] my grave misgivings, first on the basis of my belief that Japan was already defeated and that dropping the bomb was completely unnecessary and secondly, because I thought our country should avoid shocking world opinion by the use of a weapon whose employment was, I thought, no longer necessary as a measure to save American lives. It was my belief that Japan was, at the very moment, seeking some way to surrender with a minimum loss of 'face.' . . . It wasn't necessary to hit them with that awful thing."

Admiral W.D. Leahy, *I Was There* (1950), p. 441:

"It was my opinion that the use of this barbarous weapon at Hiroshima and Nagasaki was of no material assistance in our war against Japan. The Japanese were already defeated and ready to surrender."

Air Force Chief of staff LeMay, *New York Herald Tribune*, September 21, 1945:

"The atomic bomb had nothing to do with the end of the war."

Historian B

Dropping atomic bombs on Hiroshima and Nagasaki helped the United States avoid a costly invasion of Japan. It therefore saved lives in the long run, which makes it a justifiable action.

It is true that the United States received some indication in the summer of 1945 that Japan was trying to surrender. Japan would not surrender unconditionally, however, and that was very important to the United States. The Germans had not surrendered unconditionally at the end of World War I and, as a result, they rose again to bring on World War II. The United States was not going to let that mistake happen again. As President Roosevelt said, "This time there will be no doubt about who defeated whom."[1]

Although the Japanese military situation in July 1945 was approaching total defeat, many Japanese leaders hoped for one last ditch victory in order to get softer peace terms.[2] One of their hopes was to divide the Grand Alliance by getting Russia (which was not at the time at war with Japan) to be the intermediary for peace negotiations. Maybe the Allies would begin to disagree, the Japanese militarists reasoned, and Japan would get off easy. Their other hope was that they could inflict enough casualties on the American troops, or hold out long enough, to get the American public to pressure their leaders to accept something less than unconditional surrender.[3]

Some historians argue that the only issue which prevented the Japanese from accepting unconditional surrender was their fear that the emperor would be removed by the Americans. American leaders, however, believed that allowing this one condition would encourage the militarists in Japan to further resistance. Americans also felt that it would weaken the war effort in the United States since we would be deviating from our well-publicized policy of unconditional surrender.[4]

Some Japanese leaders wanted much more, however, than just the one condition of keeping their emperor. They wanted their troops to surrender to them, and they wanted no occupation of Japan or war crimes trials of Japanese leaders. Even on August 9, after the bombing of Hiroshima and Nagasaki, and after the Russian declaration of war against them, the Japanese leaders still could not agree to surrender.[5] This shows that the bombs were necessary—anything less than the bombs or invasion would not have brought about unconditional surrender.

Some people believe that the dates of dropping the bombs (August 6 and 9) show that the United States dropped them to stop Russian entry into the war (August 8). There are two problems with this line of reasoning. First, the United States did not know the exact date of Russian entry. Second, the bombs were to be dropped when a military officer decided that the weather was right.[6] If Truman wanted to beat the Russians, why didn't he order the bombs to be dropped sooner, or why didn't he give in on unconditional surrender?

The argument that the United States dropped the bombs in order to threaten the Russians is also weak. The fact that we were so unsuccessful in getting the Russians to agree to our policies in Europe shows that the bomb was not used for that reason. It must have been used to shorten the war. It certainly did not scare the Russians.

Some American scientists opposed using the bomb on civilian or military targets, preferring to demonstrate it on an uninhabited island. This recommendation was studied carefully by a committee (the Interim Committee) set up to consider how to use the bomb. The committee said that a demonstration could have had a lot of problems, which would have wasted one of the bombs and precious time. In light of the fact that it took two bombs dropped on cities to bring about a surrender, the demonstration idea does not seem like it would have been effective. The committee recommended the bombs be used against military targets.[7]

It is important to remember that on July 26, 1945, the United States warned the Japanese that we would use the atomic bomb against them unless they accepted unconditional surrender.[8] The fanatical Japanese leaders would not give in. They said they would ignore the warning.[9] Thus, the loss of life from atomic bombings was the responsibility of the Japanese leaders, not the Americans.

The United States was right in insisting on unconditional surrender. Since the Japanese would not surrender unconditionally, and since a demonstration bombing would not have been effective, the only alternative to using the atomic bombs was continuing the war. This would have cost hundreds of thousands more lives. In the long run, the use of the atomic bombs on Hiroshima and Nagasaki shortened the war and saved lives.

Endnotes for Historian B

(All are quotes from the sources cited except bracketed portions.)

[1] President Roosevelt at a press conference, *F.D.R.: Public Papers of the Presidents,* Vol. XIII, p. 210:

> "Practically all Germans deny the fact they surrendered in the last war, but this time they are going to know it. And so are the Japs."

[2] *Command Decisions* (a history of World War II), p. 504, quotes a study done by Brigadier General George A. Lincoln, 4 June 1945:

> "In allied intelligence Japan was portrayed as a defeated nation whose military leaders were blind to defeat. . . . Japan was still far from surrender. She had ample reserves of weapons and ammunition and an army of 5,000,000 troops, 2,000,000 of them in the home islands. . . . In the opinion of the intelligence experts, neither blockade nor bombing alone would produce unconditional surrender before the date set for invasion [November 1945]. And the invasion itself, they believed, would be costly and possibly prolonged."

[3] *Command Decisions,* p. 517:

> "The militarists [in the Japanese Government] could and did minimize the effects of the bomb, but they could not evade the obvious consequences of Soviet intervention, which ended all hope of dividing their enemies and securing softer peace terms."

[4] *Command Decisions,* pp. 512–13, summarizing former Secretary of State Cordell Hull, *Memoirs,* Vol. II, p. 1593:

> "[Cordell] Hull's view . . . was the proposal [by Secretary of War Stimson to let the Japanese keep the Emperor] smacked of appeasement. . . . The proposal to retain the imperial system might well encourage resistance [by the Japanese] and have 'terrible political repercussions' in the United States."

[5] Robert Butow (a historian), *Japan's Decision to Surrender* (1959), pp. 161, 163, 164. (Describing the debate among the six Japanese leaders about whether to surrender, August 9, 1945.)

> "While Suzuki [Prime Minister], Togo [Foreign Minister] and Yonai [Navy Minister] were committed in varying degrees to an outright acceptance [of the Potsdam Declaration demanding unconditional surrender] on the basis of the sole reservation that the Imperial house would be maintained, Anami [War Minister], Umezu [Army

Chief of Staff], and Toyoda [Navy Chief of Staff], felt quite differently. . . . What gagged these men—all true 'Samurai' bred in an
uncompromising tradition—were the other points Yonai had mentioned. They wanted either to prevent a security occupation entirely or to exclude at least the metropolis of Tokyo. . . . So far as
war criminals were concerned, they felt it should be Japan and not
the victorious enemy who must try such cases. In effect, they also
wanted to accept the surrender of their own men. . . .

"From the standpoint of making postwar rationalizations and of
'opening up the future of the country' it was psychologically vital
for the Japanese army and navy to make it appear as if they had
voluntarily disbanded their military might in order to save the
nation and the world at large from the continued ravages of war.
If they could do this, they could very easily later plant an appealing suggestion to the effect that the imperial forces of Great Japan
had not really suffered defeat at all. For this reason, too, a security
occupation and war crimes trials conducted by Allied tribunals
had to be avoided at all costs. . . .

"Togo pointedly asked whether Japan could win the war if a col-
lapse of the type [of negotiations] occurred. To this the military
heads could only reply that although they were not certain of ultimate victory, they were still capable of one more campaign—a 'de-
cisive' battle in the homeland. . . . The Council was deadlocked."

[6] Memorandum to Major General I.R. Groves from Brigadier General T.F.
Farrell

Subject: Report on Overseas Operations—Atomic Bomb:

27 September 1945

"After the Hiroshima strike we scheduled the second attack for 11
August [local time]. On learning that bad weather was predicted
for that time, we reviewed the status of the assembly work for the
Fat Man [the second atomic bomb], our uncompleted test program,
and readiness of the planes and crews. It was determined that with
an all-out effort, everything could be ready for takeoff on the early
morning of 9 August [local time], provided our final test of the Fat
Man proved satisfactory, which it did. The decision turned out to
be fortunate in that several days of bad weather followed 9
August."

[7] Interim Committee report, June 1, 1945, from Harry S Truman, *Year of Decisions*, p. 419:

> "Recommend unanimously:
>
> "1. The bomb should be used against Japan as soon as possible.
>
> "2. It should be used against a military target surrounded by other buildings.
>
> "3. It should be used without prior warning of the nature of the weapon."

[8] Proclamation for Unconditional Surrender, July 26, 1945. *Foreign Relations Papers of the United States: Potsdam Papers*, Vol. II, p. 1258:

> "Section 13: We call upon the government of Japan to proclaim now the unconditional surrender of the Japanese armed forces, and to provide proper and adequate assurance of their good faith in such action. The alternative for Japan is prompt and utter destruction."

[9] *Foreign Relations Papers of the United States: Potsdam Papers*, Document 12518, July 28, 1945.

Japanese Prime Minister Suzuki to reporters:

> "I believe the Joint Proclamation [the Potsdam Proclamation—warning Japan to accept unconditional surrender] by the three countries is nothing but a rehash of the Cairo Declaration [which also called on Japan to surrender]. As for the [Japanese] Government, it does not find any important value in it, and there is no other recourse but to ignore it entirely and resolutely fight for the successful conclusion of the war." ∎

Questions for Analysis

1. Describe the main arguments, reasons, and evidence that support the perspective of Historian A.

2. Describe the main arguments, reasons, and evidence that support the perspective of Historian B.

3. Imagine that you were in the position of the United States president, Harry Truman. Explain what action you would have taken with respect to the atomic bombs and explain the rationale for your decision. ◀

THINKING PASSAGE

This section is taken from the book *Working: People Talk About What They Do All Day and How They Feel About What They Do* by Studs Terkel. Terkel traveled throughout the United States interviewing people from a wide range of occupations, including farmers, steelworkers, corporate executives, and prostitutes. In his narrative, Roberto Acuna describes how he became an organizer for the United Farm Workers of America. At the beginning of his narrative, Acuna says, "The things I saw shaped my life." After reading his story, ask yourself, "Did 'things' shape Acuna's life? Or did Acuna shape and reshape the things he saw into his life?"

MIGRANT WORKER
by Roberto Acuna

I walked out of the fields two years ago. I saw the need to change the California feudal system, to change the lives of farm workers, to make these huge corporations feel they're not above anybody. I am thirty-four years old and I try to organize for the United Farm Workers of America.

His hands are calloused and each of his thumbnails is singularly cut. If you're picking lettuce, the thumbnails fall off 'cause they're banged on the box. Your hands get swollen. You can't slow down because the foreman sees you're so many boxes behind and you'd better get on. But people would help each other. If you're feeling bad that day, somebody who's feeling pretty good would help. Any people that are suffering have to stick together, whether they like it or not, whether they be black, brown, or pink.

According to Mom, I was born on a cotton sack out in the fields, 'cause she had no money to go to the hospital. When I was a child, we used to migrate from California to Arizona and back and forth. The things I saw shaped my life. I remember when we used to go out and pick carrots and onions, the whole family. We tried to scratch a livin' out of the ground. I saw my parents cry out in despair, even though we had the whole family working. At the time, they were paying sixty-two and a half cents an hour. The average income must have been fifteen hundred dollars, maybe two thousand.*

This was supplemented by child labor. During those years, the growers used to have a Pick-Your-Harvest Week. They would get all the migrant

---

* "Today, because of our struggles, the pay is up to two dollars an hour. Yet we know that is not enough."

kids out of school and have 'em out there pickin' the crops at peak harvest time. A child was off that week and when he went back to school, he got a little gold star. They would make it seem like something civic to do.

We'd pick everything: lettuce, carrots, onions, cucumbers, cauliflower, broccoli, tomatoes—all the salads you could make out of vegetables, we picked 'em. Citrus fruits, watermelons—you name it. We'd be in Salinas about four months. From there we'd go down into the Imperial Valley. From there we'd go to picking citrus. It was like a cycle. We'd follow the seasons.

After my dad died, my mom would come home and she'd go into her tent and I would go into ours. We'd roughhouse and everything and then we'd go into the tent where Mom was sleeping and I'd see her crying. When I asked her why she was crying she never gave me an answer. All she said was things would get better. She retired a beaten old lady with a lot of dignity. That day she thought would be better never came for her.

One time, my mom was in bad need of money, so she got a part-time evening job in a restaurant. I'd be helping her. All the growers would come in and they'd be laughing, making nasty remarks, and make passes at her. I used to go out there and kick 'em and my mom told me to leave 'em alone, she could handle 'em. But they would embarrass her and she would cry.

My mom was a very proud woman. She brought us up without any help from nobody. She kept the family strong. They say that a family that prays together stays together. I say that a family that works together stays together—because of the suffering. . . .

I'd go barefoot to school. The bad thing was they used to laugh at us, the Anglo kids. They would laugh because we'd bring tortillas and frijoles to lunch. They would have their nice little compact lunch boxes with cold milk in their thermos and they'd laugh at us because all we had was dried tortillas. Not only would they laugh at us, but the kids would pick fights. My older brother used to do most of the fighting for me and he'd come home with black eyes all the time.

I wanted to be accepted. It must have been in sixth grade. It was just before the Fourth of July. They were trying out students for this patriotic play. I wanted to do Abe Lincoln, so I learned the Gettysburg Address inside and out. I'd be out in the fields pickin' the crops and I'd be memorizin'. I was the only one who didn't have to read the part, 'cause I learned it. The part was given to a girl who was a grower's daughter. She had to read it out of a book, but they said she had better diction. I was very disappointed. I quit about eighth grade.

Any time anybody'd talk to me about politics, about civil rights, I would ignore it. It's a very degrading thing because you can't express yourself. They wanted us to speak English in the school classes. We'd put out a real effort. I would get into a lot of fights because I spoke Spanish and they couldn't understand it. I was punished. I was kept after school for not speaking English.

We used to have our own tents on the truck. Most migrants would live in the tents that were already there in the fields, put up by the company. We got one for ourselves, secondhand, but it was ours. Anglos used to laugh at us. "Here comes the carnival," they'd say. We couldn't keep our clothes clean, we couldn't keep nothing clean, because we'd go by the dirt roads and the dust. We'd stay outside the town.

I never did want to go to town because it was a very bad thing for me. We used to go to the small stores, even though we got clipped more. If we went to the other stores, they would laugh at us. They would always point at us with a finger. We'd go to town maybe every two weeks to get what we needed. Everybody would walk in a bunch. We were afraid. (Laughs.) We sang to keep our spirits up. We joked about our poverty. This one guy would say, "When I get to be rich, I'm gonna marry an Anglo woman, so I can be accepted into society." The other guy would say, "When I get rich I'm gonna marry a Mexican woman, so I can go to that Anglo society of yours and see them hang you for marrying an Anglo." Our world was around the fields.

I started picking crops when I was eight. I couldn't do much, but every little bit counts. Every time I would get behind on my chores, I would get a carrot thrown at me by my parents. I would daydream: If I were a millionaire, I would buy all these ranches and give them back to the people. I would picture my mom living in one area all the time and being admired by all the people in the community. All of a sudden I'd be rudely awakened by a broken carrot in my back. That would bust your whole dream apart and you'd work for a while and come back to daydreaming.

We used to work early, about four o'clock in the morning. We'd pick the harvest until about six. Then we'd run home and get into our supposedly clean clothes and run all the way to school because we'd be late. By the time we got to school, we'd be all tuckered out. Around maybe eleven o'clock, we'd be dozing off. Our teachers would send notes to the house telling Mom that we were inattentive. The only thing I'd make fairly good grades on was spelling. I couldn't do anything else. Many times we never did our homework, because we were out in the fields. The teachers couldn't understand that. I would get whacked there also.

School would end maybe four o'clock. We'd rush home again, change clothes, go back to work until seven, seven-thirty at night. That's not counting the weekends. On Saturday and Sunday, we'd be there from four-thirty in the morning until about seven-thirty in the evening. This is where we made the money, those two days. We all worked.

I would carry boxes for my mom to pack the carrots in. I would pull the carrots out and she would sort them into different sizes. I would get water for her to drink. When you're picking tomatoes, the boxes are heavy. They weigh about thirty pounds. They're dropped very hard on the trucks so they have to be sturdy.

The hardest work would be thinning and hoeing with a short handled hoe. The fields would be about a half mile long. We would be bending and stooping all day. Sometimes you would have hard ground and by the time you got home, your hands would be full of calluses. And you'd have a backache. Sometimes I wouldn't have dinner or anything. I'd just go home and fall asleep and wake up just in time to go out to the fields again.

The grower would keep the families apart, hoping they'd fight against each other. He'd have three or four camps and he'd have the people over here pitted against the people over there. For jobs. He'd give the best crops to the people he thought were the fastest workers. This way he kept you going harder and harder, competing.

When I was sixteen, I had my first taste as a foreman. Handling braceros, aliens, that came from Mexico to work. They'd bring these people to work over here and then send them back to Mexico after the season was over. My job was to make sure they did a good job and pushin' 'em even harder. I was a company man, yes. My parents needed money and I wanted to make sure they were proud of me. A foreman is recognized. I was very naive. Even though I was pushing the workers, I knew their problems. They didn't know how to write, so I would write letters home for them. I would take them to town, buy their clothes, outside of the company stores. They paid me $1.10 an hour. The farm workers' wage was raised to eighty-two and a half cents. But even the braceros were making more money than me, because they were working piecework. I asked for more money. The manager said, "If you don't like it you can quit." I quit and joined the Marine Corps.

I joined the Marine Corps at seventeen. I was very mixed up. I wanted to become a first-class citizen. I wanted to be accepted and I was very proud of my uniform. My mom didn't want to sign the papers, but she knew I had to better myself and maybe I'd get an education in the services.

I did many jobs. I took a civil service exam and was very proud when I passed. Most of the others were college kids. There were only three Chicanos in the group of sixty. I got a job as a correctional officer in a state prison. I quit after eight months because I couldn't take the misery I saw. They wanted me to use a rubber hose on some of the prisoners—mostly Chicanos and blacks. I couldn't do it. They called me chicken-livered because I didn't want to hit nobody. They constantly harassed me after that. I didn't quit because I was afraid of them but because they were trying to make me into a mean man. I couldn't see it. This was Soledad State Prison.

I began to see how everything was so wrong. When growers can have an intricate watering system to irrigate their crops but they can't have running water inside the houses of workers. Veterinarians tend to the needs of domestic animals but they can't have medical care for the workers. They can have land subsidies for the growers but they can't have adequate unemployment compensation for the workers. They treat him like a farm implement. In fact, they treat their implements better and their domestic animals better. They have heat and insulated barns for the animals but the workers live in beat-up shacks with no heat at all.

Illness in the fields is 120 percent higher than the average rate for industry. It's mostly back trouble, rheumatism and arthritis, because of the damp weather and the cold. Stoop labor is very hard on a person. Tuberculosis is high. And now because of the pesticides, we have many respiratory diseases.

The University of California at Davis has government experiments with pesticides and chemicals. To get a bigger crop each year. They haven't any regard as to what safety precautions are needed. In 1964 or '65, an airplane was spraying these chemicals on the fields. Spraying rigs they're called. Flying low, the wheels got tangled on the fence wire. The pilot got up, dusted himself off, and got a drink of water. He died of convulsions. The ambulance attendants got violently sick because of the pesticides he had on his person. A little girl was playing around a sprayer. She stuck her tongue on it. She died instantly.

These pesticides affect the farm worker through the lungs. He breathes it in. He gets no compensation. All they do is say he's sick. They don't investigate the cause.

There were times when I felt I couldn't take it any more. It was 105 in the shade and I'd see endless rows of lettuce and I felt my back hurting

. . . I felt the frustration of not being able to get out of the fields. I was getting ready to jump any foreman who looked at me cross-eyed. But until two years ago, my world was still very small.

I would read all these things in the papers about Cesar Chavez and I would denounce him because I still had that thing about becoming a first-class patriotic citizen. In Mexicali they would pass out leaflets and I would throw 'em away. I never participated. The grape boycott didn't affect me much because I was in lettuce. It wasn't until Chavez came to Salinas, where I was working in the fields, that I saw what a beautiful man he was. I went to this rally, I still intended to stay with the company. But something—I don't know—I was close to the workers. They couldn't speak English and wanted me to be their spokesman in favor of going on strike. I don't know—I just got caught up with it all, the beautiful feeling of solidarity.

You'd see the people on the picket lines at four in the morning, at the camp fires, heating up beans and coffee and tortillas. It gave me a sense of belonging. These were my own people and they wanted change. I knew this is what I was looking for. I just didn't know it before.

My mom had always wanted me to better myself. I wanted to better myself because of her. Now when the strikes started, I told her I was going to join the union and the whole movement. I told her I was going to work without pay. She said she was proud of me. (His eyes glisten. A long, long pause.) See, I told her I wanted to be with my people. If I were a company man, nobody would like me any more. I had to belong to somebody and this was it right here. She said, "I pushed you in your early years to try to better yourself and get a social position. But I see that's not the answer. I know I'll be proud of you."

All kinds of people are farm workers, not just Chicanos. Filipinos started the strike. We have Puerto Ricans and Appalachians too, Arabs, some Japanese, some Chinese. At one time they used us against each other. But now they can't and they're scared, the growers. They can organize conglomerates. Yet when we try organization to better our lives, they are afraid. Suffering people never dreamed it could be different. Cesar Chavez tells them this and they grasp the idea—and this is what scares the growers.

Now the machines are coming in. It takes skill to operate them. But anybody can be taught. We feel migrant workers should be given the chance. They got one for grapes. They got one for lettuce. They have cotton machines that took jobs away from thousands of farm workers. The people wind up in the ghettos of the city, their culture, their families, their unity destroyed.

We're trying to stipulate it in our contract that the company will not use any machinery without the consent of the farm workers. So we can make sure the people being replaced by the machines will know how to operate the machines.

Working in the fields is not in itself a degrading job. It's hard, but if you're given regular hours, better pay, decent housing, unemployment and medical compensation, pension plans—we have a very relaxed way of living. But the growers don't recognize us as persons. That's the worst thing, the way they treat you. Like we have no brains.

Now we see they have no brains. They have only a wallet in their head. The more you squeeze it, the more they cry out.

If we had proper compensation, we wouldn't have to be working seventeen hours a day and following the crops. We could stay in one area and it would give us roots. Being a migrant, it tears the family apart. You get in debt. You leave the area penniless. The children are the ones hurt the most. They go to school three months in one place and then on to another. No sooner do they make friends, they are uprooted again. Right here, your childhood is taken away. So when they grow up, they're looking for this childhood they have lost.

If people could see—in the winter, ice on the fields. We'd be on our knees all day long. We'd build fires and warm up real fast and go back onto the ice. We'd be picking watermelons in 105 degrees all day long. When people have melons or cucumber or carrots or lettuce, they don't know how they got on their table and the consequences to the people who picked it. If I had enough money, I would take busloads of people out to the fields and into the labor camps. Then they'd know how that fine salad got on their table. ■

Questions for Analysis

1. *Initial Perceptions*   What were Acuna's initial perceptions of being a migrant worker? Of his future goals? Of the growers? Of his fellow migrant workers?

2. *Experiences That Shaped His Initial Perceptions*   What experiences shaped his initial perceptions about being a migrant worker? Of his future goals? Of the growers? Of his fellow migrant workers?

3. *Experiences That Raised Doubts and Questions About His Initial Perceptions*
   a. How did becoming a foreman raise doubts about his initial perceptions?
   b. How did becoming a correctional officer raise doubts about his initial perceptions?
   c. How did meeting Cesar Chavez raise doubts about his initial perceptions?
4. *Revised Perceptions He Formed About His Situation*   What were Acuna's revised perceptions of being a migrant worker? Of his future goals? Of the growers? Of his fellow migrant workers? ◄

CHAPTER

5

BELIEVING AND KNOWING

BELIEFS:
Interpretations, evaluations,
conclusions, and predictions
about the world that we
endorse as true

Beliefs based on indirect
experience (oral or written
sources of information)

Beliefs based on
direct experience

How reliable is
the information?

How reliable is
the source of
information?

DEVELOPING KNOWLEDGE
by thinking critically about
our beliefs

Are the beliefs
compelling
and coherent
explanations?

Are the beliefs
based on reliable
sources?

Are the beliefs
consistent with other
beliefs/knowledge?

Are the beliefs
supported by reasons
and evidence?

Are the beliefs
accurate predictions?

IT SEEMS TO BE a natural human impulse to try to understand the world we live in. This is the overall goal of thinking, which we have defined as the mental process by which we make sense of the world. Perceiving is an important part of this thinking process but your perceptions, taken by themselves, do not provide a reliable foundation for your understanding of the world. Your perceptions are often incomplete, distorted, and inaccurate. They are shaped and influenced by your perceiving "lenses," which reflect your own individual personality, experiences, biases, assumptions, and ways of viewing things. To clarify and validate your perceptions, you must critically examine and evaluate these perceptions.

Thinking critically about your perceptions results in the formation of your beliefs and ultimately the construction of your knowledge about the world. For example, consider the following statements and answer "Yes," "No," or "Not sure" to each.

1. Humans need to eat to stay alive.

2. Smoking marijuana is a harmless good time.

3. Every human life is valuable.

4. Developing your mind is as important as taking care of your body.

5. People should care about other people, not just themselves.

Your responses to these statements reflect certain beliefs you have, and these beliefs help you explain why the world is the way it is and how you ought to behave. In this chapter you will see that beliefs are the main tools you use to make sense of the world and guide your actions. The total collection of your beliefs represents your view of the world, your philosophy of life.

What exactly are "beliefs"? Beliefs represent an interpretation, evaluation, conclusion, or prediction about the nature of the world. For example, the statement, "I believe that the whale in the book *Moby Dick* by Herman Melville symbolizes a primal, natural force that men are trying to destroy," represents an *interpretation* of that novel. To say, "I believe that watching soap operas is unhealthy because they focus almost exclusively on the seamy side of human life," expresses an *evaluation* of soap operas. The statement, "I believe that one of the main reasons two out of three people in the world go to bed hungry each night is that industrially advanced nations like the United States have not done a satisfactory job of sharing their knowledge," expresses a *conclusion* about the problem of world hunger. To say, "If drastic environmental measures are not undertaken to slow the global warming trend, then I believe that the polar ice caps will melt and the earth will be flooded," is to make a *prediction* about events that will occur in the future.

Beliefs are the tools you use to make sense of the world and guide your actions, and the total collection of your beliefs represents your philosophy of life.

Besides expressing an interpretation, evaluation, conclusion, or prediction about the world, beliefs also express an *endorsement* of the accuracy of the beliefs by the speaker or author. In the preceding statements the speakers are not simply expressing interpretations, evaluations, conclusions, and predictions; they are also indicating that they believe these views are *true*. In other words, the speakers are saying that they have adopted these beliefs as their own because they are convinced that they represent accurate viewpoints based on some sort of evidence. This "endorsement" by the speaker is a necessary dimension of beliefs, and we assume it to be the case even if the speaker doesn't directly say, "I believe." For example, the statement, "Astrological predictions are meaningless because there is no persuasive reason to believe that the position of the stars has any effect on human affairs," expresses a belief even though it doesn't specifically include the words "I believe. "

Beliefs Interpretations, evaluations, conclusions, or predictions about the world that we endorse as true.

Describe beliefs you have in each of these categories (interpretation, evaluation, conclusion, prediction) and then explain the reason(s) you have for endorsing the beliefs.

1. **(Interpretation)** I believe that . . .
   Supporting reason(s):

2. **(Evaluation)** I believe that . . .
   Supporting reason(s):

3. **(Conclusion)** I believe that . . .
   Supporting reason(s):

4. **(Prediction)** I believe that . . .
   Supporting reason(s):

BELIEVING AND PERCEIVING

The relationship between the activities of believing and perceiving is complex and interactive. On the one hand, your perceptions form the foundation of many of your beliefs about the world. On the other hand, your beliefs about the world shape and influence your perceptions of it. Let's explore this interactive relationship by examining a variety of beliefs, including:

1. *Interpretations* ("Poetry enables humans to communicate deep, complex emotions and ideas that resist simple expression.")

2. *Evaluations* ("Children today spend too much time watching television and too little time reading.")

3. *Conclusions* ("An effective college education provides not only mastery of information and skills, but also evolving insight and maturing judgment.")

4. *Predictions* ("With the shrinking and integration of the global community, there will be an increasing need in the future for Americans to speak a second language.")

These beliefs, for people who endorse them, are likely to be based in large measure on a variety of perceptual experiences: events that people have seen and heard. The perceptual experiences by themselves, however, do not result in beliefs—they are simply experiences. For them to become beliefs, *you must think about* your perceptual experiences and then organize them into a belief structure. This thinking process of constructing beliefs is known as *cognition*, and it forms the basis of your understanding of the world. What are some of the perceptual experiences that might have led to the construction of the beliefs just described?

Example: Many times I have seen that I can best express my feelings toward someone I care deeply about through a poem.

As we noted in Chapter 4, "Perceiving," your perceptual experiences not only contribute to the formation of your beliefs; the beliefs you have formed also have a powerful influence on the perceptions you *select* to focus on, how you *organize* these perceptions, and the manner in which you *interpret* them. For example, if you are reading a magazine and come across a poem, your perception of the poem is likely to be affected by your beliefs about poetry. These beliefs may influence whether you *select* the poem as something to read, the manner in which you *organize* and *relate* the poem to other aspects of your experience, and your *interpretation* of the poem's meaning. This interactive relationship holds true for most beliefs. Assume that you endorse the four beliefs listed above. How might holding these beliefs influence your perceptions?

Example: When I find a poem I like, I often spend a lot of time trying to understand how the author has used language and symbols to create and communicate meaning.

The belief systems you have developed to understand your world help you correct inaccurate perceptions. When you watch a magician perform seemingly impossible tricks, your beliefs about the way the world operates inform you that what you are seeing is really a misperception, an illusion. In this context, you expect to be tricked, and your question is naturally, "How did he or she do that?" Potential problems arise, however, in those situations where it is not apparent that your perceptions are providing you with inaccurate information, and you use these experiences to form mistaken beliefs. For example, you may view advertisements linking youthful, attractive, fun-loving people with smoking cigarettes and form the apparently inaccurate belief that smoking cigarettes is an integral part of being youthful, attractive, and fun loving. As a critical thinker, you have a responsibility to monitor and evaluate continually both aspects of this interactive process—your beliefs and your perceptions—so that you can develop the most informed perspective on the world.

THINKING ACTIVITY 5.1

Describe an experience of a perception you had that later turned out to be false, based on subsequent experiences or reflection. Address the following questions:

1. What qualities of the perception led you to believe it to be true?
2. How did this perception influence your beliefs about the world?
3. Describe the process that led you to the conclusion that the perception was false. ◀

BELIEVING AND KNOWING

We have seen that beliefs are a major tool that helps us explain why the world is the way it is and guide us in making effective decisions. As you form and re-form your beliefs, based on your experiences and your thinking about these experiences, you usually try to develop beliefs that are as accurate as possible. The more accurate your beliefs are, the better able you are to understand what is taking place and to predict what will occur in the future. The beliefs you form vary tremendously in accuracy. For example, how accurate do you think the following beliefs are?

1. I believe that there is a very large man who lives on the moon.
2. I believe that there is life on other planets.
3. I believe that a college education will lead me to a satisfying and well-paying job.
4. I believe that there is life on this planet.

In considering these beliefs, you probably came to the conclusion that belief 1 was not accurate at all, belief 2 was possible but far from being certain, belief 3 was likely but not guaranteed to be accurate, and belief 4 was definitely accurate.

The idea of *knowing* is one of the ways humans have developed to distinguish beliefs supported by strong reasons or evidence (such as the belief that there is life on earth) from beliefs for which there is less support (such as beliefs that there is life on other planets and that college will lead to a job) or from beliefs disproved by reasons or evidence to the contrary (such as a belief in the man in the moon). Let's try replacing the word *believe* with the word *know* in the preceding statements:

1. I *know* that there is a very large man who lives on the moon.
2. I *know* that there is life on other planets.
3. I *know* that a college education will lead me to a satisfying and well-paying job.
4. I *know* that there is life on this planet.

The only statement in which it clearly makes sense to use the word *know* is the fourth one, because there is conclusive evidence that this belief is accurate. In the case of sentence 1, we would say that this person is seriously mistaken. In the case of sentence 2, we might say that, although life on other planets is a possibility, there is no conclusive evidence (at present) that supports this view. In the case of sentence 3, we might say that, although for many people a college education leads to a satisfying and well-paying job, this is not always the case.

As a result, we cannot say that we know this belief (or belief 2) is accurate. Another way of expressing the difference between "believing" and "knowing" is by means of the following saying:

> You can *believe* what is not so, but you cannot *know* what is not so.

THINKING ACTIVITY 5.2

State whether you think that each of the following beliefs is:

- *Completely accurate* (so that you would say, "I know this is the case")
- *Generally accurate* but not completely accurate (so that you would say, "This is often, but not always, the case")
- *Generally not accurate,* but sometimes accurate (so that you would say, "This is usually not the case, but is sometimes true")
- *Definitely not accurate* (so that you would say, "I know that this is not the case")

After determining the *degree of accuracy* in this way, explain why you have selected your answer.

- *Example:* I believe that if you study hard you will achieve good grades.
- *Degree of accuracy:* Generally, but not completely, accurate.
- *Explanation:* Although many people who study hard achieve good grades, this is not always true. Sometimes people have difficulty understanding the work in a certain subject no matter how hard they study. And sometimes they just don't know how to study effectively. In other cases, the student may lack adequate background or experience in a certain subject area (for example, English may be a second language), or there might be a personality conflict with the instructor.

1. I believe that essay exams are more difficult than multiple-choice exams.
2. I believe that longer prison sentences discourage people from committing crimes.
3. I believe that there are more people on the earth today than there were one hundred years ago.
4. I believe that your astrological sign determines your basic personality traits.
5. I believe that you will never get rich by playing the lottery.
6. *Your example of a belief:*

When someone indicates that he or she thinks a belief is completely accurate by saying, "I *know*," your response is often, *"How* do you know?" If the person cannot give you a satisfactory answer to this question, you are likely to say something like, "If you can't explain how you know it, then you don't *really* know it—you're just saying it." In other words, when you say that "you know" something, you mean at least two different things.

1. I think this belief is completely accurate.
2. I can explain to you the reasons or evidence that support this belief.

If either of these standards is not met, we would usually say that the person does not really "know." We work at evaluating the accuracy of our beliefs by examining the reasons or evidence that support them (known as the *justification* for the beliefs). Looked at in this way, your beliefs form a *range,* as pictured:

Beliefs that you know *are*	*Beliefs that you are* not sure *are*	*Beliefs that you* know *are*
inaccurate	accurate	accurate
unjustified	justified	justified

Just as temperature is a scale that varies from cold to hot with many degrees in between, so your beliefs can be thought of as forming a rough scale based on their accuracy and justification. As you learn more about the world and yourself, you try to form beliefs that are increasingly accurate and justified.

Of course, determining the accuracy and justification of your beliefs is a challenging business. You generally use a number of different questions to explore and evaluate your beliefs, including the following:

- How well do my beliefs *explain* what is taking place?
- How do these beliefs *relate to other beliefs* I have about the world?
- How well do these beliefs enable me to *predict* what will happen in the future?
- How well do the *reasons or evidence* support my beliefs?
- How *reliable is the information* on which my beliefs are based?

The key point is that as a critical thinker you should continually try to form and re-form your beliefs so that you can make sense of the world in increasingly effective ways. Even when you find that you maintain certain beliefs over a long period of time, you should discover that your explorations result in a deeper and fuller understanding of these beliefs.

THINKING PASSAGE

In Chapter 2 you examined the process that led you to the conclusion that the earth is round, not flat. The following article, "Is the Earth Round or Flat?" by the author and astrophysicist Alan Lightman, examines this process and provides a clear analysis of the difference between "believing" and "knowing." Read the article and answer the questions that follow.

IS THE EARTH ROUND OR FLAT?
by Alan Lightman

I propose that there are few of you who have personally verified that the Earth is round. The suggestive globe in the den or the Apollo photographs don't count. These are secondhand pieces of evidence that might be thrown out entirely in court. When you think about it, most of you simply believe what you hear. Round or flat, whatever. It's not a life-or-death matter, unless you happen to live near the edge.

A few years ago I suddenly realized, to my dismay, that I didn't know with certainty if the Earth were round or flat. I have scientific colleagues, geodesists they are called, whose sole business is determining the detailed shape of the Earth by fitting mathematical formulae to someone else's measurements of the precise locations of test stations on the Earth's surface. And I don't think those people really know either.

Aristotle is the first person in recorded history to have given proof that the Earth is round. He used several different arguments, most likely because he wanted to convince others as well as himself. A lot of people believed everything Aristotle said for 19 centuries.

His first proof was that the shadow of the Earth during a lunar eclipse is always curved, a segment of a circle. If the Earth were any shape but spherical, the shadow it casts, in some orientations, would not be circular. (That the normal phases of the moon are crescent-shaped reveals the moon is round.) I find this argument wonderfully appealing. It is simple and direct. What's more, an inquisitive and untrusting person can knock off the experiment alone, without special equipment. From any given spot on the Earth, a lunar eclipse can be seen about once a year. You simply have to look up on the right night and carefully observe what's happening. I've never done it.

Aristotle's second proof was that stars rise and set sooner for people in the East than in the West. If the Earth were flat from east to west, stars would rise as soon for Occidentals as for Orientals. With a little scribbling on a piece of paper, you can see that these observations imply a round Earth, regardless of whether it is the Earth that spins around or the stars that revolve around the Earth. Finally, northbound travelers observe previously invisible stars appearing above the northern horizon, showing the Earth is curved from north to south. Of course, you do have to accept the reports of a number of friends in different places or be willing to do some traveling.

Aristotle's last argument was purely theoretical and even philosophical. If the Earth had been formed from smaller pieces at some time in the past (or *could* have been so formed), its pieces would fall toward a common center, thus making a sphere. Furthermore, a sphere is clearly the most perfect solid shape. Interestingly, Aristotle placed as much emphasis on this last argument as on the first two. Those days, before the modern "scientific method," observational check wasn't required for investigating reality.

Assuming for the moment that the Earth is round, the first person who measured its circumference accurately was another Greek, Eratosthenes (276-195 B.C.). Eratosthenes noted that on the first day of summer, sunlight struck the bottom of a vertical well in Syene, Egypt, indicating the sun was directly overhead. At the same time in Alexandria, 5,000 stadia distant, the sun made an angle with the vertical equal to 1/50 of a circle. (A stadium equaled about a tenth of a mile.) Since the sun is so far away, its rays arrive almost in parallel. If you draw a circle with two radii extending from the center outward through the perimeter (where they become local verticals), you'll see that a sun ray coming in parallel to one of the radii (at Syene) makes an angle with the other (at Alexandria) equal to the angle between the two radii. Therefore Eratosthenes concluded that the full circumference of the Earth is 50 x 5,000 stadia, or about 25,000 miles. This calculation is within one percent of the best modern value.

For at least 600 years educated people have believed the Earth is round. At nearly any medieval university, the quadrivium was standard fare, consisting of arithmetic, geometry, music, and astronomy. The astronomy portion was based on the *Tractatus de Sphaera*, a popular textbook first published at Ferrara, Italy, in 1472 and written by a 13th century, Oxford-educated astronomer and mathematician, Johannes de Sacrobosco. The *Sphaera* proves its astronomical assertions, in part, by a set of diagrams with movable parts, a graphical demonstration of Aristotle's second method of proof. The round Earth, being the obvious center of the universe, provides a fixed pivot for the assembly. The cutout figures of the sun, the moon, and the stars revolve about the Earth.

By the year 1500, 24 editions of the *Sphaera* had appeared. There is no question that many people *believed* the Earth was round. I wonder how many *knew* this. You would think that Columbus and Magellan might have wanted to ascertain the facts for themselves before waving good-bye.

To protect my honor as a scientist, someone who is supposed to take nothing for granted, I set out with my wife on a sailing voyage in the Greek islands. I reasoned that at sea I would be able to calmly observe landmasses disappear over the curve of the Earth and thus convince myself, firsthand, that the Earth is round.

Greece seemed a particularly satisfying place to conduct my experiment. I could sense those great ancient thinkers looking on approvingly, and the layout of the place is perfect. Hydra rises about 2,000 feet above sea level. If the Earth has a radius of 4,000 miles, as they say, then Hydra should sink down to the horizon at a distance of about 50 miles, somewhat less than the distance we were to sail from Hydra to Kea. The theory was sound and comfortable. At the very least, I thought, we would have a pleasant vacation.

As it turned out, that was all we got. Every single day was hazy. Islands faded from view at a distance of only eight miles, when the land was still a couple of degrees above the horizon. I learned how much water vapor was in the air but nothing about the curvature of the Earth.

I suspect that there are quite a few items we take on faith, even important things, even things we could verify without much trouble. Is the gas we exhale the same as the gas we inhale? (Do we indeed burn oxygen in our metabolism, as they say?) What is your blood made of ? (Does it indeed have red and white "cells"?) These questions could be answered with a balloon, a candle, and a microscope.

When we finally do the experiment, we relish the knowledge. At one time or another, we have all learned something for ourselves, from the ground floor up, taking no one's word for it. There is a special satisfaction and joy in being able to tell somebody something you have pieced together from scratch, something you really know. I think that exhilaration is a big reason why people do science.

Someday soon, I'm going to catch the Earth's shadow in a lunar eclipse, or go to sea in clear air, and find out for sure if the Earth is round or flat. Actually, the Earth is reported to flatten at the poles, because it rotates. But that's another story. ■

Questions for Analysis

1. Explain why Lightman states that although he always *believed* that the earth was round, "A few years ago I suddenly realized, to my dismay, that I didn't know with certainty if the Earth were round or flat."

2. In your own words, explain how you could prove to someone else that the Earth is round.

3. Describe a conclusion about the world that you "believe" but do not "know," in Lightman's sense. Analyze your belief in terms of the criteria for determining the accuracy of beliefs.

   • How effectively do your beliefs *explain what is taking place?*
   • *To what extent are these beliefs consistent with other beliefs* you have about the world?
   • How effectively do your beliefs help you *predict what will happen* in the future?
   • To what extent are your beliefs supported by *sound reasons and compelling evidence* derived from *reliable sources?* ◀

KNOWLEDGE AND TRUTH

Most people in our culture are socialized to believe that knowledge and truth are absolute and unchanging. One major goal of social institutions, including family, school system, and religion, is to transfer the knowledge that has been developed over the ages. Under this model, the role of learners is to absorb this information passively, like sponges. As you have seen in this text, however, achieving knowledge and truth is a much more complicated process than this. Instead of simply relying on the testimony of authorities like parents, teachers, textbooks, and religious leaders, critical thinkers have a responsibility to engage *actively* in the learning process and participate in developing their own understanding of the world.

The need for this active approach to knowing is underscored by the fact that authorities often disagree about the true nature of a given situation or the best course of action. It is not uncommon, for example, for doctors to disagree about a diagnosis, for economists to differ on the state of the economy, for researchers to present contrasting views on the best approach to curing cancer, for psychiatrists to disagree on whether a convicted felon is a menace to society or a harmless victim of social forces, and for religions to present conflicting approaches to achieving eternal life.

What do we do when experts disagree? As a critical thinker, you must analyze and evaluate all the available information, develop your own well-reasoned beliefs, and recognize when you don't have sufficient information to arrive at well-reasoned beliefs. You must realize that these beliefs may evolve over time as you gain information or improve your insight.

Although there are compelling reasons to view knowledge and truth in this way, many people resist it. Either they take refuge in a belief in the absolute, unchanging nature of knowledge and truth, as presented by the appropriate authorities, or they conclude that there is no such thing as knowledge or truth and that trying to seek either is a futile enterprise. In this latter view of the world, known as *relativism,* all beliefs are considered to be "relative" to the person or context in which they arise. For the relativist, all opinions are equal in validity to all others; we are never in a position to say with confidence that one view is right and another view is wrong. Although a relativistic view is appropriate in some areas of experience—for example, in matters of taste such as fashion—in many other areas it is not. Although it is often difficult to achieve, knowledge, in the form of well-supported beliefs, does exist. Some beliefs *are* better than others, not because an authority has proclaimed them so but because they can be analyzed in terms of the following criteria:

- How effectively do your beliefs *explain what is taking place?*
- To what extent are these beliefs *consistent with other beliefs* about the world?
- How effectively do your beliefs help you *predict what will happen* in the future?
- To what extent are your beliefs supported by *sound reasons and compelling evidence* derived from *reliable sources?*

Another important criterion for evaluating certain of your beliefs is that the beliefs are *falsifiable.* This means that you can state conditions—tests—under which the beliefs could be disproved, and the beliefs *pass* those tests. For example, if you believe that you can create ice cubes by placing water-filled trays in a freezer, it is easy to see how you can conduct an experiment to determine if your belief is accurate. On the other hand, if you believe that your destiny is related to the positions of the planets and stars (as astrologers do), it is not clear how you can conduct an experiment to determine if your belief is accurate. Since a belief that is not *falsifiable* can never be *proved,* such a belief is of questionable accuracy.

A critical thinker sees knowledge and truth as ongoing goals that we are striving to achieve through exploration and analysis, not fixed destinations.

A critical thinker sees knowledge and truth as goals that we are striving to achieve, processes that we are all actively involved in as we construct our understanding of the world. Developing accurate knowledge about the world is often a challenging process of exploration and analysis in which our understanding grows and evolves over a period of time. In Chapter 4, we examined five contrasting media accounts of the assassination of Malcolm X. All five authors, we found, viewed the event through their own perceiving lenses, which shaped and influenced the information they selected, the way they organized it, their interpretations of the individuals involved, and the language they chose to describe it. Despite the differences in these accounts, we *know* that an actual sequence of events occurred on that February day in 1965. The challenge for us is to try to figure out what actually happened by investigating different accounts, evaluating the reliability of the accounts, and putting together a coherent picture of what took place. This is the process of achieving knowledge and truth that occurs in every area of human inquiry—a process of exploration, critical analysis, and evolving understanding.

THINKING ACTIVITY 5.3

Read the following passages, which purport to give factual reports about the events that were observed at the Battle of Lexington during the American Revolution.* After analyzing these accounts, construct your own version of what you believe took place on that day. Include such information as the size of the two forces, the sequence of events (for example, who fired the first shot?), and the manner in which the two groups conducted themselves (were they honorable? brave?). Use these questions to guide your analysis of the varying accounts:

- Does the account provide a convincing description of what took place?
- What reasons and evidence support the account?
- How reliable is the source?
- What are the author's perceiving lenses that might influence his account?
- Is the account consistent with other reliable descriptions of this event?

Here is some background information to aid you in your analysis:

- *Account 1* is drawn from a mainstream American history textbook.
- *Account 2* is taken from a British history textbook, written by a former prime minister of England.
- *Account 3* comes from a colonist who participated in this event with the colonial forces. He gave the account thirty years after the battle to qualify for a military pension.
- *Account 4* comes from a British soldier who participated in the event. He gave the account in a deposition while he was a prisoner of war of the colonial forces.

* This exercise was developed by Kevin O'Reilly, creator of the Critical Thinking in History Project in Boston, Massachusetts.

Four Accounts of the Battle of Lexington

In April 1775, General Gage, the military governor of Massachusetts, sent out a body of troops to take possession of military stores at Concord, a short distance from Boston. At Lexington, a handful of "embattled farmers," who had been tipped off by Paul Revere, barred the way. The "rebels" were ordered to disperse. They stood their ground. The English fired a volley of shots that killed eight patriots. It was not long before the swift-riding Paul Revere spread the news of this new atrocity to the neighboring colonies. The patriots of all of New England, although still a handful, were now ready to fight the English. Even in faraway North Carolina, patriots organized to resist them.

—Samuel Steinberg, *The United States: Story of a Free People*

At five o'clock in the morning the local militia of Lexington, seventy strong, formed up on the village green. As the sun rose the head of the British column, with three officers riding in front, came into view. The leading officer, brandishing his sword, shouted, "Disperse, you rebels, immediately!" The militia commander ordered his men to disperse. The colonial committees were very anxious not to fire the first shot, and there were strict orders not to provoke open conflict with the British regulars. But in the confusion someone fired. A volley was returned. The ranks of the militia were thinned and there was a general *melee*. Brushing aside the survivors, the British column marched on to Concord.

—Winston Churchill, *History of the English Speaking Peoples*

The British troops approached us rapidly in platoons, with a General officer on horse-back at their head. The officer came up to within about two rods of the centre of the company, where I stood.—The first platoon being about three rods distant. They there halted. The officer then swung his sword, and said, "Lay down your arms, you damn'd rebels, or you are all dead men—fire." Some guns were fired by the British at us from the first platoon, but no person was killed or hurt, being probably charged only with powder. Just at this time, Captain Parker ordered every man to take care of himself. The company immediately dispersed; and while the company was dispersing and leaping over the wall, the second platoon of the British fired, and killed some of our men. There was not a gun fired by any of Captain Parker's company within my knowledge.

—Sylvanus Wood, *Deposition*

I, John Bateman, belonging to the Fifty-Second Regiment, commanded by Colonel Jones, on Wednesday morning on the nineteenth day of April instant, was in the party marching to Concord, being at Lexington, in the County of Middlesex; being nigh the meeting-house in said Lexington, there was a small party of men gathered together in that place when our Troops marched by, and I testify and declare, that I heard the word of command given to the Troops to fire, and some of said Troops did fire, and I saw one of said small party lay dead on the ground nigh said meeting-house, and I testify that I never heard any of the inhabitants so much as fire one gun on said Troops.

—John Bateman, *Testimony* ◀

THINKING ACTIVITY 5.4

In the spring of 1989, a vigorous pro-democracy movement erupted in Beijing, the capital of China. Protesting the authoritarian control of the Communist regime, thousands of students staged demonstrations, engaged in hunger strikes, and organized marches involving hundreds of thousands of people. The geographical heart of these activities was the historic Tiananmen Square, taken over by the demonstrators who had erected a symbolic "Statue of Liberty." On June 4, 1989, the fledgling pro-democracy movement came to a bloody end when the Chinese army entered Tiananmen Square and seized control of it. The following are various accounts of this event from different sources. After analyzing these accounts, construct your own version of what you believe took place on that day. Use these questions to guide your analysis of the varying accounts:

- Does the account provide a convincing description of what took place?
- What reasons and evidence support the account?
- How reliable is the source? What are the author's perceiving lenses, which might influence his or her account?
- Is the account consistent with other reliable descriptions of this event?

SEVEN ACCOUNTS OF EVENTS AT TIANANMEN SQUARE, 1989

The New York Times (June 4, 1989)

Tens of thousands of Chinese troops retook the center of the capital from pro-democracy protesters early this morning, killing scores of students and workers and wounding hundreds more as they fired submachine guns at crowds of people who tried to resist. Troops marched along the main roads surrounding central Tiananmen Square, sometimes firing in the air and sometimes firing directly at crowds who refused to move. Reports on the number of dead were sketchy. Students said, however, that at least 500 people may have been killed in the crackdown. Most of the dead had been shot, but some had been run over by personnel carriers that forced their way through the protesters' barricades.

A report on the state-run radio put the death toll in the thousands and denounced the Government for the violence, the Associated Press reported. But the station later changed announcers and broadcast another report supporting the governing Communist party. The official news programs this morning reported that the People's Liberation Army had crushed a "counter-revolutionary rebellion." They said that more than 1,000 police officers and troops had been injured and some killed, and that civilians had been killed, but did not give details.

Deng Xiaoping, Chairman of the Central Military Commission, as reported in *Beijing Review* (July 10-16, 1989)

The main difficulty in handling this matter lay in that we had never experienced such a situation before, in which a small minority of bad people mixed with so many young students and onlookers. Actually, what we faced was not just some ordinary people who were misguided, but also a rebellious clique and a large number of the dregs of society. The key point is that they wanted to overthrow our state and the Party. They had two main slogans: to overthrow the Communist Party and topple the socialist system. Their goal was to establish a bourgeois republic entirely dependent on the West.

During the course of quelling the rebellion, many comrades of ours were injured or even sacrificed their lives. Some of their weapons were also taken from them by the rioters. Why? Because bad people mingled with the good, which made it difficult for us to take the firm measures that were necessary. Handling this matter amounted to a severe political test for our army, and what happened shows that our People's Liberation Army passed muster. If tanks were used to roll over people, this would have created a confusion between right and wrong among the people nationwide. That is why I have to thank the PLA officers and men for using this approach to handle the rebellion. The PLA losses were great, but this enabled us to win the support of the people and made those who can't tell right from wrong change their viewpoint. They can see what kind of people the PLA are, whether there was bloodshed at Tiananmen, and who were those that shed blood.

Aftermath of the bloody clash between a prodemocracy student movement and the Chinese army on June 4, 1989.

This shows that the people's army is truly a Great Wall of iron and steel of the Party and country. This shows that no matter how heavy the losses we suffer and no matter how generations change, this army of ours is forever an army under the leadership of the Party, forever the defender of the country, forever the defender of socialism, forever the defender of the public interest, and they are the most beloved of the people. At the same time, we should never forget how cruel our enemies are. For them we should not have an iota of forgiveness.

Reporter *(eyewitness account)*, reported in the *New York Times* (June 4, 1989)

Changan Avenue, or the Avenue of Eternal Peace, Beijing's main eastwest thoroughfare, echoed with screams this morning as young people carried the bodies of their friends away from the front lines. The dead or seriously wounded were heaped on the backs of bicycles or tricycle rickshaws and supported by friends who rushed through the crowds, sometimes sobbing as they ran.

The avenue was lit by the glow of several trucks and two armed personnel carriers that students and workers set afire, and bullets swooshed overhead or glanced off buildings. The air crackled almost constantly with gunfire and tear gas grenades.

Students and workers tried to resist the crackdown, and destroyed at least sixteen trucks and two armored personnel carriers. Scores of students and workers ran alongside the personnel carriers, hurling concrete blocks and wooden staves into the treads until they ground to a halt. They then threw firebombs at one until it caught fire, and set the other alight after first covering it with blankets soaked in gasoline. The drivers escaped the flames, but were beaten by students. A young American man, who could not be immediately identified, was also beaten by the crowd after he tried to intervene and protect one of the drivers.

Clutching iron pipes and stones, groups of students periodically advanced toward the soldiers. Some threw bricks and firebombs at the lines of soldiers, apparently wounding many of them. Many of those killed were throwing bricks at the soldiers, but others were simply watching passively or standing at barricades when soldiers fired directly at them.

It was unclear whether the violence would mark the extinction of the seven-week-old democracy movement, or would prompt a new phase in the uprising, like a general strike. The violence in the capital ended a period of remarkable restraint by both sides, and seemed certain to arouse new bitterness and antagonism among both ordinary people and Communist Party officials for the Government of Prime Minister Li Peng.

"Our Government is already done with," said a young worker who held a rock in his hand, as he gazed at the army forces across Tiananmen Square. "Nothing can show more clearly that it does not represent the people." Another young man, an art student, was nearly incoherent with grief and anger as he watched the body of a student being carted away, his head blown away by bullets. "Maybe we'll fail today," he said. "Maybe we'll fail tomorrow. But someday we'll succeed. It's a historical inevitability."

Official Chinese Government Accounts

"Comrades, thanks for your hard work. We hope you will continue with your fine efforts to safeguard security in the capital."

—Prime Minister Li Peng (addressing a group of soldiers after the Tiananmen Square event)

"It never happened that soldiers fired directly at the people."

—General Li Zhiyun

"The People's Liberation Army crushed a counter-revolutionary rebellion. More than 1,000 police officers and troops were injured and killed, and some civilians were killed."

—Official Chinese news program

"At most 300 people were killed in the operation, many of them soldiers."

—Yuan Mu, official government spokesman

"Not a single student was killed in Tiananmen Square."

—Chinese army commander

"My government has stated that a mob led by a small number of people prevented the normal conduct of the affairs of state. There was, I regret to say, loss of life on both sides. I wonder whether any other government confronting such an unprecedented challenge would have handled the situation any better than mine did."

—Han Xu, Chinese ambassador to the United States

The New York Times (June 5, 1989)

It was clear that at least 300 people had been killed since the troops first opened fire shortly after midnight on Sunday morning but the toll may be much higher. Word-of-mouth estimates continued to soar, some reaching far into the thousands. . . . The student organization that coordinated the long protests continued to function and announced today that 2,600 students were believed to have been killed. Several doctors said that, based on their discussions with ambulance drivers and colleagues who had been on Tiananmen Square, they estimated that at least 2,000 had died. Soldiers also beat and bayoneted students and workers after daybreak on Sunday, witnesses said, usually after some provocation but sometimes entirely at random. "I saw a young woman tell the soldiers that they are the people's army, and that they mustn't hurt the people," a young doctor said after returning from one clash Sunday. "Then the soldier shot her, and ran up and bayoneted her."

Xiao Bin *(eyewitness account immediately after the event)*

Tanks and armored personnel carriers rolled over students, squashing them into jam, and the soldiers shot at them and hit them with clubs. When students fainted, the troops killed them. After they died, the troops fired one more bullet into them. They also used bayonets. They were too cruel. I never saw such things before.

Xiao Bin *(account after being taken into custody by Chinese authorities)*
I never saw anything. I apologize for bringing great harm to the party and the country. ◀

THINKING ACTIVITY 5.5

Locate three different newspaper or magazine accounts of an important event— a court decision, a crime, and a political demonstration are possible topics. Analyze each of the accounts with the questions listed below, and then construct your own version of what you believe took place.

- Does the account provide a convincing description of what took place?
- What reasons and evidence support the account?
- How reliable is the source? What are the author's perceiving lenses, which might influence his or her account?
- Is the account consistent with other reliable descriptions of this event? ◀

BELIEFS BASED ON DIRECT EXPERIENCE

As you attempt to make sense of the world, your thinking abilities give you the means to:

- Ask questions about your experience
- Work toward forming beliefs that will enable you to answer these questions and make useful decisions

Asking questions encourages you to try to form more accurate beliefs to explain what is taking place. By questioning your experience, instead of passively accepting it, you are better able to understand the situation you are in and to take effective control of your life.

Let's explore how these activities of asking questions and forming beliefs enable you to make sense of your world. Read carefully the following passage, in which a student, Maria, describes her experiences with the "system."

A few years ago my oldest son went to a party. On his way home he was accosted by three individuals who tried to take his belongings. Seeing guns, my son's first reaction was to run away, which he did. While running he was shot and his wounds left him paralyzed from the neck down. As he lay in the intensive care unit of the hospital, I started to receive threatening phone calls telling me that if I identified them to the police, "they would finish the work."

I reported the phone calls to both the police and the telephone company, but I was irritated by the way the police handled the whole situation. They told me that there was no reason why the city should pay for having a police officer protect my son and they asked me what he was doing in the streets at this time. (The time was 11 P.M., and my son was almost eighteen years old.) Finally, I was told there was nothing that could be done. In my anger, I called the mayor's office, the senator's office, and the local councilman. I also wrote a letter to the police commissioner and mailed it registered, special delivery, as proof in case the situation didn't improve. Within a few hours, there was an officer at my son's bedside making sure that nothing further happened to him.

I learned that although there are many laws to protect citizens, if citizens don't fight for their rights, these laws will never be exercised. My opinion of the "system" changed after this experience. I believe that I shouldn't have had to go through so much red tape in order to have my legal rights. I feel that, if you don't take a stand, there is no one who will go out of the way to instruct you or to help out. I was never informed at the police headquarters about what to do and how to go about doing it. I was left standing without any hope at all. I feel sorry for those persons who are ignorant about how you can make the system work for you.

Throughout this experience, Maria's beliefs influenced her decisions. Before her son got shot, she had formed certain beliefs about the law, the police, and the legal system as a whole. After her son was shot, Maria tried to make sense of the situation in terms of her beliefs and act on their basis. However, Maria began to discover that her beliefs did not seem to explain what was happening. As Maria came to doubt the accuracy of her initial beliefs, she began to form new beliefs to explain what was happening. After taking action based on her revised beliefs, Maria received responses that seemed to support her revised beliefs about the law, the police, and the system. These revised beliefs helped her to understand and control the situation in a way her initial beliefs had not, leading her to the following conclusion: "I learned that although there are many laws to protect citizens, if citizens don't fight for their rights, these laws will never be exercised." After reflecting critically on her experiences, Maria was convinced that the revised beliefs she had formed to explain her situation and guide her actions were more accurate than her initial beliefs. As a result, she advises those who find themselves in similar circumstances to "take a stand" and "make the system work" for them.

Maria's story illustrates the process by which we form and re-form our beliefs, a process that often follows the following sequence:

1. We *form* beliefs to explain what is taking place. (These initial beliefs are often based on our past experiences.)
2. We *test* these beliefs by acting on them.
3. We *revise* (or re-form) these beliefs if our actions do not result in our desired goals.
4. We *retest* these revised beliefs by acting on them.

As you actively participate in this ongoing process of forming and reforming beliefs, you are using your critical thinking abilities to identify and critically examine your beliefs by asking the following questions:

- How effectively do my beliefs *explain what is taking place?*
- To what extent are these beliefs *consistent with other beliefs* about the world?
- How effectively do my beliefs help me *predict what will happen* in the future?
- To what extent are my beliefs supported by *sound reasons and compelling evidence* derived from *reliable sources?*

This process of critical exploration enables you to develop a greater understanding of various situations in your experience and also gives you the means to exert more effective control in these situations.

THINKING ACTIVITY 5.6

1. Interview another person about a belief he or she once held but no longer holds. Ask that person the following questions. *(Note:* Try asking the questions in the course of a conversation you have with the person rather than confronting him or her with an intimidating series of formal questions. Most people like to be asked about their beliefs and are very cooperative.)
    a. What is the belief?
    b. On what evidence did you hold that belief? (Was it based on personal perception or oral or written sources? What were they?)
    c. What caused you to change the belief?
    d. What were your feelings or attitudes when you found that changing the belief was necessary?
    e. How do you feel now about changing the belief?

2. Next, write a summary of the interview. Begin by describing the person and explaining your relationship to him or her. Then give his or her answers to the questions. Be as detailed as possible.

3. Describe your reaction to the other person's experience. What did you learn about perception and belief from that experience? ◄

THINKING PASSAGE

Examine the process of forming and re-forming beliefs by reading the following interview, which Studs Terkel conducted with C. P. Ellis, once president (Exalted Cyclops) of the Durham, North Carolina, chapter of the Ku Klux Klan. The interview traces the evolution of Ellis's limited, racist beliefs through thoughtful reflection and critical evaluation. Answer the questions that follow the passage.

WHY I QUIT THE KLAN
by C. P. Ellis

All my life, I had work, never a day without work, worked all the overtime I could get and still could not survive financially. I began to see there's something wrong with this country. I worked my butt off and just never seemed to break even. I had some real great ideas about this nation. They say to abide by the law, go to church, do right and live for the Lord, and everything'll work out. But it didn't work out. It just kept gettin worse and worse. . . .

    Tryin to come out of that hole, I just couldn't do it. I really began to get bitter. I didn't know who to blame. I tried to find somebody. Hatin

America is hard to do because you can't see it to hate it. You gotta have somethin to look at to hate. The natural person for me to hate would be black people, because my father before me was a member of the Klan. . . .

So I began to admire the Klan. . . . To be part of somethin. . . . The first night I went with the fellas . . . I was led into a large meeting room, and this was the time of my life! It was thrilling. Here's a guy who's worked all his life and struggled all his life to be something, and here's the moment to be something. I will never forget it. Four robed Klansmen led me into the hall. The lights were dim and the only thing you could see was an illuminated cross. . . . After I had taken my oath, there was loud applause goin throughout the buildin, musta been at least four hundred people. For this one little ol person. It was a thrilling moment for C. P. Ellis. . . .

The majority of [the Klansmen] are low-income whites, people who really don't have a part in something. They have been shut out as well as blacks. Some are not very well educated either. Just like myself. We had a lot of support from doctors and lawyers and police officers.

Maybe they've had bitter experiences in this life and they had to hate somebody. So the natural person to hate would be the black person. He's beginnin to come up, he's beginnin to . . . start votin and run for political office. Here are white people who are supposed to be superior to them, and we're shut out. . . . Shut out. Deep down inside, we want to be part of this *great society*. Nobody listens, so we join these groups. . . .

We would go to the city council meetings, and the blacks would be there and we'd be there. It was a confrontation every time. . . . We began to make some inroads with the city councilmen and county commissioners. They began to call us friend. Call us at night on the telephone: "C. P., glad you came to that meeting last night." They didn't want integration either, but they did it secretively, in order to get elected. They couldn't stand up openly and say it, but they were glad somebody was sayin it. We visited some of the city leaders in their homes and talked to em privately. It wasn't long before councilmen would call me up: "The blacks are comin up tonight and makin outrageous demands. How about some of you people showin up and have a little balance?". . .

We'd load up our cars and we'd fill up half the council chambers, and the blacks the other half. During these times, I carried weapons to the meetings, outside my belt. We'd go there armed. We would wind up just hollerin and fussin at each other. What happened? As a result of our fightin one another, the city council still had their way. They didn't want to give up control to the blacks nor the Klan. They were usin us.

I began to realize this later down the road. One day I was walkin downtown and a certain city council member saw me comin. I expected him to shake my hand because he was talkin to me at night on the telephone. I had been in his home and visited with him. He crossed the street [to avoid me]. . . . I began to think, somethin's wrong here.

Most of em are merchants or maybe an attorney, an insurance agent, people like that. As long as they kept low-income whites and low-income blacks fightin, they're gonna maintain control. I began to get that feelin after I was ignored in public. I thought: . . . you're not gonna use me any more. That's when I began to do some real serious thinkin.

The same thing is happening in this country today. People are being used by those in control, those who have all the wealth. I'm not espousing communism. We got the greatest system of government in the world. But those who have it simply don't want those who don't have it to have any part of it. Black and white. When it comes to money, the green, the other colors make no difference.

I spent a lot of sleepless nights. I still didn't like blacks. I didn't want to associate with them. Blacks, Jews or Catholics. My father said: "Don't have anything to do with em." I didn't until I met a black person and talked with him, eyeball to eyeball, and met a Jewish person and talked to him, eyeball to eyeball. I found they're people just like me. They cried, they cussed, they prayed, they had desires. Just like myself. Thank God, I got to the point where I can look past labels. But at that time, my mind was closed.

I remember one Monday night Klan meeting. I said something was wrong. Our city fathers were using us. And I didn't like to be used. The reactions of the others was not too pleasant: "Let's just keep fightin them niggers."

I'd go home at night and I'd have to wrestle with myself. I'd look at a black person walkin down the street, and the guy'd have ragged shoes or his clothes would be worn. That began to do something to me inside. I went through this for about six months. I felt I just had to get out of the Klan. But I wouldn't get out. . . .

[Ellis was invited, as a Klansman, to join a committee of people from all walks of life to make recommendations on how to solve racial problems in the school system. He very reluctantly accepted. After a few stormy meetings, he was elected co-chair of the committee, along with Ann Atwater, a black woman who for years had been leading local efforts for civil rights.]

A Klansman and a militant black woman, co-chairmen of the school committee. It was impossible. How could I work with her? But it was in our hands. We had to make it a success. This give me another sense of belongin, a sense of pride. This helped the inferiority feeling I had. A man who has stood up publicly and said he despised black people, all of a sudden he was willin to work with em. Here's a chance for a low-income white man to be somethin. In spite of all my hatred for blacks and Jews and liberals, I accepted the job. Her and I began to reluctantly work together. She had as many problems workin with me as I had workin with her.

One night, I called her: "Ann, you and I should have a lot of differences and we got em now. But there's something laid out here before us, and if it's gonna be a success, you and I are gonna have to make it one. Can you lay aside some of these feelings?" She said: "I'm willing if you are." I said: "Let's do it."

My old friends would call me at night: "C. P., what the hell is wrong with you? You're sellin out the white race." This begin to make me have guilt feelins. Am I doin right? Am I doin wrong? Here I am all of a sudden makin an about-face and tryin to deal with my feeling, my heart. My mind was beginnin to open up. I was beginnin to see what was right and what was wrong. I don't want the kids to fight forever. . . .

One day, Ann and I went back to the school and we sat down. We began to talk and just reflect. . . . I begin to see, here you are, two people from the far ends of the fence, havin identical problems, except hers bein black and me bein white. . . . The amazing thing about it, her and I, up to that point, has cussed each other, bawled each other, we hated each other. Up to that point, we didn't know each other. We didn't know we had things in common. . . .

The whole world was openin up, and I was learning new truths that I had never learned before. I was beginning to look at a black person, shake hands with him, and see him as a human bein. I hadn't got rid of all this stuff. I've still got a little bit of it. But somethin was happenin to me. . . .

I come to work one mornin and some guys says: "You need a union." At this time I wasn't pro-union. My daddy was anti-labor too. We're not gettin paid much, we're havin to work seven days in a row. We're all starvin to death. . . . I didn't know nothin about organizin unions, but I knew how to organize people, stir people up. That's how I got to be business agent for the union.

When I began to organize, I began to see far deeper. I begin to see people again bein used. Blacks against whites. . . . There are two things management wants to keep: all the money and all the say-so. They don't want none of these poor workin folks to have none of that. I begin to see management fightin me with everythin they had. Hire anti-union law firms, badmouth unions. The people were makin $1.95 an hour, barely able to get through weekends. . . .

It makes you feel good to go into a plant and . . . see black people and white people join hands to defeat the racist issues [union-busters] use against people. . . .

I tell people there's a tremendous possibility in this country to stop wars, the battles, the struggles, the fights between people. People say: "That's an impossible dream. You sound like Martin Luther King." An ex-Klansman who sounds like Martin Luther King. I don't think it's an impossible dream. It's happened in my life. It's happened in other people's lives in America. . . .

. . . They say the older you get, the harder it is for you to change. That's not necessarily true. Since I changed, I've set down and listened to tapes of Martin Luther King. I listen to it and tears come to my eyes cause I know what he's sayin now. I know what's happenin. ■

Questions for Analysis

1. What were C. P. Ellis's most important *initial beliefs?* From where did his stereotypes originate?
2. What were some of the *experiences* that helped form these initial beliefs?
3. What *actions* did he take based on these initial beliefs?
4. What *experiences* raised doubts and questions about his initial beliefs? Why was he able to say: "Thank God, I got to the point where I can look past labels. . . . I was beginning to look at a black person, shake hands with him, and see him as a human bein."
5. What *revised beliefs* did he form to better make sense of his experiences? ◀

C.P. Ellis's powerful interview displays how the processes of perceiving and believing continually influence each other. On the one hand, our perceptions influence what we come to believe. Thus, for example, the fact that C.P. Ellis's friends and family insulted and disparaged African Americans, Jews, and Catholics led him to form racist beliefs about these groups. On the other hand, our beliefs influence the way we perceive things; that is, they influence the perceptual lenses we use to view the world. Thus the racist beliefs that C.P. Ellis had formed were reflected in his perceptual stereotypes of African Americans, Jews, and Catholics.

Fortunately, beliefs do not stand still in the minds of critical thinkers. We continue to form and re-form our beliefs, based in part on what we are experiencing and how we think about what we are experiencing. For C. P. Ellis, the experience of meeting and working with people from other ethnic groups broke down his perceptual stereotypes of them, for he discovered: "I found they're people just like me. They cried, they cussed, they prayed, they had desires. Just like myself."

BELIEFS BASED ON INDIRECT EXPERIENCE

Until now, we have been exploring the way we form and revise beliefs based on our direct experiences. Yet no matter how much you have experienced in your life, the fact is that no one person's direct experiences are enough to establish an adequate set of accurate beliefs. Each of us is only one person. We can only be in one place at one time—and with a limited amount of time at that. As a result, we depend on the direct experience of *other people* to provide us with beliefs and also to act as foundations for those beliefs. For example, does China exist? How do you know? Have you ever been there and seen it with your own eyes? Probably not, although in all likelihood you still believe in the existence of China and its over 1 billion inhabitants. Or consider the following questions. How would you go about explaining the reasons or evidence for your beliefs?

1. Were you really born on the day that you have been told you were?
2. Do germs really exist?
3. Do you have a brain in your head?
4. Does outer space extend infinitely in all directions?

In all probability, your responses to these questions reveal beliefs that are based on reasons or evidence beyond your direct experience. Of all the beliefs each one of us has, few are actually based on our direct experience. Instead, virtually all are founded on the experiences of others, who then communicated to us these beliefs and the evidence for them in some shape or form.

Of course, some people claim they do not really believe anything unless they have personally experienced it. They say, "Seeing is believing," "The proof of the pudding is in the eating," or "Show me" (the famous slogan of the state of Missouri). A little critical reflection, however, should convince you that these people are simply being unrealistic and unreasonable. It would be impossible for you to make most of the choices or decisions you do without depending on beliefs based on the experiences and knowledge of others. For instance, if I step out into moving traffic, will I really get hurt? Do guns really kill? Do I really have to eat to survive?

As you reach beyond your personal experience to form and revise beliefs, you find that the information provided by other people is available in two basic forms: written and spoken testimony.

Of course, you should not accept the beliefs of others without question. It is crucial that you use all your critical thinking abilities to examine what others suggest you believe. In critically examining the beliefs of others, you should pursue the same goals of accuracy and completeness that you seek when examining beliefs based on your personal experience. As a result, you are interested in the reasons or evidence that support the information others are presenting. For example, when you ask directions from others, you try to evaluate how accurate the information is by examining the reasons or evidence that seem to support the information being given.

When you depend on information provided by others, however, there is a further question to be asked: How *reliable* is the person providing the infor– mation? For instance, what sort of people do you look for if you need to ask directions? Why do you look for these particular types of people? In most cases, when you need to ask directions, you try to locate someone who you think will be reliable—in other words, a person who you believe will give you *accurate* information.

During the remainder of this chapter, you will explore the various ways you depend on others to form and revise your beliefs. In each case you will try to evaluate the information being presented by asking the following questions:

1. How reliable is the *information?*
2. How reliable is the *source* of the information?

How Reliable Are the Information and the Source?

One of the main goals of your thinking is to make sense of information. Much of the information you are exposed to is from advertisers seeking to sell their products. Review the following advertisement taken from a popular magazine and then evaluate the information presented by answering the questions that follow it:

This is the new Nissan Stanza GL. A family car that seats 5 with room to spare. Room that includes luxuries like 6-speaker stereo with cassette, power windows and door locks, and plush upholstery. Now you're talking major value.

And when a family sedan has Nissan technology going for it, you get even more than room and luxuries. You also get performance. Performance from a semi-combustion engine with two spark plugs per cylinder, fed by electronic fuel-injection. Go ahead, step on it, and feel your Stanza come to life.

Another nice thing about owning a Nissan Stanza, you don't have to feel guilty every time you step on the gas. Because Stanza's highly developed Nissan engine is as gas efficient as it is responsive.

So before you buy your family's next car, compare its specifications to that of a new Stanza. Stanza thrives on comparison. After all, Stanza has Nissan technology behind it. And that takes it way beyond transportation; all the way to Major Motion.

INFORMATION EVALUATION QUESTIONS

1. *How reliable is the information?*
   a. What are the main ideas being presented?
   b. What reasons or evidence support the information?
   c. Is the information accurate? Is there anything you believe to be false?
   d. Is there anything that you believe has been left out?
2. *How reliable is the source of the information?*
   a. What is the source of the information?
   b. What are the interests or purposes of the source of this information?
   c. How have the interests and purposes of the source of the information influenced the information selected for inclusion?
   d. How have these interests and purposes influenced the way this information is presented?

As you saw in Chapter 4, each of us views the world through our own unique "lenses," which shape how we view the world and influence how we select and present information. Comparing different sources helps to make us aware of these lenses and highlights the different interests and purposes involved. For example, examine carefully this description of the Nissan Stanza GL from *Consumer Reports,* a magazine that tests various consumer products and then reports its findings.

Every source of information views situations through their own unique "lenses" that influence what information they include and the way that information is presented.

- *On the road.* The 2-liter Four started quickly and ran well. The 5-speed manual transmission shifted easily. This front-wheel drive model handled very well. Excellent brakes.
- *Comfort and convenience.* Very comfortable individual front seats. Short on driver leg room. Comfortable rear seat for two, fairly comfortable for three. Moderate noise level. Choppy ride on poor roads, satisfactory on expressways. Excellent climate-control system, controls, displays.
- *Major options.* Automatic transmission, $350. Air-conditioner, $650.
- *Fuel economy.* Mpg with 5-speed manual transmission: city, 23; expressway, 45. Gallons used in 15,000 miles, 465. Cruising range, 485 miles.
- *Predicted reliability.* Much better than average.

Analyze the information being presented here by answering the preceding Information Evaluation Questions.

After analyzing the information presented in various accounts, the next step is to compare the accounts with one another. For example, how do these two descriptions of the Nissan Stanza GL compare in terms of the information provided and the way that this information is presented?

THINKING ACTIVITY 5.7

Locate two different passages concerning the same topic and then analyze each passage using the Information Evaluation Questions from this section of the chapter. For example, you might choose two different reviews of a movie, a play, a book, an art exhibit, or a concert, or two different passages analyzing a topic of current interest such as a criminal trial result or American foreign policy issue. ◀

There are a variety of standards or criteria you can use to evaluate the reliability of the sources of information. The following criteria are useful for evaluating both written and spoken testimony.

- Was the source of the information able to make *accurate observations?*
- What do you know about the *past reliability* of the source of the information?
- How *knowledgeable or experienced* is the source of the information?

Was the Source of the Information Able to Make Accurate Observations?
Imagine that you are serving as a juror at a trial in which two youths are accused of mugging an elderly person and stealing her social security check. During the trial the victim gives the following account of the experience:

> I was walking into the lobby of my building at about six o'clock. It was beginning to get dark. Suddenly these two young men rushed in behind me and tried to grab my pocketbook. However, my bag was wrapped around my arm, and I just didn't want to let go of it. They pushed me around, yelling at me to let go of the bag. They finally pulled the bag loose and went running out of the building. I saw them pretty well while we were fighting, and I'm sure that the two boys sitting over there are the ones who robbed me.

In evaluating the accuracy of this information, you have to try to determine how reliable the source of the information is. In doing this, you might ask yourself whether the person attacked was in a good position to make accurate observations. In the case of this person's testimony, what questions could you ask in order to evaluate the accuracy of the testimony?

Example: How sharp is the person's eyesight? (Does she wear glasses? Were the glasses knocked off in the struggle?)

When trying to determine the accuracy of testimony, you should try to use the same standards you would apply to yourself if you were in a similar situation. Was there enough light to see clearly? Did the excitement of the situation influence my perceptions? Were my senses operating at full capacity?

As you work toward evaluating the reliability of the source of the information, it is helpful to locate whatever additional sources of information are available. For instance, if you can locate others who can identify the muggers, or if you find stolen items in their possession, this will serve as evidence to support the testimony given by the witness.

Finally, accurate observations depend on more than how well your senses are functioning. Accurate observations also depend on how well you understand the personal factors (your "lenses") you or someone else brings to a situation. These personal feelings, expectations, and interests often influence what you are perceiving without your being aware of it. Once you become aware of these influencing factors, you can attempt to make allowances for them in order to get a more accurate view of what is taking place. For example, imagine that you and your friends have sponsored an antiracism rally on your college campus. The campus police estimate the crowd to be 250, while your friends who organized the rally claim it was more than 500. How could you go about determining the reliability of your friends' information? What questions could you ask them to help clarify the situation? How could you go about locating additional information to gain a more accurate understanding of the situation?

What Do You Know About the Past Reliability of the Source of the Information?

As you work at evaluating the reliability of information sources, it is useful to consider how accurate and reliable their information has been in the past. If someone you know has consistently given you sound information over a period of time, you gradually develop confidence in the accuracy of that person's reports. Police officers and newspaper reporters must continually evaluate the reliability of information sources. Over time, people in these professions establish information sources who have consistently provided reliable information. Of course, this works the other way as well. When people consistently give you *inaccurate or incomplete* information, you gradually lose confidence in their reliability and the reliability of their information.

Nevertheless, few people are either completely reliable or completely unreliable in the information they offer. You probably realize that your own reliability tends to vary, depending on the situation, the type of information you are providing, and the person you are giving the information to. Thus, in trying to evaluate the information offered by others, you have to explore each of these different factors before arriving at a provisional conclusion, which may then be revised in the light of additional information. For example, imagine that a local politician comes to your school to campaign for votes. She assures you that she fully supports higher education. How would you go about determining the reliability of the politician's information by speaking to her? What questions could you ask her to help clarify the situation? How could you go about locating additional information to gain a more accurate understanding of this situation?

How Knowledgeable or Experienced Is the Source of the Information? A third step in evaluating information from other sources is to determine how knowledgeable or experienced the person is in that particular area. When you seek information from others, you try to locate people who you believe will have a special understanding of the area in which you are interested. When asking directions, you look for a policeman, a cab driver, or a resident. When seeking information in school, you try to find a school employee or another student who may be experienced in that area. When your car begins making strange noises, you search for someone who has knowledge of car engines. In each case, you try to identify a source of information who has special experience or understanding of a particular area because you believe that this person will be reliable in giving you accurate information.

Of course, there is no guarantee that the information will be accurate, even when you carefully select knowledgeable sources. Cab drivers do sometimes give the wrong directions; school personnel do occasionally dispense the wrong information; and people experienced with cars cannot always figure out the problem the first time. By seeking people who are experienced or knowledgeable rather than those who are not, however, you increase your chances of gaining accurate information. For example, suppose you are interested in finding out more information about the career you are planning to go into. Who are some of the people you would select to gain further information? What are the reasons you would select these people? Are these sound reasons?

In seeking information from others whom you believe to be experienced or knowledgeable, it is important to distinguish between the opinions of "average" sources, such as ourselves, and the opinions of experts. Experts are people who have specialized knowledge in a particular area, based on special training and experience. If you are experiencing chest pains and your friend (who is not a doctor or nurse) tells you, "Don't worry, I've had a lot of experience with this sort of thing—it's probably just gas," you may decide to seek the opinion of an expert to confirm your friend's diagnosis. (After all, you don't want to find out the hard way that your friend was mistaken.)

Who qualifies as an expert? Someone with professional expertise as certified by the appropriate standards qualifies as an expert. For instance, you do not want someone working on your teeth just because he or she has always enjoyed playing with drills or is fascinated with teeth. Instead, you insist on someone who has graduated from dental college and been professionally certified.

It is also useful to find out how up to date the expert's credentials are. Much knowledge has changed in medicine, dentistry, and automobile mechanics in the last twenty years. If practitioners have not been keeping abreast of these changes, they will have gradually lost their expertise, even though they may have an appropriate diploma. For example, identify an expert whose information and services you rely on. How could you could go about discovering how up to date and effective his or her expertise is?

You should also make sure that the experts are giving you information and opinions in their field of expertise. It is certainly all right for people like Michael Jordan or Candice Bergen ("Murphy Brown") to give their views on a product, but you should remember that they are speaking simply as human beings (and ones who have been paid a large sum of money and told exactly what to say), not as scientific experts. This is exactly the type of mistaken perception encouraged by advertisers to sell their products. For example, identify two "experts" in television or magazine advertising who are giving testimony *outside* their field of expertise. Why you think each was chosen for the particular product he or she is endorsing? Do you trust such expertise in evaluating the product?

Finally, you should not accept expert opinion without question or critical examination, even if the experts meet all the criteria that you have been exploring. Just because a mechanic assures you that you need a new transmission for $900 does not mean that you should accept that opinion at face value. Or simply because one doctor assures you that surgery is required for your ailment does not mean that you should not investigate further. In both cases, seeking a second (or even third) expert opinion makes sense.

Summary

In this chapter we have explored the way we form and revise our beliefs. The purpose of this ongoing process of forming and revising beliefs is to develop a clear understanding of what is taking place so that you can make the most effective decisions in your life. Your ability to think critically about your beliefs guides you in asking the questions necessary to explore, evaluate, and develop your beliefs.

You use both direct and indirect experience to form and re-form your beliefs. As you evaluate beliefs based on your experience, you need to use the following criteria:

- How effectively do my beliefs *explain what is taking place?*
- To what extent are these beliefs *consistent with other beliefs* about the world?
- How effectively do my beliefs help me *predict what will happen* in the future?
- To what extent are my beliefs supported by *sound reasons and compelling evidence* derived from *reliable sources?*

Your indirect experiences are based on outside sources of information, both spoken and written. To evaluate critically these outside sources of information, you have to ask the following questions:

- How reliable is the *information?* (How accurate and justified?)
- How reliable is the *source* of the information?

By thinking critically about the process by which you form and revise your beliefs about the world, you will be able to develop your understanding insightfully and creatively.

Thinking Passages

"What's your (astrological) sign?" It is likely that you have asked—and been asked—this question numerous times in your life and on occasion have checked out various horoscopes to determine predictions and advice about your life. These sorts of activities reveal an interest (and perhaps belief) in the validity of astrology—the centuries-old belief that the positions and movements of celestial bodies are integrally related to human events. Astrological beliefs fall into the general category of "paranormal beliefs"—beliefs that attempt to explain (and predict) human events by referring to forces and phenomena that go beyond "normal" human experience or scientific explanation. Other paranormal beliefs include ESP (extrasensory perception), UFOs and alien abductions, past lives and reincarnation, psychic healing, communication with spirits, witchcraft and voodoo, and near-death experiences. A 1990 Gallup survey found that 93 percent of all Americans questioned said they believe in at least one form of paranormal phenomena.

In contrast, scientists in all fields are in near agreement that paranormal beliefs are false, irrational, and not supported by sound reasons and compelling evidence. Such beliefs fall outside of the scientific domain because they cannot be replicated in controlled laboratory settings and they are not capable of making reliable predictions. As a result, most scientists are convinced that such paranormal beliefs are based on a combination of deception, hallucinations, human gullibility, and irrational faith.

The following passages address the subject of astrological beliefs. The first, "Astrology Can Guide People's Lives," by Frederick G. Levine, offers a spirited defense of astrological beliefs. The second, "Astrology Cannot Guide People's Lives," by Paul Kurtz, presents a carefully reasoned and documented analysis debunking astrological beliefs. After reading the articles, evaluate the perspectives of each of the authors by using the criteria you identified for evaluating beliefs described in this chapter:

- How effectively do astrological beliefs explain *what is taking place?*
- To what extent are astrological beliefs *consistent with other beliefs* about the world?
- How effectively do astrological beliefs help you *predict what will happen* in the future?
- To what extent are astrological beliefs supported by *sound reasons and compelling evidence* derived from *reliable sources?*
- Are astrological beliefs *falsifiable?* That is, can you state conditions— tests—under which astrological beliefs can be disproved, and can the beliefs pass these tests?

ASTROLOGY CAN GUIDE PEOPLE'S LIVES
by Frederick G. Levine

The word "psychic" is actually a misnomer when it comes to astrology, numerology, and palmistry. These systems of divination can, in some ways, actually be considered "sciences," since they represent well-ordered systems of calculation that can be learned by anyone and then applied using objective criteria, requiring no psychic ability. They are based on the idea of "correspondences"—that all phenomena in the universe, whether physical or spiritual, are interrelated on some fundamental level, and that the patterns found in the physical universe—for instance, the movement of the planets—are reflected in the realm of human endeavor. By first taking a close look at astrology you will get a better understanding of the mechanism by which these practices work.

Astrology dates back about 4,000 years to the Chaldean and Babylonian civilizations. We can be sure that human beings were observing the motions of the heavens from the time they first gazed upward, but the actual mapping of the movements of planets and stars evolved along with civilization as a way of charting the change of the seasons to facilitate agriculture. Very early on, however, stargazers also began to use the planetary cycles to mark human and cultural events—what later became known as "mundane astrology." We can speculate that at this early point in human history the connection between humanity and nature was still strong, and that on some level people were still very much aware of the intertwining of the cycles of the natural world and the human organism.

Direct Effect of the Planets

The ancient astrologers believed that the planets actually had a direct influence on human events, and although modern astronomers dismiss this idea, there is at least some evidence that a connection exists. Take, for example, the fact that the length of a woman's menstrual cycle corresponds to the phases of the moon, or that the gravitational fields of the sun and moon are strong enough to cause the rising and falling of tides on the Earth (and that the human body is 70 percent water!). Current theories of cosmology posit that at the moment before the "big bang" that created the visible universe, all matter and energy existed at a single point in space and time. This means that on a profoundly real level, everything that exists in the universe is fundamentally related. Physicists now also tell you that all matter is bound up in fields of energy, so much so that the explosion of a supernova in a distant galaxy impacts on your solar system in some way.

In spite of all these indicators that there might be some grain of truth in the ancient view of astrology, most modern astrologers believe that the mechanism by which astrology works is much more subtle. They reject the idea that celestial events assert a direct physical force on earthly occurrences and instead take a more holistic view of the process. This thinking is based upon the metaphysical axiom, "As above, so below." This means that there are larger patterns of energy that govern all interactions in the universe and that these patterns or cycles are reflected in the movements of stars and planets in the same way they are reflected in the movements of people and cultures. Thus it is not that planetary motions *cause* events on earth, but simply that those motions are *indicators of* universal patterns. Linda Hill, a New York astrological consultant of 14 years' experience, explains this relationship:

> I don't think anyone knows exactly why it works; it just works. Carl Jung used the term synchronicity. It's simply a synchronization. Ecologically, why does every microscopic protozoa affect everything else? Well, there's a chain that links it back—some kind of a relationship between the microcosm and the macrocosm. We are a part of everything *and* we are individuals. We are part of this whole solar system, and somehow we are uniquely imprinted at birth. We are somehow synchronized to the celestial patterns that were present at our birth. It's not that the planets are doing it *to* us, it's that we're synchronized *with* them. It's not a causal relationship.

The holistic patterns that astrology deals with are chiefly manifested in the dynamics of relationships. The relationships between planets reflect the relationship of the individual to the world at large. Although this relationship takes many forms, it essentially involves the ways in which a person sees the events that take place in his life. The point of astrology is not so much to try to alter or avoid those events as to put them into a context that enables an individual to use them as opportunities for growth. The astrologer does this by preparing a horoscope.

A Map of the Planets

A horoscope is basically a map of where all the planets and zodiac constellations are at a specific time. A natal horoscope charts the positions of the planets at the time of your birth. Mundane horoscopes chart the planetary positions at the time of particular world events, such as the establishment of nations or of political groups. A business or financial horoscope would fix the positions of the planets at the time a new business is launched or contract is signed. A horary ("of the hour") horoscope is designed to answer a specific question a person might have—the chart is drawn up for the moment at which the astrologer is asked the question. Synastry is the process of comparing two individual natal charts to determine the compatibility of two people. Sometimes a third chart will also be drawn up for the relationship itself, which is considered an entity in its own right.

The astrologer begins preparing your horoscope from the moment you call for your appointment. You will be asked for the *exact* time and place of your birth. (For myself, it wasn't enough to say that I was born in

New York City; the astrologer wanted to know what borough the hospital was in!) Your time of birth should be given down to the minute, since the positions of the planets are constantly changing and the entire chart changes every four minutes. (An astrologer can determine, for instance, that the sun entered the zodiac sign of Aquarius on January 20, 1959, at precisely 7:19 P.M.) Your birth time is first converted into Greenwich mean time and then into sidereal time, which is a universal time measurement based upon the stars rather than the rotation of the earth.

Blueprint of the Universe

At this point the astrologer will look up your sidereal birth time in a book called an ephemeris, to determine what the exact positions of the sun, moon, and planets were then. Your sun sign, which is the one used in magazine and daily newspaper horoscopes, is determined by the position of the sun at your time of birth. In the same way the 12 signs of the zodiac mark the path of the sun during the course of a year, they are said to embody the evolution of the individual throughout the course of his life.

The planets, which move through the signs, represent distinct archetypal energies or functions in relation to the whole person. A planet manifests its function within the context of the sign that it is in, much in the way that a person's wishes and desires are expressed through the mediation of his personality and psychological makeup. Thus planets in Aries express their energy assertively and forcefully, for example, while planets in Gemini are manifested logically and verbally.

In addition to the zodiac signs, the astrologer also charts the planets with regard to the 12 houses, which, unlike the signs and planets, are purely artificial divisions. There are different ways of dividing up a horoscope into houses, and each astrologer has his own preferred method. The houses indicate the area of your life in which a planet will manifest its energy, whereas the sign is the "style" in which the energy is asserted. The second house, for example, is the house of personal values and money; the seventh house is the house of one-on-one relationships, such as professional partnerships, marriage, or even patient-therapist.

To understand how all this comes together, take the example of someone with Venus in Aries in the second house: such a person would have a great love of personal values and money, which would be expressed forcefully and with great impulsiveness, and he would tend to attract money, since Venus is the planet of attraction. Similarly, a person with Venus in Gemini in the seventh house would have a strong desire for marriage or partnership, especially with someone who is logical and intellectual, but would find it difficult to remain with just one partner.

Ascendants, Aspects, and Transits

In addition to these elements of your chart, an astrologer will also determine your ascendant, or rising sign, the transits of the planets (their movement through the zodiac), and the aspects of the planets (the angles formed by their relationship to each other). There are also a number of other celestial movements and astronomical relationships that can be factored into the horoscope for a more precise reading.

The degree of research and calculation necessary just to prepare a horoscope is extensive, which is one of the reasons why astrologers are generally more expensive than other types of psychic readers. (It is also the reason why magazine and newspaper horoscopes, based purely upon the 12 sun signs, are at best hopelessly general and at worst, outright frauds.) The advent of personal computers, however, has enabled the skilled astrologer to cut her calculation time drastically.

When all the research and calculations are done, it is still the ability of the astrologer to synthesize all the information in a coherent manner that finally determines the accuracy of the reading.

Most astrological work involves psychological analysis—using the natal horoscope to help a person understand who he is, what his inner composition is made up of, and what patterns of behavior tend to manifest themselves most strongly, so he can work with them in dealing with life's twists and turns. Pinpointing those twists and turns is the job of predictive astrology, which relies heavily upon the transits and aspects of planets. The transits don't necessarily predict that a specific event will occur as much as they indicate a tendency for something to happen at that point in time. In this way they trigger the potentialities that are present in the natal chart. As Linda Hill explains:

> Transits are like cosmic weather conditions: which forces are impacting us at any given time; why sometimes we feel terrible and sometimes we feel great and sometimes we feel powerful and sometimes like we want a change. They begin at certain times, they end at certain times. We tend to remember, when bad things are happening, that they're going to pass, but we forget that when good things are happening, they're also going to pass. So you have to maximize the good times by knowing how long you have to get things handled before they pass and you have to know, if you're in a difficult period, when there's going to be a letup and how

it can be used positively, as opposed to just sort of caving in and going to bed with it. Because it can always be transmuted and transformed into something useful for your own growth.

Although these readings sound very cut-and-dried, a skilled astrologer relies as much upon his intuitive skills as upon his objective knowledge. So although we might not consider astrology a function of psychic ability, neither is it a pure science. In a way, we've come full circle: although there are astrologers who approach their work in a purely scientific way, at some point, every skilled reader is going to have to rely upon less tangible methods of interpretation. Whether those intuitions are purely the product of extensive study and experience or the manifestation of psychic ability depends upon the astrologer and upon how you view psychic ability as a whole. But like other methods of divination, astrology clearly integrates us with a level of knowing that lies deeper than the rational mind. Perhaps if we concern ourselves less with the mechanics of that insight and more with its content, we will come to appreciate astrology as yet one more valuable tool in the search for self-knowledge. ■

ASTROLOGY CANNOT GUIDE PEOPLE'S LIVES
by Paul Kurtz

Astrology is a cumbersome though enormously fascinating system of belief, and it continues to captivate the human imagination. With the advent of modern astronomy astrology was given a rude shock, and during the eighteenth and nineteenth centuries it seems to have been thoroughly discredited, at least among the educated classes. Yet it never disappeared entirely, and it has been revived in the twentieth century, with great popularity in even the most advanced, affluent, and highly educated societies of the Western world. Today, horoscopes appear in large-circulation newspapers and magazines, and professional astrologers outnumber professional astronomers. Why is this so? Is it because astrology is true? Are its empirical claims valid? Does it work?

Sun-Sign Astrology
We may evaluate astrology by examining the concrete empirical descriptions and prognostications of astrologers in order to ascertain whether or not they are accurate. We will do this, first, by evaluating the accuracy of sun-sign descriptions and, second, by analyzing horoscopes. Most people are familiar with sun-sign astrology, for this is what appears in popular newspaper columns. No idea is more influential in astrology than the

notion that a person's traits are determined by the position of the sun in his or her chart. Linda Goodman summarizes the effect of sun sign as follows:

> The sun is the most powerful of all the stellar bodies. It colors the personality so strongly that an amazingly accurate picture can be given of the individual who was born when it was exercising its power through the known and predictable influences of a certain astrological sign.

Following is a list of these signs and a brief description of their meanings:

The Constellations of the Zodiac, Their Symbols, Namesakes and Selected Sun-Sign Characteristics

Constellation and symbol	Animal namesake	Selected characteristics
Aries	ram	headstrong, impulsive, quick-tempered
Taurus	bull	plodding, patient, stubborn
Gemini	twins	vacillating, split personality
Cancer	crab	clinging, protective exterior shell
Leo	lion	proud, forceful, born leader
Virgo	virgin	reticent, modest
Libra	scales	just, harmonious, balanced
Scorpius	scorpion	secretive, troublesome, aggressive
Sagittarius	archer/horse	active, aims for target
Capricornus	goat/fish	tenacious
Aquarius	water carrier	humanitarian, serving mankind
Pisces	fish	attracted to sea and alcohol

Exhaustive scientific testing of sun-sign astrology has been done. The results are invariably negative. R. B. Culver and P. A. Ianna, in *The Gemini Syndrome: A Scientific Evaluation of Astrology,* examined the claims in detail. For example, people born under the sign of Aries are supposed to have the following physical characteristics, according to one astrologer: "A longish stringy neck like a sheep; a look of the symbol in the formation of eyebrows and nose; well-marked eyebrows; ruddy complexion; red hair, active walk." Focusing on red hair, Culver and Ianna point out that this would exclude blacks and Orientals, and most Hispanics, who have black or dark brown hair. They conducted a survey of 300 redheads to find out the sign under which they were born, and found (1) that only 27 of them were born under Aries, and (2) that no one sign showed a predominance of red hair. Natural red hair, which is a genetic trait, is not determined at the moment of birth.

The Astrologer's Handbook describes many physical characteristics. Scorpios are depicted as follows: "In appearance, they are generally of robust and strong build. They often possess keenly penetrating eyes and a strong aura of personal mystique and magnetism." Culver and Ianna provide an evaluation of other physical characteristics, such as neck size, skin complexion, body build, height, weight. Again they find there is no correlation with any of the signs, so that one characteristic or type predominates over the others.

An important and often dangerous element in astrology is its diagnosis of medical conditions and diseases. Yet Culver and Ianna find that there is no correlation between the sun signs and illnesses, such as diabetes, heart disease, rheumatism, or even acne. They find these distributed equally across the signs.

Much less is said today about the physical aspects of astrology because of the patent quackery associated with it, yet that is an essential part of its tradition. Most emphasis now is on personality traits, occupations, and compatibility between people. Concerning personality traits, you find the following account of those born under Capricorn:

> Because Saturn rules Capricorn, the natives have a tendency to [be] melancholic and, at times, lonely. . . . They have sensitive personalities and want very much to be appreciated. . . . They are neat and methodical in their work and tend to be slave drivers at home. . . . Capricorns are excellent executives and remain in subordinate roles for a short time only.

Those born under Libra "are intellectual, and actively seek knowledge, new ideas, and mental stimulation. . . . they frequently play the role of peacemaker. . . . Libras are ruled by the planet Venus, which gives them charm and grace . . . with a desire for popularity."

The problem with these descriptions of traits is that they are so general they can be applied to almost anyone, especially since they tend to focus on positive qualities. Of Sagittareans you read the following: They are "naturally serious thinkers, concerned with the well-being of society as a whole as well as with their own lives . . . they are honest, just, and generous . . . they are energetic and naturally outgoing."

It is difficult to measure abstract traits; they tend to be elusive. In any case, tests have shown no correlation between the predicted personality traits and the signs under which a person is born. Culver and Ianna examined traits from aggression and ambition to understanding and wisdom and found no apparent correlation.

One way to measure the accuracy of astrology is by correlating occupations and careers with sun signs. Studies have been made of sports champions, actors, army officers, men of science, politicians, artists, etc., by consulting various reference works that list occupation. Thus John D. McGervey examined the birthdays of 16,634 scientists in *American Men of Science* and 6,475 entries in *Who's Who in American Politics* and found no basis for the assertion that occupations tend to predominate under certain signs. Other thorough statistical studies done by E. Van Deusen and Culver and Ianna likewise show no correlations.

Horoscopes

So much for sun-sign astrology, which has no discernible basis in fact and yet enjoys tremendous popularity with a vast public. Most professional astrologers will admit, however, that sun-sign astrology is only part of their diagnosis, and hence unreliable by itself. They maintain that although the sun is the strongest influence on a person, the positions of the planets must be charted for a completely accurate account. Here it is not simply the monthly range, but, as we have discovered, the exact time and place of birth that must be recorded. Each horoscope is like a personal fingerprint or signature. Only a trained, professional astrologer can give a precise diagnosis. So the question can be raised: Are detailed horoscopes accurate? I am afraid that the same criticisms we made of sun-sign astrology can be raised against the more elaborate horoscopes and that they also fail the test of adequacy—but for a variety of subtle reasons.

How accurately do horoscopes analyze personality? A number of researchers have randomly distributed horoscopes in order to test their fit. The French astronomer Paul Couderc advertised in a French newspaper that free horoscopes were available for those who wished them. Every respondent was sent the same bogus horoscope. It included such phrases as "You have inner conflicts . . . life has many problems . . . You sometimes upset people," etc. He asked for comments and received them from 200 persons. A large number of people claimed that the account fit their personalities perfectly.

The next case concerns the horoscope of a person born on January 17, 1898, at 3:00 A.M. in Auxerre, France. It reads in part:

As he is a Virgo-Jovian, instinctive warmth of power is allied with the resources of the intellect, lucidity, wit. . . . He may appear as someone who submits himself to social norms, fond of property, and endowed with a moral sense which is comforting—that of a worthy, right-thinking, middle-class citizen. . . . The subject tends to belong whole-heartedly to the Venusian side. His emotional life is in the forefront—his affection towards others, his family ties, his home, his intimate circle . . . sentiments which usually find their expression in total devotion to others, redeeming love or altruistic sacrifices . . . a tendency to be more pleasant in one's own home, to love one's house, to enjoy having a charming home.

An advertisement was placed in a French newspaper by Michel Gauquelin inviting people to send in their name, address, birthday, and birthplace. About 150 replied; each person was sent a full, ten-page horoscope, from which the quotation above is taken, a return envelope, and a questionnaire. Of those who answered the questionnaire, 94 percent said they were accurately portrayed in the horoscope and 90 percent said that this judgment was shared by friends and relatives. It was the horoscope of Dr. Marcel Petoit, a mass murderer. Dr. Petoit posed as an underground agent who would help refugees fleeing from the Nazis. Instead, he lured them to his home, robbed them, and dissolved their bodies in quicklime. Indicted for twenty-seven murders, he cynically boasted of sixty-three. So much for the accuracy of horoscopes!

Why Does Astrology Persist?

The question that can be raised is why, in spite of a lack of evidence for its claims, and considerable negative evidence to the contrary, does astrology persist as a belief-system?

One explanation is that the general public has not been exposed to the benefits of scientific criticism. Generally, proastrology propaganda is far greater than any negative criticism. If many were given scientific studies, they might be persuaded to reject the claims. There is no guarantee, however, that even if many people were aware of the negative arguments, they would reject astrology.

A second explanation is that gullibility is often very strong in the human breast, and that many people tend to accept claims that appear authoritative. They are often deceived by con men and women. Here, the guru is the astrologer, who is speaking mumbo-jumbo but is quite persuasive. There is still another element that enters in, however, and that is self-deception; this applies to both the client and the practitioner.

Astrology, like religion, is a faith; it is based upon, and reinforced by, subjective validation. In other words, the prognostications and evaluations of the astrologers appeal to a kind of inner intuition. The readings are so general that they can be applied to almost anyone. The truth is in the eye of the beholder, who stretches the diagnosis to meet his own case. "You are outgoing, yet often want to be alone," or "you are sympathetic, but often not appreciated by others." Where a horoscope is cast and the astrologer meets the client on a one-to-one basis, the former is often able to adapt the reading to the context of psychological interaction, and the reading may be facilitated by what the reader observes about the person. The reading depends upon common sense and shrewd intuition.

There is a deeper and more profound lesson from your study of astrology, and that is that the transcendental temptation is probably influencing a person's attitude toward what he is being told. In his conscious or unconscious is something like the following: The universe has a plan, and this includes the heavens. The plan encompasses each and every individual, including myself. Thus, my personal character and destiny is tied up with the stars. There is something beyond, and what I am or will become is synchronized with that.

Astrology thus speaks to a person's desires and aspirations and gives a cosmic explanation for even the most trivial, inconsequential or idiosyncratic happening in the lives of individuals. The temptation to believe in a transcendental force tends to reinforce people's hopes and wishes, and allows for subjective validation. Whether astrology is empirically true or false is not the central issue. Whether it works or is *made* to work—by fulfilling a hunger for meaning is of vital significance. And that, I submit, is its psychological function, and the key to its continuing hold on the human imagination through the centuries. ■ ◀

CHAPTER
6

LANGUAGE AND THOUGHT

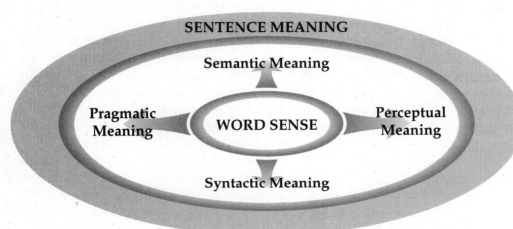

SENTENCE MEANING

Semantic Meaning

Pragmatic Meaning

WORD SENSE

Perceptual Meaning

Syntactic Meaning

LANGUAGE:
A system of symbols for thinking and communicating

TO CLARIFY THINKING
Vagueness
Ambiguity

LANGUAGE AS A TOOL

TO INFLUENCE PEOPLE
Expressions
Emotive Language
Advertising

FOR SOCIAL COMMUNICATION
Language Styles
Slang
Jargon
Dialect

UP TO THIS POINT in the book, we have been exploring the various ways we use our thinking abilities to make sense of the world: solving problems, working toward our goals, analyzing issues, perceiving, forming beliefs, and gaining knowledge. In all these cases, we have found that by *thinking critically* about the different ways in which we are trying to make sense of the world ("thinking about our thinking") we can improve our thinking abilities and perform these activities more effectively.

Throughout this process, language is the tool we have been using to understand and develop our thinking. We have been:

- Learning about the thinking of others through *reading*
- Expressing our own thinking through *writing*
- Exchanging ideas with others by *speaking* and *listening*.

We could not develop our thinking in all these ways without the ability to use language. As you will see in the pages ahead, if we lacked the ability to use language, we would not even be able to *think* in any meaningful sense. In this chapter we focus our attention on language as a means of creating and communicating our thoughts. As you develop your skill in using language, you will at the same time improve your ability to think and make sense of the world.

THE EVOLUTION OF LANGUAGE

Imagine a world without language. Imagine that you suddenly lost your ability to speak, to write, to read. Imagine that your only means of expression were grunts, shrieks, and gestures. And finally, imagine that you soon discovered that *everyone* in the world had also lost the ability to use language. What do you think such a world would be like?

As this exercise of the imagination illustrates, language forms the bedrock of your relations with others. It is the means you have to communicate your thoughts, feelings, and experiences to others, and they to you. This mutual sharing draws you together and leads to your forming relationships. Consider the social groups in your school, your neighborhood, or your community. Notice how language plays a central role in bringing people together into groups and in maintaining these groups. A loss of language would both limit the complexity of your individual relationships with others and drastically affect the entire way you live in society.

Speculation on the origin of language has excited the human imagination for ages. Herodotus, the ancient Greek, told the story of an Egyptian king who wanted to find out which language still in use at that time might have been the parent of all other languages. In order to solve this problem he arranged to have two newborn infants raised away from all hearing of human speech, so that he would know what would be the first words of humans not influenced by others' speech. After two years, the children were heard to say *bekos*. The king asked in which language this word had meaning, and learned that in Phrygian, one of the dialects spoken in Asia Minor, *bekos* meant "bread." After that time Phrygian was regarded as the parent language of all the languages of the world.

Today we know more than either the Egyptian king or Herodotus did about the evolution of language. We know that no single language was the parent of all languages. Rather, like people, languages belong to families. Languages in the same family share some characteristics with other members of their family, but they also demonstrate individual characteristics. We know that languages, like the human beings of whom they are a natural part, live, change, and die. Phrygian is no longer a living language; neither is Sanskrit, the ancient Indian language, nor is Latin.

English, like Spanish, French, Chinese, Urdu, or any of the other languages that you may speak, is a living language—and it has changed over hundreds of years. The English language has gone through four major evolutionary stages: *Old English,* 700-1050 A.D.; *Middle English,* 1050-1450 A.D.; *Early Modern English,* 1450-1700 A.D.; and *Modern English,* 1700 to the present. Because languages are systems based on sound, these evolutionary stages of English reflect variations in how the language sounds. It is difficult to represent these sounds accurately for the older periods of English because of the absence of tapes or phonograph recordings. The written symbols demonstrating early versions of the Lord's Prayer that follow are approximations based on the consensus of linguistic scholars.

The Lord's Prayer

Old English

Faeder ure
Thu the eart on heofonum,
Si thin name gehalgod.
Tobecume thin rice.
Gewurthe thin willa on eorthan swa swa on heofonum.
Urne gedaeghwamlican hlaf syle you to daeg.
And forgyf you urne gyltas, swa swa you forgyfath urum gyltendum.
And ne gelaed thu you on costnunge, ac alys you of yfele. Sothlice.

Middle English
Oure fadur
that art in hauenes,
halewid be thi name;
thi kyngdoom come to;
be thi wile don in erthe as in heuene;
zyue to vs this dai oure breed ouer othir substaunce;
and forzyue to vs oure dettis, as you forzyuen to oure dettouris;
and lede vs not in to temptacioun,
but delyuere vs from yeul. Amen.

As you read these versions of the Lord's Prayer, think about the variations in sounds, words, and sentences. With the other members of your class, discuss variations in the language(s) you speak. Could any of these be considered evolutionary changes? Why or why not?

THE SYMBOLIC NATURE OF LANGUAGE

As human beings, we are able to share our thoughts and feelings with each other because of our ability to *symbolize,* or let one thing represent something else. Words are the most common symbols we use in our daily life. Although words are only sounds or written marks that have no meaning in and of themselves, they stand for objects, ideas, and other aspects of human experience. For example, the word *sailboat* is a symbol that represents a watergoing vessel with sails that is propelled by the wind. When you speak or write *sailboat,* you are able to communicate the sort of thing you are thinking about. Of course, if other people are to understand what you are referring to when you use this symbol, they must first agree that this symbol *(sailboat)* does in fact represent that wind-propelled vessel that floats on the water. If others do not agree with you on what this symbol represents, then you will not be able to communicate what you would like to. Naturally, you could always take others to the object you have in mind and point it out to them, but using a symbol instead is much more convenient.

Language symbols (or words) can take two forms; they can be spoken sounds or written markings.* The symbol *sailboat* can be either written down or

* A unique language case is posed by American Sign Language (ASL), which is now regarded by linguists as a full-fledged language, possessing its own grammar and syntax.

spoken aloud. Either way it will communicate the sort of thing you are referring to, providing that others share your understanding of what the symbol
means.

Since using language is so natural to us, we rarely stop to realize that our
language is really a system of spoken sounds and written markings that we use
to represent various aspects of our experience. These sounds and markings enable us to communicate our thoughts and feelings to others, based on a shared
understanding of what the sounds and markings symbolize.

> **Language**   A system of symbols for thinking and communicating.

In certain respects, language is like a set of symbolic building blocks. The
basic blocks are sounds, which may be symbolized by letters:

Letters — A T C Q Y N, etc. — symbolize sounds

Sounds form the phonetic foundation of a language, and this explains why different languages have such distinctly different "sounds." Try having members
of the class who speak other languages speak a word or a few sentences in the
language. Listen to how the sound of each language differs from the others.
When humans are infants, they are able to make all the sounds of all languages.
As they are continually exposed to the specific group of sounds of their society's
language, they gradually concentrate on making only those sounds while discarding or never developing others.

Sounds combine to form larger sets of blocks called words. Words are used
to represent the various aspects of our experience—they symbolize objects,
thoughts, feelings, actions, and concepts. When you read, hear, or think about a
word, then, it usually elicits in you a variety of ideas and feelings. Describe the
ideas or feelings that the following words arouse in you: *college education, happiness, freedom, creative, love.*

The combination of all the ideas and feelings that a word arouses in your
mind comprises the "meaning" of that word to you. For instance, the ideas and
feelings that you just described reflect the meaning that each of those words
has for you as an individual. And although the meanings that these words have
for you is likely similar in many respects to the meanings they have for other
people, there are also many differences. Consider the different meanings these
words have for the two people in the following dialogue:

A: For me, a *college education* represents the most direct path to my dreams. It's the only way I can develop the knowledge and abilities required for my career.

B: I can't agree with you. I pursued a *college education* for a while, but it didn't work out. I found that most of my courses consisted of large classes with professors lecturing about subjects that had little relation to my life. The value of a college education is overblown. I know many people with college degrees who have not been able to find rewarding careers.

A: Don't you see? An important part of achieving *happiness* is learning about things you aren't familiar with, expanding your horizons about the world, developing new interests. That's what college can give you.

B: I have enough interests. As far as I'm concerned, *happiness* consists of having the opportunity to do the things that I enjoy doing with the people I enjoy doing them with. For me, happiness is *freedom!*

A: *Freedom* to do what? Freedom is meaningful only when you have worthwhile options to select and the wisdom to select the right ones. And a college education can help provide you both!

B: That sounds very idealistic, but it's also naive. Many of the college graduates I have met are neither wise nor happy. In order to be truly happy, you have to be involved in *creative* activities. Every day should be a surprise, something different to look forward to. Many careers pay well, but they don't provide creative opportunities.

A: Being *creative* means doing things you *love*. When you really love something you're doing, you are naturally creative. For example, I love to draw and paint, and this provides a creative outlet for me. I don't need to be creative at work—I have enough creative opportunities outside of work.

B: You're wrong! *Creativity* doesn't simply mean being artistic. We should strive to be creative in every part of our lives, keep looking for new possibilities and unique experiences. And I think that you are misusing the word *love.* You can only really love things that are alive, like people and pets.

A: That's a very weird idea of *love* you have. As far as I'm concerned, love is a word that expresses a strong positive emotion that can be directed toward objects ("I love my car"), activities ("I love to dance"), or people. I don't see what's so complicated about that.

B: To be able to *love* in any meaningful sense, the object of your love has to be able to respond to you, so that the two of you can develop a relationship together. When was the last time that your car responded to your love for it?

A: Very funny. I guess that we just have different ideas about the word *love*—as well as the words *happiness, freedom,* and *creative.*

As this dialogue suggests, words are not simple entities with one clear meaning that everyone agrees on. Instead, most words are complex, multidimensional carriers of meaning; their exact meaning often varies from person to person. These differences in meaning can lead to disagreements and confusion as illustrated in the previous dialogue. To clarify your understanding about the way words function in your language and your thinking, you have to examine the way words serve as vehicles to express meaning.

Words arouse in each of us a variety of ideas, feelings, and experiences. Taken together, these ideas, feelings, and experiences express the *total meaning* of the words for the individual person. Linguists believe that this total meaning is actually composed of four different types of meaning:

- Semantic meaning
- Perceptual meaning
- Syntactic meaning
- Pragmatic meaning

Let us examine each of them in turn.

Semantic Meaning

The *semantic meaning* of a word expresses the relationship between a linguistic event (speaking or writing) and a nonlinguistic event (an object, idea, or feeling). For example, saying "chair" relates to an object you sit in, while saying "college education" relates to the experience of earning an academic degree through postsecondary study. What events (ideas, feelings, objects) relate to happiness? Freedom? Creative? Love?

The semantic meaning of a word expresses the general properties of the word, and these properties determine how the word is used within its language system. How do you discover the general properties that determine word usage? Besides examining your own knowledge of the meaning and use of words, you can also check dictionary definitions. Dictionary definitions tend to focus on the general properties that determine word usage. For example, a dictionary definition of "*chair*" might be "a piece of furniture consisting of a seat, legs, and back, and often arms, designed to accommodate one person."

However, to understand clearly the semantic meaning of a word, you often need to go beyond defining its general properties to identifying examples of the word that embody those properties. If you are sitting in a chair or can see one from where you are, examine its design. Does it embody all the properties identified in the definition? (Sometimes unusual examples embody most, but not all, of the properties of a dictionary definition—for example, a "beanbag chair" lacks legs and arms.) If you are trying to communicate the semantic meaning of a word to someone, it is generally useful to provide both the general properties of the word and examples that embody the general properties. For example, identify the general properties and examples for the following words: *happiness, freedom, creative, love.*

Perceptual Meaning

The total meaning of a word also includes its perceptual meaning. The *perceptual meaning* of a word expresses the relationship between a linguistic event and an individual's consciousness. For each of us, words elicit unique and personal thoughts and feelings based on previous experiences and past associations. For example, I might relate saying "chair" to my favorite chair in my living room or the small chair that I built for my daughter. Perceptual meaning also includes an individual's positive and negative responses to the word. When you read or hear the word *book,* for example, what positive or negative feelings does it arouse in you? What about the word *textbook? Mystery book? Comic book? Cookbook?* In each case, the word probably elicited distinct feelings in your mind, and these feelings contribute to the meaning each word has for you.

Think about the words you considered earlier and describe what personal perceptions, experiences, associations, and feelings they evoke in your mind: *college education, happiness, freedom, creative, love.*

Syntactic Meaning

A third component of a word's total meaning is its syntactic meaning. The *syntactic meaning* of a word defines its relation to other words in the sentence. Syntactic relationships extend among all the words of the sentence that are spoken or written, or which will be spoken or written. The syntactic meaning defines three relationships among words:

- Content: words that express the major message of the sentence
- Description: words that elaborate or modify the major message of the sentence
- Connection: words that join the major message of the sentence

The syntax of language shapes and forms our thoughts, relating one idea to others so that their combinations, many and varied, can create meaning that no one idea could convey alone.

For example, in the sentence "The two novice hikers crossed the ledge cautiously," *hikers* and *crossed* represent the content, or major message, of the sentence. *Two* and *novice* define a descriptive relationship to *hikers,* and *cautiously* defines a descriptive relationship to *crossed.* At first, you may think that this sort of relationship among words involves nothing more than semantic meaning. The following sentence, however, clearly demonstrates the importance of syntactic meaning in language: "Invisible fog rumbles in on lizard legs." Although *fog* does not *rumble,* and it is not *invisible,* and the concept of moving on *lizard legs* instinctively seems incompatible with *rumbling,* still the sentence "makes sense" at some level of meaning—namely, at the syntactic level. One reason it does is that, in this sentence, you still have three basic content words—*fog, rumbles,* and *legs*—and you also have two descriptive words, namely *invisible* and *lizard.*

The third major syntactic relationship is that of connection. You use connective words to join ideas, thoughts, or feelings being expressed. For example, you could connect content meaning to either of your two sentences in the following fashion:

- "The two novice hikers crossed the ledge cautiously *after* one of them slipped."
- "Invisible fog rumbles in on lizard legs, *but* acid rain doesn't."

When you add content words such as *one slipped* and *rain doesn't,* you join the ideas, thoughts, or feelings they represent to the earlier expressed ideas, thoughts, or feelings *(hikers crossed* and *fog rumbles)* using connective words like *after* and *but,* as in the previous sentences.

The second reason that "invisible fog rumbles in on lizard legs" makes sense at the syntactic level of meaning is that the words of that sentence obey the syntax, or order, of English. Most speakers of English would have trouble making sense of "Invisible rumbles legs lizard on fog in"—or "Barks big endlessly dog brown the," for that matter. Because of syntactic meaning, each word in the sentence derives part of its total meaning from its combination with the other words in that sentence in order to express and join ideas, thoughts, and feelings. Look at the following sentences and explain the difference in meaning between each pair of sentences:

1a. The process of achieving an *education at college* changes a person's future possibilities.
 b. The process of achieving a *college education* changes a person's future possibilities.
2a. She felt *happiness* for her long-lost brother.
 b. She felt the *happiness* of her long-lost brother.
3a. The most important thing to me is *freedom from* the things that restrict my choices.
 b. The most important thing to me is *freedom to* make my choices without restrictions.
4a. Michelangelo's painting of the Sistine Chapel represents his *creative* genius.
 b. The Sistine Chapel represents the *creative* genius of Michelangelo's greatest painting.

5a. I *love* the person I have been involved with for the past year.
  b. I am *in love* with the person I have been involved with for the past year.

Pragmatic Meaning

The fourth element that contributes to the total meaning of a word is its pragmatic meaning. The *pragmatic meaning* of a word involves the person who is speaking and the situation in which the word is spoken. For example, the sentence "That student likes to borrow books from the library" allows a number of pragmatic interpretations:

1. Was the speaker outside looking at *that student* carrying books out of the library?
2. Did the speaker have this information because he or she was a classmate of *that student* and didn't see him/her carrying books?
3. Was the speaker in the library watching *that student* check the books out?

The correct interpretation or meaning of the sentence depends on what was actually taking place in the situation—in other words, its pragmatic meaning. For example, describe a pragmatic context for each of the following sentences that identifies the person speaking and the situation in which it is being spoken.

1. A *college education* is currently necessary for many careers that formerly required high school preparation.
2. The utilitarian ethical system is based on the principle that the right course of action is that which brings the greatest *happiness* to the greatest number of people.
3. The laws of this country attempt to balance the *freedom* of the individual with the rights of society as a whole.
4. "You are all part of things, you are all part of *creation*, all kings, all poets, all musicians, you have only to open up, to discover what is already there." (Henry Miller)
5. "If music be the food of *love*, play on." (William Shakespeare)

After completing the activity, compare your answers with those of your classmates. In what ways are the answers similar or different? Analyze the way different pragmatic contexts (persons speaking and situations) affect the meanings of the italicized words.

The four meanings you just examined— semantic, perceptual, syntactical, pragmatic—create the total meaning of a word. That is to say, all the dimensions of any word—all the relationships that connect linguistic events with nonlinguistic events, your consciousness, other linguistic events, and situations in the world—make up the meaning *you* assign to a word.

SENTENCE MEANING

It is said that the word is the basic element of language, and you have just discussed the importance of word meaning to language. Word meaning is important to your ability to organize experience and express concepts. But you rarely use single words alone. "Oh!" or "Help!" may be exceptions, but when you use even those words alone, the pragmatic meaning (or situation) is usually unmistakable. That is why you could argue that the *sentence*, not the word, is the basic unit of speech.

When you relate concepts and ideas to each other, and when you speak or write about events, you use sentences that may be combined in a variety of structural combinations, or in other words, "grammatical constructions." You may have learned to think of grammar as "how you should speak or write." In this view, known as *prescriptive grammar*, "grammar" is an artificial mechanism that prescribes speakers' and writers' use of language. In contrast to prescriptive grammar, *descriptive grammar* reflects the structure of natural language—the way we actually use language in our everyday lives. Because language and thinking are so closely related, the knowledge about language that descriptive grammar provides is essentially related to the structure of thinking. As a result, the process of becoming a sophisticated thinker is integrally involved in the process of mastering the complex structure of language.

Sentence Units: Verb Phrases and Noun Phrases

Natural language sentences are made up of *sentence units* that can be arranged in a variety of patterns. The sentences may:

- Stand alone (in *simple sentence* construction)
- Combine in a linear fashion (in *coordinate* construction)
- Combine hierarchically (in *subordinate* construction)

Each sentence unit is made up of two basic structural units: *verb phrases* and *noun phrases.*

Verb phrases consist of the verb, the representative of action or existence. For example, the verb phrase in the simple sentence unit "I swim" is *swim*. The

Words are complex carriers of meaning that evoke in people a variety of ideas and feelings. Some meanings people share, forming the basis of communication, while other meanings vary from person to person.

verb phrase also includes all the words that help describe or clarify the meaning represented by the verb. That means that in the simple sentence unit "I swim in the summer," the verb phrase includes the group of words *in the summer* along with the verb *swim.*

Noun phrases consist of the noun, the representative of people and objects. Noun phrases also include all the words that describe or add to the meaning of the noun. In the simple sentence unit "I swim," the noun phrase includes only *I.* The same is true for the simple sentence unit "I swim in the summer." If we add the group of words *My friend and* to make the simple sentence unit "My friend and I swim in the summer," then the noun phrase becomes *My friend and I.*

Simple Sentences

We mentioned that sentence units, made up of noun phrases and verb phrases, combine in three major constructions, or forms: *simple, coordinate,* or *subordinate.* The sentence forms we use when we speak or write reflect the connections of our thoughts, and these connections are influenced by the context in which they occur. These sentence forms also influence the connections of the thoughts of our listeners and readers. As an example, in the course of our discussion, the following situation narrated by a traveler will be explained from three perspectives. These perspectives illustrate the varying relationships of simple, coordinate, and subordinate sentence forms with patterns of thinking. Here is the first version:

> It was Memorial Day 1993 and a lovely time to take a leisurely trip up the coast. I looked forward to the relaxing prospect of browsing around the lazy town and maybe catching an old-time parade. As I drove along the scenic route, dividing my attention between the gentle curves of the road and the spectacular view to my right, I came upon a police car blocking the road. The officer standing outside his vehicle flagged me off the road.
>
> "Stop right here. No traffic's goin' through," he told me.
>
> "I just want to get into town."
>
> "Then park yer car over there." (He pointed.) "Walk down that street. Take yer first right. Then take a left. You'll be standing in Dock Square."
>
> "Okay."
>
> "Wait a minute, ma'am. Let me see yer handbag."
>
> "What?"
>
> "Well, he's givin' a speech in the square in just about an hour. We've got to check everything." (He smiled.) "Hurry up now. You'll miss the whole thing."

In this account, the officer's "explanation" consists of *simple* sentences, with the exception of "We've got to check everything." The simple sentence contains only one *sentence unit,* that is, one noun phrase and one verb phrase. Remember that both the noun phrase and the verb phrase may contain a number of words (and phrases) that enhance the meaning of the noun—as in *your first right*—or the verb—as in *givin' a speech in the square.*

Coordinate and Subordinate Sentences

Language is rich and complex. Usually, sophisticated speakers don't think or write only in simple sentences; they use more complex types of sentences as well. Although language and thinking are distinct processes, they are closely and inextricably intertwined at an early stage of development. As a result, complexity of language goes hand in hand with complexity of thought. Combining sentences in complex and varied ways encourages thinking that joins and juxtaposes thoughts and ideas from various perspectives.

Coordinate sentences and *subordinate sentences* are the two types of complex sentence structures that the English language uses, and they are common in both our speech and writing. Coordinate sentences and subordinate sentences both include more than one sentence unit, composed of a noun phrase and verb phrase. The difference between these two major sentence types is the way in which the sentence units are connected to each other.

In *coordinate sentences*, neither sentence unit is more important or carries more weight in terms of the meaning of the whole sentence. Here are some examples:

- Our dog's name is Harry, but we didn't name him.
- Harry loves dog biscuits, and he eats them daily.

Let's see how coordinate sentence construction works in the continuing narrative of our traveler's situation.

> It was only a couple of minutes before I reached the center of town and spied an appealing little restaurant, a sign proclaiming "Allison's" over it—a perfect place for a much-needed cup of coffee. As I made myself comfortable at a small window table, I began to absorb the conversation going on around me.
>
> "I heard Hillary put 'im up to it, and Barbara's mad as a wet hen."
>
> "Well, you know George. He's generous with his invitations, but he never thought he'd hafta honor this one."
>
> "Well, they're gonna be heah now, and George will hafta play second fiddle this weekend."
>
> "Ayuh. Same as he did last Novemba, and he can just like it or lump it!"

The conversation between local residents that our traveler overheard was composed largely of coordinate sentences such as: "Well, they're gonna be heah now, and George will hafta play second fiddle this weekend" and "I heard Hillary put 'im up to it, and Barbara's mad as a wet hen." Just as in the case of the simple sentence, the degree of description in the noun or verb phrase has nothing to do with making a sentence coordinate. A sentence is a coordinate sentence if it contains two or more sentence units that carry the same weight in the meaning of the entire sentence.

Coordinate sentence construction is often used to express a number of important thinking patterns, which will be examined in Chapter 8, "Relating and Organizing":

- *Chronological* thinking patterns: relating events in time sequence
- *Process* thinking patterns: relating aspects of the growth, development, or change of an act, event, or object
- *Comparative* thinking patterns: relating things in the same general category in terms of their similarities and dissimilarities
- *Analogical* thinking patterns: relating things belonging to different categories in terms of each other

The following chart describes some of the language-thinking links between these syntactic patterns and thinking patterns:

Syntactic Patterns:	Language-Thinking Links (Connectors):	Thinking Patterns:
Sentence coordination	*and, or, but, nor, either, neither, like, as, -er, more, similar to*	Chronological, process, comparative, analogical

In *subordinate* sentences, two or more sentence units are joined in hierarchical relationships, that is, one sentence unit is considered to be more important to the meaning being expressed than the other sentence unit. One of the sentence units always carries the main idea or meaning of the sentence, whereas the other sentence units add to or modify that meaning.

- *When* we got our dog, his name was Harry.
- Harry is happy *if* we give him dog biscuits daily.

When we *subordinate* sentence units, we are relating ideas so closely that they rely on each other to express the full meaning of the sentence—the entire meaning that the speaker or writer wants to convey. When we use subordinate sentences, we reveal the relationships of our thoughts to each other in a specific way, just as we do with simple and coordinate sentences. In other words, our syntax reflects and influences our thinking processes.

Let's examine the final explanation of the roadblock situation faced by our traveler—this time in *subordinate* sentence form.

—Hillary? Barbara? George? Then it clicked. This was Kennebunkport, the location of the president's summer house. He must have come Down East and invited the new White House residents as his guests. Although as I left Allison's I could catch only a glimpse of a black limousine winding through Dock Square, I could recognize my situation in the article in the next day's local newspaper.

Residents and Tourists Cram K'port for Memorial

When media hype hit Kennebunkport during George Bush's first presidential summer at Walker's Point, it drew even more vacationers than usual to a town that has catered to tourists since the turn of the century. When George Bush lost the presidential election to Bill Clinton, the town resigned itself to a return to normalcy. This weekend will undoubtedly stand out as its "Last Hurrah." Kennebunkport police officer William Redman noted that traffic this weekend suggests the Clintons' visit marks a historical event.

Monday morning, authorities blocked off roads so that no one would know which route Clinton was taking to Dock Square, where he was scheduled to deliver the annual Memorial Day address. Increased concern with security required all those who wanted to observe the holiday in town to have their handbags and packages examined after parking their cars outside the commercial area. Despite minor inconvenience, all went smoothly, and townfolk and visitors alike seemed to appreciate presidential participation in a long-standing local tradition.

A sentence like "Increased concern with security required all those who wanted to observe the holiday in town to have their handbags and packages examined after parking their cars outside the commercial area" is subordinate because it is composed of sentence units that, although dependent on each other to express the full meaning of the sentence, are unequal in importance.

Connections among sentence units in subordinate sentences often reflect a number of important thinking concepts.

- Time concepts: relating things in time sequence
- Condition concepts: relating events when the occurrence of one event depends on the occurrence of another event
- Causal concepts: relating events in terms of the way some event(s) are responsible for bringing about other event(s)

In the sentence we are examining, for example, the sentence unit "who wanted to observe the holiday in town" reflects a *condition* on "having their handbags and packages examined," whereas the sentence unit "after parking their cars outside the commercial area" reflects an element of *time* related to "having their handbags and packages examined." If the sentence had read, "People going into town had to have their handbags and packages examined because the police were concerned about security," the sentence unit beginning with the word *because* would have reflected an element of *cause*. The following chart demonstrates the language-thinking links between subordinate linguistic forms and thinking patterns.

Syntactic Patterns:	Language-Thinking Links (Connectors):	Thinking Patterns:
S Subordination Time	when, until after, before, since	Chronological, process
S Subordination Condition	when, until, unless, if	Comparative, analogical
S Subordination Cause	because, so, so that, since	Causal

Sentence subordination is particularly important because whenever we change a *connector* (language-thinking link) or change the order of a sentence unit, the focus of meaning and thinking expressed by the sentence also changes. Review the three accounts of the Kennebunkport traveler and analyze them by answering these questions:

- How do the various syntactic forms influence the thoughts and actions expressed?
- What thinking patterns are linked to each of the different accounts?

We have just examined some of the interrelationships between syntactic patterns and thinking patterns. Earlier in the chapter we discussed the connection between types of word meaning and the ideas, feelings, and experiences being expressed. Besides syntax and word choice, vocal signals such as emphasis, pausing, and inflection offer strong support to meaning. Even a single word like "Oh!" can be spoken to suggest a number of meanings. The same is true of simple sentences. For example, the question "Where is the waiter?" asked in a restaurant can convey a variety of thoughts depending on the emphasis the speaker places on the individual words and his or her inflection of the question. In coordinate and subordinate sentences, emphasis, pausing, and in-flection signals help clarify meaning and make it precise, and in this way vocal attributes contribute to linking syntactic and thinking patterns. These links complete the holistic process of thought and language connection.

USING LANGUAGE EFFECTIVELY

To develop your ability to use language effectively to communicate your thoughts, feelings, and experiences, you have to understand how language functions when it is used well. One way to do this is to read widely. By reading as much good writing as you possibly can, you get a "feel" for how language can be used effectively. You can get more specific ideas by analyzing the work of highly regarded writers, who use semantic and syntactical meanings accurately. They also often use many action verbs, concrete nouns, and vivid adjectives to communicate effectively. By doing so, they appeal to your senses and help you understand clearly what is being communicated. Good writers may also vary sentence length to keep the reader's attention and create a variety of sentence styles to enrich meaning. An equally important strategy is for you to write yourself and then have others evaluate your writing and give you suggestions for improving it. You will be using both of these strategies in the pages that follow.

THINKING PASSAGE

The following selection is from *Blue Highways,* a book written by a young man of Native American heritage named William Least Heat Moon. After losing his teaching job at a university and separating from his wife, he decided to explore America. He outfitted his van (named "Ghost Dancing") and drove around the country using back roads (represented on the maps by blue lines) rather than superhighways. During his travels, he saw fascinating sights, met intriguing people, and developed some significant insights about himself. Read the passage carefully and then do Thinking Activity 6.1.

FROM BLUE HIGHWAYS
by William Least Heat Moon

Back at Ghost Dancing, I saw a camper had pulled up. On the rear end, by the strapped-on aluminum chairs, was something like "The Wandering Watkins." Time to go. I kneeled to check a tire. A smelly furry white thing darted from behind the wheel, and I flinched. Because of it, the journey would change.

"Harmless as a stuffed toy." The voice came from the other end of the leash the dog was on. "He's nearly blind and can't hear much better. Down just to the nose now." The man, with polished cowboy boots and a part measured out in the white hair, had a face so gullied even the Soil Conservation Commission couldn't have reclaimed it. But his eyes seemed lighted from within.

"Are you Mr. Watkins?" I asked.

"What's left of him. The pup's what's left of Bill. He's a Pekingese. Chinese dog. In dog years, he's even older than I am, and I respect him for that. We're two old men. What's your name?"

"Same as the dog's.".

"I wanted to give him a Chinese name, but old what's-her-face over there in the camper wouldn't have it. Claimed she couldn't pronounce Chinese names. I says, 'You can't say Lee?' She says, 'You going to name a dog Lee?' 'No,' I says, 'but what do you think about White Fong?' Now, she's not a reader unless it's a beauty parlor magazine with a Kennedy or Hepburn woman on the cover, so she never understood the name. You've read your Jack London, I hope. She says, 'When I was a girl we had a horse called William, but that name's too big for that itty-bitty dog. Just call him Bill.' That was that. She's a woman of German descent and a decided person. But when old Bill and I are out on our own, I call him White Fong."

Watkins had worked in a sawmill for thirty years, then retired to Redding; now he spent time in his camper, sometimes in the company of Mrs. Watkins.

"I'd stay on the road, but what's-her-face won't have it."

As we talked, Mrs. What's-her-face periodically thrust her head from the camper to call instructions to Watkins or White Fong. A finger-wagging woman, full of injunctions for man and beast. Whenever she called, I watched her, Watkins watched me, and the dog watched him. Each time he would say, "Well, boys, there you have it. Straight from the back of the horse."

"You mind if I swear?" I said I didn't. "The old biddy's in there with her Morning Special—sugar doughnut, boysenberry jam, and a shot of Canadian Club in her coffee. In this beauty she sits inside with her letters."

"What kind of work you in?" he asked.

That question again. "I'm out of work," I said to simplify.

"A man's never out of work if he's worth a damn. It's just sometimes he doesn't get paid. I've gone unpaid my share and I've pulled my share of pay. But that's got nothing to do with working. A man's work is doing what he's supposed to do, and that's why he needs a catastrophe now and again to show him a bad turn isn't the end, because a bad stroke never stops a good man's work. Let me show you my philosophy of life." From his pressed Levi's he took a billfold and handed me a limp business card. "Easy. It's very old."

The card advertised a cafe in Merced when telephone numbers were four digits. In quotation marks was a motto: "Good Home Cooked Meals."

"'Good Home Cooked Meals' is your philosophy?"

"Turn it over, peckerwood."

Imprinted on the back in tiny, faded letters was this:

> I've been bawled out, balled up, held up, held down, hung up, bull-dozed, blackjacked, walked on, cheated, squeezed and mooched; stuck for war tax, excess profits tax, sales tax, dog tax, and syntax, Liberty Bonds, baby bonds, and the bonds of matrimony, Red Cross, Blue Cross, and the double cross; I've worked like hell, worked others like hell, have got drunk and got others drunk, lost all I had, and now because I won't spend or lend what little I earn, beg, borrow or steal, I've been cussed, discussed, boycotted, talked to, talked about, lied to, lied about, worked over, pushed under, robbed, and damned near ruined. The only reason I'm sticking around now is to see WHAT THE HELL IS NEXT.

"I like it," I said.

"Any man's true work is to get his boots on each morning. Curiosity gets it done about as well as anything else." ∎

THINKING ACTIVITY 6.1

After reading the passage from *Blue Highways,* create your own description of an experience you have had. Try to use language to communicate as effectively as possible the thoughts, feelings, and experiences you are trying to share. ◀

USING LANGUAGE TO CLARIFY YOUR THINKING

Every time you use language you send a message about your thinking. We have just examined in some detail the creature we call *language.* You have seen that it is composed of small cells, or units, pieces of sound that combine to form larger units called *words.* When words are combined into groups allowed by the rules of the language to form sentences, the creature grows by leaps and bounds. Various types of sentence structure not only provide multiple ways of expressing the same ideas, thoughts, and feelings, but also help to structure those thoughts, weaving into them nuances of focus. In turn, your patterns of thinking breathe life into language, giving both processes power.

Language is a tool, then, powered by patterns of thinking. With its power to represent your thoughts, feelings, and experiences symbolically, language is the most important tool your thinking process has. Although research shows that thinking and communicating are two distinct processes, these two processes are so closely related that they are often difficult to separate or distinguish.*

For example, when you speak or write, you are not simply making sounds or writing symbols; you are using language to communicate your thinking by conveying ideas, sharing feelings, and describing experiences. When you read, you are actively using your mind to comprehend the thinking of others. At the same time, the process of using language generates ideas, and the language you (or others) use shapes and influences your thinking. In short, the development and use of your thinking abilities is closely tied to the development and use of your language abilities—and vice versa.

Thinking and communicating in language enable you to identify, represent, and give form to your thoughts, feelings, and experiences. By representing your thoughts, feelings, and experiences, you can share them with others who use the same language system. The key to effective thinking and communication, however, lies in using language clearly and precisely, a vital requirement if other people are going to be able to understand the thoughts you are trying to communicate. At the same time, using language clearly and precisely leads in turn to clear and precise thinking.

Because language and thinking are so closely related, how well you perform one process is directly related to how well you perform the other. In most cases, when you are thinking clearly, you are able to express your ideas clearly in language. For instance, try to develop a clear and precise thought about a subject you are familiar with and express this thought in language. On the other hand, if you are *not* able to develop a clear and precise idea of what you are thinking about, then you have great difficulty in expressing your thinking in language. When this happens, you may say something like this:

---

* Seminal works on this topic are *Thought and Language,* by Lev Vygotsky, and *Cognitive Development: Its Cultural and Social Foundation,* by A. R. Luria.)

"I know what I want to say, but I just can't find the right words."

Of course, when this happens, you usually *don't* "know" exactly what you want to say—if you did, you would say it! When you have unclear thoughts, it is usually because you lack a clear understanding of the situation or you do not know the right language to give form to these thoughts. When your thoughts are truly clear and precise, this means that you know the words to give form to these thoughts and so are able to express them in language.

The relationship between thinking and language is *interactive*; both processes are continually influencing each other in many ways. This is particularly true in the case of language, as the writer George Orwell points out in the following passage from his classic essay "Politics and the English Language":

> A man may take to drink because he feels himself to be a failure, and then fail all the more completely because he drinks. It is rather the same thing that is happening to the English language. It becomes ugly and inaccurate because our thoughts are foolish, but the slovenliness of our language makes it easier for us to have foolish thoughts. The point is that the process is reversible. Modern English, especially written English, is full of bad habits which spread by imitation and which can be avoided if one is willing to take the necessary trouble. If one gets rid of these habits one can think more clearly.

Just as the drunk falls into a vicious cycle that keeps getting worse, so too can language and thinking. When your use of language is sloppy—that is, vague, general, indistinct, imprecise, foolish, inaccurate, and so on—it leads to thinking of the same sort. And the reverse is also true. Clear and precise language leads to clear and precise thinking:

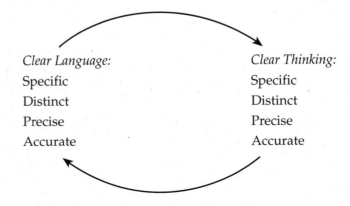

Clear Language:
Specific
Distinct
Precise
Accurate

Clear Thinking:
Specific
Distinct
Precise
Accurate

THINKING PASSAGE

In the following article, the columnist Tom Wicker analyzes what he sees as former President George Bush's lack of precision in language and thought. After reading the article, complete the questions that follow.

LIKE TOO BAD, YEAH
by Tom Wicker

Asked at a news conference about his refusal to support a ban on semiautomatic rifles, President Bush promised to take "a hard look." Beyond that, he said little and said it badly:

"But I also want to have—be the President that protects the rights of, of people to, to have arms. And that—so you don't go so far that the legitimate rights on some legislation are, are, you know, impinged on.

It was discouraging enough to hear the President expressing banalities ("I am in the mode of being deeply concerned and would like to be a part of finding a national answer") on one of the deadliest problems Americans face; or reaching for political advantage ("I'd like to find a way to be supportive of the police who are out there on the line all the time") when he has been unwilling even to endorse a ban on "copkiller" bullets.

But could he not express himself at least in, like, maybe, you know, sixth- or seventh-grade English, rather than speaking as if he were Dan Quayle trying to explain the Holocaust?

Here is more Bushspeak, concerning Middle East policy:

"Now you want to see that there's some follow on there. So the policy is set, I campaigned on what the policy is. . . . So the principles are there and I think we're, we know, we've got to, now, flesh that out and figure out what we do specifically."

Does that "figure out what we do specifically" remind you of an earlier Bush puzzlement? Perhaps his not having "sorted out" what the penalties should be for women who engage in what he had called, in a debate with Michael Dukakis, the crime of abortion?

Mr. Bush also has a way of saying nothing at numbing length—this, for example, on whether or not his support for former President Reagan's Strategic Defense Initiative was "conditional" on a 90-day review (my boldfacing of his clichés):

"I'm not ruling anything in or not. I have stated my **support for the principle** of S.D.I. I have not favored what some would call premature deployment, but **on the other hand** I will be very interested in seeing what this **overall review comes up with.** And I'm not going to close **any doors** or open any in regards to this or any other systems. We're going to have to **make some tough choices** on defense. I'm aware of that and **so let's wait and see** what the review produces."

Read carefully—and how else could you read him?—the President may be saying that he might favor "premature deployment" if the "overall review" "comes up with" such a proposal. You betcha.

On his way to Japan, at a stopover in Alaska, Mr. Bush was in good form. Asked at a news conference if he would present "new initiatives" in Tokyo, he replied, or something:

"We're ready to roll, yeah."

Let them figure that one out at the K.G.B. If, however, "yeah" meant that Mr. Bush indeed was ready with "new initiatives," he was confounding his national security adviser, Brent Scowcroft. General Scowcroft had said in a pre-departure briefing that "the substance will not be extensive" in the President's talks with other leaders.

Mr. Bush has learned one Presidential lesson well—when in doubt, point to the press. He was asked last week if there was "nothing you can do about the murder capital of the United States [Washington, D.C.] as the No. 1 resident?"

"Well," the President ventured, "we need the help of all the press to do something about it." Then, boldly, pursuing the subject, he evoked the ghost of Willie Horton: "The answer is the criminal—do more with the criminal."

Most Americans talk about as Mr. Bush has been talking. Almost everyone lapses into clichés, leaves sentences hanging in the confidence that listeners will understand, adds meaning to utterance with eyebrows and hands, and relies on, like, you know, the vernacular and slang. But George Bush is not "most Americans." He is the President of the United States and needs to speak as well as look like a President.

For one thing, he should set a needed example, in precision of speech as well as clarity of thought, neither of which distinguishes his constituency nor many of his predecessors. Mr. Bush will find, moreover, that Americans may be briefly charmed by a President who talks as they do, but that the charm will wear off; remember Jimmy Carter's sweater. Finally, a President can't afford to be imprecise, in speech *or* thought, when his every word is weighed in the capitals of the world.

Andover, where are you when we need you? Eli Yale, speak to your favored son. ■

Questions for Analysis

1.a. Describe an example that Wicker cites as imprecise language use by President Bush.

b. Explain how the imprecise language might contribute to imprecise thinking, and vice versa.

c. Rewrite the example to make it more clear and specific.

2.a. Explain what Wicker means by the statement "A President can't afford to be imprecise, in speech *or* thought, when his every word is weighed in the capitals of the world."

b. Create a scenario in which a president's use of imprecise language could lead to an international disaster.

3. Describe an experience you had in which imprecise language led to a misunderstanding and explain how more precise communication would have avoided the problem. ◀

Vague Language

Although our ability to name and identify gives us the power to describe the world in a precise way, we often do not use words that are precise. Instead, we tend to describe the world using words that are very imprecise and general. Such general and nonspecific words are called *vague* words. Consider the following sentences:

- I had a *nice* time yesterday.
- That is an *interesting* book.
- She is an *old* person.

In each of these cases, the italicized word is vague because it does not give a precise description of the thought, feeling, or experience that the writer or speaker is trying to communicate. A word (or group of words) is vague if its meaning is not clear and distinct. That is, vagueness occurs when a word is used to represent an area of experience in such a way that the area is not clearly defined.

> **Vague Word**   A word that lacks a clear and distinct meaning.

Most words of general measurement—*short, tall, big, small, heavy, light,* and so on—are vague. The exact meanings of these words depend on the

Strong writers have the ability to communicate effectively by using language clearly and precisely.

specific situation in which they are used and on the particular perspective of the person using them. For example, give specific definitions for the following words in italics by filling in the blanks. Then compare your responses with those of other members of the class. Can you account for the differences in meaning?

1. A *middle-aged* person is one who is _____ years old.
2. A *tall* person is one who is over _____ feet _____ inches tall.
3. It's *cold* outside when the temperature is _____ degrees.
4. A person is *wealthy* when he or she is worth _____ dollars.

Although the vagueness of general measurement terms can lead to confusion, other forms of vagueness are more widespread and often more problematic. Terms such as *nice* and *interesting,* for example, are imprecise and unclear. Vagueness of this sort permeates every level of human discourse, undermines clear thinking, and is extremely difficult to combat. To use language clearly and precisely, you must develop an understanding of the way language functions and commit yourself to breaking the entrenched habits of vague expression.

For example, read the following opinion of a movie and circle all the vague, general words that do not express a clear meaning.

> *Pulp Fiction* is a really funny movie about some really unusual characters in California. The movie consists of several different stories that connect up at different points. Some of the stories are nerve-racking and others are hilarious, but all of them are very well done. The plots are very interesting, and the main characters are excellent. I liked this movie a lot.

Because of the vague language in this passage, it expresses only general approval—it does not explain in exact or precise terms what the experience was like. Thus the writer of the passage is not successful in communicating the experience.

Strong language users have the gift of symbolizing their experiences so clearly that you can actually relive those experiences with them. You can identify with them, sharing the same thoughts, feelings, and perceptions that they had when they underwent (or imagined) the experience. Consider how effectively the passages written by William Least Heat Moon on pages 000 communicates the thoughts, feelings, and experiences of the author.

One useful strategy for clarifying vague language often used by journalists is to ask and try to answer the following questions: *Who? What? Where? When? How? Why?* Let's see how this strategy applies to the movie vaguely described above.

- *Who* were the people involved in the movie? (actors, director, producer, characters portrayed)
- *What* took place in the movie? (setting, events, plot development)
- *Where* does the movie take place? (physical location, cultural setting)
- *When* do the events in the movie take place? (historical situation)
- *How* does the film portray its events? (How do the actors create their characters? How does the director use film techniques to accomplish his or her goals?)
- *Why* do I have this opinion of the film? (What are the reasons that I formed that opinion?)

Even if we don't give an elaborate version of our thinking, we can still communicate effectively by using language clearly and precisely. For example, examine this review summary of *Pulp Fiction* by the professional film critic David Denby. Compare and contrast it with the earlier review.

> An ecstatically entertaining piece of suave mockery by Quentin Tarantino that revels in every manner of pulp flagrancy—murder and betrayal, drugs, sex, and episodes of sardonically distanced sadomasochism —-all told in three overlapping tales. It's a very funky, American sort of pop master-piece: improbable, uproarious, with bright colors and danger and blood right on the surface.

THINKING ACTIVITY 6.2

Write a review of a movie that you saw recently, concentrating on expressing your ideas clearly and precisely. Use the following questions to guide your analysis.

1. *Who* were the people involved with the movie?
2. *What* took place in the movie?
3. *Where* does the movie take place?
4. *When* do the events in the movie take place?
5. *How* does the film portray its events?
6. *Why* did you form this particular opinion about the film? ◀

Virtually all of us use vague language extensively in our day-to-day conversations. In many cases, it is natural that your immediate reaction to an experience would be fairly general ("That's nice," "She's interesting," etc.). If you are truly concerned with sharp thinking and meaningful communication, however, you should follow up these initial general reactions with a more precise clarification of what you really mean.

- I think that she is a nice person *because* . . .
- I think that he is a good teacher *because* . . .
- I think that this is an interesting class *because* . . .

Vagueness is always a matter of degree. In fact, you can think of your descriptive/informative use of language as falling somewhere on a scale between extreme generality and extreme specificity. For example, the following statements move from the general to the specific.

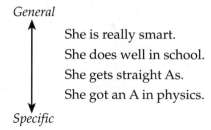

General

She is really smart.
She does well in school.
She gets straight As.
She got an A in physics.

Specific

Although different situations require various degrees of specificity, you should work at becoming increasingly precise in your use of language. For example, examine the following response to the assignment, "Describe what you think about the school you are attending." Circle the vague words.

> I really like it a lot. It's a very good school. The people are nice and the teachers are interesting. There are a lot of different things to do, and students have a good time doing them. Some of the courses are pretty hard, but if you study enough, you should do all right.

Notice how general the passage is. The writer says, for example, that "the people are nice," but gives no concrete and specific descriptions of why he thinks the people are nice. The writer would have been more specific if he had used statements such as the following:

- Everyone says hello.
- The students introduced themselves to me in class.
- I always feel welcome in the student lounge.
- The teachers take a special interest in each student.

Although these statements are more precise than saying, "The people are nice," they can also be made more specific. To illustrate this, create more specific descriptions for each of these statements.

Ambiguous Language

Ambiguity is another obstacle that can interfere with clear expression of your thoughts and feelings. We have noted that words are used to represent various areas of experience. We sometimes make the mistake of thinking that each word stands for one distinct area of experience—an object, thought, or feeling. In fact, a word may represent various areas of experience and so have a number of different meanings. When a word has more than one distinct meaning and we are not sure which meaning is being intended, then we say that the word is *ambiguous*. For example, the word *rich* can mean having lots of money (like a millionaire), or it can mean having lots of sugar and calories (like chocolate cream pie). Thus *rich* is a potentially ambiguous word.

> **Ambiguous Word**   A word with more than one meaning that is open to different interpretations.

How do you know to which of its multiple meanings an ambiguous word is referring? Usually you can tell by *how* the word is used—the situation, or context, in which it is employed. When someone asks you if you are "rich," you can be pretty certain that that person is not asking if you are full of sugar and calories. As an example, give at least two meanings for the following potentially ambiguous words:

exercise   critical   major   bar   cool

Groups of words can also be ambiguous. If someone tells you, "I hope you get what you deserve!" you may not be sure if the speaker is wishing you well or ill unless the context of the remark makes clear his or her intention. Think of two meanings for each of the following sentences.

- He fed her dog biscuits.
- The duck is ready to eat.
- Flying planes can be dangerous.
- The shooting of the hunter disturbed him.

THINKING PASSAGE

Using language imprecisely can lead to miscommunication, sometimes with disastrous results. For example, on January 29, 1990, an Avianca Airlines flight from Colombia, South America, to New York City crashed, killing seventy-three persons. After circling Kennedy Airport for 45 minutes, the plane ran out of fuel before it could land, apparently the result of imprecise communication between the plane's pilot and the air traffic controllers. Read the following excerpts from the *New York Times* account of the incident on January 30, 1990, and then answer the questions that follow.

AN ACCOUNT OF AVIANCA FLIGHT 52

The Federal Aviation Administration today defended the controllers who guided a Colombian jetliner toward Kennedy International Airport, releasing the first verbatim transcripts of communications in the hour before the jet crashed. The officials suggested that the plane's pilot should have used more precise language, such as the word "emergency," in telling controllers how seriously they were short of fuel. They made the statements a day after Federal investigators said that regional controllers never told local controllers the plane was short of fuel and had asked for priority clearance to land.

The transcripts show that the crew of Avianca Flight 52 told regional controllers about 45 minutes before the plane crashed that "we would run out of fuel" if the plane was redirected to Boston instead of being given priority to land at Kennedy. The crew said it would be willing to continue in its holding pattern 40 miles south of Kennedy for "about five minutes— that's all we can do" before the plane would have to move onward to Kennedy. But the regional controllers who gave that message to the local controllers who were to guide the plane on its final descent to Kennedy did not tell them that there was a problem with fuel supplies on the jet or that the plane had requested priority handling, the transcripts recorded by the F.A.A. confirmed.

Taken by itself, the information that the plane could circle for just five more minutes would not make the immediate danger of the plane clear to the local controllers. Without being told that the plane did not have enough fuel to reach Boston or that its crew had asked for priority clearance, the local controllers might have assumed that it had reached a point where it could still land with adequate reserves of fuel still on board.

Despite the apparent lapse in communications among controllers, an F.A.A. spokesman said they acted properly because the plane's crew had not explicitly declared a fuel emergency. An emergency would require immediate clearance to land.

R. Steve Bell, president of the National Air Traffic Controllers Association, called the safety board's statements during its inquiry "highly misleading and premature." Mr. Bell, in a statement issued today, said the pilots of the plane should have made known to controllers the extent of their problem in order to obtain immediate clearance to land the plane.

"The Avianca pilot never declared a 'fuel emergency' or 'minimum fuel,' both of which would have triggered an emergency response by controllers," he said. "Stating that you are low on fuel does not imply an immediate problem. In addition, this information would not necessarily be transmitted when one controller hands off to another." ■

Questions for Analysis

1. If the pilot of the airplane was alive (all crew died in the crash), how do you think he would analyze the cause of the crash?
2. How do the air traffic controllers and the FAA analyze the cause of the crash?
3. How do you analyze the cause of the crash? What reasons led you to that conclusion?
4. Describe a situation that you were involved in, or that you heard about, in which a misunderstanding resulted from an ambiguous use of language. ◀

USING LANGUAGE IN SOCIAL CONTEXTS

Language Styles

Language is always used in a context. That is, you always speak or write with a person or group of people in mind. The group may include friends, co-workers, strangers, or only yourself! You also always use language in a particular situation. You may converse with your friends, meet with your boss, or carry out a business transaction at the bank or supermarket. In each of these cases, you use the *language style* that is appropriate to the social situation. For example, describe how you usually greet the following people when you see them:

> *A good friend:*
> *A teacher:*
> *A parent:*
> *An employer:*
> *A waiter/waitress:*

When greeting a friend, you are likely to say something like, "Hey, Richard, how ya been!" or "Hi, Sue, good to see ya." When greeting your employer, however, or even a co-worker, something more like, "Good morning, Mrs. Jones," or "Hello, Dan, how are you this morning?" is in order. The reason for this variation is that the two social contexts, personal friendship and the workplace, are very different and call for different language responses. In a working environment, no matter how frequently you interact with co-workers or employers, your language style tends to be more formal and less abbreviated than it is in personal friendships. Conversely, the more familiar you are with someone, the better you know him or her, the more abbreviated your *style* of language will be in that context. The language you use with someone is more abbreviated when you share a variety of ideas, opinions, and experiences with that person. The language style identifies this shared thinking and consequently *restricts* the group of people who can communicate within this context.

We all belong to social groups in which we use styles that separate "insiders" from "outsiders." When you use an abbreviated style of language with your friend, you are identifying that person as a friend and sending a social message that says, "I know you pretty well, and I can assume many common perspectives between us." On the other hand, when you are speaking to someone at the office in a more elaborate language style, you are sending a different social message, namely, "I know you within a particular context (this workplace), and I can assume only certain common perspectives between us."

In this way we use language to identify the social context and to define the relationship between the people communicating. Language styles vary from *informal*, in which we abbreviate not only sentence structure but also the sounds that form words—as in "ya" in the examples—to increasingly *formal*, in which we use more complex sentence structure as well as complete words in terms of sound patterns.

Slang

Read the following dialogue and then rewrite it in your own style.

Girl 1: "Hey, did you see that new guy? He's a dime. I mean, really diesel."

Girl 2: "All the guys in my class are busted. They are tore up from the floor up. Punks, crack-heads, low-lifes. Let's exit. There's a jam tonight that is going to be the bomb, really fierce. I've got to hit the books so that I'll still have time to chill."

How would you describe the style of the original dialogue? How would you describe the style of your version of the dialogue? The linguist Shoshana Hoose writes:

As any teen will tell you, keeping up with the latest slang takes a lot of work. New phrases sweep into town faster than greased lightning, and they are gone just as quickly. Last year's "hoser" is this year's "dweeb" (both meaning somewhat of a "nerd"). Some slang consists of everyday words that have taken on a new, hip meaning. "Mega" for instance, was used mainly by astronomers and mathematicians until teens adopted it as a way of describing anything great, cool, and unbelievable. Others are words such as *gag* that seem to have naturally evolved from one meaning (to throw up) to another (a person or thing that is gross to the point of making one want to throw up). And then there are words that come from movies, popular music, and the media. "Rambo, " the macho movie character who singlehandedly defeats whole armies, has come to mean a muscular, tough, adventurous boy who wears combat boots and fatigues.

As linguists have long known, cultures create the most words for the things that preoccupy them the most. For example, Eskimos have more than seventy-six words for *ice* and *snow*, and Hawaiians can choose from scores of variations on the word *water*. Most teenage slang falls into one or two categories: words meaning "cool" and words meaning "out of it." A person who is really out of it could be described as a *nerd*, a *goober*, a *geek*, a *fade*, or a *pinhead*, to name just a few possibilities.

THINKING ACTIVITY 6.3

Review the slang terms and definitions in the following glossary. How do your terms match up? For each term, list a word that you use or have heard of to mean the same thing.

Word:	Your Word:	Meaning:
a dime, buff, diesel		a good-looking guy
phat, shorty, fly, all that		a good-looking girl
busted		gross, disgusting
crack-head, punk		someone who hangs out, takes drugs
hip, fierce		cool, awesome
the bomb		really cool
trifling		showoff
played		stupid, out of date
exit, be out, step off		leave

If your meanings did not match those in the glossary or if you did not recognize some of the words in the glossary, what do you think was the main reason? ◀

Slang is a restrictive style of language that limits its speakers to a particular group. As Hoose points out, age is usually the determining factor in using slang. But there are special forms of slang that are not determined by age; rather, they are determined by profession or interest group. Let's look at this other type of language style.

Jargon

Jargon is made up of words, expressions, and technical terms that are intelligible to professional circles or interest groups but not to the general public.

Consider the following interchanges:

1. *A:* Breaker 1-9. Com'on, Little Frog.
   B: Roger and back to you, Charley.
   A: You got to back down, you got a Smokey ahead.
   B: I can't afford to feed the bears this week. Better stay at 5-5 now.
   A: That's a big 10-4.
   B: I'm gonna cut the coax now.
2. OK A1, number six takes two eggs, wreck 'em, with a whiskey down and an Adam and Eve on a raft. Don't forget the Jack Tommy, express to California.
3. Please take further notice, that pursuant to and in accordance with Article II, Paragraph Second and Fifteen of the aforesaid Proprietary Lease Agreement, you are obligated to reimburse Lessor for any expense Lessor incurs including legal fees in instituting any action or proceeding due to a default of your obligations as contained in the Proprietary Lease Agreement.

Word meaning in these interchanges is shared by (1) CB operators, (2) restaurant/diner cooks, and (3) attorneys. Most of the rest of you would be confused listening to these forms of English, or in other words, these types of *jargon*—even if you speak English fluently!

Dialects

Within the boundaries of geographical regions and ethnic groups, the form of a language used may be so different from the usual (or standard) in terms of its sound patterns, vocabulary, and sentence structure that it either is noticeably different or cannot be understood by people outside the specific regional or ethnic group. In this case, we are no longer talking about variations in language *style*, we are talking instead about distinct *dialects*. Consider these sentences from three different dialects of English:

Dialect A: Dats allabunch of byoks at de license bureau. He fell out de rig and broke his leg boon.

Dialect B: My teacher she said I passed on the skin of my teeth. My sisters and them up there talkie' 'bout I should stayed back.

Dialect C: I went out to the garden to pick the last of them Kentucky Wonder pole beans of mine, and do you know, there on the grass was just a little mite of frost.

Probably you can recognize these sentences as English, but you may not recognize all of the words, sentence structures, and sound patterns that these speakers used.

Dialects differ from language styles in being generally restricted to geographical and/or ethnic groups. They also vary from the standard language to a greater degree than language styles do. Dialects vary not only in words but also in sound patterns and in syntax. In the following four examples of dialect, how do the sound patterns, vocabulary, and sentence structure differ from that of standard English?

1. Ah don lak to fly in dem big jet arrowpleen. Dey had a bad wreck on de hairline. Tie loose de boat!

2. I can skate better than Lois and I be only eight. If you be goin' real fast, hold it. You be goin, too fast, well, you don't be in the ring. You be outside if you be goin, too fast. That man he a clip you up. I think they call him Sonny.

3. *A:* Mornin' Alf, 'ow're yer goin?
   B: Not bad, me ol' mate, not bad. Ow's yerself ?
   A: Oh, same as usual, can't complain.
   B: 'Ow much are yer Herberts then?
   A: To you me ol' son, an Alan Whicker for a bag.
   B: Gawdelpus! An Alan Whicker! Yer goin' orf yer head. That's too dear. I'll give yer ten bob, not a penny more.
   A: Alrigh, mate—let's not have a bull and cow—gimme the bees and honey and take yer bag of Herberts.
   B: Cheers! An give me regards to yer carving knife.

Can you interpret the meaning conveyed by these passages? What words or syntactic forms contributed to your difficulty in interpreting the meaning? If you speak a dialect of your language as well as the standard dialect, write one or two sentences in that dialect and share them with your classmates. How does your dialect vary from the standard in terms of words and syntactic forms?

The Social Boundaries of Language

As you have seen, a language is a system of communication, by sounds and markings, among given groups of people. Within each language community, members' thinking patterns are defined in many respects by the specific patterns of meaning that language imposes. Smaller groups within language communities display distinctive language patterns. When there are some differences from the norm, mainly in vocabulary and length of sentences, we say the speakers are using a specific *language style*. When the form of the language spoken by these smaller groups shows many differences from the "usual" or "regular" form in words and sentence structure, we call this language form a *dialect*. Often language style is determined by the context, but sometimes speakers who differ from each other in terms of age, sex, or social class will also differ from each other in their speech—even in the same social context. This is called *social variation*.

We cannot, however, overlook the tie between language and thinking. That is, we cannot ignore the way in which our thoughts about a social situation determine the variety of language we use. The connection between language and thought turns language into a powerful social force that separates us as well as binds us together. The language that you use and the way you use it serve as important clues to your social identity. For example, dialect identifies your geographical area or group; slang marks your age group and subculture; jargon often identifies your occupation; and accent typically suggests the place you grew up and your socioeconomic class. Social dimensions of language are important influences in shaping your response to others. Sometimes they can trigger stereotypes you hold about someone's interests, social class, intelligence, personal attributes, and so on. The ability to think critically gives you the insight and the intellectual ability to distinguish people's language use from their individual qualities, to correct inaccurate beliefs about people and avoid stereotypical responses in the future.

THINKING ACTIVITY 6.4

1. Describe examples, drawn from individuals in your personal experience, of each of the following: dialect, accent, jargon, slang.

2. Describe your immediate responses to the examples you just provided. For example, what is your immediate response to someone speaking in each of the dialects on page 284? To someone with a British accent? To someone speaking "computerese"? To someone speaking a slang that you don't understand?

3. Analyze the responses you just described. How did they get formed? Do they represent an accurate understanding of the person or a stereotyped belief ?

4. Identify strategies for using critical thinking abilities to overcome inaccurate and inappropriate responses to others based on their language usage. ◀

THINKING PASSAGE

Recently gender differences in language use have reached the forefront of social research, even though variation in language use between the sexes has been observed for centuries. Proverbs such as "A woman's tongue wags like a lamb's tail" historically attest to supposed differences—usually inferiorities—in women's speech, and by implication their thinking, as opposed to men's. Vocabulary, swearing and taboo language, pronunciation, verbosity have all been pointed to as contexts that illustrate gender differences in language. Only within the last two decades, however, have scholars of the social use of language paid serious attention to variation between men's and women's language and the social factors that contribute to these differences. The excerpt on page 305 at the conclusion of this chapter from the work of Deborah Tannen reflects current interest in sociolinguistic variations between women and men. After reading the selection, answer the questions that follow. ◀

USING LANGUAGE TO INFLUENCE

The intimate relationship between language and thinking makes it natural that people use language to influence the thinking of others. As you have seen, within the boundaries of social groups people use a given language style or dialect to emphasize shared information and experience. Not only does this sharing socially identify the members of the group, it also provides a base for them to influence each other's thinking. The expression, "Now you're speaking my language!" illustrates this point. Some people make a profession of using language to influence people's thinking. In other words, many individuals and groups are interested in influencing—and sometimes controlling—your thoughts, your feelings, and (as a result) your behavior. To avoid being unconsciously manipulated by these efforts, you must have an understanding and awareness of how language functions. Such an understanding will help you distinguish actual arguments, information, and reasons from techniques of persuasion that others use to try to get you to accept their viewpoint without critical thought. Three types of language are often used to promote the uncritical acceptance of viewpoints:

- Euphemistic language
- Emotive language
- The language of advertising

By developing insight into these language strategies, you will strengthen your abilities to function as a critical thinker.

Euphemistic Language

The term *euphemism* derives from a Greek word meaning "to speak with good words," and involves substituting a more pleasant, less objectionable way of saying something for a blunt or more direct way. For example, an entire collection of euphemisms exists to disguise the unpleasantness of death: "passed away," "went to her reward," "departed this life," and "blew out the candle."

Why do people use euphemisms? Probably to help smooth out the "rough edges" of life, to make the unbearable bearable and the offensive inoffensive. Sometimes people use them to make their occupations seem more important. For example, a garbage collector may be called a "sanitation engineer," a traveling salesman a "field representative," and a police officer a "law enforcement official."

Euphemisms can become dangerous when they are used to create misperceptions of important issues. For example, an alcoholic may describe himself or herself as a "social drinker," thus ignoring the problem and the help he or she needs. Or a politician may indicate that one of his or her other statements was "somewhat at variance with the truth"—meaning that he or she lied. Even more serious examples would include describing rotting slums as "substandard housing," making the deplorable conditions appear reasonable and the need for action less important. One of the most devastating examples of the destructive power of euphemisms was Nazi Germany's characterization of the slaughter of over 12 million men, women, and children by such innocuous phrases as the "final solution" and the "purification of the race."

George Orwell, the author of the futuristic novel *1984*, describes how governments often employ euphemisms to disguise and justify wrongful policies in the following passage taken from his classic essay "Politics and the English Language."

> In our time, political speech and writing are largely the defense of the indefensible. Things like the continuance of British rule in India, the Russian purges and deportations, the dropping of the atom bombs on Japan, can indeed be defended, but only by arguments which are too brutal for most people to face, and which do not square with the professed aims of political parties. Thus political language has to consist largely of euphemism, question-begging and sheer cloudy vagueness. Defenseless villages are bombarded from the air, the inhabitants driven out into the countryside, the cattle machine-gunned, the huts set on fire with incendiary bullets: this is called *pacification*. Millions of peasants are robbed of their farms and sent trudging along the roads with no more than they can carry: this is called *transfer of population* or *rectification of frontiers*. People are imprisoned for years without trial, or shot in the back of the neck or sent to die of scurvy in Arctic lumber camps: this is called *elimination of unreliable elements*. Such phraseology is needed if one wants to name things without calling up mental pictures of them.

THINKING ACTIVITY 6.5

Read the following passage by *New York Times* columnist Bob Herbert dealing with the euphemisms that are being used for "getting fired." Why do you think these bureaucratic euphemisms are so prevalent?

Select an important social problem, such as drug use, crime, poverty, juvenile delinquency, support for wars in other countries, racism, unethical or illegal behavior in government and so on. Identify several euphemisms used to describe the problem and explain how the euphemisms can lead to dangerous misperceptions and consequences.

"SEPARATION ANXIETY"

The euphemism of choice for the corporate chopping block is downsizing, but variations abound. John Thomas, a 59-year-old AT&T employee, was told on Tuesday that his job was "not going forward." One thinks of a car with transmission trouble, or the New York Jets offense, not the demise of a lengthy career.

Other workers are discontinued, involuntarily severed, surplussed. There are men and women at AT&T who actually talk about living in a "surplus universe."

There are special leaves, separations, rebalances, bumpings and, one of my favorites, cascade bumpings. A cascade bumping actually sounds like a joyful experience.

In the old days some snarling ogre would call you into the office and say, "Jack, you're fired." It would be better if they still did it that way because that might make the downsized, discontinued, surplussed or sev-ered employee mad as hell. And if enough employees got mad they might get together and decide to do something about the ever-increasing waves of corporate greed and irresponsibility that have capsized their lives and will soon overwhelm many more.

Instead, with the niceties scrupulously observed, and with employ-ment alternatives in extremely short supply, the fired workers remain fear-ful, frustrated, confused, intimidated and far too docile. . . . The staggering job losses, even at companies that are thriving, are rationalized as neces-sary sacrifices to the great gods of international competition. Little is said about the corrosive effect of rampant corporate greed, and even less about peculiar notions like corporate responsibility and accountability—not just to stockholders, but to employees and their families, to the local commu-nity, to the social and economic well-being of the country as a whole.

New York Times, January 19, 1996 ■

Emotive Language

What is your *immediate* reaction to the following words?

sexy	peaceful	disgusting	God	filthy
mouthwatering	bloodthirsty	whore	Nazi	

Most of these words probably stimulate certain feelings in you. In fact, this ability to evoke feelings in people accounts for the extraordinary power of lan-guage.

Making sense of the way that language can influence your thinking and behavior means understanding the emotional dimension of language. Special words (like those just listed) are used to stand for the emotive areas of your experience. These emotive words symbolize the whole range of human feelings, from powerful emotions ("I adore you!") to the subtlest of feeling, as revealed in this passage spoken by Chief Seattle in 1855, responding to a U.S. government proposal to buy his tribe's land and place the tribe on a reservation:

> Every part of this soil is sacred in the estimation of my people. Every hillside, every valley, every plain and grove, has been hallowed by some sad or happy event in days long vanished. . . . The very dust upon which you now stand responds more lovingly to their footsteps than to yours, because it is rich with the blood of our ancestors and our bare feet are conscious of the sympathetic touch. . . . And when the last red man shall have perished, and the memory of my tribe shall have become a myth among the white men, these shores will swarm with the invisible dead of my tribe. . . . At night when the streets of your cities and villages are silent and you think them deserted, they will throng with the returning hosts that once filled and still love this beautiful land. The white man will never be alone. Let him be just and deal kindly with my people, for the dead are not powerless. Dead, did I say? There is no death, only a change of worlds.

Emotive language often plays a double role—it not only symbolizes and expresses our feelings but also arouses or *evokes* feelings in others. When you say "I love you" to someone, you usually are not simply expressing your feelings toward the person—you also hope to inspire similar feelings in that person toward you. Even when you are communicating factual information, you make use of the emotive influence of language to interest other people in what you are saying. For example, compare the factually more objective account by the *New York Times* (page 169) of Malcolm X's assassination with the more emotive/action account by *Life* magazine (page 169). Which account do you find more engaging? Why?

Although an emotive statement may be an *accurate* description of how you feel, it is *not* the same as a factual statement, because it is true only for you—not for others. For instance, even though you may feel that a movie is tasteless and repulsive, someone else may find it exciting and hilarious. By describing your feelings about the movie, you are giving your personal evaluation, which often differs from the personal evaluation of others (consider the case of conflicting reviews of the same movie). A factual statement, on the other hand, is a statement with which all "rational" people will agree, providing that suitable evidence for its truth is available (for example, the fact that mass transit uses less energy than automobiles).

In some ways, symbolizing your emotions is more difficult than representing factual information about the world. Expressing your feelings toward a person you know well often seems considerably more challenging than describing facts about the person.

When emotive words are used in larger groups (such as sentences, paragraphs, compositions, poems, plays, novels, and so on) they become even more powerful. The pamphlets of Thomas Paine helped inspire American patriots in the Revolutionary War, and Abraham Lincoln's Gettysburg Address has endured as an expression of our most cherished values. On the other hand, it was the impassioned oratory of Adolf Hitler that helped influence the German people before and during World War II.

One way to think about the meaning and power of emotive words is to see them on a scale or continuum, from mild to strong. For example:

>   *overweight/plump*
>   *fat*
>   *obese*

The thinker Bertrand Russell used this feature of emotive words to show how we perceive the same trait in various people:

- I am firm.
- You are stubborn.
- He/she is pigheaded.

We usually tend to perceive ourselves favorably ("I am firm"). I am speaking to you face to face, so I view you only somewhat less favorably ("You are stubborn"). But since a third person is not present, you can use stronger emotive language ("He/she is pigheaded"). Try this technique with two other emotive words:

1. I am . . . .   You are . . . .   He/she is . . . .
2. I am . . . .   You are . . . .   He/she is . . . .

Finally, emotive words can be used to confuse opinions with facts, a situation that commonly occurs when we combine emotive uses of language with informative uses. Although people may appear to be giving *factual* information, they actually may be adding personal evaluations that are not factual. These opinions are often emotional, biased, unfounded, or inflammatory. Consider the following statement: "New York City is a filthy and dangerous pigpen—only idiots would want to live there." Although the speaker is pretending to give factual information, he or she is really using emotive language to advance an opinion. But emotive uses of language are not always negative. The statement, "She's the most generous, wise, honest, and warm friend that a person could have" also illustrates the confusion of the emotive and the informative uses of language, except that in this case the feelings are positive.

The presence of emotive words is usually a sign that a personal opinion or evaluation rather than a fact is being stated. Speakers occasionally do identify their opinions as opinions with such phrases as "In my opinion . . ." or "I feel that . . ." Often, however, speakers do *not* identify their opinions as opinions because they *want* you to treat their judgments as *facts*. In these cases the combination of the informative use of language with the emotive use can be misleading and even dangerous.

THINKING ACTIVITY 6.6

Identify examples of emotive language in the following passages and explain how it is used by the writer to influence people's thoughts and feelings.

I draw the line in the dust and toss the gauntlet before the heel of tyranny, and I say segregation now, segregation tomorrow, segregation forever.

—Governor George C. Wallace, 1963

We dare not forget today that we are heirs of that first revolution. Let the word go forth from this time and place, to friend and foe alike, that the torch has been passed to a new generation of Americans—born in this century, tempered by war, disciplined by a hard and bitter peace, proud of our ancient heritage—and unwilling to witness or permit the slow undoing of those human rights to which this nation has always been committed, and to which we are committed today at home and around the world.

—President John F. Kennedy, Inaugural Address, 1961

Every criminal, every gambler, every thug, every libertine, every girl ruiner, every home wrecker, every wife beater, every dope peddler, every moonshiner, every crooked politician, every pagan Papist priest, every shyster lawyer, every white slaver, every brothel madam, every Romecontrolled newspaper, every black spider—is fighting the Klan. Think it over. Which side are you on?

—From a Ku Klux Klan circular

We need another and a wiser and perhaps a more mystical concept of animals. Remote from universal nature, and living by complicated artifice, man in civilization surveys the creature through the glass of his knowledge and sees thereby a feather magnified and the whole image in distortion. We patronize them for their incompleteness, for their tragic fate of having taken form so far below ourselves. And therein we err, and greatly err. For the animal shall not be measured by man. In a world older and more complete than ours they move finished and complete, gifted with extensions of the senses you have lost or never attained, living by voices you shall never hear. They are not brethren, they are not underlings; they are other nations, caught with ourselves in the net of life and time, fellow prisoners of the splendour and travail of the earth.

—Henry Beston, *The Outermost House* ◀

The Language of Advertising

Advertisers have nearly made a science out of using language to influence people's perceptions, beliefs, and actions. Most advertisements blend visual images and written messages to influence us to buy the products. One basic advertising strategy is to associate positive or negative thoughts and emotions with the product or service being sold. If the strategy succeeds, you are likely to recall these associations (although you are not always conscious of this) when you see the product on your next shopping trip and buy it as a result of the associations. Many people buy products not because they are of better quality than another, but because of associations that have absolutely *nothing* to do with the products. Here are some products and some of the associations for which their advertisers aim:

Product Name	*Associations*
Coca-Cola	"It just *feels* right!"—young, attractive people having fun
Nike tennis shoes	"Just do it!"—muscular, superbly conditioned, young, attractive men and women exercising and sweating with looks of grim determination

Marlboro cigarettes	"Marlboro Country"—macho, strong, rug-gedly handsome, independent cowboy riding on the range
Virginia Slim cigarettes	"You've come a long way, baby!"—young, attractive, healthy, smiling woman smoking a cigarette against a background depicting past discrimination against women
Lottery tickets	"Hey. You never know!"—average people fulfilling their fantasies by winning jackpot

Modern advertising thus appeals to fundamental human *fears* and *desires,* offering *magic potions* and *sacred objects* that will help us avoid the things we dread (aging, dependence, personal embarrassment, etc.) and gain the things we want (youth and beauty, independence, social grace, personal comfort, etc.). It appeals to our cultural values: dependability, tradition, excellence, sexual at-tractiveness, and pleasure. In these strategies advertisers are often no differ-ent from the "snake oil" salesmen of a century ago who "guaranteed" relief from "all human ills and maladies."

THINKING ACTIVITY 6.7

Examine the advertisements beginning on page 295. Analyze them by answer-ing the questions that follow.

1. Describe your subjective response to each ad—what are your first impres-sions and emotional reactions? What does the ad *do* for you? How do you look at it? Do you focus on the images or begin to read the text? Do you read it carefully or skim over it? What parts attract your attention most? Do you find yourself staring at a certain portion of it?

2. Analyze the way the ads are designed to create the responses that you de-scribed in the first question.

   a. What is the major theme of each ad?

   b. What words and phrases in the ad express that idea? Identify the action verbs, concrete nouns, and vivid adjectives.

   c. What images in each ad express its major theme? Why were these images selected?

3. To what audience does each ad appeal? What assumptions does each ad make about the tastes, habits, hopes, weaknesses, and fears of its audience? ◀

There are over 50 species of fish in the Chicago River. To find out what you can do to keep their river clean, call FRIENDS OF THE CHICAGO RIVER at (312) 939-0490.

NO MATTER
WHO LIVES THERE,
IT'LL ALWAYS
BE YOUR HOUSE.

You don't live in it. You live with it. Every day. Referrals. Reputation. Callbacks,
or worse. Houses don't forget. So remember Andersen® Windows. Whether you build
a hundred, a dozen or one, one thing's sure. If you built it, it's yours.

To learn more, call us at 1-800-426-4261, Ext. 1001

SUMMARY

This chapter on language explores the essential role of language in developing sophisticated thinking abilities. The goal of clear, effective thinking and communication—avoiding ambiguity and vagueness—is accomplished through the joint efforts of thought and language. Learning to use the appropriate language style, depending on the social context in which you are operating, requires both critical judgment and flexible expertise with various language forms. Critically evaluating the pervasive attempts of advertisers and others to bypass your critical faculties and influence your thinking involves insight into the way language and thought create and express meaning.

Its link with thinking makes language so powerful a tool that we not only rely on it as a vehicle for expressing our thoughts and feelings and for influencing others, we use language to provide a structure for learning. Like a choreographer who creates a dance, language shapes and forms our thoughts. It organizes them. It relates one idea to the other so that their combinations, many and varied, can be reported with strength and vitality, creating meaning that no one idea could convey alone. Used expertly, language *expresses* our thinking in

It's Said They Were Replaced By The Car.

Do You Really Believe It?

America Was Discovered On Horseback. It's Still The Best Way.
THE NORTH SHORE EQUESTRIAN CENTER ( ) HAMILTON, MASSACHUSETTS 508-468-5063

a way that clearly evokes the images, feelings, and ideas that we as speakers and writers want to present. It also *communicates* your thinking in such a way that others can comprehend our meaning, making in turn appropriate inferences and judgments and thereby expanding their own thinking. We will be examining these further relationships between language and thought in the ensuing chapters.

THINKING PASSAGE

One arena where the power and influence of language has become an issue of controversy is whether to prohibit racist, sexist, and otherwise offensive speech on college campuses. (This issue is graphically illustrated in the reading "Young Hate" on page 137). In the following article, "On Racist Speech," Stanford University law professor Charles R. Lawrence III contends that racial insults do not deserve to be protected under the First Amendment's protection of free speech because the intention of the speaker "is not to discover truth or initiate dialogue but to injure the victim." Therefore, he believes it is reasonable for colleges to enact rules that punish people who use this sort of speech. In contrast, the article "Free Speech on the Campus," by Nat Hentoff, contends that these attempts to restrict free expression pose a grave threat to our freedom of speech. As a writer and champion of First Amendment rights, Hentoff believes that such prohibitions not only violate the Constitution, they are counterproductive: "After all, if students are to be 'protected' from bad ideas, how are they going to learn to identify and cope with them? Sending such ideas underground simply makes them stronger and more dangerous." After carefully reading the two articles, answer the questions that follow.

On Racist Speech
by Charles R. Lawrence III

I have spent the better part of my life as a dissenter. As a high-school student, I was threatened with suspension for my refusal to participate in a civil-defense drill, and I have been a conspicuous consumer of my First Amendment liberties ever since. There are very strong reasons for protecting even racist speech. Perhaps the most important of these is that such protection reinforces our society's commitment to tolerance as a value, and that by protecting bad speech from government regulation, we will be forced to combat it as a community.

But I also have a deeply felt apprehension about the resurgence of racial violence and the corresponding rise in the incidence of verbal and symbolic assault and harassment to which blacks and other traditionally subjugated and excluded groups are subjected. I am troubled by the way the debate has been framed in response to the recent surge of racist incidents on college and university campuses and in response to some universities' attempts to regulate harassing speech. The problem has been framed as one in which the liberty of free speech is in conflict with the elimination of racism. I believe this has placed the bigot on the moral high ground and fanned the rising flames of racism.

Above all, I am troubled that we have not listened to the real victims, that we have shown so little understanding of their injury, and that we have abandoned those whose race, gender, or sexual preference continues to make them second-class citizens. It seems to me a very sad irony that the first instinct of civil libertarians has been to challenge even the smallest, most narrowly framed efforts by universities to provide black and other minority students with the protection the Constitution guarantees them.

The landmark case of *Brown v. Board of Education* is not a case that we normally think of as a case about speech. But *Brown* can be broadly read as articulating the principle of equal citizenship. *Brown* held that segregated schools were inherently unequal because of the *message* that segregation conveyed—that black children were an untouchable caste, unfit to go to school with white children. If we understand the necessity of eliminating the system of signs and symbols that signal the inferiority of blacks, then we should hesitate before proclaiming that all racist speech that stops short of physical violence must be defended.

University officials who have formulated policies to respond to incidents of racial harassment have been characterized in the press as "thought police," but such policies generally do nothing more than impose sanctions against intentional face-to-face insults. When racist speech takes the form of face-to-face insults, catcalls, or other assaultive speech aimed at an individual or small group of persons, it falls directly within the "fighting words" exception to First Amendment protection. The Supreme Court has held that words which "by their very utterance inflict injury or tend to incite an immediate breach of the peace" are not protected by the First Amendment.

If the purpose of the First Amendment is to foster the greatest amount of speech, racial insults disserve that purpose. Assaultive racist speech functions as a preemptive strike. The invective is experienced as a blow, not as a proffered idea, and once the blow is struck, it is unlikely that a dialogue will follow. Racial insults are particularly undeserving of First Amendment protection because the perpetrator's intention is not to discover truth or initiate dialogue but to injure the victim. In most situations, members of minority groups realize that they are likely to lose if they respond to epithets by fighting and are forced to remain silent and submissive.

Courts have held that offensive speech may not be regulated in public forums such as streets where the listener may avoid the speech by moving on, but the regulation of otherwise protected speech has been permitted when the speech invades the privacy of the unwilling listener's home or when the unwilling listener cannot avoid the speech. Racist posters, fliers, and graffiti in dormitories, bathrooms, and other common living spaces would seem to clearly fall within the reasoning of these cases. Minority students should not be required to remain in their rooms in order to avoid racial assault. Minimally, they should find a safe haven in their dorms and in all other common rooms that are a part of their daily routine.

I would also argue that the university's responsibility for insuring that these students receive an equal educational opportunity provides a compelling justification for regulations that insure them safe passage in all common areas. A minority student should not have to risk becoming the target of racially assaulting speech every time he or she chooses to walk across campus. Regulating vilifying speech that cannot be antici- pated or avoided would not preclude announced speeches and rallies— situations that would give minority-group members and their allies the chance to organize counter-demonstrations or avoid the speech altogether.

The most commonly advanced argument against the regulation of racist speech proceeds something like this: we recognize that minority groups suffer pain and injury as the result of racist speech, but we must allow this hate mongering for the benefit of society as a whole. Freedom of speech is the lifeblood of our democratic system. It is especially impor- tant for minorities because often it is their only vehicle for rallying sup- port for the redress of their grievances. It will be impossible to formulate a prohibition so precise that it will prevent the racist speech we want to suppress without catching in the same net all kinds of speech that it would be unconscionable for a democratic society to suppress.

Whenever we make such arguments, we are striking a balance on the one hand between our concern for the continued free flow of ideas and the democratic process dependent on that flow, and, on the other, our desire to further the cause of equality. There can be no meaningful discus- sion of how we should reconcile our commitment to equality and our com- mitment to free speech until it is acknowledged that there is real harm inflicted by racist speech and that this harm is far from trivial.

To engage in a debate about the First Amendment and racist speech without a full understanding of the nature and extent of that harm is to risk making the First Amendment an instrument of domination rather than a vehicle of liberation. We have not known the experience of victimization by racist, misogynist, and homophobic speech, nor do we equally share the burden of the societal harm it inflicts. We are often quick to say that we have heard the cry of the victims when we have not.

The *Brown* case is again instructive because it speaks directly to the psychic injury inflicted by racist speech by noting that the symbolic mes- sage of segregation affected "the hearts and minds" of Negro children "in a way unlikely ever to be undone." Racial epithets and harassment often cause deep emotional scarring and feelings of anxiety and fear that per- vade every aspect of a victim's life.

Brown also recognized that black children did not have an equal op- portunity to learn and participate in the school community if they bore the additional burden of being subjected to the humiliation and psychic assault contained in the message of segregation. University students bear an analogous burden when they are forced to live and work in an envi- ronment where at any moment they may be subjected to denigrating verbal harassment and assault. The same injury was addressed by the Supreme Court when it held that sexual harassment that creates a hostile or abusive work environment violates the ban on sex discrimination in employment of Title VII of the Civil Rights Act of 1964.

Carefully drafted university regulations would bar the use of words as assault weapons and leave unregulated even the most heinous of ideas when those ideas are presented at times and places and in manners that provide an opportunity for reasoned rebuttal or escape from immediate injury. The history of the development of the right to free speech has been one of carefully evaluating the importance of free expression and its effects on other important societal interests. We have drawn the line between protected and unprotected speech before without dire results. (Courts have, for example, exempted from the protection of the First Amendment obscene speech and speech that disseminates official secrets, that defames or libels another person, or that is used to form a conspiracy or monopoly.)

Blacks and other people of color are skeptical about the argument that even the most injurious speech must remain unregulated because, in an unregulated marketplace of ideas, the best ones will rise to the top and gain acceptance. Our experience tells us quite the opposite. We have seen too many good liberal politicians shy away from the issues that might brand them as being too closely allied with us.

Whenever we decide that racist speech must be tolerated because of the importance of maintaining societal tolerance for all unpopular speech, we are asking blacks and other subordinated groups to bear the burden for the good of all. We must be careful that the ease with which we strike the balance against the regulation of racist speech is in no way influenced by the fact that the cost will be borne by others. We must be certain that those who will pay that price are fairly represented in our deliberations and that they are heard.

At the core of the argument that we should resist all government regulation of speech is the ideal that the best cure for bad speech is good, that ideas that affirm equality and the worth of all individuals will ultimately prevail. This is an empty ideal unless those of us who would fight racism are vigilant and unequivocal in that fight. We must look for ways to offer assistance and support to students whose speech and political participation are chilled in a climate of racial harassment.

Civil rights lawyers might consider suing on behalf of blacks whose right to an equal education is denied by a university's failure to insure a nondiscriminatory educational climate or conditions of employment. We must embark upon the development of a First Amendment jurisprudence grounded in the reality of our history and our contemporary experience. We must think hard about how best to launch legal attacks against the most indefensible forms of hate speech. Good lawyers can create exceptions and narrow interpretations that limit the harm of hate speech without opening the floodgates of censorship.

Everyone concerned with these issues must find ways to engage actively in actions that resist and counter the racist ideas that we would have the First Amendment protect. If we fail in this, the victims of hate speech must rightly assume that we are on the oppressors' side. ■

Free Speech on the Campus
by Nat Hentoff

A flier distributed at the University of Michigan some months ago proclaimed that blacks "don't belong in classrooms, they belong hanging from trees."

At other campuses around the country, manifestations of racism are becoming commonplace. At Yale, a swastika and the words WHITE POWER! were painted on the building housing the University's Afro-American Cultural Center. At Temple University, a White Students Union has been formed with some 130 members.

Swastikas are not directed only at black students. The Nazi symbol has been spray-painted on the Jewish Student Union at Memphis State University. And on a number of campuses, women have been singled out as targets of wounding and sometimes frightening speech. At the law school of the State University of New York at Buffalo, several women students have received anonymous letters characterized by one professor as venomously sexist.

These and many more such signs of the resurgence of bigotry and know-nothingism throughout the society—as well as on campus—have to do solely with speech, including symbolic speech. There have also been physical assaults on black students and on black, white, and Asian women students, but the way to deal with physical attacks is clear: call the police and file a criminal complaint. What is to be done, however, about speech alone—however disgusting, inflammatory, and rawly divisive that speech may be?

At more and more colleges, administrators—with the enthusiastic support of black students, women students, and liberal students—have been answering that question by preventing or punishing speech. In public universities, this is a clear violation of the First Amendment. In private colleges and universities, suppression of speech mocks the secular religion of academic freedom and free inquiry.

The Student Press Law Center in Washington, D.C.—a vital source of legal support for student editors around the country—reports, for example, that at the University of Kansas, the student host and producer of a radio news program was forbidden by school officials from interviewing a leader of the Ku Klux Klan. So much for free inquiry on that campus.

In Madison, Wisconsin, the *Capital Times* ran a story in January about Chancellor Sheila Kaplan of the University of Wisconsin branch at Parkside, who ordered her campus to be scoured of "some anonymously placed white supremacist hate literature." Sounding like the legendary Mayor Frank ("I am the law") Hague of Jersey City, who booted "bad speech" out of town, Chancellor Kaplan said, "This institution is not a lamppost standing on the street corner. It doesn't belong to everyone."

Who decides what speech can be heard or read by everyone? Why, the Chancellor, of course. That's what George III used to say, too.

University of Wisconsin political science professor Carol Tebben thinks otherwise. She believes university administrators "are getting confused when they are acting as censors and trying to protect students from bad ideas. I don't think students need to be protected from bad ideas. I think they can determine for themselves what ideas are bad."

After all, if students are to be "protected" from bad ideas, how are they going to learn to identify and cope with them? Sending such ideas underground simply makes them stronger and more dangerous.

Professor Tebben's conviction that free speech means just that has become a decidedly minority view on many campuses. At the University of Buffalo Law School, the faculty unanimously adopted a "Statement Regarding Intellectual Freedom, Tolerance, and Political Harassment." Its title implies support of intellectual freedom, but the statement warned students that once they enter "this legal community," their right to free speech must become tempered "by the responsibility to promote equality and justice."

Accordingly, swift condemnation will befall anyone who engages in "remarks directed at another's race, sex, religion, national origin, age, or sex preference." Also forbidden are "other remarks based on prejudice and group stereotype."

This ukase is so broad that enforcement has to be alarmingly subjective. Yet the University of Buffalo Law School provides no due process procedures for a student booked for making any of these prohibited remarks. Conceivably, a student caught playing a Lenny Bruce, Richard Pryor, or Sam Kinison album in his room could be tried for aggravated insensitivity by association.

When I looked into this wholesale cleansing of bad speech at Buffalo, I found it had encountered scant opposition. One protester was David Gerald Jay, a graduate of the law school and a cooperating attorney for the New York Civil Liberties Union. Said the appalled graduate: "Content-based prohibitions constitute prior restraint and should not be tolerated."

You would think that the law professors and administration at this public university might have known that. But hardly any professors dissented, and among the students only members of the conservative Federalist Society spoke up for free speech. The fifty-strong chapter of the National Lawyers Guild was on the other side. After all, it was more important to go on record as vigorously opposing racism and sexism than to expose oneself to charges of insensitivity to these malignancies.

The pressures to have the "right" attitude—as proved by having the "right" language in and out of class—can be stifling. A student who opposes affirmative action, for instance, can be branded a racist.

At the University of California at Los Angeles, the student newspaper ran an editorial cartoon satirizing affirmative action. (A student stops a rooster on campus and asks how the rooster got into UCLA. "Affirmative action," is the answer.) After outraged complaints from various minority groups, the editor was suspended for violating a publication policy against running "articles that perpetuate derogatory or cultural stereotypes." The art director was also suspended.

When the opinion editor of the student newspaper at California State University at Northridge wrote an article asserting that the sanctions against the editor and art director at UCLA amounted to censorship, he was suspended too.

At New York University Law School, a student was so disturbed by the pall of orthodoxy at that prestigious institution that he wrote to the school newspaper even though, as he said, he expected his letter to make him a pariah among his fellow students.

Barry Endick described the atmosphere at NYU created by "a host of watchdog committees and a generally hostile classroom reception regarding any student comment right of center." This "can be arguably viewed as symptomatic of a prevailing spirit of academic and social intolerance of . . . any idea which is not 'politically correct.'"

He went on to say something that might well be posted on campus bulletin boards around the country, though it would probably be torn down at many of them: "You ought to examine why students, so anxious to wield the Fourteenth Amendment, give short shrift to the First. Yes, Virginia, there are racist assholes. And you know what, the Constitution protects them, too."

Not when they engage in violence or vandalism. But when they speak or write, racist assholes fall right into this Oliver Wendell Holmes definition—highly unpopular among bigots, liberals, radicals, feminists, sexists, and college administrators: "If there is any principle of the Constitution that more imperatively calls for attachment than any other, it is the principle of free thought—not free only for those who agree with you, but freedom for the thought you hate."

The language sounds like a pietistic Sunday sermon, but if it ever falls wholly into disuse, neither this publication nor any other journal of opinion—right or left—will survive. ∎

Questions for Analysis

1. Summarize the main reasons and arguments that each of the authors uses to support his position.

2. Describe an experience in which you witnessed an example of racist, sexist, or other offensive speech on your campus. What was your reaction to this event? What are some of the destructive consequences of behavior like this?

3. Adopt the perspective of Charles R. Lawrence and analyze this incident, explaining what the college ought to do in response to this sort of behavior.

4. Now adopt the perspective of Nat Hentoff and analyze this incident, explaining why the college should do nothing in response to this type of behavior.

5. Identify what approaches can be used to discourage and prevent racist, sexist, and offensive speech, other than enacting campus rules. ◀

SEX, LIES AND CONVERSATION
WHY IS IT SO HARD FOR MEN AND WOMEN TO
TALK TO EACH OTHER?
by Deborah Tannen

I was addressing a small gathering in a suburban Virginia living room—a women's group that had invited men to join them. Throughout the evening, one man had been particularly talkative, frequently offering ideas and anecdotes, while his wife sat silently beside him on the couch. Toward the end of the evening, I commented that women frequently complain that their husbands don't talk to them. This man quickly concurred. He gestured toward his wife and said, "She's the talker in our family." The room burst into laughter; the man looked puzzled and hurt. "It's true," he explained. "When I come home from work I have nothing to say. If she didn't keep the conversation going, we'd spend the whole evening in silence."

This episode crystallizes the irony that although American men tend to talk more than women in public situations, they often talk less at home. And this pattern is wreaking havoc with marriage.

The pattern was observed by political scientist Andrew Hacker in the late '70s. Sociologist Catherine Kohler Riessman reports in her new book *Divorce Talk* that most of the women she interviewed—but only a few of the men—gave lack of communication as the reason for their divorces. Given the current divorce rate of nearly 50 percent, that amounts to millions of cases in the United States every year—a virtual epidemic of failed conversation.

In my own research, complaints from women about their husbands most often focused not on tangible inequities such as having given up the chance for a career to accompany a husband to his, or doing far more than their share of daily life-support work like cleaning, cooking, social arrangements and errands. Instead, they focused on communication: "He doesn't listen to me," "He doesn't talk to me." I found, as Hacker observed years before, that most wives want their husbands to be, first and foremost, conversational partners, but few husbands share this expectation of their wives.

In short, the image that best represents the current crisis is the stereotypical cartoon scene of a man sitting at the breakfast table with a newspaper held up in front of his face, while a woman glares at the back of it, wanting to talk.

Linguistic Battle of Sexes

How can women and men have such different impressions of communication in marriage? Why the widespread imbalance in their interests and expectations?

In the April issue of *American Psychologist*, Stanford University's Eleanor Maccoby reports the results of her own and others' research showing that children's development is most influenced by the social structure of peer interactions. Boys and girls tend to play with children of their own gender, and their sex-separate groups have different organizational structures and interactive norms.

I believe these systematic differences in childhood socialization make talk between women and men like cross-cultural communication, heir to all the attraction and pitfalls of that enticing but difficult enterprise. My research on men's and women's conversations uncovered patterns similar to those described for children's groups.

For women, as for girls, intimacy is the fabric of relationships, and talk is the thread from which it is woven. Little girls create and maintain friendships by exchanging secrets; similarly, women regard conversation as the cornerstone of friendship. So a woman expects her husband to be a new and improved version of a best friend. What is important is not the individual subjects that are discussed but the sense of closeness, a life shared, that emerges when people tell their thoughts, feelings, and impressions.

Bonds between boys can be as intense as girls', but they are based less on talking, more on doing things together. Since they don't assume talk is the cement that binds a relationship, men don't know what kind of talk women want, and they don't miss it when it isn't there.

Boys' groups are larger, more inclusive, and more hierarchical, so boys must struggle to avoid the subordinate position in the group. This may play a role in women's complaints that men don't listen to them. Some men really don't like to listen, because being the listener makes them feel one-down, like a child listening to adults or an employee to a boss.

But often when women tell men, "You aren't listening," and the men protest, "I am," the men are right. The impression of not listening results from misalignments in the mechanics of conversation. The misalignment begins as soon as a man and a woman take physical positions. This became clear when I studied videotapes made by psychologist Bruce Dorval of children and adults talking to their same-sex best friends. I found that at every age, the girls and women faced each other directly, their eyes anchored on each other's faces. At every age, the boys and men sat at angles to each other and looked elsewhere in the room, periodically glancing at each other. They were obviously attuned to each other, often mirroring each other's movements. But the tendency of men to face away can give women the impression they aren't listening even when they are. A young woman in college was frustrated: Whenever she told her boyfriend she wanted to talk to him, he would lie down on the floor, close his eyes, and put his arm over his face. This signaled to her, "He's taking a nap." But he insisted he was listening extra hard. Normally, he looks around the room, so he is easily distracted. Lying down and covering his eyes helped him concentrate on what she was saying.

Analogous to the physical alignment that women and men take in conversation is their topical alignment. The girls in my study tended to talk at length about one topic, but the boys tended to jump from topic to topic. Girls exchanged stories about people they knew. The second-grade boys teased, told jokes, noticed things in the room and talked about finding games to play. The sixth-grade girls talked about problems with a mutual friend. The sixth-grade boys talked about 55 different topics, none of which extended over more than a few turns.

Listening to Body Language

Switching topics is another habit that gives women the impression men aren't listening, especially if they switch to a topic about themselves. But the evidence of the 10th-grade boys in my study indicates otherwise. The 10th-grade boys sprawled across their chairs with bodies parallel and eyes straight ahead, rarely looking at each other. They looked as if they were riding in a car, staring out the windshield. But they were talking about their feelings. One boy was upset because a girl had told him he had a drinking problem, and the other was feeling alienated from all his friends.

Now, when a girl told a friend about a problem, the friend responded by asking probing questions and expressing agreement and understanding. But the boys dismissed each other's problems. Todd assured Richard that his drinking was "no big problem" because "sometimes you're funny when you're off your butt." And when Todd said he felt left out, Richard responded, "Why should you? You know more people than me."

Women perceive such responses as belittling and unsupportive. But the boys seemed satisfied with them. Whereas women reassure each other by implying, "You shouldn't feel bad because I've had similar experiences," men do so by implying, "You shouldn't feel bad because your problems aren't so bad."

There are even simpler reasons for women's impression that men don't listen. Linguist Lynette Hirschman found that women make more listener-noise, such as "mhm," "uhuh," and "yeah," to show "I'm with you." Men, she found, more often give silent attention. Women who expect a stream of listener-noise interpret silent attention as no attention at all.

Women's conversational habits are as frustrating to men as men's are to women. Men who expect silent attention interpret a stream of listener-noise as overreaction or impatience. Also, when women talk to each other in a close, comfortable setting, they often overlap, finish each other's sentences and anticipate what the other is about to say. This practice, which I call "participatory listenership," is often perceived by men as interruption, intrusion and lack of attention.

A parallel difference caused a man to complain about his wife, "She just wants to talk about her own point of view. If I show her another view, she gets mad at me." When most women talk to each other, they assume a conversationalist's job is to express agreement and support. But many men see their conversational duty as pointing out the other side of an argument. This is heard as disloyalty by women, and refusal to offer the requisite support. It is not that women don't want to see other points of view, but that they prefer them phrased as suggestions and inquiries rather than as direct challenges.

In his book *Fighting for Life,* Walter Ong points out that men use "agonistic" or warlike, oppositional formats to do almost anything; thus discussion becomes debate, and conversation a competitive sport. In contrast, women see conversation as a ritual means of establishing rapport. If Jane tells a problem and June says she has a similar one, they walk away feeling closer to each other. But this attempt at establishing rapport can backfire when used with men. Men take too literally women's ritual "troubles talk," just as women mistake men's ritual challenges for real attack.

The Sounds of Silence

These differences begin to clarify why women and men have such different expectations about communication in marriage. For women, talk creates intimacy. Marriage is an orgy of closeness: you can tell your feelings and thoughts, and still be loved. Their greatest fear is being pushed away. But men live in a hierarchical world, where talk maintains independence and status. They are on guard to protect themselves from being put down and pushed around.

This explains the paradox of the talkative man who said of his silent wife, "She's the talker." In the public setting of a guest lecture, he felt challenged to show his intelligence and display his understanding of the lecture. But at home, where he has nothing to prove and no one to defend against, he is free to remain silent. For his wife, being home means she is free from the worry that something she says might offend someone, or spark disagreement, or appear to be showing off; at home she is free to talk.

The communication problems that endanger marriage can't be fixed by mechanical engineering. They require a new conceptual framework about the role of talk in human relationships. Many of the psychological explanations that have become second nature may not be helpful, because they tend to blame either women (for not being assertive enough) or men (for not being in touch with their feelings). A sociolinguistic approach by which male-female conversation is seen as cross-cultural communication allows us to understand the problem and forge solutions without blaming either party.

Once the problem is understood, improvement comes naturally, as it did to the young woman and her boyfriend who seemed to go to sleep when she wanted to talk. Previously, she had accused him of not listening, and he had refused to change his behavior, since that would be admitting fault. But then she learned about and explained to him the differences in women's and men's habitual ways of aligning themselves in conversation. The next time she told him she wanted to talk, he began, as usual, by lying down and covering his eyes. When the familiar negative reaction bubbled up, she reassured herself that he really was listening. But then he sat up and looked at her. Thrilled, she asked why. He said, "You like me to look at you when you talk, so I'll try to do it." Once he saw their differences as cross-cultural rather than right and wrong, he independently altered his behavior.

Women who feel abandoned and deprived when their husbands won't listen to or report daily news may be happy to discover their husbands trying to adapt once they understand the place of small talk in women's relationships. But if their husbands don't adapt, the women may still be comforted that for men, this is not a failure of intimacy. Accepting the difference, the wives may look to their friends or family for that kind of talk. And husbands who can't provide it shouldn't feel their wives have made unreasonable demands. Some couples will still decide to divorce, but at least their decisions will be based on realistic expectations.

In these times of resurgent ethnic conflicts, the world desperately needs cross-cultural understanding. Like charity, successful cross-cultural communication should begin at home. ■

Questions for Analysis

1. Identify the distinctive differences between the communication styles of men and women, according to Deborah Tannen, and explain how these differences can lead to miscommunication and misunderstanding.

2. Based on your experience, explain whether you believe Dr. Tannen's analysis of these different communication styles is accurate. Provide specific examples to support your viewpoint.

3. Describe a situation in which you had a miscommunication with a person of the opposite sex. Analyze this situation based on what you read in the Tannen article.

4. Identify strategies that both men and women can use to help avoid the miscommunication that can result from these contrasting styles. ◄

FORMING AND APPLYING CONCEPTS

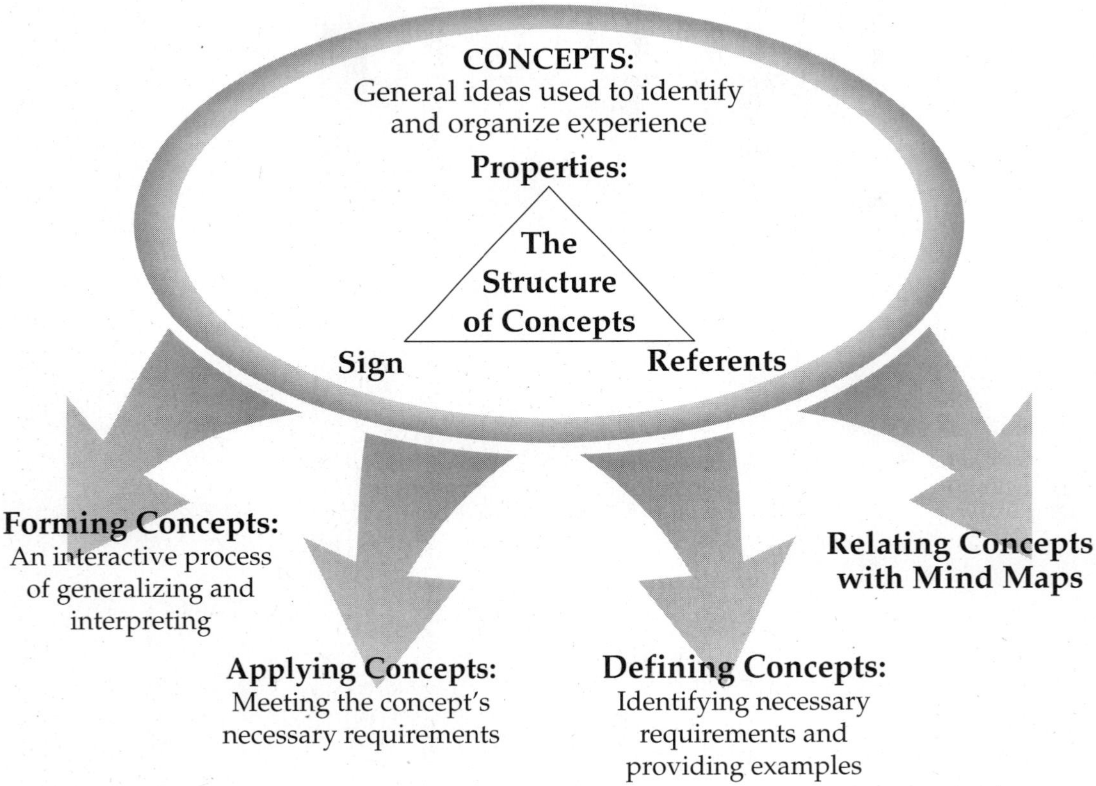

CONCEPTS:
General ideas used to identify
and organize experience

Properties:

The
Structure
of Concepts

Sign   **Referents**

Forming Concepts:
An interactive process
of generalizing and
interpreting

Applying Concepts:
Meeting the concept's
necessary requirements

Defining Concepts:
Identifying necessary
requirements and
providing examples

**Relating Concepts
with Mind Maps**

WE LIVE IN A WORLD FILLED WITH CONCEPTS. A large number of the words you use to represent your experience express concepts you have formed. *Music video, person, education, computer, sport, situation comedy, elated,* and *thinking* are only a few examples of concepts. Your academic study involves learning new concepts as well, and in order to be successful in college and your career, you need to master the conceptualizing process. For example, when you read textbooks or listen to lectures and take notes, you are required to grasp the key concepts and follow them as they are developed and supported. When you write papers or homework assignments, you are usually expected to focus on certain concepts, develop a thesis around them, present the thesis (itself a concept!) with carefully argued points, and back it up with specific examples. Many course examinations involve applying key concepts you have learned to new sets of circumstances.

WHAT ARE CONCEPTS?

Concepts are general ideas you use to organize your experience and, in so doing, bring order and intelligibility to your life. In the same way that words are the vocabulary of language, concepts are the vocabulary of thought. As organizers of your experience, concepts work in conjunction with language to identify, describe, distinguish, and relate all the various aspects of your world.

> **Concepts**   General ideas that we use to identify and organize our experience.

To become a sophisticated thinker, you must develop expertise in the conceptualizing process, improving your ability to *form, apply,* and *relate* concepts. This complex conceptualizing process is going on all the time in your mind, enabling you to think in a distinctly human way.

How do you use concepts to organize and make sense of experience? Think back to the first day of the semester. For most students, this is a time to evaluate their courses by trying to determine which concepts apply.

- Will this course be interesting? Useful? A lot of work?
- Is the teacher stimulating? Demanding? Entertaining?
- Are the students friendly? Intelligent? Conscientious?

Each of these words or phrases represents a concept you are attempting to apply so that you can understand what is occurring at the moment and also anticipate what the course will be like in the future. As the course progresses, you gather further information from your actual experiences in the class. This information may support your initial concepts, or it may conflict with these initial concepts. If the information you receive supports these concepts, you tend to maintain them ("Yes, I can see that this is going to be a difficult course"). On the other hand, when the information you receive conflicts with these concepts, you tend to find new concepts to explain the situation ("No, I can see that I was wrong—this course isn't going to be as difficult as I thought at first"). A diagram of this process might look something like that shown below.

Experience: Attending the first day of class

$\downarrow$

   leads to

$\downarrow$

Applying a concept to explain the situation: This course will be very difficult and I might not do very well

$\downarrow$

   leads to

$\downarrow$

Looking for information to support or conflict with our concept.

$\swarrow$ $\searrow$

Supporting Information:	*Conflicting Information:*
The teacher is very demanding.	I find that I am able to keep up with the work.
	$\downarrow$
There are lots of writing assignments.	leads to
	$\downarrow$
The reading is challenging.	Forming a new concept to explain the situation: This course is difficult, but I will be able to handle the work and do well.
	$\downarrow$
	leads to
	action

Concepts are general ideas we use to organize our experience and so bring order and intelligibility to our lives and the world around us.

To take another example, imagine that you are a physician and that one of your patients comes to you complaining of shortness of breath and occasional pain in his left arm. After he describes his symptoms, you would ask a number of questions, examine him, and perhaps administer some tests. Your ability to *identify* the underlying problem would depend on your knowledge of various human diseases. Each disease is identified and described by a different concept. Identifying these various diseases means that you can *distinguish* different concepts and that you know in what situations to apply a given concept correctly. In addition, when the patient asks, "What's wrong with me, doctor?" you are able to describe the concept (for example, heart disease) and explain how it is related to his symptoms. Fortunately, modern medicine has developed (and is continuing to develop) remarkably precise concepts to describe and explain the diseases that afflict us. In the patient's case, you may conclude that the problem is heart disease. Of course, there are different kinds of heart disease, represented by different concepts, and success in treating the patient will depend on figuring out exactly which type of disease is involved.

THINKING ACTIVITY 7.1

Identify an initial concept you had about an event in your life (a new job, attending college, etc.) that changed as a result of your experiences. After identifying your initial concept, describe the experiences that led you to change or modify the concept, and then explain the new concept you formed to explain the situation. Your response should include the following elements:

- Initial concept
- New information provided by additional experiences
- New concept formed to explain the situation ◀

Learning to master concepts will help you in every area of your life: academic, career, and personal. In college study, each academic discipline or subject is composed of many different concepts that are used to organize experience, give explanations, and solve problems. Here is a sampling of college-level concepts: *entropy, subtext, Gemeinschaft, cell, metaphysics, relativity, unconscious, transformational grammar, aesthetic, minor key, interface, health, quantum mechanics, schizophrenia*. To make sense of how disciplines function, you need to understand what the concepts of that discipline mean, how to apply them, and the way they relate to other concepts. You also need to learn the methods of investigation, patterns of thought, and forms of reasoning that various disciplines use to form larger conceptual theories and methods. We will be exploring these subjects in the next several chapters of the text.

Regardless of their specific knowledge content, all careers require conceptual abilities, whether you are trying to apply a legal principle, develop a promotional theme, or devise a new computer program. Similarly, expertise in forming and applying concepts helps you make sense of your personal life, understand others, and make informed decisions. It was the Greek philosopher Aristotle who once said that the intelligent person is a "master of concepts."

THE STRUCTURE OF CONCEPTS

Concepts are general ideas you use to identify, distinguish, and relate the various aspects of your experience. Concepts allow you to organize your world into patterns that make sense to you. This is the process by which you discover and create meaning in your life.

In their role as organizers of experience, concepts act to group aspects of your experience based on their similarity to one another. Consider the thing that you usually write with: a pen. The concept *pen* represents a type of object that you use for writing. But look around the classroom at all other instruments people are using to write. You use the concept *pen* to identify these things as well, even though they may look very different from the one you are using.

Thus the concept *pen* not only helps you make distinctions in your experience by indicating how pens differ from pencils, crayons, or magic markers, but it also helps you determine which items are similar enough to each other to be called pens. When you put items into a group with a single description—like "pen"—you are focusing on the *similarities* between the items:

- They use ink.
- They are used for writing.
- They are held with a hand.

Being able to see and name the similarities between certain things in your experience is the way you form concepts and is crucial for making sense of your world. If you were not able to do this, then everything in the world would be different, with its own individual name.

The process by which you group things based on their similarities is known as *classifying.* Classifying is a natural human activity that goes on all the time. In most cases, however, you are not conscious that you are classifying something in a particular sort of way; you do so automatically. The process of classifying is one of the main ways that you order, organize, and make sense of your world. Because no two things or experiences are exactly alike, your ability to classify things into various groups is what enables you to recognize things in your experience. When you perceive a pen, you recognize it as a *kind of thing* you have seen before. Even though you may not have seen this particular pen, you recognize that it belongs to a group of things that you are familiar with.

The best way to understand the structure of concepts is to visualize them by means of a model. Examine the following figure:

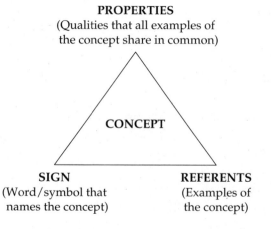

PROPERTIES
(Qualities that all examples of
the concept share in common)

CONCEPT

SIGN
(Word/symbol that
names the concept)

REFERENTS
(Examples of
the concept)

The *sign* is the word or symbol used to name or designate the concept; for example, the word *triangle* is a sign. The *referents* represent all the various examples of the concept; the three-sided figure we are using as our model is an example of the concept *triangle*. The *properties* of the concept are the features that all things named by the word or sign share in common; all examples of the concept *triangle* share the characteristics of being a polygon and having three sides. These are the properties that we refer to when we *define* concepts; thus, "A triangle is a three-sided polygon."

Let's take another example. Suppose you wanted to explore the structure of the concept *automobile*. The *sign* that names the concept is the word *automobile* or the symbol 🚗 . *Referents* of the concept include the 1954 MG "TF" currently residing in the garage as well as the Ford Explorer parked in front of the house. The *properties* that all things named by the sign *automobile* include are wheels, a chassis, an engine, seats for passengers, and so on. The following figure is a conceptual model of the concept *automobile*:

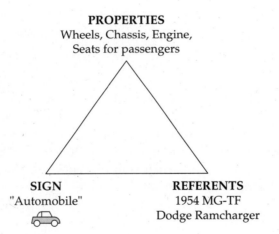

PROPERTIES
Wheels, Chassis, Engine,
Seats for passengers

SIGN
"Automobile"
🚗

REFERENTS
1954 MG-TF
Dodge Ramcharger

THINKING ACTIVITY 7.2

Using the model we have developed, diagram the structure of the following concepts, as well as two concepts of your own choosing: *table, dance, successful, student, religion, music, friend,* _____, _____. ◀

FORMING CONCEPTS

Throughout your life you are engaged in the process of forming—and apply-ing—concepts to organize your experience, make sense of what is happening at the moment, and anticipate what may happen in the future. You form concepts by the interactive process of *generalizing* (focusing on the common properties shared by a group of things) and *interpreting* (finding examples of the concept). The common properties form the necessary requirements that must be met in order to apply the concept to your experience. If you examine the diagrams of concepts in the last section, you can see that the process of forming concepts involves moving back and forth between the *referents* (examples) of the concept and the *properties* (common features) shared by all examples of the concept. Let's explore further the way this interactive process of forming concepts operates.

Consider the following sample conversation between two people trying to form and clarify the concept *philosophy.*

A: What is your idea of what *philosophy* means?

B: Well, I think philosophy involves expressing important beliefs that you have—like discussing the meaning of life, assuming that there is a mean-ing.

A: Is explaining my belief about who's going to win the Super Bowl engag-ing in philosophy? After all, this is a belief that is very important to me— I've got a lot of money riding on the outcome!

B: I don't think so. A philosophical belief is usually a belief about something that is important to *everyone*—like what standards we should use to guide our moral choices.

A: What about the message that was in my fortune cookie last night: "Eat, drink, and be merry, for tomorrow we diet!"? This is certainly a belief that most people can relate to, especially during the holiday season! Is this philosophy?

B: I think that's what my grandmother used to call "foolosophy"! Philosophi-cal beliefs are usually deeply felt views that we have given a great deal of thought to—not something plucked out of a cookie.

A: What about my belief in the Golden Rule: "Do unto others as you would have them do unto you," because if you don't, "What goes around comes around." Doesn't that have all of the qualities that you mentioned?

B: Now you've got it!

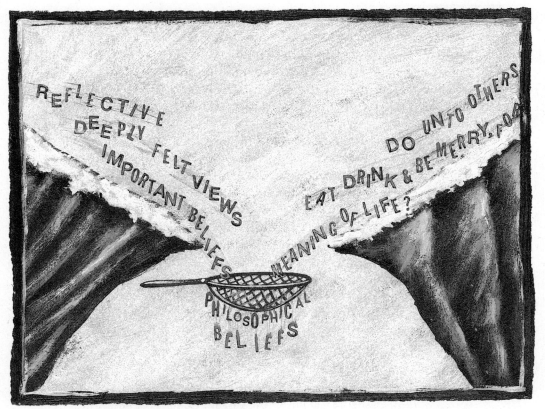

*We form concepts by **generalizing** the defining properties of the concept and **interpreting** as we try to identify examples of the concept.*

As we review this dialogue, we can see that *forming* the concept "philosophical belief" works hand in hand with *applying* the concept to different examples. When two or more things work together in this way, we say that they interact. In this case, there are two parts of this interactive process.

We form concepts by *generalizing*, by focusing on the similar features among different things. In the dialogue just given, the things from which generalizations are being made are kinds of beliefs—beliefs about the meaning of life or standards we use to guide our moral choices. By focusing on the similar features among these beliefs, the two people in the dialogue develop a list of properties philosophical beliefs share, including

- Beliefs that deal with important issues in life that everyone is concerned about

- Beliefs that reflect deeply felt views we have given a great deal of thought to

These common properties act as the *requirements* an area must meet to be considered a philosophical belief.

We apply concepts by *interpreting*, by looking for different examples of the concept and seeing if they meet the requirements of the concept we are developing. In the conversation, one of the participants attempts to apply the concept "philosophical belief" to the following examples:

- A belief about the outcome of the Super Bowl
- A fortune cookie message: "Eat, drink, and be merry, for tomorrow we diet."

Each of the proposed examples suggests the development of new requirements for the concept to help clarify how the concept can be applied. Applying a concept to different possible examples thus becomes the way we develop and gradually sharpen our idea of the concept. Even when a proposed example turns out *not* to be an example of the concept, our understanding of the concept is often clarified. For example, although the proposed example—a belief about the outcome of the Super Bowl—in the dialogue turns out not to be an example of the concept "philosophical belief", examining it as a possible example helps clarify the concept and suggests other examples.

The process of developing concepts involves a constant back-and-forth movement between these two activities:

Generalizing: Focusing on certain similar features among things to develop the requirements for the concept.

Interpreting: Looking for different things to apply the concept to, in order to determine if they "meet the requirements" of the concept we are developing.

As the back-and-forth movement progresses, we gradually develop a specific list of requirements that something must have to be considered an example of the concept and, at the same time, give ourselves a clearer idea of how it is defined. We are also developing a collection of examples that embody the qualities of the concept and demonstrate situations in which the concept applies. This *interactive* process is illustrated in the following figure:

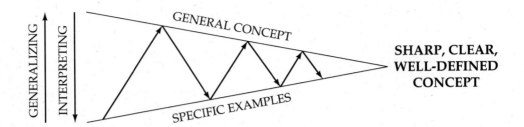

THINKING ACTIVITY 7.3

Select a type of music with which you are familiar (e.g., jazz) and write a dialogue similar to the one just examined. In the course of the dialogue, be sure to include

1. Examples that you are generalizing from (e.g., cool, big band).
2. General properties shared by various types of this music (e.g., jazz's audience spans many generations).
3. Examples to which you are trying to apply the developing concept (e.g., music of Miles Davis or Thelonius Monk). ◀

Forming concepts involves performing both of these operations (generalizing and interpreting) together, because:

- You cannot form a concept unless you know how it might apply. If you have absolutely no idea what *jazz* or *philosophy* might be examples of, then you cannot begin to form the concept, even in vague or general terms.
- You cannot gather up examples of the concept unless you know what they might be examples of. Until you begin to develop some idea of what the concepts *jazz* or *philosophy* might be (based on certain similarities between various things), you will not know where to look for examples of the concept (or how to evaluate them).

This interactive process is the way that you usually form all concepts, particularly the complicated ones. In school, much of your education is focused on carefully forming and exploring key concepts such as *democracy*, *dynamic equilibrium*, and *personality*. This book has also focused on certain key concepts, such as:

- Thinking critically
- Solving problems

- Perceiving
- Believing
- Knowing
- Language

In each case, you have carefully explored these concepts through the interactive process of *generalizing* the properties/requirements of the concept and *interpreting* the concept by examining examples to which the concept applies.

APPLYING CONCEPTS

Making sense of our experience means finding the right concept to explain what is going on. To determine whether the concept we have selected fits the situation, we have to determine whether the requirements that form the concept are being met. For example, the original television series "Superman" used to begin with the words: "Look—up in the sky! It's a bird! It's a plane! No! It's Superman!"

To figure out which concept applies to the situation (so that we can figure out what is going on), we have to

1. Be aware of the properties that form the boundaries of the concept.
2. Determine whether the experience meets those requirements, for only if it does can we apply the concept to it.

In the opening line from "Superman, what are some of the requirements for using the concepts being identified?

- Bird:
- Plane:
- Superman:

If we have the requirements of the concept clearly in mind, we can proceed to figure out which of these requirements are met by the experience—whether it is a bird, a plane, or the "man of steel" himself. This is the way we apply concepts, which is one of the most important ways we figure out what is going on in our experience.

In determining exactly what the requirements of the concept are, we can ask ourselves:

Would something still be an example of this concept if it did not meet this requirement?

The heart of education is learning to form and apply key concepts that enable us to understand the world.

If the answer to this question is no—that is, something would *not* be an example of this concept if it did not meet this requirement—then we can say the requirement is a necessary part of the concept.

Consider the concept *dog*. Which of the following descriptions are requirements of the concept that must be met to say that something is an example of the concept *dog*?

1. Is an animal
2. Normally has four legs and a tail
3. Bites the mail carrier

It is clear that descriptions 1 and 2 are requirements that must be met to apply the concept *dog*, because if we apply our test question—"Would something be an example of this concept if it did not meet this requirement?"— we can say that something would not be an example of the concept *dog* if it did not fit the first two descriptions: if it was not an animal and did not normally have four legs and a tail.

This does not seem to be the case, however, with description 3. If we ask ourselves the same test question, we can see that something might still be an example of the concept *dog even if* it did not bite the mail carrier. This is because even though *some* dogs *do* in fact bite, this is *not* a requirement for being a dog.

Of course, there may be other things that meet these requirements but are not dogs. For example, a cat is an animal (description 1) that normally has four legs and a tail (description 2). What this means is that the requirements of a concept tell us only what something *must* have to be an example of the concept. As a result, we often have to identify additional requirements that will define the concept more sharply. This point is clearly illustrated as children form concepts. Not identifying a sufficient number of the concept's requirements leads to such misconceptions as "All four-legged animals are doggies," or "All yellow-colored metal is gold."

This is why it is so important for us to have a very clear idea of the greatest possible number of specific requirements of each concept. These requirements determine when the concept can be applied and indicate those things that qualify as examples of it. When we are able to identify *all* of the requirements of the concept, we say these requirements are both *necessary* and *sufficient* for applying the concept.

Although dealing with concepts like *dog* and *cat* may seem straightforward, things quickly become more confusing when you start analyzing the more complex concepts that you encounter in your academic study. For example, consider the concepts of *masculinity* and *femininity*, two of the more emotionally charged and politically contentious concepts in our culture. There are many different perspectives on what these concepts mean, what they should mean, or whether we should be using them at all. Identify what you consider to be the essential properties (specific requirements that must be met to apply the concept) for each of these concepts, as well as examples of people or behavior that illustrate these properties. For example, you might identify "physical strength" as a property of the concept *masculinity*, and identify Arnold Swartzenegger as a person who illustrates this quality. Or you might identify "intuitive" as a property of the concept *femininity,* and illustrate this with the behavior of "being able to predict what someone is going to do or say before it occurs."

General Properties   *Specific Examples*

Femininity

1.   1.

2.   2.

3.   3.

Masculinity

1.   1.

2.   2.

3.   3.

Compare your responses to those of the other students in the class. What are the similarities and differences in your concepts? What factors might account for these similarities and differences?

THINKING PASSAGES

The following passages by Susan Brownmiller and Michael Norman deal with the concepts of masculinity and femininity. After reading the passages, analyze the authors' concepts of masculinity and femininity by answering the questions that follow. How do their perspectives on these concepts compare and contrast with your concepts and those of the other members of the class?

It is fashionable in some quarters to describe the feminine and masculine principles as polar ends of the human continuum, and to sagely profess that both polarities exist in all people. Sun and moon, yin and yang, soft and hard, active and passive, etcetera, may indeed be opposites, but a linear continuum does not illuminate the problem. What, then, is the ba-

Some people think that the concepts of masculinity *and* femininity *are outdated relics of earlier cultures, while other people believe that these concepts reflect basic qualities of the human species that are still relevant today.*

sic distinction? The masculine principle is better understood as a driving ethos of superiority designed to inspire straightforward, confident success, while the feminine principle is composed of vulnerability, the need for protection, the formalities of compliance and the avoidance of conflict—in short, an appeal of dependence and good will that gives the masculine principle its romantic validity and admiring applause. Femininity pleases men because it makes them appear more masculine by contrast; and, in truth, conferring an extra portion of unearned gender distinction on men, and unchallenged space in which to breathe freely and feel stronger, wiser, more competent, is femininity's special gift. One could say that masculinity is often an effort to please women, but masculinity is known to please by displays of mastery and competence while femininity pleases by suggesting that these concerns, except in small matters, are beyond its intent. Whimsy, unpredictability and patterns of thinking and behavior that are dominated by emotion, such as tearful expressions of sentiment and fear, are thought to be feminine precisely because they lie outside the established route to success.

—Susan Brownmiller, *Femininity*

From analyst's couch to tavern booth, the message is the same: The male animus is out of fashion. The man of the hour is supposed to be gentle, thoughtful, endearing and compassionate, a wife to his woman, a mother to his son, an androgynous figure with the self-knowledge of a hermaphrodite. He takes his lumps on the psyche, not the chin, and bleeds with emotion. Yes, in the morning, he still puts on a three-piece suit, but his foulard, the finishing touch, is a crying towel. He is so ridden with guilt, so pained about the sexist sins of his kind, he bites at his own flanks. Not only does he say that he dislikes being a man, but broadly proclaims that the whole idea of manhood in America is pitiful. He wants to free himself from the social conditioning of the past, to cast off the yoke of traditional male roles and rise above the banality of rituals learned at boot camp or on the practice field. If science could provide it, he would swallow an antidote of testosterone, something to stop all this antediluvian thumping and bashing. But the fashion for reform, the drive to emasculate macho, has produced a kind of numbing androgyny and has so blurred the lines of gender that I often find myself wanting to emulate some of the women I know—bold, aggressive, vigorous role models.

—Michael Norman, *Standing His Ground* ■

Questions for Analysis

1. According to Susan Brownmiller, what are the properties of the concept *femininity?* What are some examples of this concept?

2. Explain whether you agree with the conceptual properties Brownmiller has identified. What properties of the concept of *femininity* do you think should be included that she has not addressed? Give at least one example of each property you identify.

3. According to Michael Norman, what are the properties of the concept *masculinity?* What are some examples of this concept?

4. Explain whether you agree with the conceptual properties he has identified. What properties of the concept *masculinity* do you think should be included that Norman has not addressed? For each property you identify, give at least one example.

5. Some people feel that the concepts *masculinity* and *femininity* were formed by earlier cultures, are outdated in our current culture, and should be revised. Other people believe that these concepts reflect basic qualities of the human species, just like the sexual differences in other species, and should

not be excessively tampered with. Explain where you stand on this issue and describe the reasons that support your position. ◀

Using Concepts to Classify

When you apply a concept to an object, idea, or experience, you are in effect *classifying* the object, idea, or experience by placing it into the group of things defined by the properties/requirements of the concept. The individual objects, ideas, or experiences belong to no particular class, however, until you classify them. In fact, the same things can often be classified in many different ways. For example, if someone handed you a tomato and asked: "Which class does this tomato belong in, fruit or vegetable?" how would you respond? The fact is, a tomato can be classified as *both* a fruit and a vegetable, depending on your purposes. (Interestingly enough, the government tried at one point to have tomato catsup classified as a vegetable for the school lunch program so that it would not have to provide a regular vegetable as part of a balanced meal!)

Let us consider another example. Imagine that you are walking on undeveloped land with some other people when you come across an area of soggy ground with long grass and rotting trees. One person in your group surveys the parcel and announces: "That's a smelly marsh. All it does is breed mosquitoes. It ought to be covered with landfill and built on, so that we can use it productively." Another member of your group disagrees with the classification "smelly marsh," stating: "This is a wetland of great ecological value. There are many plants and animals that need this area and other areas like it to survive. Wetland areas also help prevent the rivers from flooding by absorbing excess water during heavy rains." Which person is right? Should the wet area be classified as a "smelly marsh" or a "valuable wetland"? Actually, the wet area can be classified both ways. The classification that you select depends on your needs and your interests. Someone active in construction and land development may tend to view the parcel through perceptual lenses that reflect his or her interests and experience and classify it accordingly. On the other hand, someone involved in preserving natural resources will tend to view the same parcel through different lenses and place it in a different category. The diagram on page 330 illustrates how a tree might be "seen" from a variety of perspectives, depending on the interest and experience of those involved.

These examples illustrate that the way you classify reflects and influences the way you see the world, the way you think about the world, and the way you behave in the world. This is true for virtually all the classifications you

From PULP! *Used by permission of Louis Hellman.*

make. Consider the race horse Secretariat, who won the Triple Crown in 1973 and was one of the most famous race horses that ever lived. Which classification should Secretariat be placed into?

- A magnificent thoroughbred
- A substantial investment
- An animal ill equipped for farming
- A descendant of Bold Ruler
- A candidate for the glue factory

You classify many of the things in your experience differently than others do because of your individual needs, interests, and values. For instance, smoking marijuana might be classified by some as "use of a dangerous drug" and by others as a "harmless good time." Some view large cars as "gas guzzlers"; others see the same cars as "safer, more comfortable vehicles." Some people categorize the latest music as "meaningless noise," while others think of it as "creative expression." And so on. The way you classify aspects of your experience reflects the kind of individual you are and the way you think and feel about the world.

You also place people into various classifications. The specific classifications you select depend on who you are and how you see the world. Similarly, each of us is placed into a variety of classifications by different people. For example, here are some of the classifications into which certain people placed me:

Classification	People Who Classify Me
First-born son	My parents
Taxpayer	Internal Revenue Service
Tickler	My son/daughter
Bagel with cream cheese	Restaurant where I pick up my breakfast

List some of the different ways that you can be classified, and identify the people who would classify you that way.

Finally, besides classifying the same thing or event in a variety of different ways, you can classify most *collections* of things in various ways. For example, consider the different ways the members of your class can be classified. You could group them according to their majors, their ages, their food preferences, and so on. The specific categories you would use depend on the purposes of your classification. If you were trying to organize career counseling, then classifying according to majors makes sense. On the other hand, if you were trying to plan the menu for a class party, then food preferences would be the natural category for classification.

Not only do you continually classify things and people into various groups based on the common properties you choose to focus on, you also classify ideas, feelings, actions, and experiences. Explain, for instance, why the killing of another person might be classified in different ways, depending on the circumstances.

Classification	Circumstance	Example
1. Manslaughter	Killing someone accidentally	Driving while intoxicated
2. Self-defense		
3. Premeditated		
4. Mercy killing		
5. Diminished capacity		

Each of these classifications represents a separate legal concept, with its own properties and referents (examples). Of course, even when you understand clearly what the concept means, the complexity of the circumstances often makes it difficult to determine which concept applies. For example, in Chapter 1, "Thinking," you considered a court case that raised complex and disturbing issues. In circumstances like these, trying to identify the appropriate concepts and then to determine which of the further concepts, "guilty" or "innocent," also applies, is a challenging process. This is true of many of life's complex situations: You must work hard at identifying the appropriate concepts to apply to the situations you are trying to make sense of and then be prepared to change or modify these concepts based on new information or better insight.

DEFINING CONCEPTS

When you define a concept, you usually identify the necessary properties/ requirements that determine when the concept can be applied. In fact, the word *definition* is derived from the Latin word meaning "boundary" because that is exactly what a definition does: It gives the boundaries of the territory in your experience that can be described by the concept. For example, a definition of the concept *horse* might include the following requirements:

- Large, strong animal
- Four legs with solid hoofs
- Flowing mane and tail
- Domesticated long ago for drawing or carrying loads, carrying riders, etc.

By understanding the requirements of the concept *horse*, you understand what conditions must be met in order for something to qualify as an example of the concept. This lets you know in what situations you can apply the concept: to the animals running around the racetrack, the animals pulling wagons and carriages, the animals being ridden on the range, and so on. In addition, understanding the requirements lets you know to which things the concept can be applied. No matter how much a zebra looks like a horse, you won't apply the concept *horse* to it if you really understand the definition of the concept involved.

Definitions also often make strategic use of *examples* of the concept being defined. Consider the following definition by Ambrose Bierce:

An edible: Good to eat and wholesome to digest, as a worm to a toad, a toad to a snake, a snake to a pig, a pig to a man, and a man to a worm.

Contrast this definition with the one illustrated in the following passage from Charles Dickens's *Hard Times:*

> "Bitzer" said Thomas Gradgrind. "Your definition of a horse." "Quadruped. Graminivorous. Forty teeth, namely twenty-four grinders, four eye teeth, and twelve incisive. Sheds coat in the spring; in marshy countries shed hoofs, too. Hoofs hard, but requiring to be shod with iron. Age known by marks in mouth." That (and much more) Bitzer. "Now girl number twenty," said Mr. Gradgrind, "you know what a horse is."

Although Bitzer has certainly done an admirable job of listing some of the necessary properties/requirements of the concept *horse*, it is unlikely that "girl number twenty" has any better idea of what a horse is than she had before because the definition relies exclusively on a technical listing of the properties characterizing the concept *horse* without giving any examples that might illustrate the concept more completely. Definitions like this that rely exclusively on a technical description of the concept's properties are often not very helpful unless you already know what the concept means. A more concrete way of communicating the concept *horse* would be to point out various animals that qualify as horses and other animals that do not. You could also explain why they do not. (For example, "That can't be a horse because it has two humps and its legs are too long and skinny.")

Although examples do not take the place of a clearly understood definition, they are often very useful in clarifying, supplementing, and expanding such a definition. If someone asked you, "What is a horse?" and you replied by giving examples of different kinds of horses (thoroughbred racing horses, plow horses for farming, quarter horses for cowboys, hunter horses for fox hunting, circus horses), you certainly would be communicating a good portion of the meaning of *horse.* Giving examples of a concept complements and clarifies the necessary requirements for the correct use of that concept. For example, provide a dictionary definition for each of the following concepts, and describe ways you could supplement and expand each definition.

Example: Smile

a. Definition: A facial expression characterized by an upward curving of the corners of the mouth and indicating pleasure, amusement, or derision.

b. Ways to expand the definition: Smiling at someone or drawing a picture of a smiling face.

- *Ambivalent*
- *Intelligent*
- *Art*
- *Thinking*
- *Work*
- *Create*

DEFINING A CONCEPT

Giving an effective definition of a concept means both

- Identifying the general qualities of the concept, which determine when it can be correctly applied.
- Using appropriate examples to demonstrate actual applications of the concept—that is, examples that embody the general qualities of the concept

---

The process of providing definitions of concepts is thus the same process you use to develop concepts. Of course, this process is often difficult and complex, and people don't always agree on how concepts should be defined. For example, consider the concepts *masculinity* and *femininity* that you explored earlier through the passages by Susan Brownmiller and Michael Norman. Notice how although areas of overlap exist between each author's definitions, there are also significant differences in the defining properties and examples that they identify.

THINKING ACTIVITY 7.4

 Review the ideas we have explored in this chapter by analyzing the concept *responsibility*. "Responsibility" is a complex idea that has an entire network of meaning. The word comes from the Latin word *respondere*, which means "to pledge or promise."

Generalizing

1. Describe two important responsibilities you have in your life and identify the qualities they embody that lead you to think of them as "responsibilities."

2. Describe a person in your life whom you think is responsible and describe a person in your life whom you think is irresponsible. In reflecting on these individuals, identify the qualities they embody that lead you to think of them as "responsible" and "irresponsible."

Interpreting

3. Consider the following situations. In each case, describe what you consider to be examples of responsible behavior and irresponsible behavior. Be sure to explain the reasons for your answer.
   a. You are a member of a group of three students who are assigned the task of writing a report on a certain topic. Your life is very hectic and in addition you find the topic dull. What is your response? Why?
   b. You are employed at a job in which you observe your supervisor and other employees engaged in activities that break the company rules. You are afraid that if you "blow the whistle" you might lose your job. What is your response? Why?

Defining

4. Using these activities of generalizing and interpreting as a foundation, define the concepts *responsible* and *irresponsible* by listing the qualities that make up the boundaries of the concept and identifying the key examples that embody and illustrate the qualities of the concept. ◀

THINKING PASSAGE

In the following article, "Suicide Solution," the columnist Anna Quindlen analyzes how the concept of *responsibility* is used—and misused—in our culture. After reading the article, answer the questions that follow.

SUICIDE SOLUTION
by Anna Quindlen

It was two days before Christmas when Jay Vance blew the bottom of his face off with a shotgun still slippery with his best friend's blood. He went second. Ray Belknap went first. Ray died and Jay lived, and people said that when you looked at Jay's face afterward it was hard to tell which of them got the worst of the deal. "He just had no luck," Ray's mother would later say of her son to a writer from Rolling Stone, which was a considerable understatement.

Jay and Ray are both dead now. They might be only two of an end-less number of American teen-agers in concert T-shirts who drop out of school and live from album to album and beer to beer, except for two things. The first was that they decided to kill themselves as 1985 drew to a close.

The second is that their parents decided to blame it on rock-and-roll.

When it was first filed in Nevada, the lawsuit brought by the fami-lies of Jay Vance and Ray Belknap against the members of the English band Judas Priest and their record company was said to be heavy metal on trial. I would love to convict heavy metal of almost anything—I would rather be locked in a room with 100 accordion players than listen to Metallica—but music has little to do with this litigation. It is a sad attempt by grieving grown-ups to say, in a public forum, what their lost boys had been saying privately for years: someone's to blame for my failures, but it can't be me.

The product liability suit, which sought $6.2 million in damages, contended that the boys were "mesmerized" by subliminal suicide mes-sages on a Judas Priest album. The most famous subliminal before this case came to trial was the section of a Beatles song that fans believed hinted at the death of Paul McCartney. The enormous interest that surrounded this seems terribly silly now, when Paul McCartney, far from being dead, has become the oldest living cute boy in the world.

There is nothing silly about the Judas Priest case, only something infinitely sad. Ray Belknap was 18. His parents split up before he was born. His mother has been married four times. Her last husband beat Ray with a belt and, according to police, once threatened her with a gun while Ray watched. Like Jay Vance, Ray had a police record and had quit high school after two years. Like Jay, he liked guns and beer and used mari-juana, hallucinogens and cocaine.

Jay Vance, who died three years after the suicide attempt, his face a reconstructed Halloween mask, had had a comparable coming of age. His mother was 17 when he was born. When he was a child, she beat him often. As he got older, he beat her back. Once, checking himself into a detox center, he was asked "What is your favorite leisure time activity?" He answered "Doing drugs." Jay is said to have consumed two six-packs of beer a day. There's a suicide note if I ever heard one.

It is difficult to understand how anyone could blame covert musical mumbling for what happened to these boys. On paper they had little to live for. But the truth is that their lives were not unlike the lives of many kids who live for their stereos and their beer buzz, who open the door to the corridor of the next 40 years and see a future as empty and truncated as a closet. "Get a life," they say to one another. In the responsibility department, no one is home.

They are legion. Young men kill someone for a handful of coins, then are remorseless, even casual: hey, man, things happen. And their parents nab the culprit: it was the city, the cops, the system, the crowd, the music. Anyone but him. Anyone but me. There's a new product on the market I call Parent In A Can. You can wipe a piece of paper on something in your kid's room and then spray the paper with this chemical. Cocaine traces, and the paper will turn turquoise. Marijuana, reddish brown. So easy to use—and no messy heart-to-heart talks, no constant parental presence. Only $44.95 plus $5 shipping and handling to do in a minute what you should have been doing for years.

In the Judas Priest lawsuit, it's easy to see how kids get the idea that they are not responsible for their actions. They inherit it. Heavy metal music is filled with violence, but Jay and Ray got plenty of that even with the stereo unplugged. The trial judge ruled that the band was not responsible for the suicides, but the families are pressing ahead with an appeal, looking for absolution for the horrible deaths of their sons. Heavy metal made them do it—not the revolving fathers, the beatings, the alcohol, the drugs, a failure of will or of nurturing. Someone's to blame. Someone else. Always someone else. ■

Questions for Analysis

1. Describe Quindlen's definition of the concept *responsibility* by listing the qualities that make up the boundaries of the concept for her and identifying the key examples she uses to illustrate the qualities of the concept.

2. Compare Quindlen's definition of the concept *responsibility* with the definition that you developed in Thinking Activity 7.4.

3. Do you think that music can influence people to commit suicide or engage in illegal activities? If so, do you believe that the people who make the music should be held legally responsible for its effects? Explain the reasons for your conclusions.

4. Teen-age depression and suicide is a significant and tragic national problem. Explain what you believe are the major factors responsible for this problem and describe what you think are effective strategies for solving this problem.

Relating Concepts with Mind Maps

Suppose someone handed you a pencil and a piece of paper with the request "Please draw me a detailed map that shows how to get to where you live from where we are now." Draw such a map on a separate sheet of paper.

Maps, like the one you just drew, are really groups of symbols organized in certain relationships. In creating your visual map, you tried both to represent *and* to organize various aspects of your experience into a pattern that made sense to you and to others. As you constructed your map, you probably traveled the route home "in your mind," trying to recall the correct turns, street names, buildings, and so on. You then symbolized these experiences and organized the symbols into a meaningful pattern—your map.

You can see that the activity of making maps draws on two skills needed for making sense of your world:

- Representing your experience with symbols
- Organizing and relating these symbols into various patterns to gain an increased understanding of your experience

Creating maps is thus a way to represent and organize experience so that you can make sense of it, and it is a strategy you can apply to many different areas of your world. For example, you can create maps of your mind—"mind maps" that express the patterns of your thinking processes.

A mind map is a visual presentation of the ways concepts can be related to one another.

Mind Map   A visual presentation of the ways concepts can be related to one another.

For example, each chapter in this book opens with a diagram—what we will call a "mind map"—that visually summarizes the chapter's basic concepts as well as the way these concepts are related to each other. These maps are a reference guide that reveals basic themes and chapter organization.

Maps for Reading

Because they clearly articulate various patterns of thought, mind maps are effective tools for helping us understand complex bodies of information, either through reading or through listening. For example, consider the first paragraph from the essay "Your Two-Sided Brain."

One of the most intriguing areas of scientific and educational exploration concerns the manner in which our brain processes information. It has been known for a long time that the brain is divided into two seemingly identical halves, usually termed the left hemisphere and the right hemisphere. Until recently, it was assumed that these two hemispheres were similar in the way that they operated. However, a variety of current research has shown conclusively that each hemisphere has a distinct "personality," processing information in its own unique way.

How would you represent the concepts and their relationships presented in this passage? Take a piece of paper and pencil and develop at least one mind map. This diagram illustrates one possible rendering:

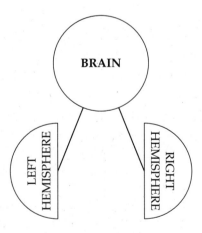

Now review the next paragraph of the essay, which focuses in on the qualities of the brain's left hemisphere.

The left hemisphere exhibits those qualities that we normally associate with higher intellectual activities. For example, the left hemisphere functions analytically, tending to break things and processes down into component parts, like taking apart an automobile engine in order to diagnose the problem. The left hemisphere is also the seat of most of our verbal activity, decoding and encoding the bulk of our language, mathematical symbols, and musical notations. Finally, the left hemisphere tends to process information in a linear, sequential way, one step at a time. This is consistent with the verbal capacities which it exhibits, since language is spoken/heard/read one word at a time, and the meaning of the words depends in large measure on the order in which the words are placed. In short, the left hemisphere is similar to a modern, digital computer in that its individual operations unfold in an orderly, logical sequence.

Expand the mind map you developed for the first paragraph of the essay to include this additional information. Your ideas should be written either on lines connected to other lines, or within shapes connected by lines, to express clearly the relationship between the various ideas. Print the ideas in capital letters so that they can be easily read and referred to. Here is a sample of how the first mind map on page 339 might be elaborated to integrate this new information. Complete the information that has been omitted.

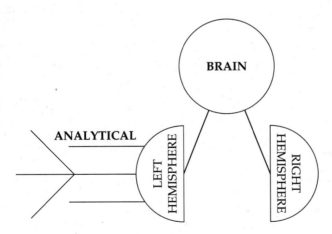

Now read the next paragraph of the essay, which describes the qualities of the right hemisphere and compares these qualities to those of the left hemisphere.

The right hemisphere operates in a much different fashion. Instead of analyzing things and processes into component parts, it seeks to synthesize by organizing parts into patterns and wholes—like arranging individual flowers into a floral arrangement. The right hemisphere normally has much less to do with verbal activity. Instead, it is much more visually oriented, focusing on shapes, arrangements, and images. It also processes information based on what you personally experience with all of your senses (including touch). So, for example, while the left hemisphere might enable you to remember people by their name, the right hemisphere might enable you to recognize them by their face or the feel of their handshake. Finally, rather than processing information in a linear, sequential fashion, the right hemisphere tends to organize information into patterns and relationships which are experienced as a whole. For instance, in listening to music, the right hemisphere focuses on the overall melody rather than the individual notes, or on the pattern of play on the chessboard rather than the individual pieces. While we compared the linear functioning of the left hemisphere to a digital computer, we might compare the functioning of the right hemisphere to a kaleidoscope, as it continually works to organize information into meaningful shapes and patterns.

Using the mind map you created for the first two paragraphs of the essay as a starting point, expand your map by including this new information. In composing your map, be sure to represent the relationships between the various qualities of the two hemispheres. Complete the missing information in the spaces provided on this sample final map:

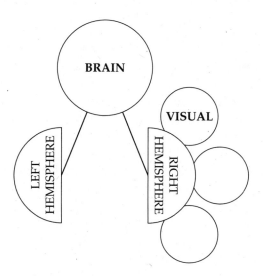

The final paragraph of the essay moves into a new direction, relating the information you have been reading (and thinking about) to education. Read this paragraph and then incorporate the ideas it presents into the mind map you have created for the essay.

> The modern research into how our brain functions has significant implications for human learning. Much of our education is structured for left hemisphere thinking—analytical, verbal, logical, and sequential. Yet much of our understanding about the world is based on the activities of the right hemisphere—synthesizing, visual, experiential, and pattern-seeking. If education is to become as effective as possible, it must introduce teaching methods that address the right hemisphere as well as the left hemisphere.

Maps for Note-taking

Clearly, creating mind maps can be a useful strategy in helping you understand complex written information. This versatile tool, however, is not limited to reading; it has other language uses as well—for example, organizing and interpreting spoken information. When people read and hear language, they normally do not try to interpret one word at a time, unless they are beginning to learn a new language. Instead, when we read and listen we typically group words together in "chunks" of meaning, trying to make sense of the *entire* meaning the words express. For instance, when you read the last two sentences, did you try to understand them one word at a time, or did you try to make sense of the complete ideas being expressed? In all likelihood, you tried to interpret the overall meaning being expressed, including the relationships among the various ideas.

The same is true when you speak. Although you pronounce the words one at a time, they form part of an entire meaning and network of relationships you are trying to express. Again, examine your thinking process as you attempt to explain an idea to someone. Are you thinking one word at a time, or do you find there is a complex process of examining, sorting, and relating the various words to express the meaning you are trying to communicate? Probably the latter.

Based on these considerations, you can see that a mapping approach offers some clear advantages in organizing the information you receive from oral communication. For instance, when you as a student take notes of what a teacher is speaking about, you may find that you try to copy down sentences and quotes the teacher has said. When you return to study these notes, you may find the notes are not adequate because they do not include the various relationships among the ideas expressed. Using a mapping approach to note-taking will help provide you with the means for identifying the key ideas and their relationships.

Maps for Oral Presentations

Mapping is also an effective aid in preparing for oral presentations. By organizing the information you want to present in this way, you have all the key ideas and their relationships in a single whole. Probably the greatest fear of people making oral presentations is that they will "get stuck" or lose their train of thought. If you have a clear map of the main ideas and their relationships either in your mind or in notes, the chances of this sort of "freeze-up" are considerably reduced.

One of the advantages of using maps is that, once you have constructed them, you can place the ideas in whatever order you may need by simply numbering them or circling them in different colors. As a result, a map not only represents all the key ideas and their relationships simultaneously, it can also be used to construct more traditional outlines or speaking notes.

Maps for Writing

Along with reading, listening, and speaking, mapping is useful for writing. *First*, the organization grows naturally, reflecting the way your mind naturally makes associations and organizes information. *Second*, the organization can be easily revised on the basis of new information and your developing understanding of how this information should be organized. *Third*, you can express a range of relationships among the various ideas. And instead of being identified once and then forgotten, each idea remains an active part of the overall pattern, suggesting new possible relationships. *Fourth*, you do not have to decide initially on a beginning, subpoints, subsubpoints, and so on; you can do this after your pattern is complete, saving time and frustration. Let's explore how mind mapping can be used in the writing process through the following activity.

Review the last paragraph of the essay "Your Two-Sided Brain" on page 342. The author's point is that effective education must involve teaching methods that make use of learning activities associated with the functions of the right hemisphere. In other words, whereas traditional education places emphasis on left-hemisphere activities (analytical, verbal, logical, and sequential), the most effective education will also include right-hemisphere activities (synthesizing, visual, experiential, and pattern-seeking). Let's explore this idea further.

A useful first step to any writing project is *brainstorming*, an activity in which, working individually or with a group of people, you write down as many ideas as you can think of related to a given theme. The goal is to produce as many ideas as possible in a specified period of time. While you are engaged in this idea-generating process, it is important to relax, let your mind run free, build on the ideas of others, and refrain from censoring or evaluating any ideas produced, no matter how marginal they seem at first. Working by yourself or with other class members, brainstorm as many examples of right hemisphere learning activities as you can think of in a five-minute period. Some initial ideas to get you started are:

View films and video	Use diagrams
Go on field trips	Engage in role-playing
Design group activities	Integrate music into lesson
Use meditation to increase concentration	Identify patterns in content

After completing your brainstorming list, create a mind map that begins to organize the ideas you have developed. Start with the main idea ("Right Hemisphere Learning Activities") in the center and then develop branches that present your ideas as well as the relationships between these ideas. As you do this, new ideas are likely to occur to you, for the act of creating mind maps also often generates ideas. In working on your map, try to relax your mind as much as possible, letting the ideas and associations flow freely. As you complete your map, look for possible connections among different branches. This strategy often suggests relationships you might not have thought of before. Here is a sample of the beginning of such a map. Once your map is more or less complete, you have laid the foundation for your writing assignment, which is described in the following Thinking Activity.

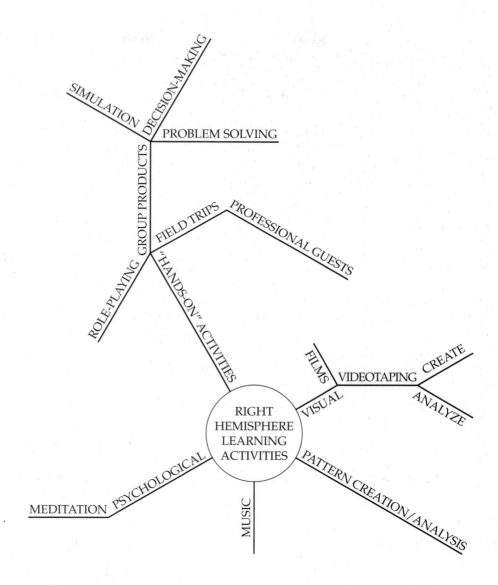

THINKING ACTIVITY 7.5

Review your map and select the ideas and relationships you want to include and how you want to organize this information. You may want to use an outline to represent this organization. Once you have made an outline, you can begin to express your ideas using full sentences and paragraphs. Use the following format to structure your assignment.

What is your point?	(Explain the concept of right-hemisphere learning activities.)
Prove it to me!	(Give examples of these learning activities and explain why you think they would be useful.)
So what!	(Conclude your paper with a closing summary.)

After writing the first draft of your paper, review it carefully to see if you can explain your ideas more clearly or provide additional examples to illustrate your points. ◀

Summary

In the same way that words are the vocabulary of language, concepts are the vocabulary of thought. Concepts are general ideas that we use to bring order and intelligibility to our experience. As organizers of our experience, concepts work in conjunction with language to identify, describe, distinguish, and relate all the various aspects of our world. They give us the means to understand our world and make informed decisions, to think critically and act intelligently.

To become a sophisticated thinker, you must develop expertise in the conceptualizing process, improving your ability to:

- *Form* concepts, through the interactive process of generalizing and interpreting
- *Apply* concepts, by matching their necessary requirements to potential examples
- *Relate* concepts to each other in various patterns

This complex conceptualizing process is going on all the time in our minds, enabling us to think in a distinctly human way.

By understanding the conceptualizing process, you can more fully appreciate the integral relationship between language and thought that you have been exploring in these last two chapters, the way in which these two processes work as one to create meaning and understanding. In the same way that words are combined according to the rules of language to produce an infinite variety of linguistic expression, so concepts are related according to the patterns of thought to create the infinite dimensions of thinking.

The remaining chapters of this text will focus on the rules and patterns of thought that determine the way concepts are combined and organized in complex relationships to produce the highest, most sophisticated levels of human thinking.

THINKING PASSAGE

There are few concepts more complex and emotionally charged than the concept of *religion.* The following passage, "What Is Religion?" is taken from the book *Ways of Being Religious,* and it presents a provocative introduction to the concepts *religion* and *religious experience.* After reading the selection, answer the questions that follow.

An African proverb, from the Ganda tribe in central Uganda, states, "He who never visits thinks his mother is the only cook." As with most proverbs, its meaning is larger than the explicit subjects referred to—in this case food and visiting. It suggests that a person is much the poorer for not having had exposure to and acquaintance with the ways of other people.

All of us have had some acquaintance with religious people, just as we have tasted our mother's food. But do we really understand very well what it means to be religious? The "Father of the Scientific Study of Religion," Max Mueller, once said: "He who knows one religion understands none." That is perhaps too extreme a statement as it stands, and yet it says about the study of religion what the African proverb says about the knowledge of life in general—that we sacrifice much if we confine ourselves to the familiar.

If a visit is to be fruitful, the "traveler" must do more than just move from place to place. He must respond to what he sees. But what is it that shapes the way we respond to new experiences? Our perception of things is often colored by our previous attitudes toward them. In this case, what do you, the reader, expect from an exposure to various expressions of religion? What sorts of things do you expect to see? How do you think you will respond to them? If you were asked to define, illustrate, or to characterize religious behavior, how would you do so? The answers to these questions, of course, reflect your pre-conceptions. To become conscious of your preconceptions, ask yourself the following four questions:

Does your definition* reduce *religion to what you happen to be acquainted with by accident of birth and socialization? Perhaps that goes without saying. It may be true of anyone's "off-the cuff" definition of religion. However, we ask this question to encourage you to consider whether your definition has sufficient *scope.* Is it broad enough to include the religious activities of human beings throughout the world? In surveying university students we have commonly gotten responses to the question, "What is religion?" as follows: "Being Christian, I would define it [religion] as personal relationship with Christ." "Religion [is]: God, Christ, and Holy Ghost and their meaning to each individual." Other students think of worship rather than belief. In this vein, one edition of Webster's dictionary, in the first of its definitions, describes religion as "the service and adoration of God or a god as expressed in forms of worship." If we were to accept any of the above definitions, many people in the world would be excluded—people who regard some of their most important activities as religious, but who do not focus upon a deity. That is to say, not all religions are theistic. It remains to be seen, of course, whether and what to extent this is true. But let us all be warned of taking our habits or our dictionary as the sole resource for defining religion. In some areas, the main lines of significant understanding are already well established. Therefore we have no serious quarrel with Webster's definition of food as "nutritive material taken into an organism for growth, work, or repair and for maintaining the vital processes." But in religion, interpretive concepts are more problematical. Therefore we are suspicious of the adequacy of the dictionary's definition of religion.

Another common way to define religion is to regard it as "morality plus stories," or "morality plus emotion." These are ways of asserting that religion has to do mainly with ethics, or that its myths merely support the particular views of a people. There are, of course, persons for whom religion has been reduced to ethics, as when Thomas Paine stated (in *The Rights of Man*): "My country is the world, and my religion is to do good." But we should be cautious in assuming that this testimony would do for all religious people.

A final example of a definition that begins with personal experience is one that claims: "Religion is a feeling of security"; or, as one student put it: "Religion is an aid in coping with that part of life which man does not understand, or in some cases a philosophy of life enabling man to live more deeply." In locating the basis of religion in man's need for a sense of security, this approach suggests that the deepest study of religion is through psychology. It has been dramatically expressed by the psychiatrist and writer C. G. Jung when he wrote: "Religion is a relationship to the highest or strongest value . . . the value by which you are possessed unconsciously. That psychological fact which is the greatest power in your system is the god, since it is always the overwhelming psychic factor which is called "god." Although this understanding of religion expresses a very important point, many theologians and religious philosophers point out that an interpretation that reduces all of religious experience to psychological, biological, or social factors omits the central reality exposed in that experience—the Sacred or Ultimate Reality. Thus, a student of religion should keep open the question of whether a familiar interpretation of religious life that fits into a conventional, social science perspective of man is adequate for interpreting the data.

Does your definition reflect a **bias** *on your part—positive or negative—toward religion as a whole, or toward a particular religion?* There are many examples of biased definitions that could be cited. Some equate religion with superstition, thus reflecting a negative evaluation. One man defined religion as "the sum of the scruples which impede the free exercise of the human faculties." Another hostile view of religion is to see religion as a device of priests to keep the masses in subjection and themselves in comfort. Similarly, Karl Marx, while not actually attempting to define religion, called it "the opiate of the people," again reflecting a bias against (all) religion.

Still others, in defining religion, are stating their concept of *true* religion as opposed to what they regard as false or pagan faiths. Henry Fielding, in his novel *Tom Jones,* has the provincial parson Mr. Thwackum saying, "When I mention religion I mean the Christian religion; and not only the Christian religion, but the Protestant religion; and not only the Protestant religion; but the Church of England." Some Christians assume that their personal conviction comprises a definition of religion, so the religion is regarded as "the worship of God through his Son Jesus Christ," or "a personal relationship with Christ." A Muslim can point out that the essence of religion is to make peace with God through complete submission to God's will, a submission that he will insist is brought to fulfillment in Islam. (In Arabic the word "Islam" means "submission," "peace," "safety," and "salvation.")

Therefore the student interested in reflecting on religious experience that includes more than a single institutional or cultural expression should remember the distinction between descriptive (neutral) and evaluative definitions. A descriptive definition attempts to be as inclusive as possible about a class of items, such as religious forms. An evaluative definition, on the other hand, reflects one's own criteria for truth or falsity, for reality or illusion. In "visiting" religious people, we suggest that you delay making an evaluation until you have understood why their expressions and processes have profound meaning for them—however strange those expressions may seem to you. In the final analysis, each person must evaluate different religious alternatives; but one of our goals in bringing together the material in this volume is to provide you with a variety of options—a variety that is reduced if you limit religion to any single historical expression.

Obviously the believer who advocates one religion to the exclusion of all others differs sharply from one who rejects all. Nevertheless, if either accepts his own convictions about what is best or worst in religion as a description of what religion in fact is everywhere and for everyone, he exhibits a common indifference to unfamiliar, and therefore potentially surprising, religious patterns. As a believer (or skeptic), you have a right to declare your own understanding of what is most important, most real, in religion. This declaration is, in fact, essential, for it guides you in your quest for whatever is most real in life. As a student, on the other hand, you have an obligation to carry your studies as far as necessary to include relevant data. In this role, your obligation is not only to your own perception of value but also to a common world of understanding in which men of many religious persuasions can converse with each other.

Does your definition **limit** *religion to what it has been in the past, and nothing else, or does your definition make it possible to speak of emerging forms of religion?* In asking this question, we should observe two striking facts of the history of religion: there was a time when some present religions did not exist, and some of the religions which once emerged no longer exist (for example, the Egyptian and Babylonian religions). Human history, then, has witnessed the emergence and abandonment of several religions.

Even religious traditions that have maintained a sense of continuity over vast stretches of time (Hinduism, Buddhism, Judaism, Christianity, for example) have undergone important changes. Is it really as obvious as we tend to think that they are essentially the same now as they were at their origins? Do the terms naming these traditions even today point to a single entity, however complex? You are familiar with at least some instances of religious warfare *within* the Christian tradition. Roman Catholics have persecuted and killed Lutherans; Lutherans have persecuted and killed Calvinists; Calvinists, Anglicans; Anglicans, Quakers; and most have returned the act with interest. Are all of these groups expressions of "the one true church"? Are some more Christian than others? Is there only one form of Christianity? Are new movements violations of the tradition? Or is the one who speaks to his own time the one who is most faithful to the genius of his tradition? These questions can be asked of all religious traditions. All have experienced change and diversity. Furthermore, it seems likely that this will continue, and that new religious traditions will emerge. Therefore, the conventions of the past cannot be regarded as the limits of future religious forms.

In part because history has witnessed the emergence and internal changes of many religions, anthropologists and cultural historians commonly suggest that religion (and human culture in general) has attained only its adolescence. Likewise, philosophers and religious thinkers in both East and West point to the anxiety and tensions today that are expressed in political, social, economic, and intellectual upheaval. They raise a question of whether or not man's moral, psychic, and evaluative resources can catch up with his self-destructive potential seen in technologically advanced weapons and psychological-chemical techniques for social control. The most hopeful of these philosophers perceive the present turmoil as a lack of "maturity" in human consciousness, and express the hope that it is not too late (quite) to change the direction of man from self-destruction to self-fulfillment.

From this perspective most of mankind's experience is still in the future. The history of religious life to the present is only a beginning. But the basis of these projections is the recognition that man's survival requires him to recognize religious dynamics and processes for evaluations as major forces in human life. Should not a definition of religion aid us in looking at contemporary phenomena to see if any new ways of being religious are emerging? At least it should not inhibit persons with an interest in this matter, and we think an introduction to religion should encourage such reflection.

Does your definition have sufficient precision? Are there any limits to the scope of religion, or are the limits so vague that they fail to mark out an object of study? In an attempt to be as broadminded as possible, many definitions are like a student's statement that religion is "the means man has of coping with his world." Or they are similar to the claim that religion is "believing in a way of life which involves understanding and caring for others," or "religion is love." Such definitions tell us a good deal, but without some qualification they might refer to many other expressions of human life than specifically religious ones. In order to find a focus and a set of limitations at the outer circumference of that focus, we need to designate what are those essential elements of religion that will expose the *religious* meaning of the evidence we look at.

When one has "visited" (seen) a wide range of religious life, from all parts of the world and throughout human history, it becomes apparent that religion is a way of life that involves many processes—all of which, in different ways, are directed toward a common end. The goal is to reach a state of being that is conceived to be the highest possible state or condition. Religion is the general term for the various ways by which people seek to become changed into that highest state. We understand *religion as a means toward ultimate transformation.* By this we are not claiming that every activity you think of as religious will in fact transform you ultimately. It might, but that is not our point. We mean that *any* reasonably specific means that *any* persons adopts with the serious hope and intention of moving toward ultimate transformation should be termed "religious." We think it possible to speak of all religious activity (Eastern and Western, past, present, and emerging) without reducing religion to what is merely familiar to us and without putting a value judgment on one or more religions. ■

Questions for Analysis

1. Describe your concept of *religion* as specifically as possible. Where did the concept originate for you? How did it evolve as you have matured? Explain the reasons or experiences that support your concept.

2. Evaluate your concept of *religion* by answering the four questions posed in the Thinking Passage:
   - Does your definition *reduce* religion to what you happen to be acquainted with by accident of birth and socialization?
   - Does your definition reflect a *bias* on your part—positive or negative— toward religion as a whole, or toward a particular religion?
   - Does your definition *limit* religion to what it has been in the past and nothing else, or does your definition make it possible to speak of emerging forms of religion?
   - Does your definition have sufficieint precision?

3. Compare your definition of religion to the definitions of other students in your class. What are the similarities? What are the differences? How do you explain these similarities and differences?

4. In the Thinking Passage, religion is defined as a "means toward ultimate transformation." What do you think this definition means? Explain how this definition relates to your definition. ◀

CHAPTER

8

RELATING AND ORGANIZING

RELATING AND ORGANIZING:
Using thinking patterns to
make sense of the world

**Chronological and
Process Relationships:**
Organizing events or ideas
in terms of time

**Comparative and
Analogical Relationships:**
Focusing on the similarities
and/or dissimilarities among
different objects, events, or ideas

Causal Relationships:
Relating events in terms of
the influence or effect they
have on one another

THROUGHOUT THIS BOOK we have been considering and experiencing the insight that each one of us is a "creator." Each of us is actively shaping—as well as discovering—the world we live in. Our world does not exist as a finished product, waiting for us to perceive it, think about it, and describe it with words and pictures. Instead, we are *active participants* in composing the world that seems so familiar to us.

The goal of this composing process is to organize your world into meaningful patterns that will help you figure out what is going on and what you ought to do. Composing your world involves all the activities that we have been exploring, including

perceiving	symbolizing	interpreting
believing	describing	conceptualizing
knowing	classifying	defining
solving problems	generalizing	analyzing

Although you are usually unaware that you are performing these activities, your ability to think critically gives you the means to examine the different ways by which you are making sense of the world so that you can develop and sharpen your understanding. As you actively discover and compose various patterns, what you are really doing is exploring the ways in which different aspects of your experience *relate* to each other.

Ideas, things, and events in the world can be related and organized in a variety of ways. For example, different individuals might take the same furniture and decorations in the same space and arrange them in many different ways, reflecting each person's needs, ways of thinking, and aesthetic preferences. Or, to take another example, a class of students may write essays about the same subject and yet create widely differing results.

All these ways of relating and organizing reflect basic thinking patterns that you rely on constantly when you think, act, or use language. These basic thinking patterns are an essential part of your process of composing and making sense of the world. We will explore three basic ways of relating and organizing in this chapter.

Chronological and Process Relationships

- Chronological—relating events in time sequence
- Process—relating aspects of the growth or development of an event or object

Comparative and Analogical Relationships

- Comparative—relating things in the same general category in terms of similarities and dissimilarities
- Analogical—relating things belonging to different categories in terms of each other

Causal Relationships

- Causal—relating events in terms of the way some event(s) are responsible for bringing about other event(s)

These basic thinking patterns (and others besides) play an active role in the way you perceive, shape, and organize your world to make it understandable to you. The specific patterns you use to organize your ideas in thinking, writing, and speaking depend on the subject you are exploring, the goals you are aiming for, the type of writing or speaking you are doing, and the audience who will be reading or listening to your work. In most cases, you will use a variety of basic patterns in thinking, writing, and speaking to organize and relate the ideas you are considering.

CHRONOLOGICAL AND PROCESS RELATIONSHIPS

Chronological and process patterns of thinking organize events or ideas in terms of their occurrence in time, though the two patterns tend to differ in focus or emphasis. The *chronological* pattern of thinking organizes something into a series of events in the sequence in which they occurred. For example, when you describe an experience you have had in the order it occurred, you are describing it chronologically. On the other hand, the *process* mode of thinking organizes an activity into a series of steps necessary for reaching a certain goal. Here the focus is on describing aspects of the growth, development, or change of something, as you might do when explaining how to prepare your favorite dish or perform a new dance.

Chronological Relationships

The simplest examples of chronological descriptions are logs or diaries, in which people record things that occurred at given points in time. The oldest and most universal form of chronological expression is the *narrative*, a way of thinking and communicating in which someone tells a story about experiences he or she has had. (Of course, the person telling the story can be a *fictional* character, created by a writer who is using a narrative form.) Every human culture has used narratives to pass on values and traditions from one generation to the next, exemplified by such enduring works as the *Odyssey* and the Bible. The word *narrative* is derived from the Latin word for "to know." Narrators are people who "know" what happened because they were there to experience it firsthand (or spoke to people who were there) and who share this experience with you.

One of America's great storytellers, Mark Twain, once said that a good story has to accomplish something and arrive somewhere. In other words, if a story is to be effective in engaging the interest of the audience, it has to have a purpose. The purpose may be to provide more information on a subject, to illustrate an idea, to lead us to a particular way of thinking, or merely to entertain us. An effective story does not merely record the complex, random, and often unrelated events of life. Instead, it has focus and purpose, possesses an ordered structure (a *plot)*, and expresses a meaningful point of view.

THINKING PASSAGE

Review the following narrative by Maria Muniz, which uses chronological examples of thinking and expression, and then answer the questions that follow.

BACK, BUT NOT HOME
by Maria Muniz

With all the talk about resuming diplomatic relations with Cuba, and with the increasing number of Cuban exiles returning to visit friends and relatives, I am constantly being asked, "Would you ever go back?" In turn, I have asked myself, "Is there any reason for me to go? I have had to think long and hard before finding my answer. Yes.

I came to the United States with my parents when I was almost five years old. We left behind grandparents, aunts, uncles and several cousins. I grew up in a very middle-class neighborhood in Brooklyn. With one exception, all my friends were Americans. Outside of my family, I do not know many Cubans. I often feel awkward visiting relatives in Miami because it is such a different world. The way of life in Cuban Miami seems very strange to me and I am accused of being too "Americanized." Yet, although I am now an American citizen, whenever anyone has asked me my nationality, I have always and unhesitatingly replied, "Cuban."

Outside American, inside Cuban.

I recently had a conversation with a man who generally sympathizes with the Castro regime. We talked of Cuban politics and although the discussion was very casual, I felt an old anger welling inside. After 16 years of living an "American" life, I am still unable to view the revolution with detachment or objectivity. I cannot interpret its results in social, political or economic terms. Too many memories stand in my way.

And as I listened to this man talk of the Cuban situation, I began to remember how as a little girl I would wake up crying because I had dreamed of my aunts and grandmothers and I missed them. I remembered my mother's trembling voice and the sad look on her face whenever she spoke to her mother over the phone. I thought of the many letters and photographs that somehow were always lost in transit. And as the conversation continued, I began to remember how difficult it often was to grow up Latina in an American world.

It meant going to kindergarten knowing little English. I'd been in this country only a few months and although I understood a good deal of what was said to me, I could not express myself very well. On the first day of school I remember one little girl's saying to the teacher: "But how can we play with her? She's so stupid she can't even talk!" I felt so helpless because inside I was crying, "Don't you know I can understand everything you're saying?" But I did not have words for my thoughts and my inability to communicate terrified me.

As I grew a little older, Latina meant being automatically relegated to the slowest reading classes in school. By now my English was fluent, but the teachers would always assume I was somewhat illiterate or slow. I recall one teacher's amazement at discovering I could read and write just as well as her American pupils. Her incredulity astounded me. As a child, I began to realize that Latina would always mean proving I was as good as the others. As I grew older, it became a matter of pride to prove I was better than the others.

As an adult I have come to terms with these memories and they don't hurt as much. I don't look or sound very Cuban. I don't speak with an accent and my English is far better than my Spanish. I am beginning my career and look forward to the many possibilities ahead of me.

But a persistent little voice is constantly saying, "There's something missing. It's not enough." And this is why when I am now asked, "Do you want to go back?" I say "yes" with conviction.

I do not say to Cubans, "It is time to lay aside the hurt and forgive and forget." It is impossible to forget an event that has altered and scarred all our lives so profoundly. But I find I am beginning to care less and less about politics. And I am beginning to remember and care more about the child (and how many others like her) who left her grandma behind. I have to return to Cuba one day because I want to know that little girl better.

When I try to review my life during the past 16 years, I almost feel as if I've walked into a theater right in the middle of a movie. And I'm afraid I won't fully understand or enjoy the rest of the movie unless I can see and understand the beginning. And for me, the beginning is Cuba. I don't want to go "home" again; the life and home we all left behind are long gone. My home is here and I am happy. But I need to talk to my family still in Cuba.

Like all immigrants, my family and I have had to build a new life from almost nothing. It was often difficult, but I believe the struggle made us strong. Most of my memories are good ones.

But I want to preserve and renew my cultural heritage. I want to keep "la Cubana" within me alive. I want to return because the journey back will also mean a journey within. Only then will I see the missing piece. ■

Questions for Analysis

1. Because chronological thinking patterns represent a sequence of events in time, they can be visually represented with mind maps structured like the diagram on page 359. Using this form as a guide, create a mind map that expresses the key events in the author's life and their relationship to one another.

2. Explain the purpose(s) you think the narrator is trying to achieve in writing this essay.

3. Identify the key points the author makes in trying to achieve her purpose(s). ◀

THINKING ACTIVITY 8.1

Using a mind map that you create as a guide, write a narrative describing an event or experience that had special significance in your life. After completing your narrative, explain what you think is the most important point that you are trying to share with your audience. Read your narrative to the other members of the class and then discuss it with them, comparing the meaning you intended with the meaning they derived. ◀

**CHRONOLOGICAL
RELATIONSHIPS**

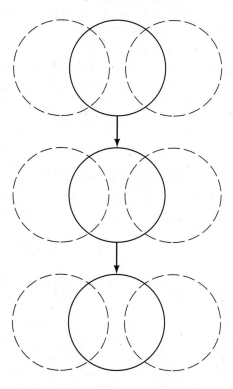

Process Relationships

A second type of time-ordered thinking pattern is the process relationship, which focuses on relating aspects of the growth and development of an event or experience. From birth onward, you are involved with processes in every facet of your life. The processes you are involved with can be classified in various ways: natural (e.g., growing physically), mechanical (e.g., assembling a bicycle), physical (e.g., learning a sport), mental (e.g., developing your thinking), creative (e.g., writing a poem), and so on.

Performing a *process analysis* involves two basic steps. The first step is to divide the process or activity you are analyzing into parts or stages. The second step is to explain the movement of the process through these parts or stages from beginning to end. The stages you have identified should be separate and distinct and should involve no repetition or significant omissions.

In performing a process analysis, you are typically trying to achieve one or both of two goals. The first goal is to give people step-by-step instruction in how to perform an activity, such as taking a photograph, changing a tire, or writing an essay. The second goal is simply to give information about a process, not to teach someone how to perform it. For example, your biology teacher might explain the process of photosynthesis to help you understand how green plants function, not to teach you how to go about transforming sunlight into chlorophyll!

Process thinking patterns relate aspects of the growth and development of an event or experience.

THINKING ACTIVITY 8.2

Review the following passages, which are examples of the process-analysis pattern of thinking. For each passage:

1. Identify the purpose of the passage.
2. Describe the main stages in the process identified by the author.
3. List questions you still have about how the process operates.

Jacketing was a sleight-of-hand I watched with wonder each time, and I have discovered that my father was admired among sheepmen up and down the valley for his skill at it: *He was just pretty catty at that, the way he could get that ewe to take on a new lamb every time.* Put simply, jacketing was a ruse played on a ewe whose lamb had died. A substitute lamb quickly would be singled out, most likely from a set of twins. Sizing up the tottering newcomer, Dad would skin the dead lamb, and into the tiny pelt carefully snip four leg holes and a head hole. Then the stand-in lamb would have the skin fitted onto it like a snug jacket on a poodle. The next step of disguise was to cut out the dead lamb's liver and smear it several times across the jacket of pelt. In its borrowed and bedaubed skin, the new baby lamb then was presented to the ewe. She would sniff the baby impostor endlessly, distrustful but pulled by the blood-smell of her own. When in a few days she made up her dim sheep's mind to accept the lamb, Dad snipped away the jacket and recited his victory: *Mother him like hell now, don't ye? See what a hellava dandy lamb I got for ye, old sister? Who says I couldn't jacket day onto night if I wanted to, now-I-ask-ye?*

—Ivan Doig, *This House of Sky*

If you are inexperienced in relaxation techniques, begin by sitting in a comfortable chair with your feet on the floor and your hands resting easily in your lap. Close your eyes and breathe evenly, deeply, and gently. As you exhale each breath let your body become more relaxed. Starting with one hand direct your attention to one part of your body at a time. Close your fist and tighten the muscles of your forearm. Feel the sensation of tension in your muscles. Relax your hand and let your forearm and hand become completely limp. Direct all your attention to the sensation of relaxation as you continue to let all tension leave your hand and arm. Continue this practice once or several times each day, relaxing your other hand and arm, your legs, back, abdomen, chest, neck, face, and scalp. When you have this mastered and can relax completely, turn your thoughts to scenes of natural tranquility from your past. Stay with your inner self as long as you wish, whether thinking of nothing or visualizing only the loveliest of images. Often you will become completely unaware of your surroundings. When you open your eyes you will find yourself refreshed in mind and body.

—Laurence J. Peter, *The Peter Prescription* ■ ◀

THINKING ACTIVITY 8.3

We tend to be most acutely aware of process analysis when we are learning a new activity for the first time, such as preparing formula for an infant or installing a new oil filter in a car. Identify such an occasion in your own life and then complete the following activities.

1. Create a mind map of the process, similar in form to the diagram on page 363.
2. Describe the steps or stages in the process.
3. Write a passage explaining how the stages fit together in an overall sequence.
4. Describe any special problems you had to solve, the manner in which you went about solving them, and the feelings you experienced in learning this process. ◀

THINKING PASSAGE

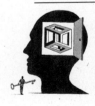

At the conclusion of this chapter (page 385) is an essay, "We Are Breaking the Silence About Death" by the psychologist Daniel Goleman, that focuses on the process of dying. He describes how the work of Dr. Elisabeth Kübler-Ross has helped change social attitudes toward dying and reviews her formulation of the psychological stages people typically go through once they know they are soon to die. After reading the article, do the Thinking Activity that follows it. ◀

COMPARATIVE AND ANALOGICAL RELATIONSHIPS

Both comparative and analogical patterns of thinking focus on the similarities and/or dissimilarities among different objects, events, or ideas. Comparative

**PROCESS
RELATIONSHIPS**

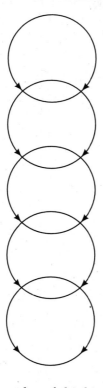

modes of thinking relate things in the *same* general category in terms of their similarities and differences. For example, when you shop for something important, like a car, you generally engage in a process of organized *comparing* (evaluating similarities and differences) as you examine the various makes and models. On the other hand, analogical modes of thinking relate things in entirely *different* categories in terms of their similarities. For example, on your shopping expedition for a car, you might say of a used car badly in need of repair: "That car is a real lemon." Obviously cars and lemons are in different categories, but the analogy brings out some similarities between the two (a sense of "sourness" or "bitterness").

Comparative Relationships

Think of an item you shopped for and bought in the past month. It might have been an article of clothing, a good book or a new record, a radio, and so on. Identify the item you selected, noting as much specific information about it as you can remember—brand, color, size, cost, and so on. (The Levi's jeans information is included as an example.)

Item purchased: Levi's jeans, size 31 x 31, blue, straight cut, $39.00

Item purchased:

When you went shopping, you probably spent a fair amount of time examining other items of the same type, things that you looked at but *did not buy.* Identify one of these competing items:

Item not purchased:

As you made your decision to purchase the item you did, you probably compared the various brands before making your selection. Identify some of the factors you took into consideration in comparing the different items. For example:

Item Purchased	Comparative Factors	Item Not Purchased
Levi's jeans	Brand	Girbaud jeans
$39.00	Price	$50.00
Straight cut	Style	Designer cut
Unwashed denim	Material	Prewashed denim

You compare in this way all the time, usually without even realizing it. Whenever you select an item on a menu or in a store, or a seat in a theater or on a bus, you are automatically looking for similarities and differences among the various items from which you are selecting, and these similarities and differences guide you in making your decision.

Of course, you do not always engage in a systematic process of comparison. In many cases, the selections and decisions you make seem to be unconscious. This may be so because you have already performed an organized comparison some time in the past and already know what you want and why you want it (e.g., "I always choose an aisle seat so I don't have to climb over people").

Sometimes, however, you make decisions impulsively, without any thought or comparative examination. Maybe someone told you to, maybe you were influenced by a commercial you saw, or maybe you simply said, "What the heck, let's take a chance." Sometimes these impulsive decisions work out for you, but often they do not because they are simply a result of rolling the dice. On the other hand, when you engage in a critical and comparative examination, you gain information that can help you make intelligent decisions.

Standards for Comparison   Naturally, not all of the factors you use in comparing are equally important in your decision-making. In any comparison, some similarities and differences outweigh others. How do you determine which factors are more important than others, and which information is more relevant than other information? Unfortunately, there is no simple formula for answering these questions. For example, review the lists you completed previously and place a check next to the factors that played an important part in your decision to buy the item. These factors represent the comparative information you found to be most important and relevant and probably reflect your needs and purposes. If you are on a limited budget, price differences may play a key role in your decision. If money is no object, your decision may have been based solely on the quality of the item or on some other consideration.

Even though there is no hard and fast way to determine which areas of comparison are most important, it does help you to become *aware* of the factors that are influencing your perceptions and decisions. These areas of comparison represent the standards you use to come to conclusions, and a critical and reflective examination of these standards can help you sharpen, clarify, and improve them.

When making comparisons, there are pitfalls you should try to avoid:

- *Incomplete comparisons.* This difficulty arises when you focus on too few points of comparison. For example, in looking for a competent surgeon to operate on you, you might decide to focus only on the fee that each doctor charges. Even though this may be an important area for comparative analysis, you would be foolish to overlook other areas of comparison, such as medical training, experience, recommendations, and success rates.
- *Selective comparisons.* This problem occurs when you take a one-sided view of a comparative situation—when you concentrate on the points favoring one side of the things being compared but overlook the points favoring the other side. For example, in selecting a dependable friend to perform a favor for you, you may focus on Bob because he is your best friend and you have known him the longest but overlook that he let you down the last few times you asked him to do something for you.

THINKING ACTIVITY 8.4

Review the following passages, which use comparative patterns of thinking to organize the ideas being presented. For each passage:

1. Identify the key ideas being compared.
2. Analyze the points of similarity and dissimilarity between the ideas being presented by using a mind map like the diagram on page 367.
3. Describe the conclusions the passage leads you to.

The difference between an American cookbook and a French one is that the former is very accurate and the second exceedingly vague. American recipes look like doctors' prescriptions. Perfect cooking seems to depend on perfect dosage. You are told to take a teaspoon of this and a tablespoon of that, then to stir them together until thoroughly blended. A French recipe seldom tells you how many ounces of butter to use to make *crepes suzette*, or how many spoonfuls of oil should go into a salad dressing. French cookbooks are full of unusual measurements such as *a pinch* of pepper, a *suspicion* of garlic, or a *generous sprinkling* of brandy. There are constant references to seasoning *to taste*, as if the recipe were merely intended to give a general direction, relying on the experience and art of the cook to make the dish turn out right.

—Raoul de Roussy de Sales, "American and French Cookbooks"

The rapidity of change and the speed with which new situations are created follow the impetuous and heedless pace of man rather than the deliberate pace of nature. Radiation is no longer merely the background radiation of rocks, the bombardment of cosmic rays, the ultraviolet of the sun that have existed before there was any life on earth; radiation is now the unnatural creation of man's tampering with the atom. The chemicals to which life is asked to make its adjustment are no longer merely the calcium and silica and copper and all the rest of the minerals washed out of the rocks and carried in rivers to the sea; they are the synthetic creations of man's inventive mind, brewed in his laboratories, and having no counterparts in nature. To adjust to these chemicals would require time on the scale that is nature's; it would require not merely the years of a man's life but the life of generations. And even this, were it by some miracle possible, would be futile, for the new chemicals come from our laboratories in an endless stream; almost five hundred annually find their way into actual use in the United States alone.

—Rachel Carson, *Silent Spring*

COMPARATIVE RELATIONSHIPS

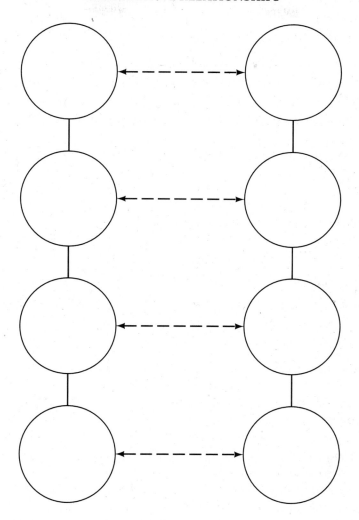

Physically and psychically women are by far the superior of men. The old chestnut about women being more emotional than men has been forever destroyed by the facts of two great wars. Women under blockade, heavy bombardment, concentration camp confinement, and similar rigors withstand them vastly more successfully than men. The psychiatric casualties of civilian populations under such conditions are mostly masculine, and there are far more men in our mental hospitals than there are women. The steady hand at the helm is the hand that has had the practice at rocking the cradle. Because of their greater size and weight, men are physically more powerful than women—which is not the same thing as saying that they are stronger. A man of the same size and weight as a woman of comparable background and occupational status would probably not be any more powerful than a woman. As far as constitutional strength is concerned, women are stronger than men. Many diseases from which men suffer can be shown to be largely influenced by their relation to the male Y-chromosome. More males die than females. Deaths from almost all causes are more frequent in males of all ages. Though women are more frequently ill than men, they recover from illnesses more easily and more frequently than men.

—Ashley Montagu, *The Natural Superiority of Women* ■ ◀

Analogical Relationships

We noted earlier that comparative relationships involve examining the similarities and differences of two items in the same general category, such as items on a menu or methods of birth control. There is another kind of comparison, however, that does not focus on things in the same category. Such comparisons are known as *analogies,* and their goal is to clarify or illuminate a concept from one category by saying that it is the same as a concept from a very different category.

The purpose of an analogy is not the same as the purpose of the comparison we considered in the last section. At that time, we noted that the goal of comparing similar things is usually to make a choice and that the process of comparing can provide you with information on which you can base an intelligent decision. The main goal of analogies, however, is not to choose or decide; it is to illuminate our understanding. Identifying similarities between very different things can often stimulate you to see these things in a new light, from a different perspective than you are used to. This can result in a clearer and more complete understanding of the things being compared. Consider the following example:

> Life's but a walking shadow, a poor player
> That struts and frets his hour upon the stage
> And then is heard no more.

—William Shakespeare, *Macbeth*

In this famous quotation, Shakespeare is comparing two things that at first glance don't seem to have anything in common at all: life and an actor. Yet as you look

closer at the comparison, you begin to see that even though these two things are unlike in many ways, there are also some very important similarities between them. What are some of these similarities?

> **Analogy**   A comparison between things that are basically dissimilar made for the purpose of illuminating our understanding of the things being compared.

We ourselves often create and use analogies to get a point across to someone else. Used appropriately, analogies can help you illustrate and explain what you are trying to communicate. This is particularly important when you have difficulty in finding the right words to represent your experiences. Powerful or complex emotions can make you speechless, or make you say things like "words cannot describe what I feel." Imagine that you are trying to describe your feelings of love and caring for another person. To illustrate and clarify the feelings you are trying to communicate, you might compare your feelings of love to "the first rose of spring," noting the following similarities:

- Like the first rose, this is the first great love of my life.
- Like the fragile yet supple petals of the rose, my feelings are tender and sensitive.
- Like the beauty of the rose, the beauty of my love should grow with time.

What are some other comparisons of love to a rose?

- Like the color of the rose, . . .
- Like the fragrance of the rose, . . .
- Like the thorns of the rose, . . .

Another favorite subject for analogies is the idea of the meaning or purpose of life, which the simple use of the word *life* does not communicate. You have just seen Shakespeare's comparison of life to an actor. Here are some other popular analogies involving life. What are some points of similarity in each of those comparisons?

- Life is just a bowl of cherries.
- Life is a football game.
- Life is like a box of chocolates.
- "Life is a tale told by an idiot, full of sound and fury, signifying nothing." (Shakespeare)

Create an analogy for life representing some of your feelings, and explain the points of similarity.

- Life is . . . .

In addition to communicating experiences that resist simple characterization, analogies are also useful when you are trying to explain a complicated concept. For instance, you might compare the eye to a camera lens or the immunological system of the body to the National Guard (corpuscles are called to active duty and rush to the scene of danger when undesirable elements threaten the well-being of the organism).

Analogies possess the power to bring things to life by evoking images that illuminate the points of comparison. Consider the following analogies and explain the points of comparison that the author is trying to make.

- "Laws are like cobwebs, which may catch small flies, but let wasps and hornets break through." (Jonathan Swift)
- "I am as pure as the driven slush." (Tallulah Bankhead)
- "He has all the qualities of a dog, except its devotion." (Gore Vidal)

Analogical thinking patterns clarify or illuminate a concept from one category by relating it to a concept from a very different category.

Similes and Metaphors   From the examples discussed so far, you can see that analogies have two parts: an *original subject* and a *compared subject* (what the original is being likened to). In comparing your love to the first rose of spring, the *original subject* is your feelings of love and caring for someone, whereas the *compared subject* is what you are comparing those feelings to in order to illuminate and express them—namely, the first rose of spring.

In analogies, the connection between the original subject and the compared subject can be either obvious (explicit) or implied (implicit). For example, you can echo the lament of the great pool hustler Minnesota Fats and say:

"A pool player in a tuxedo is like a hotdog with whipped cream on it."

This is an obvious analogy (known as a *simile)* because you have explicitly noted the connection between the original subject (man in tuxedo) and the compared subject (hotdog with whipped cream) by using the comparative term *like.* (Sometimes the structure of the sentence calls for *as* in a similar position.)

> **Simile**   An explicit comparison between basically dissimilar things made for the purpose of illuminating our understanding of the things being compared.

You could also have used other forms of obvious comparison, such as "is similar to," "reminds me of," or "makes me think of." On the other hand, you could say:

"A pool player in a tuxedo is a hotdog with whipped cream on it".

In this case, you are making an implied analogy (known as a *metaphor),* because you have not included any words that point out that you are making a comparison. Instead, you are stating that the original subject *is* the compared subject. Naturally, you are assuming that most people will understand that you are making a comparison between two different things and not describing a biological transformation.

> **Metaphor**   An implied comparison between basically dissimilar things made for the purpose of illuminating our understanding of the things being compared.

Create a *simile* (obvious analogy) for a subject of your own choosing, noting at least two points of comparison.

Subject

1.

2.

Create a *metaphor* (implied analogy) for a subject of your own choosing, noting at least two points of comparison.

Subject

1.

2.

THINKING ACTIVITY 8.5

Read the following passage, which uses an analogical pattern of thinking. Identify the major ideas being compared and describe the points of similarity between them. Explain how the analogy helps illuminate the subject being discussed.

> The mountain guide, like the true teacher, has a quiet authority. He or she engenders trust and confidence so that one is willing to join the endeavor. The guide accepts his leadership role, yet recognizes that success (measured by the heights that are scaled) depends upon the close cooperation and active participation of each member of the group. He has crossed the terrain before and is familiar with the landmarks, but each trip is new and generates its own anxiety and excitement. Essential skills must be mastered; if they are lacking, disaster looms. The situation demands keen focus and rapt attention; slackness, misjudgment, or laziness can abort the venture. The teacher is not a pleader, not a performer, not a huckster, but a confident, exuberant guide on expeditions of shared responsibility into the most exciting and least-understood terrain on earth—the mind itself.
>
> —Nancy K. Hill, "Scaling the Heights: The Teacher as Mountaineer" ◀

Extended Analogies   The analogies considered so far have been of a fairly simple sort, designed for limited purposes and displaying relatively few points of resemblance. You can also use analogies for more ambitious purposes, however, such as extended discussions of a subject. In these cases, an analogy can provide the framework for the discussion as you try to explain an idea by comparing it in some detail to something else.

THINKING PASSAGE

The following essay, "The Rivet Poppers," uses an extended analogy to dramatize how the progressive destruction of the earth's delicate ecological balance by humans is contributing to a catastrophe from which we will all suffer. The authors, Paul and Anne Ehrlich, are well known for their distinguished work on the subjects of global ecology, population control, and environmental concerns. After reading the essay, answer the questions that follow.

THE RIVET POPPERS
by Paul and Anne Ehrlich

As you walk from the terminal toward your airliner, you notice a man on a ladder busily prying rivets out of its wing. Somewhat concerned, you saunter over to the rivet popper and ask him just what the hell he's doing.

"I work for the airline—Growthmania Intercontinental," the man informs you, "and the airline has discovered that it can sell these rivets for two dollars apiece."

"But how do you know you won't fatally weaken the wing doing that?" you inquire.

"Don't worry," he assures you. "I'm certain the manufacturer made this plane much stronger than it needs to be, so no harm's done. Besides, I've taken lots of rivets from this wing and it hasn't fallen off yet. Growthmania Airlines needs the money; if we didn't pop the rivets, Growthmania wouldn't be able to continue expanding. And I need the commission they pay me—fifty cents a rivet!"

"You must be out of your mind!"

"I told you not to worry; I know what I'm doing. As a matter of fact, I'm going to fly on this flight also, so you can see there's absolutely nothing to be concerned about."

Any sane person would, of course, go back into the terminal, report the gibbering idiot and Growthmania Airlines to the FAA, and make reservations on another carrier. You never *have* to fly on an airliner. But unfortunately all of you are passengers on a very large spacecraft—one on which you have no option but to fly. And, frighteningly, it is swarming with rivet poppers behaving in ways analogous to that just described.

The rivet poppers on Spaceship Earth include such people as the President of the United States, the Chairman of the Soviet Communist Party, and most other politicians and decision makers; many big businessmen and small businessmen; and, inadvertently, most other people on the planet, including you and me. Philip Handler, the president of the United States National Academy of Sciences, is an important rivet popper, and so are industrialist Daniel Ludwig (who is energetically chopping down the Amazon rainforest) and Senator Howard Baker, enemy of the Snail Darter. Others prominent on the rivet-popper roster include Japanese whalers and woodchippers, many utility executives, the auto moguls of Detroit, the folks who run the AMAX corporation, almost all economists, the Brazilian government, Secretary of the Interior James Watt, the editors of *Science*, *Scientific American*, and the *Wall Street Journal*, the bosses of the pesticide industry, some of the top bureaucrats of the U.S. Department of Agriculture and some of those in the Department of the Interior, the officers of the Entomological Society of America, the faculties of every engineering school in the world, the Army Corps of Engineers, and the hierarchy of the Roman Catholic Church.

Now all of these people (and especially you and we) are certainly not crazy or malign. Most of them are in fact simply uninformed—which is one reason for writing a book on the processes and consequences of rivet-popping.

Rivet-popping on Spaceship Earth consists of aiding and abetting the extermination of species and populations of nonhuman organisms. The European Lion, the Passenger Pigeon, the Carolina Parakeet, and the Sthenele Brown Butterfly are some of the numerous rivets that are now irretrievably gone; the Chimpanzee, Mountain Gorilla, Siberian Tiger, Right Whale, and California Condor are prominent among the many rivets that are already loosened. The rest of the perhaps ten million species and billions of distinct populations still more or less hold firm. Some of these species supply or could supply important direct benefits to humanity, and all of them are involved in providing free public services without which society could not persist.

The natural ecological systems of Earth, which supply these vital services, are analogous to the parts of an airplane that make it a suitable vehicle for human beings. But ecosystems are much more complex than wings or engines. Ecosystems, like well-made airplanes, tend to have redundant subsystems and other "design" features that permit them to continue functioning after absorbing a certain amount of abuse. A dozen rivets, or a dozen species, might never be missed. On the other hand, a thirteenth rivet popped from a wing flap, or the extinction of a key species involved in the cycling of nitrogen, could lead to a serious accident.

In most cases an ecologist can no more predict the consequences of the extinction of a given species than an airline passenger can assess the loss of a single rivet. But both can easily foresee the long-term results of continually forcing species to extinction or of removing rivet after rivet. No sensible airline passenger today would accept a continuous loss of rivets from jet transports. Before much more time has passed, attitudes must be changed so that no sane passenger on Spaceship Earth will accept a continuous loss of populations or species of nonhuman organisms.

Over most of the several billion years during which life has flourished on this planet, its ecological systems have been under what would be described by the airline industry as "progressive maintenance." Rivets have dropped out or gradually worn out, but they were continuously being replaced; in fact, over much of the time our spacecraft was being strengthened by the insertion of more rivets than were being lost. Only since about ten thousand years ago has there been any sign that that process might be more or less permanently reversed. That was when a single species, *Homo sapiens*, began its meteoric rise to planetary dominance. And only in about the last half-century has it become clear that humanity has been forcing species and populations to extinction at a rate greatly exceeding that of natural attrition and far beyond the rate at which natural processes can replace them. In the last twenty-five years or so, the disparity between the rate of loss and the rate of replacement has become alarming; in the next twenty-five years, unless something is done, it promises to become catastrophic for humanity.

The form of the catastrophe is, unfortunately, difficult to predict. Perhaps the most likely event will be an end of civilization in T. S. Eliot's whimper. As nature is progressively impoverished, its ability to provide a moderate climate, cleanse air and water, recycle wastes, protect crops from pests, replenish soils, and so on will be increasingly degraded. The human population will be growing as the capacity of Earth to support people is shrinking. Rising death rates and a falling quality of life will lead to a crumbling of post-industrial civilization. The end may come so gradually that the hour of its arrival may not be recognizable, but the familiar world of today will disappear within the life span of many people now alive.

Of course, the "bang" is always possible. For example, it is likely that destruction of the rich complex of species in the Amazon basin could trigger rapid changes in global climate patterns. Agriculture remains heavily dependent on stable climate, and human beings remain heavily dependent on food. By the end of the century the extinction of perhaps a million species in the Amazon basin could have entrained famines in which a billion human beings perished. And if our species is very unlucky, the famines could lead to a thermonuclear war, which could extinguish civilization.

Fortunately, the accelerating rate of extinctions can be arrested. It will not be easy; it will require both the education of, and concerted action by, hundreds of millions of people. But no tasks are more important, because extinctions of other organisms must be stopped before the living structure of our spacecraft is so weakened that at a moment of stress it fails and civilization is destroyed. ■

Questions for Analysis

1. Create a mind map that illustrates the various points of comparison that the Ehrlichs are making between the original subject and the compared subject. Elaborate your map by including the points of similarity (and dissimilarity) between the original and the compared subjects.

2. Describe some of the changes in the environment that you have noticed during the course of your life. What behavior on the part of humans has contributed to these changes? If this environmental deterioration continues at its current pace, what will be the result during the next twenty years?

3. Identify five strategies people can use to help ensure that Spaceship Earth continues to be a healthy home for future generations. ◀

CAUSAL RELATIONSHIPS

Causal patterns of thinking involve relating events in terms of the influence or effect they have on one another. For example, if you were right now to pinch yourself hard enough to feel it, you would be demonstrating a cause and effect relationship. Stated very simply, a *cause* is anything that is responsible for bringing about something else—usually termed the *effect*. The *cause* (the pinch) brings about the *effect* (the feeling of pain). When you make a causal statement, you are merely stating that a causal relationship exists between two or more things:

The pinch *caused* the pain in my arm.

Of course, when you make (or think) causal statements, you do not always use the word *cause*. For example, the following statements are all causal statements. In each case, underline the cause and circle the effect.

- Since I was the last person to leave, I turned off the lights.
- Taking lots of vitamin C really cured me of that terrible cold I had.
- I accidentally toasted my hand along with the marshmallows by getting too close to the fire.

In these statements, the words *turned off, cured,* and *toasted* all point to the fact that something has caused something else to take place. Our language contains thousands of these causal "cousins." Create three statements that express a causal relationship without actually using the word *cause*.

1.

2.

3.

You make causal statements all the time, and you are always thinking in terms of causal relationships. In fact, the goal of much of your thinking is to figure out why something happened or *how* something came about. For if you can figure out how and why things occur, you can then try to predict what will happen in the future. These predictions of anticipated results form the basis of many of your decisions. For example, the experience of toasting your hand along with the marshmallows might lead you to choose a longer stick for toasting—simply because you are able to figure out the causal relationships involved and then make predictions based on your understanding (namely, a longer stick will keep my hand further away from the fire, which will prevent it from getting toasted).

Consider the following activities, which you probably performed today. Each activity assumes that certain causal relationships exist, which influenced your decision to perform them. Explain one such causal relationship for each activity.

- Brushing your teeth *Causal relationship:*
- Locking the door *Causal relationship:*
- Studying for an exam *Causal relationship:*

Causal Chains

Although you tend to think of causes and effects in isolation—A caused B—in reality causes and effects rarely appear by themselves. Causes and effects generally appear as parts of more complex patterns, including three that we will examine here:

- Causal chains
- Contributory causes
- Interactive causes

Consider the following scenario:

> Your paper on the topic "Is there life after death?" is due on Monday morning. You have reserved the whole weekend to work on it, and are just getting started when the phone rings—your best friend from your childhood is in town, and wants to stay with you for the weekend. You say yes. By Sunday night, you've had a great weekend, but have made little progress on your paper. You begin writing, when suddenly you feel stomach cramps—it must have been those raw oysters that you had for lunch! Three hours later, you are ready to continue work. You brew a pot of coffee and get started. At 3:00 (A.M.) you are too exhausted to continue. You decide to get a few hours of sleep, and set the alarm clock for 6:00 (A.M.), giving you plenty of time to finish up. When you wake up, you find that it's nine o'clock—the alarm failed to go off! Your class starts in forty minutes, and you have no chance of getting the paper done on time. As you ride to school, you go over the causes for this disaster in your mind. You are no longer worried about life after death—you are now worried about life after this class!

- What causes in this situation are responsible for your paper being late?
- What do you think is the single most important cause?
- What do you think your teacher will identify as the most important cause? Why?

A *causal chain*, as you can see from these examples, is a situation in which one thing leads to another, which then leads to another, and so on. There is not just *one* cause for the resulting effect; there is a whole string of causes. Which cause in the string is the "real" cause? Your answer often depends on your perspective on the situation. In the example of the unfinished paper on the topic "Is there life after death?" you might see the cause as a faulty alarm clock. The teacher, on the other hand, might see the cause of the problem as an overall lack of planning. Proper planning, he or she might say, does not leave things until the last minute, when unexpected problems can prevent you from reaching your goal. You can illustrate this causal structure with the following diagram:

CAUSAL CHAIN

CAUSE **A**

↓

EFFECT **B** CAUSE

↓

CAUSE **C** **EFFECT**

↓

EFFECT **D** CAUSE

↓

CAUSE **E** **EFFECT**

↓

EFFECT **F**

THINKING ACTIVITY 8.6

1. Create a similar scenario of your own, detailing a chain of causes that results in being late for class, standing someone up for a date, failing an exam, or an effect of your own choosing.

2. Review the scenario you have just created. Explain how the "real" cause of the final effect could vary depending on your perspective on the situation. ◀

Contributory Causes

In addition to operating in causal chains over a period of time (A leads to B, which leads to C, which leads to D, etc.), causes can also act simultaneously to produce an effect. When this happens (as it often does), you have a situation in which a number of different causes are instrumental in bringing something about. Instead of working in isolation, each cause *contributes* to bringing about the final effect. When this situation occurs, each cause serves to support and reinforce the action of the other causes, a structure illustrated in the following diagram:

CONTRIBUTORY CAUSES

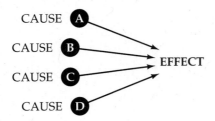

CAUSE **A**

CAUSE **B**

              EFFECT

CAUSE **C**

CAUSE **D**

Consider the following situation:

> It is the end of the term, and you have been working incredibly hard at school—writing papers, preparing for exams, finishing up course projects. You haven't been getting enough sleep, and you haven't been eating regular or well-balanced meals. To make matters worse, you have been under intense pressure in your personal life, having serious arguments with the person you have been dating. You find that this is constantly on your mind. It is the middle of the flu season and many of the people you know have been sick with various bugs. Walking home from school one evening, you get soaked by an unexpected shower. By the time you get home, you are shivering. You soon find yourself in bed with a thermometer in your mouth—you are sick!

What was the "cause" of your getting sick? In this situation, you can see it probably was not just *one* thing that brought about your illness. It was probably *a combination* of different factors that led to your physical breakdown: low resistance, getting wet and chilled, being exposed to various germs and viruses, physical exhaustion, lack of proper eating, and so on. Taken by itself, no one factor might have been enough to cause your illness. Working together, they all contributed to the final outcome.

THINKING ACTIVITY 8.7

Create a similar scenario of your own, detailing the contributory causes that led to asking someone for a date, choosing a major, losing or winning a game you played in, or an effect of your own choosing. ◀

Causal thinking patterns relate events in terms of the influence or effect they have on one another.

Interactive Causes

Our examination of causal relationships has revealed that causes rarely operate in isolation but instead often influence (and are influenced by) other factors. Imagine that you are scheduled to give a speech to a large group of people. As the time for your moment in the spotlight approaches, you become anxious, which results in a dry mouth and throat, making your voice sound more like a croak. The prospect of sounding like a bullfrog increases your anxiety, which in turn dries your mouth and constricts your throat further, reducing your croak to something much worse—silence.

This not uncommon scenario reveals the way different factors can relate to one another through reciprocal influences that flow back and forth from one to the other. This type of causal relationship, which involves an *interactive* thinking pattern, is an extremely important way to organize and make sense of your experiences. For example, to understand social relationships, such as families, teams, groups of friends, and so on, you have to understand the complex ways each individual influences—and is influenced by—all the other members of the group.

Understanding biological systems and other systems is similar to understanding social systems. To understand and explain how an organ like your heart, liver, or brain functions, you have to describe its complex, interactive relationships with all the other parts of your biological system. The diagram on page 383 illustrates these dynamic causal relationships.

THINKING ACTIVITY 8.8

Read the following passages, which illustrate causal patterns of thinking. For each passage:

1. Create mind maps that illustrate cause(s) and effect(s) relationships.
2. Identify the *kind* of causal relationship (direct, chain, contributory, or interactive).

Nothing posed a more serious threat to the bald eagle's survival than a modern chemical compound called DDT. Around 1940, a retired Canadian banker named Charles L. Broley began keeping track of eagles nesting in Florida. Each breeding season, he climbed into more than 50 nests, counted the eaglets and put metal bands on their legs. In the late 1940's, a sudden drop-off in the number of young produced led him to conclude that 80 percent of his birds were sterile. Broley blamed DDT. Scientists later discovered that DDE, a breakdown product of DDT, causes not sterility, but a fatal thinning of eggshell among birds of prey. Applied on cropland all over the United States, the pesticide was running off into waterways where it concentrated in fish. The bald eagles ate the fish and the DDT impaired their ability to reproduce. They were not alone, of course. Ospreys and pelicans suffered similar setbacks.

—Jim Doherty, "The Bald Eagle and DDT"

It is popularly accepted that Hitler was the major cause of World War II, but the ultimate causes go much deeper than one personality. First, there were longstanding German grievances against reparations levied on the nation following its defeat in World War I. Second, there were severe economic strains that caused resentment among the German people. Third, there were French and English reluctance to work out a sound disarmament policy and American noninvolvement in the matter. Finally, there was the European fear that communism was a much greater danger than National Socialism. These factors contributed to the outbreak of World War II.

—Gilbert Muller, *The American College Handbook*

You crunch and chew your way through vast quantities of snacks and confectioneries and relieve your thirst with multicolored, flavored soft drinks, with and without calories, for two basic reasons. The first is simple; the food tastes good, and you enjoy the sensation of eating it. Second, you associate these foods, often without being aware of it, with the highly

INTERACTIVE CAUSES

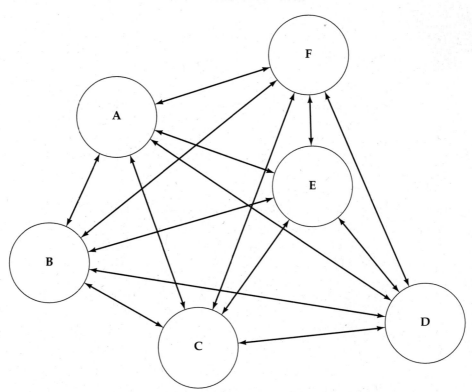

pleasurable experiences depicted in the advertisements used to promote their sale. Current television advertisements demonstrate this point: people turn from grumpiness to euphoria after crunching a corn chip. Others water ski into the sunset with their loved ones while drinking a popular soft drink. People entertain on the patio with friends, cook over campfires without mosquitoes, or go to carnivals with granddad munching away at the latest candy or snack food. The people portrayed in these scenarios are all healthy, vigorous, and good looking; one wonders how popular the food they convince you to eat would be if they would crunch or drink away while complaining about low back pain or clogged sinuses.

—Judith Wurtman, *Eating Your Way Through Life* ◀

THINKING PASSAGE

 Many of the discussions you engage in and the essays you write are based on an extended analysis of a cause-and-effect situation. When this happens, the concept of causality is used both to help you explain your viewpoint and to give you a means of organizing and structuring the topic you are examining. The article on page 391, "College Women and Alcohol" by Nancy Gleason, analyzes some of the complex causal relationships that contribute to the problem of alcohol abuse on college campuses, particularly among women. After completing the article, answer the questions that follow. ◀

SUMMARY

Concepts are the vocabulary of thought, the general ideas that we use to represent our world; thinking patterns are the vehicles we use to relate and organize concepts so that we can make sense of our world. In this chapter you have examined a number of basic thinking patterns that enable you to organize your experiences into relationships that have meaning to you:

- Chronological and process relationships
- Comparative and analogical relationships
- Causal relationships

Each of these thinking patterns helps you figure out what has happened in the past, what is occurring in the present, and what will happen in the future. You use these patterns to reveal the way the world is and also to impose your own interpretation on the events of your experience. In this sense we are all scientists and artists, both deciphering the mysteries of the world and composing our own unique perspectives on it. All of us perform these activities in distinctive ways and so construct a view of the world that is uniquely our own. As you refine your abilities to relate and organize the conceptual vocabulary of your mind, you are improving the power and creativity of your thinking processes, while at the same time developing a more accurate understanding of the world.

We Are Breaking the Silence About Death
by Daniel Goleman

Psychiatrist Elisabeth Kübler-Ross and I were to meet and fly together to Colorado Springs, where she was to give a workshop for nurses, doctors and volunteers who work with dying patients. Our flight was soon to board, but there was no sign of Kübler-Ross. Then she appeared, bustling down the corridor, a small, wiry woman carrying two huge shoulder bags. After the briefest exchange of amenities, she explained that she was concerned that one of her patients might be late for the flight. The patient was to be one of 12 dying people at the seminar. They would teach those who work with the dying by sharing their private fears and hopes.

At the last minute her patient, an emaciated but smiling woman, showed up at the gate. Kübler-Ross and I had planned to talk on the plane, but instead she spent the entire flight giving her patient emergency oxygen. Later I learned that Kübler-Ross had met her patient the week before. She saw that the woman had only a few more weeks or months to live, and learned that she had never traveled far from her hometown. So, on the spur of the moment, Kübler-Ross invited her to come along as her guest. She should, the doctor felt, live her remaining days fully.

Kübler-Ross began her work with the dying in the mid '60s when she decide to interview a dying patient for a medical-school seminar she was teaching. She searched the school's 600-bed hospital, asking the staff on each ward if there were any dying patients. On every ward she got the same answer: No. Yet on any given day in a hospital that size, many patients are near death. When she then went back and asked about specific patients, their doctors reluctantly admitted that they were terminally ill.

Medical schools in those days avoided the topic of death and dying. Medical staffs treated the physical problems of their dying patients but, more often than not, ignored the fact of approaching death. Virtually no one, the doctor included, was comfortable with the fact of death. It was taboo, best kept out of sight and out of mind.

Once a patient died, he vanished. One of Kübler-Ross's students realized that in all her months as a hospital resident she could hardly recall seeing a dead person. In part she chose to avoid them, but there was also "the remarkable disappearing act that occurs as the body is cleverly whisked out of sight . . . "

In the decade since Kübler-Ross first gave her seminar on dying, the taboo has weakened. Death is in vogue as a topic of books, seminars, scholarly articles, and classes at every level from college down to elementary school. There are two professional journals devoted to the study of death, dozens of volunteer groups working with the dying, and one or two medical facilities geared solely to helping people die with dignity.

There is no single cause for this change, but Elisabeth Kübler-Ross has done more to further it than any other person. Through her 1969 best seller *On Death and Dying,* her seminars for physicians, clergy, and others who work with dying people, and her public talks, Kübler-Ross has alerted us to a new way of handling dying.

Kübler-Ross is Chairman of the National Advisory Council to Hospice in New Haven, Connecticut, which leads the way in humane care of the dying. Modeled on a similar center in London, New Haven Hospice puts Kübler-Ross's advice into practice with a team on call around-the-clock to help people die in their own homes rather than in a strange hospital. Hospice has plans for building a center for dying patients. In contrast to policy at most hospitals, family members will be encouraged to join the medical staff in caring for their dying relatives. Visiting hours will be unlimited, and patients' children and even pets will be free to visit.

Kübler-Ross's natural openness toward the dying reflects her experience as a child in rural Switzerland. In her community, she saw death confronted with honesty and dignity. She also has the authority of one whose medical practice has been limited for the last decade to dying patients and their families; lately, her practice has been restricted to dying children. Her public life as an author and a lecturer allows her a rare luxury in her medical work; she charges no one for her services.

Kübler-Ross's career has been unusually humanitarian from the start. Before entering medical school in Switzerland, she worked at the close of the Second World War in eastern Europe, helping the survivors of bombed-out cities and death camps. After becoming a psychiatrist, she gravitated to treating chronic schizophrenics, and then to work with retarded children, whose mental slowness was compounded by being deaf, dumb or blind.

From the thousands of hours she has spent with patients facing death, Kübler-Ross has charted the psychological stages people typically go through once they know they are soon to die. Though any single person need not go through the entire progression, most everyone facing death experiences at least one of these stages. The usual progression is from denial of death through rage, bargaining, depression, and finally, acceptance.

These reactions are not restricted to dying, but can occur with a loss of any kind. We all experience them to some degree in the ordinary course of life changes. Every change is a loss, every beginning an end. In the words of the Tibetan poet Milarepa, "All worldly pursuits end in sorrow, acquisition in dispersion, buildings in destruction, meetings in separation, birth in death."

A person's first reaction to the news that he has a terminal disease is most often denial. The refusal to accept the fact that one is soon to die cushions death's impact. It gives a person time to come to grips with the loss of everything that has mattered to him.

Psychoanalysts recognize that at the unconscious level, a person does not believe he will die. From this refusal to believe in one's own death springs the hope that, despite a life-threatening illness, one will not die. This hope can take many forms: that the diagnosis is wrong, that the illness is curable, that a miracle treatment will turn up. As denial fades into a partial acceptance, the person's concern shifts from the hope of longer life to the wish that his or her family will be well and his affairs taken care of after his death.

Denial too often typifies the hospital staff's reaction to a patient who faces death. Doctors and nurses see themselves as healers; a dying patient threatens this role. Further, a person who cannot contemplate his own death, even if he is a physician, feels discomfort with someone who is dying. For this reason hospital staffs often enclose the dying patient in a cocoon of medical details that keeps death under wraps.

Sociologists Barney Glaser and Anselm Strauss studied the mutual pretense that often exists when patient and staff know the patient is dying. A staff member and a terminal patient might safely talk about his disease, they found, so long as they skirt its fatal significance. But they were most comfortable when they stuck to safe topics like movies and fashions—anything, in short, that signifies life going on as usual.

This is a fragile pretense, but not one that either party can easily break. Glaser and Strauss found that a patient would sometimes send cues to the staff that he wanted to talk about dying, but the nurses and doctors would decide not to talk openly with him because they feared he would go to pieces. The patient would openly make a remark acknowledging his death, but the doctor or nurse would ignore him. Then, out of tact or empathy for the embarrassment or distress he caused, the patient would resume his silence. In this case, it is the staff's uneasiness that maintains the pretense, not the patient's.

In the reverse instance, a doctor may give the patient an opening to talk about dying, and have the patient ignore it. Kübler-Ross urges hospital staff members to let the patient know that they are available to talk about dying, but not to force the subject on the patient. When he no longer needs to deny his death, the patient will seek out a staff member and open the topic.

When the family knows a patient is dying and keeps the secret from him, they create a barrier that prevents both patient and family from preparing for the death. The dying patient usually sees through a make-believe, smiling mask. Genuine emotions are much easier on the patient, allowing relatives to share his feelings. When his family can be open about the seriousness of the illness, there is time to talk and cry together and to take care of important matters under less emotional pressure.

A student nurse hospitalized for a fatal illness wrote her professional colleagues in a nursing journal: "You slip in and out of my room, give me medications and check my blood pressure. Is it because I am a student nurse myself that I sense your fright? If only we could be honest, both admit our fears, touch one another. Then it might not be so hard to die—in a hospital—with friends close by."

Denial becomes increasingly hard as the patient's health deteriorates. Although mutual pretense avoids embarrassment and emotional strains, it sacrifices valuable time in which the dying patient and his family could take care of unfinished emotional and practical matters, like unsettled arguments or unwritten wills, that death will forestall forever.

Kübler-Ross feels that a period of denial is useful if it gives the patient and his family time to find a way to deal with the stark truth of death. But when denial persists until the person dies, the survivors' grief is needlessly prolonged by the guilts and regrets. Often patients near death say they wished they had been told they were dying sooner so that they could have prepared themselves and their families.

A few rare patients, though, need to cling to denial because the reality is too much to bear. When those closest to the person offer no love or comfort, as when children of the dying patients blame the parent for deserting them, the patient may deny the inevitable to the very end. But this is rare; of 500 patients, Kübler-Ross found only four who refused to the last to admit that they were dying.

Once a dying patient accepts the invitation to talk about his death, Kübler-Ross tries to help him recognize any unfinished business that needs his attention. Straightforward truth helps the dying person fully live the time left. She tries to elicit their hidden hopes and needs, then find someone who can fulfill these needs.

Physical pain sometimes prevents a dying patient from making the best use of his remaining days. When his pain is overwhelming, he either becomes preoccupied with it or dependent on painkillers that leave him groggy. Kübler-Ross controls pain with Brompton's mixture. This old-time formula of morphine, cocaine, alcohol, syrup, and chloroform water dulls the patient's pain without dimming his alertness.

When a patient stops denying his impending death, the feelings that most often well up are rage and anger. The question, "Why me?" is asked with bitterness. The patient aims his resentment at whoever is handy, be it staff, friends or family. Healthy people remind the patient that he will die while they live. The unfairness of it all arouses his rage. He may be rude, uncooperative, or downright hostile. For example, when a nurse was late with his pain medication, the patient snapped "why are you late? You don't care if I suffer. Your coffee break is more important to you than my pain."

As the rage abates the patient may start to bargain with God or fate, trying to arrange a temporary truce. The question switches from "Why me?" to "Why now?" He hopes for more time to finish things, to put his house in order, to arrange for his family's future needs, to make a will. The bargain with God takes the form of the patient promising to be good or to do something in exchange for another week, month, or year of life.

With full acceptance of his approaching death, a person often becomes depressed. Dying brings him a sense of hopelessness, helplessness and isolation. He mourns past losses, and regrets things left undone or wrongs he's committed. One of Kübler-Ross's patients, for example, regretted that when his daughter was small and needed him, he was on the road making money to provide a good home. Now that he was dying, he wanted to spend every moment he could with her, but she was grown and had her own friends. He felt it was too late. At this stage the dying person starts to mourn his own death, the loss of all the people and things he has found meaningful, the plans and hopes never to be fulfilled. Kübler-Ross calls this kind of depression a "preparatory grief." It allows a person to get ready for his death by letting go of his attachments to life.

During this preparatory grief, the patient may stop seeing family and friends, and become withdrawn and silent. His outer detachment matches the inner renouncement of what once mattered to him. Family members sometimes misinterpret his detachment as a rejection. Kübler-Ross helps them to see that the patient is beginning to accept his death. Hence, he needs much less contact with family and friends.

After this preparatory mourning, the dying person can reach a peaceful acceptance. He is no longer concerned with the prolongation of his life. He has made peace with those he loves, settled his affairs, relinquished his unfinished dreams. He may feel an inner calm, and become mellow in outlook. He can take things as they come, including the progress of his illness. People bring him pleasure, but he no longer speaks of plans for the future. His focus becomes the simple joys of everyday life; he enjoys today without waiting for tomorrow. At this stage, the person is ready to live his remaining days fully and die well.

The story of modern Zen master's death shows this frame of mind. As the master lay dying, one of his students brought him a special cake, of which he had always been fond. With a wan smile the master slowly ate a piece of cake. As he grew weaker still, his students leaned close and asked if he had any final words for them. "Yes," he said, as they leaned forward eagerly, "My, but this cake is delicious."

What the dying teach us, says Kübler-Ross, is how to live. In summing up what she has learned from her dying patients, she likes to recite a poem by Richard Allen that goes:

> . . . as you face your death,
> it is only the love
> you have given
> and received
> which will count . . .
> if you have loved well
> then it will have been worth it . . .
> but if you have not
> death will always come too soon
> and be too terrible to face.* ∎

* Reprinted with permission from *Psychology Today*. Copyright © 1976. (P.T. Partners, Lip.).

THINKING ACTIVITY 8.9

1. Create a mind map that illustrates the psychological stages most people undergo during the process of dying, according to Dr. Kübler-Ross.

2. Drawing on your own experiences with people you know who have died, analyze whether you believe that the stages Dr. Kübler-Ross has identified are accurate descriptions of the dying process.

3. Imagine that you just found out that you had six months to live.

   a. Create a mind map that illustrates the psychological stages that you think you would go through.

   b. Using this map as a guide, write a passage that explains your thoughts on this subject.

   c. The author of this article, Daniel Goleman, gives the example of a dying man whose main regret was that he had not spent enough time with his daughter and now wanted to spend every minute with her. Describe how you would live the last six months of your life.

   d. Explain why thinking and writing about dying, a topic we usually try to avoid, can have a productive impact on our lives. ◀

COLLEGE WOMEN AND ALCOHOL: A RELATIONAL PERSPECTIVE
Nancy A. Gleason, MSW, LICSW, BCD

A day or two after a first-year female student arrives at college, she will be invited to a fraternity party or other mixer to meet men, and her college involvement with alcohol will begin. Whether served legally or not, alcohol will be available, and her new dormitory friends will most likely be drinking. Feeling anxious, uncomfortable, and somewhat overwhelmed, the new student will find it difficult to refuse to drink—even if she wants to refuse.

Here, on a superficial level, are ingredients for drinking—peer pressure, the wish to feel more relaxed and to appear sophisticated, perhaps even seductive. If our student has had no experience with alcohol, it won't take much persuasion to get her to try it. If she feels shy, she will be told that a drink will help her relax and feel less inhibited. If she is used to drinking, she will feel right at home. The evening's activity may produce no more than a hangover or a decision never to go to another mixer, but it could also influence her future social or drinking life.

During her college years, a student will encounter a variety of hurdles and stresses that will challenge her coping skills. At the same time, there will be many opportunities to party, to unwind, or to celebrate, and she may find that alcohol is easily available and provides an adjunct to most occasions. And college has the reputation of being the "best years of our lives," perhaps a last fling before taking on adult responsibilities.

Is something wrong with this scenario?

Despite growing research and media attention to alcohol abuse during college years and to the consequences of alcohol consumption for young women, the role that alcohol plays in the psychology of college-age women has received limited consideration. We are finally acknowledging that men and women, use and abuse alcohol for different reasons—and with different results. New theories about the psychology of women stress the importance of relational competence in their healthy development and the distress created by lack of success in relationships. These insights can help us understand why and how women use and abuse alcohol and the variety of consequences to which alcohol use makes women vulnerable.[1]

The Problem

Although rates of illicit drug use in college have decreased since 1980, women's alcohol use has remained relatively constant.[2] Ninety percent of both college men and women consistently state they have used alcohol during the previous year. Although the number of college women who drink heavily has increased in the last 20 years, [3,4] only half as many women as men in college drink daily (3% of the women *v* 6% of men). Thirty-five percent of the women describe "occasions of heavy drinking" (five or more drinks in a row) within the past 2-week period, compared with 52% of the men.[5] Wechsler and Isaac[6] expressed concern about binge drinking (also described as five drinks in a row), finding that it is generally on the increase. They found that more than twice as many college women were getting drunk in 1992 as were doing so in 1977 and that more of the women were drinking to get drunk. Men were still drinking more than women each time they drank (close to twice as much), and men drank to intoxication nearly twice as often.[3,7,8] Analyzing the results of the Fund for the Improvement of Post-Secondary Education (FIPSE) Core Survey, which included 54,361 students from 78 colleges and universities, Presley and Meilman found women binge drinking less frequently than men did, but nevertheless found that 36% of the women had binged in the previous 2 weeks.[9] Fourteen percent of those surveyed at a woman's college in 1988 had been intoxicated five or more times in the previous 30 days (N.A.G., unpublished data, 1990). Berkowitz and Perkins[10] still found men drank more on each drinking occasion, although not necessarily more frequently than did women. They concluded that 29% of male college students have drinking problems, compared with 11% of college women.

Statistics do not tell the whole story. Perhaps because women are less likely than men to engage in destructive behavior or to get into trouble with authorities,[11] the women's drinking problems have not received adequate attention. Perkins,[12] who analyzed studies done over a 10-year period, confirmed the gender differential in destructive actions associated with binge drinking in college but emphasized other consequences in which drinking women reach close to equal incidence with men: unintended sexual activity, memory loss, damaged relationship, and physical injury to themselves.

In addition to the risks everyone faces when abusing alcohol (addiction, driving accidents, and alcohol poisoning), women confront risks that appear to be different from those faced by men. These risks may result from the use of alcohol, and they may lead to increased drinking. They include depression and failure in relationships. Not least is the risk of sexual victimization, which is so destructive to women's self-esteem and so intimately connected to the use of alcohol, both as a factor leading to abuse[13] and as a coping mechanism following abuse.[14]

In this context, perspectives in the psychology of women can help us understand college women's alcohol use and resulting problems. This is a new inquiry. Interest in gender issues is increasing rapidly as recognition of gender differences gains acceptance in the psychological arena and in the popular press.[15] Researchers are studying moral development, learning styles, relationship patterns, concepts of mutuality, and more. At the same time, attention is now being paid to female alcoholics and their treatment. Research on college women's use of alcohol has focused to a large extent on such negative consequences as susceptibility to rape. Several studies have investigated how personality factors are related to alcohol abuse and have identified issues of power, dominance, and dependence,[16] fear of failure and sensation seeking,[17] and assertiveness and self-expression.[18] In an earlier study, Jones[19] found that women who drank moderately were socially isolated and depressed. Jones did not make clear whether drinking was the result or the cause of the isolation. These studies failed to examine the importance to women of their sense of capacity in making meaningful connections with others. Research into the link or correlation between the relational needs of women and their use of substances is remarkably rare.

Relational Theory
With recent exploration of gender differences, psychologists, sociologists, educators, and other researchers are recognizing that traditional psychological theories have undervalued women's attributes and skills and have

had a negative impact on women's self-esteem.[20-22] Qualities such as sensitivity, empathy, dependence, emotionality, and putting the needs of others before one's own have traditionally been seen as "female" and therefore as deficiencies—suggesting the conclusion that women may be inherently less competent and that these qualities are roadblocks on the path to success.[20] Women are described as inadequate in academia and the marketplace if they are not clear thinking, rational, capable of simplifying ethical problems into rights and wrongs, competitive, ambitious, and career-oriented.[21] American society, Western culture, and some feminists have reinforced these messages. To date, women have not had the societal support and acknowledgment that help them feel good about who they are.

At the same time, women are encouraged to be good caretakers, mothers, and nurturers of others. They are supposed to be self-effacing yet attentive to their bodies, their clothes, their makeup and their behavior so that they are attractive to others, especially to men. No wonder women are confused about who they are and what is expected of them. They are continually reminded of their failure to achieve the expectations set for them—expectations they often incorporate as their own.

Women's psychological development does not appear to move toward the traditionally accepted goal of independence, autonomy, and separation. Recent theoretical formulations, sometimes referred to as "self-in-relation,"[23] suggest that a woman's sense of self is organized around her capacity to make and maintain relationships built on mutuality in connection, recognizing and valuing one's impact on another as well as that other's effect on oneself. The relational framework suggests responsiveness and openness to the other and activity to engage the other. Miller describes the components of "growth-fostering relationships" as "zest" and empowerment to act, leading to a more accurate image of the self and of the other, an increased sense of worth, and a greater connection to the other, with the motivation then to connect more fully to people in general.[24]

Mutuality is a key component to satisfying relationships within this framework. Jordan defines a "mutuality exchange" in which "one is both affecting the other and being affected by the other. . . . There is openness to influence, emotional availability and a constantly changing pattern of responding to and affecting the other's state."[25] Genero et al further describe a "bi-directional movement of feelings, thought, and activity between persons in relationships"[26] and demonstrate the connection of mutuality to relationship satisfaction and to social supports. Where mutuality is lacking, the individual experiences a sense of isolation and increased susceptibility to depression.

The study of friendship provides another approach to understanding how relationships work for women. Research on adult friendships has produced limited results, especially when the research seeks to evaluate the interaction between friends and the experience of friendship. In general terms, researchers have found that women tend to relate in a more personal and "expressive" way, whereas men tend to be more "instrumental."[27] Although Duck and Wright[28] do not confirm that women are less instrumental, they have found that women are more affective in their relational style and that they value their friendships more and invest more in them than men do. DeVries and Parker[29] expand the discussion of difficulties in studying friendships to include the failure in most research to discuss both the giving and receiving inherent in close relationships. Looking at the contribution of both self and others in relationships, their findings suggest that women experience themselves as giving more and that both men and women find more emphatic understanding and connectedness from their women friends.

It is not our purpose here to examine men's styles of relationships or to contrast them with those of women, but some comparison is unavoidable. All who do research on the subject are careful to point out, and it needs to be stressed, that their findings offer the possibility for generalizations that do not account for a wide variety on all measures within each gender.

Some people have been studying friendships, whereas others have looked at communication styles, especially as they may create difficulties in communication between men and women.[30] Surrey[31] described a couple's problems with communication:

> When she spoke of her own needs and perceptions, she wanted him to listen actively, playing a part in the developing movement of ideas to a stage of increased focus and clarity. He was ready for debate. "When I argue and debate with her, it is because I treat her like an equal who knows what she feels and can argue effectively on her own position." She found that his position created confusion, disorganization and a feeling of disconnection, rather than fostering her idea of communication. She was asking from him what she feels she does for him—going "with him" on his line of thinking at that time, temporarily taking herself "out of the picture." Each had difficulty understanding the other's model of relationship (pp. 62–63)

Describing the different communication styles of men and women, Deborah Tannen[32] wrote

Intimacy is key in a world of connection where individuals negotiate complex networks of friendship, minimize differences, try to reach consensus, and avoid the appearance of superiority, which would highlight differences. In a world of status, independence is key, because a primary means of establishing status is to tell others what to do, and taking orders is a marker of low status. Though all humans need both intimacy and independence, women tend to focus on the first and men on the second. It is as if their lifeblood ran in different directions (p. 26). . . . If women speak and hear a language of connection and intimacy, while men speak and hear a language of status and independence, then communication between men and women can be like cross-cultural communication, prey to a class of conversational styles. (p. 42)

Studying patterns of intimacy can offer another route to exploring the relational process. Reis and Shaver,[33] doing so in detail (their analysis closely resembles that of Miller[24]), emphasize that "intimacy is a dynamic process whose operation is best observed in the pattern of communication and reaction between two people."[33] Their interactional model omits one important dimension—the sense of agency and empowerment that each person achieves in finding the capacity for giving as well as receiving in a relationship, contributing to the process as well as responding.

Looking at intimacy in terms of emotion and activity, Orosan and Schilling[34] found that

When women described their impressions of intimacy within their relationships, they spoke first about trust, dependency, closeness and self-disclosure, and secondarily about sharing experiences and doing things with the other person. . . . Men in this study tended to describe their experiences of intimacy in their personal relationships primarily by talking about activities and experiences they engaged in with one or more others, and secondarily by describing intimacy as involving trust and closeness. (p. 209)

Bergman,[35] writing about "self-in-relation" from a male perspective, notes that men may strive to be relational and search for intimacy, but that societal messages and developmental hurdles have made it particularly difficult for men to allow themselves to move away from the competitive and hierarchical stance they know.

In sum, these studies lend credence to the theory that women expect to give more in their relationships, that they value their friendships more, that they are capable of giving and receiving in mutual relationships, that they are capable and desirous of greater intimacy.

Yet when a woman strives for intimacy and mutuality, she may be disappointed, whether because her problems interfere with her capacity for intimacy or because she is in a relationship with someone who cannot reciprocate. One can wonder also if women of college age, in late adolescence, carry concepts of intimacy and mutuality that come more from an idealized wish than from genuine experience. What they search for in their relationships, whether intimacy or mutuality, is an elusive quality most often found lacking. And because women's identified role, as society has claimed it, is to be responsible for relationships, women absorb the blame when relationships fail.

Women's Normal Psychological Development

Theorists of this recent relational perspective identify self-esteem and identity for women as growing out of engaging in and facilitating mutual relationships. From birth onward, women grow by and through their connections with other people. "Self-in-relation" theory stresses the interaction between infant and mother and the empowerment that results from feeling one has an impact on the other.[36] It suggests that the infant experiences her effect on her mother, that she already finds the interaction and connection enhancing, and that the engagement is not merely a means to an end but is an end in itself.

Girls are especially encouraged to be sensitive to their emotional interplay with others—mothers first, then father and other family members, and ultimately peers. It is not clear how much expectations create the kind of responsiveness seen in infants, toddlers, and young girls, but that kind of sensitivity is seldom encouraged in boys, and those boys who do develop these qualities may be characterized as "Momma's boy," or, later in life, perhaps as "effeminate." Traditionally, boys have been expected to engage in active behavior that demonstrates their independence, and they have been rewarded for taking risks. Girls tend to be more collaborative.[37]

Adolescence is a complex time for a woman. She sees pleasing others as a way to feel affirmed, to be popular, even at the expense of her freedom of expression or achievement.[38] For instance, when a young woman feels that her striving for academic excellence conflicts with her relational needs, she may not yet have the ability to modulate the conflict and will instead opt out of the race. This is the time when girls cease to excel in math and science—fearing that competition with their male classmates will interfere with their friendships, bringing disapproval and, perhaps, rejection.[39]

New research by Gilligan and her colleagues has outlined a major crisis period for girls' entry into adolescence. Adolescent girls are under increased social pressure to accept a view of the world that may contradict their own experience. "If girls know what they know and bring themselves into relationships, they will be in conflict with prevailing authorities. If girls do not know what they know and take themselves out of relationships, they will be in trouble with themselves."[40] Peer pressure on girls emphasizes actions that lead to greater acceptance by boys (or men), and teenage girls are expected to accept the male view. Now, perhaps for the first time, girls discover that the world is not defined by their experience but by a male model. Even more, they find they must submerge those parts of themselves that do not fit the expectations that they sense others have for them. The conflict between what they "should" be and how they see themselves may end with the "suppression of the full participation of the woman's way of seeing and acting."[40] Jack[41] confirms that this loss of voice is experienced by women in adulthood and that it is a major factor in depression.

College Women and Drinking—Facilitating Relationships

The relational model of psychological development can help us understand how and why women's search for mutual and intimate relationships can sometimes go awry. The model can help us understand peer influence on drinking patterns, as well as the external and internal pressures women students encounter in making responsible choices about using alcohol.

In women's attempts to create or find satisfying relationships, especially in their search for intimacy, alcohol may become a vehicle that is readily available and offers the promise of being helpful. As Kilbourne[47] points out, women are constantly bombarded by messages from the media that alcohol is necessary if one is to achieve happiness and success and be attractive to men.

Drinking may start as a way of being with others. For teenagers, peers and peer culture are particularly important—probably more important than family.[10] The need to be accepted does not stop when the young person enters college. The wish to fit in leads most people to adapt to the cultural norms. One college norm may be a certain level of drinking, another may be popularity through cliques or subgroups.

Peer pressure may be overt—a direct request, invitation, or challenge to drink—or it may be covert—the subtle sense that to "belong" means going along with others. A drink or two may make one feel sophisticated, relaxed, and better able to fit in. Relationships may be formed through drinking at parties or other social events. When alcohol is not involved, some relationships survive, others do not.

If a student is with a drinker, she may choose to drink to be companionable. And if she does not drink when others are drinking, she may not only feel isolated or disgusted, but she may also fear ridicule that those who are drinking may think she is a "goody-goody."

To some extent, gender differences in the way peers influence each other's alcohol use follow traditional role delineations. Downs,[48] studying adolescents aged 13 to 17, found

> adolescent males exerting control over their social environment. These sex differences reflect underlying sex roles in our society. While males are taught to be active, to be independent, and to influence others, females are taught to be passive, to be dependent, and to be influenced by others. These sex differences also reflect the view that females in our society are more sensitive and attentive to interpersonal relationships than are males. Consequently, these sex differences indicate that the present generation of adolescents has not rejected traditional sex roles, at least in regard to peer pressure and alcohol use. (p. 484)

Putting it slightly differently, Berkowitz and Perkins stated that "because of greater interest in group harmony and cohesion, women may be likely to accommodate group norms and less willing than men are to assert their personal viewpoints and values in group situations."[49] Both of these statements, although they value women's sensitivities, suggest a "weakness" in women that causes them to compromise to maintain the community.

Certainly friendships and affiliation are important, and success in making peer relationships enhances the female student's sense of herself. An additional concern about the young adolescent girl's suppression of her independent voice as she conforms to the expectations of the larger world is sounded by Miller[36] and by Brown and Gilligan's[38] description of girls' entry into adolescence. As they might describe it, she is caught in a struggle to deny unacceptable thoughts and feelings as she makes an effort to appear "nice and kind." It is possible that drinking not only brings a young woman together with others, but that it also helps ease her discomfort with the alienation she may be feeling with herself. In this way, alcohol offers the promise of alleviating the pain.

College Women and Drinking—Hampering Relationships

A woman may start to drink as she seeks to enhance her sense of herself as attractive and as successful in her relationships. If she drinks too much, she achieves the opposite result. It is not easy to understand, or accept, that one's drinking is disturbing to others. It may be more difficult for the drinking woman to admit the impact her drinking has on her relationships. She may drink, or may have started drinking, to facilitate her relationships, so she cannot easily recognize that her drinking interferes with them. Because of the difficulty in acknowledging her responsibility, the drinker may work out another rationale for disconnection or abandonment. If she senses failure in the relationship, she cannot help but feel worse about her relational self as she experiences increasing isolation.[46] Allowing others to see these "failures" is likely to lead her to believe that she will, indeed, be abandoned as completely unworthy.

Surrey[50] describes four components to women's drinking from a relational perspective. Although she may start to drink as a way of feeling energized, loved, or loving, a woman is also likely to turn to alcohol to help her with "the impact of nonmutuality, the effects of abuse and violence, the effect of isolation and shaming, and/or the impact of distorted images of self and of relationships." As Surrey describes it, the culture tells her what she should look like, how she should behave, and how she should feel to be "worthy of connection." Alcohol becomes a way to manage or alter the way she believes she looks, acts, and feels.

Popular belief has it that drinking reduces inhibitions. Superficially, alcohol may make communication easier by helping people feel that they are relating better. If a woman feels shy or inhibited in social situations, she may drink too much as she seeks to relax. If a student feels more attractive when she has had a drink, she is also saying that she does not feel at ease with herself when she is sober.

Alcohol may help her overcome sexual inhibitions, reduce guilt and conflict over sexual activity, feel more seductive, and believe that she can enjoy sex more. Intoxication usually reduces sexual responsiveness, however, and may confuse cues. Drinking women may have more difficulty distinguishing between real and fantasied feelings of warmth and affection and physiological arousal.[51] Using alcohol to enhance sexual responsiveness is clearly risky. In her search for intimacy or heightened sexuality, a woman may find that too much alcohol dampens her responsiveness and interferes with her judgment. There is a sense, as Sandmaier[52] states, that it is okay to take advantage of a drunk woman. After all, everyone knows that drunk women are sexually "irresponsible."

Sexual overtures are a part of college life and frequently occur when alcohol is present. Women at mixers, fraternity parties, and other social occasions receive many invitations, overt and covert, for sex. Men may find sexual activity without intimacy acceptable, with or without the involvement of alcohol.[53] Women who are in relationships with men may also feel pressure for sex before they are ready. Some will consent, believing it is the only way to keep the man involved. Others will be confused when their intimacy-seeking behavior is misinterpreted as seductive; a man may interpret a woman's desire for a relationship as an invitation to sex—his way of expressing intimacy. Bergman states that "men may use sexuality to try to connect; they can be surprised to find that women may need connection to be fully sexual."[35] Confusing sex and intimacy, a problem for both men and women, is made more serious by alcohol,[13] and drinking too much makes the achievement of mutuality virtually impossible.

Sexual violence on campus is well documented. Benson et al,[54] in a thorough discussion of acquaintance rape, review the statistics, myths, and social expectancies that connect alcohol use and rape. One study of date rape and sexual aggression among college students found that more than 77% of the women (65% during college) and 57% of the men (51% during college) had been involved in some form of "male-against-female sexual aggression," and that 15% of the women had had unwanted sexual intercourse.[55] Risk factors for date rape and sexual aggression were identified as unfamiliar partners; power differential, including age, who paid, and who drove; miscommunication about sex; alcohol or drug use; dating activity or location; and popular myths that assert that women ask for and/or enjoy rape. Ogletree,[56] broadening the definition to "sexual coercion" and adding "menacing verbal pressure and misuse of authority" to the normal definitions of rape and attempted rape, found that 42% of the college women sampled had experienced sexual coercion. Alcohol was involved in 31% of these situations. In addition, when a woman has been drinking, her behavior is considered suspect, and she is less likely to be taken seriously if she complains.[57]

Ehrhart and Sandler[58] stress the damage that acquaintance rape has on a woman's ability to trust others and on her own capacity to distinguish who is safe and who is not. Her youth and inexperience increase her vulnerability and offer some men an opportunity to establish their masculinity, they maintain.

Berkowitz[59] discussed the multiplicity of factors involved in the man's role and, like Bergman,[35] found that social factors have had a major impact on how men perceive the use of power and sexuality. Looking more closely at the techniques used by men to obtain sex from an unwilling partner, Gray et al[60] found that lying, or "sexual manipulation," including threats to end the relationship and continuing arguments, were more frequently used than was physical force.

Date rape is an extreme example of relationships gone awry. It is easy to see how good intentions can lead to bad results—how a woman's attempt to make a relationship mutual or intimate can lead to her being abused—or how, whether drinking or not, a woman may stay in a destructive relationship with the hope that, if she can just be a better partner, the other person will stop abusing. It is also natural to assume that she will, subsequently, have far more difficulty trusting others or engaging in the "relational authenticity" and mutuality described earlier.

Traditionally, it has often been concluded that a woman, whether drinking or not, encouraged or seduced the man she claims raped her. If she was drinking, one can say the rape victim was not thoughtful or prepared and that her judgment and her capacity to resist were diminished. That she may have got high in response to his encouragement seems just another indication of the lengths to which a woman will go to be attractive to a man or to make a relationship work. It is ironic that we risk blaming women for what we want them to be good at.

Summary

Recent theory about women's psychological development contradicts the male-oriented view that autonomy and separation are the signposts of maturity. Instead, we stress the importance of the capacity for creating authentic, mutual relationships in establishing women's identity and self-esteem. These gender distinctions are important in understanding women's use of alcohol.

For college women, drinking is often a way of making friends and of lubricating social interactions, and may also seem helpful in establishing more intimate relationships. Peer influence is a strong persuader. As a woman's sense of herself is organized around her capacity to enter into meaningful, mutual relationships, so her failure to be able to find and maintain such relationships creates pain that, in turn, may lead to depressions and/or to the abuse of alcohol. The wish to belong, combined with the avoidance of subjective pain, may push women into excessive drinking.

At the same time, alcohol contributes to many relational failures, and college women who are careless in their use of alcohol may encounter additional problems.

References

1. Gleason N. Prevention of alcohol abuse by women in college: A relational perspective. *J Am Coll Health.* In press

2. Wilsnack SC, Wilsnack RW. Epidemiology of women's drinking. *J Subst Abuse.* 1991;3:133–157.

3. Engs R, Hanson D. The drinking patterns and problems of college students. *J Alcohol Drug Educ.* 1982;35:65–83.

4. Gomberg ES. *Alcohol and Women.* New Brunswick, NJ: Rutgers University Center of Alcohol Studies Pamphlet Series; 1989.

5. Johnston LD, O'Malley PM, Bachman JG. *Smoking, Drinking, and Illicit Drug Use Among American Secondary School Students, College Students, and Young Adults, 1975–1991.* Washington, DC: National Institute on Drug Abuse; 1992.

6. Wechsler H, Isaac N. "Binge" drinkers at Massachusetts colleges: Prevalence, drinking style, time trends, and associated problems. *JAMA.* 1992;267(21):2929–2931.

7. Meilman PW, Stone, JE, Gaylor MS, Turco JH. Alcohol consumption by college undergraduates: Current use and 10-year trends. *J Stud Alcohol.* 1990;51(5):389–395.

8. O'Hare TM. Drinking in college: Consumption patterns, problems, sex differences and legal drinking age. *J Stud Alcohol.* 1990;51(6):536–541.

9. Presley CA, Meilman PW. *Alcohol and Drugs on American College Campuses: A Report to College Presidents.* Carbondale: Southern Illinois University; 1992.

10. Berkowitz AD, Perkins HW. Problem drinking among college students: A review of recent research. *J Am Coll Health.* 1986;35(1):21–28.

11. Wechsler H. Summary of literature. *Alcoholism and Alcohol Abuse Among Women: Research Issues.* Research Monograph No.1. Rockville:US Dept of HEW, ADAMHA; 1980.

12. Perkins HW. Gender patterns in consequences of collegiate alcohol abuse: A 10-year study of trends in an undergraduate population *J Stud Alcohol.* 1992;53(5):458–462.

13. Abbey M. Acquaintance rape and alcohol consumption on college campuses: How are they linked? *J Am Coll Health.* 1991;39(4):165–169.

14. Stewart M. *Women, Addiction and Trauma: A Model for Recovery.* Northhampton, MA: Smith College School for Social Work; 1986. Thesis

15. *Time Magazine,* January 20, 1992; *Mademoiselle,* February 1992; and many more.

16. Canetto SS. Gender roles, suicide attempts, and substance abuse. *J Psychol.* 1991;125(6):605–620.

17. Johnson PB. Personality correlates of heavy and light drinking female college students. *J Alcohol Drug Educ.* 1989; 34(2):33–37.

18. Bailly RC, Carman RS, Forslund MA. Gender differences in drinking motivations and outcomes. *J Psychol.* 1991;125(6):649–656.

19. Jones MC. Personality antecedents and correlates of drinking patterns in women. *J Couns Clin Psychol.* 1971;36(1):61–69.

20. Miller JB. *Toward a New Psychology of Women,* 2nd ed. Boston: Beacon Press; 1986.

21. Gilligan C. *In a Different Voice: Psychological Theory and Women's Development.* Cambridge: Harvard University Press; 1982.

22. Belenky MF, Clinchy BM, Goldberger NR, Tarule JM. *Women's Ways of Knowing: The Development of Self, Voice and Mind.* New York: Basic Books; 1986.

23. Jordan JV, Kaplan AG, Miller JB, Stiver IP, Surrey JL. *Women's Growth in Connection.* New York: Guilford Press; 1991.

24. Miller JB. What do we mean by relationships? *Work in Progress #22.* Wellesley, MA: Stone Center; 1986.

25. Jordan J. The meaning of mutuality. In: Jordan JV, Kaplan AG, Miller JB, Stiver IP, Surrey JL, eds. *Women's Growth in Connection.* New York: Guilford Press; 1991:81–96.

26. Genero NP, Miller JB, Surrey J, Baldwin LM. Measuring perceived mutuality in close relationships: Validation of the Mutual Psychological Development Questionnaire. *J Fam Psychol.* 1992;6(1):36–48.

27. Bell RR. Friendships of women and men. *Psychol Women Q.* 1981;5(3):402–417.

28. Duck S, Wright PH. Re-examining gender differences in same-gender friendships: A close look at two kinds of data. In: Duck S, Wright PH, eds. *Sex Roles.* 1993;28:709–727.

29. De Vries B., Parker S. Men's and women's friendships with men and women. Presented at the International Network Conference on Personal Relationships. Vancouver, BC; 1991.

30. Brehm SS. *Intimate Relationships.* New York: Random House; 1985.

31. Surrey JL. The "self-in-relation": A theory of women's development. In: Jordan JV, Kaplan AG, Miller JB, Stiver IP, Surrey JL, eds. *Women's Growth in Connection.* New York: Guilford Press; 1991:51–67.

32. Tannen D. *You Just Don't Understand: Women and Men in Conversation.* New York: Morrow; 1990.

33. Reis HT, Shaver P. Intimacy as an interpersonal process. In: Duck S, ed. *Handbook of Personal Relationships.* New York: Wiley; 1988:367–390.

34. Orosan PG, Schilling KM. Gender differences in college students' definitions and perceptions of intimacy. *Women & Therapy.* 1992;12(1/2):201–212.

35. Bergman S. Men's psychological development: A relational perspective. *Work in Progress #48.* Wellesley, MA: Stone Center; 1991.

36. Miller JB. The development of women's sense of self. In: Jordan JV, Kaplan AG, Miller JB, Stiver IP, Surrey JL, eds. *Women's Growth in Connection.* New York: Guilford Press; 1991:11–26.

37. Lever J. Sex differences in the complexity of children's play and games. *Am Sociol Rev.* 1978;43:471–483.

38. Brown LM, Gilligan C. The psychology of women and the development of girls. Presented at the Laurel-Harvard Conference on the Psychology of Women and the Education of Girls. Cleveland, OH; April 1990.

39. Balkin J. Contributions of friends to women's fear of success in college. *Psychol Rep.* 1987;61:39–42.

40. Gilligan C. Joining the resistance: Psychology, politics, girls and women. *Mich Q Rev.* 1990;29(4):501–536.

41. Jack DC. *Silencing the Self: Women and Depression.* Cambridge: Harvard University Press; 1991. . . .

46. Kaplan AG. The "self-in-relation": Implications for depression in women. In: Jordan JV, Kaplan AG. Miller JB, Stiver IP, Surrey JL, eds. *Women's Growth in Connection.* New York: Guilford Press; 1991:206–222.

47. Kilbourne J. *Calling the Shots: The Advertising of Alcohol* [film and videotape]. Cambridge, MA: Cambridge Documentary Films; 1982, 1991.

48. Downs WR. Using panel data to examine sex differences in causal relationships among adolescent alcohol use, norms, and peer alcohol use. *J Youth Adoles.* 1985;14(6):469–486.

49. Berkowitz AD, Perkins HW. Recent research on gender differences in collegiate alcohol use. *J Am Coll Health.* 1987;36(2):123–129.

50. Surrey J. Women, addiction and codependency. Presented at the Stone Center Colloquium, Wellesley, MA, February 6, 1991.

51. Wilsnack SC. Drinking, sexuality, and sexual dysfunction in women. In: Wilsnack SC, Beckman LJ, eds. *Alcohol Problems in Women.* New York: Guilford Press; 1984;189–227.

52. Sandmaier M. *The Invisible Alcoholics–Women and Alcohol Abuse in America.* New York: McGraw-Hill; 1980.

53. Leigh BC, Aramburu B, Norris J. The morning after: Gender differences in attributions about alcohol-related sexual encounters. *J Appl Soc Psychol.* 1992;22(5):343–357.

54. Benson D, Charlton C, Goodhart F. Acquaintance rape on campus: A literature review. *J Am Coll Health.* 1992;40(4):157–165.

55. Muehlenhard CL, Linton MA. Date rape and sexual aggression in dating situations: Incidence and risk factors. *J Couns Psychol.* 1987:34(2):186–196.

56. Ogletree RJ. Sexual coercion experience and help-seeking behavior of college women. *J Am Coll Health.* 1993;41(4):149–153.

57. Norris J, Cubbins LA. Dating, drinking and rape: Effects of victim's and assailant's alcohol consumption on judgments of their behavior and traits. *Psychol Women Q.* 1992;16(2):179–191.

58. Ehrhart JK, Sandler BR. Campus gang rape: Party games? *Project on the Status and Education of Women.* Washington, DC: Association of American Colleges; 1985.

59. Berkowitz A. College men as perpetrators of acquaintance rape and sexual assault: A review of recent research. *J Am Coll Health.* 1992;40(4):175–181.

60. Gray MD, Lesser D, Rebach H, Hooks B, Bounds C. Sexual aggression and victimization: A local perspective. *Response.* 1988;11(3):9–13. ∎

Questions for Analysis

1. Describe the use of alcohol at your college. Is it widespread? Is it excessive? Have you had any personal experience with alcohol at college?

2. Using these articles and your own experiences as resources, analyze the reasons that many college students drink too much.

3. Identify three approaches that you believe would be most effective in solving this problem and explain why you suggested them.

4. According to some college administrators, alcohol is still the No. 1 source of discipline problems and other emotional or physical problems on campus. Describe some of the negative effects of drinking that you have observed at your college. ◀

9

REPORTING, INFERRING, AND JUDGING

Identify
the basis.

Evaluate
the sources.

Evaluate
the probability.

Identify
the inference.

**REPORTING
FACTUAL INFORMATION**
Describing information
that can be verified
through investigation

INFERRING:
Going beyond factual
information to describe what
is not currently known

JUDGING:
Expressing an evaluation
based on certain criteria

Evaluate
supporting
evidence/reasons.

Identify
the criteria.

THE MAIN GOAL of your thinking process is to organize the world into intelligible relationships that help you understand what is going on. The relationships that you compose and discover express the basic thinking patterns you use to make sense of the world. In the last chapter we critically examined the following basic thinking patterns:

- Chronological and process
- Comparative and analogical
- Causal

In this chapter we will be exploring the way that we use these thinking patterns, and others, to organize our beliefs and knowledge about the world. Beliefs are the main tools you use to make sense of the world and guide your actions, as explained in Chapter 5. The total collection of your beliefs represents your view of the world, your philosophy of life. More specifically, beliefs are interpretations, evaluations, conclusions, and predictions about the world that you endorse as true.

All beliefs are not equal. In fact, beliefs differ from one another in many kinds of ways, including their accuracy. The belief "The earth is surrounded by stars and planets" is considerably more certain than the belief "The positions of the stars and planets determine our personalities and destinies."

Beliefs differ in other respects besides accuracy. Review the following beliefs and then describe some of their differences:

1. I believe that I have hair on my head.
2. I believe that the sun will rise tomorrow.
3. I believe that there is some form of life after death.
4. I believe that dancing is more fun than jogging, and jogging is preferable to going to the dentist.
5. I believe that you should always act toward others in ways that you would like to have them act toward you.

In this chapter you will be thinking critically about three basic types of beliefs you use to make sense of the world:

- Reports
- Inferences
- Judgments

These beliefs are expressed in both your thinking and your use of language, as illustrated in the following sentences:

1. My bus was late today.
   Type of belief: reporting
2. My bus will probably be late tomorrow.
   Type of belief: inferring
3. The bus system is unreliable.
   Type of belief: judging

Now try the activity with a different set of statements.

1. Each modern atomic warhead has over one hundred times the explosive power of the bomb dropped on Hiroshima.
   Type of belief:
2. With all of the billions of planets in the universe, the odds are that there are other forms of life in the cosmos.
   Type of belief:
3. In the long run, the energy needs of the world will best be met by solar energy technology rather than nuclear energy or fossil fuels.
   Type of belief:

As you examine these various statements, you can see that they provide you with different types of information about the world. For example, the first statement in each list reports aspects of the world that you can verify—that is, check for accuracy. By doing the appropriate sort of investigating, you can determine whether the bus was actually late today and whether modern atomic warheads really have the power attributed to them. When you describe the world in ways that can be verified through investigation, you are said to be *reporting* factual information about the world.

Reporting Factual Information   Describing the world in ways that can be verified through investigation.

Looking at the second statement in each list, you can see immediately that each provides a different sort of information from the first one. These statements cannot be verified. There is no way to investigate and determine with certainty whether the bus will indeed be late tomorrow or whether there is in fact life on other planets. Although these conclusions may be based on factual information, they go beyond factual information to make statements about what is not currently known. When you describe the world in ways based on factual information yet go beyond this information to make statements regarding what is not currently known, you are said to be *inferring* conclusions about the world.

> **Inferring**   Describing the world in ways that are based on factual information yet going beyond this information to make statements about what is not currently known.

Finally, as you examine the third statement in both lists, it is apparent that these statements are different from both factual reports and inferences. They describe the world in ways that express the speaker's evaluation—of the bus service and of energy sources. These evaluations are based on certain standards (criteria) that the speaker is using to judge the bus service as unreliable and solar energy as more promising than nuclear energy or fossil fuels. When you describe the world in ways that express your evaluation based on certain criteria, you are said to be *judging*.

> **Judging**   Describing the world in ways that express an evaluation based on certain criteria.

You continually use these various ways of describing and organizing your world—reporting, inferring, judging—to make sense of your experience. In most cases, you are not aware that you are actually performing these activities, nor are you usually aware of the differences among them. Yet these three activities work together to help you see the world as a complete picture.

THINKING ACTIVITY 9.1

1. Compose six sentences that embody these three types of beliefs: two reports, two inferences, and two evaluations.

2. Locate a short article from a newspaper or magazine and identify the reports, inferences, and judgments it contains.

3. Carefully examine the photograph on page 412. Write five statements based on your observations. Then identify each of your statements as reporting, inferring, or judging and explain why you classify them as such. ◀

Courtesy of Frankel Gallery, San Franciso and © The Estate of Gary Winogrand.

REPORTING FACTUAL INFORMATION

The statements that result from the activity of reporting express the most accurate beliefs you have about the world. Factual beliefs have earned this distinction because they are verifiable, usually with one or more of your senses. For example, consider the following factual statement:

That young woman is wearing a brown hat in the rain.

This statement about an event in the world is considered to be factual because it can be verified by your immediate sense experience—what you can (in principle or in theory) see, hear, touch, feel, or smell. It is important to say *in principle* or *in theory,* because you often do not use all of your relevant senses to check out what you are experiencing. Look again at your example of a factual statement: You would normally be satisfied to *see* this event, without insisting on touching the hat or giving the person a physical examination. If necessary, however, you could perform these additional actions—in principle or in theory.

You use the same reasoning when you believe factual statements from other people that you are not in a position to check out immediately. For instance:

- The Great Wall of China is more than fifteen hundred miles long.
- There are large mountains and craters on the moon.
- Your skin is covered with germs.

You consider these to be factual statements because, even though you cannot verify them with your senses at the moment, you could in principle or in theory verify them with your senses *if* you were flown to China, *if* you were rocketed to the moon, or *if* you were to examine your skin with a powerful microscope. The process of verifying factual statements involves *identifying* the sources of information on which they are based and *evaluating* the reliability of these sources, topics examined in some detail in Chapter 5.

You communicate factual information to others by means of reports. *A report is* a description of something that has been experienced, then communicated in as accurate and complete a way as possible. Through reports you can share your sense experiences with other people, and this mutual sharing enables you to learn much more about the world than if you were confined to knowing only what you experience. The *recording* (making records) of factual reports also makes possible the accumulation of knowledge learned by previous generations.

Because factual reports play such an important role in our exchange and accumulation of information about the world, it is important that they be as accurate and complete as possible. This brings us to a problem. We have already seen in previous chapters that our perceptions and observations are often *not* accurate or complete. What this means is that often when we think we are making true factual reports, our reports are actually inaccurate or incomplete. For instance, consider our earlier "factual statement":

That young woman is wearing a brown hat in the rain.

Here are some questions you could ask concerning the accuracy of the statement:

- Is the woman really young, or does she merely look young?
- Is the woman really a woman, or a man disguised as a woman?
- Is that really a hat the woman/man is wearing, or something else (e.g., a paper bag)?

Of course, there are methods you could use to clear up these questions with more detailed observations. Can you describe some of these methods?

Besides difficulties with observations, the "facts" that you see in the world actually depend on more general *beliefs* that you have about how the world operates. Consider the question:

Why did the man's body fall from the top of the building to the sidewalk?

Having had some general science courses, you might say something like, "The body was simply obeying the law of gravity," and you would consider this to be a "factual statement." But how did people account for this sort of event before Newton formulated the law of gravity? Some popular responses might have included the following:

- Things always fall down, not up.
- The spirit in the body wanted to join with the spirit of the earth.

When people made statements like these and others, such as, "Humans can't fly," they thought that they were making "factual statements." Increased knowledge and understanding have since shown these "factual beliefs" to be inaccurate, and so they have been replaced by "better" beliefs. These "better beliefs" are able to explain the world in a way that is more accurate and predictable. Will many of the beliefs you now consider to be factually accurate also be replaced in the future by beliefs that are *more* accurate and predictable? If history is any indication, this will most certainly happen. (Already Newton's formulations have been replaced by Einstein's, based on the latter's theory of relativity. And Einstein's have been refined and modified as well and may be replaced someday.)

THINKING ACTIVITY 9.2

1. Locate and carefully read an article that deals with an important social issue.

2. Summarize the main theme and key points of the article.

3. Describe the factual statements that are used to support the major theme.

Factual reports play an essential role in our exchange and accumulation of informa-tion about the world, and it is important that they be as accurate and complete as possible.

4. Evaluate the accuracy of the factual information.

5. Evaluate the reliability of the sources of the factual information. ◀

THINKING PASSAGE

At the conclusion of the chapter (page 430) is an essay by N. Scott Momaday, "The Way to Rainy Mountain," which illustrates the way in which reporting factual information can help us understand significant historical events, memo-rable people, and the spiritual mystery of certain places. After reading the se-lection, answer the questions that follow. ◀

INFERRING

Imagine yourself in the following situations:

1. It is 2 (A.M.) and your roommate comes crashing through the door into the room. He staggers unsteadily to his bed and falls across it, dropping (and breaking) a nearly empty whiskey bottle. You rush over and ask, "What happened?" With alcoholic fumes blasting from his mouth, your roommate mumbles: "I juss wanna hadda widdel drink!" What do you conclude?

2. Your roommate has just learned that she passed a math exam for which she had done absolutely no studying. Humming the song "I Did It My Way," she comes bouncing over to you with a huge grin on her face and says: "Let me buy you dinner to celebrate!" What do you conclude about how she is feeling?

3. It is midnight and the library is about to close. As you head for the door, you spy your roommate shuffling along in an awkward waddle. His coat bulges out in front like he's pregnant. When you ask, "What's going on?" he gives you a glare and hisses, "Shhh!" Just before he reaches the door, a pile of books slides from under his coat and crashes to the floor. What do you conclude?

In these examples, it would be reasonable to make the following conclusions:

1. Your roommate is drunk.

2. Your roommate is happy.

3. Your roommate is stealing library books.

Although these conclusions are reasonable, they are not factual reports; they are *inferences*. You have not directly experienced your roommate's "drunkenness," "happiness," or "stealing." Instead, you have *inferred* it based on your roommate's behavior and the circumstances. What are the clues in these situations that might lead to these conclusions?

One way of understanding the inferential nature of these views is to ask yourself the following questions:

1. Have you ever pretended to be drunk when you weren't? Could other people tell?

2. Have you ever pretended to be happy when you weren't? Could other people tell?

3. Have you ever been accused of stealing something when you were perfectly innocent? How did this happen?

From these examples you can see that whereas factual beliefs can in principle be verified by direct observation, *inferential beliefs* go beyond what can be directly observed. For instance, in the examples given, your observation of certain of your roommate's actions led you to infer things that you were *not* observing directly—"He's drunk," "She's happy," "He's stealing books." Making such simple inferences is something you do all the time. It is so automatic that usually you are not even aware that you are going beyond your immediate observations, and you may have difficulty drawing a sharp line between what you *observe* and what you *infer.* Making such inferences enables you to see the world as a complete picture, to fill in the blanks and round out the fragmentary sensations being presented to your senses. In a sense, you become an artist, painting a picture of the world that is consistent, coherent, and predictable.

Your picture also includes *predictions* of what will be taking place in the near future. These predictions and expectations are also inferences because you attempt to determine what is currently unknown from what is already known.

Of course, your inferences may be mistaken, and in fact they frequently are. You may infer that the woman sitting next to you is wearing two earrings and then discover that she has only one. Or you may expect the class to end at noon and find that the teacher lets you go early—or late. In the last section we concluded that not even factual beliefs are ever absolutely certain. Comparatively speaking, inferential beliefs are a great deal more uncertain than factual beliefs, and it is important to distinguish between the two.

For example, do you ever cross streets with cars heading toward you, expecting them to stop for a red light or because you have the right of way? Is this a factual belief or an inference? Considered objectively, are you running a serious risk when you do this? In evaluating the risk, think of all the motorists who may be in a hurry, not paying attention, drunk, ill, and so on.

Consider the following situations, analyzing each one by asking these questions: Is the action based on a factual belief or an inference? In what ways might the inference be mistaken? What is the degree of risk involved?

- Placing your hand in a closing elevator door to reopen it
- Taking an unknown drug at a party
- Jumping out of an airplane with a parachute on
- Riding on the back of a motorcycle
- Taking a drug prescribed by your doctor

Having an accurate picture of the world depends on your being able to evaluate how *certain* your beliefs are. Therefore it is crucial that you *distinguish* inferences from factual beliefs and then *evaluate* how certain or uncertain your inferences are. This is known as "calculating the risks," and it is very important to solving problems successfully and deciding what steps to take.

The distinction between what is observed and what is inferred is paid particular attention in courtroom settings, where defense lawyers usually want witnesses to describe *only what they observed*—not what they *inferred* as part of the observation. When a witness includes an inference such as "I saw him steal it," the lawyer may object that the statement represents a "conclusion of the witness" and move to have the observation stricken from the record. For example, imagine that you are a defense attorney listening to the following testimony. At what points would you make the objection: "This is a conclusion of the witness"?

I saw Harvey running down the street, right after he knocked the old lady down. He had her purse in his hand and was trying to escape as fast as he could. He was really scared. I wasn't surprised because Harvey has always taken advantage of others. It's not the first time that he's stolen either, I can tell you that. Just last summer he robbed the poor box at St. Anthony's. He was bragging about it for weeks.

Developing an accurate picture of the world means we must **distinguish** *inferences from factual beliefs and then* **evaluate** *how certain or uncertain our inferences are.*

Finally, you should be aware that even though in *theory* facts and inferences can be distinguished, in *practice* it is almost impossible to communicate with others by sticking only to factual observations. A reasonable approach is to state your inference *along with* the observable evidence on which the inference is based (e.g., John *seemed* happy because . . .). Our language has an entire collection of terms (*seems, appears, is likely,* etc.) that signal we are making an inference and not expressing an observable fact.

Many of the predictions that you make are inferences based on your past experiences and the information that you presently have. Even when there appears to be sound reasons to support these inferences, they are often wrong due to incomplete information or unanticipated events. The fact that even people considered by society to be "experts" regularly make inaccurate predictions with absolute certainty should encourage you to exercise caution when making your own inferences. Here are some examples:

- *"So many centuries after the Creation, it is unlikely that anyone could find hitherto unknown lands of any value. "* —The advisory committee to King Ferdinand and Queen Isabella of Spain, before Columbus's voyage in 1492

- *"What will the soldiers and sailors, what will the common people say to 'George Washington, President of the United States'? They will despise him to all eternity."* —John Adams, 1789

- *"What use could the company make of an electrical toy?"* —Western Union's rejection of the telephone in 1878

- *"The actual building of roads devoted to motor cars is not for the near future in spite of many rumors to that effect."* — a 1902 article in *Harper's Weekly*

- *"This game will never be successful because it contains 38 major errors in design."* —Parker Brothers' initial rejection of the proposed game Monopoly in 1931, which went on to become the most successful board game of the twentieth century

- *"The energy produced by the breaking down of the atom is a very poor kind of thing. Anyone who expects a source of power from the transformation of the atom is talking moonshine."* —Lord Rutherford, Nobel Laureate, after the first experimental splitting of the atom, 1933

- *"The [atom] bomb will never go off, and I speak as an expert in explosives."* —Vannevar Bush, presidential adviser, 1945

- *"Among the really difficult problems of the world, (the Arab-Israeli conflict is) one of the simplest and most manageable."* —Walter Lippmann, newspaper columnist, 1948

- *"Space travel is utter bilge."* —British astronomer Dr. R. Woolsey, 1958

- *"The Wankel will . . . dwarf such major post-war technological developments as xerography, the Polaroid camera and color television."* —A statement by General Motors announcing its commitment to the rotary engine, 1969

- *"You ain't goin' nowhere, son. You ought to go back to driving a truck."* —Jim Denny, Grand Ole Opry manager, firing Elvis Presley after one performance, 1954

Examine the following list of statements, noting which statements are *factual beliefs* (based on observations) and which are *inferential beliefs* (conclusions that go beyond observations). For each factual statement, describe how you might go about verifying the information. For each inferential statement, describe a factual observation on which the inference could be based. *(Note:* Some statements may contain *both* factual beliefs and inferential beliefs.)

- When my leg starts to ache, that means snow is on the way.

- The grass is wet—it must have rained last night.

- I think that it's pretty clear from the length of the skid marks that the accident was caused by that person driving too fast.

- Fifty men lost their lives in the construction of the Queensboro Bridge.

- Nancy said she wasn't feeling well yesterday—I'll bet that she's out sick today.

Now consider the following situations. What inferences might you be inclined to make based on what you are observing? How could you investigate the accuracy of your inference?

- A student in your class is consistently late for class.

- You see a friend of yours driving a new car.

- A teacher asks the same student to stay after class several times.

- You don't receive any birthday cards.

So far we have been exploring relatively simple inferences. Many of the inferences people make, however, are much more complicated. In fact, much of our knowledge about the world rests on our ability to make complicated inferences in a systematic and logical way. However, just because an inference is more complicated does not mean that it is more accurate; in fact, the opposite is often the case. One of the masters of inference is the legendary Sherlock Holmes. In the following passage, Holmes makes an astonishing number of inferences on meeting Dr. Watson. Study carefully the conclusions he comes to. Are they reasonable? Can you explain how he reaches these conclusions?

"You appeared to be surprised when I told you, on our first meeting, that you had come from Afghanistan."

"You were told, no doubt."

"Nothing of the sort. I *knew* you came from Afghanistan. From long habit the train of thoughts ran so swiftly through my mind that I arrived at the conclusion without being conscious of intermediate steps. There were such steps, however. The train of reasoning ran, 'Here is a gentleman of a medical type, but with the air of a military man. Clearly an army doctor, then. He is just come from the tropics, for his face is dark, and that is not the natural tint of his skin, for his wrists are fair. He has undergone hardship and sickness, as his haggard face says clearly. His left arm has been injured. He holds it in a stiff and unnatural manner. Where in the tropics could an English army doctor have seen much hardship and got his arm wounded? Clearly in Afghanistan.' The whole train of thought did not occupy a second. I then remarked that you came from Afghanistan, and you were astonished."

—Sir Arthur Conan Doyle, *A Study in Scarlet*

THINKING ACTIVITY 9.3

Describe an experience in which you made an *in*correct inference that resulted in serious consequences. For example, it might have been a situation in which you mistakenly accused someone, an accident based on a miscalculation, a poor decision based on an inaccurate prediction, or some other event. Analyze that experience by answering the following questions:

1. What was (were) your mistaken inference(s)?
2. What was the factual evidence on which you based your inference(s)?
3. Looking back, what could you have done to avoid the erroneous inference(s)? ◄

THINKING PASSAGE

The essay at the conclusion of this chapter (page 435) entitled "Evolution as Fact and Theory" was written by Stephen Jay Gould, a professor of geology at Harvard University who also writes widely on scientific themes for nonscientific audiences. This essay illustrates the ongoing process by which natural scientists use inferences to discover factual information and to construct theories explaining this factual information. Read the selection carefully and then answer the questions that follow. ◄

JUDGING

Identify and describe a friend you have, a course you have taken, and the college you attend. Be sure your descriptions are specific and include *what you think* about the friend, the course, and the college.

1. _____ is a friend that I have.

   He/she is . . .

2. _____ is a course I have taken.

   It was . . .

3. _____ is the college I attend.

   It is . . .

Now review your responses. Do they include *factual* descriptions? For each response, note any factual information that can be verified.

In addition to factual reports, your descriptions may contain *inferences* about them based on factual information. Can you identify any inferences? In addition to inferences, your descriptions may also include *judgments* about the person, course, and school—descriptions that express your evaluation based on certain criteria. Facts and inferences are designed to help you figure out what is actually happening (or will happen); the purpose of judgments is to express your evaluation about what is happening (or will happen). For example:

- My new car has broken down three times in the first six months. *(Factual report)*
- My new car will probably continue to have difficulties. *(Inference)*
- My new car is a lemon. *(Judgment)*

When you pronounce your new car a "lemon," you are making a judgment based on certain criteria you have in mind. For instance, a "lemon" is usually a newly purchased item with which you have repeated problems—generally an automobile. To take another example of judging, consider the following statements:

- Carla always does her work thoroughly and completes it on time. *(Factual report)*
- Carla will probably continue to do her work in this fashion. *(Inference)*
- Carla is a very responsible person. *(Judgment)*

By judging Carla to be responsible, you are evaluating her on the basis of the criteria or standards that you believe indicate a responsible person. One such criterion is completing assigned work on time. Can you identify additional criteria for judging someone to be responsible?

Review your previous descriptions of a friend, a course, and your college. Can you identify any judgments in your descriptions?

1. Judgments about your friend:

2. Judgments about your course:

3. Judgments about your college:

For each judgment you have listed, identify the criteria on which the judgment is based.

1. Criteria for judgments about your friend:

2. Criteria for judgments about your course:

3. Critieria for judgments about your college:

When we judge, we are often expressing our feelings of approval or disapproval. Sometimes, however, we make judgments that conflict with what we personally approve of. For example:

- I think a woman should be able to have an abortion if she chooses to, although I don't believe it's right.
- I can see why you think that person is very beautiful, even though she is not the type that appeals to me.

Critical thinkers make explicit the standards used as a basis for their judgments and establish the reasons that justify these standards.

In fact, at times it is essential to disregard your personal feelings of approval or disapproval when you judge. For instance, a judge in a courtroom should render evaluations based on the law, not on his or her personal preferences.

Differences in Judgments

Many of our disagreements with other people focus on differences in judgments. As a critical thinker, you need to approach such differences in judgments intelligently. You can do so by following these guidelines:

- *Make explicit the criteria* or standards used as a basis for the judgment.
- Try to *establish the reasons* that justify these criteria.

For instance, if I make the judgment "Professor Andrews is an excellent teacher," I am basing my judgment on certain criteria of teaching excellence. Once these standards are made explicit, we can discuss whether they make sense, and what the justification is for them. Identify some of your standards for teaching excellence.

Of course, your idea of what makes an excellent teacher may be different from someone else's, a conclusion you can test by comparing your criteria with those of other class members. When these disagreements occur, your only hope for resolution is to use the two steps previously identified:

- Make explicit the standards you are using.
- Give reasons that justify these standards.

For example, "Professor Andrews really gets my mind working, forcing me to think through issues on my own and then defend my conclusions. I earn what I learn, and that makes it really 'mine.'"

In short, not all judgments are equally good or equally poor. The credibility of a judgment depends on the criteria used to make the judgment and the evidence or reasons that support these criteria. For example, there may be legitimate disagreements about judgments on the following points:

- Who was the greatest United States president?
- Which movie deserves the Oscar this year?
- Who should win the Miss America Pageant or the Mr. America Contest?
- Which is the best baseball team this year?
- Which music is best for dancing?

However, in these and countless other cases, the quality of judgments depends on identifying the criteria used for the competing judgments and then demonstrating that your candidate best meets those criteria by providing supporting evidence and reasons. With this approach, you can often engage in intelligent discussion and establish which judgments are best supported by the evidence.

Understanding how judgments function is also important to encourage you to continue thinking critically about a situation. For instance, the judgment "This course is worthless!" does not encourage further exploration and critical analysis. In fact, it may prevent such an analysis by *discouraging* further exploration. Judgments seem to summarize the situation in a final sort of way. And because judgments are sometimes made *before* you have a clear and complete understanding of the situation, they can serve to *prevent* you from seeing the situation as clearly and completely as you might. Of course, if you understand that all judgments are based on criteria that may or may not be adequately justified, you can explore these judgments further by making the criteria explicit and examining the reasons that justify them.

THINKING ACTIVITY 9.4

Review the following passages, which illustrate various judgments. For each passage:

1. Identify the evaluative criteria on which the judgments are based.
2. Describe the reasons or evidence the author uses to support the criteria.
3. Explain whether you agree or disagree with the judgments and give your rationale.

One widely held misconception concerning pizza should be laid to rest. Although it may be characterized as fast food, pizza is *not* junk food. Especially when it is made with fresh ingredients, pizza fulfills our basic nutritional requirements. The crust provides carbohydrates; from the cheese and meat or fish comes protein; and the tomatoes, herbs, onions, and garlic supply vitamins and minerals.

—Louis Philip Salamone, "Pizza: Fast Food, Not Junk Food"

Let us return to the question of food. Responsible agronomists report that before the end of the year millions of people if unaided might starve to death. Half a billion deaths by starvation is not an uncommon estimate. Even though the United States has done more than any other nation to feed the hungry, our relative affluence makes us morally vulnerable in the eyes of other nations and in our own eyes. Garrett Hardin, who has argued for a "lifeboat" ethic of survival (if you take all the passengers aboard, everybody drowns), admits that the decision *not* to feed all the hungry requires of us "a very hard psychological adjustment." Indeed it would. It has been estimated that the 3.5 million tons of fertilizer spread on American golf courses and lawns could provide up to 30 million tons of food in overseas agricultural production. The nightmarish thought intrudes itself. If we as a nation allow people to starve while we could, through some sacrifice, make more food available to them, what hope can any person have for the future of international relations? If we cannot agree on this most basic of values—feed the hungry—what hopes for the future can we entertain?

—James R. Kelly, "The Limits of Reason" ■ ◀

THINKING PASSAGE

Many of the judgments you are involved with are *moral* or *ethical* judgments, or judgments that concern the ways you should and should not behave toward other people. These judgments are often based on criteria you have absorbed from your parents. If you have critically examined the ethical beliefs you were raised with, however, you may have found that some of your views diverge from those of your parents. Of course, critical evaluation may also strengthen your endorsement of your parents' beliefs by deepening your understanding of the reasons on which they are based.

In the article on page 442, the psychologist Robert Coles examines the moral awareness of children. Coles claims that our society clings to the idea of children as pure innocents and does not see the ethical decisions they make or the complicated moral issues they confront. Through examples of the many children he has met, Coles argues for the need for parents to teach their children moral values. After carefully reading the article, answer the questions that follow. ◀

DISTINGUISHING REPORTS, INFERENCES, AND JUDGMENTS

Although the activities of reporting, inferring, and judging tend to be woven together in your experience, it is important for you to be able to distinguish them. Each of these activities plays a different role in helping you make sense of your world, and you should be careful not to confuse these roles. For example, although people may appear to be reporting factual information, they may actually be expressing personal evaluations, which are not factual. Consider the statement "Los Angeles is a smog-ridden city drowning in automobiles." Although seeming to be reporting factual information, the speaker is really expressing his or her personal judgment. Of course, speakers can identify their judgments with such phrases as "in my opinion," "my evaluation is," and so forth. Sometimes, however, speakers do not identify their judgments. In some cases they do not do so because the context within which they are speaking or writing (such as a newspaper editorial) makes clear that the information is judgment rather than fact. In other cases, however, they want you to treat their judgments as factual information. Confusing the activities of reporting, inferring, and judging can be misleading and even dangerous.

Confusing factual information with judgments can be personally damaging as well. For example, there is a big difference between the statements:

- I failed my exam today. *(Factual report)*
- I am a failure. *(Judgment)*

Stating the fact "I failed my exam today" describes your situation in a concrete way, enabling you to see it as a problem you can hope to solve through reflection and hard work. On the other hand, if you make the judgment "I am a failure," this sort of general evaluation does not encourage you to explore solutions to the problem or improve your situation.

Finally, another important reason for distinguishing the activities of reporting, inferring, and judging concerns the accuracy of statements. For instance, we noted that factual statements tend to be reasonably accurate since they are by nature verifiable, whereas inferences are usually much less certain. As a result, it is crucial for you to know what type of belief you are dealing with so that you can accurately evaluate the probability of its being true. If you treat an inference—for instance, "I don't think that this exam will be very difficult so I'm not going to bother to study"—as if it had the certainty of a factual statement, you may find yourself in an unexpected predicament.

THINKING ACTIVITY 9.5

Select a neighborhood you are familiar with and write a one-page passage describing it. Your passage should contain the following information:

- A description of the physical appearance of the neighborhood—what it looks like, sounds like, smells like, and so on. Give specific details.

- A description of some of the individuals or types of people who live in the neighborhood and their usual activities.
- Your thoughts and feelings about the neighborhood.
- Your prediction of what will happen to the neighborhood in the future.

After completing your passage, identify reports, inferences, and judgments that are contained in your essay. A student sample follows. ◀

The residents of Greenwich Village form a richly diverse parade each morning: young professionals moving purposefully off to work; children in Osh-Kosh overalls and parochial school plaids skipping energetically to a day of education; mothers with strollers mingling with the self-employed, the unemployed, and the retired, easing into the day at a leisurely pace; and finally, the shopkeepers, hard-working and friendly people from six continents preparing for a day of business.

One of the striking differences between Greenwich Village and other parts of Manhattan is the size of the buildings. Instead of towering structures that blot out the sky and diminish your sense of significance, the architecture of the Village is on a human scale, creating the distinct impression that this is a neighborhood in which people are considered to be more important than the buildings that they occupy.

Many of the small businesses in Greenwich Village— mom-and-pop groceries, tailors, coffee shops with soda fountains—have been replaced with expensive restaurants and exclusive boutiques. Significant increases in commercial rents have driven out the small businesses that can't pay these rents. I think that the trend away from small, privately owned businesses is unfortunate because it reduces the diversity of the neighborhood, it makes residents walk further for needed services, and it decreases your sense of being a member of a social community.

Greenwich Village has a rich history as a unique and creative part of New York City. However, I'm afraid that this creative tradition will be lost in the future as only the wealthy will be able to live there.

As you worked through this exercise, you probably became aware of the way that you continually use the activities of reporting, inferring, and judging to organize and make sense of your world. In addition, you probably experienced some difficulty distinguishing these different kinds of activities. This is because we rarely make an effort to try to separate them. Instead, the thinking processes we call reporting, inferring, and judging tend to be woven together, organizing our world into a seamless fabric. Only when we make a special effort to reflect and think critically are we able to recognize these activities as being distinct.

SUMMARY

This chapter has explored the thinking processes that create three of the fundamental types of beliefs that you use to make sense of your world. These processes are

Reporting	Describing information that can be verified through investigation
Inferring	Going beyond factual information to describe what is not known
Judging	Expressing an evaluation based on certain criteria

Each of these types of beliefs has an important and distinctive role to play in your ongoing efforts to organize and make sense of your world. As a critical thinker, you must learn to recognize each of these different types of beliefs and use them properly. Of course, it is often difficult and confusing to distinguish these types of beliefs because you rarely make an effort to try to separate them. Instead, the thinking activities of reporting, inferring, and judging tend to be woven together, organizing your world into a seamless fabric. Only when you make a special effort to reflect and think critically are you able to recognize these activities as being distinct.

In addition to recognizing and using these types of beliefs appropriately, thinking critically about these beliefs involves evaluating their basis and reliability: What is the reliability of the sources providing information for the *factual reports*? What is the probability that the *inference* is correct? What are the

evidence and reasons that support the criteria used in the *judgment?* By distinguishing and critically evaluating these fundamental types of beliefs, you are
able to improve their accuracy and effectiveness as you seek to make sense of
your world.

THE WAY TO RAINY MOUNTAIN
by N. Scott Momaday

A single knoll rises out of the plain in Oklahoma, north and west of the
Wichita range. For my people, the Kiowas, it is an old landmark, and they
gave it the name Rainy Mountain. The hardest weather in the world is
there. Winter brings blizzards, hot tornadic winds arise in the spring, and
in summer the prairie is an anvil's edge. The grass turns brittle and brown,
and it cracks beneath your feet. There are green belts along the rivers and
creeks, linear groves of hickory and pecan, willow and witch hazel. At a
distance in July or August the steaming foliage seems almost to writhe in
fire. Great green and yellow grasshoppers are everywhere in the tall grass,
popping up like corn to sting the flesh, and tortoises crawl about on the
red earth, going nowhere in the plenty of time. Loneliness is an aspect of
the land. All things in the plain are isolate; there is no confusion of objects
in the eye, but *one* hill or *one* tree or *one* man. To look upon that landscape
in the early morning, with the sun at your back, is to lose the sense of
proportion. Your imagination comes to life, and this, you think, is where
Creation was begun.

I returned to Rainy Mountain in July. My grandmother had died in
the spring, and I wanted to be at her grave. She had lived to be very old
and at last infirm. Her only living daughter was with her when she died,
and I was told that in death her face was that of a child.

I like to think of her as a child. When she was born, the Kiowas were
living the last great moment of their history. For more than a hundred
years they had controlled the open range from the Smoky Hill River to the
Red, from the headwaters of the Canadian to the fork of the Arkansas and
Cimarron. In alliance with the Comanches, they had ruled the whole of
the Southern Plains. War was their sacred business, and they were the
finest horsemen the world has ever known. But warfare for the Kiowas
was pre-eminently a matter of disposition rather than of survival, and
they never understood the grim, unrelenting advance of the U.S. Cavalry.
When at last, divided and ill provisioned, they were driven onto the Staked
Plains in the cold of autumn, they fell into panic. In Palo Duro Canyon

they abandoned their crucial stores to pillage and had nothing then but their lives. In order to save themselves, they surrendered to the soldiers at Fort Sill and were imprisoned in the old stone corral that now stands as a military museum. My grandmother was spared the humiliation of those high gray walls by eight or ten years, but she must have known from birth the affliction of defeat, the dark brooding of old warriors.

Her name was Aho, and she belonged to the last culture to evolve in North America. Her forebears came down from the high country in western Montana nearly three centuries ago. They were a mountain people, a mysterious tribe of hunters whose language has never been classified in any major group. In the late seventeenth century they began a long migration to the south and east. It was a journey toward the dawn, and it led to a golden age. Along the way the Kiowas were befriended by the Crows, who gave them the culture and religion of the Plains. They acquired horses, and their ancient nomadic spirit was suddenly free of the ground. They acquired Tai-me, the sacred sundance doll, from that moment the object and symbol of their worship, and so shared in the divinity of the sun. Not least, they acquired the sense of destiny, therefore courage and pride. When they entered upon the Southern Plains they had been transformed. No longer were they slaves to the simple necessity of survival; they were a lordly and dangerous society of fighters and thieves, hunters and priests of the sun. According to their origin myth, they entered the world through a hollow log. From one point of view, their migration was the fruit of an old prophecy, for indeed they emerged from a sunless world.

Though my grandmother lived out her long life in the shadow of Rainy Mountain, the immense landscape of the continental interior lay like memory in her blood. She could tell of the Crows, whom she had never seen, and of the Black Hills, where she had never been. I wanted to see in reality what she had seen more perfectly in the mind's eye, and drove fifteen hundred miles to begin my pilgrimage.

A dark mist lay over the Black Hills, and the land was like iron. At the top of a ridge I caught sight of Devil's Tower upthrust against the gray sky as if in the birth of time the core of the earth had broken through its crust and the motion of the world was begun. There are things in nature that engender an awful quiet in the heart of man; Devil's Tower is one of them. Two centuries ago, because of their need to explain it, the Kiowas made a legend at the base of the rock. My grandmother said:

"Eight children were there at play, seven sisters and their brother. Suddenly the boy was struck dumb; he trembled and began to run upon his hands and feet. His fingers became claws, and his body was covered with fur. There was a bear where the boy had been. The sisters were terrified; they ran, and the bear after them. They came to the stump of a great tree, and the tree spoke to them. It bade them climb upon it, and as they did so, it began to rise into the air. The bear came to kill them, but they were just beyond its reach. It reared against the tree and scored the bark all around with its claws. The seven sisters were borne into the sky, and they became the stars of the Big Dipper." From that moment, and so long as the legend lives, the Kiowas have kinsmen in the night sky. Whatever they were in the mountains, they could be no more. However tenuous their well-being, however much they had suffered and would suffer again, they had found a way out of the wilderness.

My grandmother had a reverence for the sun, a holy regard that now is all but gone out of mankind. There was a wariness in her, and an ancient awe. She was a Christian in her later years, but she had come a long way about, and she never forgot her birthright. As a child she had been to the sun dances; she had taken part in that annual rite, and by it she had learned the restoration of her people in the presence of Tai-me. She was about seven when the last Kiowa sun dance was held in 1887 on the Washita River above Rainy Mountain Creek. The buffalo were gone. In order to consummate the ancient sacrifice—to impale the head of a buffalo bull upon the Tai-me tree—a delegation of old men journeyed into Texas, there to beg and barter for an animal from the Goodnight herd. She was ten when the Kiowas came together for the last time as a living sun-dance culture. They could find no buffalo; they had to hang an old hide from the sacred tree. Before the dance could begin, a company of soldiers rode out from fort Sill under orders to disperse the tribe. Forbidden without cause the essential act of their faith, having seen the wild herds slaughtered and left to rot upon the ground, the Kiowas backed away forever from the tree. That was July 20, 1890, at the great bend of the Washita. My grandmother was there. Without bitterness, and for as long as she lived, she bore a vision of deicide.

Now that I can have her only in memory, I see my grandmother in the several postures that were peculiar to her: standing at the wood stove on a winter morning and turning meat in a great iron skillet; sitting at the south window, bent above her beadwork, and afterwards, when her vision failed, looking down for a long time into the fold of her hands; going out upon a cane, very slowly as she did when the weight of age came upon her; praying. I remember her most often at prayer. She made long, rambling prayers out of suffering and hope, having seen many things. I was never sure that I had the right to hear, so exclusive were they of all mere custom and company. The last time I saw her she prayed standing by the side of her bed at night, naked to the waist, the light of a kerosene lamp moving upon her dark skin. Her long black hair, always drawn and braided in the day, lay upon her shoulders and against her breasts like a shawl. I did not speak Kiowa, and I never understood her prayers, but there was something inherently sad in the sound, some merest hesitation upon the syllables of sorrow. She began in a high and descending pitch, exhausting her breath to silence; then again and again—and always the same intensity of effort, of something that is, and is not, like urgency in the human voice. Transported so in the dancing light among the shadows of her room, she seemed beyond the reach of time. But that was illusion; I think I knew then that I should not see her again.

Houses are like sentinels in the plain, old keepers of the weather watch. There, in a very little while, wood takes on the appearance of great age. All colors wear soon away in the wind and rain, and then the wood is burned gray and the grain appears and the nails turn red with rust. The window panes are black and opaque; you imagine there is nothing within, and indeed there are many ghosts, bones given up to the land. They stand here and there against the sky, and you approach them for a longer time than you expect. They belong in the distance; it is their domain.

Once there was a lot of sound in my grandmother's house, a lot of coming and going, feasting and talk. The summers there were full of excitement and reunion. The Kiowas are a summer people; they abide the cold and keep to themselves, but when the season turns and the land becomes warm and vital they cannot hold still; an old love of going returns upon them. The aged visitors who came to my grandmother's house when I was a child were made of lean and leather, and they bore themselves upright. They wore great black hats and bright ample shirts that shook in the wind. They rubbed fat upon their hair and wound their braids with strips of colored cloth. Some of them painted their faces and carried the scars of old and cherished enmities. They were an old council of warlords, come to remind and be reminded of who they were. Their wives and daughters served them well. The women might indulge themselves; gossip was at once the mark and compensation of their servitude. They made loud and elaborate talk among themselves, full of jest and gesture, fright and false alarm. They went abroad in fringed and flowered shawls, bright beadwork and German silver. They were at home in the kitchen, and they prepared meals that were banquets.

There were frequent prayer meetings, and nocturnal feasts. When I was a child I played with my cousins outside, where the lamplight fell upon the ground and the singing of the old people rose up around us and carried away into the darkness. There were a lot of good things to eat, a lot of laughter and surprise. And afterwards, when the quiet returned, I lay down with my grandmother and could hear the frogs away by the river and feel the motion of the air.

Now there is a funereal silence in the rooms, the endless wake of some final word. The walls have closed in upon my grandmother's house. When I returned to it in mourning, I saw for the first time in my life how small it was. It was late at night, and there was a white moon, nearly full. I sat for a long time on the stone steps by the kitchen door. From there I could see out across the land; I could see the long row of trees by the creek, the low light upon the rolling plains, and the stars of the Big Dipper. Once I looked at the moon and caught sight of a strange thing. A cricket had perched upon the handrail, only a few inches away. My line of vision was such that the creature filled the moon like a fossil. It had gone there, I thought, to live and die, for there, of all places, was its small definition made whole and eternal. A warm wind rose up and purled like the longing within me.

The next morning, I awoke at dawn and went out on the dirt road to Rainy Mountain. It was already hot, and the grasshoppers began to fill the air. Still, it was early in the morning, and birds sang out of the shadows. The long yellow grass on the mountain shone in the bright light, and a scissortail hied above the land. There, where it ought to be, at the end of a long and legendary way, was my grandmother's grave. She had at last succeeded to that holy ground. Here and there on the dark stones were ancestral names. Looking back once. I saw the mountain and came away. ■

Questions for Analysis

1. a. The first paragraph of the essay concludes with the statement, "Your imagination comes to life, and this, you think, is where creation was begun." Identify Momaday's descriptions of the Oklahoma landscape that lead him to this conclusion.

    b. Think of a place that has special meaning for you. Write a passage in which you use descriptive reports to create the atmosphere and meaning that the place has for you.

2. a. Momaday's grandmother, Aho, represents one of the main themes that ties this essay together. Identify the key descriptions regarding her life that help us understand her personality.

   b. Think about a person with distinctive qualities who occupies a special place in your life. Communicate the unique personality of that person by providing illuminating descriptions about him or her.

3. a. In many ways the history of the Kiowas mirrored that of the other Native American tribes. Describe the key events that shaped their history, concluding with the last aborted sun dance in 1890.

   b. Research the history of your own family by interviewing family members and reviewing written records. After collecting your factual information, compose a "brief history" of your family that includes the key events that shaped their lives. ◀

EVOLUTION AS FACT AND THEORY
by Stephen Jay Gould

Kirtley Mather, who died last year at age 89, was a pillar of both science and the Christian religion in America and one of my dearest friends. The difference of half a century in our ages evaporated before our common interests. The most curious thing we shared was a battle we each fought at the same age. For Kirtley had gone to Tennessee with Clarence Darrow to testify for evolution at the Scopes trial of 1925. When I think that we are enmeshed again in the same struggle for one of the best documented, most compelling and exciting concepts in all of science, I don't know whether to laugh or cry.

According to idealized principles of scientific discourse, the arousal of dormant issues should reflect fresh data that give renewed life to abandoned notions. Those outside the current debate may therefore be excused for suspecting that creationists have come up with something new, or that evolutionists have generated some serious internal trouble. But nothing has changed; the creationists have not a single new fact or argument. Darrow and Bryan were at least more entertaining than we lesser antagonists today.* The rise of creationism is politics, pure and simple; it represents one issue (and by no means the major concern) of the resurgent evangelical right. Arguments that seemed kooky just a decade ago have re-entered the mainstream.

---

* Darrow and Bryan: Clarence Darrow (1857–1938) was the defense attorney in the 1925 trial of John Thomas Scopes for teaching evolution; William Jennings Bryan (1860–1925) was an orator and politician who aided the prosecution in the Scopes trial. [Eds.]

Creationism Is Not Science

The basic attack of the creationists falls apart on two general counts before we even reach the supposed factual details of their complaints against evolution. First, they play upon a vernacular misunderstanding of the word "theory" to convey the false impression that we evolutionists are covering up the rotten core of our edifice. Second, they misuse a popular philosophy of science to argue that they are behaving scientifically in attacking evolution. Yet the same philosophy demonstrates that their own belief is not science, and that "scientific creationism" is therefore meaningless and self-contradictory, a superb example of what Orwell† called "newspeak."‡

In the American vernacular, "theory" often means "imperfect fact"—part of a hierarchy of confidence running downhill from fact to theory to hypothesis to guess. Thus the power of the creationist argument: evolution is "only" a theory, and intense debate now rages about many aspects of the theory. If evolution is less than a fact, and scientists can't even make up their minds about the theory, then what confidence can we have in it? Indeed, President Reagan echoed this argument before an evangelical group in Dallas when he said (in what I devoutly hope was campaign rhetoric): "Well, it is a theory. It is a scientific theory only, and it has in recent years been challenged in the world of science—that is, not believed in the scientific community to be as infallible as it once was."

Well, evolution *is* a theory. It is also a fact. And facts and theories are different things, not rungs in a hierarchy of increasing certainty. Facts are the world's data. Theories are structures of ideas that explain and interpret facts. Facts do not go away when scientists debate rival theories to explain them. Einstein's theory of gravitation replaced Newton's, but apples did not suspend themselves in mid-air pending the outcome. And human beings evolved from apelike ancestors whether they did so by Darwin's proposed mechanism or by some other, yet to be discovered.

Moreover, "fact" does not mean "absolute certainty." The final proofs of logic and mathematics flow deductively from stated premises and achieve certainty only because they are *not* about the empirical world. Evolutionists make no claim for perpetual truth, though creationists often do (and then attack us for a style of argument that they themselves favor). In science, "fact" can only mean "confirmed to such a degree that it would

---

†George Orwell (1903–1950): English journalist and novelist, author of *Animal Farm* and *1984*. [Eds.]

‡"Newspeak": the official language in Orwell's *1984*, devised to meet the ideological needs of the ruling party and to make all other modes of thought impossible. [Eds.]

be perverse to withhold provisional assent." I suppose that apples might start to rise tomorrow, but possibility does not merit equal time in physics classrooms.

Evolutionists have been clear about this distinction between fact and theory from the very beginning, if only because we have always acknowledged how far we are from completely understanding the mechanisms (theory) by which evolution (fact) occurred. Darwin continually emphasized the difference between his two great and separate accomplishments: establishing the fact of evolution, and proposing a theory—natural selection—to explain the mechanism of evolution. He wrote in *The Descent of Man:* "I had two distinct objects in view; firstly, to show that species had not been separately created, and secondly, that natural selection had been the chief agent of change. . . . Hence if I have erred in . . . having exaggerated its [natural selection's] power . . . I have at least, as I hope, done good service in aiding to overthrow the dogma of separate creations."

Thus Darwin acknowledged the provisional nature of natural selection while affirming the fact of evolution. The fruitful theoretical debate that Darwin initiated has never ceased. From the 1940s through the 1960s, Darwin's own theory of natural selection did achieve a temporary hegemony that it never enjoyed in his lifetime. But renewed debate characterizes our decade, and while no biologist questions the importance of natural selection, many now doubt its ubiquity. In particular, many evolutionists argue that substantial amounts of genetic change may not be subject to natural selection and may spread through populations at random. Others are challenging Darwin's linking of natural selection with gradual, imperceptible change through all intermediary degrees; they are arguing that most evolutionary events may occur far more rapidly than Darwin envisioned.

Scientists regard debates on fundamental issues of theory as a sign of intellectual health and a source of excitement. Science is—and how else can I say it?—most fun when it plays with interesting ideas, examines their implications, and recognizes that old information may be explained in surprisingly new ways. Evolutionary theory is now enjoying this uncommon vigor. Yet amidst all this turmoil no biologist has been led to doubt the fact that evolution occurred; we are debating *how* it happened. We are all trying to explain the same thing: the tree of evolutionary descent linking all organisms by ties of genealogy. Creationists pervert and caricature this debate by conveniently neglecting the common conviction that underlies it, and by falsely suggesting that we now doubt the very phenomenon we are struggling to understand.

Using another invalid argument, creationists claim that "the dogma of separate creations," as Darwin characterized it a century ago, is a scientific theory meriting equal time with evolution in high school biology curricula. But a prevailing viewpoint among philosophers of science belies this creationist argument. Philosopher Karl Popper has argued for decades that the primary criterion of science is the falsifiability of its theories. We can never prove absolutely, but we can falsify. A set of ideas that cannot, in principle, be falsified is not science.

The entire creationist argument involves little more than a rhetorical attempt to falsify evolution by presenting supposed contradictions among its supporters. Their brand of creationism, they claim, is "scientific" because it follows the Popperian model in trying to demolish evolution. Yet Popper's argument must apply in both directions. One does not become a scientist by the simple act of trying to falsify another scientific system; one has to present an alternative system that also meets Popper's criterion—it too must be falsifiable in principle.

"Scientific creationism" is a self-contradictory, nonsense phrase precisely because it cannot be falsified. I can envision observations and experiments that would disprove any evolutionary theory I know, but I cannot imagine what potential data could lead creationists to abandon their beliefs. Unbeatable systems are dogma, not science. Lest I seem harsh or rhetorical, I quote creationism's leading intellectual, Duane Gish, Ph.D., from his recent (1978) book *Evolution? The Fossils Say No!* "By creation we mean the bringing into being by a supernatural Creator of the basic kinds of plants and animals by the process of sudden, or flat, creation. We do not know how the Creator created, what processes He used, *for He used processes which are not now operating anywhere in the natural universe* [Gish's italics]. This is why we refer to creation as special creation. We cannot discover by scientific investigations anything about the creative processes used by the Creator." Pray tell, Dr. Gish, in the light of your last sentence, what then is "scientific" creationism?

The Fact of Evolution

Our confidence that evolution occurred centers upon three general arguments. First, we have abundant, direct, observational evidence of evolution in action, from both the field and the laboratory. It ranges from countless experiments on change in nearly everything about fruit flies subjected to artificial selection in the laboratory to the famous British moths that turned black when industrial soot darkened the trees upon which they rest. (The moths gain protection from sharp-sighted bird predators by blending into the background.) Creationists do not deny these observations; how could they? Creationists have tightened their act. They now argue that God only created "basic kinds," and allowed for limited evolutionary meandering within them. Thus toy poodles and Great Danes come from the dog kind and moths can change color, but nature cannot convert a dog to a cat or a monkey to a man.

The second and third arguments for evolution—the case for major changes—do not involve direct observation of evolution in action. They rest upon inference, but are no less secure for that reason. Major evolutionary change requires too much time for direct observation on the scale of recorded human history. All historical sciences rest upon inference, and evolution is no different from geology, cosmology, or human history in this respect. In principle, we cannot observe processes that operated in the past. We must infer them from results that still survive: living and fossil organisms for evolution, documents and artifacts for human history, strata and topography for geology.

The second argument—that the imperfection of nature reveals evolution—strikes many people as ironic, for they feel that evolution should be most elegantly displayed in the nearly perfect adaptation expressed by some organisms—the chamber of a gull's wing, or butterflies that cannot be seen in ground litter because they mimic leaves so precisely. But perfection could be imposed by a wise creator or evolved by natural selection. Perfection covers the tracks of past history. And past history—the evidence of descent—is our mark of evolution.

Evolution lies exposed in the *imperfections* that record a history of descent. Why should a rat run, a bat fly, a porpoise swim, and I type this essay with structures built of the same bones unless we all inherited them from a common ancestor? An engineer, starting from scratch, could design better limbs in each case. Why should all the large native mammals of Australia be marsupials, unless they descended from a common ancestor isolated on this island continent? Marsupials are not "better," or ideally suited for Australia; many have been wiped out by placental mammals imported by man from other continents. This principle of imperfection extends to all historical sciences. When we recognize the etymology of September, October, November, and December (seventh, eighth, ninth, and tenth, from the Latin), we know that two additional items (January and February) must have been added to an original calendar of ten months.

The third argument is more direct: transitions are often found in the fossil record. Preserved transitions are not common—and should not be, according to our understanding of evolution . . . —but they are not entirely wanting, as creationists often claim. The lower jaw of reptiles contains several bones, that of mammals only one. The nonmammalian jawbones are reduced, step by step, in mammalian ancestors until they become tiny nubbins located at the back of the jaw. The "hammer" and "anvil" bones of the mammalian ear are descendants of these nubbins. How could such a transition be accomplished? The creationists ask. Surely a bone is either entirely in the jaw or in the ear. Yet paleontologists have discovered two transitional lineages or therapsids (the so-called mammal-like reptiles) with a double jaw joint—one composed of the old quadrate and articular bones (soon to become the hammer and anvil), the other of the squamosal and dentary bones (as in modern mammals). For that matter, what better transitional form could we desire than the oldest human, *Australopithecus afarensis,* with its apelike palate, its human upright stance, and a cranial capacity larger than any ape's of the same body size but a full 1,000 cubic centimeters below ours? If God made each of the half dozen human species discovered in ancient rocks, why did he create an unbroken temporal sequence of progressively more modern features—increasing cranial capacity, reduced face and teeth, larger body size? Did he create a mimic evolution and test our faith thereby?

Conclusion

I am both angry at and amused by the creationists; but mostly I am deeply sad. Sad for many reasons. Sad because so many people who respond to creationist appeals are troubled for the right reason, but venting their anger at the wrong target. It is true that scientists have often been dogmatic and elitist. It is true that we have often allowed the white-coated, advertising image to represent us—"Scientists say that Brand X cures bunions ten times faster than. . . ." We have not fought it adequately because we derive benefits from appearing as a new priesthood. It is also true that faceless bureaucratic state power intrudes more and more into our lives and removes choices that should belong to individuals and communities. I can understand that requiring that evolution be taught in the schools might be seen as one more insult on all these grounds. But the culprit is not, and cannot be, evolution or any other fact of the natural world. Identify and fight your legitimate enemies by all means, but we are not among them.

I am sad because the practical result of this brouhaha will not be expanded coverage to include creationism (that would also make me sad), but the reduction or excision of evolution from high school curricula. Evolution is one of the half dozen "great ideas" developed by science. It speaks to the profound issues of genealogy that fascinate all of us—the "roots" phenomenon writ large. Where did we come from? Where did life arise? How did it develop? How are organisms related? It forces us to think, ponder, and wonder. Shall we deprive millions of this knowledge and once again teach biology as a set of dull and unconnected facts, without the thread that weaves diverse material into a supple unity?

But most of all I am saddened by a trend I am just beginning to discern among my colleagues. I sense that some now wish to mute the healthy debate about theory that has brought new life to evolutionary biology. It provides grist for creationist mills, they say, even if only by distortion. Perhaps we should lie low and rally round the flag of strict Darwinism, at least for the moment—a kind of old-time religion on our part.

But we should borrow another metaphor and recognize that we too have to tread a straight and narrow path, surrounded by roads to perdition. For if we ever begin to suppress our search to understand nature, to quench our own intellectual excitement in a misguided effort to present a united front where it does not and should not exist, then we are truly lost. ■

Questions for Analysis

1. According to Gould, evolution is both a scientific "fact" and a scientific "theory" asserting that all life forms are the result of a process of gradual development and differentiation over time, much like the progressive growth of tree branches from the central trunk. In contrast, creationism asserts that all basic forms of life were brought into being in a sudden act by a supernatural creator. Explain what you understand about the theory of evolution and creationism based on your reading of the article.

2. Gould defines "facts" as the "world's data," like observing an apple fall from a tree, as Isaac Newton is alleged to have done. Describe some of the facts Gould gives as evidence to support the theory of evolution.

3. Gould defines "theories" as "structures of ideas that explain and interpret facts," such as Newton's theory of gravitation introduced to explain facts like falling apples. In addition to facts, Gould states that the theory of evolution is supported by reasonable inferences. Describe the inferences he cites as evidence.

4. According to Gould, creationism is neither a scientific fact nor a scientific theory. Describe the reasons he gives to support this belief.

5. At the beginning of the article. Gould gives the example of Kirtley Mather as "a pillar of both science and the Christian religion." Explain how you think it might be possible to believe in both of these viewpoints with respect to the origins of life. ◀

I LISTEN TO MY PARENTS AND I WONDER WHAT THEY BELIEVE
By Robert Coles

Not so long ago children were looked upon in a sentimental fashion as "angels" or as "innocents." Today, thanks to Freud and his followers, boys and girls are understood to have complicated inner lives; to feel love, hate, envy and rivalry in various and subtle mixtures; to be eager participants in the sexual and emotional politics of the home, neighborhood and school. Yet some of us parents still cling to the notion of childhood innocence in another way. We do not see that our children also make ethical decisions every day in their own lives, or realize how attuned they may be to moral currents and issues in the larger society.

In Appalachia I heard a girl of eight whose father owns coal fields (and gas stations, a department store and much timberland) wonder about "life" one day: "I'll be walking to the school bus, and I'll ask myself why there's some who are poor and their daddies can't find a job, and there's some who are lucky like me. Last month there was an explosion in a mine my daddy owns, and everyone became upset. Two miners got killed. My daddy said it was their own fault, because they'll be working and they get careless. When my mother asked if there was anything wrong with the safety down in the mine, he told her no and she shouldn't ask questions like that. Then the Government people came and they said it was the owner's fault—Daddy's. But he has a lawyer and the lawyer is fighting the Government and the union. In school, kids ask me what I think, and I sure do feel sorry for the two miners and so does my mother—I know that. She told me it's just not a fair world and you have to remember that. Of course, there's no one who can be sure there won't be trouble; like my daddy says, the rain falls on the just and the unjust. My brother is only six and he asked Daddy awhile back who are the 'just' and the 'unjust,' and Daddy said there are people who work hard and they live good lives, and there are lazy people and they're always trying to sponge off others. But I guess you have to feel sorry for anyone who has a lot of trouble, because it's poured-down, heavy rain."

Listening, one begins to realize that an elementary-school child is no stranger to moral reflection—and to ethical conflict. This girl was torn between her loyalty to her particular background, its values and assumptions, and to a larger affiliation—her membership in the nation, the world. As a human being whose parents were kind and decent to her, she was inclined to be thoughtful and sensitive with respect to others, no matter what their work or position in society. But her father was among other things a mineowner, and she had already learned to shape her concerns to suit that fact of life. The result: a moral oscillation of sorts, first toward nameless others all over the world and then toward her own family. As the girl put it later, when she was a year older: "You should try to have 'good thoughts' about everyone, the minister says, and our teacher says that too. But you should honor your father and mother most of all; that's why you should find out what they think and then sort of copy them. But sometimes you're not sure if you're on the right track."

Sort of copy them. There could be worse descriptions of how children acquire moral values. In fact, the girl understood how girls and boys all over the world "sort of" develop attitudes of what is right and wrong, ideas of who the just and the unjust are. And they also struggle hard and long, and not always with success, to find out where the "right track" starts and ends. Children need encouragement or assistance as they wage that struggle.

In home after home that I have visited, and in many classrooms, I have met children who not only are growing emotionally and intellectually but also are trying to make sense of the world morally. That is to say, they are asking themselves and others about issues of fair play, justice, liberty, equality. Those last words are abstractions, of course—the stuff of college term papers. And there are, one has to repeat, those in psychology and psychiatry who would deny elementary-school children access to that "higher level" of moral reflection. But any parent who has listened closely to his or her child knows that girls and boys are capable of wondering about matters of morality, and knows too that often it is their grown-up protectors (parents, relatives, teachers, neighbors) who are made uncomfortable by the so-called "innocent" nature of the questions children may ask or the statements they may make. Often enough the issue is not the moral capacity of the children but the default of us parents who fail to respond to inquiries put to us by our daughters and sons—and fail to set moral standards for both ourselves and our children.

Do's and don'ts are, of course, pressed upon many of our girls and boys. But a moral education is something more than a series of rules handed down, and in our time one cannot assume that every parent feels able—sure enough of her own or his own actual beliefs and values—to make even an initial explanatory and disciplinary effort toward a moral education. Furthermore, for many of us parents these days it is a child's emotional life that preoccupies us.

In 1963, when I was studying school desegregation in the South, I had extended conversations with Black and white elementary-school children caught up in a dramatic moment of historical change. For longer than I care to remember, I concentrated on possible psychiatric troubles, on how a given child was managing under circumstances of extreme stress, on how I could be of help—with "support," with reassurance, with a helpful psychological observation or interpretation. In many instances I was off the mark. These children weren't "patients"; they weren't even complaining. They were worried, all right, and often enough they had things to say that were substantive—that had to do not so much with troubled emotions as with questions of right and wrong in the real-life dramas taking place in their worlds.

Here is a nine-year-old white boy, the son of ardent segregationists, telling me about his sense of what desegregation meant to Louisiana in the 1960s: "They told us it wouldn't happen—never. My daddy said none of us white people would go into schools with the colored. But then it did happen, and when I went to school the first day I didn't know what would go on. Would the school stay open or would it close up? We didn't know what to do; the teacher kept telling us that we should be good and obey the law, but my daddy said the law was wrong. Then my mother said she wanted me in school even if there were some colored kids there. She said if we all stayed home she'd be a 'nervous wreck.' So I went.

"After a while I saw that the colored weren't so bad. I saw that there are different kinds of colored people, just like with us whites. There was one of the colored who was nice, a boy who smiled, and he played real good. There was another one, a boy, who wouldn't talk with anyone. I don't know if it's right that we all be in the same school. Maybe it isn't right. My sister is starting school next year, and she says she doesn't care if there's 'mixing of the races.' She says they told her in Sunday school that everyone is a child of God, and then a kid asked if that goes for the colored too and the teacher said yes, she thought so. My daddy said that it's true, God made everyone—but that doesn't mean we all have to be living together under the same roof in the home or the school. But my mother said we'll never know what God wants of us but we have to try to read His mind, and that's why we pray. So when I say my prayers I ask

God to tell me what's the right thing to do. In school I try to say hello to the colored, because they're kids, and you can't be mean or you'll be 'doing wrong,' like my grandmother says."

Children aren't usually long-winded in the moral discussions they have with one another or with adults, and in quoting this boy I have pulled together comments he made to me in the course of several days. But everything he said was of interest to me. I was interested in the boy's changing racial attitudes. It was clear he was trying to find a coherent, sensible moral position too. It was also borne in on me that if one spends days, weeks in a given home, it is hard to escape a particular moral climate just as significant as the psychological one.

In many homes parents establish moral assumptions, mandates, priorities. They teach children what to believe in, what not to believe in. They teach children what is permissible or not permissible—and why. They may summon up the Bible, the flag, history, novels, aphorisms, philosophical or political sayings, personal memories—all in an effort to teach children how to behave, what and whom to respect and for which reasons. Or they may neglect to do so, and in so doing teach their children *that*—a moral abdication, of sorts—and in this way fail their children. Children need and long for words of moral advice, instruction, warning, as much as they need words of affirmation or criticism from their parents about other matters. They must learn how to dress and what to wear, how to eat and what to eat; and they must also learn how to behave under X or Y or Z conditions, and why.

All the time, in 20 years of working with poor children and rich children, Black children and white children, children from rural areas and urban areas and in every region of this country, I have heard questions— thoroughly intelligent and discerning questions—about social and historical matters, about personal behavior, and so on. But most striking is the fact that almost all those questions, in one way or another, are moral in nature: Why did the Pilgrims leave England? Why didn't they just stay and agree to do what the king wanted them to do? . . . Should you try to share all you've got or should you save a lot for yourself? . . . What do you do when you see others fighting—do you try to break up the fight, do you stand by and watch or do you leave as fast as you can? . . . Is it right that some people haven't got enough to eat? . . . I see other kids cheating and I wish I could copy the answers too; but I won't cheat, though sometimes I feel I'd like to and I get all mixed up. I go home and talk with my parents, and I ask them what should you do if you see kids cheating—pay no attention, or report the kids or do the same thing they are doing?

Those are examples of children's concerns—and surely millions of American parents have heard versions of them. Have the various "experts" on childhood stressed strongly enough the importance of such questions—and the importance of the hunger we all have, no matter what our age or background, to examine what we believe in, are willing to stand up for, and what we are determined to ask, likewise, of our children?

Children not only need our understanding of their complicated emotional lives; they also need a constant regard for the moral issues that come their way as soon as they are old enough to play with others and take part in the politics of the nursery, the back yard and the schoolroom. They need to be told what they must do and what they must not do. They need control over themselves and a sense of what others are entitled to from them—co-operation, thoughtfulness, an attentive ear and eye. They need discipline not only to tame their excesses of emotion but discipline also connected to stated and clarified moral values. They need, in other words, something to believe in that is larger than their own appetites and urges and, yes, bigger than their "psychological drives." They need a larger view of the world, a moral context, as it were—a faith that addresses itself to the meaning of this life we all live and, soon enough, let go of.

Yes, it is time for us parents to begin to look more closely at what ideas our children have about the world; and it would be well to do so before they become teen-agers and young adults and begin to remind us, as often happens, of how little attention we did pay to their moral development. Perhaps a nine-year-old girl from a well-off suburban home in Texas put it better than anyone else I've met:

"I listen to my parents, and I wonder what they believe in more than anything else. I asked my mom and my daddy once: What's the thing that means most to you? They said they didn't know but I shouldn't worry my head too hard with questions like that. So I asked my best friend, and she said she wonders if there's a God and how do you know Him and what does He want you to do—I mean, when you're in school or out playing with your friends. They talk about God in church, but is it only in church that He's there and keeping an eye on you? I saw a kid steal in a store, and I know her father has a lot of money—because I hear my daddy talk. But stealing's wrong. My mother said she's a 'sick girl,' but it's still wrong what she did. Don't you think?"

There was more—much more—in the course of the months I came to know that child and her parents and their neighbors. But those observations and questions—a "mere child's"—reminded me unforgettably of the aching hunger for firm ethical principles that so many of us feel. Ought we not begin thinking about this need? Ought we not all be asking our-selves more intently what standards we live by—and how we can satisfy our children's hunger for moral values? ■

Questions for Analysis

1. In this article, Coles gives a number of examples of children struggling to develop a set of ethical standards that make sense to them.

   a. Identify some of the ethical standards that are illustrated.

   b. Explain how these standards agree and disagree with standards their parents believe in.

   c. In those cases where the children's ethical standards diverge from those of their parents, describe the reasons that support the children's beliefs.

2. Using this article as a resource, define your own understanding of the concept *moral awareness*.

   a. Describe one or more examples from your own experience that illustrate the concept *moral awareness*.

   b. Based on these examples, identify the necessary requirements of the concept *moral awareness*.

3. At the end of the article, Coles calls for the need to think about how we teach moral awareness:

   . . . those observations and questions—a "mere child's"—reminded me unforgettably of the aching hunger for firm ethical principles that so many of us feel. Ought we not begin thinking about this need? Ought we not all be asking ourselves more intently what standards we live by—and how we can satisfy our children's hunger for moral values?

   Explain what you see as the connection between developing moral aware-ness and our ability to think critically, as suggested by Coles.

4. a. Identify a moral issue that you feel strongly about and describe your be-liefs about this issue.

   b. Describe how you developed your beliefs about this moral issue, based on your experience (education, family, friends, critical reflection, etc.).

   c. Explain how you would teach this moral issue to someone else. ◄

10

CONSTRUCTING ARGUMENTS

Recognizing Arguments
Cue words

Constructing Arguments
Decide
Explain
Predict
Persuade

ARGUMENT:
A form of thinking in which certain reasons are offered to support a conclusion

Composing an Argumentative Paper
Generating ideas
Defining a main idea
Conducting research
Organizing ideas
Revising

Distinguishing Forms of Arguments
Deductive
Inductive

Evaluating Arguments
Truth
Validity
Soundness

CONSIDER CAREFULLY the following dialogue about whether marijuana should be legalized:

Dennis: Did you hear about the person who was sentenced to fifteen years in prison for possessing marijuana? I think this is one of the most outrageously unjust punishments I've ever heard of! In most states, people who are convicted of armed robbery, rape, or even murder don't receive fifteen-year sentences. And unlike the possession of marijuana, these crimes violate the rights of other people.

Caroline: I agree that this is one case in which the punishment doesn't seem to fit the crime. But you have to realize that drugs pose a serious threat to the young people of our country. Look at all the people who are addicted to drugs, who have their lives ruined, and who often die at an early age of overdoses. And think of all the crimes committed by people to support their drug habits. As a result, sometimes society has to make an example of someone—like the person you mentioned—to convince people of the seriousness of the situation.

Dennis: That's ridiculous. In the first place, it's not right to punish someone unfairly just to provide an example. At least not in a society that believes in justice. And in the second place, smoking marijuana is nothing like using drugs such as heroin or even cocaine. It follows that smoking marijuana should not be against the law.

Caroline: I don't agree. Although marijuana might not be as dangerous as some other drugs, smoking it surely isn't good for you. And I don't think that anything that is a threat to your health should be legal.

Dennis: What about cigarettes and alcohol? We *know* that they are dangerous. Medical research has linked smoking cigarettes to lung cancer, emphysema, and heart disease, and alcohol damages the liver. No one has proved that marijuana is a threat to our health. And even if it does turn out to be somewhat unhealthy, it's certainly not as dangerous as cigarettes and alcohol.

Caroline: That's a good point. But to tell you the truth, I'm not so sure that cigarettes and alcohol should be legal. And in any case, they are already legal. Just because cigarettes and alcohol are bad for your health is no reason to legalize another drug that can cause health problems.

Dennis: Look—life is full of risks. We take chances every time we cross the street or climb into our car. In fact, with all of these loonies on the road, driving is a lot more hazardous to our health than any of the drugs around. And many of the foods we eat can kill. For example, red meat contributes to heart disease, and artificial sweeteners can cause cancer. The point is, if people want to take chances with their health, that's up to them. And many people in our society like to mellow out with marijuana. I read somewhere that over 70 percent of the people in the United States think that marijuana should be legalized.

Caroline: There's a big difference between letting people drive cars and letting them use dangerous drugs. Society has a responsibility to protect people from themselves. People often do things that are foolish if they are encouraged or given the opportunity to. Legalizing something like marijuana encourages people to use it, especially young people. It follows that many more people would use marijuana if it were legalized. It's like society saying "This is all right—go ahead and use it."

Dennis: I still maintain that marijuana isn't dangerous. It's not addictive—like heroin is—and there is no evidence that it harms you. Consequently, anything that is harmless should be legal.

Caroline: Marijuana may not be physically addictive like heroin, but I think that it can be psychologically addictive, because people tend to use more and more of it over time. I know a number of people who spend a lot of their time getting high. What about Carl? All he does is lie around and get high. This shows that smoking it over a period of time definitely affects your mind. Think about the people you know who smoke a lot—don't they seem to be floating in a dream world? How are they ever going to make anything of their lives? As far as I'm concerned, a pothead is like a zombie—living but dead.

Dennis: Since you have had so little experience with marijuana, I don't think that you can offer an informed opinion on the subject. And anyway, if you do too much of anything it can hurt you. Even something as healthy as exercise can cause problems if you do too much of it. But I sure don't see anything wrong with toking up with some friends at a party or even getting into a relaxed state by yourself. In fact, I find that I can even concentrate better on my school work after taking a little smoke.

Caroline: If you believe that, then marijuana really *has* damaged your brain. You're just trying to rationalize your drug habit. Smoking marijuana doesn't help you concentrate—it takes you away from reality. And I don't think that people can control it. Either you smoke and surrender control of your life, or you don't smoke because you want to retain control. There's nothing in between.

Dennis: Let me point out something to you. Because marijuana is illegal, organized crime controls its distribution and makes all the money out of it.

If marijuana were legalized, the government could tax the sale of it—like cigarettes and alcohol—and then use the money for some worthwhile purpose. For example, many states have legalized gambling and use the money to support education. In fact, the major tobacco companies have already copyrighted names for different marijuana brands—like "Acapulco Gold." Obviously they believe that marijuana will soon become legal.

Caroline: Just because the government can make money out of something doesn't mean that they should legalize it. We could also legalize prostitution or muggings, and then tax the proceeds. Also, simply because the cigarette companies are prepared to sell marijuana doesn't mean that it makes sense to. After all, they're the ones who are selling us cigarettes.

Continue this dialogue, incorporating other views on the subject of legalizing marijuana.

RECOGNIZING ARGUMENTS

The preceding discussion is an illustration of two people engaging in *dialogue,* which we have defined (in Chapter 2) as the systematic exchange of ideas. Participating in this sort of dialogue with others is one of the keys to thinking critically because it stimulates you to develop your mind by carefully examining the way you make sense of the world. Discussing issues with others encourages you to be mentally active, to ask questions, to view issues from different perspectives, and to develop reasons to support conclusions. It is this last quality of thinking critically—supporting conclusions with reasons—that we will focus on in this chapter and the next.

When we offer reasons to support a conclusion, we are considered to be presenting an *argument.*

Argument	A form of thinking in which certain statements (reasons) are offered in support of another statement (a conclusion).

At the beginning of the dialogue, Dennis presents the following argument against imposing a fifteen-year sentence for possession of marijuana (argument 1):

Reason: Possessing marijuana is not a serious offense because it hurts no one.

Reason: There are many other more serious offenses in which victims' basic rights are violated—such as armed robbery, rape, and murder—for which the offenders don't receive such stiff sentences.

Conclusion: Therefore a fifteen-year sentence is an unjust punishment for possessing marijuana.

Can you identify an additional reason that supports this conclusion?

Reason:

The definition of *argument* given here is somewhat different from the meaning of the concept in our ordinary language. In common speech, "argument" usually refers to a dispute or quarrel between people, often involving intense feelings. (For example: "I got into a terrible argument with the idiot who hit the back of my car.") Very often these quarrels involve people presenting arguments in the sense we have defined the concept, although the arguments are usually not carefully reasoned or clearly stated because the people are so angry. Instead of this common usage, in this chapter we will use its more technical meaning.

Using our definition, we can define the main ideas that make up an argument:

Reasons	Statements that support another statement (known as a conclusion), justify it, or make it more probable.

Conclusion	A statement that explains, asserts, or predicts on the basis of statements (known as reasons) that are offered as evidence for it.

The type of thinking that uses argument—reasons in support of conclusions—is known as *reasoning*, and it is a type of thinking you have been doing throughout this book, as well as in much of your life. We are continually trying to explain, justify, and predict things by the process of reasoning.

Of course, our reasoning—and the reasoning of others—is not always correct. For example, the reasons someone offers may not really support the conclusion they are supposed to. Or the conclusion may not really follow from the

Constructing sound arguments involves supporting our conclusions with strong and compelling reasons.

reasons stated. These difficulties are illustrated in a number of the arguments contained in the discussion on marijuana. Nevertheless, whenever we accept a conclusion as likely or true based on certain reasons or whenever we offer reasons to support a conclusion, we are using arguments to engage in reasoning— even if our reasoning is weak or faulty and needs to be improved. In this chapter and the next, we will be exploring both the way we construct effective arguments and the way we evaluate arguments to develop and sharpen our reasoning ability.

Let us return to the discussion about marijuana. After Dennis presents the argument with the conclusion that the fifteen-year prison sentence is an unjust punishment, Caroline considers that argument. Although she acknowledges that in this case "the punishment doesn't seem to fit the crime," she goes on to offer another argument (argument 2), giving reasons that lead to a conclusion that conflicts with the one Dennis made:

Reason: Drugs pose a very serious threat to the young people of our country.

Reason: Many crimes are committed to support drug habits.

Conclusion: As a result, sometimes society has to make an example of someone to convince people of the seriousness of the situation.

Can you identify an additional reason that supports this conclusion?

Reason:

Cue Words for Arguments

Our language provides guidance in our efforts to identify reasons and conclusions. Certain key words, known as *cue words*, signal that a reason is being offered in support of a conclusion or that a conclusion is being announced on the
basis of certain reasons. For example, in response to Caroline's conclusion that
society sometimes has to make an example of someone to convince people of
the seriousness of the situation, Dennis gives the following argument (argument 3):

Reason: In the first place, it's not right to punish someone unfairly just to
provide an example.

Reason: In the second place, smoking marijuana is nothing like using drugs
such as heroin or even cocaine.

Conclusion: It follows that smoking marijuana should not be against the law.

In this argument, the phrases "In the first place" and "In the second place"
signal that reasons are being offered in support of a conclusion. Similarly, the
phrase "It follows that" signals that a conclusion is being announced on the
basis of certain reasons. Here is a list of the most commonly used cue words for
reasons and conclusions:

Cue Words Signaling Reasons

since	in view of
for	first, second
because	in the first (second) place
as shown by	may be inferred from
as indicated by	may be deduced from
given that	may be derived from
assuming that	for the reason that

Cue Words Signaling Conclusions

therefore	then
thus	it follows that
hence	thereby showing
so	demonstrates that
(which) shows that	allows us to infer that
(which) proves that	suggests very strongly that
implies that	you see that
points to	leads me to believe that
as a result	allows us to deduce that
consequently	

Of course, identifying reasons, conclusions, and arguments involves more than looking for cue words. The words and phrases listed here do not always signal reasons and conclusions, and in many cases arguments are made without the use of cue words. Cue words, however, do help alert us that an argument is being made.

THINKING ACTIVITY 10.1

1. Review the discussion on marijuana and underline any cue words signaling that reasons are being offered or that conclusions are being announced.

2. With the aid of cue words, identify the various arguments contained in the discussion on marijuana. For each argument, describe:

   a. The *reasons* offered in support of a conclusion

   b. The *conclusion* announced on the basis of the reasons

   Before you start, review the three arguments we have examined so far in this chapter.

3. Go back to the additional arguments you wrote on page 451. Reorganize and add cue words if necessary to clearly identify your reasons as well as the conclusion you draw from those reasons. ◀

THINKING PASSAGES

The following two essays discuss the issue of whether drugs should be legalized. The first passage, "Drugs," is written by Gore Vidal, a well-known essayist and novelist. The second, "The Case for Slavery," is authored by the *New York Times* editor and columnist A. M. Rosenthal. After carefully reading the essays, answer the questions that follow.

DRUGS
by Gore Vidal

It is possible to stop most drug addiction in the United States within a very short time. Simply make all drugs available and sell them at cost. Label each drug with a precise description of what effect—good and bad— the drug will have on the taker. This will require heroic honesty. Don't say that marijuana is addictive or dangerous when it is neither, as millions of people know—unlike "speed," which kills most unpleasantly, or heroin, which is addictive and difficult to kick.

For the record, I have tried—once—almost every drug and liked none, disproving the popular Fu Manchu theory that a single whiff of opium will enslave the mind. Nevertheless many drugs are bad for certain people to take and they should be told why in a sensible way.

Along with exhortation and warning, it might be good for our citizens to recall (or learn for the first time) that the United States was the creation of men who believed that each man has the right to do what he wants with his own life as long as he does not interfere with his neighbor's pursuit of happiness. (That his neighbor's idea of happiness is persecuting others does confuse matters a bit.)

This is a startling notion to the current generation of Americans. They reflect a system of public education which has made the Bill of Rights, literally, unacceptable to a majority of high school graduates who now form the "silent majority"—a phrase which that underestimated wit Richard Nixon took from Homer who used it to describe the dead.

Now one can hear the warning rumble begin: If everyone is allowed to take drugs everyone will and the GNP will decrease, the Commies will stop us from making everyone free, and we shall end up a race of zombies, passively murmuring "groovy" to one another. Alarming thought. Yet it seems most unlikely that any reasonably sane person will become a drug addict if he knows in advance what addiction is going to be like.

Is everyone reasonably sane? No. Some people will always become drug addicts just as some people will always become alcoholics, and it is just too bad. Every man, however, has the power (and should have the legal right) to kill himself if he chooses. But since most men don't, they won't be mainliners either. Nevertheless, forbidding people things they like or think they might enjoy only makes them want those things all the more. This psychological insight is, for some mysterious reason, perennially denied our governors.

It is a lucky thing for the American moralist that our country has always existed in a kind of time-vacuum: We have no public memory of anything that happened before last Tuesday. No one in Washington today recalls what happened during the years alcohol was forbidden to the people by a Congress that thought it had a divine mission to stamp out Demon Rum—launching, in the process, the greatest crime wave in the country's history, causing thousands of deaths from bad alcohol, and creating a general (and persisting) contempt among the citizenry for the laws of the United States.

The same thing is happening today. But the government has learned nothing from past attempts at prohibition, not to mention repression.

Last year when the supply of Mexican marijuana was slightly curtailed by the Feds, the pushers got the kids hooked on heroin and deaths increased dramatically, particularly in New York. Whose fault? Evil men like the Mafiosi? Permissive Dr. Spock? Wild-eyed Dr. Leary? No.

The Government of the United States was responsible for those deaths. The bureaucratic machine has a vested interest in playing cops and robbers. Both the Bureau of Narcotics and the Mafia want strong laws against the sale and use of drugs because if drugs are sold at cost there would be no money in it for anyone.

If there was no money in it for the Mafia, there would be no friendly playground pushers, and addicts would not commit crimes to pay for the next fix. Finally, if there was no money in it, the Bureau of Narcotics would wither away, something they are not about to do without a struggle.

Will anything sensible be done? Of course not. The American people are as devoted to the idea of sin and its punishment as they are to making money—and fighting drugs is nearly as big a business as pushing them. Since the combination of sin and money is irresistible (particularly to the professional politician), the situation will only grow worse. ■

The Case for Slavery
by A. M. Rosenthal

Across the country, a scattered but influential collection of intellectuals is intensely engaged in making the case for slavery.

With considerable passion, these Americans are repeatedly expounding the benefits of not only tolerating slavery but legalizing it:

It would make life less dangerous for the free. It would save a great deal of money. And since the economies could be used to improve the lot of the slaves, in the end they would be better off.

The new antiabolitionists, like their predecessors in the nineteenth century, concede that those now in bondage do not themselves see the benefits of legalizing their status.

But in time they will, we are assured, because the beautiful part of legalization is that slavery would be designed so as to keep slaves pacified with the very thing that enslaves them!

The form of slavery under discussion is drug addiction. It does not have every characteristic of more traditional forms of bondage. But they have enough in common to make the comparison morally valid—and the campaign for drug legalization morally disgusting.

Like the plantation slavery that was a foundation of American society for so long, drug addiction largely involves specifiable groups of people. Most of the enchained are children and adolescents of all colors and black and Hispanic adults.

Like plantation slavery, drug addiction is passed on from generation to generation. And this may be the most important similarity: Like plantation slavery, addiction can destroy among its victims the social resources most valuable to free people for their own betterment—family life, family traditions, family values.

In plantation-time America, mothers were taken from their children. In drug-time America, mothers abandon their children. Do the children suffer less, or the mothers?

Antiabolitionists argue that legalization would make drugs so cheap and available that the profit for crime would be removed. Well-supplied addicts would be peaceful addicts. We would not waste billions for jails and could spend some of the savings helping the addicted become drug-free.

That would happen at the very time that new millions of Americans were being enticed into addiction by legalization—somehow.

Are we really foolish enough to believe that tens of thousands of drug gang members would meekly steal away, foiled by the marvels of the free market?

Not likely. The pushers would cut prices, making more money than ever from the ever-growing mass market. They would immediately increase the potency and variety beyond anything available at any Government-approved narcotics counters.

Crime would increase. Crack produces paranoid violence. More permissiveness equals more use equals more violence.

And what will legalization do to the brains of Americans drawn into drug slavery by easy availability?

Earlier this year, an expert drug pediatrician told me that after only a few months babies born with crack addiction seemed to recover. Now we learn that stultifying behavioral effects last at least through early childhood. Will they last forever?

How long will crack affect neurological patterns in the brains of adult crack users? Dr. Gabriel G. Nahas of Columbia University argues in his new book, *Cocaine: The Great White Plague,* that the damage may be irreversible. Would it not be an act of simple intelligence to drop the legalization campaign until we find out?

Then why do a number of writers and academicians, left to right, support it? I have discussed this with antidrug leaders like Jesse Jackson, Dr. Mitchell Rosenthal of Phoenix House, and William J. Bennett, who search for answers themselves.

Perhaps the answer is that the legalizers are not dealing with reality in America. I think the reason has to do with class.

Crack is beginning to move into the white middle and upper classes. That is a tragedy for those addicted.

However, it has not yet destroyed the communities around which their lives revolve, not taken over every street and doorway. It has not passed generation to generation among them, killing the continuity of family.

But in ghetto communities poverty and drugs come together in a catalytic reaction that is reducing them to social rubble.

The antiabolitionists, virtually all white and well-to-do, do not see or do not care. Either way they show symptoms of the callousness of class. That can be a particularly dangerous social disorder. ■

Questions for Analysis

1. Identify and rewrite the arguments that each of the authors uses to support his position regarding the legalization of drugs, using the following format:

   Reason:

   Reason:

   Conclusion:

   Use cue words to help you identify arguments.

2. Construct one new argument to support each side of this issue, using the form shown in question 1.

3. State whether you believe drugs should be legalized and provide reasons to support your conclusion. ◀

ARGUMENTS ARE INFERENCES

When you construct arguments, you are composing and relating the world by means of your ability to infer. As you saw in Chapter 9, *inferring* is a thinking process that we use to reason from what we already know (or believe to be the case) to new knowledge or beliefs. This is usually what you do when you construct arguments. You work from reasons you know or believe in to conclusions based on these reasons.

Just as you can use inferences to make sense of different types of situations, so you can also construct arguments for different purposes. In a variety of situations, you construct arguments to do the following:

- Decide
- Explain
- Predict
- Persuade

An example of each of these different types of arguments is given in the following sections. After examining each example, construct an argument of the same type related to issues in your own life.

We Construct Arguments to Decide

Reason: Throughout my life, I've always been interested in all different kinds of electricity.

Reason: There are many attractive job opportunities in the field of electrical engineering.

Conclusion: I will work toward becoming an electrical engineer.

Reason:

Reason:

Conclusion:

We Construct Arguments to Explain

Reason: I was delayed leaving my house because my dog needed an emergency walking.

Reason: There was an unexpected traffic jam caused by motorists slowing down to view an overturned chicken truck.

Conclusion: Therefore I was late for our appointment.

Reason:

Reason:

Conclusion:

We Construct Arguments to Predict

Reason: Some people will always drive faster than the speed limit allows, no matter whether the limit is 55 or 65 mph.

Reason: Car accidents are more likely at higher speeds.

Conclusion: It follows that the newly reinstated 65 mph limit will result in more accidents.

Reason:

Reason:

Conclusion:

We Construct Arguments to Persuade

Reason: Chewing tobacco can lead to cancer of the mouth and throat.

Reason: Boys sometimes are led to begin chewing tobacco by ads for the product that feature sports heroes they admire.

Conclusion: Therefore, ads for chewing tobacco should be banned.

Reason:

Reason:

Conclusion:

EVALUATING ARGUMENTS

To construct an effective argument, you must be skilled in evaluating the effectiveness, or soundness, of arguments already constructed. You must investigate two aspects of each argument independently to determine the soundness of the argument as a whole:

1. How true are the reasons being offered to support the conclusion?
2. To what extent do the reasons support the conclusion, or to what extent does the conclusion follow from the reasons offered?

We will first examine each of these ways of evaluating arguments separately and then see how they work together.

Truth: How True Are the Supporting Reasons?

The first aspect of the argument you must evaluate is the truth of the reasons that are being used to support a conclusion. Does each reason make sense? What evidence is being offered as part of each reason? Do I know each reason to be true based on my experience? Is each reason based on a source that can be trusted? You use these questions and others like them to analyze the reasons offered and to determine how true they are. As you saw in Chapter 5, "Believing and Knowing," evaluating the sort of beliefs usually found as reasons in arguments is a complex and ongoing challenge. Let us evaluate the truth of the reasons presented in the discussion at the beginning of this chapter about whether marijuana should be legalized.

Argument 1

Reason: Possessing marijuana is not a serious offense.

Evaluation: As it stands, this reason needs further evidence to support it. The major issue of the discussion is whether possessing (and using) marijuana is in fact a serious offense or no offense at all. This reason would be strengthened by stating: "Possessing marijuana is not as serious an offense as armed robbery, rape, and murder, according to the overwhelming majority of legal statutes and judicial decisions."

Reason: There are many other more serious offenses—such as armed robbery, rape, and murder—that don't receive such stiff sentences.

Evaluation: The accuracy of this reason is highly doubtful. It is true that there is wide variation in the sentences handed down for the same offense. The sentences vary from state to state and also vary within states and even within the same court. Nevertheless, on the whole, serious offenses like armed robbery, rape, and murder do receive long prison sentences.

The real point here is that a fifteen-year sentence for possessing marijuana is extremely unusual when compared with other sentences for marijuana possession.

Argument 2

Reason: Drugs pose a very serious threat to the young people of our country.

Evaluation: As the later discussion points out, this statement is much too vague. "Drugs" cannot be treated as being all the same. Some drugs (such as aspirin) are beneficial, while other drugs (such as heroin) are highly dangerous. To strengthen this reason, we would have to be more specific, stating "Drugs like heroin, amphetamines, and cocaine pose a very serious threat to the young people of our country." We could increase the accuracy of the reason even more by adding the qualification "*some* of the young people of our country," because many young people are not involved with dangerous drugs.

Reason: Many crimes are committed to support drug habits.

Evaluation:

Argument 3

Reason: It's not right to punish someone unfairly just to provide an example.

Evaluation: This reason raises an interesting and complex ethical question that has been debated for centuries. The political theorist Machiavelli stated that "The ends justify the means," which implies that if we bring about desirable results it does not matter how we go about doing it. He would therefore probably disagree with this reason, since using someone as an example might bring about desirable results, even though it might be personally unfair to the person being used as an example. In our society, however, which is based on the idea of fairness under the law, most people would probably agree with this reason.

Reason: Smoking marijuana is nothing like using drugs such as heroin or even cocaine.

Evaluation:

THINKING ACTIVITY 10.2

Review the other arguments from the discussion on marijuana that you identified in Thinking Activity 10.1 (page 455). Evaluate the truth of each of the reasons contained in the arguments. ◀

Validity: Do the Reasons Support the Conclusion?

In addition to determining whether the reasons are true, evaluating arguments involves investigating the *relationship* between the reasons and the conclusion. When the reasons support the conclusion, so that the conclusion follows from the reasons being offered, the argument is *valid*.* If, however, the reasons do *not* support the conclusion so that the conclusion does *not* follow from the reasons being offered, the argument is *invalid*.

Valid Argument	An argument in which the reasons support the conclusion so that the conclusion follows from the reasons offered.
Invalid Argument	An argument in which the reasons do not support the conclusion so that the conclusion does *not* follow from the reasons offered.

One way to focus on the concept of validity is to *assume* that all the reasons in the argument are true and then try to determine how probable they make the conclusion.

The following is an example of one type of valid argument:

Reason: Anything that is a threat to our health should not be legal.

Reason: Marijuana is a threat to our health.

Conclusion: Therefore marijuana should not be legal.

This is a valid argument because if we assume that the reasons are true, then the conclusion necessarily follows. Of course, we may not agree that either or both of the reasons are true and so not agree with the conclusion. Nevertheless, the *structure* of the argument is valid. This particular form of thinking is known as *deduction,* and we will examine deductive reasoning more closely in the pages ahead.

The following is a different type of argument:

---

* In formal logic, the term *validity* is reserved for deductively valid arguments in which the conclusions follow necessarily from the premises. (See the discussion of deductive arguments later in this chapter.)

Reason: As part of a project in my social science class, we selected 100 students in the school to be interviewed. We took special steps to ensure that these students were representative of the student body as a whole (total students: 4,386). We asked the selected students whether they thought the United States should actively try to overthrow foreign governments that the United States disapproves of. Of the 100 students interviewed, 88 students said the United States should definitely *not* be involved in such activities.

Conclusion: We can conclude that most students in the school believe the United States should not be engaged in attempts to actively overthrow foreign governments that the United States disapproves of.

This is a persuasive argument because if we assume that the reason is true, then it provides strong support for the conclusion. In this case, the key part of the reason is the statement that the 100 students selected were representative of the entire 4,386 students at the school. To evaluate the truth of the reason, we might want to investigate the procedure used to select the 100 students to determine whether this sample was in fact representative of all the students. This particular form of thinking is an example of *induction,* and we will explore inductive reasoning more fully in Chapter 11, "Reasoning Critically."

The following argument is an example of an invalid argument.

Reason: Bill Clinton believes that the Stealth Bomber should be built to ensure America's national defense, providing the capability of undetected bombing attacks.

Reason: Bill Clinton is the president of the United States.

Conclusion: Therefore the Stealth Bomber should be built.

This argument is *not* valid because even if we assume that the reasons are true, the conclusion does not follow. Although Bill Clinton is the president of the United States, the fact does not give him any special expertise on the subject of sophisticated radar designs for weapon systems. Indeed, this is a subject of such complexity and global significance that it should not be based on any one person's opinion, no matter who that person is. This form of invalid thinking is a type of *fallacy,* and we will investigate fallacious reasoning in Chapter 11.

The Soundness of Arguments

When an argument includes both true reasons and a valid structure, the argument is considered to be *sound.* When an argument has either false reasons or an invalid structure, however, the argument is considered to be *unsound.*

True reasons Valid structure	} ————————————→	Sound argument
False reasons Valid structure	} ————————————→	Unsound argument
True reasons Invalid structure	} ————————————→	Unsound argument
False reasons Invalid structure	} ————————————→	Unsound argument

From this chart, we can see that, in terms of arguments, "truth" and "validity" are not the same concepts. An argument can have true reasons and an invalid structure or false reasons and a valid structure. In both cases the argument is *unsound.* To be sound, an argument must have *both* true reasons and a valid structure. For example, consider the following argument:

Reason: For a democracy to function most effectively, the citizens should be able to think critically about the important social and political issues.

Reason: Education plays a key role in developing critical thinking abilities.

Conclusion: Therefore education plays a key role in ensuring that a democracy is functioning most effectively.

A good case could be made for the soundness of this argument because the reasons are persuasive and the argument structure is valid. Of course, someone might contend that one or both of the reasons are not completely true, which illustrates an important point about the arguments we construct and evaluate. Many of the arguments we encounter in life fall somewhere between complete soundness and complete unsoundness because we are often not sure if our reasons are completely true. Throughout this book we have found that developing accurate beliefs is an ongoing process and that our beliefs are subject to clarification and revision. As a result, the conclusion of any argument can be only as certain as the reasons supporting the conclusion.

To sum up, evaluating arguments effectively involves both the truth of the reasons and the validity of the argument structure. The degree of soundness an argument has depends on how accurate our reasons turn out to be and how valid the argument's structure is.

Forms of Arguments

We use a number of basic argument forms to organize, relate, and make sense of the world. As already noted, two of the major types of argument forms are *deductive arguments* and *inductive arguments.* In the remainder of this chapter we will explore various types of deductive arguments, reserving our analysis of inductive arguments for Chapter 11.

Deductive Arguments

The deductive argument is the one most commonly associated with the study of logic. Though it has a variety of valid forms, they all share one characteristic: If you accept the supporting reasons (also called *premises*) as true, then you must necessarily accept the conclusion as true.

Deductive Argument An argument form in which one reasons from premises that are known or assumed to be true to a conclusion that follows necessarily from these premises.

For example, consider the following famous deductive argument:

Reason/Premise: All men are mortal.

Reason/Premise: Socrates is a man.

Conclusion: Therefore Socrates is mortal.

In this example of deductive thinking, accepting the premises of the argument as true means that the conclusion necessarily follows; it cannot be false. Many deductive arguments, like the one just given, are structured as *syllogisms,* an argument form that consists of two supporting premises and a conclusion. There are also, however, a large number of *invalid* deductive forms, one of which is illustrated in the following syllogism:

Reason/Premise: All men are mortal.

Reason/Premise: Socrates is a man.

Conclusion: Therefore all men are Socrates.

Deductive arguments *involve reasoning from general premises to specific conclusions, while* **inductive arguments** *involve reasoning from specific instances to general conclusions.*

In the next several pages, we will briefly examine some common valid deductive forms.

Applying a General Rule   Whenever we reason with the form illustrated by the valid Socrates syllogism, we are using the following argument structure:

Premise: All *A* (men) are *B* (mortal).

Premise: *S* is an *A* (Socrates is a man).

Conclusion: Therefore *S* is *B* (Socrates is mortal).

This basic argument form is valid no matter what terms are included. For example:

Premise: All politicians are untrustworthy.

Premise: Bill White is a politician.

Conclusion: Therefore, Bill White is untrustworthy.

Notice again that, with any valid deductive form, *if* we assume that the premises are true, then we must accept the conclusion. Of course, in this case there is considerable doubt that the first premise is actually true.

When we diagram this argument form, it becomes clear why it is a valid way of thinking:

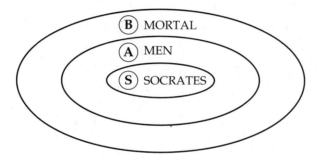

The *first premise* states that classification *A* (men) falls within classification *B* (mortal).

The *second premise* states that *S* (Socrates) is a member of classification *A* (men).

The *conclusion* simply states what has now become obvious—namely, that *S* (Socrates) must fall within classification *B* (mortal).

Although we are usually not aware of it, we use this basic type of reasoning whenever we apply a general rule in the form *All A is B*. For instance:

Premise: All children eight years old should be in bed by 9:30 P.M.

Premise: You are an eight-year-old child.

Conclusion: Therefore you should be in bed by 9:30 P.M.

Review the dialogue at the beginning of this chapter and see if you can identify a deductive argument that uses this form.

Premise:

Premise:

Conclusion:

Describe an example from your own experience in which you use this deductive form.

Modus Ponens   Another valid deductive form that we commonly use in our thinking goes by the name *modus ponens*—that is, "affirming the antecedent"—and is illustrated in the following example:

Premise: If I have prepared thoroughly for the final exam, then I will do well.

Premise: I prepared thoroughly for the exam.

Conclusion: Therefore I will do well on the exam.

When we reason like this, we are using the following argument structure:

Premise: If *A* (I have prepared thoroughly), then *B* (I will do well).

Premise: *A* (I have prepared thoroughly).

Conclusion: Therefore *B* (I will do well).

Like all valid deductive forms, this form is valid no matter what specific terms are included. For example:

Premise: If the Democrats are able to register 20 million new voters, then they will win the presidential election.

Premise: The Democrats were able to register more than 20 million new voters.

Conclusion: Therefore the Democrats will win the presidential election.

As with other valid argument forms, the conclusion will be true *if* the reasons are true. Although the second premise in this argument expresses information that can be verified, the first premise would be more difficult to establish.

Review the dialogue at the beginning of this chapter and see if you can identify any deductive arguments that use this form.

Modus Tollens   A third commonly used valid deductive form has the name *modus tollens*—that is, "denying the consequence"—and is illustrated in the following example:

Premise: If Michael were a really good friend, he would lend me his car for the weekend.

Premise: Michael refuses to lend me his car for the weekend.

Conclusion: Therefore Michael is not a really good friend.

When we reason in this fashion, we are using the following argument structure:

Premise: If *A* (Michael is a really good friend), then *B* (He will lend me his car).

Premise: Not *B* (He won't lend me his car).

Conclusion: Therefore not *A* (He's not a really good friend).

Again, like other valid reasoning forms, this form is valid no matter what subject is being considered. For instance:

Premise: If Iraq were genuinely interested in world peace, it would not have invaded Kuwait.

Premise: Iraq did invade Kuwait (that is, Iraq did not "not invade" Kuwait).

Conclusion: Therefore Iraq is not genuinely interested in world peace.

This conclusion—and any other conclusion produced by this form of reasoning—can be considered accurate if the reasons are true. In this case, the second premise would be easier to verify than the first.

Review the dialogue at the beginning of this chapter and see if you can identify any deductive arguments that use this reasoning form.

Disjunctive Syllogism   A fourth common form of a valid deductive argument is known as a *disjunctive syllogism.* The term *disjunctive* means presenting several alternatives. This form is illustrated in the following example:

Premise: Either I left my wallet on my dresser or I have lost it.

Premise: The wallet is not on my dresser.

Conclusion: Therefore I must have lost it.

When we reason in this way, we are using the following argument structure:

Premise: Either *A* (I left my wallet on my dresser) or *B* (I have lost it).

Premise: Not *A* (I didn't leave it on my dresser).

Conclusion: Therefore *B* (I have lost it).

This valid reasoning form can be applied to any number of situations and still yield valid results. For example:

Premise: Either your stomach trouble is caused by what you are eating or it is caused by nervous tension.

Premise: You tell me that you have been taking special care with your diet.

Conclusion: Therefore your stomach trouble is caused by nervous tension.

To determine the accuracy of the conclusion, we must determine the accuracy of the premises. If they are true, then the conclusion must be true.

Review the dialogue at the beginning of this chapter and see if you can identify any deductive arguments that use this reasoning form.

All these basic argument forms—applying a general rule, *modus ponens,* *modus tollens,* and disjunctive syllogism—are found not only in informal, everyday conversations but also at more formal levels of thinking. They appear in academic disciplines, in scientific inquiry, in debates on social issues, and so on. Many other argument forms—both deductive and inductive—also constitute human reasoning. By sharpening your understanding of these ways of thinking, you will be better able to make sense of the world by constructing and evaluating effective arguments.

THINKING ACTIVITY 10.3

Analyze the following arguments by completing the following steps.

1. Summarize the reasons and conclusions given.
2. Identify which, if any, of the following deductive argument forms are used.
   * Applying a general rule
   * *Modus ponens* (affirming the antecedent)
   * *Modus tollens* (denying the consequence)
   * Disjunctive syllogism
3. Evaluate the truth of the reasons that support the conclusion.

For if the brain is a machine of ten billion nerve cells and the mind can somehow be explained as the summed activity of a finite number of chemical and electrical reactions, [then] boundaries limit the human prospect—we are biological and our souls cannot fly free.

—Edward O. Wilson, *On Human Nature*

The state is by nature clearly prior to the family and to the individual, since the whole is of necessity prior to the part.

—Aristotle, *Politics*

There now is sophisticated research that strongly suggests a deterrent effect [of capital punishment]. Furthermore, the principal argument against the deterrent effect is weak. The argument is that in most jurisdictions where capital punishment has been abolished there has been no immediate, sharp increase in what had been capital crimes. But in those jurisdictions, the actual act of abolition was an insignificant event because for years the death penalty had been imposed rarely, if at all. Common sense—which deserves deference until it is refuted—suggests that the fear of death can deter some premeditated crimes, including some murders.

—George F. Will, *Cleveland Plain-Dealer,* March 13, 1981

If the increased power which science has conferred upon human volitions is to be a boon and not a curse, the ends to which these volitions are directed must grow commensurately with the growth of power to carry them out. Hitherto, although we have been told on Sundays to love our neighbor, we have been told on weekdays to hate him, and there are six times as many weekdays as Sundays. Hitherto, the harm that we could do to our neighbor by hating him was limited by our incompetence, but in the new world upon which we are entering there will be no such limit, and the indulgence of hatred can lead only to ultimate and complete disaster.

—Bertrand Russell, "The Expanding Mental Universe"

The extreme vulnerability of a complex industrial society to intelligent, targeted terrorism by a very small number of people may prove the fatal challenge to which Western states have no adequate response. Counterforce alone will never suffice. The real challenge of the true terrorist is to the basic values of a society. If there is no commitment to shared values in Western society—and if none are imparted in our amoral institutions of higher learning—no increase in police and burglar alarms will suffice to preserve our society from the specter that haunts us—not a bomb from above but a gun from within.

—James Billington, "The Gun Within"

To fully believe in something, to truly understand something, one must be intimately acquainted with its opposite. One should not adopt a creed by default, because no alternative is known. Education should prepare students for the "real world" not be segregating them from evil but by urging full confrontation to test and modify the validity of the good.

—Robert Baron, "In Defense of 'Teaching' Racism, Sexism, and Fascism"

The inescapable conclusion is that society secretly *wants* crime, *needs* crime, and gains definite satisfactions from the present mishandling of it! We condemn crime; we punish offenders for it; but we need it. The crime and punishment ritual is a part of our lives. We need crimes to wonder at, to enjoy vicariously, to discuss and speculate about, and to publicly deplore. We need criminals to identify ourselves with, to envy secretly, and to punish stoutly. They do for us the forbidden, illegal things we *wish* to do and, like scapegoats of old, they bear the burdens of our displaced guilt and punishment—"the iniquities of us all."

—Karl Menninger, "The Crime of Punishment" ◀

COMPOSING AN ARGUMENTATIVE PAPER

The purpose of mastering the forms of argument is to become a sophisticated critical thinker who can present your ideas to others effectively. The art of discussing and debating ideas with others was explored in Chapter 2. We saw then that effective discussion involves:

- Listening carefully to other points of view
- Supporting views with reasons and evidence
- Responding to the points being made
- Asking—and trying to answer—appropriate questions
- Working to increase understanding, not simply to "win the argument"

Although learning to discuss ideas with others in an organized, productive fashion is crucial for thinking critically, it is equally important to present your ideas in written form. When you write your ideas, you are creating a record that can be shared with many people, not simply those you are speaking directly with. Also, in many academic and professional contexts, communicating ideas in writing is essential. Term papers, interoffice memos, research analyses, grant proposals, legal briefs, evaluation reports, and countless other situations that you are likely to encounter require that you develop the skills of clear, persuasive writing. Finally, composing your ideas develops your mind in distinctive, high-level ways. When you express your ideas in writing, you tend to organize them in more complex relationships, select your terms with more care, and revise your work after an initial draft. As a result, your writing is often a more articulate and comprehensive expression of your ideas than you could achieve in verbal discussions. And the process of expressing your ideas in such clear and coherent fashion has the simultaneous effect of sharpening your thinking. As you saw in Chapter 6, language and thinking are partners that work together to create meaning and communicate ideas. How well you perform one of these activities is directly related to how well you perform the other.

Learning to compose argumentative papers is one of the most important forms of writing that you need to develop. Since an argument is a form of thinking in which you are trying to present reasons to support a conclusion, it is likely that much of your writing will fall into this category. Composing thoughtfully reasoned and clearly written papers is very challenging, and few people are able to do it well. In the same way that many discussions are illogical, disorganized, and overly emotional, much of argumentative writing is also ineffective. In this section, you will examine how to present your ideas in this essential form.

The papers that you write in college and many careers range from short one- to two-page papers to very elaborate research papers. Yet despite these different writing contexts, the basic stages in the writing process remain relatively constant.

- Generating ideas
- Defining a main idea
- Conducting research (for research papers)
- Organizing ideas
- Revising

Generating Ideas

Ideas are not created in isolation but are almost always related to a particular subject. We develop ideas by exploring that subject. Some of the papers assigned to you will have very specific requirements, while others may be more open-ended. In most cases, however, you will be expected to come up with your own ideas. Even when the paper topic is fairly straightforward, you will be expected to bring your own individual perspective to the subject being explored. There are several strategies to help you generate ideas.

1. *Familiarize yourself with the subject.* There is no simple formula for developing original ideas for your writing assignments. However, the place to begin is by thoroughly immersing yourself in the subject and then letting your subconscious work on the project of making connections and generating creative ideas. In a way, developing creative ideas is like gardening: you have

to prepare the soil, plant the seeds, ensure that there is sufficient food, water, and sunlight—and then wait. Once the ideas begin to emerge, you have to be ready to seize on them. The creative process is a natural process that works according to its own schedule and rhythm. Familiarize yourself with the subject, allow time for "incubation," and then be prepared to recognize and act on the ideas once they occur to you.

2. *Brainstorm.* Brainstorming is an activity in which, working individually or with a group of people, you write down as many ideas as the group can think of related to a given theme. The goal is to produce as many ideas as possible in a specified period of time. While you are engaged in this idea-generating process, it is important to relax, let your mind run free, build on the ideas of others, and refrain from censoring or evaluating any ideas produced, no matter how marginal they seem at first. Brainstorming stimulates your creative juices, and you will be surprised at how many ideas you are able to come up with. And if you work with other people, you will be exposed to fresh perspectives and the synergy of people working together as a team.

3. *Create mind maps.* Mind maps are visual presentations of the various ways ideas can be related to one another. For example, each chapter in this book opens with a "mind map" that visually summarizes the chapter's basic concepts as well as the way these concepts are related to each other. As you saw in Chapter 7, mind maps are an effective tool for taking notes on your reading assignments. However, mind maps are also a powerful approach for writing, helping you generate ideas and begin organizing them into various relationships. They are well suited for the writing process for a number of reasons. First, the organization grows naturally, reflecting the way your mind naturally makes associations and organizes information. Second, the organization can be easily revised on the basis of new information and your developing understanding of how this information should be organized. Third, you can express a range of relationships among the various ideas. And instead of being identified once and then forgotten, each idea remains an active part of the overall pattern, suggesting new possible relationships. Fourth, you do not have to decide initially on a beginning, subpoints, subsubpoints, and so on; you can do this after your pattern is complete, saving time and frustration.

The best way to explore the process of generating ideas is to actually engage in it. Imagine that you are assigned the following topic for a research paper.

There are many problems that students face on college campuses. Identify one such problem and then write a research paper that analyzes the causes and possible solutions of the problem. Why does the problem occur and what can be done to deal with it? Your paper should include relevant research findings as well as your own perspective on this problem.

Using the brainstorming strategy with a friend, you might come up with a list that includes the following student problems on your campus:

parking	poor quality of campus food
cafeteria too noisy	classes too large
library closes too early	no comfortable places to study
racial tensions	date rape
abuse of alcohol	use of other drugs
registration is a nightmare	tests and papers come in clumps
not enough social activities	some teachers just lecture
thefts are increasing	books are too expensive
not sufficient financial aid	the curriculum is not well organized

Can you identify additional problems faced by students on your campus?

Defining a Main Idea

After generating possible ideas for your paper, the next step is to define a working main idea suggested by the information and ideas you have been considering. Once selected, your main idea—known as a thesis—will act to focus your thinking on a central theme. It will also guide your future explorations and suggest new ideas and other relationships. Of course, a variety of main ideas can usually develop out of any particular situation. And, your initial working idea will probably need redefining as you explore your material further. In the preceding example, you might feel that some of the topics are not significant enough for a substantive paper; for example, "the poor quality of campus food." On the other hand, some topics might seem to be too large and complex; for example, "the curriculum is not well organized." It is also important to select a topic which you find compelling, as people perform better when they are actively engaged in the issues they are investigating. In this case you decide to select "abuse of alcohol" as your topic.

Once identified, your topic needs to be defined. There are many different ways you can approach a topic like "abuse of alcohol," and you need to specify the one you want to take. Since this is an argumentative paper, you need to develop at least two contrasting perspectives on your topic. Creating mind maps is a very useful strategy to use in this stage of the writing process. A sample mind map for the topic of "abuse of alcohol" appears on page 479.

Conducting Research

Research papers are more elaborate versions of the standard papers that are typically assigned. In writing a research paper, you will be using the same approach to the composing process and writing papers that we just explored. The difference is that research papers involve gathering relevant information from appropriate sources, integrating this information into your paper, and then documenting your sources with footnotes and a bibliography. Most professors who assign research papers will expect you to bring your perspective to the subject: it's just that you are also expected to support your point of view with factual information and evidence drawn from authoritative sources.

Sometimes students writing research papers make the mistake of simply reporting the information from research sources, excluding their own perspective entirely. Other times students make the opposite mistake, including mainly their own ideas with little support from research sources. A properly balanced research paper integrates both.

Research Sources   Once you have defined your main idea, the next stop is the library for your research. You can spend anywhere from a few hours to a few days in the library, depending on how familiar you are with library resources. The research sources that you are looking for will be contained in books, newspaper articles, and scholarly journal articles. All of these sources have their own indexes that will help you track down the information needed.

- *Encyclopedias:* Depending on your topic, encyclopedias can be a useful place to begin your investigations, serving as a launching pad for more extensive research. In libraries, bound encyclopedias are being replaced by computerized CD-ROM versions, including ones like *Encarta* and *Grolier Encyclopedia.* These computerized versions make searching for information simple, as they have many illustrations and even animated sequences, and you can print out useful information, saving you from taking notes or standing in line at the copier.

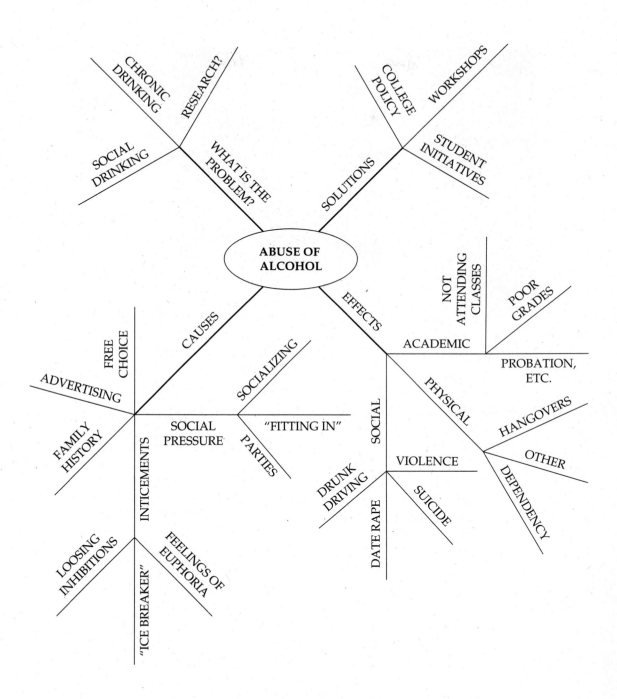

Composing informed argumentative papers involves researching relevant information from authoritative sources and integrating this information into the paper in appropriate ways.

- *Card catalogs:* This is the basic index system of the library, referencing the collection of books by author, subject, and title. Increasingly the traditional index cards are being replaced by computerized versions.
- *Periodical indexes:* The term periodicals refers to magazines and journals that are published at regular intervals. In addition to common magazines like *Time* and *Newsweek,* there are many "scholarly" journals that contain articles and research findings in all the major fields of human inquiry. Periodical indexes are both bound—like the *Reader's Guide to Periodical Literature*—and computerized. You will also find that in addition to general indexes, there are indexes relating to specific fields, such as the *Social Science Index.* These indexes are usually organized by subject, although you may have to use a number of variations on your topic to ensure that you are locating all of the appropriate references. For example, in looking for information about college drinking, you will likely have to explore a number of different subjects such as "college life" and "alcohol drinking." The computerized indexes enable you to conduct these searches with great ease by using the "Key Word search" and the "Boolean search," which enables you to combine several key words, like "college" and "drinking."

- *Newspaper indexes:* A number of the larger newspapers, like the *New York Times,* have their own indexes.

Research Notes   Once you collect a listing of potential references that you think look promising, the next step is to investigate. Although you will find bound copies of the major periodicals, many of your sources will be available only in microfilm or microfiche, so you will have to become familiar with using this technology. The newer machines also give you the means to make copies of the articles while you are viewing them (for a price, of course!). If you're not making a copy, you should make out a 4x6 index card that contains the title, author, publishing information, and your notes detailing the important information contained in it. Using index cards will give you flexibility when you are organizing and writing your paper. A sample note card is pictured below.

"Bad Times at Hangover U"
Debra Rosenberg Newsweek 11/19/90 Pg 81
At Boston College, the number of students hospitalized for alcohol related problems has doubled.
At U Mass, 80% of weekend visits to health services are alcohol related.
Study of 1,600 freshman by Harvard School of Public Health found that among those who drink at least once a week, 92% men and 82% women consume at least 5 drinks in a row. 50% said they wanted to get drunk.

After you have gathered what seems to be enough information (you may go back for additional research once you begin writing the paper), you need to organize your ideas and start writing. When the ideas, research, or information that you are expressing is based on one of your sources, you need to reference that source with a footnote or a citation right in the body of the text. Your teacher will likely provide guidelines. If you are expressing the information in the exact words of the author, then you need to use quotation marks. Students sometimes commit plagiarism by not providing sufficient credit with citations and quotation marks. This sort of "idea stealing" is a primary sin in academic writing, whether the theft is intentional or not, and you should avoid anything close to it. If in doubt, give credit.

Organizing Ideas

Argumentative papers generally include three essential elements:

- Defending the main idea
- Refuting the opposing view(s)
- Reaching a conclusion or proposing a solution

Just as the same ingredients can be combined in different amounts to create varying recipes, these elements can be organized in a variety of different ways. For example, here are some possible organizations:

1. Your paper can focus on the viability of your main idea, emphasizing the supporting reasons and evidence and providing modest treatment of opposing views.
2. Your paper can focus on key issues one at a time, supporting your view and refuting opposing views in each instance.
3. Your paper can focus on the inadequacy of the opposing views, identifying each weakness and explaining why your view is superior.
4. Your paper can take a balanced approach, examining various perspectives in an objective and evenhanded fashion, and then concluding with your own conclusion and solution.

In the case of dealing with the topic "abuse of alcohol," let's suppose you discover that in conducting your research there seem to be a number of legitimate perspectives on this complex problem. As a result, instead of emphasizing the pro/con, adversarial approach evident in organizations 1, 2, and 3, you decide to use organization 4, leading you to the following format:

- Part 1: one perspective on this problem, supported by appropriate research
- Part 2: a contrasting perspective on this problem, supported by relevant research
- Part 3: your own well-reasoned perspective, including what approaches might be effective in addressing the problem

A sample draft of the paper on student drinking follows.

Critical Thinking about Uncritical Drinking

There is widespread agreement that excessive student drinking is a serious problem on many college campuses. However, there are different views on the causes of this problem and the best solutions for dealing with it. In this paper I will present two contrasting perspectives on the problem of student drinking and conclude with my own analysis of how best to deal with this serious threat to student heath and success.

Perspective 1:

Why do college students drink to excess? According to many experts it is mainly due to the influence of the people around them. When most students enter college, they do not have a drinking problem. However, although few realize it, these unwary people are entering a culture in which alcohol is often the drug of choice. It is a drug that can easily destroy their lives. According to some estimates, between 80 percent and 90 percent of the students on many campuses drink alcohol (1). Many of these students are heavy drinkers (2). One study found that nearly 30 percent of university students are heavy drinkers, consuming more that 15 alcoholic drinks a week (3). Another study found that among those who drink at least once a week, 92 percent of the men and 82 percent of the women consume at least five drinks in a row, and half said they wanted to get drunk (4). The results of all this drinking are predictably deadly. Virtually all college administrators agree that alcohol is the most widely used drug among college students and that its abuse is directly related to emotional problems and violent behavior, ranging from date rape to death (5), (6). For example, at one university, a 20-year-old woman became drunk at a fraternity party and fell to her death from the third floor

(7). At another university, two students were killed in a drunk-driving accident after drinking alcohol at an off-campus fraternity house. The families of both students have filed lawsuits against the fraternity (8). When students enter a college or university, they soon become socialized into the alcohol-sodden culture of "higher education," typically at formal and informal parties. The influence of peer pressure is enormous. When your friends and fellow students are encouraging you to drink, it is extremely difficult to resist giving in to these pressures.

Perspective 2:

Other experts believe that although peer pressure is certainly a factor in excessive college drinking, it is only one of a number of factors. They point out that the misuse of alcohol is a problem for all youth in our society, not just college students. For example, a recent study by the surgeon general's office shows that 1 in 3 teenagers consumes alcohol every week. This is an abuse that leads to traffic deaths, academic difficulties, and acts of violence (9). Another study based on a large, nationally representative sample indicates that although college students are more likely to use alcohol, they tend to drink less quantity per drinking day than nonstudents of the same age (10). In other words, college students are more social drinkers than problem drinkers. Another sample of undergraduate students found that college drinking is not as widespread as many people think (11). The clear conclusion is that although drinking certainly takes place on college campuses, it is no greater a problem than in the population at large. What causes the misuse of alcohol? Well, certainly the influence of friends, whether in college or out, plays a role. But it is not the only factor. To begin with, there is evidence that family history is related to alcohol abuse. For example, one survey of college students found greater problem drinking among students whose parent or grandparent had been diagnosed (or treated) for alcoholism (12). Another study found that college students who come from families with high degrees of conflict display a greater potential for alcoholism (13). Another important factor in the misuse of alcohol by young people is advertising. A recent article entitled "It Isn't Miller Time Yet, and This Bud's Not for You" underscores the influence advertisers exert on the behavior of our youth (14). By portraying beer drinkers as healthy, fun-loving, attractive young people, they create role models that many youths imitate. In the same way that cigarette advertisers used to encourage smoking among our youth—without regard to the health hazards—so alcohol advertisers try to sell as much booze as they can to whoever will buy it—no matter what the consequences. A final factor in the abuse of alcohol is the people themselves. Although young people are subject to a huge number of influences, in the final analysis, they are free to choose what they want to do. They don't have to drink, no matter what the social pressures. In fact, many students resist these pressures and choose not to drink excessively or at all. In short, some students choose to think critically, while others choose to drink uncritically.

Part 3: My Perspective

In my opinion, both of these perspectives on excessive drinking on college campuses have merit. I believe that there are a complex variety of factors that are responsible for this problem, and the specific explanation varies from context to context, and individual to individual. With this in mind, I believe that there are a number of strategies that would be effective in solving this problem.

(1) Colleges should create orientation and education programs aimed at preventing alcohol abuse, and colleges

should give campaigns against underage drinking top priority.

(2) Advertising and promotion of alcoholic beverages on college campuses and in college publications should be banned. Restrictions should be imposed on liquor distributors that sponsor campus events. In addition, alcohol beverage companies should be petitioned not to target young people in their ads.

(3) Students at residential colleges should be able to live in "substance free" housing, offering them a voluntary haven from drugs, alcohol, and peer pressure.

(4) Colleges should ban or tightly restrict alcohol use on campus, and include stiffer penalties for students who violate the rules.

(5) Colleges should create alcohol-free clubs to combat alcohol abuse and find alternatives for students who are under 21.

(6) The drinking age should be reduced to 18, so that students won't be forced to move parties off-campus. At off-campus parties there is no college control, and as a result students tend to drink greater quantities and more dangerous concoctions like spiked alcohol.

(7) Colleges should ban the use of beer kegs, the symbol of cheap and easy availability of alcohol.

(8) Fraternities should eliminate pledging in order to stop alcohol abuse and hazing.

In conclusion, I believe that alcohol abuse on college campuses is an extremely important problem that is threatening the health and college careers of many students. As challenging as this problem is, I believe that it is a problem that can be solved if students, teachers and college officials work together in harmony and with determination.

1. *Chronicle of Higher Education:* Jan 17/90; pp A33-A35
2. *Journal of Studies on Alcohol:* Nov/90
3. *Chronicle of Higher Education:* April 12/89; p A43
4. *Newsweek:* Nov 19/90; p81
5. *Chronicle of Higher Education:* Jan 17/90; p A33,35
6. *Chronicle of Higher Education:* Jan 31/90; p A33-35
7. *Chronicle of Higher Education:* Jan 31/90; p 3
8. *Chronicle of Higher Education:* June 12/91; p A29-30
9. *Time:* Dec 16/91; p 64
10. *Journal of Studies on Alcohol:* Vol: 52 Iss: 1 Jan/91
11. *Journal of Studies on Alcohol:* Vol: 51 Iss: 6 Nov/90
12. *Journal of Counseling and Development:* Vol: 69 Jan/91 p 237-40
13. *Adolescence:* Vol: 26 Iss: 102 Summer/91 p 341-47
14. *Business Week:* June 24/91 p 52

Note the numbers in parentheses used in this essay. Each number (known as a *callout*) directs the reader to a note that credits the source of either the information used or the language quoted. If the writer is using a footnote style, each note would appear at the bottom of the page on which it is called out. In endnote style, the notes are listed together, in order, after the conclusion of the essay. However, some documentation methods use parenthetical style, in which each source is credited in parentheses, directly after it is used. Whatever style of documentation is used, the last element of the essay will be the bibliography, or reference list. Here, all sources are listed alphabetically. The difference between a note and a reference citation is that the note contains specific information (such as the exact page that was used for a quotation) and the reference citation includes complete information about the source: page range, place of publication, etc.

Revising

This book emphasizes that thinking is an interactive process, constantly moving back and forth between various activities in order to make sense of things—forming and applying concepts, defining and exemplifying key terms, generating and developing ideas. This same interactive process is part of the writing process. Most writers find it natural to move back and forth between the various aspects of the writing process as they follow out the line of their thinking. In fact, you will probably discover that the process of writing does not merely express your thinking: it also *stimulates* your thoughts, bringing new ideas and ways to explore them to the surface.

Because thinking and writing are interactive, in a sense you are continually revising your thinking and writing. The first draft of your writing is usually just that—a first draft. Having expressed your thinking in language, it is important to go back and "re-see" (the origin of the word *revise*) your writing from a fresh perspective. In addition, it is helpful to have others read what you have written and give their reactions.

Improving sentence structure and correcting spelling and punctuation are of course part of the revising process. However, you also want to take a fresh look at the *thinking* that is being expressed. One useful strategy is to create an outline or map of the first draft, because it enables you to identify the main ideas and express their relationships. This, in turn, may suggest ways you can clarify your thinking by rearranging different parts, developing certain points further, or deleting what is repetitious or not central to the main ideas of the paper.

After completing a draft of your essay, you should re-view how you have developed and organized your ideas and information by following these steps:

REVISION STEPS

1. Create a map that expresses the main points being considered in your paper and their various relationships.
2. Examine your map carefully, looking for ways to clarify and improve your ideas. Determine whether you should:
   - Rearrange the sequence of your ideas
   - Develop certain ideas further
   - Delete points that are repetitious or not central to the subject
   Revise your map (or create a new one to reflect these changes).
3. Compose a revised draft of your paper, using your revision map as a guide.

THINKING ACTIVITY 10.4

Select a current issue of interest to you. (Possible choices are animal rights, mandatory AIDS testing, and so on.) Following the guidelines in this section, construct an argumentative essay that explores the issue by:

- Generating ideas
- Defining a main idea

- Conducting research (*Locate at least two articles about the issue you have selected and use them as resources.*)
- Organizing ideas (*List arguments on both sides of the issue, organizing them into premises and conclusions. Make notes evaluating the strengths and weaknesses of each argument. Identify the most important arguments and make an outline.*)
- Revising

Before composing your essay, examine the two sets of argumentative essays included in this chapter on legalizing drugs (page 456) and the death penalty (page 490). Note how each author organizes the essay and examine the types of arguments used. Your essay should begin with a paragraph that introduces the issue and should end with a paragraph that sums up and concludes it. ◀

Summary

In this chapter we have focused mainly on deductive arguments, an argument form in which it is claimed that the premises constitute conclusive evidence for the truth of the conclusion. In a correct deductive argument, which is organized into a valid deductive form, if the premises are true, the conclusion must be true; it cannot be false.

Although *deductive* forms of reasoning are crucial to our understanding the world and making informed decisions, much of our reasoning is nondeductive. The various nondeductive argument forms are typically included under the general category of *inductive* reasoning. In contrast to deductive arguments, inductive arguments rarely provide conclusions that are totally certain. The premises offer evidence in support of the conclusion, but the conclusion does not follow necessarily from the premises.

We will explore the area of inductive reasoning more fully in the next chapter, "Reasoning Critically."

Thinking Passages

The following articles present two opposing sets of arguments regarding capital punishment. The first article, written by former New York City Mayor Edward I. Koch, gives reasons for supporting capital punishment. The second article, written by South Carolina attorney David Bruck (who recently defended Susan Smith, the South Carolina woman convicted of drowning her two children), gives reasons for opposing capital punishment. Read the articles and complete the activities that follow.

Death and Justice: How Capital Punishment Affirms Life
by Edward I. Koch

Last December a man named Robert Lee Willie, who had been convicted of raping and murdering an 18-year-old woman, was executed in the Louisiana state prison. In a statement issued several minutes before his death, Mr. Willie said: "Killing people is wrong. . . . It makes no difference whether it's citizens, countries, or governments. Killing is wrong." Two weeks later in South Carolina, an admitted killer named Joseph Carl Shaw was put to death for murdering two teenagers. In an appeal to the governor for clemency, Mr. Shaw wrote: "Killing is wrong when I did it. Killing is wrong when you do it. I hope you have the courage and moral strength to stop the killing."

It is a curiosity of modern life that we find ourselves being lectured on morality by cold-blooded killers. Mr. Willie previously had been convicted of aggravated rape, aggravated kidnapping, and the murders of a Louisiana deputy and a man from Missouri. Mr. Shaw committed another murder a week before the two for which he was executed, and admitted mutilating the body of the 14-year-old girl he killed. I can't help wondering what prompted these murderers to speak out against killing as they entered the deathhouse door. Did their newfound reverence for life stem from the realization that they were about to lose their own?

Life is indeed precious, and I believe the death penalty helps to affirm this fact. Had the death penalty been a real possibility in the minds of these murderers, they might well have stayed their hand. They might have shown moral awareness before their victims died, and not after. Consider the tragic death of Rosa Velez, who happened to be home when a man named Luis Vera burglarized her apartment in Brooklyn. "Yeah, I shot her," Vera admitted. "She knew me, and I knew I wouldn't go to the chair."

During my twenty-two years in public service, I have heard the pros and cons of capital punishment expressed with special intensity. As a district leader, councilman, congressman, and mayor, I have represented constituencies generally thought of as liberal. Because I support the death penalty for heinous crimes of murder, I have sometimes been the subject of emotional and outraged attacks by voters who find my position reprehensible or worse. I have listened to their ideas. I have weighed their objections carefully. I still support the death penalty. The reasons I maintain my position can be best understood by examining the arguments most frequently heard in opposition.

1. *The death penalty is "barbaric."* Sometimes opponents of capital punishment horrify with tales of lingering death on the gallows, of faulty electric chairs, or of agony in the gas chamber. Partly in response to such protests, several states such as North Carolina and Texas switched to execution by lethal injection. The condemned person is put to death painlessly, without ropes, voltage, bullets, or gas. Did this answer the objections of death penalty opponents? Of course not. On June 22, 1984, the *New York Times* published an editorial that sarcastically attacked the new "hygienic" method of death by injection, and stated that "execution can never be made humane through science." So it's not the method that really troubles opponents. It's the death itself they consider barbaric.

Admittedly, capital punishment is not a pleasant topic. However, one does not have to like the death penalty in order to support it any more than one must like radical surgery, radiation, or chemotherapy in order to find necessary these attempts at curing cancer. Ultimately we may learn how to cure cancer with a simple pill. Unfortunately, that day has not yet arrived. Today we are faced with the choice of letting the cancer spread or trying to cure it with the methods available, methods that one day will almost certainly be considered barbaric. But to give up and do nothing would be far more barbaric and would certainly delay the discovery of an eventual cure. The analogy between cancer and murder is imperfect, because murder is not the "disease" we are trying to cure. The disease is injustice. We may not like the death penalty, but it must be available to punish crimes of cold-blooded murder, cases in which any other form of punishment would be inadequate and, therefore, unjust. If we create a society in which injustice is not tolerated, incidents of murder—the most flagrant form of injustice—will diminish.

2. *No other major democracy uses the death penalty.* No other major democracy—in fact, few other countries of any description—are plagued by a murder rate such as that in the United States. Fewer and fewer Americans can remember the days when unlocked doors were the norm and murder was a rare and terrible offense. In America the murder rate climbed 122 percent between 1963 and 1980. During that same period, the murder rate in New York City increased by almost 400 percent, and the statistics are even worse in many other cities. A study at M.I.T. showed that based on 1970 homicide rates a person who lived in a large American city ran a

greater risk of being murdered than an American soldier in World War II ran of being killed in combat. It is not surprising that the laws of each country differ according to differing conditions and traditions. If other countries had our murder problem, the cry for capital punishment would be just as loud as it is here. And I daresay that any other major democracy where 75 percent of the people supported the death penalty would soon enact it into law.

3. *An innocent person might be executed by mistake.* Consider the work of Hugo Adam Bedau, one of the most implacable foes of capital punishment in this country. According to Mr. Bedau, it is "false sentimentality to argue that the death penalty should be abolished because of the abstract possibility that an innocent person might be executed." He cites a study of the 7,000 executions in this country from 1893 to 1971, and concludes that the record fails to show that such cases occur. The main point, however, is this. If government functioned only when the possibility of error didn't exist, government wouldn't function at all. Human life deserves special protection, and one of the best ways to guarantee that protection is to assure that convicted murderers do not kill again. Only the death penalty can accomplish this end. In a recent case in New Jersey, a man named Richard Biegenwald was freed from prison after serving 18 years for murder; since his release he has been convicted of committing four murders. A prisoner named Lemuel Smith, who, while serving four life sentences for murder (plus two life sentences for kidnapping and robbery) in New York's Green Haven Prison, lured a woman corrections officer into the chaplain's office and strangled her. He then mutilated and dismembered her body. An additional life sentence for Smith is meaningless. Because New York has no death penalty statute, Smith has effectively been given a license to kill.

But the problem of multiple murder is not confined to the nation's penitentiaries. In 1982, 91 police officers were killed in the line of duty in this country. Seven percent of those arrested in the cases that have been solved had a previous arrest for murder. In New York City in 1976 and 1977, 85 persons arrested for homicide had a previous arrest for murder. Six of these individuals had two previous arrests for murder, and one had four previous murder arrests. During those two years the New York police were arresting for murder persons with a previous arrest for murder on the average of one every 8.5 days. This is not surprising when we learn that in 1975, for example, the median time served in Massachusetts for homicide was less than two and a half years. In 1976 a study sponsored by the Twentieth Century Fund found that the average time served in the United States for first-degree murder is ten years. The median time served may be considerably lower.

4. *Capital punishment cheapens the value of human life.* On the contrary, it can be easily demonstrated that the death penalty strengthens the value of human life. If the penalty for rape were lowered, clearly it would signal a lessened regard for the victims' suffering, humiliation, and personal integrity. It would cheapen their horrible experience, and expose them to an increased danger of recurrence. When we lower the penalty for murder, it signals a lessened regard for the value of the victim's life. Some critics of capital punishment, such as columnist Jimmy Breslin, have suggested that a life sentence is actually a harsher penalty for murder than death. This is sophistic nonsense. A few killers may decide not to appeal a death sentence, but the overwhelming majority make every effort to stay alive. It is by exacting the highest penalty for the taking of human life that we affirm the highest value of human life.

5. *The death penalty is applied in a discriminatory manner.* This factor no longer seems to be the problem it once was. The appeals process for a condemned prisoner is lengthy and painstaking. Every effort is made to see that the verdict and sentence were fairly arrived at. However, assertions of discrimination are not an argument for ending the death penalty but for extending it. It is not justice to exclude everyone from the penalty of the law if a few are found to be so favored. Justice requires that the law be applied equally to all.

6. *Thou Shalt Not Kill.* The Bible is our greatest source of moral inspiration. Opponents of the death penalty frequently cite the sixth of the Ten Commandments in an attempt to prove that capital punishment is divinely proscribed. In the original Hebrew, however, the Sixth Commandment reads "Thou Shalt Not Commit Murder," and the Torah specifies capital punishment for a variety of offenses. The biblical viewpoint has been upheld by philosophers throughout history. The greatest thinkers of the 19th century—Kant, Locke, Hobbes, Rousseau, Montesquieu, and Mill—agreed that natural law properly authorizes the sovereign to take life in order to vindicate justice. Only Jeremy Bentham was ambivalent. Washington,

Jefferson, and Franklin endorsed it. Abraham Lincoln authorized executions for deserters in wartime. Alexis de Tocqueville, who expressed profound respect for American institutions, believed that the death penalty was indispensable to the support of social order. The United States Constitution, widely admired as one of the seminal achievements in the history of humanity, condemns cruel and inhuman punishment, but does not condemn capital punishment.

7. *The death penalty is state-sanctioned murder.* This is the defense with which Messrs. Willie and Shaw hoped to soften the resolve of those who sentenced them to death. By saying in effect, "You're no better than I am," the murderer seeks to bring his accusers down to his own level. It is also a popular argument among opponents of capital punishment, but a transparently false one. Simply put, the state has rights that the private individual does not. In a democracy, those rights are given to the state by the electorate. The execution of a lawfully condemned killer is no more an act of murder than is legal imprisonment an act of kidnapping. If an individual forces a neighbor to pay him money under threat of punishment, it's called extortion. If the state does it, it's called taxation. Rights and responsibilities surrendered by the individual are what give the state its power to govern. This contract is the foundation of civilization itself.

Everyone wants his or her rights, and will defend them jealously. Not everyone, however, wants responsibilities, especially the painful responsibilities that come with law enforcement. Twenty-one years ago a woman named Kitty Genovese was assaulted and murdered on a street in New York. Dozens of neighbors heard her cries for help but did nothing to assist her. They didn't even call the police. In such a climate the criminal understandably grows bolder. In the presence of moral cowardice, he lectures us on our supposed failings and tries to equate his crimes with our quest for justice.

The death of anyone—even a convicted killer—diminishes us all. But we are diminished even more by a justice system that fails to function. It is an illusion to let ourselves believe that doing away with capital punishment removes the murderer's deed from our conscience. The rights of society are paramount. When we protect guilty lives, we give up innocent lives in exchange. When opponents of capital punishment say to the state, "I will not let you kill in my name," they are also saying to murderers: "You can kill in your *own* name as long as I have an excuse for not getting involved."

It is hard to imagine anything worse than being murdered while neighbors do nothing. But something worse exists. When those same neighbors shrink back from justly punishing the murderer, the victim dies twice. ■

The Death Penalty
by David Bruck

Mayor Ed Koch contends that the death penalty "affirms life." By failing to execute murderers, he says, we "signal a lessened regard for the value of the victim's life." Koch suggests that people who oppose the death penalty are like Kitty Genovese's neighbors, who heard her cries for help but did nothing while an attacker stabbed her to death.

This is the standard "moral" defense of death as punishment: even if executions don't deter violent crime any more effectively than imprisonment, they are still required as the only means we have of doing justice in response to the worst of crimes.

Until recently, this "moral" argument had to be considered in the abstract, since no one was being executed in the United States. But the death penalty is back now, at least in the southern states, where every one of the more than 30 executions carried out over the last two years has taken place. Those of us who live in those states are getting to see the difference between the death penalty in theory, and what happens when you actually try to use it.

South Carolina resumed executing prisoners with the electrocution of Joseph Carl Shaw. Shaw was condemned to death for helping to murder two teenagers while he was serving as a military policeman at Fort Jackson, South Carolina. His crime, propelled by mental illness and PCP, was one of terrible brutality. It is Shaw's last words ("Killing was wrong when I did it. It is wrong when you do it. . . .") that so outraged Mayor Koch: he finds it "a curiosity of modern life that we are being lectured on morality by cold-blooded killers." And so it is.

But it was not "modern life" that brought this curiosity into being. It was capital punishment. The electric chair was J. C. Shaw's platform. (The mayor mistakenly writes that Shaw's statement came in the form of a plea to the governor for clemency: actually Shaw made it only seconds before his death, as he waited, shaved and strapped into the chair, for the switch to be thrown.) It was the chair that provided Shaw with celebrity and an opportunity to lecture us on right and wrong. What made this weird moral reversal even worse is that J. C. Shaw faced his own death with undeniable dignity and courage. And while Shaw died, the TV crews re-corded another "curiosity" of the death penalty—the crowd gathered out-side the deathhouse to cheer on the executioner. Whoops of elation greeted the announcement of Shaw's death. Waiting at the penitentiary gates for the appearance of the hearse bearing Shaw's remains, one demonstrator started yelling, "Where's the beef?"

For those who had to see the execution of J. C. Shaw, it wasn't easy to keep in mind that the purpose of the whole spectacle was to affirm life. It will be harder still when Florida executes a cop-killer named Alvin Ford. Ford has lost his mind during his years of death-row confinement, and now spends his days trembling, rocking back and forth, and muttering unintelligible prayers. This has led to litigation over whether Ford meets a centuries-old legal standard for mental competency. Since the Middle Ages, the Anglo-American legal system has generally prohibited the ex-ecution of anyone who is too mentally ill to understand what is about to be done to him and why. If Florida wins its case, it will have earned the right to electrocute Ford in his present condition. If it loses, he will not be executed until the state has first nursed him back to some semblance of mental health.

We can at least be thankful that this demoralizing spectacle involves a prisoner who is actually guilty of murder. But this may not always be so. The ordeal of Lenell Jeter—the young black engineer who recently served more than a year of a life sentence for a Texas armed robbery that he didn't commit—should remind us that the system is quite capable of making the very worst sort of mistake. That Jeter was eventually cleared is a fluke. If the robbery had occurred at 7 P.M. rather than 3 P.M., he'd have had no alibi, and would still be in prison today. And if someone had been killed in that robbery, Jeter probably would have been sentenced to death. We'd have seen the usual execution-day interviews with state officials and the victim's relatives, all complaining that Jeter's appeals took too long. And Jeter's last words from the gurney would have taken their place among the growing literature of death-house oration that so irritates the mayor.

Koch quotes Hugo Adam Bedau, a prominent abolitionist, to the ef-fect that the record fails to establish that innocent defendants have been executed in the past. But this doesn't mean, as Koch implies, that it hasn't happened. All Bedau was saying was that doubts concerning executed prisoners' guilt are almost never resolved. Bedau is at work now on an effort to determine how many wrongful death sentences may have been imposed: his list of murder convictions since 1900 in which the state even-tually *admitted* error is some 400 cases long. Of course, very few of these cases involved actual executions: the mistakes that Bedau documents were uncovered precisely because the prisoner was alive and able to fight for his vindication. The cases where someone is executed are the very cases in which we're least likely to learn that we got the wrong man.

I don't claim that executions of entirely innocent people will occur very often. But they will occur. And other sorts of mistakes already have. Roosevelt Green was executed in Georgia two days before J. C. Shaw. Green and an accomplice kidnapped a young woman. Green swore that his companion shot her to death after Green had left, and that he knew nothing about the murder. Green's claim was supported by a statement that his accomplice made to a witness after the crime. The jury never resolved whether Green was telling the truth, and when he tried to take a polygraph examination a few days before his scheduled execution, the state of Georgia refused to allow the examiner into the prison. As the pressure for symbolic retribution mounts, the courts, like the public, are losing patience with such details. Green was electrocuted on January 9, while members of the Ku Klux Klan rallied outside the prison.

Then there is another sort of arbitrariness that happens all the time. Last October, Louisiana executed a man named Ernest Knighton. Knighton had killed a gas station owner during a robbery. Like any murder, this was a terrible crime. But it was not premeditated, and is the sort of crime that very rarely results in a death sentence. Why was Knighton electrocuted when almost everyone else who committed the same offense was not? Was it because he was black? Was it because his victim and all 12 members of the jury that sentenced him were white? Was it because Knighton's court-appointed lawyer presented no evidence on his behalf at his sentencing hearing? Or maybe there's no reason except bad luck. One thing is clear: Ernest Knighton was picked out to die the way a fisherman takes a cricket out of a bait jar. No one cares which cricket gets impaled on the hook.

Not every prisoner executed recently was chosen that randomly. But many were. And having selected these men so casually, so blindly, the death penalty system asks us to accept that the purpose of killing each of them is to affirm the sanctity of human life.

The death penalty states are also learning that the death penalty is easier to advocate than it is to administer. In Florida, where executions have become almost routine, the governor reports that nearly a third of his time is spent reviewing the clemency requests of condemned prisoners. The Florida Supreme Court is hopelessly backlogged with death cases. Some have taken five years to decide, and the rest of the Court's work waits in line behind the death appeals. Florida's death row currently holds more than 230 prisoners. State officials are reportedly considering building a special "death prison" devoted entirely to the isolation and electrocution of the condemned. The state is also considering the creation of a special public defender unit that will do nothing else but handle death penalty appeals. The death penalty, in short, is spawning death agencies.

And what is Florida getting for all of this? The state went through almost all of 1983 without executing anyone: its rate of intentional homicide declined by 17 percent. Last year Florida executed eight people—the most of any state, and the sixth highest total for any year since Florida started electrocuting people back in 1924. Elsewhere in the U.S. last year, the homicide rate continued to decline. But in Florida, it actually rose by 5.1 percent.

But these are just the tiresome facts. The electric chair has been a centerpiece of each of Koch's recent political campaigns, and he knows better than anyone how little the facts have to do with the public's support for capital punishment. What really fuels the death penalty is the justifiable frustration and rage of people who see that the government is not coping with violent crime. So what if the death penalty doesn't work? At least it gives us the satisfaction of knowing that we got one or two of the sons of bitches.

Perhaps we want retribution on the flesh and bone of a handful of convicted murders so badly that we're willing to close our eyes to all of the demoralization and danger that come with it. A lot of politicians think so, and they may be right. But if they are, then let's at least look honestly at what we're doing. This lottery of death both comes from and encourages an attitude toward human life that is not reverent, but reckless.

And that is why the mayor is dead wrong when he confuses such fury with justice. He suggests that we trivialize murder unless we kill murderers. By that logic, we also trivialize rape unless we sodomize rapists. The sin of Kitty Genovese's neighbors wasn't that they failed to stab her attacker to death. Justice does demand that murderers be punished. And common sense demands that society be protected from them. But neither justice nor self-preservation demands that we kill men whom we have already imprisoned.

The electric chair in which J. C. Shaw died earlier this year was built in 1912 at the suggestion of South Carolina's governor at the time, Cole Blease. Governor Blease's other criminal justice initiative was an impassioned crusade in favor of lynch law. Any lesser response, the governor insisted, trivialized the loathsome crimes of interracial rape and murder.

In 1912 a lot of people agreed with Governor Blease that a proper regard for justice required both lynching and the electric chair. Eventually we are going to learn that justice requires neither. ■

Questions for Analysis

For each article on capital punishment:

1. Identify the arguments that were used and summarize the reasons and conclusion for each.
2. Describe the types of argument forms that you identified.
3. Evaluate the truth of the reasons that support the conclusion for each of the arguments that you identified.
4. Construct additional arguments on both sides of this issue, using the argument forms described in this chapter. ◄

11

REASONING CRITICALLY

INDUCTIVE REASONING:
Reasoning from premises assumed
to be true to a conclusion supported
(but not logically) by the premises

Empirical Generalization:
Drawing conclusions about a target
population based on observing
a sample population.

Is the sample known?
Is the sample sufficient?
Is the sample representative?

Causal Reasoning:
Concluding that an event is
the result of another event.

Scientific Method

1. Identify an event for investigation.
2. Gather information.
3. Develop a theory/hypothesis.
4. Test/experiment.
5. Evaluate results.

FALLACIES:
Unsound arguments
that can appear logical

**Fallacies of
Generalization:**
Hasty generalization
Sweeping generalization
False dilemma

Causal Fallacies:
Slippery slope

Fallacies of Relevance:
Appeal to authority
Appeal to pity
Appeal to fear
Appeal to ignorance
Appeal to personal
attack

THE CRITICAL THINKER'S GUIDE TO REASONING

REASONING IS THE TYPE OF THINKING that uses arguments—reasons in support of conclusions—to decide, explain, predict, and persuade. Effective reasoning involves using all of the intellectual skills and critical attitudes you have been developing in this book, and in this chapter you will further explore various dimensions of the reasoning process.

Chapter 10 focused primarily on *deductive reasoning*, an argument form in which one reasons from premises that are known or assumed to be true to a conclusion that follows necessarily from the premises. In this chapter we will examine *inductive reasoning*, an argument form in which one reasons from premises that are known or assumed to be true to a conclusion that is supported by the premises but does not follow logically from them.

Inductive Reasoning	An argument form in which one reasons from premises that are known or assumed to be true to a conclusion that is supported by the premises but does not follow necessarily from them.

When you reason inductively, your premises provide evidence that makes it more or less probable (but not certain) that the conclusion is true. The following statements are examples of conclusions reached through inductive reasoning.

1. A recent Gallup poll reported that 74 percent of the American public believes that abortion should remain legalized.
2. On the average, a person with a college degree will earn over $830,000 more in his or her lifetime than a person with just a high school diploma.
3. In a recent survey, twice as many doctors interviewed stated that if they were stranded on a desert island they would prefer Bayer Aspirin to Extra Strength Tylenol.
4. The outbreak of food poisoning at the end-of-year school party was probably caused by the squid salad.
5. The devastating disease AIDS is caused by a particularly complex virus that may not be curable.
6. The solar system is probably the result of an enormous explosion—a "big bang"—that occurred billions of years ago.

The first three statements are forms of inductive reasoning known as *empirical generalization*, a general statement about an entire group made on the basis of observing some members of the group. The final three statements are examples of *causal reasoning*, a form of inductive reasoning in which it is claimed that an event (or events) is the result of the occurrence of another event (or events). We will be exploring the ways each of these forms of inductive reasoning function in our lives and in various fields of study.

In addition to examining various ways of reasoning logically and effectively, we will also explore certain forms of reasoning that are not logical and, as a result, usually not effective. These ways of pseudo-reasoning (false reasoning) are often termed *fallacies:* arguments that are not sound because of various errors in reasoning. Fallacious reasoning is typically used to influence others. It seeks to persuade not on the basis of sound arguments and critical thinking but rather on the basis of emotional and illogical factors.

Fallacies   Unsound arguments that are often persuasive because they can appear to be logical, because they usually appeal to our emotions and prejudices, and because they often support conclusions that we want to believe are accurate.

EMPIRICAL GENERALIZATION

One of the most important tools used by both natural and social scientists is empirical generalization. Have you ever wondered how the major television and radio networks can accurately predict election results hours before the polls close? These predictions are made possible by the power of empirical generalization, which is defined as reasoning from a limited sample to a general conclusion based on this sample.

Empirical Generalization   A form of inductive reasoning in which a general statement is made about an entire group (the "target population") based on observing some members of the group (the "sample population").

Network election predictions, as well as public opinion polls that occur throughout a political campaign, are based on interviews with a select number of people. Ideally, pollsters would interview everyone in the *target population* (in this case, voters), but this, of course, is hardly practical. Instead, they select a relatively small group of individuals from the target population, known as a *sample*, who they have determined will adequately represent the group as a whole. Pollsters believe that they can then generalize the opinions of this smaller group to the target population. And with a few notable exceptions (such as in the 1948 presidential election, when New York Governor Thomas Dewey went to bed believing he had been elected president and woke up a loser to Harry Truman), these results are highly accurate. (Polling techniques are much more sophisticated today than they were in 1948.)

There are three key criteria for evaluating inductive arguments:

- Is the sample known?
- Is the sample sufficient?
- Is the sample representative?

Is the Sample Known?

An inductive argument is only as strong as the sample on which it is based. For example, sample populations described in vague and unclear terms—"highly placed sources" or "many young people interviewed," for example—provide a treacherously weak foundation for generalizing to larger populations. In order for an inductive argument to be persuasive, the sample population should be explicitly *known* and clearly identified. Natural and social scientists take great care in selecting the members in the sample groups, and this is an important part of the data that is available to outside investigators who may wish to evaluate and verify the results.

Is the Sample Sufficient?

The second criterion for evaluating inductive reasoning is to consider the *size* of the sample. It should be sufficiently large to give an accurate sense of the group as a whole. In the polling example discussed earlier, we would be concerned if only a few registered voters were interviewed and the results of these interviews were generalized to a much larger population. Overall, the larger the sample, the more reliable the inductive conclusions. Natural and social scientists have developed precise guidelines for determining the size of the sample needed to achieve reliable results. For example, poll results are often

Empirical generalizations are general statements made about an entire group based on observing some members of the group. Although an important form of reasoning, care must be taken to avoid the fallacy of **hasty generalization.**

accompanied by a qualification such as "These results are subject to an error factor of ± 3 percentage points." This means that if the sample reveals that 47 percent of those interviewed prefer candidate X, then we can reliably state that 44 to 50 percent of the target population prefer candidate X. Because a sample is usually a small portion of the target population, we can rarely state that the two match each other exactly—there must always be some room for variation. The exceptions to this are situations in which the target population is completely homogeneous. For example, tasting one cookie from a bag of cookies is usually enough to tell us whether or not the entire bag is stale.

Is the Sample Representative?

The third crucial element in effective inductive reasoning is the *representativeness* of the sample. If we are to generalize with confidence from the sample to the target population, then we have to be sure the sample is similar to the larger group from which it is drawn in all relevant aspects. For instance, in the polling example, the sample population should reflect the same percentage of men and women, of Democrats and Republicans, of young and old, and so on, as the target population. It is obvious that many characteristics, such as hair color, favorite food, and shoe size are not relevant to the comparison. The better the sample reflects the target population in terms of *relevant* qualities, however, then the better the accuracy of the generalizations. On the other hand, when the sample is *not* representative of the target population—for example, if the election pollsters interviewed only females between the ages of thirty and thirty-five—then the sample is termed *biased*, and any generalizations about the target population will be highly suspect.

How do we ensure that the sample is representative of the target population? One important device is *random selection*, a selection strategy in which every member of the target population has an equal chance of being included in the sample. For example, the various techniques used to select winning lottery tickets are supposed to be random—each ticket is supposed to have an equal chance of winning. In complex cases of inductive reasoning—such as polling—random selection is often combined with the confirmation that all of the important categories in the population are adequately represented. For example, an election pollster would want to be certain that all significant geographical areas are included, and then would randomly select individuals from within those areas to compose the sample.

Understanding the principles of empirical generalization is of crucial importance to effective thinking because we are continually challenged to construct and evaluate this form of inductive arguments in our lives.

THINKING ACTIVITY 11.1

Review the following examples of inductive arguments. For each argument, evaluate the quality of the thinking by answering the following questions:

1. Is the sample known?
2. Is the sample sufficient?
3. Is the sample representative?
4. Do you believe the conclusions are likely to be accurate? Why or why not?

In a study of a possible relationship between pornography and antisocial behavior, questionnaires went out to 7,500 psychiatrists and psychoanalysts, whose listing in the directory of the American Psychological

Association indicated clinical experience. Over 3,400 of these professionals responded. The result: 7.4 percent of the psychiatrists and psychologists had cases in which they were convinced that pornography was a causal factor in antisocial behavior; an additional 9.4 percent were suspicious; 3.2 percent did not commit themselves; and 80 percent said they had no cases in which a causal connection was suspected.

A survey by the Sleep Disorder Clinic of the VA hospital in La Jolla, California (involving more than one million people), revealed that people who sleep more than ten hours a night have a death rate 80 percent higher than those who sleep only seven or eight hours. Men who sleep less than four hours a night have a death rate 180 percent higher, and women with less [than four hours] sleep have a rate 40 percent higher. This might be taken as indicating that too much and too little sleep cause death.

"U.S. Wastes Food Worth Millions." Americans in the economic middle waste more food than their rich and poor counterparts, according to a study published Saturday. Carried out in Tucson, Arizona, by University of Arizona students under the direction of Dr. William L. Rathje, the study analyzed 600 bags of garbage each week for three years from lower-, middle-, and upper-income neighborhoods. They found that city residents throw out around 10 percent of the food they brought home—about 9,500 tons of food each year. The figure amounts to $9 to $11 million worth of food. Most of the waste occurred in middle-class neighborhoods. Both the poor and the wealthy were significantly more frugal.

Being a general practitioner in a rural area has tremendous drawbacks— being on virtually 24-hour call 365 days a year; patients without financial means or insurance; low fees in the first place; inadequate facilities and assistance. Nevertheless, America's small town G.P.s seem fairly content with their lot. According to a survey taken by *Country Doctor*, fully 50 percent wrote back that they "basically like being a rural G.P." Only 1 in 15 regretted that he or she had not specialized. Only 2 out of 20 rural general practitioners would trade places with their urban counterparts, given the chance. And only 1 in 30 would "choose some other line of work altogether."

A recent survey of 5,012 students from 4th grade through high school yields important insights about how young people make moral decisions. Asked how they would decide what to do if "unsure of what was right or wrong in a particular situation," these were the responses and how they were described by the researchers:

- 23% said they would "do what was best for everyone involved," an orientation the researchers labeled "civic humanist."
- 20% would "follow the advice of an authority, such as a parent, teacher, or youth leader"—"conventionalist."
- 18% of respondents said they would do what would make them "happy"—"expressivist."
- 16% would "do what God or Scriptures" say "is right"—"theistic."
- 10% would "do what would improve their own situations"—"utilitarian."
- 9% did not know and 3% wrote that they would follow their "conscience."

When young people were asked their beliefs about anything from lying, stealing and using drugs to abortion or reasons for choosing a job, these rudimentary ethical systems or "moral compasses" turned out to be more important than the background factors that social scientists habitually favor in their search for explanations, like economic status, sex, race, and even religious practice. ◀

THINKING ACTIVITY 11.2

Select an issue that you would like to poll a group of people about—for example, the population of your school or your neighborhood. Describe in specific terms how you would go about constructing a sample both large and representative enough for you to generalize the results to the target population accurately. ◀

FALLACIES OF FALSE GENERALIZATION

In Chapter 7, "Forming and Applying Concepts," we explored the way that we form concepts through the interactive process of generalizing (identifying the common qualities that define the boundaries of the concept) and interpreting (identifying examples of the concept). This generalizing and interpreting process is similar to the process involved in constructing empirical generalizations, as we seek to reach a general conclusion based on a limited number of examples and then apply this conclusion to other examples. Although generalizing and interpreting are useful in forming concepts, they also can give rise to fallacious ways of thinking, including the following:

- Hasty generalization
- Sweeping generalization
- False dilemma

Hasty Generalization

Consider the following examples of reasoning. Do you think that the arguments are sound? Why or why not?

My boyfriends have never shown any real concern for my feelings. My conclusion is that men are insensitive, selfish, and emotionally superficial.

My mother always gets upset over insignificant things. This leads me to believe that women are very emotional.

In both of these cases, a general conclusion has been reached that is based on a very small sample. As a result, the reasons provide very weak support for the conclusions that are being developed. It just does not make good sense to generalize from a few individuals to all men or all women. Our conclusion is *hasty* because our sample is not large enough and/or not representative enough to provide adequate justification for our generalization.

Of course, many generalizations are more warranted than the two given here because the conclusion is based on a sample that is larger and more representative of the group as a whole. For example:

I have done a lot of research in a variety of automotive publications on the relationship between the size of cars and the gas mileage they get. In general, I think it makes sense to conclude that large cars tend to get fewer miles per gallon than smaller cars.

In this case, the conclusion is generalized from a larger and more representative sample than those in the preceding two arguments. As a result, the reason for the last argument provides much stronger support for the conclusion.

Fallacies are unsound arguments that are often persuasive because they appeal to our emotions and prejudices in order to support illogical conclusions. Choosing fallacious reasoning leads to oversimplified and inaccurate conclusions, while choosing logical reasoning results in sound, intelligent conclusions.

Unfortunately, many of the general conclusions we reach about the world are not legitimate because they are based on samples that are too small or are not representative. In these cases, the generalization is a distortion because it creates a false impression of the group that is being represented. These illegitimate generalizations sometimes result in *stereotypes*. Stereotypes affect our perception of the world because they encourage us to form an inaccurate idea of an entire group based on insufficient evidence ("Men are insensitive and selfish"). Even if we have experiences that conflict with our stereotype ("This man is not insensitive and selfish"), we tend to overlook the conflicting information in favor of the stereotype ("All men are insensitive and selfish—except for this one").

THINKING ACTIVITY 11.3

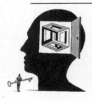

1. Have you ever been the victim of a stereotyped generalization? Describe the experience and explain why you believe that you were subjected to this kind of generalization.

2. There are many stereotypes in our culture—in advertising, in the movies, on television, in literature, and so on.

   • Describe one such stereotype.

   • Identify some specific examples of places where this stereotype is found.

   Explain the reasons why you think this stereotype developed. ◀

Sweeping Generalization

Whereas the fallacy of hasty generalization deals with errors in the process of generalizing, the fallacy of *sweeping generalization* focuses on difficulties in the process of interpreting. Consider the following examples of reasoning. Do you think that the arguments are sound? Why or why not?

Vigorous exercise contributes to overall good health. Therefore vigorous exercise should be practiced by recent heart attack victims, people who are out of shape, and women who are about to give birth.

People should be allowed to make their own decisions, providing that their actions do not harm other people. Therefore people who are trying to commit suicide should be left alone to do what they want.

In both of these cases, generalizations that are true in most cases have been deliberately applied to instances that are clearly intended to be exceptions to the generalizations because of special features that the exceptions possess. Of course, the use of sweeping generalizations stimulates us to clarify the generalization, rephrasing it to exclude instances, like those given here, that have special features. For example, the first generalization could be reformulated as "Vigorous exercise contributes to overall good health, *except for* recent heart attack victims, people out of shape, and women who are about to give birth." Sweeping generalizations become dangerous only when they are accepted without critical analysis and reformulation.

Review the following examples of sweeping generalizations, and in each case (a) explain *why* it is a sweeping generalization, and (b) reformulate the statement so that it becomes a legitimate generalization.

1. A college education stimulates you to develop as a person and prepares you for many professions. Therefore, all persons should attend college, no matter what career they are interested in.

2. Drugs such as heroin and morphine are addictive and therefore qualify as dangerous drugs. This means that they should never be used, even as painkillers in medical situations.

3. Once criminals have served time for the crimes they have committed, they have paid their debt to society and should be permitted to work at any job they choose.

False Dilemma

The fallacy of the false dilemma—also known as the either/or fallacy or the black-or-white fallacy—occurs when we are asked to choose between two extreme alternatives without being able to consider additional options. For example, we may say, "Either you're for me or against me," meaning that a choice has to be made between these alternatives. Sometimes giving people only two choices on an issue makes sense ("If you decide to swim the English Channel, you'll either make it or you won't"). At other times, however, viewing situations in such extreme terms may be a serious oversimplification—for it would mean viewing a complicated situation in terms that are too simple.

The following statements are examples of false dilemmas. After analyzing the fallacy in each case, suggest different alternatives than those being presented.

Example: "Everyone in Germany is a National Socialist—the few outside the party are either lunatics or idiots." (Adolf Hitler, quoted by the *New York Times*, April 5, 1938)

Analysis: This is an oversimplification. Hitler is saying that if you are not a Nazi, then you are a lunatic or an idiot. By limiting the population to these groups, Hitler was simply ignoring all the people who did not qualify as Nazis, lunatics, or idiots.

1. "America—love it or leave it!"
2. "She loves me; she loves me not."
3. "Live free or die."
4. "If you're not part of the solution, then you're part of the problem." (Eldridge Cleaver)
5. "If you know about BMW, you either own one or you want to."

CAUSAL REASONING

A second major type of inductive reasoning is causal reasoning, in which an event (or events) is claimed to be the result of the occurrence of another event (or events).

> **Causal Reasoning**   A form of inductive reasoning in which an event (or events) is claimed to be the result of another event (or events).

As you use your thinking abilities to try to understand the world you live in, you often ask the question, "Why did that happen?" For example, if the engine of your car is running roughly, your natural question is, "What's wrong?" If you wake up one morning with an upset stomach, you usually ask yourself, "What's the cause?" Or maybe the softball team you belong to has been losing recently. You typically wonder, "What's going on?" In each of these cases you assume that there is some factor (or factors) responsible for what is occurring, some *cause* (or causes) that results in the *effect* (or effects) you are observing (the rough engine, the upset stomach).

As you saw in Chapter 8, "Relating and Organizing," causality is one of the basic patterns of thinking we use to organize and make sense of our experience. For instance, imagine how bewildered you would feel if a mechanic looked at your car engine and told you there was no explanation for the poorly running engine. Or suppose you take your upset stomach to the doctor, who examines you and then concludes that there is no possible causal explanation for the malady. In each case you would be understandably skeptical of the diagnosis and would probably seek another opinion.

The Scientific Method

Causal reasoning is also the backbone of the natural and social sciences; it is responsible for the remarkable understanding of our world that has been achieved. The *scientific method* works on the assumption that the world is constructed in a complex web of causal relationships that can be discovered through systematic investigation. Scientists have devised an organized approach for discovering causal relationships and testing the accuracy of conclusions. The sequence of steps is as follows:

1. Identify an event or relationship between events to be investigated.
2. Gather information about the event (or events).
3. Develop a theory or hypothesis to explain what is happening.

4. Test the theory or hypothesis through experimentation.

5. Evaluate the theory or hypothesis.

How does this sequence work when applied to the situation of the rough-running engine mentioned earlier?

1. *Identify an event to be investigated.* In this case, the event is obvious—your car engine is running poorly and you want to discover the cause of the problem so you can fix it.

2. *Gather information about the event.* This step involves locating any relevant information about the situation that will help solve the problem. You initiate this step by asking and trying to answer a variety of questions: When did the engine begin running poorly? Was it abrupt or gradual? When did the car last have a tune-up? Are there other mechanical difficulties that might be related? Has anything unusual occurred with the car recently?

3. *Develop a theory or hypothesis to explain what is happening.* After reviewing the relevant information, you want to identify the most likely explanation of what has happened. This possible explanation is known as a *hypothesis*. (A *theory* is normally a more complex model that involves a number of inter-connected hypotheses, such as the theory of quantum mechanics in physics.)

> **Hypothesis**   A possible explanation that is introduced to account for a set of facts and that can be used as a basis for further investigation.

Although your hypothesis may be suggested by the information you have, it goes beyond the information as well and so must be tested before you commit yourself to it. In this case the hypothesis you might settle on is "water in the gas." This hypothesis was suggested by your recollection that the engine troubles began right after you bought gas in the pouring rain. This hypothesis may be correct or it may be incorrect—you have to test it to find out.

When you devise a plausible hypothesis to be tested, you should keep three general guidelines in mind:

- *Explanatory power:* The hypothesis should effectively explain the event you are investigating. The hypothesis that damaged windshield wipers are causing the engine problems doesn't seem to provide an adequate explanation of the difficulties.

- *Economy:* The hypothesis should not be unnecessarily complex. The explanation that your engine difficulty is the result of sabotage by an unfriendly neighbor is possible but unlikely. There are simpler and more direct explanations you should test first.
- *Predictive power:* The hypothesis should allow you to make various predictions to test its accuracy. If the "water in the gas" hypothesis is accurate, you can predict that removing the water from the gas tank and gas line should clear up the difficulty.

4. *Test the theory or hypothesis through experimentation.* Once you identify a hypothesis that meets these three guidelines, the next task is to devise an experiment to test its accuracy. In the case of your troubled car, you would test your hypothesis by pouring several containers of "dry-gas" into the tank, blowing out the gas line, and cleaning the carburetor. By removing the moisture in the gas system, you should be able to determine whether your hypothesis is correct.

5. *Evaluate the theory or hypothesis.* After reviewing the results of your experience, you usually can assess the accuracy of your hypothesis. If the engine runs smoothly after you remove moisture from the gas line, then this strong evidence supports your hypothesis. On the other hand, if the engine does *not* run smoothly after your efforts, then this persuasive evidence suggests that your hypothesis was not correct. There is, however, a third possibility. Removing the moisture from the gas system might improve the engine's performance somewhat but not entirely. In that case, you might want to construct a *revised* hypothesis along the lines of "Water in the gas system is partially responsible for my rough-running engine, but another cause (or causes) might be involved as well."

If the evidence does not support your hypothesis or supports a revised version of it, you then begin the entire process again by identifying and testing a new hypothesis. The natural and social sciences engage in an ongoing process of developing theories and hypotheses and testing them through experimental design. Many theories and hypotheses are much more complex than our "moisture in the gas" example and take years of generating, revising, and testing. Determining the subatomic structure of the universe and finding cures for various kinds of cancers, for example, have been the subjects of countless theories and hypotheses, as well as experiments to test their accuracy. We might diagram this operation of the scientific process as follows:

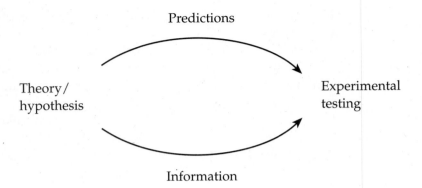

Predictions

Theory/
hypothesis

Experimental
testing

Information

(Acceptance, rejection, or revision of the
theory/hypothesis)

THINKING ACTIVITY 11.4

Select one of the following situations or describe a situation of your own choosing. Then analyze the situation by working through the various steps of the scientific method listed directly after.

- Situation 1: You wake up in the morning with an upset stomach.
- Situation 2: Your grades have been declining all semester.
- Situation 3: (Your own choosing)

1. *Identify an event or a relationship between events to be investigated.* Describe the situation you have selected.

2. *Gather information about the event.* Elaborate the situation by providing additional details. Be sure to include a variety of possible causes for the event. (For example, an upset stomach might be the result of food poisoning, the flu, anxiety, etc.).

3. *Develop a theory or hypothesis to explain what is happening.* Based on the information you have described, identify a plausible hypothesis that (a) explains what occurred, (b) is clear and direct, and (c) leads to predictions that can be tested.

4. *Test the theory or hypothesis through experimentation.* Design a way of testing your hypothesis that results in evidence proving or disproving it.

5. *Evaluate the theory or hypothesis.* Describe the results of your experiment and explain whether the results lead you to accept, reject, or revise your hypothesis. ◀

In designing the experiment in Thinking Activity 11.4, you may have used one of the two common reasoning patterns.

Reasoning pattern 1: *A* caused *B* because *A* is the only relevant common element shared by more than one occurrence of *B*.

For example, imagine you are investigating your upset stomach and you decide to call two friends who had dinner with you the previous evening to see if they have similar symptoms. You discover they also have upset stomachs. Because dining at "Sam's Seafood" was the only experience shared by the three of you that might explain the three stomach problems, you conclude that food poisoning may in fact be the cause. Further, although each of you ordered a different entrée, you all shared an appetizer, "Sam's Special Squid," which suggests that you may have identified the cause. As we can see, this pattern of reasoning looks for the common thread linking different occurrences of the same event to identify the cause; stated more simply, "The cause is the common thread."

Reasoning pattern 2:   *A* caused *B* because *A* is the only relevant difference between this situation and other situations in which *B* did not take place.

For example, imagine that you are investigating the reasons that your team, which has been winning all year, has suddenly begun to lose. One way of approaching this situation is to look for circumstances that might have changed at the time your team's fortunes began to decline. Your investigation yields two possible explanations. First, your team started wearing new uniforms about the time it started losing. Second, one of your regular players was sidelined with a foot injury. You decide to test the first hypothesis by having the team begin wearing the old uniforms again. When this doesn't change your fortunes, you conclude that the missing player may be the cause of the difficulties, and you anxiously await the player's return to see if your reasoning is accurate. As you can see, this pattern of reasoning looks for relevant differences linked to the situation you are trying to explain; stated more simply, "The cause is the difference."

Controlled Experiments

Although our analysis of causal reasoning has focused on causal relationships between specific events, much of scientific research concerns causal factors influencing populations composed of many individuals. In these cases, the causal relationships tend to be much more complex than the simple formulation *A* causes *B*. For example, on every package of cigarettes sold in the United States appears a message such as: "Surgeon General's Warning: Smoking Causes Lung Cancer, Heart Disease, Emphysema, And May Complicate Pregnancy." This does not mean that every cigarette smoked has a direct impact on one's health, nor does it mean that everyone who smokes moderately, or even heavily, will die prematurely of cancer, heart disease, or emphysema. Instead, the statement means that if you habitually smoke, your chances of developing one of the diseases normally associated with smoking are significantly higher than are those of someone who does not smoke or who smokes only occasionally. How were scientists able to arrive at this conclusion?

The reasoning strategy scientists use to reach conclusions like this one is the *controlled experiment*, and it is one of the most powerful reasoning strategies ever developed. There are three different kinds of controlled experiment designs:

1. Cause-to-effect experiments (with intervention)
2. Cause-to-effect experiments (without intervention)
3. Effect-to-cause experiments

Cause-to-Effect Experiments (with Intervention)   The first of these forms of reasoning is illustrated by the following example. Imagine that you have developed a new cream you believe will help cure baldness in men and women and you want to evaluate its effectiveness. What do you do? To begin with, you have to identify a group of people who accurately represent all of the balding men and women in the United States, because testing it on all balding people simply isn't feasible. This involves following the guidelines for inductive reasoning described in the last section. It is important that the group you select to test be *representative* of all balding people (known as the *target population*), because you hope your product will grow hair on all types of heads. For example, if you selected only men between the ages of twenty and thirty to test, the experiment would establish only whether the product works for men of these ages. Additional experiments would have to be conducted for women and other age groups. This representative group is known as a *sample*. Scientists have developed strategies for selecting sample groups to ensure that they mirror fairly the larger group from which they are drawn.

Once you have selected your sample of balding men and women—say you have identified 200 people—the next step is to divide the sample into two groups of 100 people that are alike in all relevant respects. The best way to ensure that the groups are essentially alike is through the technique we examined earlier called *random selection*, which means that each individual selected has the same chance of being chosen as everyone else. You then designate one group as the *experimental group* and the other group as the *control group*. You next give the individuals in the experimental group treatments of your hair-growing cream, and you give either no treatments or a harmless, non-hair-growing cream to the control group. At the conclusion of the testing period, you compare the experimental group with the control group to evaluate hair gain and hair loss.

Suppose that a number of individuals in the experimental group do indeed show evidence of more new hair growth than the control group. How can we be sure this is because of the cream and not simply a chance occurrence? Scientists have developed a statistical formula based on the size of the sample and the frequency of the observed effects. For example, imagine that 13 persons in your experimental group show evidence of new hair growth, whereas no one in the control group shows any such evidence. Statisticians have determined that we can say with 95 percent certainty that the new hair growth was caused by your new cream; that the results were not merely the result of chance. This type of experimental result is usually expressed by saying that the experimental results were significant at the 0.05 level, a standard criterion in experimental research. The diagram on page 520 shows the cause-to-effect experiment (with intervention).

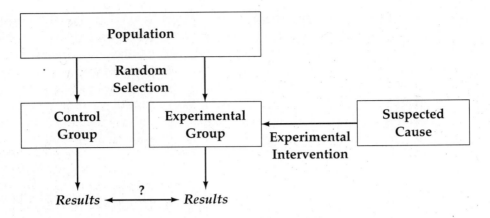

CAUSE-TO-EFFECT EXPERIMENTS (WITH INTERVENTION)

Cause-to-Effect Experiments (without Intervention)   The second form of controlled experiment is known as the *cause-to-effect experiment (without intervention)*. This form of experimental design is similar to the one just described except that the experimenter does not intervene to expose the experimental group to a proposed cause (like the hair-growing cream). Instead, the experimenter identifies a cause that a population is already exposed to and then constructs the experiment. For example, suppose you suspect that the asbestos panels and insulation in some old buildings cause cancer. Because it would not be ethical to expose people intentionally to something that might damage their health, you would search for already existing conditions in which people are being exposed to the asbestos. Once located, these individuals (or a representative

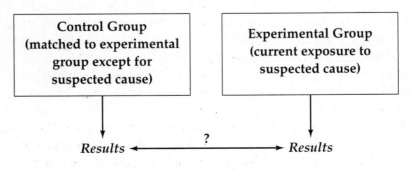

**CAUSE-TO-EFFECT EXPERIMENTS
(WITHOUT INTERVENTION)**

sample) could be used as the experimental group. You could then form a control group of individuals who are not exposed to asbestos but who match the experimental group in all other relevant respects. You could then investigate the health experiences of both groups over time, thereby evaluating the possible relationship between asbestos and cancer. The diagram on page 521 illustrates the procedure used in cause-to-effect experiments (without intervention).

Effect-to-Cause Experiments   A final form of reasoning employing the controlled experimental design is known as the *effect-to-cause experiment*. In this case the experimenter works backward from an existing effect to a suspected cause. For example, imagine that you are investigating the claim by many Vietnam veterans that exposure to the chemical defoliant Agent Orange has resulted in significant health problems for them and for children born to them. Once again, you would not want to expose people to a potentially harmful substance just to test the hypothesis. And unlike the asbestos case we just examined, people are no longer being exposed to Agent Orange as they were during the war. As a result, investigating the claim involves beginning with the effect (health problems) and working back to the suspected cause (Agent Orange). In this case the target population would be Vietnam veterans who were exposed to Agent Orange, so you would draw a representative sample from this group. You would form a matching control group from the population of Vietnam veterans who were *not* exposed to Agent Orange. Next, you would compare the incidence of illnesses claimed to have been caused by Agent Orange in the two groups and evaluate the proposed causal relation. The diagram below illustrates the procedure used in effect-to-cause experiments.

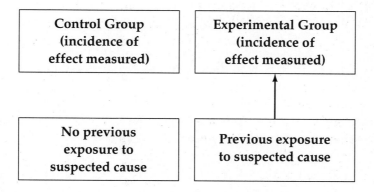

THINKING ACTIVITY 11.5

Read the following experimental situations. For each situation:

1. Describe the proposed causal relationship (the theory or hypothesis).
2. Identify which kind of experimental design was used.
3. Evaluate:
   a. The representativeness of the sample
   b. The randomness of the division into experimental and control groups
4. Explain how well the experimental results support the proposed theory or hypothesis.

New studies reported in the *Journal of the American Medical Association* indicate that vasectomy is safe. A group headed by Frank Massey of UCLA paired 10,500 vasectomized men with a like number of men who had not had the operation. The average follow-up time was 7.9 years, and 2,300 pairs were followed for more than a decade. The researchers reported that, aside from inflammation in the testes, the incidence of diseases for vasectomized men was similar to that in their paired controls.

Canadian researchers led by D. G. Perrin of the department of pathology at the Hospital for Sick Children in Toronto have found an important biochemical difference in the bodies of children who died from sudden infant death syndrome (SIDS), compared with infants who died from other causes. According to the scientists, the research suggests that infants at high risk for SIDS may manufacture the brain chemical transmitter dopamine at abnormally high levels. Theoretically, if the results of the investigation are borne out, a child at risk might be treated with dopamine-blocking drugs as a preventive measure, but the scientists caution it is too early to consider doing that. "Just because (dopamine) is abnormal does not necessarily mean it's a primary cause," says Perrin. "It may be a secondary cause."

Perrin and his colleagues examined the carotid bodies of 13 SIDS babies and five infants who died from other causes. All but two of the SIDS babies had dopamine levels far in excess of those in the controls.

SIDS claims about ten thousand infants between two months and four months of age each year in the United States. All SIDS deaths involve the mysterious cessation of breathing during sleep.

A study released last week indicates that Type A individuals, who are characteristically impatient, competitive, insecure and short-tempered, can halve their chances of having a heart attack by changing their behavior with the help of psychological counseling.

In 1978, scientists at Mt. Zion Hospital and Medical Center in San Francisco and Stanford University School of Education began their study of 862 predominantly male heart attack victims. Of this number, 592 received group counseling to ease their Type A behavior and improve their self-esteem. After three years, only 7 percent had another heart attack, compared with 13 percent of a matched group of 270 subjects who received only cardiological advice. Among 328 men who continued with the counseling for the full three years, 79 percent reduced their Type A behavior. About half of the comparison group was similarly able to slow down and cope better with stress.

This is the first evidence "that a modification program aimed at Type A behavior actually helps to reduce coronary disease," says Redford Williams of Duke University, an investigator of Type A behavior.

A new study, based on 2,745,149 deaths from natural causes, has found that men tend to die just before their birthdays, while women tend to die just after their birthdays. Thus an approaching birthday seems to prolong the life of women and precipitate death in men. The study, published in the journal *Psychosomatic Medicine*, found 3 percent more deaths than expected among women in the week after a birthday and a slight decline the week before. For men, deaths peaked just before birthdays and showed no rise above normal afterward.

"Experts in sleep behavior and sleep disorders have found that a majority of people are sleeping at least an hour to 90 minutes less each night than they should, based on a series of studies of several hundred college and graduate students between the ages of 18 and 30. In one representative experiment with young adults who were generally healthy and got an average of seven to eight hours sleep a night, sleep researchers discovered that 20 percent of these apparently normal students could fall asleep almost instantaneously throughout the day if allowed to lie down in a darkened room, evidence that they were sleep deprived. Researchers further discovered that even the students who seemed alert and did not quickly fall asleep under test conditions could benefit from more sleep. If they spent one week getting to bed an hour to 90 minutes earlier than usual, the students improved their performance markedly on psychological and cognitive tests. Such results seem to suggest that most people who think they are sleeping enough would be better off with an extra portion of rest.

A survey of 5000 people by Stanley Coren found that while 15 percent of the population at age 10 was left-handed, there was a pronounced drop-off as people grew older, leaving 5 percent among 50-year-olds and less than 1 percent for those aged 80 and above. Where have all the lefties gone? They seem to have died. Lefties have a shorter life expectancy than righties, by an average of 9 years in the general population, apparently due to the ills and accidents they are more likely to suffer by having to live in a "righthanded world."

The ads seem too good to be true: Slap a patch on the arm, change it every day, and two or three months later, you've kicked the habit. However, the truth is more elusive. Studies submitted to the F.D.A. indicated that smokers who used nicotine patches for 8 to 12 weeks were about twice as likely to have quit at the end of that period as were those who used dummy patches without nicotine. But as any smoker will testify, quitting is easy; the problem is that starting up again is even easier. So smokers wonder whether the patches will conquer their craving for nicotine and help them quit permanently or whether they will have to continue to purchase the patches at a cost of $300 for the 12-week supply. So far, research suggests that those who quit with the help of patches relapse at about the same rate as anyone else. In one series of follow-up studies, the share of individuals still smoke-free six months after they stopped using patches ranged from zero to 48 percent, as compared with a six-month success rate of zero to 40 percent for those who did not use them. Other studies indicate that success rates then continue to drop for at least a year, with patch users retaining some of their initial edge. Taken together, the figures suggest that the patches can help a small fraction of smokers. Each year 17 million Americans try to quit smoking, but only 1.3 million manage to do so. ◄

THINKING ACTIVITY 11.6

Construct an experimental design to investigate a potential causal relationship of your own choosing. Be sure that your experimental design follows the guidelines established:

- A clearly defined theory or hypothesis expressing a proposed relationship between a cause and an effect in a population of individuals
- Representative samples
- Selection into experimental and control groups

- A clear standard for evaluating the evidence for or against the theory or hypothesis ◀

THINKING PASSAGE

Human history is filled with examples of misguided causal thinking—bleeding people's veins and applying leeches to reduce fever, beating and torturing emotionally disturbed people to drive out the devils thought to possess them, sacrificing young women to ensure the goodwill of the gods, and so on. When the bubonic plague ravaged Europe in the fourteenth century, the lack of scientific understanding led to causal explanations like "God's punishment of the unholy" and "the astrological position of the planets."

Contrast this fourteenth-century plague with what some people have termed the plague of the twentieth century—acquired immune deficiency syndrome (AIDS). We now have the knowledge, reasoning, and technical capabilities to investigate the disease in an effective fashion, though no cure or preventative inoculation has yet been developed. Read the following article describing the scientific battle against AIDS and then answer the questions that follow.

FOR A NATIONAL EFFORT TO DEVELOP A VACCINE TO COUNTERACT AIDS
by Robert E. Pollack

The time has come for the Government to underwrite a nationwide effort to produce an effective vaccine against HTLV III, the virus that causes AIDS. Though a frightening new disease, AIDS is no longer so novel that such an effort would be premature.

Samples of the virus have been isolated and their entire sets of genes decoded. The human populations for testing and eventual inoculation with a vaccine exist and are ready to volunteer. Yet the communities of physicians, and of public and corporate researchers, seem unable to organize the process. Why is the nation unwilling or unable to expend the effort and money to launch an applied-biology and bioengineering effort to develop and test a vaccine?

Let's examine what is know about viruses. Most viruses cannot "find" just any human cell; they have to attach to a cell's surface, and the attachment has to be a specific match between a portion of the cell's surface membrane and a portion of the virus's coat. HTLV III is ordinary in its habits much like other viruses. It is remarkable only for the fastidious way in which it chooses the cell it will attach to, enter and take over.

HTLV III must find and attach to a particular kind of white blood cell. This sort of cell is the very one everyone's body needs in order to recognize and reject a multiplicity of micro-organisms, fungi, parasites, yeasts and bacteria. That is the reason AIDS patients suffer from so many different diseases. As the virus takes over these cells, the body loses its defenses and eventually succumbs to one or many of a host of infectious agents.

Two scientific reasons are given for the reluctance to begin a national effort to develop a vaccine. One is that AIDS might be caused by a family of closely related variants of the same virus and that therefore no vaccine could be effective. The other is that there are no animals suitable for initial testing of a vaccine and thus no way to be sure a vaccine is safe for testing in people.

It seems to me and to some colleagues that these objections, though sound, are not conclusive. The exquisite specificity of HTLV III's recognition of certain white blood cells suggests that all variants of the virus will have in common at least one part of their outer coat—the region that finds and binds to this specific kind of cell.

Gene-splicing is the answer to the second objection and the key to making a vaccine. HTLV III is a new virus, but its known properties so far suggest that it is not so exotic as to be beyond the grasp of recombinant DNA techniques. All the genes of more than one AIDS virus have been isolated and chemically identified. This knowledge should permit scientists to put genes from an AIDS virus into a bacterium. Once they are there, the bacterium, grown in large quantities, can be the source of material for testing as a vaccine. And vaccines produced this way would be totally incapable of causing AIDS.

In the absence of an animal model for AIDS, such vaccines could not now be tested in volunteers, because Government regulations require that new vaccines be first tested in an animal. These rules no longer make sense for vaccines produced by recombinant techniques.

There is at least one other reason for our nation's inability to act: irrational fear and hostility directed at a minority. The population at risk and ready to volunteer for testing is largely homosexual. Our political leaders apparently do not wish to be involved with this minority. As a result, the clock runs out on thousands of victims without even the beginning of an effort to develop the vaccine that might prevent new cases from occurring. This is a social disaster.

Consider what we could be doing. We have a population of homosexuals available for prospective study of such vaccines. These men, like the estimated million or so Americans who already have antibodies to HTLV III, are highly motivated to participate in the large-scale studies necessary to develop an optimal vaccine.

We have as well as population of perhaps 100,000* people with what is known medically as "AIDS-related complex"—a syndrome in which a person has an AIDS virus in his blood but does not show the full set of symptoms characteristic of AIDS. In addition, there are perhaps 10,000 people with AIDS whose white cells are drastically reduced. These 10,000 have a currently irreversible disease, and many have repeatedly offered themselves for any experimental treatments.

A vaccine for any virus-caused cancer will have to be made by recombinant techniques in order to separate the gene for the vaccine from all cancer-causing genes in the virus. Therefore, if we proceed immediately to organize biotechnology for the production and testing of recombinant AIDS vaccines, we gain time on the eventual production of vaccines for leukemias, lymphomas and other human tumors that are likely to be caused by viruses.

All physicians have taken an oath to do no harm. But in fact they do harm by sitting quietly by, or referring AIDS victims to another physician or hoping the disease will quietly go away after it destroys a few thousand homosexual men and narcotics addicts. It is not enough to offer succor and solace. Physicians and scientists should lobby actively for a nationwide effort to develop an AIDS vaccine. ■

Questions for Analysis

1. Explain the process by which the HTLV III virus causes the AIDS syndrome.

2. Construct an experimental design that would test the AIDS vaccine that Dr. Pollack thinks should be developed. Be sure that your experimental design follows the guidelines detailed in Thinking Activity 11.6 on page 524.

3. Dr. Pollack believes that a national effort to develop a vaccine to deal with the AIDS epidemic is overdue and states: "All physicians have taken an oath to do no harm. But in fact they do harm by sitting quietly by. . . ." Explain

* This figure represents the estimate in 1985. In 1990, estimates of persons with AIDS-related complex in the United States ranged as high as 1 million (Editor's note).

whether you agree with this view or not and state the reasons that support your position.

CAUSAL FALLACIES

Because causality plays such a dominant role in the way we make sense of the world, it is not surprising that people make many mistakes and errors in judgment in trying to determine causal relationships. The following are some of the most common fallacies associated with causality:

- Questionable cause
- Misidentification of the cause
- *Post hoc ergo propter hoc*
- Slippery slope

Questionable Cause

The fallacy of *questionable cause* occurs when someone presents a causal relationship for which no real evidence exists. Superstitious beliefs, such as "If you break a mirror, you will have seven years of bad luck," usually fall into this category. Some people feel that astrology, a system of beliefs tying one's personality and fortunes in life to the position of the planets at the moment of birth, also falls into this category.

Consider the following passage from St. Augustine's *Confessions*. Does it seem to support or deny the causal assertions of astrology? Why or why not?

Firminus had heard from his father that when his mother had been pregnant with him, a slave belonging to a friend of his father's was also about to bear. It happened that since the two women had their babies at the same instant, the men were forced to cast exactly the same horoscope for each newborn child down to the last detail, one for his son, the other for the little slave. Yet Firminus, born to wealth in his parents' house, had one of the more illustrious careers in life whereas the slave had no alleviation of his life's burden.

Other examples of this fallacy include explanations like those given by fourteenth-century sufferers of the bubonic plague who claimed that "the Jews are poisoning the Christians' wells." This was particularly nonsensical since an equal percentage of Jews were dying of the plague as well. The evidence did not support the explanation.

Misidentification of the Cause

In causal situations we are not always certain about what is causing what—in other words, what is the cause and what is the effect. *Misidentifying the cause* is easy to do. For example, which are the causes and which are the effects in the following pairs of items? Why?

- Poverty and alcoholism
- Headaches and tension
- Failure in school and personal problems
- Shyness and lack of confidence
- Drug dependency and emotional difficulties

Of course, sometimes a third factor is responsible for both of the effects we are examining. For example, the headaches and tension we are experiencing may both be the result of a third element—such as some new medication we are taking. When this occurs, we are said to commit the fallacy of *ignoring a common cause*. On the other hand, there also exists the fallacy of *assuming a common cause*—for example, assuming that both our sore toe and our earache stem from the same cause.

Post Hoc Ergo Propter Hoc

The translation of the Latin phrase *post hoc ergo propter hoc* is "After it, therefore because of it." It refers to those situations in which, because two things occur close together in time, we assume that one caused the other. For example, if your team wins the game each time you wear your favorite shirt, you might be tempted to conclude that the one event (wearing your favorite shirt) has some influence on the other event (winning the game). As a result, you might continue to wear this shirt "for good luck." It is easy to see how this sort of mistaken thinking can lead to all sorts of superstitious beliefs.

Consider the following causal conclusion arrived at by Mark Twain's fictional character Huckleberry Finn in the following passage. How would you analyze the conclusion that he comes to?

I've always reckoned that looking at the new moon over your left shoulder is one of the carelessest and foolishest things a body can do. Old Hank

Bunker done it once, and bragged about it; and in less than two years he got drunk and fell off a shot tower and spread himself out so that he was just a kind of layer. . . . But anyway, it all come of looking at the moon that way, like a fool.

Can you identify any of your own superstitious beliefs or practices that might have been the result of *post hoc* thinking?

Slippery Slope

The causal fallacy of *slippery slope* is illustrated in the following advice:

Don't smoke that first marijuana cigarette. If you do, it won't be long before you are smoking hashish. Then you will soon be popping pills and snorting cocaine. Before you know it, you will be hooked on heroin and you will end your life with a drug overdose in some rat-infested hotel room.

Slippery slope thinking asserts that one undesirable action will inevitably lead to a worse action, which will necessarily lead to a worse one still, all the way down the "slippery slope" to some terrible disaster at the bottom. Although this progression may indeed happen, there is certainly no causal guarantee that it will. Create slippery slope scenarios for one of the following warnings:

1. If you get behind on one credit card payment . . .
2. If you fail that first test . . .
3. If the United States lets gay men and women serve in the military . . .

Review the causal fallacies described above and then identify and explain the reasoning pitfalls illustrated in the following examples:

1. The person who won the lottery says that she dreamed the winning numbers. I'm going to start writing down the numbers in my dreams.
2. Yesterday I forgot to take my vitamins and I immediately got sick. That mistake won't happen again!
3. I'm warning you—if you start missing classes, it won't be long before you flunk out of school and ruin your future.
4. I always take the first seat in the bus. Today I took another seat, and the bus broke down. And you accuse me of being superstitious!
5. I think the reason I'm not doing well in school is because I'm just not interested. Also, I simply don't have enough time to study.

The fallacy of **slippery slope** *thinking suggests that one undesirable action will inevitably lead to a worse action, which will necessarily lead to a worse one still, all the way down the "slippery slope" to some unavoidable terrible disaster at the bottom.*

Many people want us to see the cause-and-effect relationships that they believe exist, and they often utilize questionable or outright fallacious reasoning. Consider the following examples:

1. Politicians assure us that a vote for them will result in "a chicken in every pot and a car in every garage."

2. Advertisers tell us that using this detergent will leave our wash "cleaner than clean, whiter than white."

3. Doctors tell us that eating a balanced diet will result in better health.

4. Educators tell us that a college degree is worth an average of $830,000 additional income over an individual's life.

5. Scientists inform us that nuclear energy will result in a better life for all of us.

In each of these examples, certain causal claims are being made about how the world operates in an effort to persuade us to adopt a certain point of view. As critical thinkers, it is our duty to evaluate these various causal claims in an effort to figure out whether they are sensible ways of organizing the world.

Explain how you might go about evaluating whether each of the following causal claims makes sense.

- *Example:* Taking the right vitamins will improve health.
- *Evaluation:* Review the medical research that examines the effect of taking vitamins on health; speak to a nutritionist; speak to a doctor.

1. Sweet Smell deodorant will keep you drier all day long.
2. Allure perfume will cause men to be attracted to you.
3. Natural childbirth will result in a more fulfilling birth experience.
4. Aspirin Plus will give you faster, longer-lasting relief from headaches.
5. Radial tires will improve the gas mileage of your car.

FALLACIES OF RELEVANCE

Many fallacious arguments appeal for support to factors that have little or nothing to do with the argument being offered. In these cases, false appeals substitute for sound reasoning and a critical examination of the issues. Such appeals, known as *fallacies of relevance*, include the following kinds of fallacious thinking:

- Appeal to authority
- Appeal to pity
- Appeal to fear
- Appeal to ignorance
- Appeal to personal attack

Appeal to Authority

In Chapter 5, "Believing and Knowing," we explored the ways in which we sometimes appeal to various authorities to establish our beliefs or prove our points. At that time, we noted that to serve as a basis for beliefs, authorities must have legitimate expertise in the area in which they are advising—like an experienced mechanic diagnosing a problem with your car. People, however, often appeal to authorities who are not qualified to give an expert opinion. Consider the reasoning in the following advertisements. Do you think the arguments are sound? Why or why not?

Hi. You've probably seen me out on the football field. After a hard day's work crushing halfbacks and sacking quarterbacks, I like to settle down with a cold, smooth Maltz beer.

SONY. Ask anyone.

Over 11 million women will read this ad. Only 16 will own the coat.

Each of these arguments is intended to persuade us of the value of a product through the appeal to various authorities. In the first case, the authority is a well-known sports figure; in the second, the authority is large numbers of people; and in the third, the authority is a select few, appealing to our desire to be exclusive ("snob appeal"). Unfortunately, none of these authorities offers legitimate expertise about the product. Football players are not beer experts; large numbers of people are often misled; and exclusive groups of people are frequently mistaken in their beliefs. To evaluate authorities properly, we have to ask:

- What are the professional credentials on which the authorities' expertise is based?
- Is their expertise in the area they are commenting on?

Appeal to Pity

Consider the reasoning in the following arguments. Do you think that the arguments are sound? Why or why not?

I know that I haven't completed my term paper, but I really think that I should be excused. This has been a very difficult semester for me. I caught every kind of flue that came around. In addition, my brother has a drinking problem, and this has been very upsetting to me. Also, my dog died.

I admit that my client embezzled money from the company, your honor. However, I would like to bring several facts to your attention. He is a family man, with a wonderful wife and two terrific children. He is an important member of the community. He is active in the church, coaches a little league baseball team, and has worked very hard to be a good person who cares about people. I think that you should take these things into consideration in handing down your sentence.

In each of these arguments, the reasons offered to support the conclusions may indeed be true. They are not, however, relevant to the conclusion. Instead of providing evidence that supports the conclusion, the reasons are designed to make us feel sorry for the person involved and so agree with the conclusion out of sympathy. Although these appeals are often effective, the arguments are not sound. The probability of a conclusion can be established only by reasons that support and are relevant to the conclusion.

Appeal to Fear

Consider the reasoning in the following arguments. Do you think that the arguments are sound? Why or why not?

> I'm afraid I don't think you deserve a raise. After all, there are many people who would be happy to have your job at the salary you are currently receiving. I would be happy to interview some of these people if you really think that you are underpaid.

> If you continue to disagree with my interpretation of *The Catcher in the Rye*, I'm afraid you won't get a very good grade on your term paper.

In both of these arguments, the conclusions being suggested are supported by an appeal to fear, not by reasons that provide evidence for the conclusions. In the first case, the threat is that if you do not forgo your salary demands, your job may be in jeopardy. In the second case, the threat is that if you do not agree with the teacher's interpretation, you will fail the course. In neither instance are the real issues—Is a salary increase deserved? Is the student's interpretation legitimate?—being discussed.

People who appeal to fear to support their conclusions are interested only in prevailing, regardless of which position might be more justified.

Appeal to Ignorance

Consider the reasoning in the following arguments. Do you think that the arguments are sound? Why or why not?

> You say that you don't believe in God. But can you prove that He doesn't exist? If not, then you have to accept the conclusion that He does in fact exist.

> Greco Tires are the best. No others have been proved better.

> "With me, abortion is not a problem of religion. It's a problem of the Constitution. I believe that until and unless someone can establish that the

Instead of sound reasoning and a critical examination of the issues, fallacies of **false** **appeal** *substitute emotional appeals to irrelevant factors like pity, fear, authority, ignorance, and personal attack.*

unborn child is not a living human being, then that child is already pro-tected by the Constitution, which guarantees life, liberty, and the pursuit of happiness to all of us."

—Ronald Reagan

When this argument form is used, the person offering the conclusion is asking his or her opponent to *disprove* the conclusion. If the opponent is unable to do so, then the conclusion is asserted to be true. This argument form is not valid because it is the job of the person proposing the argument to prove the conclusion. Simply because an opponent cannot *dis*prove the conclusion offers no evidence that the conclusion is in fact justified. In the first example, for instance, the fact that someone cannot prove that God does not exist provides no persuasive reason for believing that he does.

Appeal to Personal Attack

Consider the reasoning in the following arguments. Do you think that the arguments are valid? Why or why not?

Your opinion on this issue is false. It's impossible to believe anything you say.

How can you have an intelligent opinion about abortion? You're not a woman, so this is a decision that you'll never have to make.

"Well, I guess I'm reminded a little bit of what Will Rogers once said about Hoover. He said it's not what he doesn't know that bothers me, it's what he knows for sure just ain't so."

—Walter Mondale characterizing Ronald Reagan

This argument form has been one of the most frequently used fallacies through the ages. Its effectiveness results from ignoring the issues of the argument and focusing instead on the personal qualities of the person making the argument. By trying to discredit the other person, the effort is being made to discredit the argument—no matter what reasons are offered. This fallacy is also referred to as the *ad hominem* argument, which means "to the man" rather than to the issue, and *poisoning the well*, because we are trying to ensure that any water drawn from our opponent's well will be treated as undrinkable.

The effort to discredit can take two forms, as illustrated in the preceding examples. The fallacy can be *abusive* in the sense that we are directly attacking the credibility of our opponent (as in the third example). In addition, the fallacy can also be *circumstantial* in the sense that we are claiming that the person's circumstances, not character, render his or her opinion so biased or uninformed that it cannot be treated seriously (as in the second example). Other examples of the circumstantial form of the fallacy would include disregarding the views on nuclear plant safety given by an owner of one of the plants or ignoring the views of a company comparing a product it manufactures with competing products.

THINKING ACTIVITY 11.7

Locate (or develop) an example of each of the following kinds of false appeals. For each example, explain why you think that the appeal is not warranted.

1. Appeal to authority
2. Appeal to pity
3. Appeal to fear
4. Appeal to ignorance
5. Appeal to personal attack ◀

THE CRITICAL THINKER'S GUIDE TO REASONING

This book has provided you with the opportunity to explore and develop many of your critical thinking and reasoning abilities. As you have seen, these abilities are complex and difficult to master. The process of becoming an accomplished critical thinker and effective reasoner is a challenging quest that requires ongoing practice and reflection. This section will present a critical thinking/reasoning model that will help you pull together the important themes of this book into an integrated perspective. This model is illustrated on page 540.* In order to become familiar with the model, you will be thinking through an

* A modified version of a schema originally devised by Ralph H. Johnson; design and layout by J.A. Blair.

important issue that confronts every human being: "Are people capable of choosing freely?"

What Is My Initial Point of View?

Reasoning always begins with a point of view. As a critical thinker, it is important for you to take thoughtful positions and express your views with confidence. Using this statement as a starting point, respond as specifically as you can:

- *I believe (or don't believe) that people can choose freely because . . .*

Here is a sample response:

> *I believe that people are capable of choosing freely because when I am faced with choosing among a number of possibilities, I really have the feeling that it is up to me to make the choice that I want to.*

How Can I Define My Point of View More Clearly?

After stating your initial point of view, the next step is to define the issues more clearly and specifically. As you have seen, the language that we use has multiple levels of meaning, and it is often not clear precisely what meaning(s) people are expressing. To avoid misunderstandings and sharpen your own thinking, it is essential that you clarify the key concepts as early as possible. In this case, the central concept is "choosing freely." Respond by beginning with the following statement:

- *From my point of view, the concept of "choosing freely" means . . .*

Here is a sample response:

> *From my point of view, the concept of "choosing freely" means that when you are faced with a number of alternatives, you are able to make your selection based solely on what you decide, not because you are being forced by other influences.*

What Is an Example of My Point of View?

Once your point of view is clarified, it's useful to provide an example that illustrates your meaning. As you saw in Chapter 7, the process of forming and defining concepts involves the process of *generalizing* (identifying general qualities) and the process of *interpreting* (locating specific examples). Respond to the issue we have been considering by beginning with the following statement:

- *An example of a free choice I made (or was unable to make) was . . .*

Here is a sample response:

An example of a free choice I made was deciding whom I would date. There are a number of people who I could have chosen to go out with, but I chose the person I did entirely on my own, without being forced by other influences.

What Is the Origin of My Point of View?

To fully understand and critically evaluate your point of view, it's important to review its history. How did the point of view develop? Have you always held this view, or did it develop over time? This sort of analysis will help you understand how your perceiving "lenses" regarding this issue were formed. Respond to the issue of free choice by beginning with the following statement:

- *I formed my belief regarding free choice . . .*

Here is a sample response:

I used to believe that everything happened because it had to, because it was determined. Then when I was in high school, I got involved with the "wrong crowd" and developed some bad habits. I stopped doing schoolwork and even attending most classes. I was on the brink of failing out when I suddenly came to my senses and said to myself, "This isn't what I want for my life." Through sheer willpower, I turned everything around. I changed my friends, improved my habits, and ultimately graduated with flying colors. From that time on I knew that I had the power of free choice and that it was up to me to make the right choices.

What Are My Assumptions?

Assumptions are beliefs, often unstated, that underlie your point of view. Many disputes occur and remain unresolved because the people involved do not recognize or express their assumptions. For example, in the very emotional debate over abortion, when people who are opposed to abortion call their opponents "murderers," they are assuming the fetus, at *any* stage of development from the

ORIGIN

How did I
form this point
of view?

LOOK BEHIND

ASSUMPTIONS

What are
my unstated
beliefs?

LOOK BEHIND

POINT OF VIEW

Initial description
Clear definition
Examples

**OTHER POINT
OF VIEW**

Strong? | Reasons
Evidence
Arguments | Valid?

Relevant?

*LOOK TO
ONE SIDE*

**OTHER POINT
OF VIEW**

Strong? | | Valid?

Relevant?

*LOOK TO THE
OTHER SIDE*

SUPPORT

Strong? | Reasons
Evidence
Arguments | Valid?

Relevant?

Inference

**CONCLUSION
DECISION
SOLUTION
PREDICTION**

Prediction

CONSEQUENCES

What will happen
if the conclusion
is adopted

A modified version of a schema
originally devised by Ralph H.
Johnson; design and layout by
J.A. Blair.

fertilized egg onward, is a "human life," since murder refers to the taking of a human life. On the other hand, when people in favor of abortion call their opponents "moral fascists," they are assuming that antiabortionists are merely interested in imposing their narrow moral views on others.

Thus it's important for all parties to identify clearly the assumptions that form the foundation of their points of view. They may still end up disagreeing, but at least they will know what they are arguing about. Thinking about the issue that we have been exploring, respond by beginning with the following statement:

- *When I say that I believe (or don't believe) in free choice, I am assuming . . .*

Here is a sample response:

When I say that I believe in free choice, I am assuming that people are often presented with different alternatives to choose from, and I am also assuming that they are able to select freely any of these alternatives independent of any influences.

What Are the Reasons, Evidence, and Arguments That Support My Point of View?

Everybody has opinions. What distinguishes informed opinions from uninformed opinions is the quality of the reasons, evidence, and arguments that support the opinions. Respond to the issue of free choice by beginning with the following statement:

- *There are a variety of reasons, evidence, and arguments that support my belief (or disbelief) in free choice. First . . . Second . . . Third . . .*

Here is a sample response:

There are a variety of reasons, evidence, and arguments that support my belief in free choice. First, I have a very strong and convincing personal intuition when I am making choices that my choices are free. Second, freedom is tied to responsibility. If people make free choices, then they are responsible for the consequences of their choices. Since we often hold people responsible, that means that we believe that their choices are free. Third, if people are not free, and all of their choices are determined by external forces, then life would have little purpose and there would be no point in trying to improve ourselves. But we do believe that life has purpose and we do try to improve ourselves, suggesting that we also believe that our choices are free.

What Are Other Points of View on This Issue?

One of the hallmarks of critical thinkers is that they strive to view situations from perspectives other than their own, to "think empathetically" within other viewpoints, particularly those that disagree with them. If we stay entrenched in our own narrow way of viewing the world, the development of our minds will be severely limited. This is the only way to achieve a deep and full understanding of life's complexities. In working to understand other points of view, we need to identify the reasons, evidence, and arguments that have brought people to these conclusions. Respond to the issue we have been analyzing by beginning with the following statement:

- *A second point of view on this issue might be . . . A third point of view on this issue might be . . .*

Here is a sample response:

A second point of view on this issue might be that many of our choices are conditioned by experiences that we have had in ways that we are not even aware of. For example, you might choose a career because of someone you admire or because of the expectations of others, although you may be unaware of these influences on your decision. Or you might choose to date someone because he or she reminds you of someone from your past, although you believe you are making a totally free decision. A third *point of view on this issue might be that our choices are influenced by people around us, although we may not be fully aware of it. For example, we may go along with a group decision of our friends, mistakenly thinking that we are making an independent choice.*

What Is My Conclusion, Decision, Solution, or Prediction?

The ultimate purpose of reasoning is to reach an informed and successful conclusion, decision, solution, or prediction. Chapters 1 and 3 describe reasoning approaches for making decisions and solving problems; Chapters 2 and 5 analyze reaching conclusions; and Chapter 9 explores the inferences we use to make predictions. With respect to the sample issue we have been considering—determining whether we can make free choices—the goal is to achieve a thoughtful conclusion. This is a complex process of analysis and synthesis in which we consider all points of view; evaluate the supporting reasons, evidence, and arguments; and then construct our most informed conclusion. Respond to our sample issue by using the following statement as a starting point:

- *After examining different points of view, and critically evaluating the reasons, evidence, and arguments that support the various perspectives, my conclusion about free choice is . . .*

Here is a sample response:

After examining different points of view, and critically evaluating the reasons, evidence, and arguments that support the various perspectives, my conclusion about free choice is that we are capable of making free choices, but that our freedom is sometimes limited. For example, many of our actions are conditioned by our past experience, and we are often influenced by other people without being aware of it. In order to make free choices, we need to become aware of these influences and then decide what course of action we want to choose. As long as we are unaware of these influences, they can limit our ability to make free, independent choices.

What Are the Consequences?

The final step in the reasoning process is to determine the *consequences* of our conclusion, decision, solution, or prediction. The consequences refer to what is likely to happen if our conclusion is adopted. Looking ahead in this fashion is helpful not simply for anticipating the future but also for evaluating the present. Identify the consequences of your conclusion regarding free choice by beginning with the following statement:

- *The consequences of believing (or disbelieving) in free choice are . . .*

Here is a sample response:

The consequences of believing in free choice are increasing personal responsibility and showing people how to increase their freedom. The first consequence is that if people are able to make free choices, then they are responsible for the results of their choices. They can't blame other people, bad luck, or events "beyond their control." They have to accept responsibility. The second consequence is that although our freedom can be limited by influences of which we are unaware, we can increase our freedom by becoming aware of these influences and then deciding what we want to do. On the other hand, if people are not able to make free choices, then they are not responsible for what they do, nor are they able to increase their freedom. This could lead people to adopt an attitude of resignation and apathy.

THINKING ACTIVITY 11.8

Identify an important issue in which you are interested and apply "The Critical Thinker's Guide to Reasoning" to analyze it:

- What is my initial point of view?
- How can I define my point of view more clearly?
- What is an example of my point of view?
- What is the origin of my point of view?
- What are my assumptions?
- What are the reasons, evidence, and arguments that support my point of view?
- What are other points of view on this issue?
- What is my conclusion, decision, solution, or prediction?
- What are the consequences? ◀

THINKING PASSAGE

The following reading selection by John Sabini and Maury Silver demonstrates graphically the destructive effects of *failing* to think critically and suggests ways to avoid these failures. After reading this provocative selection, answer the questions that follow.

CRITICAL THINKING AND OBEDIENCE TO AUTHORITY
by John Sabini and Maury Silver

In his 1974 book, *Obedience to Authority*, Stanley Milgram reports experiments on destructive obedience. In these experiments the subjects are faced with a dramatic choice, one apparently involving extreme pain and perhaps injury to someone else. When the subject arrives at the laboratory, the experimenter tells him (or her) and another subject—a pleasant, avuncular, middle-aged gentleman (actually an actor)—that the study concerns the effects of punishment on learning. Through a rigged drawing, the lucky subject wins the role of teacher and the experimenter's confederate becomes the "learner."

In the next stage of the experiment, the teacher and learner are taken to an adjacent room; the learner is strapped into a chair and electrodes are attached to his arm. It appears impossible for the learner to escape. While strapped in the chair, the learner diffidently mentions that he has a heart condition. The experimenter replies that while the shocks may be painful, they cause no permanent tissue damage. The teacher is instructed to read to the learner a list of word pairs, to test him on the list, and to administer punishment—an electric shock—whenever the learner errs. The teacher is given a sample shock of 45 volts (the only real shock administered in the course of the experiment). The experimenter instructs the teacher to increase the level of shock one step on the shock generator for each mistake. The generator has thirty switches labeled from 15 to 450 volts. Beneath these voltage readings are labels ranging from "SLIGHT SHOCK" to "DANGER: SEVERE SHOCK," and finally "XX."

The experiment starts routinely. At the fifth shock level, however, the confederate grunts in annoyance, and by the time the eighth shock level is reached, he shouts that the shocks are becoming painful. Upon reaching the tenth level (150 volts), he cries out, "Experimenter get me out of here! I won't be in the experiment any more! I refuse to go on!" This response makes plain the intensity of the pain and underscores the learner's right to be released. At the 270-volt level, the learner's response becomes an agonized scream, and at 300 volts the learner refuses to answer further. When the voltage is increased from 300 volts to 330 volts, the confederate shrieks in pain at each shock and gives no answer. From 330 volts on, the learner is heard from no more, and the teacher has no way of knowing whether the learner is still conscious or, for that matter, alive (the teacher also knows that the experimenter cannot tell the condition of the victim since the experimenter is in the same room as the teacher).

Typically the teacher attempts to break off the experiment many times during the session. When he tries to do so, the experimenter instructs him to continue. If he refuses, the experimenter insists, finally telling him, "You must continue. You have no other choice." If the subject still refuses, the experimenter ends the experiment.

We would expect that at most only a small minority of the subjects, a cross section of New Haven residents, would continue to shock beyond the point where the victim screams in pain and demands to be released. We certainly would expect that very, very few people would continue to the point of administering shocks of 450 volts. Indeed, Milgram asked a sample of psychiatrists and a sample of adults with various occupations to predict whether they would obey the orders of the experimenter. All of the people asked claimed that they would disobey at some point. Aware that people would be unwilling to admit that they themselves would obey such an unreasonable and unconscionable order, Milgram asked another sample of middle-class adults to predict how far other people would go in such a procedure. The average prediction was that perhaps one person in a thousand would continue to the end. The prediction was wrong. In fact, 65 percent (26/40) of the subjects obeyed to the end.

It is clear to people who are not in the experiment what they should do. The question is, *What features of the experimental situation make this clear issue opaque to subjects?* Our aim is to suggest some reasons for such a failure of thinking and action and to suggest ways that people might be trained to avoid such failures—not only in the experiment, of course, but in our practical, moral lives as well. What are some of the sources of the failure?

The experimental conditions involve entrapment, and gradual entrapment affects critical thought. One important feature inducing obedience is the gradual escalation of the shock. Although subjects in the end administered 450-volt shocks, which is clearly beyond the limits of common morality and, indeed, common sense, they began by administering 15-volt shocks, which is neither. Not only did they begin with an innocuous shock, but it increased in innocuous steps of 15 volts. This gradualness clouds clear thinking: we are prepared by our moral training to expect moral problems to present themselves categorically, with good and evil clearly distinguished. But here they were not. By administering the first shock, subjects did two things at once—one salient, the other implicit. They administered a trivial shock, a morally untroublesome act, and they in that same act committed themselves to a policy and procedure which ended in clear evil.

Surely in everyday life, becoming entrapped by gradual increases in commitment is among the most common ways for us to find ourselves engaging in immoral acts, not to mention simple folly. The corrective cannot be, of course, refusing to begin on any path which *might* led to immorality, but rather to foresee where paths are likely to lead, and to arrange for ourselves points beyond which we will not go. One suspects that had the subjects committed themselves—publicly—to some shock level they would not exceed, they would not have found themselves pushing the 450-volt lever. We cannot expect to lead, or expect our young to lead, lives without walking on slopes: our only hope is to reduce their slipperiness.

Distance makes obedience easier. Another force sustaining obedience was the *distance* between the victim and the subject. Indeed, in one condition of the experiment, subjects were moved physically closer to the victim; in one condition they had to hold his hand on the shock plate (through Mylar insulation to protect the teachers from shock). Here twelve out of forty subjects continued to the end, roughly half the number that did so when the subjects were farther from their victim.

Being closer to the victim did not have its effect by making subjects think more critically or by giving them more information. Rather it intensified their *discomfort* at the victim's pain. Still, being face to face with someone they were hurting probably caused them at least to focus on their victim, which might well be a first step in their taking seriously the pain they were causing him.

Both the experimenter's presence and the objective requirements of the situation influenced decisions to obey authority. The experimenter's *presence* is crucial to the subjects' obedience. In one version of the experiment he issued his commands at a distance, over the phone, and obedience was significantly reduced—to nine out of forty cases. The experimenter, then, exerts powerful *social influence* over the subjects.

One way to think about the experimenter's influence is to suppose that subjects uncritically cede control of their behavior to him. But this is too simple. We suggest that if the experimenter were to have told the subjects, for example, to shine his shoes, every subject would have refused. They would have refused because shining shoes is not a sensible command within the experimental context. Thus, the experimenter's ability to confuse and control subjects follows from his issuing commands which make sense given the ostensible purpose of the experiment; he was a guide, for them, to the experiment's objective requirements.

This interpretation of the experimenter's *role* is reinforced by details of his behavior. For example, his language and demeanor were cold—bureaucratic rather than emotional or personal. The subjects were led to see his commands to them as his dispassionate interpretations of something beyond them all: the requirements of the experiment.

Embarrassment plays a key role in decisions to obey authority. The experimenter entrapped subjects in another way. Subjects could not get out of the experiment without having to explain and justify their abandoning their duty to the experiment and to him. And how were they to do this?

Some subjects attempted to justify their leaving by claiming that they could not bear to go on, but such appeals to "personal reasons" were rebutted by the experimenter's reminding them of their duty to stay. If the subjects could not escape the experiment by such claims, then how could they escape? *They could fully escape his power only by confronting him on moral grounds.* It is worth noting that this is something that virtually none of the hundreds of subjects who took part in one condition or another fully did. Failing to address the experimenter in moral terms, even "disobedient" subjects just passively resisted; they stayed in their seats refusing to continue until the experimenter declared the experiment over. They did *not* do things we might expect them to: leave, tell the experimenter off, release the victim from his seat, and so on. Why did even the disobedient subjects not confront the experimenter?

One reason seems too trivial to mention: confronting the experimenter would be embarrassing. This trivial fact may have much to do with the subjects' obedience. To confront the experimenter directly, on moral grounds, would be to disrupt in a profound way implicit expectations that grounded this particular, and indeed most, social interaction: namely, that the subject and experimenter would behave as competent moral actors. Questioning these expectations is on some accounts, at least, the source of embarrassment.

Subjects in Milgram's experiment probably did not realize that it was in part embarrassment that we keeping them in line. Had they realized that—had they realized that they were torturing someone to spare themselves embarrassment—they might well have chosen to withstand the embarrassment to secure the victim's release. But rather we suspect that subjects experience their anticipation of embarrassment as a nameless force, a distressing emotion they were not able to articulate. Thus the subjects found themselves unable to confront the experimenter on moral grounds and unable to comprehend why they could not confront the experimenter.

Emotional states affect critical thought. Obviously the emotions the subjects experienced because of the embarrassment they were avoiding and the discomfort produced by hearing the cries of the victim affected their ability to reason critically. We do not know much about the effects of emotion on cognition, but it is plausible that it has at least one effect—a focusing of attention. Subjects seem to suffer from what Milgram has called "Tunnel Vision": they restricted their focus to the technical requirements of the experimental task, for these, at least, were clear. This restriction of attention is both a consequence of being in an emotional state more generally, and it is a strategy subjects used to avoid unwanted emotional intrusions. This response to emotion is, no doubt, a formidable obstacle to critical thought. To reject the experimenter's commands, subjects had to view their situation in a perspective different from the technical one the experimenter offered them. But their immediate emotional state made it particularly difficult for them to do just that: to look at their own situation from a broader, moral perspective.

How can we train individuals to avoid destructive obedience? Our analysis leads to the view that obedience in the Milgram experiment is *not* primarily a result of a failure of knowledge, or, at least knowledge of the crucial issue of what is right or wrong to do in this circumstance. People do not need to be told that torturing an innocent person is something they should not do—even in the context of the experiment. Indeed, when the experimenter turns his back, most subjects are able to apply their moral principles and disobey. The subjects' problem instead is not knowing *how* to break off, how to make the moral response without social stickiness. If the subjects' defect is not primarily one of thinking correctly, then how is education, even education in critical thinking, to repair the defect? We have three suggestions.

First, we must teach people how to confront authority. We should note as a corollary to this effort that teaching has a wide compass: we teach people how to ride bikes, how to play the piano, how to make a sauce. Some teaching of how to do things we call education: we teach students how to do long division, how to parse sentences, how to solve physics problems. We inculcate these skills in students not by, or not only by, giving them facts or even strategies to remember, but also by giving them certain sorts of experiences, by correcting them when they err, and so on. An analogy would be useful here. Subjects in the Milgram experiment suffered not so much from a failure to remember that as center fielders they should catch fly balls as they did from an inability to do so playing under lights at night, with a great deal of wind, and when there is ambiguity about whether time-out has been called. To improve the players' ability to shag fly balls, in game conditions, we recommend practice rather than lectures, and the closer the circumstances of practice to the conditions of the actual game, the more effective the practice is likely to be.

Good teachers from Socrates on have known that the intellect must be trained; one kind of training is in criticizing authority. We teachers are authorities and hence can provide practice. Of course, we can only do that if we *remain* authorities. Practice at criticizing us if we do not respect our own authority is of little use. We do not have a recipe for being an authority who at the same time encourages criticism, but we do know that is what is important. And sometimes we can tell when we are either not encouraging criticism or when we have ceased being an authority. Both are equally damaging.

Practice with the Milgram situation might help too; it might help for students to "role play" the subjects' plight. If nothing else, doing this might bring home in a forcible way the embarrassment that subjects faced in confronting authority. It might help them develop ways of dealing with this embarrassment. Certainly, it would at least teach them that doing the morally right thing does not always "feel" right, comfortable, natural. There is no evidence about whether such experiences generalize, but perhaps they do.

If they are to confront authority assertively individuals must also be taught to use social pressure in the service of personal values. Much of current psychology and education sees thought, even critical thought, as something that goes on within individuals. But we know better than this. Whether it be in science, law, or the humanities, scholarship is and must be a public, social process. To train subjects to think critically is to train them to expose their thinking to others, to open *themselves* to criticism, from their peers as well as from authority. We insist on this in scholarship because we know that individual thinking, even the best of it, is prey to distortions of all kinds, from mere ignorance to "bad faith."

Further, the support of others is important in another way. We know that subjects who saw what they took to be two other naive subjects disobey, and thus implicitly criticize the action of continuing, were very likely to do so themselves. A subject's sense that the experimenter had the correct reading was undermined by the counter reading offered by the "other subjects." Public reinforcement of our beliefs can liberate us from illegitimate pressure. The reason for this is twofold.

Agreement with others clarifies the cognitive issue and helps us see the morally or empirically right answer to questions. But it also can have another effect—a nonrational one.

We have claimed that part of the pressure subjects faced in disobeying was produced by having to deal with the embarrassment that might emerge from confrontation. Social support provides a counter-pressure. Had the subjects committed themselves publicly to disobedience before entering the experiment then they could have countered pressures produced by disobedience (during the experiment) by considering the embarrassment of admitting to others (after the experiment) that they had obeyed. Various self-help groups like Alcoholics Anonymous and Weight Watchers teach individuals to manage social pressures to serve good ends.

Social pressures are forces in our lives whether we concede them or not. The rational person, the person who would keep his action in accord with his values, must learn to face or avoid those pressures when they act to degrade his action, but equally important he ought to learn to *employ* the pressure of public commitment, the pressure implicit in making clear to others what he values, in the service of his values.

Students should know about the social pressures that operate on them. They should also learn how to use those pressures to support their own values. One reason we teach people to think critically is so that they may take charge of their own creations. We do not withhold from engineers who would create buildings knowledge about gravity or vectors or stresses. Rather we teach them to enlist this knowledge in their support.

A second area requires our attention. We need to eliminate intellectual illusions fostering nonintellectual obedience. These are illusions about human nature which the Milgram experiment renders transparent. None of these illusions is newly discovered; others have noticed them before. But the Milgram experiment casts them in sharp relief.

The most pernicious of these illusions is the belief, perhaps implicit, that only evil people do evil things and that evil announces itself. This belief, in different guises, bewildered the subjects in several ways.

First, the experimenter looks and acts like the most reasonable and rational of people: a person of authority in an important institution. All of this is, of course, irrelevant to the question of whether his commands are evil, but it does not seem so to subjects. The experimenter had no personally corrupt motive in ordering subjects to continue, for he wanted nothing more of them than to fulfill the requirements of the experiment. So the experimenter was not seen as an evil man, as a man with corrupt desires. He was a man, like Karl Adolf Eichmann, who ordered them to do evil because he saw that evil as something required of him (and of them) by the requirements of the situation they faced together. Because we expect our morality plays to have temptation and illicit desire arrayed against conscience, our ability to criticize morally is subverted when we find evil instructions issued by someone moved by, of all things, duty. [For a fuller discussion of this point, see Hannah Arendt's *Eichmann in Jerusalem* (1965), where the issue is placed in the context of the Holocaust.]

And just as the experimenter escaped the subjects' moral criticism because he was innocent of evil desire, the subjects escaped their own moral criticism because *they too* were free of evil intent: they did not *want* to hurt the victim; they really did not. Further, some subjects, at least, took action to relieve the victim's plight—many protested the experimenter's commands, many tried to give the victim hints about the right answers— thus further dramatizing their purity of heart. And because they acted out of duty rather than desire, the force of their conscience against their own actions was reduced. But, of course, none of this matters in the face of the evil done.

The "good-heartedness" of people, their general moral quality, is something very important to us, something to which we, perhaps rightly, typically pay attention. But if we are to think critically about the morality of our own and others' acts, we must see through this general fact about people to assess the real moral quality of the acts they do or are considering doing.

A second illusion from which the subjects suffered was a confusion about the notion of responsibility. Some subjects asked the experimenter who was responsible for the victim's plight. And the experimenter replied that he was. We, and people asked to predict what they would do in the experiment, see that this is nonsense. We see that the experimenter cannot discharge the subjects' responsibility—no more than the leader of a bank-robbing gang can tell his cohorts, "Don't worry. If we're caught, I'll take full responsibility." We are all conspirators when we participate in planning and executing crimes.

Those in charge have the right to assign *technical* responsibility to others, responsibility for executing parts of a plan, but moral responsibility cannot be given, taken away, or transferred. Still, these words—mere words—on the part of the experimenter eased subjects' "sense of responsibility." So long as the institutions of which we are a part are moral, the need to distinguish technical from moral responsibility need not arise. When those institutions involve wanton torture, we are obliged to think critically about this distinction.

There is a third illusion illustrated in the Milgram experiment. When subjects threatened to disobey, the experimenter kept them in line with prods, the last of which was, "You have no choice; you must go on." Some subjects fell for this, believed that they had no choice. But this is also nonsense. There may be cases in life when we *feel* that we have no choice, but we know we always do. Often feeling we have no choice is really a matter of believing that the cost of moral action is greater than we are willing to bear—in the extreme we may not be willing to offer our lives, and sometimes properly so. Sometimes we use what others have done to support the claim that we have no choice; indeed, some students interpret the levels of obedience in the Milgram experiment as proof that the subjects had no choice. But we all know they did. Even in extreme situations, we have a choice, whether we choose to exercise it or not. The belief that our role, our desires, our past, or the actions of others preclude our acting morally is a convenient but illusory way of distancing ourselves from the evil that surrounds us. It is an illusion from which we should choose to disabuse our students. ■

Questions for Analysis

1. The authors of this article describe the reasons they believe that the majority of subjects in the Stanley Milgram experiment were willing to inflict appar-

ent pain and injury on an innocent person. Explain what you believe were the most significant reasons for this disturbing absence of critical thinking and moral responsibility.

2. The authors argue that the ability to think critically must be developed within a social context, that we must expose our thinking to the criticism of others because "individual thinking, even the best of it, is prey to distortions of all kinds, from mere ignorance to 'bad faith.'" Evaluate this claim, supporting your answer with examples and reasons.

3. The authors contend that in order to act with critical thinking and moral courage, people must be taught to confront authority. Explain how you think people could be taught and encouraged to confront authority in a constructive way.

4. "Even in extreme situations, we have a choice, whether we choose to exercise it or not. The belief that our role, our desires, our past, or the actions of others preclude our acting morally is a convenient but illusory way of distancing ourselves from the evil that surrounds us." Evaluate this claim and give examples and reasons to support your view. ◄

12

THINKING CRITICALLY, LIVING CREATIVELY

Trust the creative process.

Make creativity a priority.

LIVING CREATIVELY

THINKING CREATIVELY
Developing ideas that are unique, useful, and worthy of further elaboration

Eliminate the voice of judgment.

Establish a creative environment.

THINKING CRITICALLY
Carefully examining our thinking in order to clarify and improve understanding

Creating a Life Philosophy
What are my values?
How should I create
my moral compass?

THINKING CRITICALLY AND THINKING CREATIVELY are two essential and tightly interwoven dimensions of the thinking process. These two forms of thinking work as partners to produce effective thinking, enabling us to make informed decisions and lead successful lives.

Thinking Creatively	The cognitive process we use to develop ideas that are unique, useful, and worthy of further elaboration.

Thinking Critically	The cognitive process we use to carefully examine our thinking (and the thinking of others) in order to clarify and improve our understanding.

For example, imagine that you are confronted with a problem to solve. *Thinking critically* enables you to identify and accept the problem. When you generate alternatives for solving the problem you are using your *creative thinking* abilities, while when you evaluate the various alternatives and select one or more to pursue you are *thinking critically*. Developing ideas for implementing your alternative(s) involves *thinking creatively*, while constructing a practical plan of action and evaluating the results depends on *thinking critically*.

It is apparent that *thinking creatively* and *thinking critically* interact in continuous and complex relationships in the mind of an effective thinker. Although this text has emphasized critical thinking abilities, creative thinking has been involved in every part of our explorations of the mind. In this chapter, we will shift the emphasis to creative thinking, working to gain insight into this powerful and mysterious dimension of the thinking process.

LIVING CREATIVELY

You are an artist, creating your life portrait, and your paints and brush strokes are the choices you make each day of your life. This metaphor provides you with a way to think about your personal development and underscores your responsibility for making the most intelligent decisions possible.

Sometimes students become discouraged about their lives, concluding that their destinies are shaped by forces beyond their control. Although difficult circumstances *do* hamper our striving for success, this fatalistic sentiment can also reflect a passivity that is the opposite of thinking critically. As a critical thinker, you should be confident that you can shape the person that you want to become through insightful understanding and intelligent choices.

In this book you have been developing the abilities and attitudes needed to become an educated thinker and a successful person. In this final chapter, we will integrate these goals into a larger context, exploring how to live a life that is creative, professionally successful, and personally fulfilling. By using both your creative and your critical thinking abilities, you can develop informed beliefs and an enlightened life philosophy. In the final analysis, the person who looks back at you in the mirror is the person you have created.

THINKING ACTIVITY 12.1

1. Describe a portrait of yourself as a person. What sort of person are you? What are your strengths and weaknesses? In what areas do you feel you are creative?
2. Describe some of the ways you would like to change yourself. ◀

Every day you encounter a series of choices, forks in your life path that have the cumulative effect of defining you as a person. For example: What will be my schedule for the day? Whom will I seek out and what will I say? Will I participate in class? What will be my social agenda for the day? How will I approach my studying? What will I do after school: exercise? sleep? watch television? write in my journal? compose a poem?

In thinking about these questions, you may discover that there are habitual patterns in your life that rarely change. If you find that your life is composed of a collection of similar activities and routines, don't despair; this is typical, not unusual. However, it may be an indication that you are not living your life in the most creative fashion possible, that your choices have become automatic, and that your experiences are fixed in certain "ruts." If this is the case, it may be time to reflect on your life, reevaluate the choices you are making, and consider living your life in a more creative fashion.

Over 2,000 years ago the Greek philosopher Socrates said: "The unexamined life is not worth living." In saying this, he was suggesting that if you live unreflectively, simply reacting to situations and not trying to explore

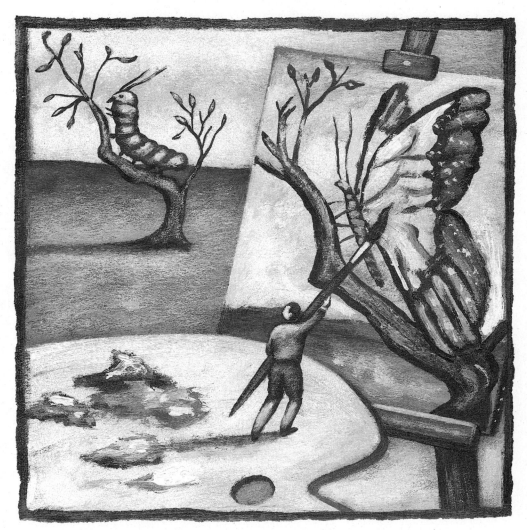

You are an artist, creating your life portrait, and your paints and brush strokes are the choices that you make each day of your life.

life's deeper meanings, then your life has diminished value. An unreflective person is not making use of the distinctive human capacity to think deeply about important issues and develop thoughtful conclusions about herself and her world.

Conversely, humans have a nearly limitless capacity to be creative, our imaginations giving us the power to conceive of new possibilities and put these innovative ideas into action. Using creative resources in this way enriches our lives and brings a special meaning to our activities. Although we might not go to the extreme of saying that "The *uncreative* life is not worth living," it is surely preferable to live a life enriched by the qualities of creativity.

Can I Be Creative?

The first day of my course, "Creative Thinking: Theory and Practice," I always ask the students in the class if they think they are creative. Typically less than half of the class members raise their hands. One reason for this is that people often confuse being "creative" with being "artistic"—skilled at art, music, poetry, creative writing, drama, dance. Although artistic people are certainly creative, there are an infinite number of ways to be creative that are *not* artistic. This is a mental trap that I fell into growing up. In school, I always dreaded art class because I was so inept. My pathetic drawings and art projects were always good for a laugh for my friends, and I felt no overwhelming urges to write poetry, paint, or compose music. I was certain that I had simply been born "uncreative" and accepted this "fact" as my destiny. It wasn't until I graduated from college that I began to change this view of myself. I was working as a custom woodworker to support myself, designing and creating specialized furniture for people when it suddenly struck me: I was being creative! I then began to see other areas of my life in which I was creative: playing sports, decorating my apartment, even writing research papers. I finally understood that being creative was a state of mind and a way of life. As the writer Eric Gill expresses it: "The artist is not a different kind of person, but each one of us is a different kind of artist."

Are you creative? Yes! Think of all of the activities that you enjoy doing: cooking, creating a wardrobe, raising children, playing sports, cutting or braiding hair, dancing, playing music. Whenever you are investing your own personal ideas, putting on your own personal stamp, you are being creative. For example, imagine that you are cooking your favorite dish. To the extent that you are expressing your unique ideas developed through inspiration and experimentation, you are being creative. Of course, if you are simply following someone else's recipe without significant modification, your dish may be tasty—but it is not creative. Similarly, if your moves on the dance floor or the basketball court express your distinctive personality, you are being creative, as you are when you stimulate the original thinking of your children or make your friends laugh with your unique brand of humor.

Living your life creatively means bringing your unique perspective and creative talents to all of the dimensions of your life. The following passages are written by students about creative areas in their lives. After reading the pas-

"If you do not expect the unexpected you will not find it, for it is not to be reached by search or trail." —Heraclitus

sages, complete Thinking Activity 12.2, which gives you the opportunity to describe a creative area from your own life.

One of the most creative aspects of my life is my diet. I have been a vegetarian for the past five years, while the rest of my family has continued to eat meat. I had to overcome many obstacles to make this lifestyle work for me, including family dissension. The solution was simple: I had to learn how to cook creatively. I have come to realize that my diet is an ongoing learning process. The more I learn about and experiment with different foods, the healthier and happier I become. I feel like an explorer setting out on my own to discover new things about food and nutrition. I slowly evolved from a person who could cook food only if it came from a can into someone who could make bread from scratch and grow yogurt cultures. I find learning new things about nutrition and cooking healthful foods very relaxing and rewarding. I like being alone in my house baking bread; there is something very comforting about the aroma. Most of all I like to experiment with different ways to prepare foods, because the ideas are my own. Even when an effort is less than successful, I find pleasure in the knowledge that I gained from the experience. I discovered recently, for example, that eggplant is terrible in soup! Making mistakes seems to be a natural way to increase creativity, and I now firmly believe that people who say that they do not like vegetables simply have not been properly introduced to them!

As a tropical fish hobbyist, I create an ecosystem most suited to the variety of fish I keep. My most recent choice of fish has been pacus, a close cousin of the Piranha native to South America and Africa. I then added two barracuda of the same approximate size. These two genera are nervous, aggressive fish not ordinarily found together in nature. As "dither fish," which are used as a distraction between two or more genera, I chose two Jack Dempseys, which are large, territorial cichlids. Since these fish require different habitats it was necessary to create a blend of environments. The pacus need an area to be well planted, providing cover, which I placed in the corners of the aquarium. The Dempseys require rocks, caves, and tree branches to do their cavorting and establish their domain. The barracuda, being the most dominant and aggressive of the lot, got the center area of the tank to swim about freely. When raising fish, you become familiar with their distinct personalities, and you have to be both knowledgeable and creative to develop appropriate habitats for them.

As any parent knows, children have an abundance of energy to spend, and toys or television do not always meet their needs. In response, I create activities to stimulate their creativity and preserve my sanity. For example, I involve them in the process of cooking, giving them the skin from peeled vegetables and a pot so they make their own "soup." Using catalogs, we cut out pictures of furniture, rugs, and curtains, and they paste them onto cartons to create their own interior decors: vibrant living rooms, plush bedrooms, colorful family rooms. I make beautiful boats from aluminum paper, and my children spend hours in the bathtub playing with them. We "go bowling" with empty soda cans and a ball, and they star in "track meets" by running an obstacle course we set up. When it comes to raising children, creativity is a way of survival!

After quitting the government agency I was working at because of too much bureaucracy, I was hired as a carpenter at a construction site, although I had little knowledge of this profession. I learned to handle a hammer and other tools by watching other co-workers, and within a matter of weeks I was skilled enough to organize my own group of workers for projects. Most of my fellow workers used the old-fashioned method of construction carpentry, building panels with inefficient and poorly made bracings. I redesigned the panels in order to save construction time and materials. My supervisor and site engineer were thrilled with my creative ideas, and I was assigned progressively more challenging projects, including the construction of an office building that was completed in record time.

My area of creativity is hair braiding, an activity that requires skill, talent, and patience that is difficult for most people to accomplish. Braiding hair in styles that are being worn today consists of braiding small to tiny braids, and it may include adding artificial hair to make the hair look fuller. It takes anywhere from ten to sixteen hours depending on the type of style that is desired: the smaller the braids, the longer it takes. In order to braid, I had to learn how to determine the right hair and color for people who wanted extensions, pick out the right style that would fit perfectly on my customers' faces, learn to cut hair in an asymmetric fashion, put curls in the braids, and know the sequence of activities. Doing hair is a rewarding experience for me because when I am through with my work, my customers think the result is gorgeous!

THINKING ACTIVITY 12.2

1. Describe a creative area of your life in which you are able to express your unique personality and talents. Be specific and give examples.

2. Analyze your creative area by answering the following questions:
   - Why do you feel that this activity is creative? Give examples.
   - How would you describe the experience of being engaged in this activity? Where do your creative ideas come from? How do they develop?
   - What strategies do you use to increase your creativity? What obstacles block your creative efforts? How do you try to overcome these blocks? ◄

Becoming More Creative

Although we each have nearly limitless potential to live creatively, most people use only a small percentage of their creative gifts. In fact, there is research to suggest that people typically achieve their highest creative point as young children, after which there is a long, steady decline into uncreativity. Why? Well, to begin with, young children are immersed in the excitement of exploration and discovery. They are eager to try out new things, act on their impulses, and make unusual connections between disparate ideas. They are not afraid to take risks in trying out untested solutions, and they are not compelled to identify the socially acceptable "correct answer." Children are willing to play with ideas, creating improbable scenarios and imaginative ways of thinking without fear of being ridiculed.

All of this tends to change as we get older. The weight of "reality" begins to smother our imagination, and we increasingly focus our attention on the nuts and bolts of living rather than playing with possibilities. The social pressure to conform to group expectations increases dramatically. Whether the group is our friends, schoolmates, or fellow employees, there are clearly defined "rules" for dressing, behaving, speaking, and thinking. When we deviate from these rules, we risk social disapproval, rejection, or ridicule. Most groups have little tolerance for individuals who want to think independently and creatively. As we become older, we also become more reluctant to pursue untested courses of action, because we become increasingly afraid of failure. Pursuing creativity inevitably involves failure, because we are trying to break out of established ruts and go beyond traditional methods. For example, going beyond the safety of a proven recipe to create an innovative dish may involve some disasters, but it's the only way to create something genuinely unique. The history of creative discoveries is littered with failures, a fact we tend to forget when we are debating whether we should risk an untested idea. Those people who are courageous enough to risk failure while expressing their creative impulses are rewarded with unique achievements and an enriched life.

THINKING ACTIVITY 12.3

Reflect on your own creative development and describe some of the fears and pressures that inhibit your own creativity. For example, have you ever been penalized for trying out a new idea that didn't work out? Have you ever suffered the wrath of the group for daring to be different and violate the group's unspoken rules? Do you feel that your life is so filled with responsibilities and the demands of reality that you don't have time to be creative? ◀

Our creativity is often inhibited by the social pressure to conform to group expectations, and deviations from the established social "rules" often involves risking social disapproval, rejection, or ridicule. However, when we are able to resist group pressure and express our own creative impulses, it enriches our lives.

Although the forces that discourage us from being creative are powerful, they can nevertheless be overcome with the right approaches. We are going to explore four productive strategies:

- Understand and trust the creative process
- Eliminate the "Voice of Judgment"
- Establish a creative environment
- Make creativity a priority

Understand and Trust the Creative Process Discovering your creative talents requires that you understand how the creative process operates and then have confidence in the results it produces. There are no fixed procedures or formulas for generating creative ideas because creative ideas *by definition* go beyond established ways of thinking to the unknown and the innovative. As the ancient Greek philosopher Heraclitus once said: "You must expect the unexpected, because it cannot be found by search or trail."

Although there is no fixed path to creative ideas, there are activities you can pursue that make the birth of creative ideas possible. In this respect, generating creative ideas is similar to gardening. You need to prepare the soil, plant the seeds, ensure proper water, light, and food, and then be patient until the ideas begin to sprout. Here are some steps for cultivating your creative garden:

- *Absorb yourself in the task*: Creative ideas don't occur in a vacuum. They emerge after a great deal of work, study, and practice. For example, If you want to come up with creative ideas in the kitchen, you need to become knowledgeable about the art of cooking. The more knowledgeable you are, the better prepared you are to create valuable and innovative dishes. Similarly, if you are trying to develop a creative perspective for a research paper in college, you need to immerse yourself in the subject, developing an in-depth understanding of the central concepts and issues. Absorbing yourself in the task "prepares the soil" for your creative ideas.
- *Allow time for ideas to incubate:* After absorbing yourself in the task or problem, the next stage in the creative process is to *stop* working on the task or problem. Although your conscious mind has stopped actively working on the task, the unconscious dimension of your mind continues working—processing, organizing, and ultimately generating innovative ideas and solutions. This process is known as *incubation* because it mirrors the process in which baby chicks gradually evolve inside the egg until the moment comes when they break out through the shell. In

the same way, your creative mind is at work while you are going about your business until the moment of *illumination,* when the incubating idea finally erupts to the surface of your conscious mind. People report that these illuminating moments—when their mental light bulbs go on— often occur when they are engaged in activities completely unrelated to the task. One of the most famous cases was that of the Greek thinker Archimedes, whose moment of illumination came while he was taking a bath, causing him to run naked through the streets of Athens shouting "Eureka" ("I have found it").

- *Seize on the ideas when they emerge and follow them through:* Generating creative ideas is of little use unless you recognize them when they appear and then act on them. Too often people don't pay much attention to these ideas when they occur, or they dismiss them as too impractical. You have to have confidence in the ideas you create, even if they seem wacky or far out. Many of the most valuable inventions in our history started as improbable ideas, ridiculed by the popular wisdom. For example, the idea of Velcro started with burrs covering the pants of the inventor as he walked through a field, and Post-It Notes resulted from the accidental invention of an adhesive that was weaker than normal. In other words, thinking effectively means thinking creatively *and* thinking critically. After you use your *creative thinking* abilities to generate innovative ideas, you then must employ your *critical thinking* abilities to evaluate and refine the ideas and design a practical plan for implementing them.

Eliminate the "Voice of Judgment"   The biggest threat to our creativity lies within ourselves, the negative Voice of Judgment (VOJ).* The VOJ can undermine your confidence in every area of your life, including your creative activities, with statements like:

> "This is a stupid idea and no one will like it."

> "Even if I could pull this idea off, it probably won't amount to much."

> "Although I was successful the last time I tried something like this, I was lucky and I won't be able to do it again."

These statements, and countless others like them, have the ongoing effect of making us doubt ourselves and the quality of our creative thinking. As we lose

---

* This is a term coined by Michael Ray and Rochelle Myers, authors of *Creativity in Business,* a book on creativity based on a Stanford University course.

confidence, we become more timid, reluctant to follow through on ideas and present them to others. After a while our cumulative insecurity discourages us from even generating ideas in the first place, and we end up simply conforming to established ways of thinking and the expectations of others. And in so doing we surrender an important part of ourselves, the vital and dynamic creative core of our personality that defines our unique perspective on the world.

Where do these negative voices come from? Often they originate in the negative judgments we experienced while growing up, destructive criticisms that become internalized as a part of ourselves. In the same way that praising children helps make them feel confident and secure, consistently criticizing them does the opposite. Although parents, teachers, and acquaintances often don't intend these negative consequences with their critical judgments and lack of positive praise, the unfortunate result is still the same: a Voice of Judgment that keeps hammering away at the value of ourselves, our ideas, and our creations. As a teacher, I see the VOJ evident when students present their creative projects to the class, with apologies like: "This isn't very good and it probably doesn't make sense."

How do we eliminate this unwelcome and destructive voice within ourselves? There are a number of effective strategies you can use, although you should be aware that the fight, while worth the effort, will not be easy.

- *Become aware of the VOJ:* You have probably been listening to the negative messages of the VOJ for so long that you may not even be consciously aware of it. To conquer the VOJ you need to first recognize when it speaks. In addition, it is helpful to analyze the negative messages, try to figure out how and why they developed, and then create strategies to overcome them. A good strategy is to keep a VOJ journal, described in Thinking Activity 12.4.
- *Restate the judgment in a more accurate or constructive way:* Sometimes there is an element of truth in our self-judgments, but we have blown the reality out of proportion. For example, if you fail a test, your VOJ may translate this as "I'm a failure." Or if you ask someone for a date and get turned down, your VOJ may conclude: "I'm a social misfit with emotional bad breath!" In these instances, you need to translate the reality accurately: "I failed this test—I wonder what went wrong and how I can improve my performance in the future," and "This person turned me down for a date—I guess I'm not his/her type, or maybe he/she just doesn't know me well enough."
- *Get tough with the VOJ:* You can't be a wimp if you hope to overcome the VOJ. Instead, you have to be strong and determined, telling yourself as

soon as the VOJ appears: "I'm throwing you out and not letting you back in!" This attack might feel peculiar at first, but it will soon become an automatic response when those negative judgments appear. Don't give in to the judgments, even a little bit, by saying, "Well, maybe I'm just a little bit of a jerk." Get rid of the VOJ entirely, and good riddance to it!

- *Create positive voices and visualizations:* The best way to destroy the VOJ for good is to replace it with positive encouragements. As soon as you have stomped on the judgment "I'm a jerk," you should replace it with "I'm an intelligent, valuable person with many positive qualities and talents." Similarly, you should make extensive use of positive visualization, as you "see" yourself performing well on your examinations, being entertaining and insightful with other people, and succeeding gloriously in the sport or dramatic production in which you are involved. If you make the effort to create these positive voices and images, they will eventually become a natural part of your thinking. And since positive thinking leads to positive results, your efforts will become self-fulfilling prophecies.

- *Use other people for independent confirmation:* The negative judgments coming from the VOJ are usually irrational, but until they are dragged out into the light of day for examination, they can be very powerful. Sharing our VOJ with others we trust is an effective strategy because they can provide an objective perspective that reveals to us the irrationality and destructiveness of these negative judgments. This sort of "reality testing" strips the judgments of their power, a process that is enhanced by the positive support of concerned friends we have developed relationships with over a period of time.

THINKING ACTIVITY 12.4

1. Take a small notebook or pad with you one day and record every negative judgment that you make about yourself. At the end of the day, classify your judgments by category. For example: negative judgments about your physical appearance, your popularity with others, your academic ability, and so on.

2. Analyze the judgments in each of the categories and try to determine where they came from and how they developed.

3. Use the strategies described in this section, and others of your own creation, to start fighting these judgments when they occur. ◀

Establish a Creative Environment   An important part of eliminating the negative voices in our mind is to establish environments in which our creative resources can flourish. This means finding or developing physical environments conducive to creative expression as well as supportive social environments. Sometimes working with other people is stimulating and energizing to our creative juices; other times we require a private place where we can work without distraction. For example, I have a specific location in which I do much of my writing: sitting on a comfortable couch, with a calm, pleasing view, music on the stereo, a cold drink, a supply of Tootsie Roll Pops. I'm ready for creativity to strike me, although I sometimes have to wait for some time! Different environments work for different people: you have to find the environment(s) best suited to your own creative process and then make a special effort to do your work there.

The people in our lives who form our social environment play an even more influential role in encouraging or inhibiting our creative process. When we are surrounded by people who are positive and supportive, this increases our confidence and encourages us to take the risk to express our creative vision. They can stimulate our creativity by providing us with fresh ideas and new perspectives. By engaging in *brainstorming* (described on page 000) they can work with us to generate ideas and then later help us figure out how to refine and implement the most valuable ones.

However, when the people around us tend to be negative, critical, or belittling, then the opposite happens: we lose confidence and are reluctant to express ourselves creatively. Eventually, we begin to internalize these negative judgments, incorporating them into our own VOJ. When this occurs, we have the choice of telling people that we will not tolerate this sort of destructive behavior, or, if they can't improve their behavior, moving them out of our lives. Of course, sometimes this is difficult because we work with them or they are related to us. In this case, we have to work at diminishing their negative influence and spending more time with those who support us.

Make Creativity a Priority   Having diminished the voice of negative judgment in your mind, established a creative environment, and committed yourself to trusting your creative gifts, you are now in a position to live more creatively. How do you actually do this? Start small. Identify some habitual patterns in your life and break out of them. Choose new experiences whenever possible—for example, unfamiliar items on a menu or getting to know people outside of your circle of friends—and strive to develop fresh perspectives on things in your life. Resist falling back into the ruts you were previously in by remembering that living things are supposed to be continually growing, changing, and evolving, not acting in repetitive patterns like machines. The

Using creative resources enriches our lives and brings a special meaning to our activities.

following student essay summarizes many of the reasons why choosing to live creatively may be one of the most fulfilling decisions that you make.

CREATIVITY
by Michelle Austin

Creativity is an energizing force: powerful, generative, productive. Sadly, for the most part, its potential remains unused, as men and women circle the periphery of its domain. The author Kahlil Gibran writes: "For the self is a sea, boundless and measureless," and for many of us that sea remains largely undiscovered. Creativity is a treasure that if nurtured can become a harvest of possibilities and riches. Why is creativity important? Very simply, creativity brings fulfillment and enrichment to every dimension of our lives. A creative disposition sees difficulties not as problems but as challenges to be met. The intuitive thinker draws upon the combined resources of insight, illumination, imagination and an inner strength. He puts ideas and strategies into effect, while developing a sense of competency and control over his environment. Creativity fosters limitless opportunities because it draws upon the power of discovery and invention.

Creativity's realm is in the vast uncharted portions of the mind. What we call full consciousness is a very narrow thing, and creativity springs from the unknown and unconscious depths of our being. In the words of Gibran: "Vague and nebulous is the beginning of all things." Creativity always begins with a question and we must abandon preconceived ideas and expectations. But while the phenomenon of creativity involves innovating, developing, playing and speculating, there must ultimately be a point of synthesis. Ideas in flight are of little use; a convergence and application gives substance to our visions. Fostering our creative gifts is a lifelong project. The Buddhists use the term "mindfulness" to describe the creative state of being. Mindfulness involves developing an openness to ideas, suggestions and even once discarded thoughts. The goal is to increase our sensitivity and awareness to the mystery and beauty of life. We must adopt a playful attitude, a willingness to fool around with ideas, with the understanding that many of these fanciful notions will not be relevant or practical. But some will, and these creative insights can lead to profound and wondrous discoveries. At the same time, cultivating a creative attitude stretches our imaginations and makes our lives vibrant and unique.

Worry and mental striving create anxiety that clogs rather than stimulates the flow of ideas. It is impossible to impose one's will with brute force on the chaos. We must be gentle with ourselves, harmonize rather than try to conquer, and in the words of Albert Einstein, "The solution will present itself quietly and say 'Here I am.'" And while we need critical evaluation to provide direction and focus for our creative efforts, a premature and excessive critical judgment suppresses, overpowers and smothers creative spontaneity. This "Voice of Judgment" shrinks our creative reservoir and undermines our courage to take creative risks. The author Napoleon Hill has stated, "Whatever the mind can conceive and believe, it can achieve." Similarly, if we approach our lives with a mindful sense of discovery and invention, we can continually create ourselves in ways that we can only imagine. In such lives, there are no predetermined outcomes, only creativity searching for seeds of progress.

THINKING ACTIVITY 12.5

Select an area of your life in which you would like to be more creative: it can be in school, on your job, an activity you enjoy, or your relationship with someone. Make a special effort to inject a fresh perspective and new ideas into your area and keep a journal recording your efforts and their result. Be sure to allow yourself sufficient time to break out of your ruts and establish new patterns of thinking, feeling, and behaving. Focus on your creative antennae as you "expect the unexpected" and pounce on new ideas when they emerge from the depths of your creative resource. ◄

CREATING A LIFE PHILOSOPHY

The purpose of this text has been to introduce the thinking abilities you need to become successful, not just in your studies but in all areas of your life. Creating yourself as a person is a lifelong process that involves developing your intellectual abilities and your creative potentials. And becoming a critical thinker involves using these abilities to develop informed beliefs, make intelligent decisions, and empathize genuinely with viewpoints other than your own. It is a process tied to your personal growth as a mature and socially responsible individual.

The important decisions that you make in life reflect your *values*, the principles that you consider to be most important. For example, in Chapter 1 (page 32) you explored the case of Mary Barnett, a woman accused of second-degree murder in the death of her young child. The decision that you made regarding Mary Barnett's guilt or innocence expresses values that you have. If you decided that Mary Barnett was *guilty,* you might have explained your decision by saying:

- I believe it is important that adults be held responsible for their actions without excuses or complaints.

On the other hand, if you decided that Mary Barnett was *innocent*, your decision might have expressed the value:

- I believe it is important that we make a special effort to understand people who have been victimized by emotional problems.

When you make decisions regarding "right" and "wrong" behavior in your relationships with others, the values that these decisions express are *moral* values, such as the values just identified regarding the Mary Barnett case. Reflect on the reasoning you used in reaching a verdict in this case and then identify the moral values expressed in your verdict.

- Reasoning that led to my verdict
- Moral values expressed in my verdict

Each one of us possesses a "moral compass" that we use to guide our decisions in moral situations, and the values you just identified are part of your moral compass. In Chapter 11 (page 507), we quoted from a research study that analyzed the moral compasses young people use to guide their decisions in moral situations. Students were asked: "If you were unsure of what was right or wrong in a particular situation, how would you decide what to do?" Describe how you would respond to this question:

According to the researcher, here's how the students interviewed responded:

- 23 percent: I would do what is best for everyone involved.
- 20 percent: I would follow the advice of an authority, such as a parent or teacher.
- 18 percent: I would do whatever made me happy.
- 16 percent: I would do what God or Scriptures say is right.
- 10 percent: I would do whatever would improve my own situation.
- 9 percent: I do not know what I would do.
- 3 percent: I would follow my conscience.

Each of these guiding principles represents a different moral theory that describes the way people reason and make decisions about moral issues. However, moral values do not only *describe* the way people behave; they also suggest that this is the way people *ought to* behave. For example, if I say, "Abusing children is morally wrong," I am not simply describing what *I* believe, I am also suggesting that abusing children is morally wrong for *everyone*. Let's briefly examine the moral theories represented by each of the responses just listed.

I would follow my conscience. We could describe this as a *psychological* theory of morality because it holds that we should determine right and wrong based on our psychological moral sense. Our "conscience" is that part of our mind formed by internalizing the moral values we were raised with, generally from our parents, but from other authority figures and peers as well. If that moral upbringing has been intelligent, empathetic, and fair-minded, then our conscience can serve as a fairly sound moral compass of determining right and wrong. The problem with "following our conscience" occurs when the moral values we have internalized are *not* intelligent, empathetic, or fair-minded. For example, if we were raised in an environment that encouraged racist beliefs or condoned child abuse, then our "conscience" might "tell us" that these are morally acceptable behaviors.

I do not know what I would do. This statement expresses a *moral agnostic* theory of morality that holds there is no way to determine clearly what is "right" or "wrong" in moral situations. This view is a form of *relativism*, because it suggests that there is no universal common standard to determine how we ought to behave toward each other. Although there are often times when we are confused about the right course of action in complex moral situations, the *moral agnostic* theory is problematic because it does not permit us to evaluate the conduct of others. For example, if someone robs you and beats you up, you have no basis on which to say, "That was a morally wrong thing for you to do."

Instead, you have to tolerate such conduct because there is no ultimate "right" or "wrong."

I would do whatever would improve my situation. We could describe this viewpoint as a *pragmatic* theory of morality, because the "right" action is based on what works well for my advancing my interests, while the "wrong" action is determined by what works against my interests. For example, if you are trying to decide whether you should do volunteer work at a local drug treatment center, you might conclude that this is the "right" thing to do because it will help you in your training as a psychologist and will look good on your resume. The problem with this sort of moral reasoning is that you could also use it to justify cheating on an upcoming exam (if you were assured of not getting caught!) or hurting someone's reputation so that you could get ahead. At its heart, the "pragmatic theory" of morality can be used to justify *any* actions that serve someone's own individual interests, ranging from Mother Teresa to Adolf Hitler!

I would do whatever God or Scriptures say is right. This statement expresses a *theist* theory of morality that holds that "right" and "wrong" are determined by a supernatural Supreme Being ("God"). We determine what this Supreme Being wants us to do through divinely inspired writings (Scriptures or Holy Books) or through divinely inspired messengers (priests, ministers, prophets, the Pope). As an "absolutist" moral theory, this view holds that there are absolute moral principles that all humans should follow, determined by the Supreme Being that created us. The strength of this moral theory lies in the fact that many religions embody values that are intelligent, empathetic, and fair-minded, and the devotion of these religions' followers encourages them to act in these morally upright ways. The potential problem with this moral perspective is that all religions don't agree regarding moral values, and so we are left to determine which religion is the "right" one to base our moral views on. In addition, there have been many historical instances in which religion has been used to justify actions that by any standard are cruel and inhuman, including torture, murder, and human sacrifice. There is always a danger when we surrender our critical thinking faculties completely to another authority, as is shown by the actions of those who joined cults led by figures like David Koresh and the Reverend Jim Jones. In these instances, people who claimed to be divinely inspired messengers of God brought bizarre sexual practices, pain, and ultimately death to the followers who relied on them.

I would do whatever made me happy. This statement reflects a slightly more refined version of the *hedonist* moral theory, which advises people to do whatever brings them pleasure. Although this is certainly an understandable goal in life—almost everybody wants to be "happy," whatever that means—there are significant problems when we apply this way of thinking to the moral realm and our relationships with other people. For example, suppose you are contemplating an action that will make you very happy—stealing a new BMW convertible, for example—but will make someone else very *un*happy—the owner of the car, for example. According to this moral theory, the "right" thing to do would be to steal the car, assuming that you didn't experience feelings of guilt or risk getting caught, feelings that would interfere with your happiness. In other words, the trouble with doing "whatever makes you happy" is the same difficulty we saw with "doing whatever improves your situation." Neither moral theory takes into account the interests or rights of other people, and so when your interests conflict with someone else's, your interests always prevail. If everyone thought this way, then our world would be an even more dangerous and unpleasant place to live!

I would follow the advice of an authority, such as a parent or teacher. This *authoritarian* moral theory is analogous to the *theist* moral theory ("I would do whatever God or Scriptures say is right") in the sense that according to both theories, there are clear values of "right" and "wrong," and we should ask authorities to find out what these are. The difference is, of course, that in the *theist* view this authority is a Supreme Being, while the *authoritarian* view holds that the authority is human. And the same difficulties that the *theist* view brings carry over to the *authoritarian* perspective, for although the values of parents and teachers often reflect wisdom and insight, many times they do not. How can we tell the difference between the appropriate and inappropriate values of these authorities? And what do we do when these authorities disagree with each other, as they often do? If we have deferred our critical judgment to the authorities, then we are at their mercy. On the other hand, if we are prepared to evaluate critically the values of authorities, accepting what makes sense and discarding what doesn't, then we need another source for our moral values.

I would do what is best for everyone involved. This response expresses an *altruistic* moral theory, a view in which the interests of other people are held to be as important as our own when we are trying to decide what to do. For example, if you are trapped with other students in a burning theater, the morally "right" course of action is to work for everyone's safe escape, not simply your own. This moral perspective is an important part of many of the prominent world religions, and it is embodied in the Golden Rule: "Do unto others as you would have them do unto you." In other words, deciding on the morally right thing to do requires that we mentally and emotionally place ourselves in the positions of other people who might be affected by our action and then make our decision based on what will be best for their interests *as well as* our interests. By adopting this moral view, we eliminate many of the difficulties of other moral theories. For example, we will be reluctant to act in ways that harm other people, because if we were in their position, we wouldn't want to be harmed that way ourselves.

This is also a perspective consistent with the qualities of thinking critically, since as you saw in Chapter 2, a critical thinker is one who actively strives to view situations from different perspectives, to think empathetically within other viewpoints and try to understand them. This does not mean abandoning our own views or automatically sacrificing our own interests. It simply means that as we work toward creating a fulfilling life for ourselves we take other people's interests into consideration. We do not exist in isolation: we are members of communities to whom we are related in complex and interdependent ways. According to the *altruistic* point of view, achieving happiness and fulfillment in life does not mean pursuing our own narrow desires; instead it involves pursuing our dreams in a context of love, empathy, and understanding for other people. To become truly fulfilled as a human being involves living a life that is woven into the fabric of other lives, contributing to their happiness as they contribute to ours.

As the artist of your life, your brush strokes express your philosophy of life, a vision that incorporates your most deeply held values, aspirations, and convictions. The challenge you face is to create a coherent view of the world that expresses who you are and the person you want to become. It should be a vision that not only guides your actions but also enables you to understand the value of your experiences, the significance of your relationships, and the meaning of your life.

THINKING ACTIVITY 12.6

Following are several dilemmas that ask you to respond with decisions based on moral reasoning. After thinking carefully about each situation, do the following:

- Describe the decision that you would make in this situation and explain the reasons why.
- Identify the moral value(s) or principle(s) on which you based your decision.

- At the conclusion of the activity, compare the moral values that you used. Did you find that you consistently used the same values to make decisions, or did you use different values? If different, how did the various values used relate to each other?
- Based on this analysis, describe your general conclusions about your own "moral compass."

1. **The Captain:** Your ship struck an iceberg and sank. There are thirty survivors, but they are crowded into a lifeboat designed to hold just seven. With the weather stormy and getting worse, it is obvious that many of the passengers will have to be thrown out of the lifeboat, or it will sink and everyone will drown. Will you have people thrown over the side? If so, on what basis will you decide who will go? Age? Health? Strength? Gender? Size?

2. **The Whistle-blower:** You are employed by a large corporation that manufactures baby formula. You suspect that a flaw in the manufacturing process has resulted in contamination of the formula in a small number of cases, and this contamination can result in serious illness, even death. You have been told by your supervisor that "everything is under control" and warned that if you "blow the whistle" by going public, you will be putting the entire company in jeopardy from multimillion-dollar lawsuits. You will naturally be fired and blackballed in the industry, and as the sole provider in your household, your family depends on you.

3. **The Mad Bomber:** You are a police lieutenant heading up an investigation of a series of bombings that have resulted in extensive damage, injuries, and deaths. Your big break comes when you capture the person whom you are certain is the "mad bomber." However, he tauntingly tells you that he has placed a number of devices in public locations that will explode at the cost of many innocent lives and injuries. You believe that your only chance of extracting the location of these bombs is to torture this person until he tells. If you decide to do this, both your career and the legal case against the bomber will be placed in jeopardy. What do you do?

4. **The Patient:** As a clinical psychologist, you are committed to protecting the privacy of your patients. One afternoon a patient tells you that her husband, who has been abusing her physically and mentally for

years, has threatened to kill her, and she believes him. You try to convince her to leave him and seek professional help, but she tells you that she has decided to kill him. She is certain that he will find her wherever she goes and feels that she will be safe only when he is dead. What do you do?

5. **The Friend:** As the director of your department, you are in charge of filling an important vacancy. Many people have applied, including your best friend, who has been out of work for over a year and needs a job desperately. Although your friend would likely perform satisfactorily, there are several more experienced and talented candidates who would undoubtedly perform better. You have always prided yourself on hiring the best people, and you have earned a reputation as someone with high standards who will not compromise your striving for excellence. Whom do you hire? ◄

THINKING PASSAGES

The process of creating yourself through your choices is a lifelong one that involves all the creative and critical thinking abilities that we have been exploring in this book. The processes of creative thinking and critical thinking are related to one another in complex, interactive ways. We use the creative thinking process to develop ideas that are unique, useful, and worthy of further elaboration, and we use the critical thinking process to analyze, evaluate, and refine these ideas. Creative thinking and critical thinking work as partners, enabling us to lead fulfilling lives. The first of the following articles, "Original Spin" by Lesley Dormen and Peter Edidin, provides a useful introduction to creative thinking and suggests strategies for increasing your creative abilities. The second article, "Discovering Your Personal Myth," by Sam Keen, encourages you to discover—and create—the overarching personal "myth" that gives your life meaning and purpose. After reading each article and reflecting on its ideas, answer the questions that follow.

ORIGINAL SPIN
by Lesley Dormen and Peter Edidin

Creativity, somebody once wrote, is the search for the elusive "Aha," that moment of insight when one sees the world, or a problem, or an idea, in a new way. Traditionally, whether the discovery results in a cubist painting or an improved carburetor, we have viewed the creative instant as serendipitous and rare—the product of genius, the property of the elect.

Unfortunately, this attitude has had a number of adverse consequences. It encourages us to accept the myth that the creative energy society requires to address its own problems will never be present in sufficient supply. Beyond that, we have come to believe that "ordinary" people like ourselves can never be truly creative. As John Briggs, author of *Fire in the Crucible: The Alchemy of Creative Genius*, said, "The way we talk about creativity tends to reinforce the notion that it is some kind of arbitrary gift. It's amazing the way 'not having it' becomes wedded to people's self-image. They invariably work up a whole series of rationalizations about why they 'aren't creative,' as if they were damaged goods of some kind." Today, however, researchers are looking at creativity, not as an advantage of the human elite, but as a basic human endowment. As Ruth Richards, a psychiatrist and creativity researcher at McLean Hospital in Belmont, MA, says, "You were being creative when you learned how to walk. And if you are looking for something in the fridge, you're being creative because you have to figure out for yourself where it is." Creativity, in Richards' view, is simply fundamental to getting about in the world. It is "our ability to adapt to change. It is the very essence of human survival."

In an age of rampant social and technological change, such an adaptive capability becomes yet more crucial to the individual's effort to maintain balance in a constantly shifting environment. "People need to recognize that what Alvin Toffler called future shock is our daily reality," says Ellen McGrath, a clinical psychologist who teaches creativity courses at New York University. "Instability is an intrinsic part of our lives, and to deal with it every one of us will need to find new, creative solutions to the challenges of everyday life. I think creativity will be the survival skill of the '90s."

But can you really become more creative? If the word *creative* smacks too much of Picasso at his canvas, then rephrase the question in a less intimidating way: Do you believe you could deal with the challenges of life in a more effective, inventive and fulfilling manner? If the answer is yes, then the question becomes, "What's stopping you?"

Defining Yourself as a Creative Person

People often hesitate to recognize the breakthroughs in their own lives as creative. But who has not felt the elation and surprise that come with the sudden, seemingly inexplicable discovery of a solution to a stubborn problem? In that instant, in "going beyond the information given," as psychologist Jerome Bruner has said, to a solution that was the product of your own mind, you were expressing your creativity.

This impulse to "go beyond" to a new idea is not the preserve of genius, stresses David Henry Feldman, a developmental psychologist at Tufts University and the author of *Nature's Gambit*, a study of child prodigies. "Not everybody can be Beethoven," he says, "but it is true that all humans, by virtue of being dreamers and fantasizers, have a tendency to take liberties with the world as it exists. Humans are always transforming their inner and outer worlds. It's what I call the 'transformational imperative.'"

The desire to play with reality, however, is highly responsive to social control, and many of us are taught early on to repress the impulse. As Mark Runco, associate professor of psychology at California State University at Fullerton and the founder of the new *Creativity Research Journal*, says, "We put children in groups and make them sit in desks and raise their hands before they talk. We put all the emphasis on conformity and order, then we wonder why they aren't being spontaneous and creative."

Adults too are expected to conform in any number of ways and in a variety of settings. Conformity, after all, creates a sense of order and offers the reassurance of the familiar. But to free one's natural creative impulses, it is necessary, to some extent, to resist the pressure to march in step with the world. Begin small, suggests Richards. "Virtually nothing you do can't be done in a slightly different, slightly better way. This has nothing to do with so-called creative pursuits but simply with breaking with your own mindsets and trying an original way of doing some habitual task. Simply defer judgment on yourself for a little while and try something new. Remember, the essence of life is not getting things right, but taking risks, making mistakes, getting things *wrong*."

But it also must be recognized that the creative life is to some degree, and on some occasions, a solitary one. Psycholinguist Vera John-Steiner, author of *Notebooks of the Mind: Explorations of Thinking*, is one of many creativity researchers who believe that a prerequisite for creative success is "intensity of preoccupation, being pulled into your activity to such an extent that you forget it's dinnertime." Such concentration, John-Steiner believes, is part of our "natural creative bent," but we learn to ignore it because of a fear that it will isolate us from others. To John-Steiner, however, this fear is misplaced. Creative thought, she has written, is a "search for meaning," a way to connect our inner sense of being with some aspect of the world that preoccupies us. And she believes that only by linking these two aspects of reality—the inner and the outer—can we gain "some sense of being in control of life."

Avoiding the Myths

David Perkins, co-director of Project Zero at the Harvard Graduate School of Education, asks in *The Mind's Best Work*, "When you have it—creativity, that is—what do you have?" The very impalpability of the subject means that often creativity can be known only by its products. Indeed, the most common way the researchers define creativity is by saying it is whatever produces something that is: a. original; b. adaptive (i.e., useful); c. meaningful to others. But because we don't understand its genesis, we're often blocked or intimidated by the myths that surround and distort this mercurial subject.

One of these myths is, in Perkins's words, that creativity is "a kind of 'stuff' that the creative person has and uses to do creative things, never mind other factors." This bit of folk wisdom, that creativity is a sort of intangible psychic organ—happily present in some and absent in others— so annoys Perkins that he would like to abolish the word itself.

Another prevalent myth about creativity is that it is restricted to those who are "geniuses"—that is, people with inordinately high IQs. Ironically, this has been discredited by a study begun by Stanford psychologist Lewis Terman, the man who adapted the original French IQ test for America. In the early 1920s, Terman had California schoolteachers choose 1,528 "genius" schoolchildren (those with an IQ above 135), whose lives were then tracked year after year. After six decades, researchers found that the putative geniuses, by and large, did well in life. They entered the professions in large numbers and led stable, prosperous lives. But very few made notable creative contributions to society, and none did extraordinary creative work.

According to Dean Simonton, professor of psychology at the University of California at Davis and the author of *Genius, Creativity and Leadership* and *Scientific Genius*, "There just isn't any correlation between creativity and IQ. The average college graduate has an IQ of about 120, and this is high enough to write novels, do scientific research, or any other kind of creative work."

A third myth, voiced eons ago by Socrates, lifts creativity out of our own lives altogether into a mystical realm that makes it all but unapproachable. In this view, the creative individual is a kind of oracle, the passive conduit or channel chosen by God, or the tribal ancestors, or the muse, to communicate sacred knowledge.

Although there *are* extraordinary examples of creativity, for which the only explanation seems to be supernatural intervention (Mozart, the story goes, wrote the overture to *Don Giovanni* in only a few hours, after a virtually sleepless night and without revision), by and large, creativity begins with a long and intensive apprenticeship.

Psychologist Howard Gruber believes that it takes at least 10 years of immersion in a given domain before an eminent creator is likely to be able to make a distinctive mark. Einstein, for example, who is popularly thought to have doodled out the theory of relativity at age 26 in his spare time, was in fact compulsively engaged in thinking about the problem at least from the age of 16.

Finally, many who despair of ever being creative do so because they tried once and failed, as though the truly creative always succeed. In fact, just the opposite is true, says Dean Simonton. He sees genius, in a sense, as inseparable from failure. "Great geniuses make tons of mistakes," he says. "They generate lots of ideas and they accept being wrong. They have a kind of internal fortress that allows them to fail and just keep going. Look at Edison. He held over 1,000 patents, but most of them are not only forgotten, they weren't worth much to begin with."

Mindlessness vs. Mindfulness

"Each of us desires to share with others our vision of the world, only most of us have been taught that it's wrong to do things differently or look at things differently," says John Briggs. "We lose confidence in ourselves and begin to look at reality only in terms of the categories by which society orders it."

This is the state of routinized conformity and passive learning that Harvard professor of psychology Ellen Langer calls, appropriately enough, mindlessness. For it is the state of denying the perceptions and promptings of our own minds, our individual selves. Langer and her colleagues' extensive research over the past 15 years has shown that when we act mindlessly, we behave automatically and limit our capacity for creative response. Mired down in a numbing daily routine, we may virtually relinquish our capacity for independent thought and action.

By contrast, Langer refers to a life in which we use our affective, responsive, perceptive faculties as "mindful." When we are mindful, her research has shown, we avoid rigid, reflexive behavior in favor of a more improvisational and intuitive response to life. We notice and feel the world around us and then act in accordance with our feelings. "Many, if not all, of the qualities that make up a mindful attitude are characteristic of creative people," Langer writes in her new book, *Mindfulness*. "Those who can free themselves of mindsets, open themselves to new information and surprise, play with perspective and context, and focus on process rather than outcome are likely to be creative, whether they are scientists, artists, or cooks."

Much of Langer's research has demonstrated the vital relationship between creativity and uncertainty, or conditionality. For instance, in one experiment, Langer and Alison Piper introduced a collection of objects to one group of people by saying, "This is a hair dryer," and "This is a dog's chew toy," and so on. Another group was told "This *could be* a hair dryer," and "This *could be* a dog's chew toy." Later, the experimenters for both groups invented a need for an eraser, but only those people who had been conditionally introduced to the objects thought to use the dog's toy in this new way.

The intuitive understanding that a single thing is, or could be, many things, depending on how you look at it, is at the heart of the attitude Langer calls mindfulness. But can such an amorphous state be cultivated? Langer believes that it can, by consciously discarding the idea that any given moment of your day is fixed in its form. "I teach people to 'componentize' their lives into smaller pieces," she says. "In the morning, instead of mindlessly downing your orange juice, *taste it*. Is it what you want? Try something else if it isn't. When you walk to work, turn left instead of right. You'll notice the street you're on, the buildings and the weather. Mindfulness, like creativity, is nothing more than a return to who you are. By minding your responses to the world, you will come to know yourself again. How you feel. What you want. What you want to do."

Creating the Right Atmosphere

Understanding the genesis of creativity, going beyond the myths to understand your creative potential, and recognizing your ability to break free of old ways of thinking are the three initial steps to a more creative life. The fourth is finding ways to work that encourage personal commitment and expressiveness.

Letting employees learn what they want to do has never been a very high priority in the workplace. There, the dominant regulation has always been, "Do what you are told."

Today, however, economic realities are providing a new impetus for change. The pressure on American businesses to become more productive and innovative has made creative thinking a hot commodity in the business community. But innovation, business is now learning, is likely to be found wherever bright and eager people *think* they can find it. And some people are looking in curious places.

Financier Wayne Silby, for example, founded the Calvert Group of funds, which today manages billions of dollars in assets. Silby, whose business card at one point read Chief Daydreamer, occasionally retreats for inspiration to a sensory deprivation tank, where he floats in warm water sealed off from light and sound. "I went into the tank during a time when the government was changing money-market deposit regulations, and I needed to think how to compete with banks. Floating in the tank I got the idea of joining them instead. We wound up creating an $800-million program. Often we already have answers to our problems, but we don't quiet ourselves enough to see the solutions bubbling just below the surface." Those solutions will stay submerged, he says, "unless you create a culture that encourages creative approaches, where it's OK to have bad ideas."

Toward this goal, many companies have turned to creativity consultants, like Synectics, Inc., in Cambridge, MA. Half the battle, according to Synectics facilitator Jeff Mauzy, is to get the clients to relax and accept that they are in a safe place where the cutthroat rules of the workplace don't apply, so they can allow themselves to exercise their creative potential in group idea sessions.

Pamela Webb Moore, director of naming services (she helps companies figure out good names for their products) at Synectics, agrees. One technique she uses to limber up the minds of tightly focused corporate managers is "sleight of head." While working on a particular problem, she'll ask clients to pretend to work on something else. In one real-life example, a Synectics-trained facilitator took a group of product-development and marketing manages from the Etonic shoe corporation on an "excursion," a conscious walk away from the problem—in this case, to come up with a new kind of tennis shoe.

The facilitator asked the Etonic people to imagine they were at their favorite vacation spot. "One guy," Moore says, "was on a tropical island, walking on the beach in his bare feet. He described how wonderful the water and sand felt on his feet, and he said, 'I wish we could play tennis barefoot.' The whole thing would have stopped right there if somebody had complained that while his colleague was wandering around barefoot, they were supposed to come up with a *shoe*. Instead, one of the marketing people there was intrigued, and the whole group decided to go off to play tennis barefoot on a rented court at 10 at night."

While the Etonic people played tennis, the facilitator listed everything they said about how it felt. The next morning, the group looked at her assembled list of comments, and they realized that what they liked about playing barefoot was the lightness of being without shoes, and the ability to pivot easily on both the ball of the foot and the heel. Nine months later, the company produced an extremely light shoe called the Catalyst, which featured an innovative two-piece sole that made it easier for players to pivot.

The Payoff

In *The Courage to Create*, Rollo May wrote that for much of this century, researchers had avoided the subject of creativity because they perceived it as "unscientific, mysterious, disturbing and too corruptive of the scientific training of graduate students." But today researchers are coming to see that creativity, at once fugitive and ubiquitous, is the mark of human nature itself.

Whether in business or the arts, politics or personal relationships, creativity involves "going beyond the information given" to create or reveal something new in the world. And almost invariably, when the mind exercises its creative muscle, it also generates a sense of pleasure. The feeling may be powerfully mystical, as it is for New York artist Rhonda Zwillinger, whose embellished artwork appeared in the film *Slaves of New York*. Zwillinger reports, "There are times when I'm working and it is almost as though I'm a vessel and there is a force operating through me. It is the closest I come to having a religious experience." The creative experience may also be quiet and full of wonder, as it was for Isaac Newton, who compared his lifetime of creative effort to "a boy playing on the seashore and diverting himself and then finding a smoother pebble or prettier shell than ordinary, while the greater ocean of truth lay all undiscovered before me."

But whatever the specific sensation, creativity always carries with it a powerful sense of the mind working at the peak of its ability. Creativity truly is, as David Perkins calls it, the mind's best work, its finest effort. We may never know exactly how the brain does it, but we can feel that it is exactly what the brain was meant to do.

Aha! ■

Questions for Analysis

1. According to the authors, "Creativity . . . is the search for the elusive 'Aha,' that moment of insight when one sees the world, or a problem, or an idea, in a new way." Describe an "aha" moment that you have had recently, detailing the origin of your innovative idea and how you implemented it.

2. Identify some of the influences in your life that have inhibited your creative development, including the "myths" about creativity that are described in the article.

3. Using the ideas contained in this chapter and in this article, identify some of the strategies that you intend to use in order to become more creative in your life: for example, becoming more "mindful," destroying the "voice of judgment," and creating a more conducive atmosphere. ◀

Discovering Your Personal Myth
by Sam Keen

It seems that Americans are finally taking seriously what Carl Jung, this Swiss psychologist, said is the most important question we can ask ourselves: "What myth are we living?"

What Is a Myth?

What is a myth? Few words have been subject to as much abuse and been as ill-defined as *myth*. Journalists usually use it to mean a "lie," "fabrication," "illusion," "mistake," or something similar. It is the opposite of what is supposedly a "fact," of what is "objectively" the case, and of what is "reality." In this usage myth is at best a silly story and at worst a cynical untruth. Theologians and propagandists often use myth as a way of characterizing religious beliefs and ideologies other than their own.

Such trivialization of the notion of myth reflects false certainties of dogmatic minds, an ignorance of the mythic assumptions that underlie the commonly accepted view of "reality," and a refusal to consider how much our individual and communal lives are shaped by dramatic scenarios and "historical" narratives that are replete with accounts of the struggle between good and evil empires: our godly heroes versus the demonic enemy.

In a strict sense *myth* refers to "an intricate set of interlocking stories, rituals, rites, and customs that inform and give the pivotal sense of meaning and direction to a person, family, community, or culture." A living myth, like an iceberg, is 10 percent visible and 90 percent beneath the surface of consciousness. While it involves a conscious celebration of certain values, which are always personified in a pantheon of heroes (from the wily Ulysses to the managing Lee Iacocca) and villains (from the betraying Judas to the barbarous Moammar Kadafi), it also includes the unspoken consensus, the habitual way of seeing things, the unquestioned assumptions, the automatic stance. It is differing cultural myths that make cows sacred objects for Hindus and hamburgers meals for Methodists, or turn dogs into pets for Americans and roasted delicacies for the Chinese.

People's Myths Are Primarily Unconscious

At least 51 percent of the people in a society are not self-consciously aware of the myth that informs their existence. Cultural consensus is created by an unconscious conspiracy to consider the myth "the truth," "the way things *really* are." In other words, a majority is made up of literalists, men and women who are not critical or reflective about the guiding "truths"—myths—of their own group. To a tourist in a strange land, an anthropologist studying a tribe, or a psychologist observing a patient, the myth is obvious. But to the person who lives within the mythic horizon, it is nearly invisible.

For instance, most Americans would consider potlatch feasts, in which Northwest Indian tribes systematically destroy their wealth, to be irrational and mythic but would consider the habit of browsing in malls and buying expensive things we do not need (conspicuous consumption) to be a perfectly reasonable way to spend a Saturday afternoon. To most Americans the Moslem notion of *jihad*—holy war—is a dangerous myth. But our struggle against "atheistic communism" is a righteous duty. Ask a born-again Christian about the myth of the atonement, and you will be told it is no myth at all but a revealed truth. Ask a true believer of Marxism about the myth of the withering away of the state, and you will get a long explanation about the "scientific" laws of the dialectic of history.

I suggest two analogies that may help to counteract the popular trivialized notion of myth. The dominant myth that informs a person or a culture is like the "information" contained in DNA or the program in the systems disk of a computer. Myth is the software, the cultural DNA, the unconscious information, the metaprogram that governs the way we see "reality" and the way we behave.

Myths Can Be Creative or Destructive

The organizing myth of any culture functions in ways that may be either creative or destructive, healthful or pathological. By providing a world picture and a set of stories that explain why things are as they are, it creates consensus, sanctifies the social order, and gives the individual an authorized map of the path of life. A myth creates the plotline that organizes the diverse experiences of a person or a community into a single story.

But in the same measure that myth gives us security and identity, it also creates selective blindness, narrowness, and rigidity because it is intrinsically conservative. It encourages us to follow the faith of our fathers, to hold to the time-honored truths, to imitate the way of the heroes, to repeat the formulas and rituals in exactly the same way they were done in the good old days. As long as no radical change is necessary for survival, the status quo remains sacred, the myth and ritual are unquestioned, and the patterns of life, like the seasons of the year, repeat themselves. But when crisis comes—a natural catastrophe, a military defeat, the introduction of a new technology—the mythic mind is at a loss to deal with novelty. As Marshall McLuhan said, it tries to "walk into the future looking through a rearview mirror."

Families Have Myths

Every family, like a miniculture, also has an elaborate system of stories and rituals that differentiate it from other families. The Murphys, being Irish, understand full well that Uncle Paddy is a bit of a rogue and drinks a tad too much. The Cohens, being Jewish, are haunted each year at Passover when they remember the family that perished in the Holocaust. The Keens, being Calvinists, are predestined to be slightly more righteous and right than others, even when they are wrong. And within the family each member's place is defined by a series of stories. Obedient to the family script, Jane, "who always was very motherly even as a little girl," married young and had children immediately, while Pat, "who was a wild one and not cut out for marriage," sowed oat after oat before finding fertile ground.

Family myths, like those of the Kennedy clan, may give us an impulse to strive for excellence and a sense of pride that helps us endure hardship and tragedy. Or they may, like the myths of alcoholic or abusive families, pass a burden of guilt, shame, and failure from generation to generation as abused children, in turn, become abusive parents, ad nauseam. The sins, virtues, and myths of the fathers are passed on to the children of future generations.

Every Individual Has a Personal Myth

Finally, the entire legacy and burden of cultural and family myth comes to rest on the individual. Each person is a repository of stories. To the degree that any one of us reaches toward autonomy, we must begin a process of sorting through the trash and treasures we have been given, keeping some and rejecting others. We gain the full dignity and power of our persons only when we create a narrative account of our lives, dramatize our existence, and forge a coherent personal myth that combines elements of our cultural myth and family myth with unique stories that come from our experience. As my friend David Steere once pointed out to me, the common root of "authority" and "authorship" tells us a great deal about power. Whoever authors your story authorizes your actions. We gain personal authority and power in the measure that we question the myth that is upheld by "the authorities" and discover and create a personal myth that illuminates and informs us.

What George Santayana said about cultures is equally true for individuals: "Those who do not remember history are condemned to repeat it." If we do not make the effort to become conscious of our personal myths gradually, we become dominated by what psychologists have variously called repetition compulsion, autonomous complexes, engrams, routines, scripts, games. One fruitful way to think of neurosis is to consider it a tape loop, an oft-told story that we repeat in our inner dialogues with ourselves and with others. "Well, I'm just not the kind of person who can . . ." "I never could . . ." "I wouldn't think of . . .". While personal myths give us a sense of identity, continuity, and security, they become constricting and boring if they are not revised from time to time. To remain vibrant throughout a lifetime we must always be inventing ourselves, weaving new themes into our life-narratives, remembering our past, re-visioning our future, reauthorizing the myth by which we live. ■

Questions for Analysis

1. The author defines myth as "an intricate set of interlocking stories, rituals, rites, and customs that inform and give the pivotal sense of meaning and direction to a person, family, community or culture." Describe examples of myths from both your culture and your family and explain how these myths provide meaning and influence the behavior of the people who participate in the myth.

2. Myths, as we saw in the previous article regarding "myths of creativity," can be destructive and repressive, and they can encourage uncritical thinking. On the other hand, myths can be constructive and liberating, encouraging creative expression and independent thought. Describe one myth that is a part of your own life that is destructive and another that is constructive. Discuss how you might go about diminishing the destructive myth and enlarging the constructive myth.

3. The author concludes by saying, "To remain vibrant throughout a lifetime, we must always be inventing ourselves, weaving new themes into our life-narratives . . ." Describe new themes that you are currently trying to weave into your own personal myth as you project yourself into the future. ◄

(Continued from page iv)

ILLUSTRATION ACKNOWLEDGMENTS

Page 4: Illustration by Warren Gebert

Page 6: Illustration by Warren Gebert

Page 15: Illustration by Warren Gebert

Page 25: Illustration by Warren Gebert

Page 30: Photo by Hazel Hankin/Stock Boston

Page 48: Illustration by Warren Gebert

Page 51: Illustration by Warren Gebert

Page 58: Illustration by Warren Gebert

Page 71: Illustration by Warren Gebert

Page 97: Illustration by Warren Gebert

Page 100: Illustration by Warren Gebert

Page 107: Illustration by Warren Gebert

Page 110: Illustration by Warren Gebert

Page 119: Illustration by Warren Gebert

Page 160: Hogarth print. All rights reserved. The Metropolitan Museum of Art. Gift of Sarah Lazarus, 1891. (91.1.33).

Page 161: The Investigation. © John Jonik. Reproduced with permission. This cartoon first appeared in *Psychology Today,* February 1984.

Page 163: Photo by George Mars Cassidy/The Picture Cube

Page 173: Illustration by Warren Gebert

Page 176: Illustration by Warren Gebert

Page 186: Photo by Sygma

Page 201: Illustration by Warren Gebert

Page 212: Illustration by Warren Gebert

Page 217: Photo by Patrick Dural/Sygma

Page 231: Illustration by Warren Gebert

Page 254: Illustration by Warren Gebert

Page 257: Illustration by Warren Gebert

Page 274: Illustration by Warren Gebert

Page 295: Courtesy of Friends of the Chicago River

Page 296: Courtesy of Andersen Windows

Page 296: Courtesy of North Shore Equestrian

Page 315: Illustration by Warren Gebert

Page 320: Illustration by Warren Gebert

Page 328: From *PULP!* Used by permission of Louis Hellman.

Page 330: Photo by Jean Pierre Laffont/Sygma

Page 334: Illustration by Warren Gebert

Page 355: Illustration by Warren Gebert

Page 365: Illustration by Warren Gebert

Page 381: Illustration by Warren Gebert

Page 410: Illustration by Warren Gebert

Page 412: Photo courtesy of Frankel Gallery, San Francisco and © The Estate of Gary Winogrand.

Page 416: Illustration by Warren Gebert

Page 422: Illustration by Warren Gebert

Page 453: Illustration by Warren Gebert

Page 468: Illustration by Warren Gebert

Page 475: Illustration by Warren Gebert

Page 504: Illustration by Warren Gebert

Page 509: Illustration by Warren Gebert

Page 531: Illustration by Warren Gebert

Page 535: Illustration by Warren Gebert

Page 557: Illustration by Warren Gebert

Page 561: Illustration by Warren Gebert

Page 564: Illustration by Warren Gebert

Page 570: Illustration by Warren Gebert

ACKNOWLEDGMENTS

Page 11: From *The Autobiography of Malcolm X* by Malcolm X with the assistance of Alex Haley. Copyright © 1964 by Alex Haley and Malcolm X and copyright © 1965 by Alex Haley and Betty Shabazz. Reprinted by permission of Random House, Inc.

Page 22: From "Where Are You?" © United Technologies Corporation 1984. Used by permission.

Page 42: From "Jurors Hear Evidence and Turn It into Stories" by Daniel Goldman, *New York Times,* May 12, 1992, p. C1. Copyright © 1992 by The New York Times Company. Reprinted by permission.

Page 77: From "Life Sentence: Individual Autonomy, Medical Technology, and the 'Common Good'" by Howard Moody. Reprinted with permission. Copyright October 12, 1987, *Christianity and Crisis,* 537 West 121st St., New York, N.Y. 10027.

Page 82: From "A Step Closer to Mercy Killing" by Robert Barry. From *Medical Moral Newsletter,* February 1987. Reprinted by permission of AYD Medical Communications.

Page 86: From "Television and Reading" from *The Plug-in Drug, Revised Edition* by Marie Winn. Copyright © 1977, 1985 by Marie Winn Miller. Used by permission of Viking Penguin, a division of Penguin Books, USA Inc.

Page 137: From "Young Hate" by David Shenk, *CV Magazine.* Reprinted by permission.

Page 144: From "When Is It Rape?" by Nancy Gibbs, *Time,* June 3, 1991.

Page 169: From "On the Assassination of Malcolm X," *New York Times,* February 22, 1965. Copyright © 1965 by The New York Times Company. Reprinted by permission.

Page 335: "Suicide Solution" by Anna Quindlen, *New York Times*, September 20, 1990. Copyright © 1990 by The New York Times Company. Reprinted by permission.

Page 347: From "What Is Religion?" from introduction to *Ways of Being Religious* by F. Streung, C. Lloyd, and J. Allen, 1973.

Page 357: From "Back, But Not Home" by Maria Muniz, *New York Times,* July 13, 1979 (Op-Ed). Copyright © 1979 by The New York Times Company. Reprinted by permission.

Page 373: From "The Rivet Poppers," from *Extinction* by Paul R. Erlich and Anne H. Erlich. Copyright © 1981 by Paul R. and Anne H. Erlich. Reprinted by permission of Random House, Inc.

Page 385: From "We Are Breaking the Silence About Death" by Daniel Goleman, from *Psychology Today,* September 1976. Reprinted with permission from Psychology Today Magazine. Copyright © 1976 (Sussex Publishers, Inc.).

Page 391: From "College Women and Alcohol: A Relational Perspective" by Nancy A. Gleason, from *Journal of American College Health,* vol. 42, no. 6, May 1994.

Page 430: First published in *The Reporter,* 26 January 1967. From The Way To Rainy Mountain, by N. Scott Momaday. © 1969 the University of New Mexico Press. Reprinted by permission.

Page 435: From "Evolution as Fact and Theory," selection from *Discover,* 1981, reprinted by permission of Stephen Jay Gould.

Page 442: From "I Listen to my Parents and Wonder What They Believe," selection by Robert Coles reprinted by permission of the author.

Page 456: From "Homage to Daniel Shays: Collected Essays 1952–1972" by Gore Vidal. Copyright © 1972 by Gore Vidal. Reprinted by permission of Random House, Inc.

Page 457: From "The Case for Slavery," by A.M. Rosenthal, *New York Times,* September 26, 1989. Copyright © 1989 by The New York Times Company. Reprinted by permission.

Page 490: From "Death and Justice: How Capital Punishment Affirms Life" by Edward Koch. Selection reprinted by permission of *The New Republic* © 1985, The New Republic, Inc.

Page 495: From "The Death Penalty" by David Bruck. Article reprinted by permission of *The New Republic* © 1985, The New Republic, Inc.

Page 523: From "Infant Death Tied to Dopamine Excess," by J. Greenberg, *Science News,* September 15, 1984. Reprinted by permission from *Science News,* the weekly news magazine of science, copyright 1984 by Science Service, Inc.

Page 525: From "For a National Effort to Develop a Vaccine to Counteract AIDS" by Robert E. Pollack, *New York Times,* November 27, 1985 (Op-Ed). Copyright © 1985 by The New York Times Company. Reprinted by permission.

Page 544: From "Critical Thinking and Obedience to Authority" by John Sabini and Maury Silver, reprinted from *National Forum: The Phi Kappa Phi Journal,* Winter 1985, pp. 13–17, by permission.

Page 579: From "Original Spin" by Lesley Dormen and Peter Edidin, *Psychology Today,* July/August 1989. Reprinted with permission from Psychology Today Magazine. Copyright © 1989 (Sussex Publishers, Inc.)

Page 587: From "Discovering Your Personal Myth," from *Your Mythic Journey* by Sam Keen and Anne Valley-Fox, 1973.

Index